HUMANITIES

THE EVOLUTION OF VALUES

HUMANITIES
THE EVOLUTION OF VALUES

Lee A. Jacobus
University of Connecticut

McGraw-Hill Book Company

New York   St. Louis   San Francisco   Auckland   Bogotá   Hamburg   Johannesburg
London   Madrid   Mexico   Montreal   New Delhi   Panama   Paris   São Paulo
Singapore   Sydney   Tokyo   Toronto

This book was set in Goudy Old Style by Black Dot, Inc. (ECU).
The music examples were set by York Graphic Services, Inc.
The editors were Emily G. Barrosse and Susan Gamer;
the designer was Jo Jones;
the production supervisor was Joe Campanella.
The photo editor was Elsa Peterson.
The drawings were done by Fine Line Illustrations, Inc.
The maps were prepared by Joseph Le Monnier.
Ornamental illustrations by Joseph Gillians.
Von Hoffmann Press, Inc., was printer and binder.

Cover Credits

Front   Mark Rothko. *Untitled.* 1957. Reproduced with the
        permission of Marcia Weisman and Richard Weisman.
Back   Oscar Claude Monet. *Branch of the Seine Near Giverny, II.*
        Gift of Mrs. Walter Scott Fitz.
        Courtesy, Museum of Fine Arts, Boston.
The cover researcher was Inge King.

Acknowledgments for photographs and music appear at the
appropriate places in the text, and on this page by reference.
Photographs not otherwise credited are by the author.

Acknowledgments for quoted material appear on pages
619–623, and on this page by reference.

HUMANITIES: *The Evolution of Values*

1234567890 VNHVNH 898765

ISBN 0-07-032173-6

Library of Congress Cataloging in Publication Data

Jacobus, Lee A
    Humanities: the evolution of values.

    Bibliography: p.
    Includes index.
        1. Humanism in art.   2. Arts—History.   I. Title.
NX650.H8J32   1986   700'.1'04   85-6683
ISBN 0-07-032173-6

For
Julia and Ernest Jacobus,

who planted the seed

ABOUT THE AUTHOR

Lee A. Jacobus began teaching interdisciplinary courses in the arts in 1962 and with Joanna Jacobus now teaches an intersession course in London called "The Arts in England." Apart from his scholarly publications in seventeenth-century literature and modern Irish literature, his interests in the arts include music, (particularly playing jazz drums) and photography (he has been a recipient of an Arts Grant for photographic work from the State of Connecticut Arts Council and the University of Connecticut Research Foundation). His undergraduate and master's degrees were from Brown University; his Ph.D., in English, was from Claremont Graduate School. He was a Lackawanna Brown Club scholarship student at Brown and a Danforth Teaching Fellow while at Claremont. Among his publications are short stories, poems, and articles on literature. Currently he is writing plays. His books include *Sudden Apprehension: Aspects of Knowledge in Paradise Lost*; *John Cleveland: A Study*; *The Humanities through the Arts* (with F. David Martin); and several edited collections, among which are *Aesthetics and the Arts*, *The Longman Anthology of American Drama*, and *A World of Ideas*. He is Professor of English at the University of Connecticut, where he has taught since 1968.

CONTENTS

IN BRIEF

CONTENTS

PREFACE

Humanities: The Evolution of Values is a values-based historical survey using a case-study rather than an encyclopedic approach to the arts. Each important period in art history is treated in detail to give a full understanding of its artistic styles and the values revealed by them.

The theoretical premises used in this book are thoroughly defined in F. David Martin and Lee A. Jacobus, *The Humanities through the Arts*, third edition (McGraw-Hill, 1983). The theory of revelatory aesthetics, developed by David Martin and adapted further in our book, is the basis of the critical method used in the present text, although with some modifications and without reliance on its special terminology.

The purpose of *Humanities* is to provide information "of" rather than "about" works of art. Background information, even dates and names, is treated as less important than an immediate, critical involvement with important works of painting, sculpture, architecture, literature, photography, film, music, and dance. Not all these art forms are discussed in every chapter, but each chapter does present an analysis of the major artistic achievements of a culture or historical era.

Knowledge "of" works of art depends upon perceiving the relationship between formal elements and subject matter. The basis of revelatory aesthetics is the artist's interpretation of subject matter through form, achieving a "form-content" which is a fusion of the two. I assume that art reveals values and that one can become more sensitive to values through a scrupulous study of the arts.

PERCEPTION AND ANALYSIS

The procedure in each chapter is to provide necessary historical details, including appropriate observations on the political, religious, and philosophical background. Individual artists and their works are discussed in relationship to the movements with which they have been associated. But ultimately the focus becomes explicit, with analysis of specific elements of form: line, dynamics, rhythm, color, mass, space, bulk, depth, flatness, perspective, distortion, realistic representation, and other considerations relevant to each medium. In other words, the emphasis moves from that which can be perceived to more theoretical concepts evolving from a thorough perception of sensual elements.

Because of the nature of the case-study approach, not every artist of importance is discussed in detail. The "brief chronologies" include the names of figures of importance whose achievements are worth examining, and some of those figures are included in the "suggested readings" for each chapter. Naturally, individual study of these artists is to be encouraged, and they can be interpreted in light of the information in the chapters themselves. The primary focus of the book is on analysis of individual works by important artists rather than on recognition of every artist's achievements.

"Keys"—"perception keys," "concept keys," "comparison keys," and "listening keys"—are placed strategically throughout the text to call attention to the kinds of questions that a careful observer will ask. The content of some keys is also treated, at least in important part, within the text itself, but others are the responsibility of the reader, who by the time they are presented should have enough experience and enough background to offer shrewd responses. The "concept keys," as the name implies, ask conceptual rather than perceptual questions, usually focusing on ideas. This method, which is also used in *The Humanities through the Arts*, has been praised as a means of genuinely engaging the imagination and the intellect in responding to works of art.

The reader is invited to offer counteranalyses and to test interpretations developed by the present author or other critics. The most important thing is not who is right, but who looks closest, who perceives most completely, and—in a real sense—who asks the most interesting questions.

Analysis without historical understanding is limited. Certain eras have favored such analysis, but formal elements are not only better understood but also more fully perceived when the historical sources—the roots—of important works of art are understood. That is true, too, of the interrelationships among works of art. Important aesthetic effects are achieved by allusion or "borrowing," either direct or indirect. It is impossible to perceive, much less to appreciate, such artistic efforts without historical awareness. It is easy to overpraise an artistic achievement if one is ignorant of the history of the arts. Certain startling effects would be much less startling if their indebtedness to their genuine inventors was known.

VALUES

Every age and every culture hold different values. Examination of the arts reveals not only the values which are publically and officially praised, but often those which are "underground," or unofficial, but widely held. All eras and all cultures are vastly too complex to understand thoroughly, and any attempt to do so must be limited. But it is nonetheless worth the effort.

Values attract our attention, hold our interest, and assume great importance. They sometimes can be discussed as classes of values—for example, religious values, military values, social values, intellectual values, economic values, and values of personal freedom.

The entire study of values is complex and beyond the limits of a book such as this. Rather, this book stays with the arts themselves and examines them as a means of gaining insight into the broad range of values we call the "humanities." The humanities begin with the appreciation of beauty and the means by which to achieve it. That is why the arts come first, why they reveal our ancestors and forebears to us in the past, and why they reveal us to ourselves in the present.

ACKNOWLEDGMENTS

A project of this kind, which stretches over many years in writing and decades in gestation, is dependent on the learning and generosity of more people than can be acknowledged formally. Some of those whose contribution I am most aware of are former colleagues at Western Connecticut State University, whose program "The Nature of Man" first gave me a chance to work out my thinking on the interrelationship of the arts: H. Jonathan Greenwald, James Timmins, Richard Moryl, Elizabeth Dominy, Marceau Myers, and David Driscoll. More recently, those who had a hand in shaping this book are Gloria Kitto Lewis of GMI Engineering and Management Institute, John Werenko of Marist College, Louise Matthews Hewitt of Coastlines Community College, Allen Arnold of Lakeland Community College, Jon Thiem and Kenneth Rhoads of Colorado State University, Daniel P. Tompkins of Temple University, and Dion K. Brown of Polk Community College. Each contributed enthusiastically and each helped me make this a better book. Bruce Bellingham of the Department of Music, a colleague and friend, gave the sections on music a very thorough going over, helping me over sometimes rocky terrain. My colleague William E. Parker helped with photographic history. My discussions with other members of the University of Connecticut Art Department over a period of years naturally helped deepen my understanding of the arts. F. David Martin, my coauthor on an earlier book on the humanities, deserves special mention. We have shared ideas over a period of years concerning the arts and aesthetics. His theories of revelatory aesthetics form the foundation of our *Humanities through the Arts* (McGraw-Hill, 3d ed., 1983), and they are present in this book as well, although without the stricter terminology we were able to develop in that first book. Over the years David has been colleague, collaborator, and friend. A number of editors at McGraw-Hill shepherded this project at different times: Robert Rainier, Jan Yates, Kaye Pace, Anne Murphy, James Dodd, and Emily Barrosse; to them I am deeply grateful. Phillip Butcher oversaw the project at McGraw-Hill and was always a point of stability and a cordial guide. I am very grateful to Elsa Petersen, who handled the sometimes problematic illustration program. I am particularly grateful to Pamela Haskins, my copy editor, and to Jo Jones, whose excitement about the design of the book buoyed me from the first day I knew it would be a reality. I want to thank Susan Gamer, my editing supervisor, whose standards have improved the quality of the book and whose work was inspiring throughout the difficult final stages. Finally, no one is more aware than I of how much more there is to say about the works discussed here (as well as those that are not discussed). One book, however large, is never enough. This must be thought of as only the beginning of an endless examination of the humanities.

Lee A. Jacobus

HUMANITIES
THE EVOLUTION OF VALUES

PART ONE

MEDITERRANEAN SEA

• Jerusalem

• Gaza

SINAI PENINSULA

Heliopolis
(Cairo)

Giza •
Saqqara •
Memphis

Akhetaton (Tell-el-Am

Hermopolis •

Nile

Valley of the Kings   Lycopolis

LOWER EGYPT

0   50   100   150   200 miles

HUMANITIES: THE BEGINNINGS

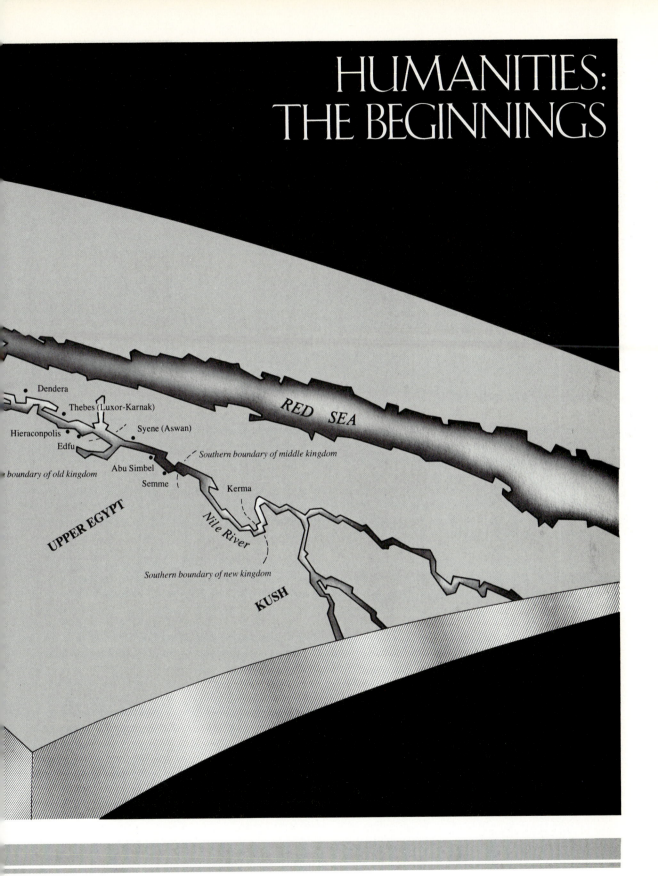

- Dendera
- Thebes (Luxor-Karnak)
- Hieraconpolis
- Edfu
- Syene (Aswan)

Southern boundary of middle kingdom

boundary of old kingdom

- Abu Simbel
- Semme
- Kerma

RED   SEA

UPPER EGYPT

Nile River

Southern boundary of new kingdom

KUSH

Because the historical record reaches back only a few thousand years and because the earliest surviving works of art are products of a long tradition, it is impossible to say when the humanities began. We know that the earliest human-like life probably developed somewhere in southern Africa, and that the humanities existed even before our own species, *Homo sapiens sapiens,* appeared.

Humans were at first herbivorous. When they became carnivorous, they gathered into hunting groups that divided the labor to guarantee efficiency. Such groups also produced a social order. Hunters and gatherers exist in parts of the world today, reminding us that human development is by no means uniform and absolute. The old ways often exist beside the new, just as they do and have done in the arts. The exciting discoveries of the great painted caves in Spain and France show that 30,000 years before Christ, people were capable of one of their most remarkable achievements: the conceptual abstraction that results in the capacity to make representations of the world outside the imagination. Obviously, such an astonishing accomplishment, shared by no other animal, took thousands of years to develop.

The art of the glacial period, from 40,000 B.C. to 1500 B.C., consists primarily of human figures in sculpture and animal figures in painting; the animal figures have been thought to have certain magical qualities. Paintings of bulls and bison were made, we think, in hopes of gaining control over them or of sharing in their power. Respect for life and its mysteries is evident everywhere in the earliest surviving artifacts, along with respect for harmony, grace, balance, and beauty. These are signs of human values.

No reliable evidence tells us anything about social organization during the ice age beyond

the fact that the people who painted the caves and carved the sculpture were dependent on reindeer for their food, clothing, and tools. The temperatures were cool, but the herds were abundant; people migrated with the herds and avoided making settlements, which would have required dependable sources of food and warmth. When the glacier receded, the herds disappeared northward, and the people of the caves may well have followed them.

Slowly, the wanderers and the tribal people who survived became agricultural and learned how to domesticate cattle, sheep, pigs, and other pastoral animals. Numerous tribal people who avoided making permanent settlements spread over northern Europe and survived long enough to be conquered by the Romans and converted by the Christians.

The great cities of Mesopotamia—the middle eastern countries now known as Iran and Iraq—and Egypt flourished as people mastered agriculture and became independent of migrating herds. Planting crops involved settling in one place. Stored crops represented wealth, which had to be protected by building walls around cities; these cities grew into individual states, which in turn became confederations. Within these cities specialized classes of workers developed, including priests, artists, and government functionaries. A rigid class structure also evolved, as did a long-term social stability.

In the middle east, great cultures developed which displayed their pride in themselves by establishing dynastic governments that seemed destined to last forever. These people built temples—great complexes for ceremonies designed to celebrate and extend their powers over nature. Their pyramids and the cities of the dead in Egypt implied a longevity that extended into eternity.

In Mexico and Central America, civilizations developed which resembled those of the

middle east. Temples elevated the priests toward the sun. These people's religious beliefs included blood sacrifice to propitiate the gods. Before and during the earliest stages of the great Mayan temple building, the Wessex people—Celts—were building Stonehenge, in England, which predicts astronomical events and thus demonstrates a control of the environment. This skill was shared by the Maya, who developed their own calendar and made their own predictions.

People in the earliest societies lived in a perilous balance between life and death. Their agricultural technology was limited, and they were at the mercy of crop failure and possible famine. Their religious faith was profound; their ceremonies, in which decorative arts played a part, were filled with music, dance, and complex ritual. Their sophisticated regard for both life and death reveals a complex and subtle system of values based on their ways of life. Our own sense of values begins with the earliest moments of human awareness.

Brief Chronology

40,000 B.C. Paleolithic period (the old stone age); some cave paintings, burial of the "Shanidar man."

20,000 B.C. Upper paleolithic period (the upper stone age); cave paintings at Altamira, Lascaux, and elsewhere; hunting-and-gathering culture.

10,000 B.C.   Mesolithic period (the middle stone age); cave painting, transition to an agricultural society; end of the glacial (ice) age.

7000 B.C.   Beginnings of cities: Çatal Huyuk; Jericho.

3100–2686 B.C.   Egypt: Thinite or early dynastic period; King Narmer unites upper and lower Egypt; step pyramid at Saqqara.

2750 B.C.   Bronze age: the beginning of Stonehenge I.

2686–2182 B.C.   Egypt: the "old kingdom," building of pyramid complex at Giza; kings: Zoser, Khafre, Khufu, Menkaure.

2181–2133 B.C.   Egypt: first intermediate period, royal tombs ransacked, social disorder, revolution.

2133–1633 B.C.   Egypt: "middle kingdom"; power shifts from Memphis to Thebes; period of great artistic splendor; king: Sesostris.

2100 B.C.   Ur: the beginning of the ziggurat.

1633–1567 B.C.   Egypt: second intermediate period; Hyksos rulers bring eastern influence to Egypt.

1567–1085 B.C.   Egypt: "new kingdom"; changes and period of greatness in Egyptian art; rulers: Amosis, Tuthmosis, Hatshepsut, Akhenaton, Tutankhamen; Rameses I–XI.

1085–341 B.C.   Egypt: late dynastic period; last flourish of Egyptian art; Assyrians, Persians invade, control Egypt temporarily.

900 B.C.   Assyrian power at its height.

332–30 B.C.   Egypt: Invasion by and rule by Greeks under Alexander the Great. Rulers: the Ptolemies, Cleopatra.

CHAPTER 1

THE IMPULSE TO ART

Valuing Life; Valuing Beauty

 The study of the humanities is a study of values, beginning with the special value of life and its concomitant, beauty. The humanities predate our own species, _Homo sapiens sapiens_, which is no more than 50,000 years old. The oldest example of human handiwork, an architectural foundation of rocks shaped into a circle, was created 2 million years ago in Africa. The Terra Amata structure, 400,000 years old (Figure 1-1), reveals a high regard for symmetry, balance, and grace. Such shelters may still be in use somewhere today. Terra Amata was found during excavations for apartments on the Riviera, in Nice, France.

Neanderthals (_Homo sapiens neandertalensis_) seem to have been capable of an emotional life similar to ours. A carefully prepared burial site discovered in Iraq at the mouth of a cave demonstrates their capacity to grieve and probably to hope. The "Shanidar man" of approximately 40,000 B.C.—almost certainly a Neanderthal—was buried with an arrange-

ment of Saint Barnaby's thistle, cornflowers, and other medicinal plants; it is believed that this "flower burial" indicates the value of this man's life and the hope that the magic or medicinal qualities of the plants would ease him in death. That hope would

Figure 1-1
Reconstruction of Terra Amata shelter. (From Richard Leakey. _Origins._ London: Macdonald and Jane's, 1977. P. 129. By permission of Rainbird Publishing Group.)

imply a belief in an afterlife, which is important in most religions. The flower arrangement also suggests that the mourners valued balance and order—and that, in turn, implies a concern for art, which excites feeling. The humanities have to do with both the education of feeling and the establishment of a system of values.

Those who mourned the "Shanidar man" understood that life was different from death and must also have understood that they, too, would die. Because we are the only creatures who expect death, we have developed a special reverence for life, revealed in the care with which many prehistoric people were buried. Care in burial is also unique to humans, and it seems to have a special power to console the living.

Cornflowers have been found in the tombs of Egyptian pharaohs, and the "Shanidar man" may, like the pharaohs, have been a special figure in his society. Such flowers have long been thought to have special properties which ease the journey into death. The fact that the Neanderthals had a funeral ritual tells us that they must have already developed a system of communication to preserve it. Recent studies of Neanderthal anatomy—it is in some respects identical to that of newborn *Homo sapiens sapiens*—suggest that the Neanderthals may not have been able to speak as we do. (If this is true, we can understand why the Neanderthals, whose brain was as large as our own, disappeared 30,000 years ago.) However, ochre pencils have been found at Terra Amata, and it is possible that the Neanderthals had a form of visual arts to aid in communication.

If the Neanderthals had a sense of magic, they may also have had some form of religion. This view is supported by the care that is evident in the Shanidar burial. And if they had a religion, then it is also possible that they had music, dance, and other arts; in fact, dance is common in hunting-and-gathering societies. We have little evidence, beyond structures and occasional burial sites, of Neanderthal art; but that would be understandable if their creativity went mostly into dance and music.

The First Sculpture: Ice Age Mysteries

The earliest visual arts, the cave paintings, teem with animal life; the earliest preserved sculpture is a mixture of human and animal forms. We know nothing of the purposes or impulses behind the creation of these works. The earliest forms of art, then, present us with an extraordinary and tantalizing mystery—and it is reasonable to suppose that if we gain more insight into the values revealed by these works, we will learn more about the human condition.

The "Venus" of Willendorf (Figure 1-2), found in Austria in 1908, is one of many similar limestone carvings dating from approximately 30,000 years ago. The "Brno man" (Figure 1-3), found in Czechoslovakia, dates from the same period. These figures are very different in appearance and seem to have played different roles in society. Another difference is that "Venus" figures have been found in France, the Ukraine, Austria, Czechoslovakia, and the Urals; but the "Brno man" is unique.

The widespread dissemination of the "Venuses" suggests that they may be relics of a cult; the impressive distortions that emphasize their sexuality, and by implication their fruitfulness, imply that it may have been a fertility cult. These small carvings have been found near the hearths of homes, reinforcing the possiblity that their function was religious. Statuettes of household deities have been found in the same locations in later cultures, such as the Greek and Roman. The "Venuses" all have distorted, enlarged breasts and buttocks, a faceless head bent forward, and footless legs; and all of them are small. Some anthropologists consider these to be ideal forms for women, and have suggested that some women actually assumed this "ideal" shape, making themselves pure sex objects and thus very limited members of society. Others consider the "Venuses" symbolic forms designed to appeal to the gods (or other

Figure 1-2
Opposite page, near right: "Venus" of Willendorf. (By permission of the Naturhistorisches Museum Wein; photo, Mazonowicz/Art Resource.)

Figure 1-3
Opposite page, far right: The "Brno man." (Moravske Muzeum, Brno, Czechoslovakia.)

Ice Age Sculpture

1. One of the sculptures in Figures 1-2 and 1-3 is female; the other is male. Are their sexual differences disguised? Are they emphasized?

2. Which of these sculptures might be a portrait? What qualities of the figure contribute to portraiture? What qualities do not?

3. The capacity of art to excite feeling is fundamental. We cannot know what feelings were excited in the creators or original owners of these figures, but it is possible to understand our own feelings. Describe your emotional reactions to each work.

4. Distortion is an enduring device for achieving emphasis and expression in art. What are the most obvious distortions in these works? What guesses can you make about their purposes?

controlling forces) and thus to ensure plenty. Still others believe that the figures are representations of a female deity—an "earth mother"— or a female ruler in a matriarchal society.

The "Brno man" shows less distortion, which may well imply that it was a less powerful figure or had a nonreligious function. It has not been taken to be a portrait; but recently some individualized figures have been found in France, wearing distinctive clothing, and all suggesting portraiture. Some of these figures are dancing; some, possibly, are praying. There is no question that representative art was technically possible for ice age sculptors. The ability to represent the world—not only in three dimensions, as in sculpture, but also in two dimensions in painting—is an important human achievement, and it is critical to our understanding of the humanities and the impulses to art, which are unique to human beings.

The threatening appearance of the "Brno man" is in large part due to the weathering of the ivory. Yet it implies a kind of terror that, for us, is not implied by the "Venus." The "Brno man" is more angular, sharper; its flatness is not as reassuring as the bulbous distortion of the "Venus." Both figures command a kind of respect—perhaps awe—although neither would strike us as an ideal masculine or feminine form. What their effect was when they were created is a mystery. But the artists who made them carved skillfully and respected symmetry, balance, and other formal values. As representations of the male and female figure, these works are clear, exact, and impressive. The sculptors were producing objects of artistic value and possibly religious or political value.

The First Painting: The Mysteries of the Caves

The most exciting discoveries of prehistoric art were made in the nineteenth century, when the great caves of Altamira in Spain and Font-de-Gaume and Niaux in France were explored. At first, in the 1880s, the paintings found in these caves were thought to be modern fakes. Eventually, however, in other caves, paintings were found that had been covered with natural deposits thousands of years old. By 1901, Abbé Breuil, the most patient student of the caves, had convinced archaeologists and art historians that the works were genuine.

The paintings are preserved in limestone caves. The most famous, Lascaux (Figure 1-4), was discovered in 1940; so far 110 caves have been found throughout Europe. Abbé Breuil, in his monumental study of the caves, asserted that they span 400 centuries. The current estimate is that cave painting lasted from 20,000 B.C. to 10,000 B.C.; this implies that the culture which produced them was relatively stable for a period of 100 centuries. The artistic style of the paintings was also stable, although it shows some distinct developments. The subject matter of the cave paintings is almost entirely animals; there are very few representations of humans, and these are usually rudimentary stick figures or hands. The hands are most often painted negatively: a hand has been placed against the wall and color blown around it through a bone tube. Some hands are missing a knuckle or finger, as if through ritual amputation. These may be the hands of important persons, or they may simply be "marks" of individuals.

The artists who painted the caves had immense skill. They concentrated on bison, oxen, horses, ibex, and elk, painting sometimes with a brush, sometimes using hollow bones through which they blew ground-up colors. They set a formidable standard of accuracy of observation and representation. Most of the paintings are far from the entrance to the caves; this means that they were created and viewed in artificial light. One theory is that the artists must have had fine visual memories; another is that they actually hauled dead animals into the caves to draw them; a third is that they sketched outdoors and painted the caves later. The artists built scaffolds to paint on. They ground natural oxides and pigments into a considerable supply of ochres, browns, blacks, and reds. Their blowing tubes and a few of their small lamps have been found.

The entrances to the caves appear to have been, in some cases, inhabited; but the deeper areas, where the most impressive paintings are, were never lived in. This means that the paintings were not created to decorate a living space; and if their value was not decorative, it may have been religious.

Because nobody lived in the caves (some sketches show huts in which the people who used the caves actually lived), it has been suggested that the caves, like our churches, were holy places. The paintings have been interpreted as talismans, a means of gaining magical control over the animals on which the culture depended. However, reindeer, on which

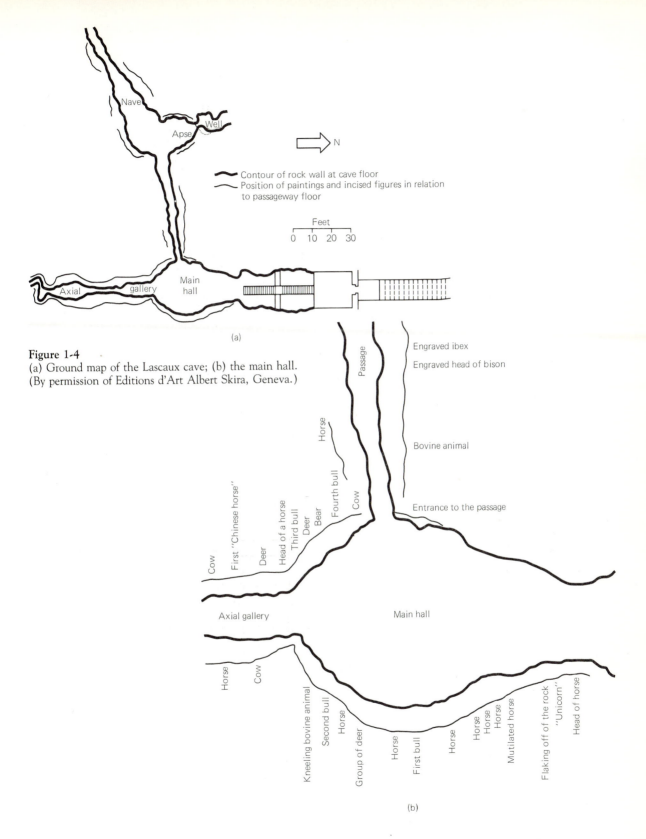

Figure 1-4
(a) Ground map of the Lascaux cave; (b) the main hall.
(By permission of Editions d'Art Albert Skira, Geneva.)

Figure 1-5
Latticework signs. (From Annette Laming. *Lascaux.* Harmondsworth, England: Penguin, 1959.)

the culture depended for food and materials, do not figure in the most important cave paintings. Could it have been that magic was reserved for scarcer animals, those which were not readily available? The evidence that the caves were sanctuaries or temples in which rituals were conducted includes the fact that the footprints which have occasionally been preserved in them are almost always those of young children; this implies that the caves were used for initiation rites.

Lascaux was discovered by four boys on September 12, 1940, when their dog fell into a brush-covered hole that had been left by a falling piece of limestone. This is now the entrance to the cave, although it may not have been during the ice age. After the war, Lascaux became a tourist attraction, but the humidity the tourists produced by breathing was so damaging to the paintings that it has now been closed. The conditions which preserved the paintings were ideal; today, however, the paintings could perish.

The ground plan of Lascaux (Figure 1-4) shows several "galleries" in which certain animals are dominant. Some of the figures in the "great hall of the bulls" (in the first bulge after the entrance) are 18 feet long; many are painted over earlier paintings. The latticework signs in Figure 1-5 may have been a kind of writing; other signs like them suggest that they had a communicative function. The vitality in the representations throughout Lascaux and in certain other caves is dazzling. Some of the figures seem to have a life of their own.

THEORIES OF THE CAVES: MAGIC, FERTILITY, AND SEX

The Caves and Magic

Theories of what the caves and their paintings mean are numerous, and certain of them have important points in common. The most persistent view is that the paintings were magical aids in hunting. All the animals shown were used as food, and many were also sources of hides and clothing, as ancient needles indicate. These people may have built their culture around the animals that supported them, as Amerindians did with the bison. The fact that the cave painters could evolve a highly developed art and practice it over an immense stretch of time tells us that the supply of food was plentiful, so that people did not need to move about and hunt all the time. They could return to or become established in a locality where nature provided them with what they needed. It may even be that Lascaux and Altamira are places in which people honored the animals who supported them so generously.

The absence of human figures supports the theory

that the representations of animals are hunting magic. Figure 1-6 shows one of the few humans in Lascaux, the "dead man." He is a bird-headed stick figure, and there is a bird-headed staff near him. He may have been killed in a hunt: the painting shows a disemboweled bison, mortally wounded, which appears to have thrown the man to the ground. If this interpretation is reasonable, then we are looking at a visual narrative, not just a representation of a figure. There is evidence that this was a late addition to the walls; and it may be a schematic message—its artistic authority is not of the same order as the representation of the cows and horse in Figure 1-7. The rhinoceros next to the "dead man" is in a still later style and appears to have been added at another time.

The schematic, clumsy rendition of the "dead man" suggests that there may be no magic in this representation; it may be simply a record of an event.

The Caves: A Sexual Theory

The most impressive new theory is that the animal representations in many of the caves constitute a symbolic language. French scholars have found that the animals fall into groups: some walls are dominated by oxen and some by horses; some caves emphasize groups of ibex, bison, and horses. Professor André Leroi-Gourhan points out that in the central locations of the caves, horses appear in almost 200 compositions. Bison dominate almost 150; oxen

Figure 1-6
The "dead man." Detail from the shaft in Lascaux. (© Arch. Phot./SPADEM/VAGA, New York; photo, SEF/Art Resource.)

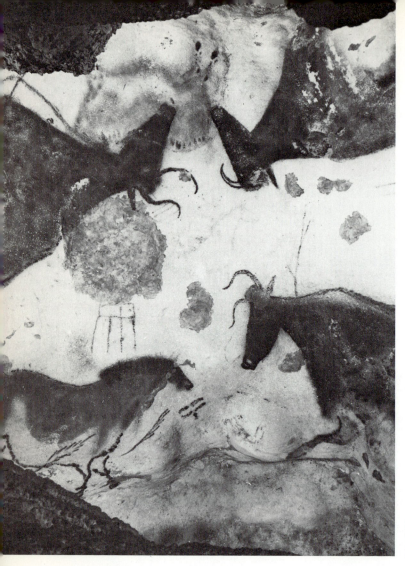

Figure 1-7
Three cows and a horse, from the "painted gallery,"
Lascaux. (© Arch. Phot./SPADEM/VAGA, New York.)

dominate 50. Leroi-Gourhan's theory is that the bison and ox are female symbols and the horse is a male symbol.

Widely separated caves share a similar vocabulary of signs, which may allow us to see the caves as temples where the mysteries of sexuality were celebrated in terms of animals—a practice that has been widespread in many cultures. The caves can then be understood as sanctuaries for sexual initiations such as those associated with puberty. The importance of the caves in their culture would be comparable to the importance of temples to the Greeks and Romans and of churches and schools in our own culture.

Leroi-Gourhan's theories are as yet untested, but they show extraordinary promise. The celebration of sexuality—which is essentially the celebration of life, its creation, and the abundance of nature—offers us an instructive starting point for the development of the institutions of culture. The art of the caves reveals a profound respect for the sources of cultural support, and a high regard for artistic skills devoted to the service of humanity and the forces of nature.

Painting of the Caves

1. Individual paintings of animals (such as those shown in Figure 1-7) show a high regard for balance and rhythm of line. We sense not only that each animal is well represented, but that the artist has tried to make its appearance pleasing to the eye. Which of the paintings shown here is most pleasing to your eye? Do you feel that it would also have been pleasing to its original viewers?

2. The "great hall of the bulls" seems to have a rudimentary "procession" of bulls, but that may be our imagination. Do you perceive a sense of composition or special relationship of separate elements in these paintings? What helps you decide one way or the other?

3. If these paintings are sexual in their content, how does their formal treatment contribute to this? Are any of these figures especially sexual? Do any suggest pregnancy or virility? Is sexual content perceptible in these works?

4. To what extent do line, shading, and composition create an illusion of reality? Is a sense of three dimensions achieved in any of these works? Do you think that three-dimensionality would enhance the magical qualities of the work?

Decoration: Ancient Rock Painting

AFRICAN ROCK PAINTING

The widespread rock painting on the African continent, dating from perhaps 900 years ago, is by no means close in time to the sculpture and painting of the ice age, but it was produced by people whose ways were close to those of the cave people. (Abbé Breuil, who studied the caves so painstakingly, also studied African rock painting from many of the thousands of identified sites.)

In some places it seems as if a rock simply demanded to be decorated with a complex design. Many of the works are representational, although usually not as finely detailed as any of the cave work. Most are schematic in the sense that the "dead man" of Lascaux is; and this may mean that the works are symbols or magic signs.

The painting found near Tizi-n'Tirlist in Algeria (Figure 1-8) may be a representation of a man and woman. It is not a standard rock painting, but neither is it an isolated example. The figures are rhythmically related to one another in what appears to be a clear sense of a composition of two separate elements, perhaps hinting at a narrative. The lines are exuberant, vital, and spontaneous. If we were not told otherwise, we might think of these works as modern. Yet their tradition is ancient. Some rock carvings by the Tassili people of the Sahara apparently refer to a time when the desert was covered with vegetation, some 60,000 years ago.

Figure 1-8
Stylized human figures from Tizi-n'Tirlist, Algeria. (From P. M. Grand. *Prehistoric Art.* New York Graphic Society, 1967. P. 51.)

AMERINDIAN ROCK PAINTING: DIGHTON ROCK

Because the Amerindians came to North America only about 15,000 years ago, the tradition in the southwest cannot be as old as that in Africa, where life existed much earlier. Even so, modern Indians have no idea who made their rock paintings, or why. Dighton Rock (Figure 1-9), found in Berkeley, Mas-

sachusetts, in 1680, was copied by John Winthrop, governor of Massachusetts. Its purpose and origin are obscure. It may be a narrative of a single event, or perhaps of several events, or it may simply be a complex record of individual moments—and could be none of these. Its lines are vigorous and sure and cover all the available space. (In the caves, by contrast, there are many spaces left unpainted, although some spaces have been painted over several times.)

Amerindians did not decorate only rocks. They also decorated their tools, their basketware, their pottery, their clothes, their houses, and their bodies. Before them, the Neanderthals even decorated their dead. The impulse to decorate is an impulse to please the senses—in these cases the senses of sight and touch. Ice age artists had a passion for decoration. They decorated throwing sticks, tools, and flints in a way that took considerable skill and time.

Decoration is sometimes thought to be less important than independent works of art; the reasoning is that art reveals values but decoration does not. It is true that art can, through form, interpret a subject and produce significant content, whereas decoration simply *is*. And it is also true that some societies developed decoration to a high degree as a way of avoiding representation in art, thus avoiding any implied magical powers of represented figures. But it must be remembered that decoration is a symptom of

Figure 1-9
Dighton Rock, Berkeley, Massachusetts. From the copy by James Winthrop. (Walker Art Center. *American Indian Art.* New York: Dutton, 1972. P. 27.)

Prehistoric Art

1. Which of the works shown in Figures 1-8 and 1-9 is most likely to have been done by a professional, full-time artist?

2. Do you agree with others concerning which of the works shown in Figures 1-1 to 1-3 and 1-5 to 1-9 is more perceptibly modern?

3. How important is representation to these artists? What does representation seem to imply to them?

4. What is the range of subject matter apparent in these works? Which works do you feel most confident about in terms of establishing content? Which have the clearest content? Which seem most decorative?

5. Distortion is fundamental to these works. What does distortion achieve in the most distorted works? What does it achieve in the least distorted works? How does distortion contribute to emphasis? How does it contribute to our own emotional responses?

value. It usually reveals—through rhythm, harmony, balance, symmetry, and vigor—a passion for organization and beauty of the kind which appealed to the people who buried the "Shanidar man." It still appeals to people the world over today.

Summary

In the treatment of the dead, we see some of the first evidence of the development of human feelings, and thus of the humanities themselves. In the concern for life and the concern for art, we see the first flowering of humanistic values. Our own species, which may once have shared the earth with its predecessors, the Cro-Magnons and Neanderthals, was not the first to feel the stirrings and perceptions that separate us from the rest of nature. Through the capacity for abstraction, creating visual signs that represent a three-dimensional, living world, humans made a leap forward—and the significance of that leap should not be underestimated. The magical emblems of the great caves, and possibly the signs of the African and Amerindian painters, may demonstrate the beginnings of religious systems. In the work of the great rock painters, we see a passion for decoration that persists, as does the passion for representative art, to the present day, linking us inexorably with our forebears. Our sense of humanity is linked to theirs and revealed to us in the values which we share with them.

Concepts in Chapter 1

The study of the humanities is a study of values.

The arts reveal values through formal interpretation of subject matter.

Prehistoric art may have had a magical function.

Prehistoric cave painting has been interpreted as having a sexual meaning.

The painting of the caves may have had a ritual function.

Distortion is one of the basic means of achieving emphasis and expressing feeling in art.

Decoration is a basic cultural impulse.

Suggested Readings

Grand, P. M. *Prehistoric Art.* Greenwich, Conn.: New York Graphic Society, 1967.

Grant, Campbell. *Rock Art of the American Indians.* New York: Promontory, 1967.

Haberland, Wolfgang. *The Art of North America.* New York: Crown, 1964.

Laming, Annette. *Lascaux.* Harmondsworth, England: Penguin, 1959.

Leakey, Richard, and Roger Lewin. *Origins.* London: Macdonald and Jane's, 1977.

National Geographic Magazine. Washington, D.C. *National Geographic* has up-to-date information about recent finds and the progress of current research on early humans.

Powell, Ann. *The Origins of Western Art.* New York: Harcourt Brace Jovanovich, 1973.

Sandars, N. K. *Prehistoric Art in Europe.* Harmondsworth, England: Penguin, 1968.

Torbrugge, Walter. *Prehistoric European Art.* New York: Abrams, 1968.

CHAPTER 2

PYRAMID BUILDERS

The Value of Community

 The change to an agricultural society permitted the growth of large communities based in a single locale and independent of the migrations of animal herds. In the middle stone age, between 7000 B.C. and 6000 B.C., people had learned how to cultivate dependable crops and how to store grain from season to season so that they would not have to fear a bad harvest. Storing grain was like storing wealth. The first cities, like Jericho, protected their wealth with walls. Cities became independent states—there were farmers, laborers, architects, artists, priests, and other specialists.

Çatal Huyuk: Agricultural Myths

Çatal Huyuk (Figure 2-1), which was discovered in Turkey in the 1960s, is the earliest city that has yet been explored.

We do not know who the neolithic people who built Çatal Huyuk were, but we do know that their city dates from 6500 B.C. and was erected on a commanding plain. The houses abut one another in

Figure 2-1
Shrine in Çatal Huyuk. (From Lloyd Seton et al. *Ancient Architecture: Mesopotamia, Egypt, Crete, Greece.* New York: Abrams, 1972. By permission of Electa Editrice, Milan.)

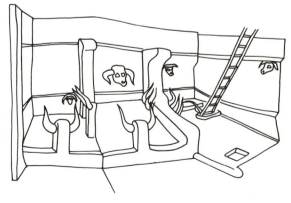

the manner of Amerindian pueblos, which permitted easy growth by means of additions. They were useful for defense as well, since anyone who penetrated an outer house still had to struggle to penetrate deeper into the city. Religion played an important part in the lives of those who lived there; each house contains a small shrine, and larger shrines or temples are spread throughout the city. Many of the walls are painted with red bulls, stags, or cattle, and the horns of the cattle are very prominent. Like many who lived before and after them, the people of Çatal Huyuk attached a special significance to the power of certain animals.

A mother goddess also seems to have been part of their religion. She appears in plaster wall reliefs as well as in small sculptures, and her features are well defined and realistic. She merges the forces of life and death: her body is round and suggestive of fecundity, but her nipples sometimes conceal the beaks of vultures, used for tearing flesh. The conjunction of life and death is also seen in the burying of the bones of ancestors in crypts within the house. This may have been a form of ancestor worship, and possibly it inspired the people in Jericho, who sometimes kept skulls on which the features were modeled in plaster.

Myths centering on rebirth were common in the earliest agricultural communities; they were probably inspired by the fact that crops are reborn each year and the sun is reborn each day. Thammus, Adonis, Attis, and the Egyptian Osiris are solar gods—gods of the sun. But Osiris is also a corn god, and gods with roots both in solar myths and in corn myths had extra power and influence. In Central America, Quetzalcoatl was such a god. Rebirth, particularly when related to crops and to the sun, is still the basis of some of our most powerful metaphors.

Ur

ARCHITECTURAL BEGINNINGS AT UR: THE ZIGGURAT TO THE HEAVENS

Temple building was widespread among ancient people. Amerindians built burial mounds that resemble the Egyptian ben-ben, the mound from which, in myth, the first Egyptian god rose, thus inspiring the pyramids of the great dynasties. Mayan temples were built high, to lift their priests toward the gods. When Nimrod built the tower of Babel, he was thought to be challenging god. Such structures reflected both ambition and arrogance.

The story of the tower of Babel is told in the Old Testament (Genesis: 11).

> Now the whole earth had one language and few words. And as men migrated in the east, they found a plain in the land of Shinar and settled there. And they said to one another, "Come, let us make bricks, and burn them thoroughly." And they had brick for stone, and bitumen for mortar. Then they said, "Come, let us build ourselves a city, and a tower with its top in the heavens, and let us make a name for ourselves, lest we be scattered abroad upon the face of the whole earth." And the Lord came down to see the city and the tower, which the sons of men had built. And the Lord said, "Behold, they are one people, and they have all one language; and this is only the beginning of what they will do; and nothing that they propose to do will now be impossible for them. Come, let us go down, and there confuse their language, that they may not understand one another's speech." So the Lord scattered them abroad from there over the face of all the earth, and they left off building the city. Therefore its name was called Babel, because there the Lord confused the language of all the earth; and from there the Lord scattered them abroad over the face of all the earth.

The biblical reference may be to the tower of Marduk in Babylon, built about 550 B.C. But such structures existed even earlier; the ziggurat at Ur (Figure 2-2), near the Persian Gulf, dates from 2100 B.C. Ur is in southern Mesopotamia (literally, "land between the waters") in the area between the Tigris and Euphrates rivers. The ziggurat at Ur must have inspired great pride and confidence, not only among the citizens of the community but also among visitors. It is a massive structure, like a brick mountain. Its lines are severe and unsoftened by curves or rounded edges; the three stairways were designed almost like a stage set to carry brilliant ceremonial groups to the central temple on the structure's topmost surface. The subject matter of the building is power expressed through massive brickwork, formidable columns set in relief, a reliance on simple geometric patterns, an absence of openings on the huge tapered surfaces, and a scale that dwarfs the individual. One can imagine that the ziggurats were designed to impress those who saw them.

Even today, standing before the pyramids is a humbling experience; but in 2100 B.C. standing

Figure 2-2
Reconstruction of the ziggurat at Ur. (Photo, Hirmer
Fotoarchiv München.)

before such a building as a ziggurat, designed to be used for ceremonial purposes as well as to be seen, must have been overwhelming. This architecture has a psychological and dramatic impact; its purpose is to affect its audience, whether that audience be citizens or gods. The ceremonies performed there reach heavenward.

Such architecture expressed the will of the king and of the state. It was designed to remind the people of the values of the state and to convince them of the inevitability of the social order in which they lived. The evidence indicates that the Mesopotamian states had a rigid social order, a powerful class system, and a proliferation of specialists.

RELIEF SCULPTURE: THE CEREMONIAL HUNT AT UR

When hunting was no longer a necessity, it became a ceremony. The great wall reliefs (see Figure 2-3) from the palace of Ashurbanipal, the Assyrian king whose armies plundered Egypt and subdued Babylon in the seventh century B.C., are highly professional works narrating a lion hunt, which was a symbolic expression of the power of the king. However, lions were by this time virtually extinct in Assyria; in the reliefs they emerge from cages, indicating that they had

been captured and brought some distance at the will of the king to be submitted to his spear.

The composition of the reliefs demonstrates a highly articulated concept of narrative and of the relationship between design elements. The powerful lions are expertly and realistically rendered, and the human figures show a great attention to detail. They are uniformly stylized; the king is portrayed wearing a regal helmet and clothing. The figures are carefully related to one another through the use of expressive repetition and lines with similar rhythms, as in the textural details of the lions' manes and the men's beards. Most of the figures are shown in profile, and there is little or no effort to portray distance through the use of perspective.

Both the ziggurat and the relief sculpture are expressions of power and control: on the one hand over the earth and the technical problems of building, and on the other hand over the animal world. The king of the human community easily subdues the king of beasts. Neither work is explicitly tender in emotional expression, a quality that some people expect in art today. But ferocity is a human expression as well, and the values expressed by these works are connected with pride, strength, victory, and power. These qualities made the Assyrians' ascendancy possible.

Figure 2-3
Reliefs from the palace of
Ashurbanipal. (By permission
of the trustees of the British
Museum.)

The details of the ziggurat are calculated to intensify its massiveness and strength. Decorative elements would have softened the lines of the building —which are long, straight, and unyielding and create a sense of inevitability—and would have produced quite a different effect. The line of the figures on the relief sculpture also reinforce the idea of inevitability: they are clear, precise, and exact, particularly in repeated forms and representations. Such inevitability reinforces the power of the monarch and the absolute authority of the government. Human control over the environment is expressed in the artists' ability to work with intractable materials such as baked brick and alabaster walls.

Ur

designus. decoration

1. What decorative elements are used on the ziggurat (Figure 2-2)? How important is decoration to this structure?

2. What formal elements of the ziggurat are most important in eliciting emotional responses on the part of the viewer? What are the most prominent geometric forms? What do you think the desired emotional responses are?

3. What function might a ritual hunt have served in a culture which did not rely upon hunting for its food and clothing? Would the existence of the wall reliefs have served that function?

4. In the ziggurat and the reliefs (Figure 2-3), how important are the formal qualities of symmetry, balance, strength of line, rhythm of line and form (particularly in *strength* repeated passages), accuracy of representation, centrality, and interrelationships of compositional elements?

5. What kinds of values are portrayed in the ziggurat? In the reliefs?

Egypt: The Traditions of Power

Egypt was an important center of civilization from the Thinite dynasty, of 3100 B.C., to the period of Cleopatra, around 30 B.C. As in other cultures, there is evidence of stone age sculpture, and unusually refined designs appear on predynastic pottery. Egypt grew independently of Assyria and other Mesopotamian civilizations into the largest and most complex civilization of early times.

EGYPTIAN ARCHITECTURE

Saqqara: The Genius of Imhotep

The step pyramid at Saqqara, c. 2600 B.C., stands as Egypt's most impressive early cultural achievement. Imhotep is credited with being the first architect to build with stone. Certain details in the Saqqara complex reveal that the models he depended upon, now lost to us, were made of mud brick and wood. If

this is true, Imhotep's genius, which must be likened to that of the more modern Leonardo da Vinci, is all the greater. The use of small stones in the walls of Saqqara suggests an imitation of mud brick, and carved supports in the shape of logs and papyrus designs in columns attached to the walls indicate that Imhotep was following earlier designs, probably those of King Zoser's complex in Memphis, which was built of mud and wood.

The complex at Saqqara (Figure 2-4) represents a permanent monument to Zoser. It was discovered in the 1920s, and efforts have been made to find Imhotep's tomb, which may be nearby. His symbol was the ibis, a common Nile bird, and thousands of mummified ibises have been found. Imhotep was remembered for millennia: he was deified 2000 years after his death.

Lauer's model (Figure 2-5) reveals an intricate and massive construction. The complex was a necropolis —a city for the dead. The outer walls, which have one real entrance and several false ones, measured 1000 by 1700 feet, encompassing almost 40 acres.

Figure 2-4
Step pyramid complex with modern reconstruction. (Photo, Hirmer Fotoarchiv München.)

The pyramid, which is 204 feet high, began as a small square structure. Imhotep's designs changed several times, however, which reveals something of the evolution of pyramids, especially as this seems to have been the first one ever made. It was built by free workers, not slaves. They took pride in their work and left their marks on the stones they installed. Employed in the "off season," while the Nile irrigated the fields, they were given housing and were paid with food.

The pyramid began as a mound resembling earlier tombs called "mastabas," meaning "benches," since the tombs looked like conventional Egyptian benches. At some point Imhotep decided on an oblong shape and placed a second mastaba on the first one, then he repeated the process until he reached the

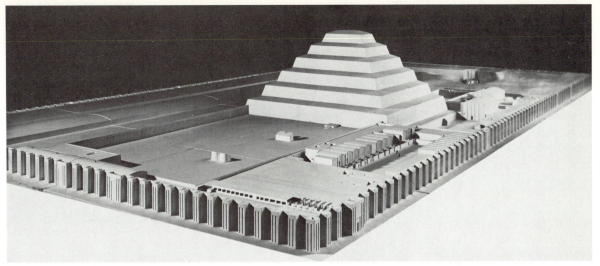

Figure 2-5
Model of Saqqara. (Reconstruction by and photo courtesy of Jean-Philippe Lauer.)

2,600 B.C.

present number of six. The workers were obviously greatly skilled in working with stone. The exterior joints are carefully fashioned, and the columns on the outer walls are delicately treated, suggesting a skill that had been thought to have developed only much later.

Saqqara: Religious Purposes

The complex at Saqqara was used as more than a city of the dead. The Egyptians assumed that the king or pharaoh was a god and that his spirit was in their care. Complex religious ceremonies involving many arts, including music and dance, were performed at Saqqara. Part of the purpose of the complex was to preserve the remains of the king. The Egyptians believed that there were two spiritual qualities of great importance: the ka and the ba. "Ka" is untranslatable; Zoser is said to have possessed a ka and to have returned to it when he died. Perhaps it is a concept something like our concept of the soul. Ba is like our concept of spirit. Because the ka was perishable, an exact likeness of the king was prepared for the ka in which it could continue its existence. One purpose of vandalism may have been to destroy the

statues so as to harm the spiritual life of the dead king.

The splendor of Saqqara helped guarantee the perpetuation of Zoser's ka. It lasted in good condition into the "new kingdom," 2000 years after it was built. Zoser was buried in a series of deeply dug chambers beneath the pyramid. They have been raided and plundered; much remains, however, including a mummified foot that may have been Zoser's. Texts which survive on the walls reveal that writing was highly developed at the time.

The heb-sed, an elaborate and detailed ceremony of ritual renewal, was performed at Saqqara. As part of the ceremony, the king demonstrated his vigor by running around the outside perimeter of the walls. It was believed that the successful completion of this feat would guarantee Zoser another thirty years of reign. Zoser planned carefully for this celebration, although he did not fear that he would be killed if he failed. The ceremony had by this time replaced the actual event, making the death of the king unnecessary. It is not surprising that the Egyptians took ceremonies of such importance seriously. They had a zeal for gigantic demonstrations in which there was dancing and music, played on horns, harps, and percussion instruments, such as sistrums, which jingled when they were shaken. Like Mesopotamian architecture, Egyptian ceremonies were designed to be impressive.

The concept of the Egyptian pyramid seems to have derived from the early creation myths told at Memphis. Creation derived from Nun, the waters of chaos; Ra, the sun god, created a ben-ben, or mound, on which to stand. On it rose the phoenix, a symbol of rebirth. There seems to be a natural progression from the ben-ben, to the mastaba, and then to the pyramid.

EGYPTIAN RELIGION: VALUING THE WORLD AFTER DEATH

The ennead of Heliopolis, the nine gods of the Egyptian town of On (it was renamed Heliopolis by the Greeks), constituted the Egyptian pantheon. Ra, the sun god, was foremost. He had several manifestations; among them were Atum, "one who creates," and Khepri, "one who brings into being." Ra-Atum-Khepri created himself from Nun, the waters of chaos, and formed the first ben-ben so that he would have something to stand on. From his own semen he begot Shu, god of the air, and Tefnut, goddess of moisture. They begot Geb, god of the earth, and Nut, goddess of the sky, who in turn begot Osiris, Isis, Set, and Nephthys. (Amen-Ra, Isis, Osiris, and Set are pictured in Figure 2-6.)

Ra's manifestations related to sunlight; he appeared as Atum in the morning sun; as Ra at high noon, and as Khepri thereafter. Conflicting claims for creation did not disturb the Egyptians. Memphite kings, for example, accepted the claim that Ptah had

created the ennead "by conceiving with his mind and uttering with his tongue," which suggests a creation by the word. The New Testament also emphasizes the concept of logos, "the word," and creation by the word. The myths about the gods are told on the walls of the pyramids. They are called "pyramid texts," and they contain many conflicting stories, which the Egyptians accepted without difficulty.

The Myth of Osiris

One myth of the ennead concerns dissension among the gods, but in terms of rebirth, it points toward hope for humankind. Isis and Osiris were married, and Nut, the sky goddess, proclaimed Osiris king of upper and lower Egypt. His jealous brother, Set, decided to kill him and fashioned a beautiful box designed to fit him perfectly. Osiris, who had been off bringing agriculture and civilization to his people, returned to a celebration. Set invited everyone to lie in the box, which he promised to give to whomever it fit. When Osiris got in, Set clamped the box shut and threw it into the Nile. Isis later found Osiris's body washed up at Byblos, in ancient Phoenicia, and brought it back to Egypt, where she hid it for proper burial. But Set accidentally found the body while he was hunting and tore it into fourteen pieces, which he threw far and wide over the kingdom. The Nile fish oxyrhynchus devoured the phallus.

Isis recovered all the pieces, preserved them, and fitted them together, except for the phallus, which she replaced with a model. Then she breathed life into Osiris; in some versions, she was made pregnant by him. Because he could not reign on earth, Osiris was made god of the underworld. Set had taken his

Figure 2-6
Amen-Ra; Isis; Osiris; Set.

throne and had imprisoned Isis for embalming Osiris, since this would make him immortal. Ra had overseen all these events; he had helped Isis embalm Osiris and had encouraged her when she covered Osiris with her wings to breathe life into him.

Isis gave birth to Horus. Set, in the form of a serpent, discovered Horus as an infant in a reed hiding place. Horus (Figure 2-7) was poisoned by Set, but he was cured through a spell cast by Ra and through the help of Thoth, god of wisdom. Horus eventually avenged his father's death and defeated Set; Set did not die, however, but became a power of evil like the more modern Satan.

The story is preserved in verses such as the following:

> O Osiris, stand up, see that which your son has done for you! Awake, hear that which Horus has done for you!
> He has caused Thoth to turn back for you the Followers of Set, and that he brings them to you all together.
> Thoth has seized your enemy for you, so that he is beheaded together with his followers; there is not one whom he has spared!
> He has beaten for you him who beats you. He has killed for you him who kills you, like a wild bull. He had bound for you him who binds you.
> . . . .
> Osiris has come forth this day at the head of the full flood. Osiris is the crocodile with the flourishing green plume, with head erect, his breast lifted, the foaming one who had come from the thigh of the Great Tail which is in the gleaming heavens.
> . . . .
> Osiris makes green and fertile the fields in both lands of the horizon. Osiris has brought the gleam to the Great Eye in the midst of the field.

The imagery of the crocodile links Osiris with the flooding Nile and the rebirth of the fields. The annual recurrence of agricultural changes must have been celebrated at Saqqara, which was built on a prominent site that erupts from the land like a natural outgrowth. Its design is similar to that of the ziggurat at Ur, but its walls resemble a fortification. The height of the structure places it on a human level, and it functioned less to awe than to protect the spirit of the king and serve as a place in which the ceremonies of the society could be performed.

Figure 2-7
The hawk god Horus with a figure of King Nectanebos. (Metropolitan Museum of Art, Rogers Fund, 1934.)

The ruthless way in which Thoth and Horus deal with Osiris's enemies reminds us of the exercise of power in Egyptian society. In the struggle Horus loses an eye; he rips Set's testicles off, for which Ra praises him. The myth was taken very seriously. It was believed that the pharaoh was Horus when he was alive and Osiris when he was dead; the symbols of Osiris—the shepherd's crook and the flail whip—are in all the mummified representations of the pharaoh.

The myth of Osiris inspired literature, music, and drama. Osiris's last resting place was supposed to be Abydos, and each year the festivals at Abydos featured ritual dancing, music, and passion plays. In the plays, the struggles of Horus and Set and the resurrection of Osiris by Isis were reenacted. Isis was celebrated as a divine, protective spirit. Fragments of the

Egyptian Beginnings

1. Does the complex at Saqqara (Figures 2-4 and 2-5) command the same kind of awe and respect as the ziggurat at Ur? Is it as severe in formal design? Does it seem, in Lauer's reconstruction, modern in concept?

2. Is the function of Saqqara as a necropolis revealed in the formal elements of its design? Is its function as a ceremonial center revealed in its formal elements?

3. What values does the myth of Osiris seem to express? What human qualities are the gods portrayed as having?

4. In the verses about Osiris, Thoth is an avenging deity. What qualities does he possess? Is revenge an appropriate religious value?

5. What is the function of the animal imagery in the verses about Osiris? Does this imagery have a connection with the agricultural implications of the last lines?

---

texts of the dramas show that Egypt preceded Greece in producing ritual drama.

The Great Pyramids at Giza: Celebrating Immortality

The pyramids at Giza (Figure 2-8) are the last of the wonders of the ancient world. They were built in the period of the "old kingdom" to preserve the remains of three great kings—Khufu (Cheops), Khafre, and Menkaure—who reigned during the fourth dynasty, from approximately 2613 B.C. to 2494 B.C. According to the classical traveler Herodotus, it took shifts of about 100,000 workers each, replaced every three months and organized in gangs and on different time schedules, ten years to build the causeway leading to the pyramid and twenty years to build the pyramid itself. Khufu's pyramid measures 755 feet on each side and is 481 feet high.

Modern theories discount the view that the pyramids were built with slave labor, and they also discount Herodotus's figures for the work gangs. Today it is estimated that no more than 3000 to 5000 people worked on the pyramids at any one time; and modern workers using ancient copper tools have quarried a typical block and had it ready for moving in an hour. The outer layer of the pyramids was a finely dressed stone which was removed, starting in the thirteenth century after Christ, for use in other buildings.

The Great Pyramid was designed to hold Khufu's preserved remains for eternity. As Figure 2-9 shows, three burial chambers were prepared for Khufu. The lowest, which was never finished, was built first; the middle chamber seems to have been prepared after a change in construction plans. When the final plans were settled on, the upper chamber was chosen as the king's resting place. The horizontal lines in the figure represent huge blocks of stone that apparently were intended to relieve the stress of the mass of stone above the vault. The huge grand gallery has a corbeled roof (a roof in which successive layers of stone are overlapped by several inches until the top layers rest against each other). The shaft leading downward contradicts the old belief that people were buried alive in the pyramid: it was the workers' exit after the tomb was sealed. Huge "plugs" of stone were used to seal all entrances when the work was finished, but they did not prevent robbers from eventually desecrating the tombs.

Figure 2-8
The pyramid complex at Giza.
(Photo, Hirmer Fotoarchiv
München.)

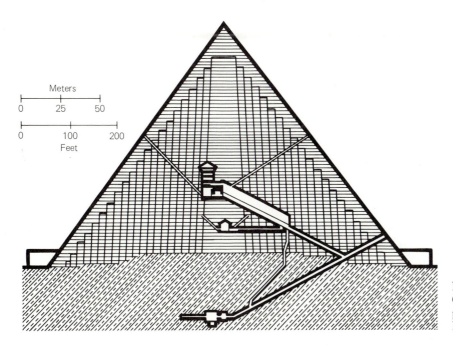

Meters
0   25   50

0   100   200
Feet

Figure 2-9
Cross-section of Khufu's
pyramid. (By permission of
Rainbird Publishing Group.)

The first robberies and destruction of monuments and mummies apparently occurred during the disorders of the first intermediary period, 2181 B.C. to 2133 B.C. There is no accounting for the turmoil of this period. Some historians insist that it represented a new attitude toward human culture and human values. It was definitely a reaction against the absolute rule of the old kings, and it did result in some democratic advances. But it began mysteriously; no outside forces or pressures and no specific leaders seem to have been involved. Some ancients thought that it was a reaction against the building of the pyramids, and one modern scholar thinks that it marked the moment in human evolution at which self-awareness came into existence. In any case, this turmoil marked the end of the period of absolute rule; the pyramids failed to achieve their purpose and were never attempted again.

EGYPTIAN SCULPTURE

The Sphinx: Holder of Mysteries

Built during the construction of the second pyramid, the Sphinx (Figure 2-10) has the body of a crouching lion and the face of King Khafre. It is a mysterious structure whose secrets have never been freed. The Sphinx was buried to its neck in sand during the twentieth dynasty and was cleared away in A.D. 1926, when archaeologists searched in vain for secret passageways. It was significantly damaged (for religious reasons) by an Arab Sufi named Saim-el-Dahr, in the early fifteenth or late fourteenth century after Christ. It is said that Napoleon's army used it for artillery practice, but that has not been verified. Holes in the Sphinx suggest that a decorative crown, or other details, may have been added to it for ceremonies. Other sphinxes, on a much smaller scale, exist; such structures do not seem to be part of burial groups.

The Sphinx had a religious value, but nothing like it is associated with the ka or the ba. Temples were built in front of the Sphinx; apparently these were places of worship used by members of several cults. In the later dynasties the Sphinx was related to the sun god; beyond this, we know very little about it.

The sculpture of King Menkaure (called "Mycerinus" by the Greeks) and his queen (Figure 2-11) was carved from one piece of slate; it was found at Giza. The faces are not disfigured and seem to be remarkable likenesses, showing family resemblances to earlier representations of King Khafre. Menkaure ruled only briefly, and—according to Herodotus—with unusual gentleness toward his people. He died suddenly, and monuments to him were finished hastily, if at all.

Such a sculpture is a welcome relief from the facelessness of the pyramids and the human-animal fusion of the Sphinx. We find ourselves touched by its representation of humanity. However, it is not universally admired as art. Some experts, such as H. A. Groenwegen-Frankfort, believe that it marks a decline in quality:

> It is not the rather charming plainness of the man, his bulbous nose, fleshy cheeks, protruding eyes (which must delight the hunters for realism in Egyptian art), that make these statues unimpressive, even a trifle common; it is the fact that they do not suggest any metaphysical awareness.

Others have suggested that statues of Menkaure, particularly the Boston statue, are devoid of feeling. Some complain because the face that appears on local goddesses portrayed with Menkaure also appears on the portrait of Khammererebty, but this may simply reveal a convention by which the queen was elevated to the status of goddess.

Egyptian Portraits: Spiritual Truths

Because the ka searched after death for a likeness of the body, Egyptian sculpture from the early dynasties attempts accurate representations of individuals. Some of the representations portray expressions and emotions that are familiar to the modern eye. In later ages, the portrait came to be valued for the degree to which it revealed the essence of the sitter. To some extent, the representations of lesser Egyptian figures accomplish this; when we feel that an Egyptian

Figure 2-10
The Sphinx at Giza. (Photo, Egyptian Tourist Authority.)

Sculpture and the Giza Group

1. The pyramids at Giza (Figure 2-8) were designed to house the dead, not the living. Is it appropriate, then, to consider them architecture? Or, because they are mostly solid, should they be thought of as sculpture?

2. If the celebration of an eternal afterlife is part of the subject matter of the pyramids, does their form reveal any insight into that subject matter? What are the principal characteristics of their form?

3. What might be the point of the conjunction in the Sphinx (Figure 2-10) of the body of a lion with the face of King Khafre? What kinds of emotions might be elicited by such a work? What kinds of emotions does the work elicit in you?

4. Do you agree with Groenwegen-Frankfort's assessment of the statue of Menkaure and Khammerernebty (Figure 2-11)? Is the work "a trifle common"? Would it merely "delight the hunters for realism"? Do you think that the sculpture was intended to reveal the character of Menkaure?

5. What seem to be the principal values expressed in these Egyptian works? Do they seem different from the Assyrian works at Ur? Consider social values, such as community pride, religious duty, and community enjoyment, as well as personal values, such as love, respect, religious devotion, and independence of spirit.

Figure 2-11
Pair statue of Mycerinus and his Queen, Khammerernebty II, from Giza. c. 2570 B.C. Slate, 56 ⅞ inches high. (Museum of Fine Arts, Boston, Harvard University-MFA Expedition.)

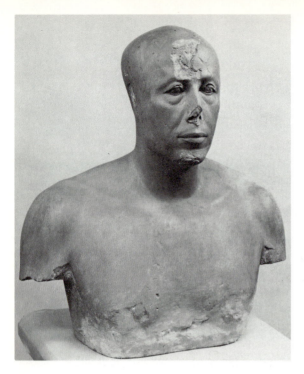

Figure 2-12
Above: Bust of the prince Ankh-haf, from Giza.
Life-size. (Museum of Fine Arts, Boston, Harvard
University-MFA Expedition.)

Figure 2-13
Right: The sheik El Beled, from his tomb in Saqqara.
Wood, approximately 43 inches high. (Cairo Museum.
Photo, Hirmer Fotoarchiv München.)

portrait makes an effort to reveal the essence of the
person whom it depicts, we find ourselves in a very
modern relationship with the work. We feel that we
are seeing not an abstract symbol but a concrete
interpretation of personality. It is not just a recepta-
cle for the ka but an evocation of the ka.

The portraits in Figures 2-12 through 2-15 are of
figures in repose. None of the faces has a highly
individual expression; none is smiling. They are all
relatively serious, in part because they were created
for serious purposes; they were not intended for casual
viewers. They were preserved in tombs and were
meant for the "eyes" of the ka. These works were
designed to entertain the spirit, not the flesh. They
were all metaphysical in their intention and were
not, like the pyramids or public sculpture, addressed

Figure 2-14
Queen Tiy. Wood, life-size. (Aegyptisches Museum, Berlin.)

Figure 2-15
Plaster funeral mask. Second century after Christ. (By permission of the trustees of the British Museum.)

PERCEPTION KEY

Egyptian Portraits

1. Which of the portraits in Figures 2-12 through 2-15 seems most realistic to you? Why?

2. Which of the portraits seems to reveal the most emotion? Which is the most emotionless? Do those qualities have any bearing on which is most realistic in appearance?

3. Are the men or the women more carefully represented?

4. Does any of these portraits seem to represent the essential personality of the sitter? How important a value does individuality seem to be in these portraits?

5. Which is the most spiritual of the portraits? Which is the most fleshly? Do the sculptors seem to place great value on such qualities?

to a fleshly humankind. Many of them were not originally placed where there was light sufficient for viewing; the ka needed no light.

KING TUTANKHAMEN AND THE AMARNA EPISODE: 1370 B.C.

The most startling discoveries in Egypt were made between the 1870s and the 1930s. They included the discovery of the city of Akhetaten, at the modern Tell El Amarna, halfway between Thebes and Memphis (the traditional capitals of Egypt) and the discovery of the only intact royal tomb, that of Tutankhamen, found in modern times. The art from this period is regarded as the "Amarna style"; the events surrounding Akhenaton are known as the "Amarna episode."

The city of Akhetaten came as a total surprise to archaelogists, since it was revealed to be the capital of Akhenaton and his wife Nefertiti. All the lists of kings made by the Egyptians had omitted Akhenaton in a traditional effort to "erase" his memory. The city was apparently abandoned to the sands as soon as Akhenaton died. Workshops were left intact; in the workshop of the master sculptor Tuthmosis, the models for royal portraits were found, including some which may have been life masks.

The famous portrait of Nefertiti (Figure 2-16) was smuggled out of the digs by its German discoverers just before World War I. We know little about Nefertiti. She was raised with Akhenaton as a sister by Queen Tiy, a woman of immense influence and strong religious convictions. The portrait is cool and detached, and yet it is powerful in line and form. The unusual crown was apparently designed to match Akhenaton's. The name Nefertiti means "the beautiful one has come," and her portrait shows how well named she was.

Figure 2-16
Tuthmosis. Bust of Nefertiti. Limestone, life-size. (Aegyptisches Museum, Berlin.)

Stirrings of Monotheism

Queen Tiy (Figure 2-14) and Nefertiti played an important role in history. Amenhotep (Akhenaton's father) and Queen Tiy made some changes in certain attitudes toward religion and art. What happened is shadowy because successive ages have destroyed the records. Apparently, the priests of the sun god Ra-Amen had become wealthy and powerful in Thebes and had gained considerable influence over the king. Before his "revolt," Akhenaton had reigned as Amenhotep IV, then changed his name to Akhenaton, "beloved of Aton," and elevated Aton to the status of god of the state. Such a move was revolutionary and dangerous.

James Breasted and others have seen this as the first move toward monotheism. An important mark of a civilization's modernity is its moving toward the worship of one god. The Greeks and Romans were polytheistic through the time of Christ. Monothe-

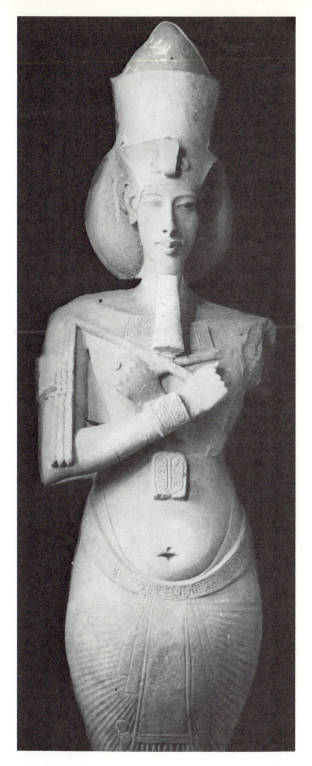

Figure 2-17
Colossal statue of Akhenaton. Sandstone. (Egyptian Antiquities Museum, Cairo.)

ism, as we know it, is derived from the Hebrews, and many people have seen a connection between Akhenaton's god, Aton, and Moses's god, Adonai, particularly since Moses came out of Egypt, as he tells us in Genesis.

However, Akhenaton held many gods in reverence, and his scholarly piety did not necessarily carry over into monotheism, although he seems to have been a gentle, truly religious man. He and his family lived an odd life, isolated in Akhetaten and far from the traditional centers of power. Akhenaton had several concubines, and Nefertiti seems to have had three of their six children by other men. The nation suffered greatly from Akhenaton's refusal to rule the state. He ordered his armies not to attack and to defend themselves without shedding blood. Essentially this meant that they could not fight, which in turn meant that earlier conquests were lost during his dynasty. Breasted called Akhenaton "the first individual in history" because he was willing to go against the established order and challenge authority.

Akhenaton's "Hymn to Aton" shows not only his piety but also his poetic skill:

> You arise beautiful in the horizon of heaven
> O living Aton, the initiator of life,
> When you shine forth in the eastern horizon
> And fill the whole earth with your beauty.
> You are beauteous, great, shining and high above
>   every land.
> Your rays encompass the lands to the limits of all that
>   you have made.
> You are the sun, and reach their limits, subduing
>   them to your beloved son.

Akhenaton's critics point out that Egypt suffered mightily under his rule and that he was foolish to lead a religious crusade which amounted to, they say, a mere change of name of the state god. But those who praise him point to the independent way in which he lived. The portraits usually show him with members of a devoted family—almost always Nefertiti and their daughters. Some reliefs show the royal couple nude. No matter how they are portrayed, the representations are obviously more relaxed and informal than those from any other dynasty.

Representations of Akhenaton (such as Figure 2-17) show him with a potbelly and with hips so wide that the first Europeans to uncover the statues thought they were of a woman. Certain representa-

The Amarna Episode

1. What are the formal distinctions between the portraits of King Menkaure and Queen Khammerernebty (Figure 2-11) and those of Akhenaton (Figure 2-17) and Nefertiti (Figure 2-16)? Which are less personalized? Which are more obviously official?

2. What evidence is there in the portrait that Akhenaton was highly individualistic?

3. What kind of conflict in values would have led Akhenaton to order his soldiers not to kill the enemy? Does this decision make sense to you? Was Akhenaton's position a desirable one? Was it appropriately religious, or is religion irrelevant in such a view?

4. To what extent does the art of the Amarna period or of King Tutankhamen's tomb reveal a new attitude toward the value of the individual or the value of human life?

tions of Akhenaton omit genitalia and do resemble a woman more than a man. Since there was a precedent—the eighteenth-dynasty Queen Hatshepsut ruled as pharaoh—the Europeans thought that they were looking at a female monarch.

Royal reliefs, statuary, and surviving records indicate that Akhenaton was developing new models of behavior, and for this he was feared and disliked. His military commanders thought him a fool, the priests of Ra-Amen considered him a serious threat, and the people were bewildered by him. Some present-day scholars regard him as a modern man; others feel that he may have had medical problems brought on by inbreeding. His sexuality was so ambiguous that it provoked concern that he was impotent. It is no wonder that he died suddenly and mysteriously and that his son-in-law, who succeeded him, changed his own name from Tutankhaten to Tutankhamen.

The Tomb of King Tutankhamen: "Wonderful Things"

The only royal tomb ever discovered intact belonged to Tutankhamen, "the living image of Amen." Al-though he was a minor king who died before he was twenty, the treasures in his tomb are such that we can only gasp to think what was lost in the greatest of the tombs. Howard Carter found the tomb in the Valley of the Kings near Thebes in 1922 and opened the sarcophagus in 1926. It was intact because its entrance had been covered with rubble from the digging for a Ramesside king's tomb. King Rameses held King Tutankhamen's entire line in contempt; ironically, he saved Tutankhamen for posterity.

King Tutankhamen's mummy was preserved in a solid gold coffin weighing 450 pounds (a detail is shown in Figure 2-18 and Color Plate 1), which was protected by two more coffins of ceramic material, in turn protected by an airtight quartzite sarcophagus placed inside four tightly fitting wooden cases. All these are decorated painstakingly, some with accurate likenesses of Tutankhamen. (The second coffin is shown in Figure 2-19.) These portraits are in the grand style that had existed before the time of Akhenaton, and the only suggestions of the Amarna style are in a few potbellied goddesses guarding the chest containing the inner organs. The Ramesside kings, Tutankhamen's successors, were rough-and-

Figure 2-18
Left: Gold coffin of Tutankhamen, detail. (Cairo Museum; photo, Lee Boltin, Croton-on-Hudson, New York.)

Figure 2-19
Below: Second coffin of Tutankhamen. (Metropolitan Museum of Art; photo, Harry Burton.)

ready military men, not of royal birth. Their struggle to hold the kingdom together failed, and King Tutankhamen seems to have lived at the zenith of Egypt's power: ahead lay 1000 years of disintegration.

Pyramids in the Americas

Materials and conditions in Mexico and Central America were right for building durable temples and tombs. The Mayan temples in Mexico date from the time of Christ, although mound building was going on 1000 years earlier. It had long been thought that the temples were not used for burial mounds, but recent research has discovered otherwise. They provided safe resting places for an honored few.

THE CITIES OF THE MAYA

The cities of the Maya have been known to us only since the 1820s, and since that time much has been learned about these people. Among all the American civilizations—including those of the Incas, the Aztecs, and the Toltecs—the Mayan was the only one to achieve a highly developed hieroglyphic writing. Mayan temples are carved with highly dramatic glyphs, many of which are not yet understood. The Maya had developed a number system and a calendar stone which helped them predict rainfall and astronomical events. The Spaniards had more trouble conquering the Maya than the more warlike Aztecs. They succeeded when a Spanish priest, Andrés de Avendano, deciphered the calendar and convinced the Mayan priests that the Mayan katun, "destruction," was at hand. The fact that a white man could unravel 1000 years of learning stunned the Maya.

The cities of the Maya are primarily in Mexico, in the Yucatan—a Mayan word for "I don't understand you," which is what the Indians answered when the Spanish asked them what the name of the place was. Their great cities were Tikal, Chichen Itza, Mayapan, and Palenque; but these were used chiefly for ceremonies and sacrifices, not as residences.

Figure 2-20 shows a burial crypt. A Mexican archaeologist, Alberto Ruz Lhuillier, noticed some holes in a flat stone on top of the temple. He removed the stone and found some steps covered with rubble. When they were cleared, he discovered the skeletons of six young people; below, he found the burial chamber of a chief. The stone lid of the

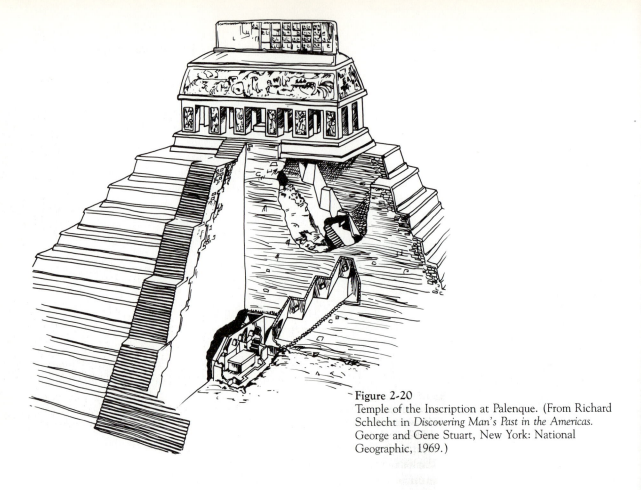

Figure 2-20
Temple of the Inscription at Palenque. (From Richard
Schlecht in *Discovering Man's Past in the Americas.*
George and Gene Stuart, New York: National
Geographic, 1969.)

sarcophagus weighed 5 tons; beneath it lay the
skeleton of the chief, buried with precious stones and
an oblong pearl 1 inch long.

PYRAMID OF THE MOON

The Pyramid of the Moon at Teotihuacan, Mexico
(Figure 2-21), is much later than the pyramids in
Egypt—by about 1500 years. It is also quite different
from the Egyptian pyramids. For one thing, Mayan
religious practices emphasized the sacrifice of humans
to the gods because the Maya thought that the gods
needed human blood, particularly the blood of children. Members of the priestly caste spent much of
their initiation fasting on top of the temples, where
they ritually cut earlobes and tongue, as well as other
parts of the body, so as to keep their blood flowing for

their gods. In comparison with the warlike Aztecs,
the Maya performed relatively few human sacrifices,
but they persisted in the practice long after the
Spaniards converted them to Christianity in the
seventeenth century.

The Pyramid of the Moon puzzled even the Aztecs, who thought it had been built by giants or gods.
We have no idea who built it or why, but we do know
that it is a recent structure, dating from the third
century after Christ. It is similar to the step pyramid
at Saqqara and the ziggurat at Ur. The emphasis is on
grandeur and colossal size: it is 200 feet high and 700
feet long, and it has a mate not far away. Its size
approximates that of the pyramid of Khufu, but it is a
total mystery. Today, like so many monuments of the
distant past, it stands as a tantalizing clue to a
message we cannot yet decipher. We know that it

Figure 2-21
Pyramid of the Moon. Teotihuacan, Mexico.
(Popperfoto.)

offers evidence that the building of pyramids and temples is a common human activity. But of the Pyramid of the Moon, we know little more than the Aztecs before us did.

Summary

Agriculture permitted the growth of stable societies, which in turn made possible the development of strong, centralized governments. Whether they were held together by tyranny or by devotion, the societies of the middle east and of Central America and South America built on a grand scale. In such societies, religion commanded the work of the entire nation, and the pyramids served a wide variety of ceremonial functions; in Egypt they were connected with the values of immortality; and in Mexico they were connected with the values of propitiating the gods with nourishing, restorative human blood. The pyramid is one of the most stable geometric forms; Egyptian society was generally stable, but there were rumblings of change and reactions against the older traditions and the upper classes. Periods of anarchy permitted the robbing and defacing of tombs. The Amarna period was marked by strong reaction against the old ways. Akhenaton may not have been the world's first individual, but he showed that even the pharaoh could have trouble with the establishment. The discoveries of the Amarna period tell us that art was one of the most important instruments of the state and of the pharaoh's will: art was expected to influence people at all levels of society and bend them to the will of the state.

Concepts in Chapter 2

Agricultural civilization began in Mesopotamia; the first cities date from at least 6500 B.C.

Reliable crops permitted the growth of complex civilizations.

Religious beliefs, often based on concepts of rebirth and eternal afterlife, dominated agricultural societies.

Assyrian, Egyptian, and other middle eastern societies became strong, monolithic, and powerful and had rigid class structures.

Architecture and other arts reveal the power of a society.

Egyptian portraiture shows an interest in depicting the essential nature of the individual.

Corn myths and solar myths reveal people's faith in their ability to control nature, as well as their fear that they might lose this ability.

During the Amarna period, a new attitude developed toward the value of the individual; this may have been associated with monotheism.

The traditions associated with pyramid and temple building in the Americas were different from the traditions associated with such building in Egypt; in the Americas, they were based on propitiating the gods through the sacrifice of human blood.

Suggested Readings

Aldred, Cyril. *Akhnaten and Nefertiti*. New York: Viking, 1973.

————. *The Development of Egyptian Art*. 3 vols. London: Academy Edition, 1949–1951, 1973.

Breasted, James. *History of Egypt*. New York: Scribner, 1956 (originally published in 1909).

Edwards, I. E. S. *The Pyramids of Egypt*. New York: Viking, 1947, 1972.

Fakhry, Ahmed. *The Pyramids*. Chicago: University of Chicago Press, 1961.

Kaster, Joseph, ed. and trans. *The Literature and Mythology of Ancient Egypt*. London: Allen Lane, Penguin, 1968.

Lange, Kurt, and Max Hirmer. *Egyptian Architecture, Sculpture, Painting in 3000 Years*. London: Phaidon, 1968.

Lauer, Jean-Philippe. *Saqqara*. New York: Scribner, 1976.

Lloyd, Seton, Hans Wolfgang Muller, and Roland Martin. *Ancient Architecture: Mesopotamia, Egypt, Crete, Greece*. New York: Abrams, 1972.

Redford, Donald B. *Akhenaten: The Heretic King*. Princeton, N.J.: Princeton University Press, 1984.

Sewell, Barbara. *Egypt under the Pharaohs*. New York: Putnam, 1968.

Vandenberg, Philipp. *Nefertiti*. New York: Lippincott, 1978.

CHAPTER 3

THE CELTS AND STONE AGE EUROPE

Celtic Culture

 Developments in the middle east produced monolithic societies with developed cities, rigid class systems, and professional artists. However, developments in northern Europe were quite different. Celtic peoples, as well as those they supplanted, were tribal and given to migration. They lived in a rugged country in which there were no centralized governments, and they had little need for professional artists. Their habits were generally agricultural and pastoral, with an emphasis on cultivating livestock, especially cattle. Much Celtic literature centers on cattle, a form of wealth, and on the raids which sometimes "distributed" this wealth.

Because they often lived in or near large forests, the Celts developed a reputation as a people of darkness, and metaphors of darkness still haunt northern legends. They used the local wood for building and for making other artifacts, most of which have perished. Even Stonehenge shows evidence of being a translation of a traditional wooden structure.

Although their origins are obscure, the Celts seem to have roamed from Turkey into France, then into Britain, and then north to Scandinavia. Julius Caesar's legions faced them shortly before the time of Christ, and Caesar observed large tribal differences among the Celts, saying that "all Gaul is divided into three parts." Their wars with Caesar were marked by great heroism and skill, but the Roman legions were highly organized, technologically superior forces which eventually conquered them (much as the United States cavalry later conquered the Amerindians).

Diodorus Siculus described the Celtic warriors:

> Their aspect is terrifying. . . . They are very tall in stature . . . their hair is blonde, but not naturally so: they bleach it, to this day, artificially, washing it in lime and combing it back from their foreheads. They look like wood-demons, their hair shaggy like a horse's mane.

They beat their lances and javelins on their shields, singing songs that sounded subhuman to dignified Roman ears. Their art was largely decorative, and their literature has contributed to many of our best-known myths: that of Tristan and Isolde, from Brittany; *The Mabinogion*, from Wales; and the *Tain bo Cuailnge* ("The Cattle Raid at Cooley"), from Ireland. These are only a fragment of what must have existed.

Stonehenge: Mysterious Computer

Stonehenge in Wessex, England, is a relic of neolithic Europe. It was built in stages, from about 2700 B.C. to at least 1800 B.C. Its trilothons—two upright stones with one lintel—range from 20 to 25 feet in height. Many of them have fallen, and the site has long been a ruin; yet it still commands a sense of wonder. Whether it should be considered architecture or sculpture — or neither—hardly matters. It is a product of human imagination and is evidence of a process of conceptual abstraction that makes us keenly aware of the complexity of the neolithic mind.

The building of Stonehenge may have been supervised by druids, the priestly caste of the Celts. However, it may also be true that the druids later appropriated the place for their rites. It may be a temple, a holy place, or a monument. It took much more of the collective labor of the Wessex people to build than the pyramids required of Egyptian workers, and it seems certainly to have been constructed by the willing hands of people who believed that they were helping their society. It was destined to serve the living, not the dead; and yet cremated remains have been found in the embankments.

Stonehenge can "calculate" several kinds of lunar and solar events (see Figure 3-1), and possibly events of even more sophisticated astronomical significance, such as recurrent comets or astral conjunctions. It predicts sunrise, sunset, moonrise, and moonset in any season, and thus it is a useful tool for planting and harvesting.

Gerald Hawkins, an American, assuming that Stonehenge was a solar and lunar calculator, fed data into his computer and found that the accuracy of

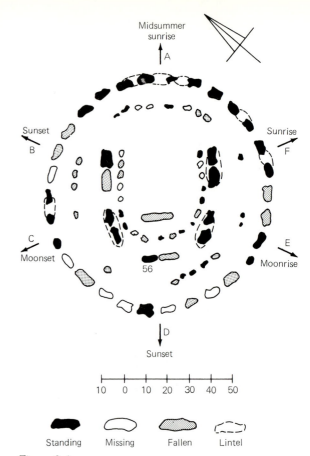

Figure 3-1
Plan of Stonehenge. (from Gerald S. Hawkins and John B. White. *Stonehenge Decoded.* Garden City, N. Y.: Doubleday, 1965. Drawing 5. Copyright © 1965 by Gerald S. Hawkins and John B. White. Reprinted by permission of Doubleday and Company, Inc.)

prediction was staggering. He even discovered that the fifty-six chalk-filled Aubrey holes, about 50 feet outside the outer rim of sarsen stones, predict a cycle of lunar eclipses that modern scientists were unaware of. This discovery—if it is accurate—is all the more astonishing because the Aubrey holes (named by James Aubrey, 1626–1697, who first proposed a connection with druids) were among the earliest segments of Stonehenge, predating the huge sarsens by centuries. Stonehenge may still be able to predict events thousands of years into the future, which would explain why it is built so durably. Hawkins's estimates of the labor involved (in man-days) are impressive.

Digging ditch, making bank: 3,500 cubic yards at 1 yard per man-day	3,500
Carrying for the above	7,000
Digging 5,000 cubic yards for avenue banks, leveling, surveying, etc.	6,000
Carrying for the above	12,000
Transporting eighty bluestones, with an average weight of 4 tons, 24 miles by land at 100 men per stone, 1 mile per day	192,000
Transporting the stones 216 miles by water at 10 men per stone, 10 miles per day	17,280
Erecting Stonehenge II at twenty man-days per stone	1,600
Transporting eighty sarsens [outer stones], with an average weight of 30 tons, 20 miles by land at 700 miles per stone, 1 mile per day	1,120,000
Cutting with stone axes, hauling 300 logs for the lattice tower, 2,000 rollers, one man-day per log	60,000
Making 60,000 yards of hide rope at one man-day per yard	60,000
Erecting Stonehenge III at 200 man-days per stone	16,000
Total man-days	1,497,000

These figures do not include planning the monument, organizing the workers, or feeding and clothing them. A thousand workers working seven days a week would have taken four years to build Stonehenge.

Stonehenge was built in three distinct stages, usually numbered I, II, and II (these are the references in Hawkin's list), with later additions even within the third stage. Some parts were left unfinished, and others were dismantled. The outer ring of sarsens was erected after the inner ring of bluestones had been dismantled. The sarsens (we do not know the meaning of the term) were found lying on the ground north of Stonehenge. Exceptionally hard, they needed a great deal of grinding, cutting, and preparation, and they had to be transported immense distances.

Figure 3-2
Trilithon, Stonehenge.

Other structures like Stonehenge exist, but none has the inner horseshoe of giant trilithons (Figure 3-2), which are still useful for sighting important settings and risings of the sun and the moon. Some of the trilithons seem to have developed "personalities," such as stone 56 (Figure 3-3), whose mate and lintel have fallen. It resembles a sentry. The knob, which looks like a head, is a tenon that fit into the lintel resting on it, a detail common to all the trilithons. Stone 56 is part of the trilithon that sighted the midsummer sunset, and it must have had special importance. Walking around it as if it were a colossal sculpture, one observes that its edges are sharp, that it has hardly weathered, and that its poise is unaffected by time. The experience of walking through Stonehenge (no longer possible for the casual visitor) leaves one suitably impressed, but totally differently from the way one is impressed by viewing Mesopotamian artifacts. One has a special

Figure 3-3
Stone 56, Stonehenge.

were a priestly caste who were thought to have magic powers, and they seem to have maintained their position in society partly as a result of their ability to predict astronomical events. The Celtic peoples must have regarded the heavens as the source of power—perhaps as the home of the gods—although their concept of gods was idiosyncratic: they believed that everything, animate and inanimate, was infused with a spirit. We call this "animism," and many peoples today hold the same belief.

The efforts of the druids or other priests at Stonehenge must have been rewarded, since no culture would expend most of its energies on a project of this sort unless the results warranted it. Crops must have been planted according to the times predicted by the instrument, and serious undertakings must have been begun or ended according to its astrological predictions. In other words, the calculator was a technical instrument that helped people plan their lives. Belief in it must have been second nature, and no sacrifice was too great for its preservation.

Stonehenge is, however, an extraordinarily abstract instrument. The caves and other sites of prehistoric art are shrouded in mystery, but at least we see the representation of life itself on the walls and in the sculpture. In Stonehenge, however, we have an abstraction somewhat like the ziggurat at Ur: the instrument stands for something symbolic, like power. But it is not power over people so much as it is power over the stars and heavenly events. Stonehenge is a dramatic piece of public sculpture; but it is also—like a compass, a sextant, or any other such instrument—an intellectual thing. It stands for an idea, a belief, and for all the systems and cultural complexities that stemmed from that idea.

regard for the mind that could produce an instrument of such subtlety and for the community that valued it so highly that it was willing to make enormous sacrifices to build it. Stonehenge is impressive if one takes it strictly as a sculptural event, but even more impressive is the fact that its real grandeur is intellectual and metaphysical. It lies beyond our capacities for perception.

The priests who presided over Stonehenge must have been powerful persuaders. Their ability to predict the seasons, weather changes, and eclipses of the sun and the moon may have been regarded as a kind of magic power. Celtic lore places great importance on magicians, such as Merlin, who (according to Welsh legend) had the stones of Stonehenge transported by magic from Ireland to Salisbury Plain to celebrate the Britons who died there. The druids

Celtic Literature and Myth

THE TAIN BO CUAILNGE: THE CATTLE RAID AT COOLEY

Classical writers report three main kinds of Celtic professionals: the druids, the fili, and the bards. The druids were highly trained writers who were skilled in magic, medicine, and telling the future. The fili were less well educated versions of the druids and were responsible for making some of the minor predictions. The bards were storytelling poets. Christianiz-

Stonehenge

1. If Stonehenge is in fact a computer for calculating solar, lunar, and astral events, what might we guess about the values of the community that built it regarding the heavens and their influence on humankind?

2. What practical value would a solar or lunar computer have had in an early pastoral-agricultural community?

3. Specialists presided over Stonehenge, directed its construction, and organized the ceremonies held there. What kind of specialists do you think they were?

4. Unlike the caves in Spain and France, Stonehenge makes no reference to animal life, human life, or sexuality. What might that imply about the Wessex people and their values?

5. The tremendous energy that went into building Stonehenge was expended in the hope of obtaining some useful "payoff" from the calculations that were to be made. What value do you feel that the Wessex people placed on the "technology" that would have produced a payoff?

---

ing the Celtic world did away with the druids. The fili survived for a while, and the bards thrived. As the first two classes of poets died out, the bards took on more of their responsibilities.

Strict classes of poets seem to have been rigidly maintained and provided for. They studied with master poets, often for ten years or more—a fact which demonstrates that the Celts had some professional artistic groups. The Celtic poets had to master an enormous number of metrical forms. And they had to create their poems while lying in tiny stone shelters in the dark. When a poem was finished, the poet left the shelter and sang it to the master; if the master did not like it, the poet went back and wrote it again.

The *Tain bo Cuailnge* (pronounced "toyn bo koo-linguh")— "The Cattle Raid at Cooley"—is a major epic; the heroine is Queen Maeve, a strong, willful woman with enormous pride. The story is told by Senchan Torpeist, an important poet. Maeve uses her sexuality to get what she wants—a fact that embarrassed the monks who preserved the *Tain*. Even modern translations have omitted some of the steamier details. The hero of the *Tain* is Cuchulain (pronounced "ku-hool-an"), a seventeen-year-old superhero who, like Conan, also a legendary Irish hero, performs unbelievable feats.

The *Tain* describes a raid by the forces of the west of Ireland, where Maeve is queen, against the forces of the north of Ireland, where Cuchulain is guardian. The action of the *Tain* is set around the time of Christ, although the story as we have it seems to date from about the seventh century after Christ. In any case, it is the oldest surviving European epic written in a nonclassical language. No one who reads it today can ignore the fact that the struggle between the two parts of Ireland still continues; there have been 2000 years of troubles.

The *Tain* begins with "pillow talk" between Maeve and her husband, Ailill. They are comparing their wealth, and Maeve insists that she is the wealthier. As they argue, they marshal their goods for comparison, and Maeve finds that she is short one prize bull, the brown bull of Cooley. (Later, she decides to invade the north of Ireland to take the bull by force.) As she is talking with Ailill, she makes a speech that shows the vitality of this literature:

> If I married a mean man our union would be wrong, because I am so full of grace and giving. It would be an insult if I were more generous than my husband, but not if the two of us were equal in this. If my husband was a timid man our union would be just as wrong because I thrive, myself, on all kinds of trouble. It is an insult for a wife to be more spirited than her husband, but not if the two are equally spirited. If I married a jealous man that would be wrong, too: I never had one man without another waiting in his shadow. So I got the kind of man I wanted: Rus Ruad's other son—yourself, Ailill, from Leinster. You aren't greedy or jealous or sluggish.

Maeve may have been a historical figure; if so, she was a powerful woman who knew how to operate in a male-dominated world. In the story, she leads the warriors into battle herself. She may have been related to the ancient people of Ireland, the Tuatha de Danaan—the followers of the goddess Dana. The influence and power of Celtic women, both real and fictional, may relate to the mother-dominated societies which existed in northern Europe, and Maeve may be a remnant of that age. These ancient heroines eventually were reduced to fairies; Maeve becomes Queen Mab in Shakespeare's play *A Midsummer Night's Dream.*

Cuchulain is Maeve's antagonist; his name means "hound of Culann." When he was a child, he slew a mighty hound of the king, Conchobar (pronounced "kon-ku-vor"), and offered to replace it by becoming the king's hound himself. Cuchulain was not born in Ulster, where Conchobar was king, and therefore he is the only warrior left to fight after a curse is placed on the warriors of Ulster. They offended a pregnant woman by forcing her to race against horses at a festival. She defeated the horses, but as she lay giving birth to twins after the race, she cursed the men of Ulster and condemned them to suffer birth pangs in the time of their greatest danger. When Maeve attacks, Ulster is suffering from such pangs, and Cuchulain has to fight alone. Because he is the

greatest of warriors, he holds off Maeve's forces long enough for Ulster to recover.

Cuchulain works himself up to fight by experiencing a "Warp-spasm" that makes him a terrifying enemy:

> The Warp-spasm overtook him: it seemed each hair was hammered into his head, so sharply they shot upright. You would swear a fire-speck tipped each hair. He squeezed one eye narrower than the eye of a needle; he opened the other wider than the mouth of a goblet. He bared his jaws to the ear; he peeled back his lips to the eye-teeth till his gullet showed. The hero-halo rose up from the crown of his head.

This transformation is unique in ancient literature. Scholars are unclear about what the "hero-halo" is. The rest of the change they treat simply as conventional overstatement.

Cuchulain kills enough of Maeve's advancing forces to get them to agree to single combat; this gives him time and provides some relief for Maeve's forces. She has several important heroes with her, Fergus and Ferdia among them. Fergus does not fight Cuchulain, but Ferdia (Cuchulain's foster brother) does, and their fight is terrible. Cuchulain wins, but he is weakened; when Ulster rises, his strength is almost gone. Still he chases after Maeve's retreating forces and catches up to her when she is weakened by her menstrual flow. Not only is there no precedent for this in early literature, but until contemporary times, literature has never been so explicit:

> Then Medb [Maeve] got her gush of blood.
> "Fergus," she said, "take over the shelter of shields at the rear of the men of Ireland until I relieve myself."
> "By god," Fergus said, "you have picked a bad time for this."
> So Fergus took over the shelter of shields at the rear of the men of Ireland and Medb relieved herself. It dug three great channels, each big enough to take a household. The place is called Fual Medba, Medb's Foul Place, ever since. Cuchulainn found her like this, but he held his hand. He wouldn't strike her from behind.
> "Spare me," Medb said.
> "If I killed you dead," Cuchulainn said, "it would only be right."
> But he spared her, not being a killer of women.

Finally Maeve retreats. But the bull which she has sought, the brown bull of Cooley, ends the *Tain* by

PERCEPTION KEY

Celtic Myth: The Tain

1. Maeve is a warrior, but she is also a woman. What is the meaning of the hero's, Cuchulain's, coming upon her when she is menstruating—when she is, in one biological sense, most womanly? Is this a testament to womanliness? To manliness?

2. Is it manly for the warrior-hero to let Maeve go at this time?

3. Do you feel that it is modern for Maeve and Ailill to be equals in marriage? Is this to be expected in a marriage that may date back almost to the time of Christ? You may be able to recall some Bible stories that will help you respond to this question. Is such equality unusual in marriages today?

4. Is the "Warp-spasm" realistic? Does realism suffer when heroes undergo such "comic book" transformations?

fighting to the death with the white bull of Connaught, Maeve's land. Thus, the war was completely pointless. The sophistication of the *Tain* impresses every reader; the irony of futile battle is particularly modern. Homer's great epics, the *Iliad* and the *Odyssey*, treat war as a noble activity. The Celtic tradition sees warriors as noble, but war, as portrayed in the *Tain*, is waged over trivial issues. Ulster and Connaught, in the final analysis, have fought for nothing but pride. In one version of the *Tain*, pig farmers begin and end the tale with their own disputes. So much for pride.

CELTIC BELIEF: THE OTHER WORLD

Celtic legend includes deities and concepts of other worlds, but the *Tain* never treats the concept of god. The *Tain* refers to the Sidhe (pronounced "shee"), a separate world of spirits who seem to specialize in changing their shape. Mananaan was the god of the sea, and so he was naturally important to an island people. Various goddesses, such as Bel and Dana, were also important, but no elaborate system, such as the Egyptian ennead, seems to have dominated

Celtic thought. This may be one reason why the Celts were Christianized quickly.

The Sidhe existed side by side with the real world; it was dominated by somewhat sinister spirits such as Fand, the woman of the Sidhe who loved Cuchulain. But another world of delight—the Land of Tir na nOg, which was brighter and happier—was the "land of heart's desire," the land of eternal youth. The Welsh Ysbaddaden, on the other hand, was dark and threatening, almost like hell. The concept that a person might live in one or the other of these worlds after death seems foreign to the Celts.

Metalwork and Decoration

LA TÈNE ART: THE GUNDESTRUP BOWL

We have little visual art to compare with Celtic literature and myth. One important piece of metalwork is the Gundestrup bowl (Figures 3-4, 3-5, and 3-6), which was found in Jutland, Denmark, and dates from the second or first century B.C. Because it is made of silver, it has survived without corrosion.

Figure 3-4
Above: Gundestrup bowl.
Silver, 16 ½ inches high, 27
inches in diameter.
(Nationalmuseet, Copenhagen;
photo, Lennart Larson.)

Figure 3-5
Right: Goddess from the
Gundestrup bowl.
(Nationalmuseet, Copenhagen;
photo, Lennart Larson.)

Figure 3-6
Cernunnos as god of the animals, from the Gundestrup bowl. (Nationalmuseet, Copenhagen; photo, Lennart Larsen.)

And the fact that it is made of silver indicates that it had special value; perhaps it was reserved for use in a religious ritual. Its interior decorations are narrative panels, suggesting that it was used in a ceremony. The figures on the outside are gods, and one of them holds two stags by the hind legs. Design and composition are more important than representation: the head is too large for the hands and the arms, and the stags are much too small for the entire figure. The design places considerable emphasis on symmetry: balancing one side with the other. The vertical line through the nose of the god implies that the left side repeats the right. The head follows the form that Ian Finlay says marks most Celtic heads: "a pear- or wedge-shaped face, a wedge-like nose, a slit mouth, generally small, and eyes which in depicting the living tend to be large and staring, slit-like when they seem to belong to the dead." This does not appear to be a portrait, but rather an accepted formula for a face. Yet its force and power are evident.

The anatomy of the goddess in Figure 3-5 is so unlikely that it almost puts us off. Her arms are attached to her shoulders in two different ways, both of which are impossible. Her left arm seems to have two articulated joints between the shoulder and the wrist. Her breasts, if that is what they are, are totally improbable. Another goddess who looks just like her sits next to her right shoulder on a ledge that seems to be an extension of the shoulder. Animals and figures proportioned to one another surround her, but we cannot make out their significance. Is the masculine figure by her left arm dead? Is the female figure holding her hair an attendant or a spirit? Do the symmetrical birds represent spirits? We do not know the answers to these questions. Yet the power of the arrangement of forms is very strong.

If this bowl does indeed date from the second or first century B.C. it falls in the period of La Tène art. La Tène, which means "the shallows," is a place-name identifying art objects found near the Lake of Neuchâtel. It is also used to indicate the beginning of the iron age in Europe. The art of the period is much more professional and polished than earlier art, and whether the Gundestrup bowl is a genuine piece of La

The Gundestrup Bowl

1. The representations shown in Figures 3-4, 3-5, and 3-6 are of gods. Are they portrayed as humans or as animals? Would this make a difference as far as the growth of humanist values is concerned?

2. The artists who worked on this bowl were decorating a surface. How does their emphasis on filling all the available space contribute to their style?

3. Does this work share any stylistic qualities with Egyptian art or with the art of the caves, discussed in Chapter 1?

4. Do these designs show an interest in abstract intellectual values of the sort illustrated by Stonehenge?

Tène art is related partly to its date (which is uncertain), to its place of origin (also uncertain), and to its style (which bears only some resemblance to the style of other examples of La Tène art). One of the exciting qualities of this bowl is that it shows influences from both the near and the far east. For this reason, N. K. Sandars sees it as having many influences, and thus she calls it "eclectic." To be eclectic, a work of art must join several different styles, usually of different periods. This bowl seems to do just that, which makes it particularly useful to someone interested in the development of the arts in Europe.

Celtic influences are clear in the development of the heads. Details such as the goddess's torque (necklace) are Celtic, as is the fact that the representations of animals are more realistic than those of people. But there is a striking fusion of Celtic and Asian art in one of the panels on the interior. This is the portrait of the god Cernunnos, "lord of the animals" (Figure 3-6). He holds a torque in his right hand and a serpent in his left. He wears a peculiar suit with pants, an Asian influence. He is wearing antlers to emphasize his involvement with the animals, and he is surrounded by stags, a fish, a boar, and other animals. The composition is asymmetrical, off balance. The god is at the left of center; his horns are placed directly next to the horns of the stag.

Some of the other animals are paired or balanced symmetrically, and they fill the space allotted to them. The spaces between the animals' legs are filled with hammered floral details, as if the artists had been afraid of wasting any available surfaces. The animals face both right and left, and there is no narrative starting point.

These figures are all represented quite independently from one another, in different scales, and in different spaces. Surprisingly, this portrait resembles portraits found in India of the god Shiva as Pashupati, "lord of beasts"; he is also antlered and sits in the squat position that Cernunnos assumes. He, too, is surrounded by animals appropriate to his environment. If the connection is not merely accidental, we have a clue to the source of one of the continental artist's powers: contact with other artistic cultures.

ISLAND ART: THE LATE PHASES

Migrating Germanic tribes ran the Celts off the continent of Europe and into the British Isles; a few clung to Brittany, Denmark, and several other havens. Many traditions in Celtic art were developed and preserved in the relative safety of the islands. Most of what we know of Celtic literature, for instance, has been recovered from the island peoples.

Even after Caesar had won his battles, Celtic traditions survived in England and Ireland. They also survived the impact of Christianization, as we can see from Celtic interpretations of Christian stories on the high crosses of Ireland.

The Battersea shield (Figure 3-7) is an example of typical Celtic decorative work. Its shape, which is graceful and beautifully proportioned, is one that has been shown to have developed during the period. Some earlier shields—called "targas"—were circular and others tended toward a lozenge shape. This may have been a ceremonial shield, made for a chief or a very important warrior, since it was not used in any battles. The decorative motif is based on circular forms. Some are complete circles, such as the circle in the center boss, the large central circle, and the two flanking circles. But each of the swirling lines, which move so gracefully from center to center, is also part of a circle. By using a compass and changing the center of a circle at different points, such designs can be reliably repeated. The circle, even keeping Stonehenge in mind, seems to have provided endless delight for the Celtic artist. Even the smallest of the circular forms on this shield is filled with small squares which form spokes, like those of a wheel (Figure 3-8).

The Battersea shield emphasizes balance and symmetry. The central circle, balanced as it is by the top and bottom circles, is linked gracefully with the main design elements. Each circle within the composition echoes the overall design, containing circles (such as the pair above the central boss) which are "multiplied" because their circumferences touch, while their centers are different. The horizontal swirling lines of the design within the central circle also repeat the shape of the entire shield. The way the details refer to, develop, and echo the structural form is typical of the Celtic approach to harmony of design. Working the bronze in this way demanded a great deal of skill, as did the laying out and the conception of the circular motifs.

Circular design patterns also dominate in the shield boss and the bowl shown in Figures 3-9 and 3-10. These works are almost simple and direct in comparison with the Battersea shield, and yet they possess all the characteristics of harmony and balance that we perceive in the shield.

Figure 3-7
Ceremonial shield from Battersea, London. c. second century B.C. Bronze, originally gilt, 31 ½ inches high. (Trustees of the British Museum.)

Figure 3-8
Central circle of the Battersea shield, detail. (Trustees of the British Museum.)

Figure 3-9
Shield boss from Wandsworth. Third century (?) after
Christ. Bronze, 13 inches in diameter. (Trustees of the
British Museum.)

Figure 3-10
Ceremonial bowl found in Ireland. Date uncertain.
Bronze, 10 inches in diameter. (Trustees of the British
Museum.)

PERCEPTION KEY

Celtic Shield Boss and Ceremonial Bowl

1. One of the works shown in Figures 3-9 and 3-10 has been described as "lyrical,"
and the other as "formal." Can you tell which work fits each description, and why?

2. Can either of these works be said to depend more heavily on the circular form, or
are they equal in this respect? Which one actually has more circles on it?

3. Can you tell from the design of the boss whether the Wandsworth shield was
circular or lozenge-shaped?

4. Is either of these works more harmonious in design than the Battersea shield?

5. Do you sense that the satisfaction the Celts derived from looking at these useful
objects may have paralleled our own? How much do you value a pleasing design?

Summary

Because the Celts were a tribal people who inhabited a rugged country and were only partly settled by agricultural habits, they were relatively easy prey for organized powers, like those of Rome. Their art seems not to have been as single-minded as that of the Egyptians, the Mesopotamians, or the Maya. All these latter peoples enjoyed stable, centralized governments and fairly rigid class systems. The Celts were more fluid and elusive. Yet they, or their predecessors in Wessex, conceived of an instrument —Stonehenge—whose powers not only fascinate us but also have illuminated us. The sense in which the Celts lived "in touch" with the stars, the sun, and the moon is strikingly modern, particularly as it enabled them to portray character in modern terms and to comment ironically on events. This is partly the result of good modern translations, but the basic matter is there in the original Celtic languages. The portrayals of Queen Maeve and the warrior Cuchulain are masterpieces of literature. And though much Celtic rock sculpture is relatively crude in appearance, the development of the La Tène style, beginning in about 500 B.C., shows that a more professional approach to art was possible. The Gundestrup bowl, which is probably from the La Tène period, is useful for observing the ways in which characteristic distortion of figures and anatomy combines with a concern for using all the available space. The bowl's "formula" Celtic heads imply a lack of interest in portraiture, while the details of the animals show a remarkable concern for accuracy. Finally, the circle-based decorations of the island peoples, the last surviving Celtic societies, show a development in terms of harmony of design elements, balance, and symmetry. They suggest a refinement of design perception, and possibly they signal a refinement of culture. These design interests survived the Christianizing of the islands and were absorbed into the mainstream of western culture.

Concepts in Chapter 3

Celtic tribes in neolithic times were pastoral and agricultural.

Celtic tribes had no cities or centralized government.

Stonehenge represents a high level of intellectual abstraction.

Stonehenge functions to predict astronomical events.

Celtic literature and myth are highly vigorous and earthy.

The *Tain* is the oldest European epic written in a nonclassical language.

Celtic religion was animistic.

The Celts studied the heavens closely and were guided by them in their actions.

Celtic art is characterized by "formula" representations of heads rather than carefully detailed portraits.

Celtic metalwork shows a strong design sense and a desire to use all the available space.

Celtic decorative work shows a fascination with balance, symmetry, and rhythm.

Because there was no professional artist class, some Celtic art seems clumsy.

Complex repetitions of circles and geometric forms show that Celtic artists were interested in abstract mathematical relationships.

Suggested Readings

Finlay, Ian. *Celtic Art.* London: Faber, 1973.

Gregory, Lady Isabella Augusta. *Gods, and Fighting Men.* London: Colin Smythe, 1970.

Hawkins, Gerald S., and John B. White. *Stonehenge Decoded.* New York: Dell, 1965.

Herm, Gerhard. *The Celts.* New York: St. Martin's, 1975.

Jackson, K. H., ed. *A Celtic Miscellany.* Harmondsworth, England: Penguin, 1971.

Jacobsthal, Paul. *Early Celtic Art.* London: Oxford University Press, 1944.

Kinsella, Thomas, trans. *The Tain Bo Cuailnge.* London: Oxford University Press, 1970.

MacCana, Proinsias. *Celtic Mythology.* London: Paul Hamlyn, 1970.

Piggott, Stuart. *The Druids.* New York: Praeger, 1968.

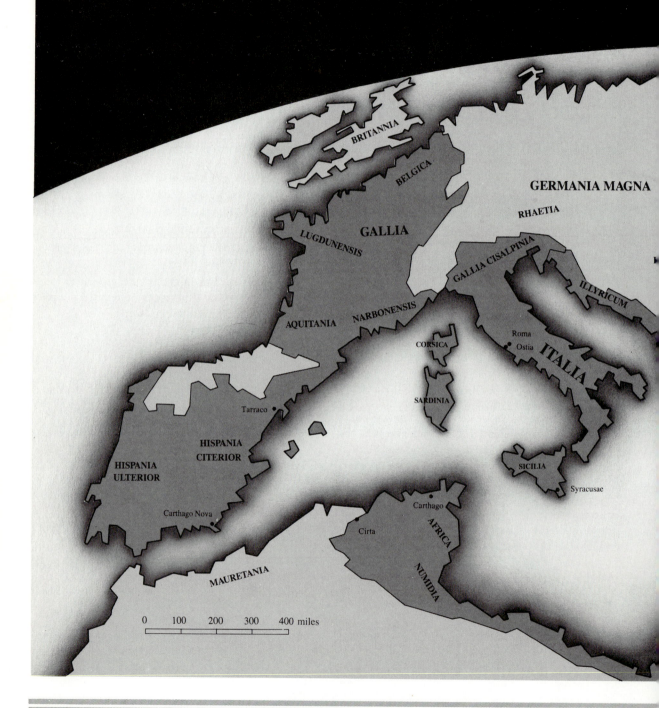

PART TWO

BRITANNIA

BELGICA

GERMANIA MAGNA

RHAETIA

GALLIA

LUGDUNENSIS

GALLIA CISALPINIA

ILLYRICUM

AQUITANIA NARBONENSIS

CORSICA

Roma
Ostia

ITALIA

HISPANIA CITERIOR

Tarraco

SARDINIA

HISPANIA ULTERIOR

SICILIA

Carthago Nova

Syracusae

Carthago

Cirta

AFRICA

MAURETANIA

NUMIDIA

0   100   200   300   400 miles

THE CLASSICAL WORLD

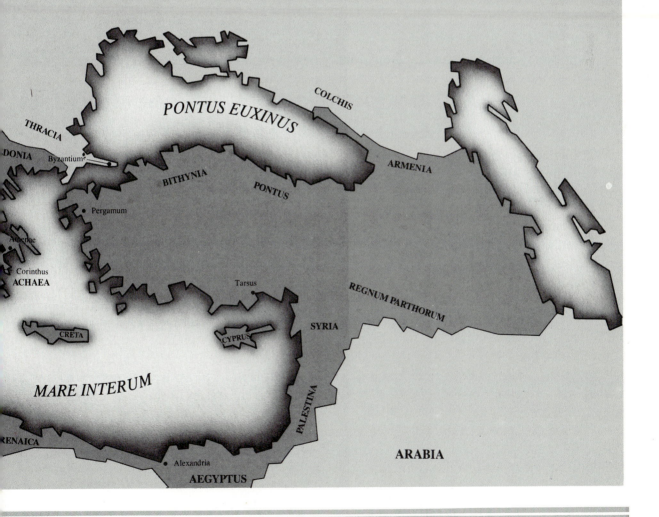

SARMATIA

THE ROMAN REPUBLIC AT THE DEATH OF CAESAR 44 B.C.

COLCHIS

PONTUS EUXINUS

THRACIA

DONIA   Byzantium

BITHYNIA   PONTUS   ARMENIA

Pergamum

Athenae

Corinthus
ACHAEA   Tarsus   REGNUM PARTHORUM

CRETA   CYPRUS   SYRIA

MARE INTERUM

PALESTINA

RENAICA   ARABIA

Alexandria
AEGYPTUS

Classical civilization began with the Mycenaeans on the Greek mainland and with the Minoans on the island of Crete. These were both bronze age cultures and were dependent on that relatively soft metal for their weaponry. Doric invaders—early Greeks with iron weapons—swept the Mycenaeans away. The iron age culture brought with it primarily military prowess, plunging Greece into a dark age that lasted for four centuries.

Gifted seafarers, the Greeks conducted a lively trade that permitted them to establish colonies modeled on the polis, or Greek city-state, in which a strong government structure based on law evolved along with the institutions of religious and martial importance that gave most Greek cities their characteristic flavor.

The Greeks were great pioneers and settlers, and their colonies helped solve the problems of overcrowding on the mainland. Ultimately, their success made them targets of the Persians, the dominant Mesopotamian civilization. The Persians tried several times, unsuccessfully, to invade and destroy Greece. They were finally turned back in 480 B.C. at the battle of Salamis by Pericles, ruler of Athens. In 340 B.C., Alexander the Great conquered Persia and brought Greek culture to Mesopotamia, Egypt, Asia Minor, and even India.

We think of Greek culture as having had a deep spiritual center and a powerful humanizing influence on civilization. Its gods were not animals or animistic forces; they were figures whose bodies resembled our own, whose patterns of living were familial (like ours), and whose angers and irritations were human and understandable. The gods were interested in human activities and sometimes took part in important events, such as the Trojan war, the subject of Homer's *Iliad.*

We see the spiritual values of Greek culture in other ways, too. The beauty of Periclean Athens—the Acropolis and its dedication to Athena, the Parthenon, and the Elgin marbles, which were once on the east pediment of the Parthenon—pleases the eye. But the pleasure

does not stop with the senses: it nurtures the spirit as well. For the Greeks, earthly beauty was a metaphor for spiritual beauty and spiritual understanding.

The philosophies of Socrates, Plato, and Aristotle reinforce the view that the world of the senses is a lesser world, only a hint of the permanent beauties of the higher world of the spirit. It may be somewhat misleading to use the word "heaven" to describe that other world of perfection, but it is the modern term that best expresses Plato's meaning. The Greeks' emphasis on the inner life, on examining the life we lead, and on moral behavior is the legacy of humanism which transformed the world. The Greeks were powerful, accomplished, and prosperous, but their culture did not worship power, skill, or material possessions.

Greek artists sought to nourish the inner spirit through balanced, symmetrical compositions that, in the time of Pericles, were idealized and aimed for perfection—at least in concept. The Parthenon is structured according to mathematical formulas that make its parts relate pleasingly to one another. Yet subtle imperfections are built into it so that it *appears* perfect to the eye, which must accept the limitations of the position from which the structure can be viewed. Greek temples were meant to be seen and appreciated from all angles.

Greek literature supplied, in the case of Homer, a form of living history and living myth. It also supplied knowledge of the gods and their concerns. Greek epic poetry was recited at special occasions by singers who had memorized the *Iliad* and the *Odyssey*, poems that were composed orally, preserved orally, and not written down for generations. Greek drama was part of celebrations of deities whose festivals were held regularly in Athens. Sophocles, Euripides, Aeschylus, Aristophanes, and other dramatists vied with one another for prizes. Their plays preserved and expanded the knowledge of the myths, which—modern psychologists tell us—are metaphoric expressions of the subconscious.

Greek influence brought about a revolution in world thought and a humanizing change in values and attitudes. However, Greek power waned in the Hellenistic age, after Alexander the

Great died and his generals fell out among themselves and carved up the world that Greece had made its own.

Legend has it that Rome was settled by Aeneas in 753 B.C. after he left Troy. The original Romans encountered an Etruscan civilization with institutions, a religion, and arts that showed both Greek and Mesopotamian influences. The Romans grew strong enough to defeat the Etruscans in 509 B.C., when Tarquin was overcome and the rest of the Etruscans were absorbed into, or evicted from, central Italy. The coastal areas of Italy had already sustained Greek settlements, and the Romans, in absorbing them, also absorbed a great deal of the Greek way. However, Rome had a special genius for centralized government which made the old concept of the polis, the independent Greek city-state, obsolete. There was too much squabbling among the cities and too little organization—and what organization there was often came too late. The Roman concept of a strong central government and a large standing army triumphed.

Rome grew from a republic to an empire, absorbing Greek styles in architecture, sculpture, and painting and spreading them throughout the world. What it could not do was to keep those ideals intact for itself. Rome enjoyed wealth and power beyond the dreams of Athens. Its builders could build larger, grander buildings. Its engineers could solve greater problems. Its gods were mightier and more profuse. Its sway was worldwide. But it could not avoid civil war, vicious tyrants, heavy taxation, and almost wholesale slavery. The irony is that the imperialism of Rome, built on the humanist values of Greece, was often expressed in violent excesses such as the infamous "entertainments" in the Colosseum and the martyrdom of the Christians, who were thought to be a threat to the empire.

But the positive achievements of Rome were enormously important. The world benefited from the spread of Roman law, from the civilizing influences of Roman rule, and from the humanizing effects of the spread of a great literature and great art. The excesses of Rome itself did not necessarily corrupt the outlying areas. The order and discipline that the Romans brought with them, as well as the language that they imposed on those they conquered, made the Roman world cosmopolitan, exciting, and huge. Its legacy, like that of Greece, is ongoing. The classical achievement is everywhere about us.

Brief Chronology

2800 B.C.   Bronze age civilization; early Minoan period: Crete.

1600 B.C.   Height of Minoan civilization.

1400 B.C.   Height of the Mycenaean civilization on mainland Greece.

1184 B.C.   Fall of Troy.

1100 B.C.   Dorian invasions, beginnings of the iron age.

800 B.C.   Homer's epics, the *Iliad* and the *Odyssey*.

753 B.C.   Legendary date for the founding of Rome.

700 B.C.   Archaic period of Greek art.

534 B.C.   Drama festivals begin at Athens.

509 B.C.   The defeat of Etruscan King Tarquin by the Romans.

480 B.C.   Persian destruction of the Acropolis; Persian defeat at Salamis.

450 B.C.   Great classical period; building of the Parthenon: 447 *B.C. to* 432 *B.C.*.

432 B.C. to 404 B.C.   Peloponnesian wars: Spartan alliance defeats the Athenian alliance.

399 B.C.   The death of Socrates.

387 B.C.   Founding of Plato's academy.

353 B.C.   Aristotle founds the Lyceum.

336 B.C.   Beginning of Alexander the Great's conquests.

323 B.C.   Death of Alexander the Great; the Hellenistic period in Greek culture; beginning of Greek decline.

86 B.C.   Roman conquest of Athens.

44 B.C.   The assassination of Julius Caesar on the Roman forum, followed by civil war.

31 B.C.   Battle of Actium: Rome takes Egypt.

30 B.C.   Augustus emperor; beginning of the Augustan age.

27 B.C. to A.D. 284   Early imperial period in Rome.

A.D. 284 to A.D. 395   Late imperial period; Constantine declares Christianity the state religion.

A.D. 410   The sack of Rome by the Visigoths; Rome falls in this century.

CHAPTER 4

GREEK HUMANISM

Archaic Greece: Mycenae

 By 2200 B.C. a form of Greek was spoken on the islands and the mainland of what is now modern Greece. By 1600 B.C., the Mycenaeans in southern Greece and the Minoans on the island of Crete had developed brilliant cultures. Great traders, they had brought ideas back from their neighbors in Egypt and Asia. At home they excelled in pottery, sculpture, metalwork, architecture, dance, and music. Soon they "exported" all these arts, along with their poetry. Homer's references to the Mycenaeans' love of gold imply wealth and political stability. As they grew more powerful, the Mycenaeans founded new cities, among which may have been Troy, whose ruins were discovered in Turkey in the 1870s by Heinrich Schliemann. Mycenaean domination, from 1600 B.C. to 1200 B.C., marked the height of the Greek bronze age. Weapons, tools, and shields were cast in bronze, which is an alloy of copper and tin but with a longer-lasting edge than copper.

The bronze daggers in Figure 4-1 have gold inlays showing men hunting lions and lions hunting deer. These dynamic scenes are intensified by a sensitivity to the space in which they must fit. The figures are lively and poised, and they express both motion and emotion. Mycenaean design was already highly developed in 1600 B.C. The same sense of design is present in the bowl in Figure 4-2—which dates from 1400 B.C. or 1300 B.C.—in the schematic portraits of a bull and its lice-seeking friend, the bird. They are not realistically portrayed; instead, areas of their bodies are filled in with solid color or various kinds of lines. The eyes, although anatomically "wrong," are compelling design features with an unusual significance.

The bronze age domination of Mycenaean culture came to an abrupt end in 1200 B.C., when iron age Dorians destroyed the Mycenaean cities. The ability of iron to hold an edge is infinitely superior to that of bronze, and no bronze age army could stand up against an enemy whose weapons were made of iron. With the end of Mycenaean culture came a 400-year-

Figure 4-1
Above and right: Mycenaean
daggers. 1500 B.C. Inlaid gold.
(National Archaeological Museum,
Athens; and Scala/Art Resource.)

Figure 4-2
Left: Bull and bird on a clay
bowl from Enkomi. 1300–1200
B.C. Diameter about 11 inches.
(Trustees of the British
Museum.)

long dark age: writing disappeared, to be reinvented centuries later. Art seems almost to have disappeared. We do not understand what caused the dark age, or what it was historically.

Perhaps because the lack of a written history or the interruption of myth telling caused a break that no one could repair, Homer reveals that the Greeks were unaware that an earlier Mycenaean culture had existed. They thought that iron had always been dominant. Even Herodotus thought that the pyramids had been built with iron tools.

Homer

Homer, who wrote in the ninth or eighth century B.C., told the story of Troy (or Ilium, its Greek name) in the *Iliad* and the *Odyssey,* proving that the story was remembered because people retold it from generation to generation. A high form of oral literature existed before Homer, whose epics were sung from memory by minstrels, a tradition that lasted until modern times: in the 1940s, bards in Yugoslavia (in the mountains northwest of Greece) sang epics as long as Homer's. Discoveries in 1985 show that Troy had its own epics, written in the Trojan language, called "Lluvian."

ARÊTE: THE VALUE OF PERSONAL HONOR

Homer's epics reveal a passion for personal honor, the Greek arête. The Trojan war was a test of honor, and despite efforts to avoid it, once the war began, it was fought in earnest. The values of honor as expressed in single combat inspired western thought until modern times. Homer's epics made war, in a just cause, a matter of utmost human seriousness, and they made valor a virtue of the highest order.

With Homer, modern literature was born. Achilles and Hector, in the *Iliad,* are three-dimensional people. Odysseus, in the *Odyssey,* is canny, skeptical, cautious, and daring. His twenty-year journey home after the Trojan war, during which he has many hair-raising adventures, became the basic model for episodic literature, both ancient and modern.

HOMER'S GODS: THE HUMAN DIMENSION

Homer's gods have human forms. The Greeks substituted the domination of humankind for the domina-

tion of bulls in the limestone caves of Europe and for the animism of the Celts. The Egyptians had almost achieved this by making gods of their pharoahs. The ultimate Greek fusion was the humanist ideal of seeing gods and humans as common shareholders in life, although with that fusion came the necessary view of the gods as superior to people. In the *Iliad,* a debate among the gods ends with the decision to honor Achilles and destroy Troy. The chief of the gods, Zeus, inspires Agamemnon to attack Troy in the beginning of Book 2:

[Zeus] cried out to the dream and addressed him in winged words: "Go forth, evil Dream, beside the swift ships of the Achaians. Make your way to the shelter of Atreus' son Agamemnon; speak to him in words exactly as I command you. Bid him arm the flowing-haired Achaians for battle in all haste; since now he might take the wide-wayed city of the Trojans. For no longer are the gods who live on Olympos arguing the matter, since Hera forced them all over by her supplication, and evils are in store for the Trojans." (Book 2.)

Like people, the gods argue; even Hera, Zeus's wife, had to argue with him to get her way. Frightening though it may be to have gods who meddle in human affairs, it implies that human life is meaningful.

The Trojan war began when Helen, wife of the Achaean Menelaus, ran off to Troy with Paris. In the *Iliad* (which deals with the events of the final days of the war), the Achaeans, under Agamemnon, gather a coalition of forces to get her back. Ultimately, the battle becomes a businesslike affair; the warriors march out daily from Troy to face warriors who march from their camps to battle. Single combat between the greatest heroes—Hector for Troy and Achilles for the Achaeans—becomes the focus of the epic. At one point, Achilles refuses to fight; he is offended because Agamemnon has taken one of his favorite slave girls, Briseis. Achilles rejoins the army only after his closest friend, Patroclus, is killed by Hector. Then Achilles, in a fury, kills Hector and drags his body behind a chariot around the walls of Troy while Andromache, his wife, wails the fate of the city.

Gods weave and interweave their way throughout the story. Athena, patron of Athens, plays an important part, as she does later in the *Odyssey,* when, as

Homer

1. To what extent does Andromache's emotional outcry in the *Iliad* seem based on a private, personal grief over losing Hector? To what extent is it a public grief? Is either kind of grief dominant?

2. Why would the Greeks imagine that the gods would come down from Mount Olympus to take part in the Trojan war? What does such a view imply about the Greeks' view of themselves? Of their gods?

3. The Greeks imagined gods who could be temporarily deceived, who were vain and sometimes petty, and who were remorseless toward the enemy. How might such beliefs have shaped Greek behavior? Is a connection to be expected between a people and the gods they honor?

4. Why should it be more desirable to worship gods who are in the form of humans than to worship, say, a god who is in the form of a bull or snake?

5. The concept of arête, or honor, applies to people. Should it apply to the Greek gods? Does it seem to?

Odysseus reminds us, she helped him in the Trojan horse:

> For Troy must perish, as ordained, that day
> she harbored the great horse of timber; hidden
> the flower of Akhaia lay, and bore
> slaughter and death upon the men of Troy.
> He sang, then, of the town sacked by Akhaians
> pouring down from the horse's hollow cave,
> this way and that way raping the steep city,
> and how Odysseus came like Arês to
> the door of Deiphobos, with Meneláos,
> and braved the desperate fight there—
> conquering once more by Athena's power. (Book 8.)

According to legend, the Greeks built a huge wooden horse in which they concealed a band of soldiers, left it on the plain before the walled city of Troy, and then pretended to sail off. The Trojans, unsure about what to do with the horse, debated among themselves and then brought it inside the city walls until they could decide. During the night Odysseus and others crept out of the horse and opened the city gates, and the rest of the Greek army

poured in to sack the town. Such deceit and cunning, as well as the mercilessness of the town's destruction, was approved by Athena. She was also the protectress of Odysseus, who was himself cunning and merciless. We must see the combination of mercilessness and tenderness as related to Greek concepts of fate. Fate is what the gods will, and people can do little more than take courage and meet their fate with dignity.

Nowhere is fate met with more emotion and resignation than in the *Iliad,* when Andromache bemoans her lost Hector. She knows that with Hector dead, Troy will fall:

> My husband, you were lost young from life, and have left me a widow in your house, and the boy is only a baby who was born to you and me, the unhappy. I think he will never come of age, for before then head to heel this city will be sacked, for you, its defender, are gone, you who guarded the city, and the grave wives, and the innocent children, wives who before long must go away in the hollow ships, and among them I shall also go, and you, my child, follow. . . . (Book 24.)

At its best, fate brought life to a cosmic level. At its

worst, it limited the role of humankind by limiting free will. Free will means nothing in the face of what Zeus or Hera desires. Greek literature, which demonstrates the concept of fate better then Greek politics, enobles characters, such as Hector and Andromache, who seem most ill-fated. It is as if the Greeks admit basic facts in order to face them better. Yes, the Greeks say, there can be greatness in our efforts to live, despite our sentence of doom. The gods dictate what we do, and yet our own efforts can, if only for a time, forestall the wishes even of the gods. Finally, if we must submit to fate, we must do so with great dignity, which makes us worthy of the respect of the gods.

Greek Myth and Greek Gods

We may never know how devoted the Greeks were to their gods. The Greeks told fortunes; they read their fate in signs, such as the appearances of birds; and they relied on oracles, such as that at Delphi, which built an enormous treasure. Battles were fought for possession of Delphi.

The gods were related: Zeus overthrew the Titans, who were led by his father, Cronus, and cast them into Tartarus, which was the Greek equivalent of hell. Zeus remained a sky god: his symbol was thunder and lightning, and his home was on Mount Olympus. His brother Poseidon became god of the sea, with a full retinue of undersea deities. The third brother, Hades, became god of the underworld. However, Hades and Poseidon sometimes displeased Zeus. Hades, for instance, took Persephone, daughter of the earth goddess Demeter (the goddess of agriculture), and would not let her go from the underworld. Eventually he was persuaded to release her for a part of each year so that she could visit her mother. Such a story is related to the seasonal growth of grains and other food crops. Countless myths are designed to explain seasonal changes and the origin of phenomena such as mountains and oceans.

The chart of the principal gods in Figure 4-3, from Edith Hamilton's *Mythology*, shows that Zeus, though not the first of the gods, was certainly the most active. His liaisons with female gods indicate his special significance. His proper wife was Hera, with whom he produced Arês, the god of war; Hebe, the goddess of youth; and Hephaestus, the god of fire and metalworking. In one version of the myth, Athena sprang fully armed from Zeus's forehead. Jealous of that, Hera gave birth miraculously to Hephaestus, who was born lame. Zeus and Demeter begot Persephone. Apollo, the god of the muses and the arts,

Figure 4-3
The principal Greek gods. (Copyright © 1942 by Edith Hamilton; copyright renewed © 1969 by Dorian Fielding Reid and Doris Fielding Reid, executrix of the will of Edith Hamilton.)

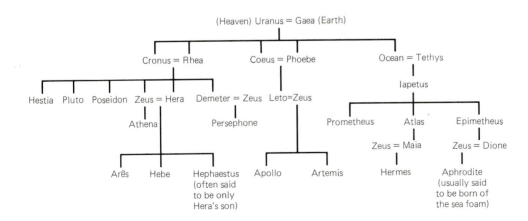

Greek Myth

1. Is the myth of Zeus antifeminist? What is the meaning of his interest in females, both divine and human?

2. How does the Greeks' view of their gods seem different from the Egyptians' concepts of their gods? What are some similarities? Consider the questions of power, authority, and internal squabbles.

3. What might one conjecture about the behavior of Greeks who believed in the gods? Might they have been tempted to behave like their gods? If so, what might their behavior have been?

4. The Greeks invented many stories about their gods. What impulse could produce a literature about the gods? Could it be an indication of an advanced civilization? Could it be a symptom of humanism?

5. Does it appear that the gods, as well as people, must submit to fate? Did Cronus have to submit to fate at the hands of Zeus? What about Zeus?

and Artemis, who is often portrayed as a huntress who protected her nymphs from all men, both came from the union of Zeus and Leto. Zeus and Maia produced Hermes, who served as messenger to the other gods. And Aphrodite, the goddess of beauty, came from the union of Zeus and Dione, although her name means "born from the foam." Zeus had many more relationships with females, not all of whom were goddesses.

Prometheus is credited with having created men. His brother Epimetheus was assigned the task of creation; he gave all the fur, talons, fangs, and natural weapons to the animals but forgot to provide for men. Prometheus then was asked to make men different from the animals and gave them fire. But he also taught them how to trick Zeus by sacrificing only the bones and fat of an ox, rather than the best part. Enraged, Zeus paid men back by creating the source of evil in their world: women. Prometheus was later fastened to a mountain in the Caucasus and was tortured by eagles, who gnawed away his liver.

Prometheus had a secret that could permit Zeus to live forever. Through the intervention of Athena, Prometheus and Zeus patched up the quarrel, and the secret was delivered over. Thus Zeus rules forever.

The Classical Period

PERICLEAN ATHENS

In a span of approximately 100 years, beginning in 776 B.C., the first Olympic games were held; Homer ahd Hesiod lived and wrote; complex musical forms came into existence; Greek architects began building in stone; and Athens was founded as an aristocratic state. In 561 B.C., Athens, no longer governed by aristocrats, became the prey of tyrants, not all of whom were bad. Peisistratus, the first of the tyrants, established an accurate written text of Homer's epic poems. Meanwhile, Persia had become a great military power and had gained control of Greek cities in

Turkey. By 507 B.C., Athens had overthrown the tyrants, had developed the democratic rule for which it is famous, and had become the largest of the Greek cities. Sparta, its much smaller rival, joined with other cities and helped repel a Persian invasion. The Persians came again a decade later, when Athens was the leader of the Delian League, a confederation of Greek states. All the cities in the league had given funds to support their defense. When the Persians attacked Athens in 480 B.C., they found the city almost empty, and after a brief but fierce battle against a handful of resisters, they destroyed it. Through a clever ruse, the main body of Athenians lured the Persians into a nearby harbor, where they waited in heavily armed ships. The Persians, taken by surprise, were routed.

In 448 B.C., Pericles (Figure 4-4) began rebuilding the Acropolis (the term means "high city"). Pericles, who helped maintain democracy in Athens, appointed the sculptor Phidias, his friend, as superviser. Ictinus and Callicrates were commissioned to build the Parthenon, and Mnesicles was commissioned to build the approaches to the Acropolis.

THE ACROPOLIS: ATHENA'S HOLY PLACE

The most important buildings of the project (a plan and a model are shown in Figures 4-5 and 4-6) are the Propylaea, the Erechtheum, and the Parthenon (Figure 4-8), which was dedicated to Athena (Figure 4-7). The smaller of its two rooms, originally called the "parthenon" and containing a throne and some small artifacts, was the treasury for the Delian League. The bigger room, the cella, contained the large gold and ivory statue of Athena Parthenos, "Athena the virgin." She stood balancing her shield with her left hand, and a spear rested against her shoulder. On her helmet was a sphinx, and on her breast the head of Medusa. Her right hand, which may at one time have rested on a pillar, cupped a smaller statue of Nike, or Victory, as is shown on many coins.

The details of the statue's construction are open to debate. To build it of wood, with ivory and gold coverings—as Phidias had been instructed—was impractical for a 37-foot statue. An extraordinary technical feat, the main part of the statue may have been constructed from a long cypress timber filled out with wooden blocks glued together. The ivory would have been glued or attached by pegs, and the gold would have been attached in thick plates with screws. It may be that the wooden core had a brass covering, to which the gold and ivory were affixed.

Plutarch mentions that Pericles told Phidias to make the gold plates removable. Pericles anticipated that certain people, trying to get to him, might attack Phidias. They did accuse him of stealing the gold, but he removed the panels and showed that their weight was unchanged. These plates and other gold images in the Parthenon suggest that they may possibly have served, in part, as a treasury for Athens.

Figure 4-4
Pericles. Roman copy, life-size. (Trustees of the British Museum.)

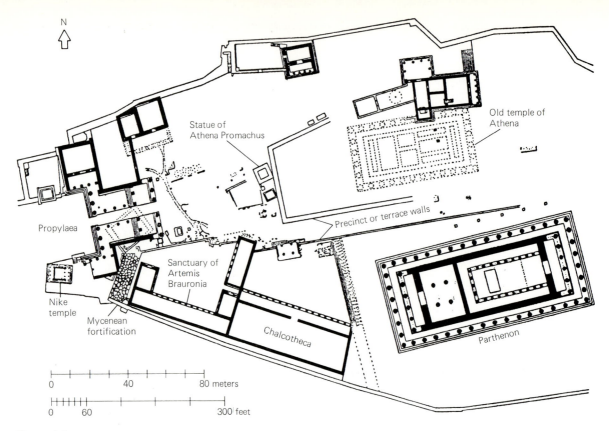

N

Statue of
Athena Promachus

Old temple of
Athena

Propylaea

Precinct or terrace walls

Sanctuary of
Artemis
Braaronia

Nike
temple

Mycenean
fortification

Chalcotheca

Parthenon

0   40   80 meters

0   60   300 feet

Figure 4-5
Above: Restored plan of the Acropolis. 400 B.C.
(From *Hesperia*. Vol. 5, 1937. Fig. 66. By permission
of *Hesperia*.)

Figure 4-6
Left: Model of the
Acropolis. (Royal
Ontario Museum,
Toronto.)

The Parthenon and Athena

1. Compare the Parthenon (Figures 4-6 and 4-8) with the ziggurat at Ur (Figure 2-2). What are the principal differences between the two in terms of surfaces, decoration, columns, and treatment of roofline? Is power an important part of the subject matter of the Parthenon?

2. What views might Pericles have shared with the builders of the American pyramid-temples? What has the Acropolis in common with Mayan or other such temples?

3. What qualities are portrayed in the Varvakeion statuette (Figure 4-7)? What values does Athena seem most to express?

4. Do the same qualities of beauty—in terms of rhythm of line, balance of composition, harmony of details, symmetry, and proportion—govern both the Parthenon and the portrayal of Athena?

5. Classical Greece held that spiritual values could be expressed through beautiful objects. Can we perceive spiritual values in the beauty of the Parthenon?

The use of Doric columns on the Parthenon softens its stony exterior. Their roundness, in contrast with the severity of the lines of the ziggurat at Ur, humanizes the structure. The decorative details and the careful attention to proportion and balance are intended to please and reward, rather than intimidate, the viewer. Like many temples, including those of the Maya, the Acropolis seeks height, moving itself closer to the habitat of the gods and making those who use it their intimates.

The Varvakeion statuette (Figure 4-7), which dates from the time of Christ, stands a little over 40 inches high and was of considerable value in an Athenian household. It may have been copied from the original. Athena's figure and her weapons emphasize her potential for warlike action. Her head is large, her neck is solid, and her arms are capable of wielding power. The posture of the statue is relatively natural; a knee shows through the drapery, and the face is impassive. Athena's helmet, with its central sphinx and flanking gryphons, inspired coin and

medal makers of the time. The serpent that coils within the shield may have been a symbol of special powers.

THE PARTHENON: SPIRITUAL VALUES EXPRESSED IN MARBLE

The ancients were impressed by the statue of Athena, but moderns have been much more impressed by the Parthenon (Figure 4-8), particularly by the architect's attention to how the eye would behold the building. Each column bulges a bit in the middle so that when one looks from below, it appears straight. This is called "entasis"; without it, the center of the column would look thinner than its ends. The fluting, added after the column was built, is designed to avoid the illusion of flatness that an unfluted column gives from a distance. The play of light on the fluting gives a roundness to the column, another possible function of entasis.

The bases of the building, both on the short east

and west pediments and on the longer north and south sides, are not straight. They rise gradually in the middle to about 4 inches on the long sides and almost 3 inches on the short sides. This is to prevent the "weight" of the building from appearing to cause the lines to sag. As it is, they seem straight. Each of the columns leans inward as much as 3 or 4 inches. This may be for strength, to support either the heavy pediments or the roof itself. Leaning columns inward would produce the same effect as using buttresses against the building. This feature may have been designed to help protect against earthquakes. No mortar or cement is used, but many of the joints are reinforced with lead or iron bars encased in lead. Modern restorers in 1909 did not understand the purpose of the lead casing and used steel to help reinforce certain sections. Sixty years later the steel had rusted and had cracked some marble. The original lead-encased iron has still not rusted.

Mathematical Beauty

The beauty of a pyramid is mathematical, and this may be true also of the beauty of the Parthenon. But if it is, the relationships between the parts of the building are more subtle than those of a pyramid. Moreover, the psychological and dramatic relationships between the subjects of the metopes and the subjects of the pediments and their individual sculptures are almost totally novel and add immensely to the harmony of the building.

Figure 4-7
Above: The Varvakeion statuette. (Deutsches Archaeologisches Institut, Athens.)

Figure 4-8
Right: Parthenon, west facade.

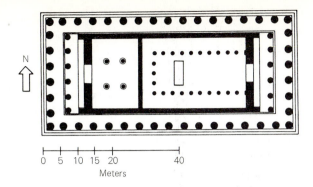

Figure 4-9
Plan of the Parthenon. (By permission of Electa Editrice, Milan.)

The Roman architect Vitruvius insisted that the perfection, in aesthetic terms, of the Parthenon was a result of the harmony of its parts: a result of its mathematical ratios. The building (a plan is shown in Figure 4-9) is dominated by one mathematical ratio. The width is 101½ feet; the length is 228 feet. The ratio of length to width is 4:9. The ratio of the diameter of the columns to the space between them is also 9:4. The ratio of the height of the columns (34¼ feet) plus the entablature (10¾ feet) to the width of the building is also 4:9. Nine is one more than twice four; hence eight columns stand on the east and west, while seventeen, one more than twice eight, stand on the north and south. Many such ratios exist in this building, and it would be tedious to enumerate them. But it is clear that the Greek architects imagined a mathematical "harmony" of elements that we still perceive directly.

The Greek Architectural Orders

The relative standardization of Greek temples was well under way by the seventh century B.C. The Greeks understood the nature of the marble and stone they used in their buildings. They knew how much stress on the entablature could be borne by the powerful columns poised on the stylobate. Egyptian architecture (the walls at Saqqara appear to have had columns) may have been an inspiration, but the Greek columns had a special, lasting value which was transmitted to the Romans and to later generations of builders.

PERCEPTION KEY

The Acropolis

1. Zeus was a masculine figure of worship. Does Athena seem to have been a feminine figure of worship? Do you think that worshiping a female deity had any effect on the architecture of the Acropolis?

2. Is the home of Athena beautiful to behold? Should it be?

3. Pericles used funds that were gathered by the Delian League and designated for mutual defense to rebuild Athens and the Acropolis after the Persians destroyed them. The league complained that the money was misspent. Do you agree?

4. The Parthenon (Figure 4-8) is the flower of Doric order architecture. By virtue of its architectural "look" or its qualities of volume and space, does it seem like a church to you? A bank? What function does it suggest most to you?

5. Find a modern building using a Greek architectural order. What is its function now? Was it ever used for any other purpose in the past? Does its use harmonize with what you know about the buildings on the Acropolis?

(a) Doric   (b) Ionic   (c) Corinthian

Figure 4-10
(a) Doric, (b) Ionic, and (c) Corinthian entabulature, capital, and base. (From M.I. Findlay. *Atlas of Classical Archaeology*. New York: McGraw-Hill, 1977. By permission of Rainbird Publishing Group.)

The Doric order (Figure 4-10*a*) has a clean but massive quality that is best revealed in the elevation of the temple of Hera (Figure 4-12), built on the plan of the Parthenon. It has the same number of columns, but the tympanum and frieze are bare. The Doric order puts the column directly on the stylobate, whereas the Ionic order (Figure 4-10*b*) and the Corinthian order (Figure 4-10*c*) use bases beneath the column. The Doric order uses an unadorned echinus and abacus, suggesting simplicity and strength, as shown in Figures 4-11 and 4-12. The more detailed orders sometimes found uses within buildings, as the Ionic may have done in the interior of the Parthenon.

Sculptures of the Parthenon: Idealized Narrative

The Parthenon was built in nine years, and its sculptures took twelve years to complete. The entire project required a little more than twenty years to finish. Phidias probably acted as overseer of the sculptures; but since he was busy with the great statue of Athena, it is probable that the other master sculptors were responsible for the execution, and maybe the design, of the other statues.

In the fifth century after Christ, the giant statue of Athena in the Parthenon was removed to Constantinople, where it stayed for some five centuries. Then it disappeared. The building and the statues on the

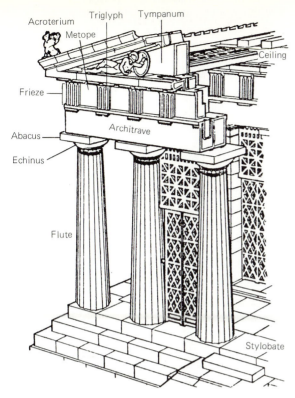

Figure 4-11
Section of a temple, Doric order (From M. I. Findlay. *Atlas of Classical Archaeology*. New York: McGraw-Hill, 1977. By permission of Rainbird Publishing Group.)

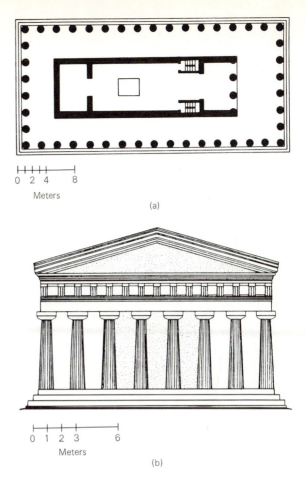

(a)

(b)

Figure 4-12
(a) Plan and (b) elevation, temple of Hera, Paestum. (From Lloyd Seton et al. *Ancient Architecture.* New York: Abrams, 1972. Figs. 360–361. By permission of Electa Editrice, Milan.)

east and west pediments remained largely intact and in place until 1687, when the Parthenon was exploded by a shell in a war between the Turks and the Venetians. A Venetian general tried to take some of the statues off the pediment with a crane, but the ropes broke and the statues were shattered. Ironically, the Venetians abandoned Athens to the Turks two days later because the Acropolis had no real military value.

A British traveler, Lord Elgin, fearing their destruction, purchased many of the remaining statues early in the nineteenth century. They are now in the British Museum in London. Elgin also removed almost half of the frieze, which is Ionic in style

(without triglyph interruptions) and continuous in action. It represents a procession of Athenians celebrating a holy day, the Panathenaic festival; heifers are coming to be sacrificed, and a figure stands ready to wear the sacred garment, the peplos. On the metopes on each side of the building are carvings in relief that tell various stories: the battle of Troy, the battle of gods and giants, the battle of Lapiths and centaurs (Figure 4-13), and the battle of the Greeks and the Amazons. Their narratives reveal an awareness that civilization is fragile and needs the protection of the gods.

Figure 4-13
Metope from the Parthenon.
(Trustees of the British
Museum.)

The Birth of Athena: Protectress

The east pediment, on which there were freestanding statues of heroic size, told of the miraculous birth of Athena. The west pediment told the story of Athena's struggle with Zeus. Because a French artist drew the arrangements of the statues on the west pediment in the 1700s, we know what they looked like. But the figures on the east pediment were not in place and were not intact, and so a great deal of guesswork has gone into reconstructing them. Since the east pediment was over the main entrance to the building, it is important to know what was on it. One of the most painstaking efforts of scholarship on the subject was the reconstruction worked out by Evelyn B. Harrison (Figure 4-14).

Zeus is at the center, sitting on his throne; he has just produced Athena, who stands fully armed at his left. On his right is Hephaestus. Each of these figures

is in a special relation to Zeus. Beginning the action on the left with Helios (the sun, rising,) and ending on the right with Selene (the moon, setting) imparts unity to the events of a single day and focuses our attention on the apex.

The existing statues from the east pediment are known as the "Elgin marbles." Like the rest of the building, they are carved from Pentelic marble, a naturally cream-colored building material. Even in their present damaged state, they have every mark of genius and show a special regard for the material in which they are worked. Once this skill in sculpture was lost, it did not return again until the late Renaissance.

The east pediment shows Athena's birth—she is full-grown and fully armed. All the gods lean slightly outward from the center of the action as if reacting to a shock wave. The attention of the nearby figures is

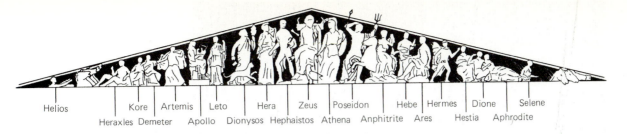

Helios   Kore   Artemis   Leto   Hera   Zeus   Poseidon   Hebe   Hermes   Dione   Selene

Heraxles Demeter   Apollo   Dionysos Hephaistos Athena Anphitrite Ares   Hestia   Aphrodite

Figure 4-14
East pediment of the Parthenon. (Drawing by Evelyn B. Harrison. From "Athena and Athens in the East Pediment of the Parthenon," *American Journal of Archaeology*, LXXI, 1967. Pp. 27–58. Plate 22, fig. 30. By permission of Evelyn B. Harrison.)

drawn to the center, while the figures who are at the ends of the pediment do not yet know what has happened.

The nude male shown in Figure 4-15 is left, or south, of Athena, with his back to the action. His identity has been in question: he is either Dionysus or Heracles, and he is lying on a lion's skin, his symbol. Whoever he may be, he is unaware of how momentous the day is. His pose suggests anticipation, and he seems to be rising from sleep. His body is fully modeled, but his midriff is relaxed and therefore does not show the idealized tension found in other male nudes.

Parallel with this male figure in the south are three female figures on the north (Figure 4-16). Evelyn Harrison has identified them as Hestia, Dione, and Aphrodite. If she is right, Aphrodite leans recumbent against her mother—echoing the idea of birth. Moreover, she seems to be getting ready for sleep, as Selene (the moon) sets to her left, paralleling the

PERCEPTION KEY

Sculptures of the Parthenon

1. Examine Evelyn Harrison's drawing of the east pediment (Figure 4-14). Take a measure of the proportion of the height of the tympanum to its width. Does it relate to the general proportion of 4:9?

2. Examine Figures 4-5 and 4-6, which show the layout of the buildings on the Acropolis. Given the Greeks' fascination with harmony and proportion, why would they permit the entire arrangement of buildings to be such a jumble?

3. Idealization of the human form dominates Phidias's treatment (Figures 4-13, 4-15, and 4-16). What constitutes such idealization? Is idealization also distortion?

4. The backs of these statues, which were never intended to be seen, are fully carved and finished. What could this mean?

5. Many people are disturbed to learn that not only were most of these statues painted in bright colors, but so was the background of the tympanum itself. Moreover, the shields were gilded, the spears were made of bronze, and the reins and bridles of the horses were fashioned from bright metal. Does this disturb you? If so, why?

action of Heracles, who is about to rise. These figures are parallel to one another in one further way. Heracles is masculine because of his strength and power. Aphrodite is feminine because of her beauty and commitment to love.

Such balance and symmetry are basic to this composition. For instance, Heracles is close to two other figures, possibly Persephone and Demeter; thus he, like Aphrodite, is part of a group of three. In each group is the figure of either Demeter or Dione, both of whom had a liaison with Zeus that produced offspring, which again reinforces the central concept of birth.

Moreover, next inward from each of these groups is a single figure: Artemis to the south and Hermes to the north. Each is a messenger to the gods and each is spreading the news. The fact that the messengers have not yet reached the ends of the pediment might explain the puzzling inattention of Heracles and Aphrodite.

Figure 4-17
Theater at Epidaurus. (Photo, Greek National Tourist Office.)

Greek Drama: Fate and Human Courage

The geniuses of Greek comedy are Aristophanes (c. 450– c. 388 B.C.) and Menander (342–292 B.C.); they are joined by the tragedians Aeschylus (525–465 B.C.), Euripides (c. 484 – 406 B.C.), and Sophocles (c. 496 – 406 B.C.). They competed in day-long festivals in Athens held in open-air theaters like the one at Epidaurus (Figure 4-17), which is cut into the rock. The plays were attended by all kinds of people, and special seats were provided for the priests of Dionysus and for the archons, or judges, who decided the winner.

Aristophanes's plays *The Frogs* and *The Clouds* are like modern farces. They portray real people, such as Socrates, and while they make fun of individuals, they never make fun of people in general. That would be going too far, since it would attack the foundation of the Greek city-state. The works of Menander, with the exception of one play and some fragments, have been totally lost. Roman copies show that he was a gifted writer of comedies of manners—polished plays that reveal some of society's faults.

The tragedies were staged during the festival of Dionysus, which celebrated death and rebirth, like the festival of Osiris. Tragedians submitted their plays to the archon, who, if he accepted them, would put them into production. The costs were usually borne by a rich private "producer." Each play was provided with a chorus, who represented the audience and commented on the action, speaking directly to the main characters of the drama, sometimes at key moments.

Sophocles's *Oedipus Rex* ("Oedipus the King") was Aristotle's model in the *Poetics* as he attempted a definition of tragic drama. Aristotle stressed unities of plot, character, and action: one story line should follow one main character, and the action should be in one place on one day. Such unities hold a play together and make it more effective. Aristotle also stressed excellence of plot, character, and language, as well as excellence of music, which accompanied the Greek tragedies.

Oedipus Rex is the story of Oedipus, who was born to a royal family. Because omens said that the boy would kill his father and marry his mother, his parents gave him to a servant with instructions to kill him. But the servant could not kill the baby. Instead, he took him to a distant place, bound a leather thong through his Achilles tendons, and abandoned him. A wandering shepherd saved Oedipus and raised him as his own child. When Oedipus grew up, he left home to avoid the omens. At a crossroads, his way was blocked by a nobleman, Laius—his true father. Neither yielded to the other, and Oedipus killed Laius. Soon he arrived at Thebes, a city which was frightened by the sphinx and which asked every traveler a riddle: "What walks on four legs in the morning, two in the afternoon, and three in the evening?" Oedipus solved the riddle: it is a human being, who crawls on all fours as a baby, walks on two legs as an adult, and uses a cane—the third leg—in old age.

In Thebes, Oedipus married Queen Jocasta, who had just lost her husband, Laius. Thus, unknown to himself, he married his own mother. The play begins with Oedipus searching for the criminal whose acts against the gods have brought a plague on the city. He does not know that he is searching for himself, and when the prophet Tiresias tells him the truth, he does not believe it. Witnesses are brought in, and when the truth becomes known, Jocasta hangs herself, and Oedipus strikes out his eyes with her gold brooch. Then he leaves Thebes, his true home, to wander as a lonely exile—a fate as bad as death.

The dominant force in this tragedy, as in most Greek tragedies, is fate and the struggle of humans against it. People watched tragedies in order to understand their own condition. Seeing that rulers can fall and be destroyed, they realized how they, too, were subdued by fate. One rule for these tragedies was that the tragic hero or heroine had to be noble; otherwise, there could be no fall from a great height. Greek tragedy showed that all things change. At one moment we might, like Oedipus, seem to have a bright future. At another, we might be ruined.

Oedipus was at fault because he killed his father and married his mother. He could not plead ignorance. The gods did not care that he did not know who Laius and Jocasta were. The real problem of the play is that Oedipus did not know himself, which refers back to the first of Socrates's instructions: "Know thyself."

Self-knowledge is fundamental to western literature as well as to much western philosophy and psychology. Freud saw the play as a model for human psychology because it revealed the male's unconscious desire to compete with his father, remove him,

and live alone with his mother. The fact that such desires are unconscious means that we are not aware of them. In the terms of Sophocles's play, this means that we do not *know* them. It does not mean that such desires do not exist. "Knowing thyself," then, implies knowing your unconscious desires.

Hellenism: The Waning of Tradition

During the Hellenistic age—which began at the time of Alexander the Great, in the fourth century B.C.—the Greeks conquered Persia and extended their rule to Pergamon, in Asia Minor (Turkey), and to Alexandria, in Egypt. When Alexander died, in 323 B.C., his generals fell out among themselves in petty squabbles, instead of securing Greek holdings. This began a long decline in Greek power and influence that was in sharp contrast to the greatness of the Periclean past.

GREEK PHILOSOPHY: VALUING THE SOUL

Greek philosophy valued the soul and deemphasized sensual experience. The tradition of the academy began with Socrates (c. 470–399 B.C.), who was the teacher of Plato (c. 428–348 or 347 B.C.), who was the teacher of Aristotle (384–322 B.C.), who was the teacher of Alexander the Great (356–323 B.C.). Philosophy had long been practiced in Greece, but Socrates became a legend. He stressed pure ideas—justice, love, and wisdom—rather than sensory perception.

Socrates: Know Thyself

In his old age, Socrates was tried and convicted of "corrupting youth." No one knows exactly what this meant, but a vague political charge of atheism was brought against him, and he argued that his belief in the spirit implied a belief in the gods. He argued well against every point, but ultimately he was forced to die.

Socrates's unusual skill as a teacher, at a time when the Greek educational system was changing, may have been the cause. Plato was soon to form his academy, the first model of the university, in the olive groves of Academe. Young men had formerly been educated at home by their relatives; now they were encouraged to leave home for instruction. For this reason, Socrates might have been considered a corrupter of youth. His most important piece of advice, "Know thyself," may have appeared to slight the gods.

By placing humanity at the center of philosophy, Socrates reflected the Greek mood, in which human affairs took first importance, implying a change from a god-centered to a human-centered culture. Perhaps nothing so definite as this polarity ever existed, but pressures toward a fuller humanism shaped Greek thought 500 years before Christ. If Socrates seemed to be moving too quickly in that direction, it would have been possible for conservative politicians to think him dangerous.

The Socratic method, a question-and-answer approach, assumes that the student already has the knowledge, which the teacher coaxes out with questions. Socrates is credited with being profoundly inspiring, a bit mystical in nature, and intensely involved in the life of the mind. As he said, "The unexamined life is not worth living," and he challenged his students to examine their own lives intensely.

Plato: The Theory of Forms

Plato, an aristocrat whose family helped govern Athens, wrote dialogues in which Socrates speaks; they offer the best insight we have into Socrates's character and method. The *Apology* records Socrates's last words to the Athenians before his death. *Crito* is set in Socrates's prison, as are the dialogues *Phaedo*, *Gorgias*, *Timaeus*, and *Symposium*. All relate discussions of an earlier time in Socrates's life. A sample of the Socratic method follows, from *Crito*. Its subject is the question whether to follow the advice of the public or that of the person of wisdom. But the real question is: Should one follow the people of Athens or the "criminal," Socrates?

Socrates: And the opinions of the wise are good, and the opinions of the unwise are evil?

Crito: Certainly.

Socrates: And what was said about another matter? Is the pupil who devotes himself to the practice of gymnastics supposed to attend to the praise and blame and opinion of every man, or of one man only—his physician or trainer, whoever he may be?

Crito: Of one man only.

Socrates: And he ought to fear the censure and welcome the praise of that one only, and not of the many?

Crito: Clearly so.

Socrates: And he ought to act and train, and eat and drink in the way which seems good to his single master who has understanding, rather than according to the opinion of all other men put together?

Crito: True.

Socrates: And if he disobeys and disregards the opinion of the many who have no understanding, will he not suffer evil?

Crito: Certainly he will.

Socrates: And what will the evil be, whither tending and what affecting in the disobedient person?

Crito: Clearly, affecting the body; that is what is destroyed by the evil.

Socrates: Very good; and is not this true, Crito, of other things which we need not separately enumerate? In questions of just and unjust, fair and foul, good and evil, which are the subjects of our present consultation, ought we to follow the opinion of the many and fear them; or the opinion of the one man who has understanding? Ought we not to fear and reverence him more than all the rest of the world: and if we desert him shall we not destroy and injure that principle in us which may be assumed to be improved by justice and deteriorated by injustice;—there is such a principle?

Crito: Certainly there is, Socrates.

Socrates: Take a parallel instance:—if, acting under the advice of those who have no understanding, we destroy that which is improved by health and is deteriorated by disease, would life be worth having? And that which has been destroyed is—the body?

Crito: Yes.

Socrates: Could we live, having an evil and corrupted body?

Crito: Certainly not.

Socrates: And will life be worth having, if that higher part of man be destroyed, which is improved by justice and depraved by injustice? Do we suppose that principle, whatever it may be in man which has to do with justice and injustice to be inferior to the body?

Crito: Certainly not.

Socrates: More honorable than the body?

Crito: Far more.

Socrates: Then, my friend, we must not regard what the many say of us: but what he, the one man who has understanding of just and unjust, will say, and what the truth will say.

Plato's thought, which is revealed in the dialogues —including his most important book-length work, *The Republic*—is highly moral, and his concerns with love, justice, and morality pleased later Christians. He held that people desire justice and virtue and that unjust, unvirtuous behavior is a failure of knowledge, temporarily obscured by the passions.

He also professed a first cause, god, and believed that the human being has an immortal soul. Like Christ, Plato emphasized the spiritual life. Instead of a church, he founded his academy, which long outlived him. Some philosophers have gone so far as to say that all later philosophy was built on Plato's work.

Plato's theory of forms insists that all things exist in their perfect, ideal form only in heaven. Things on earth are simply a shadow of heaven's reality. In *The Republic,* Plato uses the analogy of men chained to a wall in a cave. A fire behind them casts a light on the wall before them. People walk in front of the fire, and the men see only their shadows. They do not see the real people. Our senses, Plato says, are like this. We do not see the real, ideal forms. We see, instead, a sensory version, imperfect and changeable. "Heaven" is the real world—perfect and unperishable. We must aspire to it and not be taken in by the false versions of reality in our sensory world.

Plato's views produced a commitment to spiritual values. Abstract ideals of love, truth, justice, virtue, and goodness cannot be perceived by the senses. They are as close to reality as we can come because ideas do not change. Materialism—faith in things we can perceive—ceases to have meaning. A serious consequence of this view was that science could not develop, because observation depends on the senses. Platonic science was based on reason and not on observation. Consequently, western culture, because it responded to Platonism, did not soon develop a "modern" science.

Aristotle: The Value of Sensory Evidence

Aristotle, Plato's most distinguished student, entered the academy at age seventeen and stayed for twenty years. He was known as the "intellect" of the school. After traveling, he returned to start the Lyceum, where he lectured on poetics, art, psychology, rhetoric, and logic. He is credited with having invented

CONCEPT KEY

Socratic Dialogue

1. Socrates argues by analogy in the dialogue from *Crito,* comparing a physical trainer to a philosopher. What are the strengths and weaknesses of this analogy?

2. What would the Socratic order of importance—the mind as superior to the body—have meant for those who believed it? How might it have guided their lives?

3. If the mind is superior to the body, why does Socrates begin with a discussion of physical training?

4. Have you witnessed the Socratic method in teaching? Do you respect it? What are its strengths and weaknesses?

5. Are you convinced by Socrates's argument with Crito?

Greek Philosophy

1. Why would science depend more heavily on evidence gathered by the senses than it would on reasoning done in the abstract? Is it not true that scientific truths can be figured out by reasoning?

2. Why would placing special value on sensory evidence produce materialistic attitudes? Why might avoiding the "truth" of sensory evidence result in placing more value on spiritual truths? How are the sensory and the spiritual opposed?

3. Socrates, Plato, and Aristotle all conceive of a god, or a first mover. None of them talk as much about the gods as they do about people. Is that evidence of a growing humanism?

4. Is an emphasis on politics, law, ethics, and the pursuit of the good more likely to intensify the development of humanist values than, say, an emphasis on physics and biology?

5. In Athens, Greek power, Greek art, Greek architecture, and Greek thought flowered at approximately the same time. Should we think of this as unusual? What might have accounted for this? Was it to be expected?

---

logic. Because he was interested in archaeology and medicine (his father was a physician), he stressed observation and good record keeping, the tools of the modern scientist. This placed him in contradiction with Plato's theory of forms. He made an uneasy peace with it by essentially agreeing that Plato was correct—that the real world is in heaven—but he also maintained that the earthly world is knowable through careful observation.

Aristotle's comments on drama in the *Poetics* are still central to any discussion of theater. His *Analytics* is the basis of modern logic. His *On the Soul* is the first full treatise on psychology and was influential until the early twentieth century. He wrote *Physics* and *Metaphysics* and lectured on biology. In addition to works on the sciences, he also wrote *Politics* and *Ethics*, both of which provide insight into how we should live our lives. Happiness, the highest good for humans, "is a working of the soul in the way of excellence or virtue," and is achieved essentially by leading a temperate life dominated by reason.

HELLENISTIC SCULPTURE

In Hellenistic sculpture we see some of the tensions felt in the waning years of Greek culture. Some critics have held that the realism of the sculpture reflects a lowering of ideals, a lessening in faith, while others have seen in it signs of struggle and anxiety. The Romans made many copies of Hellenistic work, and some Hellenistic sculpture survives only in that form.

The dying Gaul (Figure 4-18) looks as if he is about to collapse from his wounds. This is not the figure of a godlike creature, like those of Phidias, but a real person who deserves our sympathy. The Gauls, a Celtic people, were in contact with Greek culture, as Celtic literature reveals, and the *Dying Gaul* celebrates a warlike interaction. The fact that the work is so realistic that it looks almost like a tableau has caused some critics to consider it "stagy" and artificial. Nonetheless, it influenced Roman sculpture and other works over the centuries.

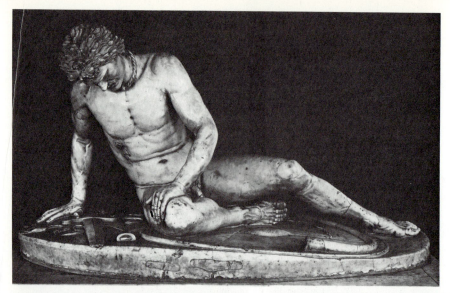

Figure 4-18
Top: *Dying Gaul.* Bronze original, Pergamon, c. 240.
Roman copy, marble, life-size. (Musei Capitolini, Rome;
photo, Barbara Malter.)

Figure 4-19
Left: Aphrodite of Melos. c. 150–100 B.C. Marble, 6 feet
10 inches high. (Louvre, Paris; photo, Musées
Nationaux.)

Figure 4-20
Above right: Agesander, Athanadoros, and
Polydoros—the Laocoön group. 40–22 B.C. (?) 8 feet
high. (Musei Vaticani.)

Hellenistic Sculpture

1. Can you see signs of degeneration in the Hellenistic works shown in Figures 4-18, 4-19, and 4-20? What qualities would make critics feel that these works are inferior to the earlier works of, say, Phidias?

2. Is the Laocoön group as concerned with balance and symmetry as the group on the east pediment of the Parthenon? Is it a realistic work?

3. What are the qualities of pose, representation, or expression that distinguish the realism of the *Dying Gaul* from the idealism of the Aphrodite of Melos? Do you agree that these works are, respectively, realistic and idealized?

4. Does Hellenistic sculpture seem to be concerned with representing or expressing human emotion? What ranges of emotion do you think are expressed in the works shown in Figures 4-18, 4-19, and 4-20?

5. What is the difference between the emotions evoked by Hellenistic sculpture and those evoked by the sculpture on the Parthenon? Is this an important difference for distinguishing between the apex of Greek sculpture and its period of decline?

The Aphrodite of Melos (Figure 4-19) seems to defy its stone, and yet it is not as dramatic or staged a work as the *Dying Gaul*. The posture is almost that of a dancer; the lines of the shoulders and of the hips tilt in different directions. The portions of the work that represent skin seem luminous, soft, and human. The face is idealized, but it is recognizably human and is much more easy, natural, and realistic than the heroic works on the Parthenon. Aphrodite, the goddess of love, seems sensual and appealing, yet chaste and proper. She is not a particular person, like the dying Gaul. Aphrodite's posture is traditional; her features seem idealized but are much closer to human features than to those of an imagined, remote goddess.

The Laocoön group (Figure 4-20) was discovered in a vineyard in Rome after Michelangelo had finished his statue of David in 1501. It had been mentioned by the Roman writer Pliny as an important work by three sculptors of Rhodes: Agesander, Athenadoros, and Polydoros. A massive sculpture, cut out of one piece of marble, it shows the Trojan priest Loacoön struggling with his sons against a serpent sent by Poseidon to kill him. His crime is vague, but it seems to have been linked to his urging the Trojans not to bring into the city the horse that the Greeks had left outside the gates of Troy. The agony and struggle in this work are sometimes seen as further evidence of the struggles of the Hellenistic Greeks to keep their culture vital.

Music and Dance

Many Greek ceremonies featured dance, particularly dancing women who appeared in costume and made use of the flow of their garments. The terra-cotta statuettes shown in Figures 4-21 and 4-22 resemble the statue of Artemis on the east pediment of the Parthenon. Motion is expressed in the lines, the swirls, and the serpentine shape of the garments. But in Figure 4-21 motion is also expressed in the posture of the dancer. Her head is poised, as if she has stopped in mid-step. Her hands create a gentle circle

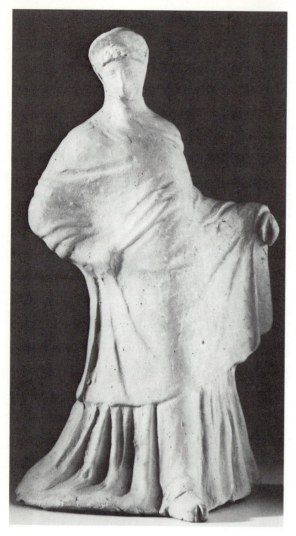

Figure 4-21
Greek dancer. c. 100 B.C. Terra-cotta, about 9 inches tall. (Trustees of the British Museum.)

Figure 4-22
Greek dancer. c. 100 B.C. Terra-cotta, about 8 inches tall. (Trustees of the British Museum.)

which seems about to break. The motion, as in most early Greek dance, begins in the solar plexus, just below the middle of the rib cage; from there it radiates outward. Both figures are moving intensely outward from the body's center.

Dance was basic to the education of every Greek. It was considered training for the body and for the spirit. Moving in time to music and musical rhythms was thought to bring people closer to the harmonies of the world, such as the movements of the planets. But the Greeks also expressed themselves in more exuberant dances. They often danced the cordax when intoxicated, a dance that naturally permitted improvisation. Some dances, such as the krinon (which was danced by the chorus) and the paradenai tettara (for four dancers), were ensemble pieces. Some dances were relatively stately—for example, the diple, which was danced to accompanying voices, and the ephilema, which was danced to instruments. Others, such as the nibadismos and the morphasmos, required the dancers to imitate animals.

Some Greek vases show dances done by nymphs and satyrs. Satyrs were half animal and half man, and they symbolized intense sexual power. Such dances were themselves intense. The bacchantes (the term is derived from the name of the god of wine, Bacchus) performed very lively dances, usually holding hands and forming a circle. Some dances told stories from Greek myths. The story of the death and rebirth of Dionysus was a particular favorite. Unfortunately, we cannot reproduce these dances, although study of vases and statues has allowed us to approximate them. Greek dance was almost surely as impressive as Greek theater and philosophy.

The Greeks' musical scales, like many of their dances, came from India. According to legend, Pythagoras (c. 580–500 B.C.), a mathematician, returned from India with a tuned string from which he could construct scales. The octave and all the intervals between notes that we rely on today were known to him. The Greeks inherited Egyptian wind instruments, the lyre (or kithera), the reed pipe (or flute), and a variety of percussion instruments. The sistrum, which made a jingling noise when shaken, had spread through Greece and even into Europe.

Greek music concentrated on melody. The octave —actually seven tones, the first of which is repeated at a higher level—was called the "diapason" by the Greeks. However, they relied on a smaller musical unit called the "tetrachord," which consisted of four tones. Two tetrachords could represent an octave. The kithera had four strings, like the lyre.

Different ways of organizing tones, starting with different notes, gave rise to different scales or modes. The Greek modes were associated with their emotional effect on the listener, and their names implied much more than just the scale of tones; they referred to the kinds of music best suited to those scales. Each mode had its own ethos, or character. The Dorian mode, for instance, like the Doric architectural order, was stately and chaste. The Lydian mode was racy and considered possibly "dangerous."

Some of the major Greek modes, with the approximate ranges of notes, are as follows: f down to F, hypolydian; e down to E, Dorian; d down to D, Phrygian; c down to C, Lydian; and a down to A, Aeolian. Each produced music suitable for different purposes. During the Middle Ages, the Greek modes survived in European church modes. Today, the singing of cantors in synagogues also preserves some of the ancient traditions. The Greek modes are the basis of modern scales and musical keys.

Summary

The defeat of Athens in the Peloponnesian wars, resulting in the Spartan alliance, marked the end of the age of classical innovation. Thereafter, the Greeks seemed to spread their influence and achievements throughout the near east, India, Sicily, Turkey, Italy, and north Africa. Like Aristotle, Alexander the Great was not Athenian, but Macedonian. His forces spread Greek civilization and art throughout the known world: from Egypt to the Danube and from Turkey to Armenia, Syria, Iran, and Afghanistan and almost to China. His victories began in 334 B.C., and his empire grew steadily until his death in 323 B.C. Thereafter it crumbled slowly, but it was clear that Greek influence had permeated all the areas he conquered. There is even evidence that the great religious statues of India, such as those of Buddha, were based on portraits of Greek gods.

Greek Doric columns, Greek sculptured heads, Greek dance, Greek thought, and Greek ideals expressed less a conquest than a revolution in thought and feeling. The Greeks had absorbed what they could from their nearest neighbors; then they added their own genius for humanizing the arts that they knew. Other peoples, in seizing on the Greeks' achievement, gave proof that what the Greeks had done was good. The classical ideal, based on the ultimate worth of the human being, dominated the works of Greek artists and thinkers. Humanism, which celebrates the value of humankind, transformed the world.

Concepts in Chapter 4

Archaic Greece was originally dominated by the bronze age culture of the Mycenaeans on the mainland and the Minoans on Crete.

Iron age invaders, the Dorians, brought a dark age that lasted for 400 years.

Homer's epics demonstrate that the stories of some historical events, such as the Trojan war, were preserved orally.

Homer's epics celebrate arête, or honor, and the virtues of individual combat in a "just" war.

Homer portrays the gods as being keenly concerned with human activities. Classical Greece, in the age of Pericles, was a nation powerful enough to hold off Persian invaders.

Classical Greek art idealizes the gods, as in Phidias's sculpture for the Parthenon.

The Parthenon, sacred to Athena, the patron goddess of Athens, was built to satisfy the senses; a mathematical ratio of 4:9 was used to accomplish this.

The Greeks believed that spiritual values were expressible in sensory terms; thus perceptual beauty was an avenue toward spiritual awareness.

The Greek architectural orders reveal complex patterns of expression with moral implications.

The Parthenon sculptures are narrative compositions.

The Ionic frieze on the Parthenon narrates the Panathenaic festival.

The metopes on the Parthenon narrate important struggles that threatened Greek civilization.

Phidias's east pediment narrates the miraculous birth of Athena.

Phidias's sculpture represents an idealization of the gods in human form.

Greek drama was presented in contests held during festivals.

Tragedies celebrating death and rebirth were performed at the feast of Dionysus.

The consequences of fate dominate Greek drama.

Greek culture spread throughout the world as a result of Alexander's conquests.

Greek philosophy, which had a long tradition, reached its apex in the humanist teachings of Socrates, who valued ideas.

Socrates valued the soul and self-knowledge.

Plato devalued sensory experience; his theory of forms insisted that the only reality is the ideal in heaven.

Aristotle valued sensory experience as a means of acquiring true knowledge.

Greek influence spread throughout the world, bringing a humanist revolution in thought and feeling.

Suggested Readings

Cook, Albert, and Edward Dolin, eds. *An Anthology of Greek Tragedy.* Indianapolis: Bobbs-Merrill, 1972.

Finley, M. I. *The Ancient Greeks.* New York: Viking, 1964.

Frankel, Hermann. *Early Greek Poetry and Philosophy.* New York: Harcourt Brace Jovanovich, 1962, 1973.

Harsh, Philip Whaley. *A Handbook of Classical Drama.* Stanford, Calif.: Stanford, 1944.

Homer. *The Iliad.* Robert Fitzgerald, trans. New York: Doubleday, 1974.

———. *The Odyssey.* Richmond Lattimore, trans. New York: Harper and Row, 1967.

Hopper, R. J. *The Acropolis.* New York: Macmillan, 1971.

Kitto, H. D. F. *The Greeks.* Baltimore: Penguin, 1957.

Lawrence, A. W. *Greek Architecture.* 3d ed. Harmondsworth, England: Penguin, 1973.

Lullies, R., and M. Hirmer. *Greek Sculpture.* New York: Abrams, 1957.

Rodenwaldt, Gerhart. *The Acropolis.* 2d ed. Norman: University of Oklahoma Press, 1957.

Schoder, Raymond V., S. J. *Masterpieces of Greek Art.* Greenwich, Conn.: New York Graphic Society, 1960.

CHAPTER 5

THE ROMAN EMPIRE: EXTENDING GREEK VALUES

Etruscan Beginnings

According to Virgil's epic poem the *Aeneid*, Rome was founded in 753 B.C. by Romulus and Remus, descendants of Aeneas, who had fled Troy in 1184 B.C. These dates cannot be validated, but they are quite possibly accurate. Aeneas settled in Latium, a center of the Etruscan civilization, and eventually selected a site on the river Tiber as a good place to build a city. The Romans defeated the Etruscan general Tarquin in 509 B.C., after which they declared a republic and cast out the remaining Etruscans.

ETRUSCAN ARCHITECTURE AND PAINTING

Despite our limited knowledge of Etruscan culture, one fact is clear: Etruscan buildings definitely had a dominant side—the front—from which they were to be viewed. That tradition, rather than the tradition of the Greeks, was passed on to the Romans.

Surviving Etruscan tombs (such as those shown in Figures 5-1 and 5-2) are decorated with replicas of the houses in which the dead once lived. In some of the tombs, there are even stone or stucco replicas of furniture and other household items, and some have interesting square columns with a flared archaic capital.

The tombs were built as houses for the dead, like the Egyptian necropolises, which demonstrates that the Etruscans had a similar religious attitude toward the afterlife. Most of the paintings in the tombs portray young people engaged in activities which might have absorbed them in life. Some paintings show that the Etruscans had a knowledge of Greek myths; other paintings depict scenes from funeral games, some of which involved men in combat to the death.

The scene of hunters and fishermen in Figure 5-2 has analogues more in Egyptian tomb painting than in Greek or Roman painting. Humans and animals are shown in sharp profile, and numerous scenes are

87

Figure 5-1
Above: The tomb of the reliefs, Caere
(Cerveteri). Fifth to fourth century
A.D. (Photo, Scala/Art Resource.)

Figure 5-2
Right: Seascape from the tomb of
hunting and fishing, Tarquinia. c. 510
B.C. (Archaeological Museum,
Florence; photo, SEF/Art Resource.)

Figure 5-3
Apollo from Veii. c. 510 B.C. Terra-cotta, about 70 inches high. (Museo Nazionale di Villa Giulia, Rome; Archivo Fotografico, Soprintendenza alle Antichita dell/Etruria Meridionale.)

gathered together in one composition. Still, the composition is sparse—not crowded with detail, as it might be in an Egyptian version—and attention is paid to each figure rather than to the balance and symmetry achieved by the entire composition. Design is not the primary element, nor is the value of decoration. Instead, this painting serves as a record of activity—a memento and a reminder to the dead of the activities of life.

ETRUSCAN SCULPTURE

The Etruscans preferred bronze and terra-cotta—clay that has been baked and is therefore hard—but some sculpture in stone exists as well. Most works are not carved but are modeled, which gives them a novel easiness, as opposed to the formalized or conventional poses of Egyptian sculpture and the polished idealization of Greek sculpture. Figures 5-3 and 5-4 are examples.

While neither work is as realistic as late Hellenistic sculpture, they are both relaxed, informal, and direct. The statue of Apollo (Figure 5-3) is a representation of a god; mildly idealized, the figure strides forward as it might in a wall painting. The figures on the sarcophagus (Figure 5-4) are less idealized in terms of anatomy, but their faces are stylized in the same manner as that of Apollo. These are not likenesses of the people inside the sarcophagus, but rather emblems of them. The poses of the figures are neither dramatic nor stiff and formal: the figures assume positions which may have been characteristic in life—perhaps, as has been suggested, at a banquet. Their hands gesture as if they were in lively conversation.

Rather than evoking awe or fear, these works establish an easy relationship with the viewer, who seems to have been expected to see them from the front. The qualities of Mesopotamian and Egyptian formal funerary sculpture are absent, as are the qualities of portraiture evident in the less important Egyptian figures. These works are definitely stylized, like Celtic representations, and thus appear archaic. They reveal a culture in which the individual was important, in which the gods were represented as approachable, and in which the delights of life were so great that people could not bear the thought of a time when they would not be able to enjoy them.

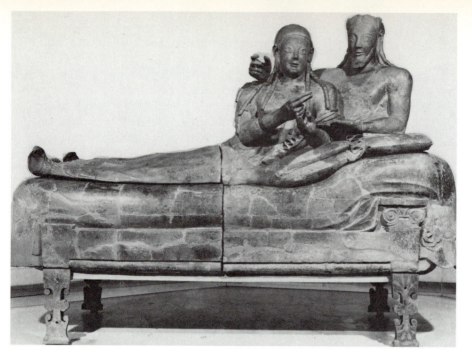

Figure 5-4
Sarcophagus of the married couple from Caere (Cerveteri). c. 520 B.C.
Terra-cotta, about 6 feet 7 inches long. (Museo Nazionale di Villa Giulia,
Rome; Archivo Fotografico, Soprintendenza alle Antichita dell/Etruria
Meridionale.)

PERCEPTION KEY

Etruscan Sculpture

1. Do the sculptures in Figures 5-3 and 5-4 appear to be realistic or idealized? Are they portraits?

2. Are the sculptures intended to be looked at from a single position, or are they meant to be seen from all sides?

3. Certain later Hellenistic works are dramatic, highly personal, and revealing of daily life. Is that true of these works?

4. The statue of Apollo (Figure 5-3) is a representation of a god, while the figures on the sarcophagus (Figure 5-4) probably represent those buried within it. Is there a clear distinction between the styles of representation of gods and people?

5. Does a sense of power seem to be part of the subject matter of either sculpture? What emotions seem to be evoked or expressed by these works?

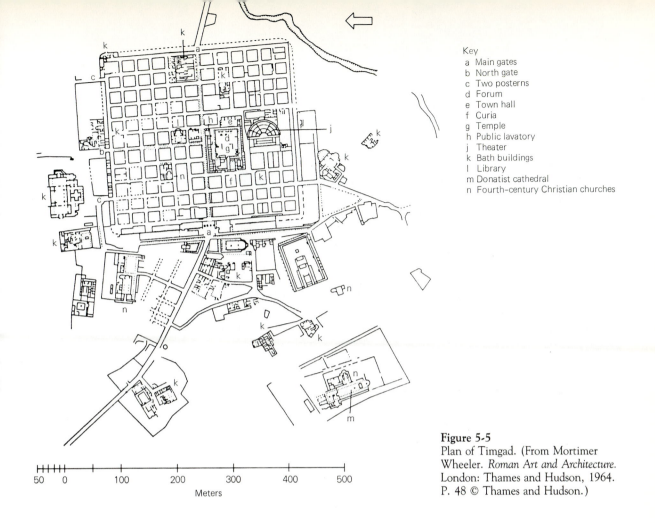

Key
a Main gates
b North gate
c Two posterns
d Forum
e Town hall
f Curia
g Temple
h Public lavatory
j Theater
k Bath buildings
l Library
m Donatist cathedral
n Fourth-century Christian churches

50 0   100   200   300   400   500
                      Meters

Figure 5-5
Plan of Timgad. (From Mortimer
Wheeler. *Roman Art and Architecture*.
London: Thames and Hudson, 1964.
P. 48 © Thames and Hudson.)

The Romans

ARCHITECTURE

City Planning and the Roman Forum

The practical, take-charge quality of the Romans is
evident in their approach to city planning and
architecture. They were efficient and depended on
chessboard grids, which are rectangular, clear, and
logical. Timgad, in north Africa (Figure 5-5), was
built for veterans of one of the Roman legions by the
emperor Trajan in A.D. 100.

Rome, by comparison, is a magnificent disorder.
In the fourth century after Christ, when it was at its
height, it must have been overwhelming. A model of
the city in the year 350 (Figure 5-6) shows a
metropolitan density which would equal that of most
modern cities. The buildings, large and small, are
virtually all of stone. Huge places of entertainment—
such as the circular Colosseum and the oblong Circus
Maximus, the site of chariot races—dominate the
city. Temples dot it liberally: the temple of Aescula-
pius on the island in the river, the temple of Jupiter
on the Capitoline hill, and the temple of Venus and
Roma near the Colosseum. As the city grew, it
accumulated forums, large public spaces, most of
which were built by emperors as a means of celebrating victories or other great achievements. The Romans were public-minded. Many emperors built for
themselves, but most built for the people, for Rome.

The first Roman forum (Figure 5-7), like the agora

Figure 5-6
Above: Model of Rome in A.D. 350.
(Museo del Civilta Romana; photo,
Barbara Malter.)

Figure 5-7
Right: The Roman forum.

in Athens, was a place where business could be conducted, where the Senate met, and where great public events took place. Today it is a ruin, but like so many ruins, it has a romantic splendor. In it Romulus is said to be buried. The "golden milestone," from which all the great roads of the Roman empire began, was there. The architecture of the first forum was copied throughout the empire and throughout Rome itself.

The forum reveals a great deal of borrowing from the Greeks, such as Greek columns, most of which use the Corinthian order. Modern historians associate Greek styles primarily with the Doric order because it is strong, simple, and unpretentious. They associate Roman styles with the Corinthian order, which is ornate, flowery, splashy, and regal. The Corinthian order became associated with imperial design and imperial values. It was a symbol of Roman materialism.

Another sign of materialism, and a technique of building that still persists, is the use of cheap materials reinforced by concrete. The Greeks knew about cement, but they rarely used it. The Romans rarely did without it. Concrete made it possible to build cheaper, larger structures. Some modern critics sneer at the Romans because they built of cheap concrete and brick and then faced their buildings with marble. The Greeks, who had more of it, usually built of solid marble.

The Roman Arch

The triumphal arches that grace every important Roman city have a message. For the Romans they memorialized various victories and triumphs of Roman armies, but we see them as an architectural victory, an architectural declaration of freedom and independence. Greek post-and-lintel construction—such as was used for the facade of the Parthenon, where Doric posts support horizontal marble lintels—was limited. The posts could never be far apart, or the lintels would break. The buildings could never be more than one story high, or the posts would crumble. The arch, by contrast, can sustain enormous weights because the rounding spreads the weight evenly from post to post. Therefore, when one added another post, one spread the weight further. As long as the posts were adequately buttressed—supported by an opposing weight—an unlimited number of arches could be added. That is why colossal Roman aqueducts, such as the Pont du Gard at Nîmes in France (Figure 5-8), are still standing. These struc-

Figure 5-8
Pont du Gard, Nîmes, France.
(Photo, Jean Roubier, Paris.)

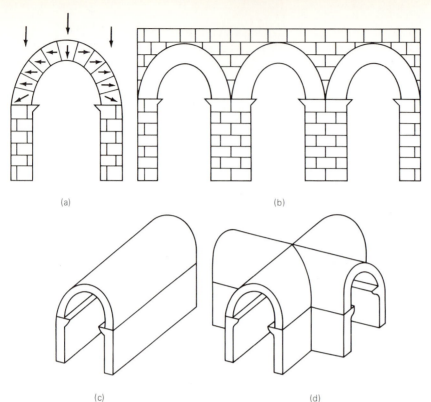

Figure 5-9
(a) Stress pattern of the arch;
(b) series of arches; (c) barrel
vault; (d) groin vault.

tures carried water to the cities, and some still do so today.

Not only could arches be strung out indefinitely; they also permitted building second and third stories on top of them because the arch could be raised very high, with a great deal of open space between the masonry. Therefore, a second or third story would not contain so much stone that the weight would crush the level below. This is why Roman buildings look like modern structures. Greek buildings, by contrast, rarely seem modern to our eyes. Their relentless one-story designs mark them as ancient.

A further victory for the arch was achieved in terms of light. The open spaces of the arch permitted huge window areas: interiors could be filled with light and relieved by airiness. By contrast, the Greek Parthenon was noted for its darkness. The Romans, because of their confidence in the arch, were able to build many round structures whose continuous arches

counterbalanced one another. Sometimes, as in the Colosseum and the Pantheon, the arches were not used primarily for ventilation or for light. The Colosseum was an open-air structure and needed no special light sources. The Pantheon has a circular opening in its dome, the oculus, that admits almost all its light.

In Figure 5-9a, the pattern of stress shows how the weight is distributed from the center of the arch to the buttressed posts. The impost tabs supported the wooden form, on top of which the stones were balanced until the keystone was fitted in. Once the keystone was in place, the wooden form could be moved to the next prepared imposts, and the process was repeated (b). The barrel vault (c) is a series of arches joined together to cover a large space. Its virtue is that it can cover a great distance; however, it does not admit much light. For this reason, intersecting arches—forming two barrel vaults and called a "groin vault"—were devised (d). They are still strong. They disperse the stress, as all arches do, and they admit plenty of light. Later, this became a chief feature of the great medieval cathedrals.

The Pantheon

The Pantheon ("Place of All the Gods") was built, or rebuilt, by the emperor Hadrian between A.D. 118 and A.D. 128. Most of the great architectural triumphs of Roman times are in ruins. We must reconstruct them in the mind or on the drawing board. We cannot experience them as we can the Pantheon, which stands in Rome much as it was when it was built. As a rule, we have little sense of Roman interior spaces or their effects on human sensibilities —except, of course, for the Pantheon. It still dazzles all who enter.

Figure 5-10
(a) Cross section and (b) plan of the Pantheon.

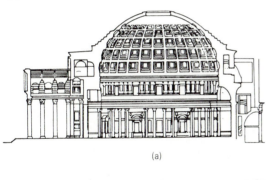

(a)

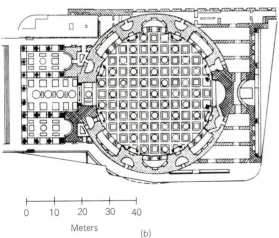

```
0   10  20  30  40
        Meters
```

(b)

The Pantheon (a plan is shown in Figure 5-10) is a round, drumlike structure 142 feet in diameter. Above the drum rises a dome, 142 feet high. The symmetry was intentional and was important to the architect. Instances of numerical repetition, such as that found in the Parthenon, appear in the Pantheon. The significance of patterns of eight and of seven, which show up with regularity in inner decorations and details, is unknown; yet, like most of the details in the building, they had meaning.

The exterior of the building does not prepare one for the interior. The portico, which consists of eight Corinthian pillars of Egyptian marble, supports a peaked roof (Figure 5-11) like that of the Parthenon. But one passes through that Greek entryway into a novel circular Roman space (Figures 5-12 and 5-13). The light that enters through the single round oculus, 27 feet in diameter, is theatrical. The first level is dominated by Corinthian freestanding pillars and the squared-off, attached versions called "pilasters." But there are also suggestions of arches in three large arched alcoves.

Above the first level is a narrow band of blank frames alternating with windowlike niches on which there are repetitions of the Greek pitched roof outside the portico. Finally, on top of that rises the dome itself, which is inset with coffers that angle up to the top and also recede in three or four steps into the masonry of the dome. The coffers reinforce the feeling of space receding, virtually radiating away from one's position. The "waffle" structure implies extraordinary strength. The dome is much thicker at the base than at the top, as the waffling suggests. And on the outside of the building, the third level still rises drumlike from the base in order to give the dome adequate support.

At first, like so many other features of the building, the archwork is virtually invisible. However, if you examine the rounding of the drum in the photograph in Figure 5-11, you will see that there are arches embedded in the stonework. They are filled in because of the architect's decisions about interior light and spaces. Yet they are there, and they function all around the building to give it strength and height. Finally, the dome itself is a circular succession of arches whose keystones ring the edge of the oculus; this permits the open space at the top, something that is possible with all such domes. The arch is the basis of the dramatic style of this building.

Figure 5-11
Facade (left) and side (below left) of the Pantheon.

Figure 5-12
Below: Interior of the Pantheon.

The Pantheon is very nearly intact because it became a Christian church in the seventh century after Christ and has been in continuous use since then. The features of the building lend themselves to Christian purposes. One passes through the Greek portico into a new order, a new religious space. The dome is a metaphor for the heaven that Christ promises, and the light streaming through the single oculus is a metaphor for the one God. The Pantheon reinforces the Bible's dramatic emphasis on light.

Domus Augustana: The Palace of Domitian

The emperors built great personal residences during the first and second centuries after Christ. Nero's Domus Aurea ("Golden House") was built in the heart of Rome after the fire of A.D. 64. It used

Figure 5-13
Giovanni Paolo Pannini. A painting of the interior of the Pantheon. c. 1750. Oil on canvas. (National Gallery of Art, Washington, Samuel H. Kress Collection.)

PERCEPTION KEY

The Pantheon

1. Do you know of any buildings whose exteriors "disguise" their interiors? If so, can you explain what these exteriors would lead one to expect? What upsets those expectations?

2. What buildings do you know of whose interior spaces are dramatic? What makes them dramatic? Do they please you? Are they meant to? What effects do you think such drama is intended to have?

3. Examine the diagram and the photographs of the Pantheon (Figures 5-10 through 5-13). What conclusions can you draw about the fusion of Greek style with Roman style? Is it an easy fusion, or is it uneasy? Is there a natural relation between the two elements in this building? At what points might some strain be detected?

4. Does the Pantheon's exterior make it look like a religious building? Does its interior? Which suggests religious values? Why?

5. What is most Roman and least Greek about the Pantheon?

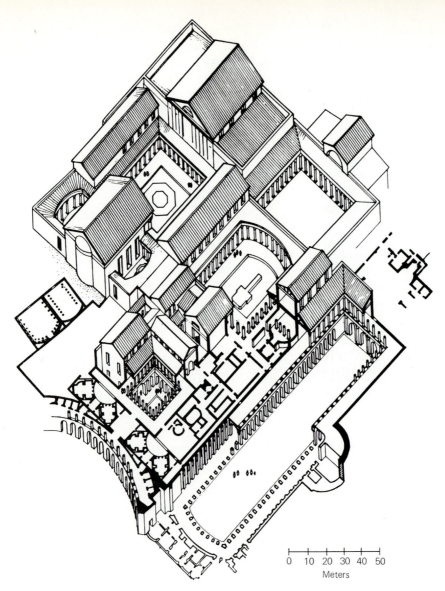

Figure 5-14
Axonometric drawing of the Domus Augustana. (From S.E. Gibson, in John B. Ward-Peters. *Roman Architecture,* New York: Abrams, 1977. Fig. 125. By permission of Electa Editrice.)

0 10 20 30 40 50
Meters

concrete, arches, and an octagonal hall with an oculus. Like most important buildings, it was covered with marble and mosaics. Today, only the raw brick and concrete remain.

The emperors' residences often featured vast covered spaces. The Domus Augustana, built by Rabirius for Domitian in A.D. 92, is on the Palatine, one of Rome's seven hills. The buildings are attached by arcades and passageways: open spaces permit good light and a variety of environments and walkways (Figure 5-14). Post-and-lintel construction is used in most spaces, but there are many arches and curved facades. The various levels of the roofs also help relieve the constant pattern of four walls and ceiling that dominates most architecture.

The tenements of the average Roman did not look like this; the Domus is representative of architecture for the wealthy. Seaside villas may have been much smaller, but they aimed at the same kinds of effects: open spaces, light, and air, along with visual variety.

The Colosseum

The Colosseum, built between A.D. 72 and A.D. 80, was one of the last public projects constructed in Rome. It is characterized by many of the older techniques of building, such as basic stone arches, limited use of concrete, and internal barrel vaults without the groin vaulting that might have let in extra light. Its marble facing is now gone. It was 620 feet long, 513 feet wide, and 160 feet high. The interior arena was originally 290 feet long and 180 feet wide, and the wooden floor was so carefully made that the entire arena could be flooded for mock naval battles. The size of the building is overwhelming, but this is not why it is called the Colosseum. On the site on which it stands, there was formerly a colossal, 120-foot-high statue of Nero; hence the name. It stands close to Nero's house, Domus Aurea.

Nero's sadism and misanthropy could be seen in the deadly spectacles of the Colosseum. It spawned many buildings dedicated to the same frightening events. Renaissance architects considered it a model of Roman techniques and copied its recurrent arch motifs liberally. It also influenced the construction of our present-day football and soccer bowls.

The exterior of the Colosseum (Figure 5-15) consists of a series of three tiers of arches of the same size capped by a solid wall of masonry. The arches have withstood centuries of earthquakes and pillage. Their posts have pillars in relief, in imitation of Greek orders. The lowest level is basically Doric, with a Roman-modified capital called "Tuscan." The second level is Ionic, and the third Corinthian. The top level uses a squared-off column with a capital in the Corinthian style. This is the pilaster, a contribution from Roman architecture that is often used today. The pattern of these arches, one on top of the other, became popular in Rome.

The interior of the Colosseum (Figure 5-16) is ingeniously designed: a series of radiating barrel-vaulted corridors allowed the arena to be emptied in a matter of minutes. The topmost level of the building can be fitted with poles that support huge awnings to protect people from sun and, on occasion, rain. The ruins now reveal the corridors, staging areas, and rooms which undoubtedly housed animals, gladiators, and victims. Apparently, the original flooring

Figure 5-15
Colosseum, exterior.

Figure 5-16
Colosseum, interior.

Roman Architecture

1. Examine your immediate environment. Do you see buildings or plans that remind you of the Roman achievement? If possible, sketch or photograph them and discuss them with others who have done the same.

2. Have you been in buildings or stadiums like the Colosseum (Figure 5-15)? What are your emotional responses to such structures? Do you think that they were designed with such responses in mind?

3. Is it possible to perceive a presence or absence of moral concern in a building like the Pantheon? The Domus Augustana (Figure 5-14)? The Colosseum? Can architecture project moral values? Can it project any values?

4. Why should concerns about economy, practicality, and efficiency conflict with human concerns in architecture? Is such a conflict inevitable? Is it still with us? How can it be avoided?

contained trapdoors and surprise entries, which thrilled the mob.

The achievement of Roman architecture, like the achievement of Roman society, is recognizably modern. The scale on which the Romans built feels comfortable to us. Greek influences are evident everywhere: instead of inventing, the Romans innovated, adapting Greek ideas and adding their own extraordinary engineering and their gift for organizing work forces. Their mastery of concrete and the arch and their use of brick and marble facing strike us as practical, intelligent, and economical—qualities that we admire today. The Romans' ability to plan cities and great public areas was also modern, perhaps even futuristic.

PAINTING AND MOSAIC: ILLUSIONISM AND DRAMA AT POMPEII

A catastrophic volcano preserved an entire Roman city, Pompeii, which contains the best surviving examples of Roman painting. Like the mosaics found in Rome, Pompeii, and elsewhere, some of the paintings are decorative, some are geometric, some are narrative, and some are portraits. Most of them are wall paintings. Many are fitted inside painted architectural details, such as pillars and frames. The painted walls, in these cases, sometimes give the illusion of great architectural space. Many of the paintings, such as that of the heroic Theseus, shown in Figure 5-17, were fitted into the walls and edged with a pliable strip of lead. Making and selling standard-format paintings was common in Pompeii and elsewhere.

Since Pompeii was completely and suddenly buried by an eruption of Mount Vesuvius in A.D. 79, we have an excellent idea of what the arts were like during the first century of the early empire. Because many of the people in Pompeii were vacationers from Rome, we have insight into Roman, not just provincial, styles.

Hellenistic Greek influence is evident in the painting shown in Figure 5-17, which depicts the moment in the Greek myth when Theseus slays the Minotaur. Theseus dominates the center as if he were on stage. His face, however, is so realistic, so far from any Greek or Roman ideal, that it is tempting to

Figure 5-17
Heroic Theseus Slaying the Minotaur. Wall painting from the house of Gavius Rufus, Pompeii. (Museo Nazionale, Napoli; photo, Scala/Art Resource.)

think of it as a portrait. Theseus was the king who went into the maze of the cave of the Minotaur—half bull and half man—to rescue Athenian virgins and youths who had been offered as sacrifices to it. By slaying the Minotaur, Theseus struck a blow for humanity over the animal lust of the man-beast. The children, in a conventional pose, kiss the hand and the foot of Theseus, and the Minotaur is shown lying dead in a lower corner. The paintings in Pompeii seem to have developed from basic models which probably had their origins in Greek wall painting.

Not all the paintings are mythological or dramatic. The landscape from the villa of Agrippa Postumus (Figure 5-18) shows people resting beneath a tree, playing music, and talking, while domestic animals

walk and browse among them. They are near a stately solitary column, behind which spreads a large tree. Behind that there are buildings, perhaps including a temple. This has been described as a highly romantic painting because it idealizes the landscape and the setting.

The fish mosaic shown in Figure 5-19 exists in many versions in Pompeii. The figures are scattered about the space almost casually, although each is perfectly balanced. The fish seem dynamic rather than static. Their scale, relative to one another, is unnatural; yet we are not troubled by scale or by their placement on the same physical plane. The composition is realistic, yet unreal. This design is a space filled for our pleasure, with no story and no recognizable scene. Our imagination and our sense of design are being appealed to in this work.

Figure 5-18
Above: Romantic landscape, wall painting from the villa of Agrippa Postumus, near Pompeii. Before A.D. 79. 61 ¼ by 39 ¼ inches. (Museo Nazionale, Napoli; photo, Andre Held, Lausanne.)

Figure 5-19
Left: Fish mosaic. (Museo Nazionale, Napoli; photo, Alinari/Art Resource.)

SCULPTURE

Many Roman sculptures are copies of Hellenistic originals which have been lost. Just as we know very few names of Roman architects, we know very few names of Roman sculptors. Phidias and Praxiteles, the great Greek sculptors, simply have no counterparts in the Roman world. Instead, the Romans produced highly gifted workers who could reproduce the Greek style with apparent ease.

Figures 5-20, 5-21, and 5-22 are Roman copies of Hellenistic works. The bodies are finely modeled, the details are realistic, and very little is idealized. The copy of the figure by Praxiteles is in a conventional pose; the specific twist of the torso, found in Asian art, is designed to show the fullness of the body and the articulation and the grace of youth. The stone is subtly worked to suggest musculature, but it is not the kind of musculature that we see in the *Heracles*. The Praxitelean figure is that of a boy, as yet undeveloped, while Heracles has a stern and powerful face, huge groin muscles, and boldly muscled legs. The figure of Eros is almost girlish. The hip, which is thrown out to one side as a result of the effort to string the bow, suggests a dance pose. Yet the serpentine twist is attractive and dynamic. Compared with the static pose of Heracles, the gentle torsos of Eros and the Praxitelean figure seem filled with motion. The *Eros* suggests the dynamics of the tensioned string, and yet there is no bulge of muscles and no disfiguring overdevelopment.

In these figures, the Romans have caught the Greek mood. The poses are filled with life and motion. The marble implies flesh, and the Hellenistic capacity to simulate human life in stone is apparent. The most Roman detail is probably the portrait quality of the head of Heracles, which is more lifelike, and yet more fully and realistically heroic, than what we see in most Greek figures.

The head of a Roman lady, Antonia (Figure 5-23), is a portrait of a specific, once-breathing, once-touchable young woman. The statue invites us to move around it. We feel that no one angle can do Antonia total justice, which is the way we often feel about people. Hers was a popular hairdo among Roman women of her time.

The memorial to Antistius Sarculo and Antistia Plutia (Figure 5-24) was set up by freed slaves in

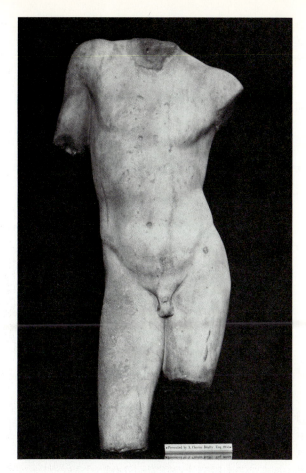

Figure 5-20
Youthful Apollo; Roman copy of a Greek work by Praxiteles, c. 350 A.D. (National Gallery of Ireland, presented by Chester Beatty.)

honor of their former owners. Each scalloped cavity holds a fine portrait bust. The male head is slightly larger. Its expression is strong and severe. This man has nothing to smile about and nothing to frown about. The jaws are chiseled, and the ears are enormous. The figure of the woman, Plutia, is perhaps less severe, but she too is neither smiling nor frowning. Theirs is a very straight, unyielding presence. Yet the portraits are riveting. Each face is strong, but together they project a special quality. Double portraits can present problems, since one often outweighs the other; but in this instance, we are aware of a balance, not only in the composition,

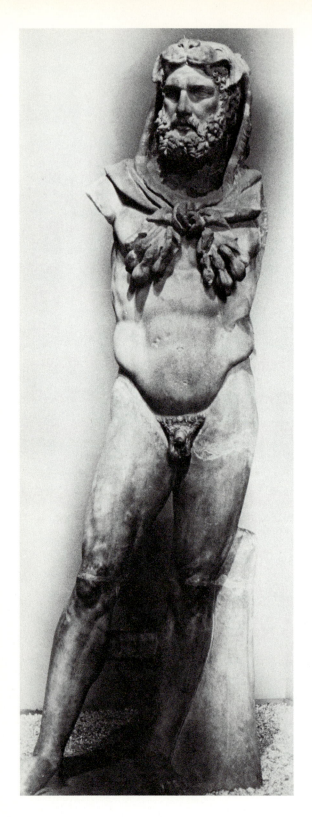

Figure 5-21
Left: Heracles; Roman copy of Greek original. Heroic size. (By permission of Metropolitan Museum of Art.)

Figure 5-22
Above right: Eros stringing his bow, Roman. (Reproduced by permission of the University Museum, University of Pennsylvania.)

which is balanced and symmetrical, but also in the evenness of the strength of the personalities. Neither seems dominant; they are complementary.

The column of Trajan (Figure 5-25), in the forum of Trajan, rising to a height of 125 feet, is now topped by a statue of Saint Peter. Formerly, the statue was a bronze of the emperor Trajan. The column was built in about A.D. 113, the approximate date of the forum of Trajan. It is important because it narrates a sequence of Trajan's victories in Dacia (Romania) through a spiral 3 feet high and 650 feet long. The sculptural relief (Figure 5-26) tells a continuous story in which there are vital, dynamic, and convincing figures; it seems to have no precedent. Trajan brought a Greek architect, Apollodorus, from Syria to build his forum.

Whoever designed the column, it stands as one of the genuinely original ideas in Roman sculpture, representing things as they happened. The struggle of Trajan and his legions is impressively tense. Armies fight back. The battles are hard-fought. The heroics of the action reinforce the epic power of Virgil. In many ways, the column of Trajan can be regarded as the most Roman of sculptural achievements.

Figure 5-23
Detail of a portrait of a Roman lady, Antonia, daughter of Marcus Antonius and Octavia. A.D. 36–38. Marble. (Trustees of the British Museum.)

Figure 5-24
Funeral relief of Antistius Sarculo and his wife Antistia Plutia. 50–30 B.C. (Trustees of the British Museum.)

Figure 5-25
Column of Trajan, Rome.

Figure 5-26
Detail of the Column of Trajan.

LITERATURE

The Love Lyric

Roman poetry was as varied, exciting, and intense as any poetry written in any age. Love poetry reflected a world of passion and intrigue, but also a world of frankness between lovers. Theirs was a cosmopolitan, beguiling, and open eroticism. Catullus (c. 84– c. 54 B.C. wrote love poetry for three years to an unscrupulous woman who was married to a Roman official. She was beautiful but gave Catullus a great deal of pain. Catullus changed her real name, Clodia, to Lesbia because of its metrical qualities. One of his poems, "Lesbia Speaks," suggests the passions that she aroused in him as well as her capacity to deceive men:

> Lesbia speaks evil of me with her husband near and
>   he (damned idiot) loves to hear her.
> Chuckling, the fool is happy, seeing nothing,
>   understanding nothing.
> If she forgetting me fell silent, her heart would be his
>   alone, content and peaceful;
> But she raves, spitting hatred upon me, all of which
>   carries this meaning:
> I am never out of her mind, and what is more, she
>   rises in fury against me

With words that make her burn, her blood passionate
  for me.

Catullus's frankness is striking. Lesbia, her husband, and her lover could be found in any modern city. Her anger, transformed as it is into passion, is human, revealing, and understandable. In matters of romance, the Romans were expert.

Propertius (c. 50–c. 15 B.C.), though he died young, wrote a number of poems about life in Rome. He, too, was a gifted love poet, as we see in "Passion's Power":

> When drowsy eyelids downwards slid
> She laid her lips on either lid,
> And when they opened at her kiss
> Said "Should a lover laze like this?"
> How various were the ways we clung!
> How long my lips on her lips hung!
> Darkness the lover's work impedes;
> In love it is the eye that leads.

Propertius loved an older woman, renamed Cynthia, who was the object of many of his better poems. Yet many of his poems are on other subjects, with titles as varied as "The Honest Whore," "The Sickness," "Cleopatra and Caesar," and "A Brawl." One, "Beyond the Grave," reveals his preoccupation with death. It is not philosophical or religious; rather, in it Propertius reacts to a vision he had of his dead mistress, whom he outlived by only a few years:

> Beyond the grave lies something, not all of us expires;
> There is a ghastly phantom that 'scapes the funeral
>   fires.
> For lo, I dreamed that Cynthia, then resting with the
>   dead
> Beside the noisy roadway, was bending o'er my bed.

Cynthia explains how she wishes her servants to be treated, and she expresses her fear that she will be too soon forgotten. She says, "My reign was long, Propertius, as mistress of your songs." She suggests that there are two ships moving in the underworld. On one, the mood is severe and cool; the other, on which there is music and laughter, is the one that she wishes to be on:

> "There lutes, and Phrygian cymbals, and Lydian lyres
>   resound,
> And turbaned dancers foot it in one delightful
>   round."

The poem ends with her being called, at cockcrow, back to Hades, which reminds Propertius that they will soon be together forever:

> "At cockcrow, all the vagrants troop back to
>   Acheron;
> The boatman keeps strict tally, and notes us one by
>   one.
> For now, let others have thee; ere long shalt be all
>   mine:
> We two shall lie together, my bones shall cling to
>   thine."
> She spoke: and in that instant, ere Yet I was aware,
> The shape my arms were clasping had vanished in
>   thin air.

Not all Roman poets were men, and not all celebrated the women they loved. One group of poems comes to us from the hand of Sulpicia (fl. 25 B.C.). She, too, has her lover, whom she celebrates in "An Avowal," a brief, passionate verse:

> Let other maids, whose eyes less prosperous prove,
> Publish my weakness, and condemn my love.
>   Exult, my heart! at last the queen of joy,
>   Won by the music of her votary's strain,
>   Leads to the couch of bliss herself the boy;
>   And bids enjoyment thrill in every vein.
> Last night entranced in ecstasy we lay,
> And chid the quick, too quick return of day!
> But stop, my hand! beware what loose you scrawl,
> Lest into curious hands the billet fall.
> No—the remembrance charms!—Begone, grimace!
> Matrons! be yours formality of face.
> Know with a youth of worth the night I spent.
> And cannot, cannot for my soul, repent!

Love poetry was only a small part of the Roman poetic output. Other writers chose very high themes. Lucretius wrote "On the Nature of Things," a long philosophical poem that examines astronomy, zoology, and physics. Ovid's *Metamorphoses* tells many of the most important Roman myths, such as the stories of the origins of the world, of Narcissus, and of Pygmalion. Horace celebrated serious themes. His odes were inspiring to later poets writing in many languages. One, "The Roman Way," celebrates Regulus, the Roman general who was captured by the Punic forces during the Punic wars. He was released on his promise as a Roman that he would return to captivity. His mission was to tell Rome to give up in the Punic wars, but instead he urged Rome to

Roman Sculpture and Poetry

1. If possible, read a selection of the poems of Ovid, Catullus, Propertius, Sulpicia, or Horace. What are their subjects? What Roman values are expressed in the works you read?

2. Most of the sculpture shown in Figures 5-20 through 5-24 tends toward portraiture. Is there a relationship between Roman sculpture and Roman poetry? Are the poets and sculptors equally interested in individual personality?

3. Compare Roman portraits with those of the Greeks and the Egyptians. There was a great deal of cultural infiltration of all these traditions, as well as many others, and therefore some similarity is evident. But how do the portraits vary? Choose one from each era for comparison. Do they imply changes in terms of respect for the individual?

4. Which of the sculptures and which of the poems seem most realistic? Are they also the works that seem most modern? Is there general agreement among your peers with your choices?

5. Much of the sculpture and the poetry of the Romans can be described as realistic. Does valuing realism in sculpture or poetry imply special ways of valuing this world? Of valuing a world to come? What might it imply concerning an attitude toward the afterlife?

---

continue fighting. Then, heading toward certain torture and death, Regulus mounted: "He knew the tortures that barbaric hate/ Had stored for him. Exulting in his fate/ With kindly hand he waved away/ The crowds that strove his course to stay." This was the Roman way: honor before all.

Roman moral views may be different from ours, but we can see in Horace the values that were important to the Romans. One was honor. Another was bravery and courage. Steadfastness, fidelity, suffering quietly, keeping one's word, and remaining steady were also qualities that the Romans valued.

The Epic: Virgil and the Glory of the Empire

Virgil (70–19 B.C.) lived in Rome's imperial age. Julius Caesar was killed in the forum on the ides of March, 44 B.C. Augustus Caesar, his successor, commissioned the *Aeneid,* which he hoped would be an epic to rival Homer's and a history to rival that of Thucydides. Augustus was like Pericles, but his Phidias worked in words instead of stone.

The *Aeneid* was begun when Rome was at relative peace. Civil war had raged since the death of Julius Caesar, and peace was not restored until Augustus finally triumphed. Virgil expressed his gratitude and that of Rome in an epic consisting of twelve books. The opening words—"Arma virumque cano," "Of arms and the man I sing"—state immediately the theme of war and the celebration of a warlike hero. Rome, whose empire was built on the prowess of its centurions, could not have hoped for a more honest account of itself than the one Virgil was to offer. His hero, Aeneas, wanders from Troy all through the known world—from Turkey, to Greece, to northern Africa, to Italy—until he finds his new home.

Through Aeneas's wanderings, Virgil explained how Rome came to be founded. Its pedigree went back to the heroes of Troy—even to Hector, whose offspring eventually ruled in Rome.

Traditions of heroism, such as Aeneas's journey through the underworld (paralleling Odysseus's journey to Hades) and his love affair with the African queen Dido (paralleling Odysseus's idyll with Nausicaa), have become standard in the epic. Virgil's technique was so perfect that later Roman scholars considered it the basis of all education in language. Even though Virgil died before he could put the last finishing touches on the poem, it stands as a monument to Roman ambition and Roman values.

The gods smile on Rome in Venus's speech. She is the goddess of love, like the Greek Aphrodite, and she implores Jove:

> Oh Ruler of Gods and men with laws eternal,
> Who wields the terrible thunderbolt, now tell me
> What crime have my Aeneas and the Trojans
> Committed against you? What can they have done,
> Who have suffered so many deaths, and now it seems
> The entire world is a barrier against
> Them reaching Italy, and yet you promised
> In the full course of time the rule of the world
> To the Romans, a people sprung from Trojan blood.

She pleads with him to fulfill his pledge and to relieve the suffering of the Romans. After listening, Jove answers:

> Have no fear, Cytherean; the destiny of your people
> Remains unaltered, you shall see your city,
> And see Lavinia's walls as I have promised.
> You shall bear great-heart Aeneas to the height
> Of the highest of heaven's stars.
>   I have no thought
> Of change of mind. But since you are so consumed
> With anxiety for Aeneas I shall turn forward far
> The hidden pages of fate and speak of the future.
> He shall conduct a great campaign for you
> And conquer all Italy and its haughty peoples.
> ·

PERCEPTION KEY

The Aeneid

1. The god of war, Mars, and the goddess of love, Venus, both seem intensely interested in Aeneas. What does this tell us about his character? What kind of a national representative would Aeneas make?

2. The evidence does not suggest that Virgil was personally involved in war. He never married, and he lived a life as sheltered as that of a monk. He seems not to have been interested in the entertainments of the time. How might such a background have helped him portray Roman values? What kinds of values would you expect him to portray?

3. Read either Book 4 of the *Aeneid*, which tells of Aeneas's adventure with Dido, or Book 6, in which Aeneas visits the underworld. What can you determine of Aeneas's character? Is he humane and gentle, or is he self-centered and cruel?

4. How does Virgil define Aeneas's heroism? What kind of lover is he? How does he face death?

5. What Roman qualities does Aeneas display?

The seed of Hector for three hundred years
Shall reign and reign till Ilia, a priestess
Of royal blood, bear twins begotten by Mars;
And one of these, Romulus, fostered by a she-wolf,
And joyfully wearing her tawny hide, shall rule
And found a city for Mars, a new city,
And call his people Romans, after his name.
For them I see no measure nor date, I grant them
Dominion without end. (Book 1).

Virgil's vision of the founding of Rome is based on legend. Romulus and Remus, children of the god of war, Mars, supposedly were raised by a she-wolf. An Etruscan statue shows the wolf suckling the twins; it dates from 400 B.C. Jove, Venus, and Mars all show great interest in Aeneas and Rome. The theory that Aeneas, or anyone else, emigrated from Troy to Italy is based on legend, but it is possible. In the Greek and Roman periods, cultures were not sealed off from one another. They mixed, met, and borrowed; their meetings, whether peaceful or warlike, stimulated new growth and new developments.

DRAMA AND PHILOSOPHY

Dramatists

Like most of their arts and institutions, the Romans' drama and philosophy depended on the achievements of the Greeks. The great Roman dramatists were Plautus (c. 254–184 B.C.), a comedian whose work resembles that of the Greek Aristophanes; Terence (186 or 185– c. 159 B.C.), also a comedian, whose work is based on that of the Greek Menander; and Seneca (c. 4 B.C.–A.D. 65), whose work develops themes from Greek tragedies. Even Terence's contemporaries complained that he plagiarized Menander's work, his defense was that nothing that anyone wrote was original. His works—which include *The Woman of Andros, Phormio,* and *The Mother-in Law*— are in a tradition known as "new comedy," which stressed social criticism. It showed the audience its own vices while making it laugh. It was an instrument of change: by criticizing society, even mildly, new comedy could help reform it. Ordinarily it relied on a chief character with stereotypical qualities— such as a mother-in-law. Most of the other characters were also types. A major source of the humor was in the audience's recognition of personality types among its own acquaintances.

The tradition known as "old comedy," begun by Aristophanes and carried on in Roman times by Plautus, was slapstick, sidesplitting, rollicking, and often low-down. Instead of depending on type characters, it depended on impossible situations out of which ridiculous complications arose. Plautus sometimes used type characters, as in *The Braggart Warrior,* which influenced Shakespeare and George Bernard Shaw (and many other writers in between). The play depends on trickery, mistaken identity, and deception. Like all Plautus's comedies, it contains elements of farce and burlesque. *Amphitryon, The Haunted House,* and *The Pot of Gold* are also important plays by Plautus, whose influence is still felt today in modern drama.

Seneca and Stoicism

Seneca was both a dramatist and a philosopher; he followed the Greek philosophy of stoicism, which was particularly relevant in a time of rapid change. Seneca, Cicero (106 – 43 B.C.), and Marcus Aurelius (A.D. 121–180) were all famous stoics. Stoicism was well suited to Roman life, since it stressed the ability of the individual to adapt to sudden change. It did not offer hope of an afterlife. It was founded on a belief in law, in understanding nature so as to live in accord with it, in the personal qualities of courage and steadfastness, and in the reliability of sensory perception as a means of acquiring true knowledge of things. The ideal of this philosophy was human happiness, which was achievable by living in accord with nature, both human and cosmic. It was a philosophy based on public action, and the three most famous stoics were all public men.

Not only did Seneca write philosophy; he also took part in the government of Nero's time. A businessman, he was a millionaire many times over, which contradicted his philosophy and undermined the acceptance of some of his works. But he showed the seriousness of his views when Nero commanded him to kill himself because of a scandal. Seneca died calmly, without showing fear or a loss of his beliefs. His death has become a model of stoic behavior.

Seneca's most famous play, *The Trojan Women,* is the story of the women who were captured after the fall of Troy. As is true of most of his plays, the theme had been treated by many Greek playwrights. The version by Euripides has survived, and it shows that

Seneca relied on it. He probably also relied on other versions that have been lost. The play focuses on the sufferings of the women of Troy, particularly those of Hecuba, the queen; and of Andromache, the wife of Hector, Troy's greatest hero. These women face their fate with the kind of strength and dignity that Seneca defended in his writings on stoicism. The play is a defense of stoic attitudes. When Polyxena refuses Pyrrhus, the Greek, she chooses death rather than the indignity of a forced marriage:

> Then numbing dread
> Seized Greeks and Trojans all, as they beheld
> The maid. She walked with downcast, modest eyes,
> But on her face a wondrous beauty glowed
> In flaming splendour, as the setting sun
> Lights up the sky with beams more beautiful,
> When day hangs doubtful on the edge of night.
> All gazed in wonder. Some her beauty moved,
> And some her tender age and hapless fate;
> But all, her dauntless courage in the face
> Of death. Behind the maid grim Pyrrhus came;
> And as they looked, the souls of all were filled
> With quaking terror, pity, and amaze.
> But when she reached the summit of the mound
> And stood on the lofty sepulchre,
> Still with unfaltering step the maid advanced.
> And now she turned her to the stroke of death
> With eyes so fierce and fearless that she smote
> The hearts of all, and, wondrous prodigy,
> E'en Pyrrhus' bloody hand was slow to strike.
> But soon, his right hand lifted to the stroke,
> He drove the weapon deep within her breast;
> And straight from that deep wound the blood burst
>   forth
> In sudden streams. But still the noble maid
> Did not give o'er her bold and haughty
>   mien*   *expression
> Though in the act of death.

Thus the last victim of the Trojan war met her death.

Epicureanism

Contrasted with the public-spirited courage of stoicism was the pleasure-based doctrine of Epicureanism. This, too, was a popular Roman philosophy with Greek roots. The Epicureans believed that personal happiness was the greatest good and that it was best achieved by avoiding all pain—the greatest evil. Just as stoics were most stoical when facing death, Epicureans were at their best when avoiding

it. They often retired from the world with a few friends to lead lives of satisfaction, usually avoiding participation in public affairs. Personal pleasures were highly cultivated, and sensual pleasures were greatly valued. At the time of Cicero, Julius Caesar, and Brutus—the first century B.C.—Epicureanism was in many ways the chief philosophy and was a serious obstacle to the Christian forces growing in Rome. It was self-centered; no public works were aimed at sharing the pleasures of Epicurean satisfaction with others. Like much of stoicism, it was basically a materialistic philosophy.

MYTH AND RELIGION

Roman religion often had no strong moral quality. The *Aeneid* concerns itself with what the gods desire, not with the question of ultimate good, although it prescribes good behavior and even condones self-sacrifice. Roman religion focused on finding ways of getting the gods on one's side. In the passage from the *Aeneid* quoted earlier, Venus wonders whether Jove has abandoned Aeneas. Such things could happen. To avoid being abandoned, the Romans made certain ritual gestures, including prayer, to remind the gods of their obligations. The Romans expected the allegiance of the gods in matters of revenge, in lawsuits, and in war.

The earliest Roman sense of gods or godliness had nothing to do with individual gods or human representations of gods. The early Romans were, like the Celts, animistic. They saw powers in trees, torrents, and winds. Certain locations, as Virgil's poems suggest, were considered sacred for various reasons and were the site of celebrations and rituals. Cults developed later in Rome, before Julius Caesar, and were generally tolerated. Many were imported from other cultures. Astrology—reading the signs in the heavens—was also very popular in Rome. Like modern astrology, it had no special moral qualities at all; it helped people avoid calamity, survive, and prosper.

The Romans absorbed the Greek pantheon, substituting Jupiter or Jove for Zeus, Mars for Arês, and Venus for Aphrodite. The Romans absorbed the Greek myths and saw little need to develop their own versions. They also found it easy to respond to the myths of Isis and Horus. Roman women were drawn to these myths and enacted the story of Osiris, as the Egyptians had.

The Mystery Cults and Christianity

When Christianity became influential, in the second and third centuries after Christ, two cults, those of Mani and Mithra (Figure 5-27), had spread to many parts of the empire. Mithraism was a conjunction of the teaching of both cults. It assumed that the world had two great forces. One was evil, the force of dark. The other was good, the force of light. Mithraism taught that one must join the struggle of the universe on the side of light. The Christians—particularly Saint Augustine, who had been a Manichaean—argued that belief in such a cult cast doubt on the goodness of God. If the fate of the world was really in doubt, this meant that God was weak and needed the help of humans to keep things in order.

Figure 5-27
Head of Mithras, Roman. (Museum of London.)

The simplicity of Mithraism, with its reliance on the basic forces of light and dark, made it very popular. In some forms it seems to have a moral quality, but the ways in which it has been practiced have been not moral but moralistic. Joining in on the side of the right has caused many people to kill and maim in the name of good. Mithraism, Manichaeanism, dualism—whatever name it goes by—appeals to our sense of the natural because we see light triumph over darkness each morning. Fighting on the side of the good seems appealing.

Manichaeanism and Mithraism often led to fire worship. The cult of Vesta, which was housed in a single temple in Rome (Figure 5-28), also treated fire as holy. Its priestesses were all virgins who were buried alive if they broke their vow of chastity. Theirs was a most solemn calling; it lasted for thirty years, beginning when they were small girls. Their duties included maintaining a sacred fire, which was never to go out. The building in the forum dedicated to the fire of the Vestals resembles an early circular Roman wood hut, which is what it may have been before it was built in marble.

During the first two centuries after Christ, when Christianity was becoming more and more widespread, many mystery cults thrived throughout the empire. Mithraism, which did not admit women, had a sister cult, Cybele, the cult of Isis. All cults involved initiation rites, each stage of which brought the initiate deeper into the cult. As initiates mastered more and more secret or mysterious information and performed the sacred rites, they rose in position. In the cult of Mithra, initiates performed various acts symbolic of the soul's journey through the universe, thus helping the progress of their own souls. The concept of the soul held by the cult members may have been a version of the Egyptian Ba or Ka, something related to the "I-ness" of the person.

Most mystery cults promised a rebirth in another world. Some of the language of the cults also reminds us of the language of Christianity and of the other modern religions. An Egyptian papyrus containing information on Mithraism, dating from A.D. 300, ends with this passage:

> O Lord! I have been born again and pass away in exaltation. In exaltation I die. Birth that produces life brings me into being and frees me for death. I go my way as thou has ordered, as thou has established for the law and ordained the sacrament.

Figure 5-28
Temple of the Vestals. Rome, Forum Boarium. c. 100 B.C.

This language, which echoes the language of the Bible, may show a longing for a single, personal god who is interested in deep moral views. If it does, and if such a longing was common among other mystery cults, Christianity may well have answered a spiritual need of those who had turned against the old imperial ways.

Early Christianity

During the two centuries after Christ, Christianity spread throughout the empire: to India, Spain, Italy, the main centers of Greece, the near East, and Britain. The gospels were written in Greek and were widely circulated. Christianity, which began as a Jewish cult, attracted important and eloquent converts. A religion of the people, it was based on a strong code of ethics that stressed love and forgiveness. It was particularly quick to spread because it included women—something many cults did not do. Partly because it was popular and partly because it appealed to the lower classes, Christianity was distrusted by the Romans. One of the greatest of the early Roman converts, Tertullian, the son of a Roman centurion, describes some of the ridiculous beliefs that people held about the early Christians:

> We are spoken of as utter reprobates and are accused of having sworn to murder babies and to eat them and of committing adulterous acts after the repast. Dogs, you say, pimps of darkness, overturn candles and procure license of our impious lusts.

The concept of a god who walked the earth and ascended to heaven and the practice of praying and holding meetings were things that the new religion shared with many cults. There were no initiation rites, but the early Christians performed baptism and other sacraments common among the cults. Christ was, in a sense, initiated in the name of the church; and the promise of an afterlife was one important element that Christianity shared with the mystery cults. The early Christians were unaccountably joyful people. They seemed to be at peace with themselves, and their doctrine of love—even love for scoundrels —was difficult for the right-thinking Romans to accept. However, many Romans were curious about Christians and envious of them. They were particularly envious of the Christians' assurance that salvation was possible.

Tertullian's *Apology*, written in A.D. 197, when the Christians were being persecuted widely, tells us that Christianity had begun to "conquer" more of the world than Rome. It was everywhere in the empire, and it extended beyond to parts of Britain. As Tertullian said, the Romans had the temples, but the Christians had the people. He exaggerated, but his words pointed to the future. The persecution of the

CONCEPT KEY

Mystery Cults and Christianity

1. Initiation rites and growth in stages, as one mastered holy knowledge, were important in the mystery cults. The initiate partook of mysteries that others knew nothing of. Are such practices and beliefs part of modern religions? Of modern nonreligious institutions? What is their appeal?

2. Moderns expect religion to have a deep moral center, but this is a relatively recent view. What would the features of a religion without a clear moral center be? What would it have in common with modern religions? What would it lack? Is it possible for a modern person to be religious but not moral?

3. Even today some religions condone the killing of groups of people either in religious wars or because of offenses against the religion. This was certainly true in Rome. Is it contrary to general moral views today?

4. If possible, read Romans and Acts in the Bible. Romans is a letter from Saint Paul to those who were in need of conversion to Christianity. What do these books reveal about the nature of the new religion and the nature of the old ways? What do they reveal about the conflict of Christianity and Roman law?

Christians, begun by the insane emperor Nero after the fire that burned Rome in A.D. 64, finally ended in A.D. 312, with the conversion of the emperor Constantine. The empire of the material world gave way to the spiritual world.

The reasons for the triumph of Christianity are complex and not fully understood. Generations of Roman materialism, widespread degeneracy, the lack of a deep spiritual center, and the eventual bankruptcy of belief in multiple gods all combined with admiration for the Christians themselves. The power of spokespersons like Saint Paul and of other converts like Tertullian was incalculable. Another factor was the absence of a powerful state religion to compete with Christianity. Like the Egyptian pharaohs, the Roman emperors, beginning with Augustus, considered themselves gods. Unlike the Egyptians, however, the Romans could not sustain a powerful, abiding

faith in such a belief. Imperial divinity was considered political, not religious.

MUSIC AND DANCE

Roman drama included both music and dance. Not only performers but people of high station sometimes danced. Suetonius, in *The Lives of the Caesars,* tells of wealthy women who danced for the entertainment of guests and of companies of dancing girls who performed in great houses. He describes the emperor Caligula dancing:

> Sometimes also, he danced in the night. Summoning once to the palatium, in the second watch of the night, three men of consular rank . . . he . . . then suddenly came bursting out, with a loud noise of flutes and castanets, dressed in a mantle and tunic reaching down to his heels. Having danced out a song, he retired.

Figure 5-29
Relief from Villa Quintiliana on the Appian Way, 4 miles south of Rome. A.D. 100, from a Greek original. (Trustees of the British Museum.)

Roman dance, like Greek dance, was sometimes based on a concept of abandonment or "possession." Bacchic dances—consecrated to the god of wine—were popular throughout Rome. The postures of the dancers in Figure 5-29 suggest an abandonment close to being possessed or rapt. The tambour player in the lead seems lost in the dance. The pipe player's concentration is total, and the Bacchic figure with his leopard seems likewise ecstatic. It is a processional dance, like many classical dances, and everyone is lost to the music and the movement.

Summary

The Romans built on and refined the Greek achievement not only in the arts but also in politics, religion, statecraft, and and virtually all other human activities. A practical, efficient people, they were pious and reverenced their gods. They conceived legal institutions that were international in scope. The Greek concept of the city-state gave way to the Roman concept of an imperial cosmopolitanism. In architecture, the Romans achieved great things by adopting techniques that the Greeks knew but did not much use. The arch and the use of concrete and brick faced with marble made possible huge buildings with several stories. The emphasis on personal pleasure and personal virtues in Roman philosophy bears directly on much Roman portrait art. The emphasis in the portrait is on revealing personality. In Roman portraits of great figures, certain qualities are clearly idealized. But portraits of lesser figures have the personal qualities that we associate with modern portraits. The contradictions of the society lie in the taste that even noble people had for gladiatorial contests, the sports of death and torture. Baffling though it is, the Roman achievement, like the Greek, is magnificent.

Concepts in Chapter 5

Etruscan culture, which centered on the afterlife, was supplanted by Roman culture.

The Etruscans, who were of uncertain origin but were not Greek, were influenced by Greek art and eastern art.

The ascendancy of Rome dates from the sixth century B.C.

Roman architecture and city planning derived from Etruscan and Greek models.

Roman cities were planned for the people, not just the emperors.

The arch, although not original with the Romans, made possible much of their extensive, high building.

The architecture of the Romans was one of their great achievements; it was characterized by the use of cement and cheap building materials faced with marble.

The Corinthian order became associated with Roman imperialism.

Roman painting relied on Greek themes, and possibly Greek techniques.

Much painting found in Pompeii shows a keen interest in design and decorative values.

Some painting in Pompeii is illusionistic and seems to extend interior architectural lines.

Roman sculptors at first copied Hellenistic Greek styles.

Later Roman sculpture shows a profound interest in individual portraits and in realistic portrayal.

The Romans' poetic achievement is of the highest order; Roman love poetry reveals an erotic, intense frankness between lovers.

Many long Roman poems tell the stories of gods, narrate the origin of the world, or explore philosophical questions.

Virgil's *Aeneid* celebrates the Roman virtues of virility, courage, and skill in war.

Roman drama and philosophy depended on Greek models.

Old comedy was slapstick; new comedy was a comedy of manners, based on social criticism.

Seneca professed stoicism, a public-minded philosophy that prepared one to deal with sudden changes in life.

Epicureanism, also popular in Rome, was egocentric and focused on pleasure.

Roman myths were generally based on a reworking of the Greek pantheon.

Mystery cults flourished at the time of early Christianity; they offered principles of morality and the hope of an afterlife.

Christianity flourished among the common Romans, despite the fact that Christians were persecuted; it offered a morality based on love and forgiveness.

Suggested Readings

Brilliant, Richard. *Roman Art.* London: Phaidon, 1974.

Duckworth, George E. *The Complete Roman Drama.* 2 vols. New York: Random House, 1942.

Dudley, Donald R. *The Civilization of Rome.* New York: New American Library, 1960, 1962.

Ferguson, John. *The Religions of the Roman Empire.* Ithaca, N.Y.: Cornell, 1970.

Godolphin, Francis R. B., ed. *The Latin Poets.* New York: Random House, Modern Library, 1949.

Grant, Michael. *Roman Myths.* New York: Scribner, 1971.

Kraemer, Casper J., Jr., ed. *The Complete Works of Horace*. New York: Random House, Modern Library, 1936.

Ovid. *The Metamorphoses*. Horace Gregory, trans. New York: New American Library, 1964.

Robertson, Donald Struance. *Greek and Roman Architecture*. London: Cambridge, 1943.

Strong, Donald. *Roman Art*. Harmondsworth, England: Penguin, 1976.

Virgil, *The Aeneid*. Patric Dickinson, trans. New York: New American Library, 1961.

Ward-Perkins, John B. *Roman Architecture*. New York: Abrams, 1977.

Wheeler, Mortimer. *Roman Art and Architecture*. New York: Praeger, 1964.

PART THREE

EUROPE

RUSSIAN EMPIRE

Constantinople

OTTOMAN EMPIRE

BOKHARA

PERSIA

MUG
EMPI
OF IN

Mecca

Bombay

Goa

ARABIA

0   250   500   750   1000 miles

INDIAN

AFRICA

THE ORIENT AND ISLAM

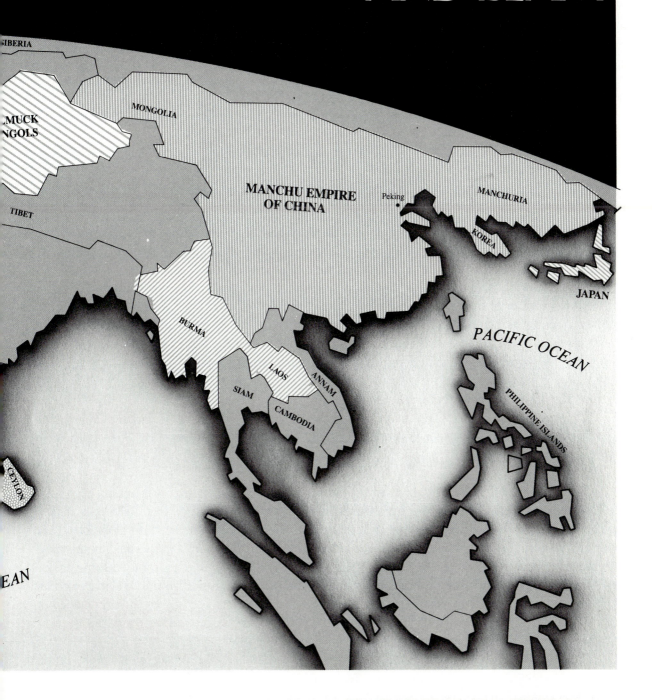

SIBERIA

KALMUCK MONGOLS

MONGOLIA

TIBET

MANCHU EMPIRE OF CHINA

Peking

MANCHURIA

KOREA

JAPAN

BURMA

LAOS

ANNAM

SIAM

CAMBODIA

PACIFIC OCEAN

PHILIPPINE ISLANDS

CEYLON

OCEAN

 Achievements in Greece and Rome were paralleled by achievements in India and China. Natural boundaries—deserts and mountains—made cultural interchange between Asia and the classical world almost impossible. Yet word had come to the west regarding Chinese jade and silk; and Indian music and mathematics were known to the Greeks. There were some cultural connections between east and west even in the days before Christ.

Buddhism dates from the sixth century after Christ, and the Han dynasty in China spans the two centuries before and the two centuries after Christ. Then, during the almost total destruction of Roman influence—dating from the seventh century after Christ—the rise of the "nation" of Islam produced architecture, music, poetry, and thought. Islamic civilization may have affected the west more than that of either China or India because Islam was close to Europe during a formative period.

Europeans marveled at Islamic attention to detail. They were awed by mosques and tombs and impressed by the splendor of ceremonies with orchestras and dancers. And they were struck by the piety of worshipers and by the extraordinary skill of warriors filled with the zeal of the Prophet.

Much that we think of as western—including many aspects of religious thought, achievements in all the arts, and inventions of many sorts—is derived from a long-standing connection with the east. Orthodoxy and mysticism have their eastern versions as well as their western versions. Our knowledge of Greek philosophers, physicians, musicians, poets, and theorizers derives in large part from translations made into Arabic of texts that, in some cases, are lost in the original. The preservation of the Greek intellectual tradition in the major cities of Islam made it possible for the west to base its Renaissance on a recovery of the knowledge of its classical heritage. If the Arabs had not preserved that knowledge, the west might have had a very different kind of "rebirth."

The instability of Chinese dynasties, in which war and revolution were common, made

the struggle against paganism and idolatry very difficult. But Confucius's humanist ideals eventually won out against magic, superstition, and forces that made humankind seem insignificant. The traditions of Buddha also elevated values concerning the inwardness of the soul and the spirit. Concerns for spiritual development also emerged early in the culture of India. Yet it, too, suffered from war and invasion as well as many other kinds of political instability. The last major battles against pagans and idolators were fought by the Prophet Muhammad in the seventh century after Christ, when the inspiration and power of the Islamic belief in Allah spread like a blaze from Asia, over north Africa, to southern Europe.

Brief Chronology

3000 B.C.   Indus Valley civilization in India.

1766 B.C. to 1122 B.C.   China: the Shang dynasty; Aryan invasion of India: period of the Rigveda.

1122 B.C. to about 256 B.C.   Chou dynasty in China.

c. 563 B.C. to c. 483 B.C.   Buddha in India.

c. 551 B.C. to c. 479 B.C.   Confucius in China.

200 B.C.   The Great Wall of China.

207 B.C. to A.D. 220   Han dynasty; Chinese call themselves "the children of Han."

A.D. 500   The Ajanta caves in India are built.

600–750   Early medieval period in Indian Art; Tang dynasty in China.

c. A.D. 570 to A.D. 632   Muhammad in Arabia.

to A.D. 750   Islamic conquest of Egypt and Spain.

1000–1500   Period of great Indian temples; Sung and Ming dynasties in China; Omar Khayyám (c. 1048– c. 1131), Islamic poet; building of the Alhambra and the Taj Mahal.

CHAPTER 6   INDIA

The Indus Valley Civilization

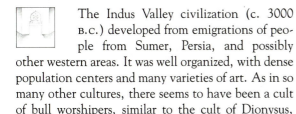

The Indus Valley civilization (c. 3000 B.C.) developed from emigrations of people from Sumer, Persia, and possibly other western areas. It was well organized, with dense population centers and many varieties of art. As in so many other cultures, there seems to have been a cult of bull worshipers, similar to the cult of Dionysus, and other echoes of cultures elsewhere.

The original inhabitants, the Dravidians—small, dark people—moved south in the face of invasions. Their beliefs have been absorbed and reexpressed in various features of the Hindu religion. The great Hindu trinity, which was a force long before the birth of Christ, consists of Brahma, the creator; Shiva, the destroyer; and Vishnu, the preserver. Shiva and Vishnu may have Dravidic roots; but this trinity, three aspects of the one god, may also have come with the invaders. Its Indian form was a result of assimilation with native traditions.

Aryans, light-skinned people, brought the Indus

civilization to a sudden end, beginning around 2000 B.C. There was little art for 1000 years after their invasion, and we have little evidence of culture during this time. It was a period of racial struggle. At the end of it came the great early books of Indian religion, the Vedas. The Rigveda ("poems of Knowledge") dates from 1500 B.C. to 1200 B.C. The Vedas are sacred texts, celebrating deities such as Indra, the chief Vedic god, and Varuna, king of the air and the sea. The "Song of Creation" begins:

> There was not non-existent nor existent. . . . All was indiscriminated chaos. . . . Thereafter rose desire in the beginning, desire, the primal seed and germ of spirit.

It ends:

> Who knows, then, whence it first came into being? / He, the first origin of this creation, whether he formed it all or did not form it, / Whose eye controls this world in highest heaven, he verily knows it, or perhaps he knows not.

The "eye" suggests the sun, and an earlier reference to a primal warmth implies that this song grew from a solar myth. The emphasis on desire, or will, helps explain some of the strongly erotic art that graces almost all Hindu temples. The mithunas, or lovers, carved on the temples celebrate creation and the one god.

Religion

HINDUISM AND BUDDHISM

Hinduism supported a caste system of groups that were almost completely sealed off from one another. The Brahmans were the priestly caste, the Kshatriyas were the warrior caste, and the Sudras were the workers. Because the Brahmans acquired so much power as a result of their claim to be the only ones to truly know the Vedas, several rival sects, supported by the Kshatriyas, grew up early in India. Hinduism was challenged by Jainism and Buddhism, both of which still flourish, although neither is as significant as Hinduism.

For a few centuries, Buddhism rivaled Hinduism as India's chief religion. The crucial difference between the two religions is in their attitude toward personal action. Hinduism demands exact performance of sacrifices, exact interpretation of scripture, and exact ritual. Buddhism recognizes that evil exists and that it can be eradicated by personal action. Evil results from an attachment to the sensory, material world and from an overemphasis on the self, or ego. Buddha preached self-denial, spiritual inwardness, and eventual salvation through reincarnation. The Hindu belief is in samsara, the eternal wandering of the soul through both good and bad karma, or actions, from incarnation to incarnation. Eventually, nirvana, a union with "all," can be achieved through practicing yoga meditation and through asceticism, or religious self-denial.

The two forms of Buddhism are Mahayana, the greater vehicle (or greater way), and Hinayana, the lesser vehicle (or lesser way). Hinayana is older. It reveres Buddhist doctrine, treats Buddha as a sage, and regards personal salvation as the most worthwhile goal of life. Mahayana, a later development, treats Buddha as the god who has existed for all time. It also developed a system of saints, or bodhisattvas, who minister the will of Buddha. They help mortals achieve salvation, and they have forgone their own salvation for the good of others. This kind of self-sacrifice is unknown to Hinayanistic Buddhism, which emphasizes personal salvation.

THE AJANTA CAVES: PAINTING CONSECRATED TO RELIGION

One of the great monuments to Mahayanistic Buddhism is the Ajanta caves, which were carved and decorated from the first to the seventh centuries after Christ. Many of the paintings portray moments in the life of Buddha and are the only examples of early Buddhist painting.

The bodhisattva in Figure 6-1 poses against a rich, teeming background. The single lotus in his hand is a symbol of spirituality. His expression is tender; his

Figure 6-1
Bodhisattva on the way to enlightenment. Ajanta, cave 1. Sixth century after Christ. (Photo, UNESCO.)

Figure 6-2
Buddha in the tushita heavens. Ajanta, cave 2. Sixth century after Christ. (Photo, UNESCO.)

eyes reflect inward, and yet they suggest unselfishness. There is nothing severe, judgmental, or unapproachable about this figure. One of its remarkable qualities is its pose. The serpentine shape of the torso and head is called the "tribhanga posture." It derives from movements in Indian dance, which is never far from the minds of Indian painters and sculptors. The bodhisattva expresses himself with his entire body, as most Indian figures do. The colors are earth tones: reddish browns; deep earthy greens; and soft blues, whites, and yellows. But the dominating color here as in most of the paintings, is reddish brown.

The portrait of Buddha preaching in the tushita heavens (Figure 6-2) shows a typical symmetrical balance: three segments are separated by the architectural device of pillars. To the left of Buddha stands a figure suggesting the tribhanga posture. Buddha himself dominates the central panel of the composition in a scene narrating a moment shortly after he has achieved buddhahood, when one of his first acts was to visit the tushita heavens in order to lead his mother, Mahamaya, and certain other gods and goddesses onto the true path of enlightenment. His head is in a nimbus, or aureole, resembling a halo. He sits on a rich thronelike chair. The walls in this section of cave 2 are a complex network of narrative, showing his mother, foreign visitors, and other gods, such as Indra and Brahma. typically, all the available space is filled with floral patterns, color, and form.

The lifelike elephant (Figure 6-3), pink against a soft green-and-white background, is from the ceiling decorations. Because it probably represents one of the earlier incarnations of Buddha, the artist has been careful to make it realistic. Yet the space over the elephant's back allows room for a huge lotus, while beneath its feet is space only for lotus petals. The curve of the trunk is proportionately too long; yet its design echoes the bend of the main part of the animal's body. The right front leg is also distorted, but it is difficult to know whether the distortion is for reasons of space or perspective. This figure is dynamic, and it almost appears to be dancing out of the pond.

Figure 6-3
Ceiling motif, elephant in a lotus pond. Ajanta, cave 1. Sixth to seventh century after Christ. (Photo, UNESCO.)

Ajanta Caves

1. Which of the paintings in the caves (Figures 6-1, 6-2, and 6-3) seems most realistic? Which seems most idealized? If possible, establish the obvious differences between these paintings and classical Greek and Roman works in terms of realistic or idealized representation.

2. One notable characteristic of much Indian art is the filling up of all the available space. Is this apparent in the Ajanta cave paintings? Is there an equal emphasis on balance, symmetry, and realistic perspective in these paintings?

3. What kinds of emotions seem to be expressed in these works? What kinds of emotions do they evoke in the viewer? Do you perceive religious values or feel a sense of religious emotions while looking at these works?

4. In the figure of the elephant (Figure 6-3), the lotus and the lotus petals are completely out of proportion to the elephant itself. Does this annoy you or make you feel that the work is less realistic? Do you find the disproportion pleasant?

5. The caves were discovered by the English in 1819. Detailed drawings of them were available in the 1880s. By that time, the Nizam's government, which was appointed by the English, was permitting minor officials to cut out heads and figures from the paintings in the Ajanta caves to give to visitors of note. Would this be a religious as well as an aesthetic offense?

Sculpture and Architecture

SANCHI: BUDDHIST SHRINE

One of the last Buddhist monuments, dating from the end of the eleventh century after Christ, is at Sanchi. Located in central India, Sanchi is also the site of one of the great stupas: burial mounds serving as memorials to Buddha. Among many in central India, no other is quite so large and impressive. In the central portion of the stupa (Figure 6-4), the dome resting on a circular pediment represents the marriage of heaven and earth. The squared-off porch on top of the dome represents the house of the gods. The triple parasol, chattra, signifies the rule of Buddha over the Vedic gods, heaven, and the world. The four gateways point to the four corners of the earth to admit worshipers from everywhere. On the gates, which are somewhat Mayan in appearance, are carvings of holy figures. They give appropriate instructions to those who enter.

The stupa has no interior space. Instead, like the Egyptian pyramid, it is almost a sculpture. Its purpose is to memorialize the dead and to inspire the living. It is a house for a god, not a person. Other Hindu temples share this characteristic with Greek temples and some Roman ones whose interior spaces are very tiny.

Two pieces of sculpture (Figures 6-5 and 6-6) from a much later period, approximately A.D. 900, come from a temple next to the great stupa at Sanchi. The "Sanchi torso" (Figure 6-5) was brought to England in 1886 by General Kincaid, who was wrongly convinced that the torso showed Greek influences. He thought this because he believed the workmanship and the angle of the body, the tribhanga posture, to be Greek. The torso, eventually and reluctantly purchased for about $400, very soon became (as the

Figure 6-4
Right: Great stupa at Sanchi. 100 feet in diameter, 50 feet high. (Photo, E. Boehm, Mainz.)

Figure 6-5
Below left: Torso of bodhisattva from Sanchi. c. ninth century after Christ. Sandstone. (Victoria and Albert Museum, London.)

Figure 6-6
Below right: Cast of Bodhisattva Maitreya. c. A.D. 900. Approximately life-size. (Victoria and Albert Museum, London.)

Victoria and Albert Museum describes it) "the most famous and widely admired piece of Indian sculpture in the Western world." For more than half a century, nothing was known of the torso, including whom it represented. Some shrewd detective work in 1971 yielded a companion figure (Figure 6-6), and further work uncovered the fact that these two figures originally flanked a seated buddha. These discoveries proved that the figures were bodhisattvas and, through interpretation of the symbols on the clothing, revealed their identities.

The Sanchi torso alone, without reference to the grouping of which it is a part, shows workmanship of the highest quality. The posture is dancelike and poetic. Viewing the piece from almost any angle gives one the impression of a deep inner beauty. The ruined condition of the torso makes it more intense than it might be if it were complete, possibly because western eyes are used to seeing great classical works in fragment.

KHAJURAHO: HINDU TEMPLE

The building of the great Hindu temples exactly paralleled the construction of the great cathedrals in western Europe—from the tenth to the thirteenth centuries after Christ—and the art of this period in India is usually called "Hindu medieval art." Buddhism had lost its vitality, and Hinduism had reasserted itself. India was being almost covered with temples. We have no idea how many were built, but many survive.

Kandariya Mahadeva, at Khajuraho (Figure 6-7), is a tenth-century temple dedicated to Shiva (Mahadeva), the destroyer. The Hindus believe that all that exists is the result of the regular rhythms of creation and destruction. Therefore, Shiva is not a sinister deity, although he is to be feared.

Every detail of temples such as this had to be carefully calculated. The dimensions were important: numbers represented magic. The position of the temple (Kandariya Mahadeva faces due west) is also important. The repetition of patterns, the number of spires, and the figures themselves—all have numerological meaning. The workers who made the temple had instruction books, called "sastras," that helped them do everything exactly right. No detail was too insignificant to heed. The priests controlled all the work and made sure that it was perfect.

Kandariya Mahadeva, the finest example of tem-

Figure 6-7
Kandariya Mahadeva temple at Khajuraho. Tenth century after Christ. 102 feet 3 inches long; 66 feet 10 inches wide; 101 feet 9 inches high. (Photo, Borromeo/Art Resource.)

ple building at Khajuraho, is the work of master artisans. Like most Hindu temples, it was based on the concept that the architects were building a mountain, the "world mountain," Meru. The constantly rising peaks (shown clearly in Figure 6-8) are allusions to the great northern mountain range. Some viewers have actually compared this temple to a specific sacred mountain, Kailasa. The highest spire, the sikhara, 101 feet 9 inches high, is also a phallic symbol and is intended to remind us of one of the forms that Shiva takes. Thus, the temple itself is a monument to creativity and the power of Shiva.

Figure 6-9 shows four main interior spaces. The garbha-griha is the equivalent of the Greek cella, where the cult figure is kept. In the case of this temple, it was a 4-foot-high marble linga, or symbolic phallus. An entryway, the anta-rala, led to it. The maha-mandapa is a large hall used for gatherings; it

Figure 6-8
Right: Kandariya Mahadeva, conjectural section. (From Eliky Zannas. *Khajuraho.* 's Gravenhage, Netherlands: Mouton, 1960.)

Figure 6-9
Below: Plan of Kandariya Mahadeva temple. (From Eliky Zannas. *Khajuraho.* 's Gravenhage, Netherlands: Mouton, 1960.)

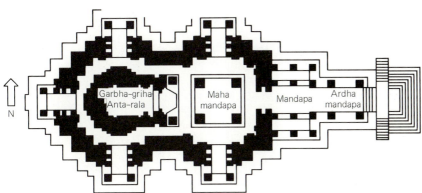

has a magnificent carved ceiling and its own rising roof spire. The mandapa and the ardhamandapa are basically the same space, an inner and outer porch, the actual entrance to the temple. Each of these spaces has its own roof and spire, culminating in a symbolic finial.

The carved decorations, both inside and out, are painstakingly executed, incredibly detailed, and similar, but they are not monotonous (Figure 6-10). The outer wall of the temple is covered with 646 carved figures ranging from 2½ to 3 feet in height. Inside there are 226 figures. Most of them are heavenly creatures, and many are in the familiar tribhanga posture. Many of the figures are shown engaged in complex sexual intercourse, which has often struck westerners as strange. Nowhere is it clearer than in these sculptures that the unity between flesh and spirit is a fact in Hindu culture.

Figure 6-11 shows Vishnu, the preserver, in his incarnation as a boar, raising the earth from the seas.

Figure 6-10
Above: Kandariya Mahadeva, south wall. (Photo, Borromeo/Art Resource.)

Figure 6-11
Right, above: Varaha—boar incarnation of Vishnu—lifting the earth goddess Bhumi from the primeval ocean. Late twelfth century. Sandstone. (Victoria and Albert Museum, London.)

Figure 6-12
Right, below: Shiva Nataraja. Late twelfth century. Chola style, brass, about 30 inches high. (Victoria and Albert Museum, London; photo: Lee Boltin, Croton-on-Hudson, New York.)

The treatment of the body of Vishnu, as well as that of the loincloth and neck jewelry, is like the treatment of the Sanchi torso. The soft fullness of the skin around the navel and the richness of the detail in the necklace, with its jewels of receding size, show a continuity of the techniques used by Buddhist workers. Such combinations as the head of a boar on a human body have been common in Indian art since the civilization of the Indus Valley.

Shiva is probably best known in his incarnation as Nataraja, "lord of the dance," in which he symbolizes the ultimate destruction of the world (Figure 6-12). His hand holds a flame and touches the circle of flame that surrounds him. Beneath his foot is a dwarf meant to symbolize all that is evil, vanquished by Shiva. This posture is still used by Indian dancers.

Indian Architecture and Sculpture

1. Do you know of any European or American equivalents of the stupa at Sanchi (Figure 6-4)? Is there any evidence of the tradition of such building in western civilization?

2. The entrance to Kandariya Mahadeva (Figure 6-8) faces due east; the cella faces due west. Great care was taken to make the positioning exact. How might the sunlight, as it changes throughout the day, change the appearance of the temple? Does the temple seem responsive to light?

3. The Hindus covered their temples with carvings of mithunas, or lovers; do you feel that this indicates a degenerate religious or moral view on their part? What emotional reactions do you have to the sculpture? Is your reaction a result of cultural attitudes, or is it universal?

4. Compare your responses to the fragmented Sanchi torso (Figure 6-5) with your responses to one of the intact sculptures shown in Figures 6-10, 6-11, and 6-12. How is your response to the Sanchi torso affected by its being in a state of ruin?

Literature

Like other Indian arts, Indian literature is steeped in religious themes. Long before the Indian medieval period, there were Indian dramas, Indian poems, and Indian tales. Poets enjoyed a prestigious place in Indian court life. However, the priests reserved the most important literature, the Vedas, for themselves, and they spent much of their time interpreting them. The great Indian epics, the Mahabharata and the Ramayana (the first is said to be the longest poem in the world), have long been influential in western literature. The best-known part of the Mahabharata is the Bhagavad Gita ("The Song of God").

The Bhagavad Gita, which dates from at least 500 B.C., has been compared to Jesus's Sermon on the Mount. A dialogue between Krishna and Prince Arjuna, it takes place during a lull in a battle in which Arjuna must reluctantly face some of his own relatives. Krishna, the divine incarnation of Vishnu and a figure whose life resembles that of Christ, takes time to instruct Arjuna in karma yoga to help him discover the meaning of his life: "The gates of hell are three: lust, rage, and greed." Krishna also urges Arjuna to continue the war and bring it to a successful conclusion. His reasoning is that all people best serve their god by doing their duty. Krishna points out that the sensory world is mere illusion; even war is illusion. Therefore, he tells Arjuna:

Thinking about sense-objects
Will attach you to sense-objects;
Grow attached, and you become addicted;
Thwart your addiction, it turns to anger;
Be angry, and you confuse your mind;
Confuse your mind, you forget the lesson of
   experience;
Forget experience, you lose discrimination;
Lose discrimination, and you miss life's only purpose.

Krishna's message is suggestive of Christian belief: the loss of self, the illusionary nature of the sensory world, and the belief in Krishna himself all have counterparts in Christian teachings. Further, Krishna insists that he can bring Arjuna closer to Brahma, the one god.

Figure 6-13
Radha and Krishna in a Grove, from the Punjab. c. 1780.
(Victoria and Albert Museum, London.)

He tells Arjuna:

But if a man will worship me, and meditate upon me with an undistracted mind, devoting every moment to me, I shall supply all his needs, and protect his possessions from loss. Even those who worship other deities, and sacrifice to them with faith in their hearts, are really worshipping me, though with a mistaken approach. For I am the only enjoyer and the only God of all sacrifices.

Krishna figures in many visual arts, along with his consort, Radha (Figure 6-13). A Bengali tradition preserves poems that celebrate the love of Krishna and Radha, who was one of the gopi, or milkmaids, who were seduced by Krishna's beautiful flute playing. The symbolism of these poems suggests that the love of Krishna is so great that it makes the lover give up the comfort of daily routine, and of social respect and position, and risk all for Krishna.

One of the Bengali poems, probably composed in the 1700s, is about Radha's decision to come to Krishna. A sexual poem, it tells of a lover who finally yields to her beloved; she comes to him in the night, overcoming her great fear of the darkness. Again, this is symbolic of the absolute devotion that Krishna demanded of his worshipers. Radha speaks:

Oh Madhava, how shall I tell you of my terror?
I could not describe my coming here
If I had a million tongues.
When I left my room and saw the darkness
I trembled:
I could not see the path,
there were snakes that writhed round my ankles!

I was alone, a woman; the night was so dark,
the forest so dense and gloomy,
and I had so far to go.
The rain was pouring down—
which path should I take?
my feet were muddy

and burning where thorns had scratched them.
But I had the hope of seeing you, none of it
   mattered,
and now my terror seems far away.
. . . .

When the sound of your flute reaches my ears
it compels me to leave my home, my friends,
it draws me into the dark toward you.

The portrayal of Krishna as warrior god in the Bhagavad Gita and as lover in the tradition preserved by the Bengali poems and in countless paintings demonstrates that Krishna is many things.

The Ramayana dates from 1500 B.C. and is the second of the great Indian epics; it tells of the fate of Rama, who is unfairly denied the throne. His father chooses Rama's brother Bharat to rule, and he instructs Rama to spend fourteen years wandering in the forest, dressed like a hermit. When Bharat offers Rama the throne after the death of their father, Rama cannot accept. He cannot offend the memory of his dead father, even though Bharat is right in offering him the throne.

He gives Bharat advice:

Make thy gifts of wealth and food,
Not to lords and proud retainers, but to worthy and
   the good
Render justice pure and spotless as befits thy royal
   line,
And to save the good and guiltless. (Book 4).

Rama wanders with his brother Lakshman in voluntary exile. His adventures include the loss of his beloved Sita to a rapacious warlord. He enlists the aid of the monkey kingdom to retrieve his beloved, but there is no way that he can be sure of her fidelity to him. Thus, when Rama finally ascends to the throne, Sita commits suicide because she can never, in the eyes of the people, appear spotless enough for him. Her death brings Rama lifelong grief. The story has obvious parallels with Homer's *Odyssey*. The concepts of the usurped home, of years of wandering and discovery, and of the fidelity of loved ones left behind are basic to many cultures and are part of growth and maturity of a hero. The Ramayana establishes the ideals of devotion to father, by Rama; to brother, by Lakshman; and to husband, by Sita. These figures remain models for people to admire. The Ramayana is filled with instructions on how to fulfill the duties expected of one throughout life.

Music and Dance

Musicologists assure us that chants sometimes heard in Indian temples—often consisting of no more than three notes—have endured for more than 3000 years. Flutes, drums, and horns are often depicted in early Indian art. Lyres, harps, the vina (or zither), hand drums, bells, and gongs existed long before the time of Christ. Modern musicians are familiar with the tambura, which is a long stringed instrument without frets that makes a droning sound. The sitar, a long stringed instrument with a gourd resonator and with frets similar to those of the guitar, has become popular in the west. So, too, have various Indian drums, particularly the tabla.

Indian classical music has roots deep in the earliest religious practices of Hinduism. But its present character probably owes most to the revival of Hinduism in the medieval period. Like the sudras who worked on the temples, musicians were trained from their earliest years. They worked, as all students did, with masters who imparted their skills. Since Indian music is not written down but constantly improvised, every musician is, in a sense, a virtuoso. There are no casual musicians in India.

The essence of Indian music is melody. There is no harmony, except in droned sounds (sustained tones), and the purpose of the music is to intensify the emotional mood of a particular moment. Indian classical music was played for an aristocratic audience, not in public concerts.

The scale of tones has twenty-two intervals instead of our twelve. Therefore, the unusual intervals —sruti, or quarter tones—make the music sound exotic to western ears. Instead of keys, like C major, there are ragas, or basic melodic plans of organization of a limited number of tones, usually six or seven, one of which is repeated often enough to make it important. "Raga" means "passion" or "emotion," and there are ragas considered appropriate for each hour of the day.

Like the paintings in the Ajanta caves and the carvings on Kandariya Mahadeva, Indian classical music "fills all the available space." The intense rhythms of the music demand quick successions of notes; only the droned sounds are sustained for a long period of time. By comparison, western music, as Coomaraswamy has said, seems to have holes in it.

A raga begins and ends with no formal warning. The tambura sounds a tone, the kharaja, which is like the tonic of western key-based music. The raga is accompanied by a tala, which is a tempo scheme, sometimes very complex. These three elements constitute the basis of the piece. Indian musicians are so thoroughly trained that they rarely have to rehearse in order to play with one another: they play much as American jazz musicians do. They already understand the basic structures of the music and can improvise with considerable skill within them.

Indian classical music derives much from Indian folk music, some of which is still played in tribal districts. In general, the music is accompanied by voice, but the words are unimportant in relation to the music itself. Some pieces use nonsense syllables so that the music can maintain total authority. As Coomaraswamy puts it:

> In the ecstasies of love and art we already receive an intimation of . . . redemption. . . . We are assured by the experience of aesthetic contemplation that Paradise is a reality.

There are many forms of Indian dance. Some are regional, and some are tribal or folk dances. Indian classical dance was already well developed four centuries before Christ, when Bharata Muni wrote the natya sastra, the sastra that contained instructions for dancers; as noted earlier, Indian sculptors also had sastras that helped them in their work. Natya is the combination of movement and acting common to almost all Indian dance. In contrast with this is nrtta, or pure dance—movements with no specific meaning. The natya, a dance that tells a story, is by far the most widespread dance in India. Plato speaks of Greek dance as consisting of gestures that tell a story; many people have observed that Greek dance and Indian have similar functions, if not similar origins and forms.

Bharata Natya is the best-known form of classic dance, but the word "bharata" is probably not derived from the name of the writer of the sastra. The widespread belief is that it is made up of the first syllables of the three most important elements in Indian dance: bhave (mood), raga (melody), and tala (tempo or rhythm). The feet of the dancer are naturally guided by the tala, while the facial expressions and the specific hand gestures (hastas) express the mood of the piece.

Apart from the general dance drama of the bharata natya, there are several specific Indian dance forms. The kathak is a very popular northern dance which shows the influence of the Muslims who invaded the north. It is sometimes acrobatic and almost always difficult. The dancer often chants meaningless syllables to the tala. The kathakali, a dance of south India, is performed only by men at night using an oil lamp for stage lighting. It is a pantomimic dance, specializing in telling the stories of the Ramayana and the Mahabharata. It is usually very vigorous. A dance performed exclusively by women is the sadir nautch, also a southern dance. The nautch includes gesture songs, with the dancer often singing the song herself. Her aim is to find the best ways of interpreting in movement the words that she sings. There are many other dance forms in India, but these are a cross section of the most important ones.

The dance in general builds upon a specific series of positions, which are associated with specific movements. Each position is called a "karana." The dance usually builds on a series of six or eight karanas, which is then called an "angahara." The angaharas build together to make the dance. The rules concerning the karanas, the hastas, and every step (cari) of the dancer are very rigid. The excellence of the dance depends on the ability of the dancer to follow the rules exactly.

There are 108 karanas and 32 angaharas. Angahara 5 is illustrated in Figure 6-14; it is called "aksipta," which means "scattering round." The fourth karana in this sequence is also called "aksipta." Its requirements are:

> The left leg is bent with the flat foot on the ground, the toes turned outwards. The right foot is raised toes downwards with the heel touching the left ankle. The left hand is raised to the shoulder level in the Pataka gesture, that is, all the fingers and the thumb stretched straight close together. The right hand is kept hanging down at a slight angle. Then there are four movements. (1) The right leg is bent, raised and moved about. (2) Then the same is done with the left leg. (3) The right hand is kept straight and still. (4) The fingers of the left hand are bent slightly, one by one, the little finger, third, second, and first fingers consecutively.

Indian dance maintains a mood which soothes rather than excites. The dancer concentrates on the movement of the arms and of the body above the waist, and the bare feet move and point in expressive

Figure 6-14
Angahara number 5: "aksipta—scattering all round." (From Enakshi Bhavnani. *The Dance in India.* 2d ed. Bombay, Taraporevala, 1970. Plates 16 and 17. By permission of D. B. Taraporevala Sons and Co. Pvt. Ltd., Bombay.)

CONCEPT KEY

Indian Literature, Music, and Dance

1. Experts say that the stories of Krishna, the incarnation of Shiva, and Rama, the incarnation of Vishnu, do not constitute a myth like the Egyptian or Greek myths. What might prevent them from being myths? Do you agree with the experts?

2. The songs of Krishna and other Indian literature argue that the self must be deemphasized and that the sensory world must be overcome through meditation. To what degree do Indian music and dance help achieve this end?

3. Indian dance is best when the dancer follows the prescriptions for the dance exactly. Could this help establish a relationship between dance and religion? Could a dance, even if secular, be considered a form of ritual if it were repeated the same way each time it was performed?

4. Do you perceive religious qualities in the literature, music, and dance of India? In which is religion most or least apparent? Or is that an irrelevant question?

5. Indian literature, music, and dance are characterized by narrative. How is narrative expressed differently in Indian literature, music, and dance? Is narrative basically literary, or can it be considered independent of literature?

patterns. In western dance, particularly ballet, the difficulties of technique are often highlighted, but in Indian dance the difficulties are assumed and are often disguised by the artistry of the dancer, who avoids projecting his or her personality into the dance and, instead, becomes thoroughly absorbed in the inwardness of the dance.

Summary

Benjamin Rowland has said that in India religion and art are one: Indian art projects spiritual and inward values. Representations are usually idealized references to heavenly beings; even sculptured erotic dancers are heavenly. Architecture always alludes to heaven, with upward-tending spires and many vertical repetitions. Sensory experience is praised insofar as it develops a sense of inwardness in the individual. Therefore, music and dance help maintain or produce an emotional response or mood which sustains an inward calm. Most Indian art devotes great attention to detail at the expense of structure. Even in architecture, such as the stupa or the Hindu temple, structural solutions are conceptually simple. The stupa's dome suggests heaven. The shape of the temple suggests the "world mountain," Meru. Our real interest is drawn toward the details of the buildings. Attention to detail is one of the sources of genius in all Indian art.

Concepts in Chapter 6

The most important religions in India have been Hinduism and Buddhism. (Hinduism and Islam are the chief religions today.)

The great Hindu trinity consists of Brahma, the creator; Shiva, the destroyer; and Vishnu, the preserver.

The Vedas, great early books of Indian religion, date from 1500 B.C.

The Ajanta caves are a monument to Buddhism.

Many of the paintings in the Ajanta caves depict different incarnations of Buddha.

The great stupa, or burial mound, at Sanchi is a Buddhist monument.

The Sanchi torso, a bodhisattva, exhibits the tribhanga posture, once thought to have been a Greek influence.

Hindu temple building at Khajuraho occurred at the same time as the Middle Ages in Europe, when the great cathedrals were built.

Erotic sculpture on Hindu temples celebrates creativity and life.

Much Hindu sculpture concentrates on the incarnations of Shiva and Vishnu.

The Ramayana (1500 B.C.) and the Mahabharata (500 B.C.) are infused with religious thought; the Ramayana resembles the *Odyssey*.

The Bhagavad Gita, part of the Mahabharata, tells of Krishna, one of the incarnations of Vishnu.

Indian music and dance are intended to produce meditative, inward experiences.

There are Indian ragas appropriate for each hour of the day; ragas evoke specific moods.

Indian music and dance are deeply influenced by religious practice.

Classical Indian dance is formalized; it was well developed by 300 B.C.

Natya is storytelling dance; nrtta is pure dance; the word "bharata" is derived from the Indian words meaning "mood," "melody," and "tempo."

Suggested Readings

Bachhofer, Ludwig. *Early Indian Sculpture.* New York: Hacker, 1972 (originally published in 1929).

Basham, Arthur L. *The Wonder That Was India.* 3d ed. Paris: Arthaud, 1976.

Bhavnani, Enakshi. *The Dance in India.* 2d ed. Bombay: Taraporevala, 1970.

Coomaraswamy, Ananda. *The Dance of Siva.* New York: Sunwise Turn, 1913.

Kramrisch, Stella. *The Art of India.* 3d ed. London: Phaidon, 1965.

————. *The Hindu Temple.* 2 vols. Delhi: Motilal Banarsidass, 1976.

Krishna, Deva. *Temples of North India.* New Delhi: National Book Trust, 1969.

La Meri (R. Meriweather Hughes). *The Gesture Language of the Hindu Dance.* New York: Benjamin Blom, 1964.

Lin Yutang. *The Wisdom of China and India.* New York: Random House, 1942.

Munsterberg, Hugo. *Art of India and Southeast Asia.* New York: Abrams, 1970.

Rawson, Philip. *Indian Art.* New York: Dutton, 1972.

Rowland, Benjamin. *The Art and Architecture of India.* Harmondsworth, England: Penguin, 1977.

Srinivasan, K. R. *Temples of South India.* New Delhi: National Book Trust, 1972.

UNESCO. *The Ajanta Caves.* New York: New American Library, 1963.

Zannas, Elly. *Khajuraho.* 's Gravenhage, Netherlands: Mouton, 1960.

Early Chinese Culture

 Archaeological finds have uncovered important information concerning the earliest Chinese cultures. Until 1926 the Shang dynasty was thought to be legendary, but recent finds of tombs and of impressive bronze objects have dated its existence from 1766 B.C. to 1122 B.C. An even earlier dynasty, the Hsia, dates from about 2200 B.C. The Chou dynasty (1122 B.C. to about 256 B.C.) produced Confucius and Mencius, great religious leaders; Taoism was also founded during the Chou dynasty. The Han dynasty (207 B.C. to A.D. 220) was a period of achievements equivalent to those of the Romans. The Tang (A.D. 618 to A.D. 907), Sung (A.D. 960 to A.D. 1280), and Ming (A.D. 1368 to A.D. 1644) dynasties were important ages of Chinese culture.

The Great Wall of China was built during the Ch'in dynasty (221 B.C. to 206 B.C.), a period of bloodshed and anguish. Natural boundaries kept China free of worry about invasions from the west, but the Mongols, Siberians, and other northerners were troublesome raiders and a threat to security. The wall, which cost a million lives to build, permitted the state of Ch'in to establish dominance in China. Meanwhile, the Chinese plundered ideas and inventions from their neighbors to the south—the Annamese, the Vietnamese, and the Koreans. China did not respect their cultures, but borrowed what it thought useful.

Religion

CONFUCIUS

The earliest Chinese religion seems to have been dominated by magic and animism. People were considered on a par with animals and the vegetable world. Modern Chinese religion is based on the beliefs of Confucius (551–479 B.C.), who was born during the Chou dynasty. His *Analects*, although carefully edited by several dynastic governments, are read as a record of his thought. His emphasis on learning pleased the studious and scholarly, while his emphasis on the exactitude of ceremonies pleased the conservatives in power.

A brief sample of sayings will show something of his range:

> Confucius said: "To silently appreciate a truth, to learn continually and to teach other people unceasingly— that is just natural with me." (Analect 16.)

Confucius said, "Men are born pretty much alike, but through their habits they gradually grow further and further apart from each other." (828.)

Tselu asked about the worship of the celestial and earthly spirits. Confucius said, "We don't know yet how to serve men, how can we know about serving the spirits?" "What about death?" was the next question, and Confucius said, "Those who are born wise are the highest type of people; those who become wise through learning are next; those who learn by sheer diligence and industry, but with difficulty, come after that. Those who are slow to learn, but still won't learn, are the lowest type of people." (842.)

The *Analects* represent a collection of thoughts rather than a system of behavior. Yet the Chinese people may still be said to be Confucian in their outlook. Like Aristotle, Confucius advocated the temperate, well-balanced life. Like Christ and Plato, he recommended personal virtue as a means of curing the evils of the world. His ideal is called "jen": humanity, charity, and benevolence—the highest ideals of human behavior. Jen, in practice, would guarantee a healthy, humane society. The precept later known as the "golden rule"—"Do as you would be done by"—was laid down by Confucius. His disciples saw the effectiveness of his teachings and their contrast with the behavior of those in power.

Confucius did not represent himself as a god or as a descendant of a god; he professed the fullness and value of humanity. In his time, people were frightened by eclipses, dreams, and prophecies, and his teachings were totally unlike anything else. But he insisted that the ceremonies of the astrologers and others were not all bad, because ceremonies, even if based on superstition, had a value in and of themselves. That was why he praised both music and dance, which were part of contemporary ceremonies.

Ancient rituals, Confucius said, were handed down from less inhumane times than his own, and thus were worthy of special attention. He spent his last years editing ancient texts, which became known as "Confucian texts." He has been accused of forging them, but there is no evidence to support that view. He praised scholarship and was himself very scholarly. He saw the will of heaven expressed in rituals, and he felt that people should align themselves with nature and the natural world in order to express that will, which could be known only through study and reflection.

Confucius's teachings have been followed in China since his death, with only brief periods when Taoism or Buddhism was dominant. Because Confucianism has returned with greater vigor after each period of lapse, it is believed that Confucius expressed something deep and permanent in Chinese thought.

TAOISM

Taoism, which is based on principles of mysticism, arose almost simultaneously with Confucianism. It is based on *The Book of Tao*, reputedly by Lao-tzu, who was about fifty years older than Confucius. It may date from two centuries earlier; scholars are not certain. Tao, which means "the way," stresses personal virtue, in contrast with Confucius's emphasis on public virtue and the public good, which stemmed from his own interest in becoming a politician. Taoism was not concerned with politics or public life, nor did it value scholarship or ritual. It praised inactivity: "See the simple, embrace primitivity;/ Reduce the self, lessen the desires" (Verse 19). This suggests much of the spirit of Taoism.

Taoism had only a brief vogue because it absorbed superstitions and rituals foreign to its central teachings. It was most influential during the fall of the Han dynasty in A.D. 220, when a long period of stability came to an end, and with it the state religion, Confucianism. However, Taoism was ignored as the official religion in favor of Buddhism.

BUDDHISM

Imported from India, Buddhism lasted for 600 years in China, until the late Tang dynasty. The buddha in Figure 7-1 is in a cave similar to those in Ajanta, in India. Some Chinese caves contained paintings of the kind found in Ajanta, but they were destroyed by vandals in relatively recent times. The caves in Yunkang were begun by a monk, T'an-yao, during a period of Buddhist persecution. The great buddha of cave 20, one of the most famous in Asia, is 45 feet high.

This work shows that some missionary influence from India was reaching China. The Han dynasty saw contact with outside influences, such as traders from Greece and Rome. Rome had an area for marketing silks; the road connecting east and west was known as the "silk road." The making of silk depended on an

Figure 7-1
Buddha from Yunkang, cave 20. A.D. 450. (Photo © Wan-go H. C. Weng.)

CONCEPT KEY

Chinese Religion

1. Why might a strong centralized government approve of a religious leader who praised ritual and ceremony?

2. Do you agree with Confucius that all ritual has an important value for human beings? Why would ritual seem valuable to people? What is its function in religion?

3. The statue of Athena in the Parthenon was about 35 feet high. The buddha in cave 20 (Figure 7-1) is 45 feet high. Why would people make such large statues in connection with their religion? Does their size contribute to their religious value?

4. The recommendation to lead a virtuous life appears in the teachings of Socrates, Christ, Buddha, Confucius, and Lao-tzu. Is a virtuous life appropriate for religion, or is it irrelevant? Is leading a virtuous life especially humanistic?

ancient technology and the presence of the mulberry tree, on which the silkworm lives. Like paper, gunpowder, the compass, and printing, silk is among the many Chinese inventions.

Bronzeware

The Chinese call themselves the "children of Han," referring to the Han dynasty. The people of the Shang dynasty, the period of the great bronzes, may have been ethnically different. The finds in Anyang in the 1920s uncovered Shang tombs (Figure 7-2), artifacts, and bronzes with designs similar to northwestern Amerindian carvings.

Burial practices in the Shang dynasty included using elaborate tombs containing personal possessions and figures, such as of warriors, which would accompany the dead in the next world. Sometimes the dead were buried with all their retainers, slaves, and advisers. Most of these seem to have been willing victims; only a few show signs of having died violently. One tomb held twenty-four female and twenty-two male skeletons, and fifty male heads were buried in a separate pit. The Chou dynasty was the last in which such practices were generally carried on.

The bronzes in these tombs are mostly ritual vessels whose purposes are unknown. They seem to have been made using the lost-wax process. In this process a model is made in wax; the model is then encased in plaster, and molten bronze is poured into the case, replacing the wax as it melts away. The process, used in European cast-bronze sculpture, has had to be reinvented several times.

The marks on these bronzes may be magical. No one knows the exact function of the ritual cups and containers called "yu," "ku," "chueh," and "fang i" (Figure 7-3). The fantastic mask, the t'ao-t'ieh, on the fang i in Figure 7-3d appears on many bronzes. China's interest in magic during this period was great, and these vessels may have been used in magical ceremonies. Religion was related to magic, and astrology and alchemy were both highly developed. Representations of fish, birds, tigers, elephants, and dragons are most common on these bronzes. The t'ao-t'ieh, a creature with a head but no body, is said to be a symbol of gluttony. Such figures appear on wood carvings of Indians in the north coastal regions of Canada and Alaska, and some art historians hold that the similarities are not accidental.

Chinese bells, called "chung," both small and gigantic, were also cast in this period. Because these were used in ceremonies, and because some bronzes are decorated with carvings of large ceremonial drums, Chinese music must have been well developed early in the Shang period. Dance was also quite advanced; talented dancers could rise to high station.

Figure 7-2
Tomb at Wuguancun, Anyang. Late Shang period. (Photo © Wan-go H. C. Weng.)

(a)

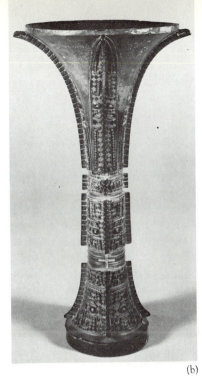

(b)

(c)

(d)

Figure 7-3
(a) Yu, (b) ku, (c) chueh, (d) fang i.
Shang period. (Freer Gallery, Smithsonian
Institution, Washington.)

Landscape Painting

Chinese landscapes like those in Figures 7-4 to 7-8 are an impression rather than a realistic representation of a scene: they aim to express essence rather than substance. People in Chinese landscapes are usually small and insignificant in relation to nature. The purpose of the Chinese landscape painter is to express the ch'i of a scene—its underlying spirit and vitality. The Chinese painter looks beneath the surface of the subject matter for a way, through form, to extract from it the spirit that will express its ch'i. The literal translation of the Chinese word for landscape is "mountain water," and Chinese landscapes rely heavily on both these elements.

Wang Wei died in A.D. 759 at the age of twenty-eight, during the period when landscape was rising in importance. He once said:

> So must a landscape painting be a symbolic language through which the painter may express not a relative, particularized aspect of nature seen at a given moment from a given viewpoint, but a genuine truth beyond time and place.

Ku K'ai-chih (c. 344–c. 406) illustrated *Admonitions of the Instructress to the Palace Ladies,* a handbook of etiquette and behavior for prominent women. His work exists in several fairly reliable copies. Most Chinese landscape paintings are not narratives, but his scroll *Nymph of the Lo River* (shown in Figure 7-4), which illustrates a poem, is an important exception.

The people in Figure 7-4 are larger than those we would ordinarily find in a Chinese landscape because this is a narrative, poetic event: the poet is bidding a sad farewell to his nymph-lover. Outlining the figures and filling the space with color are techniques basic to all Chinese figure painting. The dependence on clear line, in conjunction with the highly advanced calligraphy that existed in China (Chinese script is written with a paintbrush), led Roger Fry to say that "painting for the Chinese is a branch of handwriting."

Figure 7-4 is filled with subtle symmetries, balances, and contrasts. The three weeping willows echo the three people, one of whom stands apart from the rest. One group of trees shelters one of the willows, just as the attendant shelters the poet with a canopy. The trees seem to group in threes; the mountains explode abruptly as if symbolizing distances and separation. The water and the retreating ship, symbolic of the nymph's departure, are as disproportionate to the scene as the people are to the trees or as the mountains are to the people. Ku K'ai-chih was much less interested in exact proportion than in the ch'i of this scene.

Realism is not essential to the ch'i. There are no secure surfaces under the feet of the three people in Figure 7-4. As in most Chinese landscapes, the horizon is missing. That alone is often unsettling to western observers, since much of western painting depends on a strong horizon and a sense of receding space with clear perspective (in which a distant object is smaller than a nearby one). Such effects are dispensed with in the works of Ku K'ai-chih and those who came after him.

Wo-yun-sheng's landscape (Figure 7-5) comes from the great period of the Sung dynasty landscapes. It is a scroll, meant to be unrolled and viewed continuously; the definite, repeated rhythms of the downward or upward curves of the mountain ridges

Figure 7-4
Ku K'ai-chih. *Nymph of the Lo River.* Detail, twelfth-century copy. (Freer Gallery, Smithsonian Institution, Washington.)

Figure 7-5
Wo-yun-sheng. *Clear Day in the Valley,* detail. First half of thirteenth century.
(Museum of Fine Arts, Boston; from Mr. Okakura, May 1912.)

are matched by the rhythmic, irregular groupings of the trees. These repetitions are designed to echo the rhythms of nature. The humans are tiny, as is the house, suggesting their proper place in the valley.

Strong line and subtle shading—particularly in the rhythmic, craggy formations of the central mountain —suggest upward motion and receding distances. Atmosphere dominates the mountain peaks, which disappear in the haze, creating a powerful impression and a sense of timelessness. Timelessness was an aesthetic criterion during this period, and Figure 7-5 does aim for a sense of the eternal.

Hsieh Ho, an aesthetician and painter of the fifth century after Christ, laid down six rules for good painting. Three concern the proper technique for using the brush and color; one concerns the "proper placing of elements"; and another emphasizes fidelity in making copies. But the first rule is: "animation through spirit consonance." This is a mysterious rule which Alexander Soper has interpreted as demanding

Figure 7-6
Ma Yüan. *Bare Willows and Distant Mountains.* c. 1200.
(Museum of Fine Arts, Boston, Chinese and Japanese
Special Fund.)

that the painter capture the ch'i of the scene. In the case of the landscape in Figure 7-5, it means capturing the "mountainness" of the mountains, the "treeness" of the trees, and the "hazyness" of the haze. Everything else is secondary.

In MaYüan's landscape (Figure 7-6), a figure in the lower right, carrying a bundle, is moving toward a bridge which will take him to the house beyond the river. The barren willows suggest a cold, hard time of year, but the foliage on the far side of the river is abundant and reassuring. The curves of the willows create a rhythmic repetition across the painting, echoing the curves of the mountains. The straight, angular lines of the bridge, almost like Chinese characters, are echoed in the stiff, straight branches of the nearest tree. The painting is refined to the barest essentials: the figure is briskly painted with only a few lines, and even the bridge and the trees show economy of line. Careful shading and edging suggest the mountains, and the water is evoked without a single brushstroke. The black paint is applied to an earth-tone silk, and so no color is

Figure 7-7
Li Ch'eng (attributed). *A Solitary Temple amid Clearing Peaks.* Tenth century. Painting on silk. (Nelson-Atkins Museum of Art, Kansas City, Missouri; Nelson Fund.)

Figure 7-8
Fan K'uan. *Traveling amid Mountains and Gorges.* Sung dynasty. Ink and slight color on silk. (Collection of the National Palace Museum, Taiwan, Republic of China.)

Chinese Landscape Painting

1. What are the similarities in subject matter between Figure 7-8, Fan K'uan's landscape, and the landscapes shown in Figures 7-4 through 7-7? What does Figure 7-8 have in common with the others, and what, if anything, is different about it?

2. Do the landscapes shown in Figures 7-4 through 7-7 have a pattern of rhythmic repetition of formal details similar to that in Figure 7-8? Identify any such details and demonstrate how they echo one another.

3. Each of the landscapes depicts large natural elements: water, mountains, air. What is the relative importance of each of these in Figure 7-8? What is their relative importance in the other landscapes? Is there a relationship between the dramatic quality of an object and its importance in a painting?

4. How successful are these works in evoking the ch'i of the scenes? Which seems to you most successful? Is it possible for a non-Chinese viewer to perceive the ch'i? Are you aware of a sense of timelessness—a sense of eternity—in these works?

5. The tops of the mountains in these landscapes are darker than their bases. Is this the way mountains really appear? Do these painters use different stylistic techniques to portray mountains? Which painting is most successful in revealing the "mountain-ness" of mountains? Is this painting a realistic representation, or does it express the ch'i?

needed. Color was minimized in paintings of this period so that the artist could concentrate on essentials. The traditional seals on the right of this painting, however, are bright red.

Li Ch'eng's painting of a Buddhist temple (Figure 7-7) is much busier than earlier landscapes. The arched rooflines of the temple, in the center of the composition, are echoed in the lower buildings and in the craggy branches of the trees at the left and right. The verticality of the composition is reinforced everywhere, as the mountain in the upper portion of the painting rises higher and higher, echoing the height of the pagoda-pattern rooftops. The contrast of descending water and rising mountain is an essential part of the composition. Humans, in the lower houses and near the bridges, are dwarfed by natural forms. The lines of the painting are crisp, the shading is exact, and the entire scene is rendered with clarity. Any small segment of the composition may also be viewed separately, since the patterns of formal repetition which dominate the whole also dominate its parts. The result is an integrity of composition—a sense of unity—and an evocation of atmosphere.

Figure 7-8 shows a landscape by Fan K'uan.

Poetry

TU FU: THE IMAGE

Chinese poetry often discards narrative and argument to concentrate on the image, which insinuates itself into our unconscious and makes us respond to the poet's vision. Imagery makes a direct appeal to our senses: sight, touch, smell, taste, and sound. Tu Fu (A.D. 712–770), the master poet of the Tang dynasty, depends on the power of images in his poem "The Emperor," in which the emperor is himself impressed by the image he sees of the empress:

> On a throne of new gold the Son of the Sky is sitting among his Mandarins. He shines with jewels and is like a sun surrounded by stars.
> The Mandarins speak gravely of grave things; but the Emperor's thought has flown out by the open window.
> In her pavilion of porcelain the Empress is sitting among her women. She is like a bright flower among leaves.
> She dreams that her beloved stays too long at council, and wearily she moves her fan.
> A breathing of perfumed air kisses the face of the Emperor.
> "My beloved moves her fan, and sends me a perfume from her lips."
> Towards the pavilion of porcelain walks the Emperor, shining with his jewels; and leaves his grave Mandarins to look at each other in silence.

Tu Fu has chosen a special moment to express the essential humanity of the emperor, a moment not of power, but of love. Tu Fu's imagery emphasizes sensory perception: the emperor's shining jewels, the flowerlike beauty of the empress, the odor of perfume from her lips, and the movement of air from her fan.

Tu Fu is today generally considered first among Chinese poets. Yet in his own time he was hardly noticed. Political circumstances made his life difficult, and "The Emperor" may have been an expedient form of flattery. To survive, Tu Fu had to watch court manners very carefully. He experienced exile, separation from his family, and disappointment in his ambitions for his own advancement. Yet he developed a purer and purer sense of the poetical. He came from one of the best families in China, was a Confucian, and naturally showed an interest in public service and the exercise of power.

"Spring View" combines personal and public concerns:

The nation smashed	hills and the River endure
spring in the City	grass and trees grow deep
grief for the times	flowers tear-spattered
ache of absence	a bird's cry ruffles my mind
signal fires	for three months unending

news from home	would be worth thousands in gold
my white hairs thinner	I scratch them they grow
nearly too few	to hold the pin of my cap

David Lattimore, the translator, has structured the lines to resemble the original. The phrases are timed to the reader's breathing, intensifying the enigmatic quality of certain expressions, such as "a bird's cry ruffles my mind." The reader must make connections between the expressions; their absence communicates a sense of woe and derangement. This poem may have been written after the An Lu-Shan rebellion, which began in 755. Tu Fu stayed with the ousted emperor's court in exile, while struggles for power brought war and disorder to much of China.

In the last of his "Seven Songs Written while Living at T'ung-ku in 759," Tu Fu laments his lack of success:

> I am a man who's made no name, already I've grown old,
> Wandering hungry three years on barren mountain roads.
> In Ch'ang-an the ministers are all young men;
> Wealth and fame must be earned before a man grows old.
> In the mountains here are scholars who knew me long ago.
> We only think of the good old days, our hearts full of pain.
> Alas! this is my seventh song, oh! with sorrow I end the refrain,
> Looking up to the wide sky where the white sun rushes on.

This sad contemplation of old age reminds us of many western poets, among them William Shakespeare and John Donne. Tu Fu's anxieties center on his not having risen in the ranks of the ministers, not having achieved worldly fame and recognition. He is almost unaware of the significance of his poetry.

TU FU AND LANDSCAPE PAINTING

Tu Fu's most famous series of poems, "Autumn Thoughts," show how he aligned his imagery with that of the landscape painters of his time. The imagery of mountains and water contributes to establishing the atmosphere, much as it does in painting.

Poetry—Tu Fu

1. What connections can you make between Tu Fu's poetry and the landscape paintings discussed earlier and shown in Figures 7-4 through 7-8? How are they similar in terms of their subject matter, their patterns of repetition, and their evocation of atmosphere?

2. Which of Tu Fu's images seems most intense and realized? Which sense does he appeal to most? Is any of the five senses omitted?

3. If possible, read a poem by Li Po, about whom Tu Fu sometimes wrote. Li Po contrasts his Taoist beliefs with Tu Fu's Confucianism. Taoism stressed a deep, inward spirituality—a relief from the activity of the world. Do these qualities in Li Po's work put it in sharp contrast to Tu Fu's work?

4. Compare Tu Fu's "Autumn Thoughts" with Shakespeare's Sonnet 73, "That time of year thou may'st in me behold" (see Chapter 13). What are the differences and similarities in subject matter? In use of imagery? In attitude toward oneself?

5. Write a poem using Tu Fu's techniques. Concentrate on producing imagery that appeals directly to the senses. Choose a subject similar to his. You may refer to one of the landscape paintings as an aid to composition.

Jade dews deeply wilt and wound the maple woods;
On Witch Mountain, in Witch Gorge, the air is
    somber, desolate.
Billowy waves from the river roar and rush towards
    the sky;
Over the frontier pass, wind and clouds sink to the
    darkening earth.
These clustered chrysanthemums, twice blooming,
    evoke the tears of yesteryear;
A lonely boat, as ever, is moored to the heart that
    yearns for home.
To cut winter clothes, women everywhere ply their
    scissors and foot-rulers--
Below the White Emperor's tall city wall is heard the
    urgent pounding of the evening wash.

This poem simulates the verticality of a scroll painting. The dews settle on the mountain. The waves, the pass, the chrysanthemums, and the boat all seem beneath it. And below them are the tall city wall and the washerwomen, who are even lower. Tu Fu evokes a visual scene, a timeless moment carefully fused with nature and recurrent human events.

Tu Fu wrote during a period when many of China's greatest poets were alive. Wang Wei (699–759), also a noted landscape painter, and Li Po (701–762) were older than he; Meng Chaio (751–814), Li Ho (791–817), and Tu Mu (803–852) were younger. All were poets of great importance whose works have been well translated into English.

Architecture

PAGODA ARCHITECTURE

Pagoda-style architecture—octagonal, with multiple roofs—is associated with the introduction of Buddhism. The pagoda shown in Figure 7-9 suggests an imitation of mountains, such as that found in the Indian stupa or sikhara. The roofs are not strictly

Figure 7-9
Pagoda. (Photo © Wan-go H. C. Weng.)

"tou-kung" (Figure 7-11). Shorter beams cross one another to support the roofing. They sometimes become so complex that they resemble the Chinese puzzle—interlocking pieces that form a box. They not only support the roofing but also provide strong visual interest and permit considerable variety in appearance. In some periods, a straight roofline was most common, while in others, more flamboyant arching was preferred.

The typical Chinese wooden structure could be expanded almost endlessly. Chinese extended families sometimes numbered 100 persons. The houses had a north-south alignment, with side buildings built at right angles to the main building. The head of the family was the oldest father or, if he had died, his wife. Some of the sons would have second or third wives and their children. A flexible design that could be expanded was essential.

CITY PLANNING: ESTABLISHING COMMUNITY

The hallmark of Chinese architecture is careful planning. Careful detail work, symmetry, and rhythmic repetition of details typify Chinese buildings. But the careful planning shows up best in the cities, which were generally walled enclosures. "Ch'eng" means both "city" and "wall." The ideal was to have the cities walled and to have everyone live within the walls. This was not always possible, since new neighborhoods sometimes sprang up outside the walls as the cities grew. Whenever possible, though, new walls were constructed around the new neighborhoods so as to include them in the city.

Ch'ang-an (Figure 7-12), the capital during the Tang dynasty and the city that Tu Fu lamented, includes an imperial city, built in the northern central area of the city. Two gates to the west parallel two more to the east. Ming-te gate, the main gate to the city, lies to the south; there are two great markets—one to the east and one to the west. The segments of the city are laid out in rectangles, with roads going from east to west and from north to south; the larger, more important roads are on an east-south axis. The rigidity of the grid is softened by natural streams and their lakes. The hibiscus garden and the Ta-Ming Palace, as well as the imperial park, show that the planners were able to take advantage of the natural site. During the Tang dynasty, this may have been the largest city in the world. Its walls held

functional, but accentuate the building's vertical thrust. Some Chinese buildings with multiple roofs make use of the added protection they provide against strong light and rain.

The Kuan-yin-ko (Figure 7-10), part of a Buddhist temple complex, shows the typical construction of the roof: wooden crossbeams supporting an arched roof with a high central pitch. The lower set of eaves protects the ground floor, while the upper set protects the central porch, which runs the length of the building. In some later buildings the eaves protrude further in proportion to the building. These eaves are supported with a complex system of bracketing called

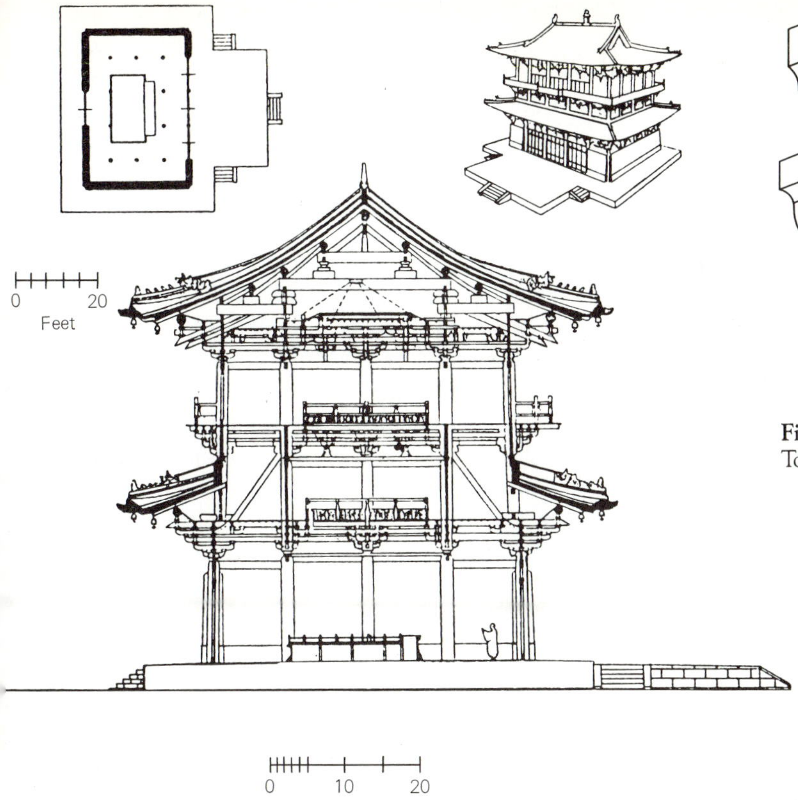
0
20
Feet
0
10
20

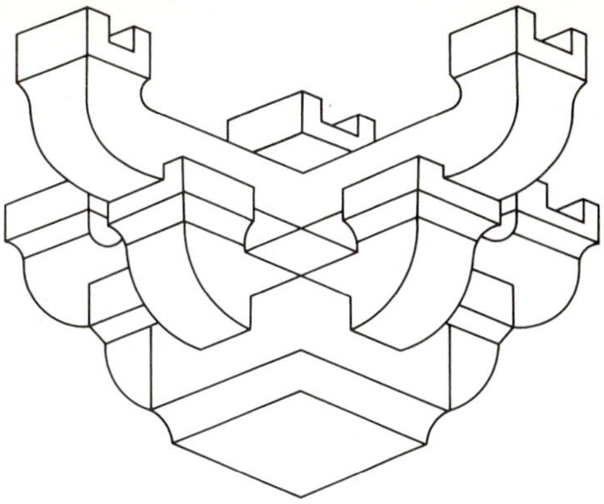

Figure 7-11
Tou-kung supports.

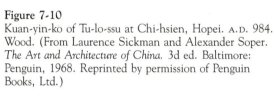

Figure 7-10
Kuan-yin-ko of Tu-lo-ssu at Chi-hsien, Hopei. A.D. 984. Wood. (From Laurence Sickman and Alexander Soper. *The Art and Architecture of China.* 3d ed. Baltimore: Penguin, 1968. Reprinted by permission of Penguin Books, Ltd.)

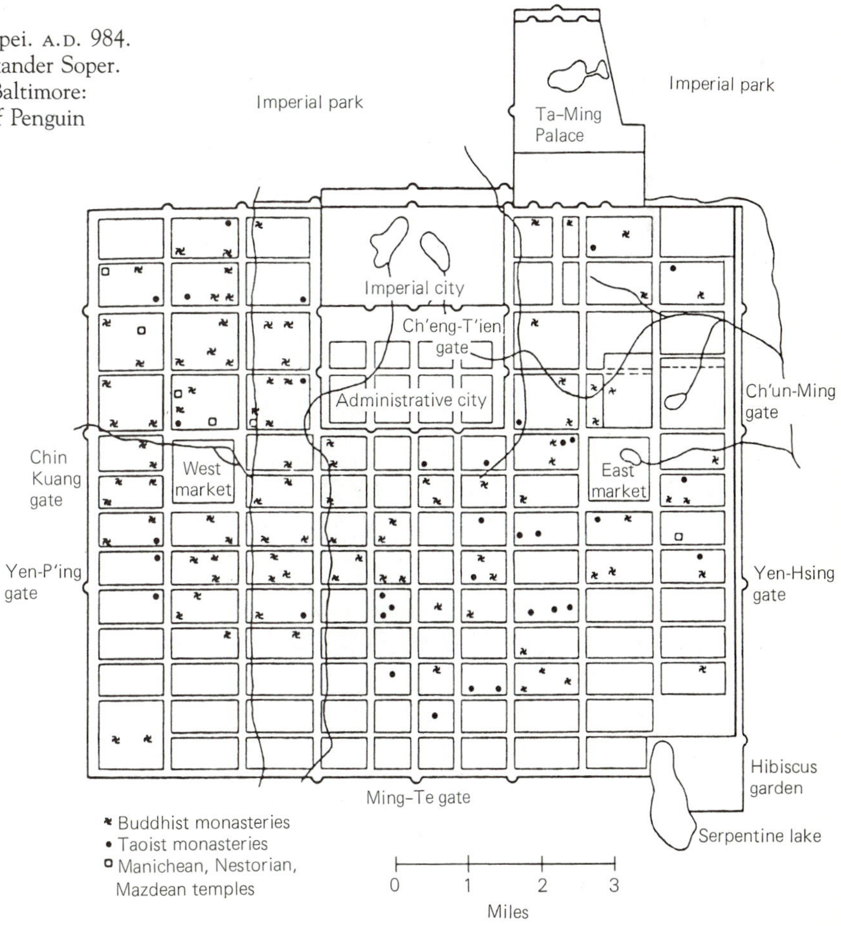
Imperial park
Ta-Ming Palace
Imperial park
Imperial city
Ch'eng-T'ien gate
Administrative city
Ch'un-Ming gate
Chin Kuang gate
West market
East market
Yen-P'ing gate
Yen-Hsing gate
Hibiscus garden
Ming-Te gate
Serpentine lake
Buddhist monasteries
Taoist monasteries
Manichean, Nestorian, Mazdean temples
0
1
2
3
Miles

Figure 7-12
Plan of Ch'ang-an. (From Conrad Schirokauer. *A Brief History of Chinese and Japanese Civilizations.* New York: Harcourt Brace Jovanovich, 1978. Reprinted by permission of the publisher; © 1978.)

at least 1 million persons, while another million sprawled into its outlying areas.

Such city planning is the norm in China. Peking follows a similar pattern; its axis of streets lies north to south, and its main gate is in the south. The inner city is the area that was originally walled; the outer city reflects the considerable growth that has taken place. Peking was built by the Mongol emperor Kublai Khan according to a Chinese plan. During the Ming dynasty (1368–1644), when China was retrieved from the Mongols, additions were built on the southern portions of the city.

The Temple and Altar of Heaven in Peking (Figure 7-13), built during the Ming dynasty, consists of three circular terraces, one on top of the other. The four openings in the balustrades are at the points of the compass: north, south, east, and west. A larger circular wall surrounds the terraces, and a square walkway is laid out to encompass all of it. The temple, the Hall of Annual Prayers, lies to the north of the altar; it has a three-tiered roof that cannot be seen by anyone who walks toward the altar on ground level. The design is similar to that of the Indian stupa, and the same attention is paid to the points of the compass and to the protection of the inner areas with walls and ritual gates.

The Leng-en Tien (Figure 7-14) is the main hall in a grouping of arched bridges, walkways, and terraces that constitute the tomb complex of the emperor Yung-lo (1360–1424). Many such subtly landscaped Ming tombs were built in Peking. Chinese houses were often set in a garden landscape of moving water, rising hillsides, and artificial islands with connecting bridges. The influence of landscape painting is evident in such complexes as the Summer Palace in Peking, most of which was built during the

Figure 7-13
Temple of Heaven, Peking. A.D. 1420, 1754. (Photo © Wan-go H. C. Weng.)

Figure 7-14
Leng-en Tien, Ming tomb, Peking. c. A.D. 1424. (Photo © Wan-go H. C. Weng.)

CONCEPT KEY

Chinese Architecture

1. What would be the advantages and disadvantages of living in a carefully planned city like Ch'ang-an (Figure 7-12)? Do you have firsthand experience with such a city?

2. What is the point of building a pagoda (such as Figure 7-9) with numerous useless roofs? Do you feel that practicality should rule architectural decisions of this sort?

3. Modern architects often insist that form should follow function. Establish the function, as best you can, of any of the buildings shown in Figures 7-10, 7-13, and 7-14, and decide to what extent the form follows the function. Do you think that Chinese architects would have agreed that form should follow function?

4. Most Chinese wooden structures were built according to a formula, with no need to consult plans. The only critical information had to do with the size of the building. What would this have meant for a person who wanted to be an architect? What would an architect's job have been?

5. Why would it be important to situate a building, or even a city, on an axis correlating with the compass? Why would it matter whether a gate or an entrance was north, south, east, or west?

Manchu dynasty in the nineteenth century. Its houses and other structures are carefully set in the landscape almost as if they were jewels in a crown. Many such complexes preserve a sense of wildness and raw natural power as a means of providing relief from the rigidity of regularly planned cities.

Jadeware and Porcelain

JADE

The Chinese have always thought that jade symbolizes certain virtues: charity, rectitude, wisdom, courage, and equity. It is as strong as steel, it comes in many colors, and it is rare. Figures 7-15 and 7-16 show examples of late carving; modeling is deep and subtle, and we are aware of the artists' confidence in working with this intractable material. These pieces might have symbolic powers for the wearer, although during the Ming dynasty they were often simply decorative.

A recent find reminds us that jade was believed to have special restorative powers. In 1968 the rumor that royalty were sometimes buried in jade suits was confirmed when a tomb from the Han dynasty was

unearthed. In it were two jade suits—one for a prince and the other for a princess. Tou Wan, who died in about 115 B.C., had a jade suit (shown in Color Plate 2). It required ten years of work on the jade, which was cut into rectangular pieces and then fitted with gold thread to make the suit.

PORCELAIN

The west has long called all dishware "china," indicating our connection of the durable, brilliant ware with the country that produces it. Chinese porcelain has been used not only for dishes but also for figurines, such as the horses in Figure 7-17, which are typical of those found in many Tang tombs. They have a dynamic quality, with iridescent surfaces and subtle colorations. They are so distinctive that when a similar horse was discovered in the caves at Lascaux, it was named the "Chinese horse."

The blue flask covered with lotus scrolls (Figure 7-18) is large but graceful. It is typical of such vessels of the Ming period; its surfaces are radiant, and the decorations are balanced as a result of careful patterning and repetition. Ming pottery is colorful; but the earlier Sung dynasty produced some of the most valued glazes and some of the most graceful shapes. The green crackleware pot shown in Figure 7-19

Figure 7-15
Jade pi disk, Ming dynasty. (By permission of the Trustees of the British Museum.)

Figure 7-16
Jade dragon ring, Ming dynasty. (By permission of the Trustees of the British Museum.)

Figure 7-17
Left: Porcelain horses: tomb figures, Tang dynasty. (By permission of the University Museum, University of Pennsylvania.)

Figure 7-18
Below left: Blue flask, Ming dynasty. (By permission of the Trustees of the British Museum.)

Figure 7-19
Below right: Green crackleware pot, Sung dynasty. (Freer Gallery of Art, Smithsonian Institution, Washington.)

exhibits the classic Sung proportions. The line is simple, combining a full, round base with cautious fluting in the upper half of the pot. The shape is at once graceful, easy, and simple. Attention to detail and grace in everyday objects reflects the passion of the Chinese for beauty and for beautiful things. Whether for the table of an emperor or a commoner, Chinese porcelain is likely to be symmetrical, balanced, well proportioned, and decorated to please the eye.

Summary

China, which is situated in such a way that its culture grew without much contact with the west, has maintained a steady tradition in all the arts. A concern for natural beauty and a sense of the individual's place in nature guided the work of the Chinese in landscape painting, in poetry, and in architecture. Humanist religious forces, beginning with Confucius, helped rout superstition and placed love of nature in a perspective that included respect for humankind. During the Buddhist period, there were important Indian influences on Chinese art and architecture. But Buddhism was soon reabsorbed into a new form of Confucianism. Confucianism respects scholarship, tradition, the laws, and the proper celebration of rituals. Its opposing religious force, Taoism, emphasized none of these; rather, it centered on the inner life, a mystical union with nature, and personal inspiration. Chinese painting penetrates the surface reality in order to portray the ch'i. The love of beautiful things is evident in Chinese silks, tapestries, jades, and porcelain.

Concepts in Chapter 7

Confucius founded Confucianism, a religion emphasizing scholarship, ritual, and public service.

Taoism, founded by Lao-tzu, stressed inner vision, personal inactivity, and communion with nature.

Buddhism, introduced through India, had a vogue that lasted for 600 years, beginning in A.D. 220.

The Shang dynasty (1766 B.C. to 1122 B.C.) is the earliest verifiable historical period in China.

Bronze objects were used in elaborate rituals during the Shang period.

Chinese painting is dominated by landscapes. Its great period was the Sung dynasty (A.D. 960 to A.D. 1279).

Chinese landscapes are not meant to be realistic, but rather are meant to represent the ch'i, or essence, of a scene.

Chinese landscapes portray mountains, water, and air.

Humans usually appear as tiny elements in a Chinese landscape.

The poetry of Tu Fu uses elaborate images.

The Tang dynasty (A.D. 618 to A.D. 907) was a great age in Chinese poetry.

Chinese poetry shows the influence of Chinese landscape painting and uses some of the same subject matter.

Pagodas are associated with Buddhism.

Chinese wooden structures were usually built without plans; the details varied according to the size of the structure.

City planning is one of the hallmarks of Chinese architecture.

Tomb complexes in the Ming dynasty (A.D. 1368 to A.D. 1644) were built according to complex plans.

Many important Chinese buildings are sited according to the four compass points.

Chinese landscape planning shows the influence of Chinese landscape painting.

Jade and porcelain objects are explicitly Chinese; everyday objects made of porcelain are usually graceful and beautifully designed.

Suggested Readings

De Bary, William Theodore, et al., eds. *Sources of Chinese Tradition.* New York: Columbia, 1960.

Fontein, Jan, and Pratapaditya Pal. *Museum of Fine Arts, Boston: Oriental Art.* Greenwich, Conn.: New York Graphic Society, 1973.

Graham, A. C. *Poems of the Late T'ang.* Baltimore: Penguin, 1965.

Lee, Sherman E. *A History of Far Eastern Art.* New York: Abrams, 1964.

Li, Dun J. *The Essence of Chinese Civilization.* Princeton, N.J.: Van Nostrand, 1967.

Liu, Wu-chi, and Irving Yucheng Lo. *Sunflower Splendor.* Bloomington: University of Indiana Press, 1975.

Reischauer, Edwin O., and John K. Fairbank. *East Asia: The Great Tradition*. Boston: Houghton Mifflin, 1960.

Schirokauer, Conrad. *A Brief History of Chinese and Japanese Civilizations*. New York: Harcourt Brace Jovanovich, 1978.

Sickman, Lawrence, and Alexander Soper. *The Art and Architecture of China*. 3d ed. Baltimore: Penguin, 1968.

Sullivan, Michael. *The Arts of China*. 2d ed. Berkeley: University of California Press, 1973.

———. *An Introduction to Chinese Art*. Berkeley: University of California Press, 1961.

CHAPTER 8   ISLAM

Religion

ISLAMIC INFLUENCE

 The pressure of overpopulation in Arabia, combined with the weakening of the Byzantine empire—the last remnant of Roman rule in the seventh century after Christ—helped Arab influence spread northward to Syria and Egypt, and then to the west. The zeal that was part of the Islamic faith—the belief that the Prophet Muhammad (c. 570–632) knew Allah and knew that Allah had prophesied greatness for his people—made conquest, once it had begun, seem inevitable.

Islam reached India in the east and Spain in the west; it even penetrated into France. Islamic influence is evident in the architecture, painting, and literature of European and Asian cultures. Because Arab artists and architects could assimilate local styles and brilliantly reexpress them in an original way, the influence of Islam is neither singular nor monolithic. Its source of energy is the faith expressed in the Koran.

THE HOLY KORAN

Like the Bible, the Koran (or Qu'ran) is held to be the revealed word of God. Muhammad received revelations for more than twenty years. He preserved them in the Koran, which, since he could not read or write, he memorized and passed on to his followers to memorize. The Koran was written down in around 660, in part because it was feared that with Muhammad's death it might be lost.

The Koran includes some of the Old and the New Testaments; it mentions Abraham and Moses as well as Jesus. Its structure reflects the fact that various revelations, covering many subjects, were made over a period of many years. Its suras, or chapters, give it the physical appearance of the Bible, and their titles—"The Angels," "Divorce," "Iron," "The Ant," "The Blood-Clot," "Jonah," "The Prophets"—show that the Koran and the Bible cover some similar topics. All the suras, both long and short, are in the form of poems written in a language which the faithful consider the purest and best Arabic that is possible.

The following passage, from Sura 25, "Salvation," is characteristic of the tone of the Koran:

> Put thy trust in the Living God,
> the Undying,
> and proclaim his praise.
> Sufficiently is He aware of His servants' sins
> who created the heavens and the earth,
> and what between them is, in six days,
> then sat Himself upon the Throne,
> the All-compassionate: ask any informed of Him!
> (Lines 60–67.)

Good and evil, Satan and evildoers, are similar in the Koran and the Bible, but the Koran stresses the will of God to the extent that personal freedom of will is brought into question. Scholars of the Koran disagree on the question whether it grants free will in any great degree to humankind.

Since the will of God is all-powerful, it must be acted out:

> And whosoever submits his will to God,
> being a good-doer, has laid hold
> of the most firm handle; and unto God is the issue of
> all affairs.
> And whoso disbelieves, let not his disbelief
> grieve thee; unto Us they shall return,
> and We shall tell them what they did.
> Surely God knows all the thoughts within the breasts.
> To them We give enjoyment a little, then
> We compel them to a harsh chastisement. (Sura 31,
> lines 20–25.)

In the strictest interpretations of the text, even the question whether one has faith in God is an expression of the will of God.

In light of such attitudes toward predestination, it

CONCEPT KEY

The Holy Koran

1. When Muhammad returned victoriously to his native Mecca, after his hegira, or forced exile in Medina, he is said to have entered an area sacred to pagandom. In it were 360 pagan idols set in a circle, representing the days of the lunar year. Muhammad rode slowly by them on his camel, tipping each one over and saying, "Truth has come." Was this an act of humanist religious reform?

2. Is it contradictory to provide clear guidelines to everyday behavior and yet demand a belief in predestination? Does a belief in predestination conflict with the idea of free will?

3. The faith of Islam was spread at the point of a sword. Does armed conquest to spread a religion seem congruent with the tenets of a humanist religion? Is it an unusual procedure for spreading a faith?

4. Is the teaching of everyday behavior central to religious faith as you understand it? Why would a religion that defined proper behavior and set limits on it have a strong appeal?

5. Read Sura 12, "Joseph," in the Koran and compare it with the story of Joseph in the Bible (in Matthew or Luke). Use A. J. Arberry's translation of the Koran (Toronto: Macmillan, 1955), which Muslims say gives the best sense of the original. What similarities and differences are there in the stories? How effective is each narrative style? How does each version treat human values and human concerns?

may seem odd that the Koran emphasizes proper behavior, but that is precisely what it does. Throughout the text, passages explain how to perform certain acts and what may and may not be done. In Sura 33, "The Confederates," the Prophet is told that he may take any woman he chooses for his wife, just as he may cast from him any wife he no longer wants. This liberal view requires, however, that he pay his wives "their wages."

Allah uses the pronoun "we" when addressing the Prophet:

O Prophet, We have sent thee as a
witness, and good tidings to bear
and warning, calling unto God by His
leave, and as a light-giving lamp.
Give good tidings to the believers that
there awaits them with God great bounty.
And obey not the unbelievers
and the hypocrites; heed not their hurt,
but put thy trust in God; God suffices as a guardian.
O believers, when you marry believing women
and then divorce them, before you touch them;
you have no period to reckon against them;
so make provision for them and set them free with
    kindliness. (Sura 33, lines 45–57.)

The fact that Muhammad stressed guidance in everyday activity helped the faith spread. Earlier pagan beliefs had focused on performing rituals to pacify or celebrate specific forces and deities; their emphasis was always on satisfying the gods. The religion of Islam offered a way—a path, a guide—to living more fully. It gave human life priority over empty ritual. That God chose a person to be his prophet, as he had done for the Jews and Christians, emphasizes the humanist import and value of the message of Islam.

Architecture

THE DOME OF THE ROCK

The earliest extant Arab building—the Dome of the Rock, in Jerusalem (Figure 8-1)—was constructed between 643 and 691. It is built on the most holy site of the ancient world: the place where Abraham was to have sacrificed Isaac, the site of the ancient temple of Solomon, and the place from which Muhammad is said to have made his night visit to heaven. By building its temple here, Islam became the successor of earlier religions. Muhammad preached that he was the last of a series of prophets who revealed first Judaism, then Christianity, and then Islam.

The temple (Figures 8-2 and 8-3 show a cross section and plan) is octagonal, with a small domed shelter covering a well; this contributed to the sanctity of the site, as a similar shelter does on the Greek acropolis. Like the Indian stupa, the dome is a metaphor for heaven; it was a common motif in Byzantine churches. The Dome of the Rock is Byzantine in pattern: a central area covered by a dome, with an octagonal outer walkway for the faithful. It has Roman arches and modified pillars in the Byzan-

Figure 8-1
Dome of the Rock, Jerusalem. 643–691.
(Photo, A. Duncan, Middle East
Archive.)

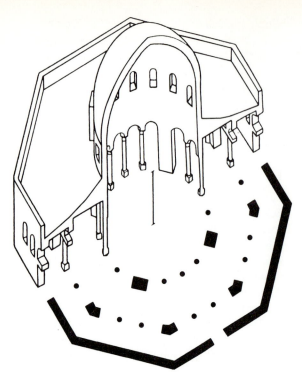

Figure 8-2
Cross section of the Dome of the Rock. (From Titus Burckhardt. *Art of Islam.* London: World of Islam Festival Trust, 1976.)

Figure 8-3
Geometrical scheme of the Dome of the Rock. (From Titus Burckhardt. *Art of Islam.* London: World of Islam Festival Trust, 1976.)

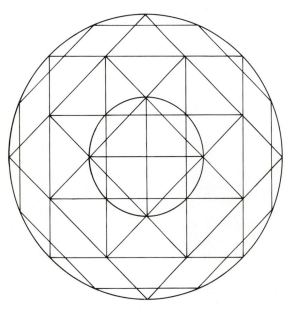

tine mode. On the outside, there are rows of Arab pointed arches with richly colored inlay decorations typical of Arab architecture.

The decorations on the Dome of the Rock are basically geometric. Like other Semitic peoples, the Arabs avoided representations of figures that could have become idols. However, the taboo against such representations has not been absolute and may not even have been in effect when the Dome of the Rock was built. Some later buildings do include representations of mythical animals. Officially, the prohibition is against making images of God, but the fear is that any representational image may be construed as an idol of God, like the golden calf mentioned in Genesis.

The rock protected by the Dome of the Rock is the sacred top of Mount Moriah. The dome is built on four piers of solid masonry, with twelve slender Roman pillars, each topped by a soft Roman arch. The four solid piers represent the corners of a square space, while the dome imposes a round form on the square. The underlying structure of the building is an elaborate but intelligible geometric pattern. The inner and outer circles, the squares, and the oblong forms intersect so as to create a star shape.

THE GREAT MOSQUE AT DAMASCUS

The Dome of the Rock assimilated a design from another culture. The Great Mosque at Damascus, built by the Umayyad rulers in 707, is more typical of Arab design; the space is low and wide, not long and high. The basic plan of a mosque (Figure 8-4 shows the plan of the Great Mosque) is usually a square or rectangle, with a long hallway built on the south side, the side of Mecca. In the outermost wall facing Mecca is an arched doorway, or mihrab. Its function is not to admit people, but to give an exact orientation to Mecca. To its right is a small pulpit, or minbar, from which passages of the Koran may be read and preached and from which a holy man may lead prayers.

Since most Muslims pray on their knees, or even lying face down, the mosque should be viewed from a low angle, as in Figure 8-5. The Great Mosque at Damascus is earth-rooted, like other mosques; it does not stress verticality, and there are no dramatic spaces overhead. Instead, the spaces are simple, wide, and designed to accommodate masses of the faithful. The minarets, towers next to mosques, are

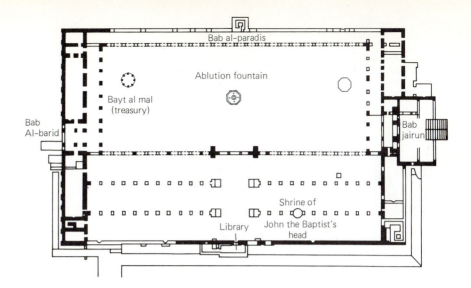

adapted from watchtowers used in time of war or when there was a threat of invasion; now they are used to call the faithful to prayer.

The word "Arab" implies nomads or wanderers, such as the Bedouin. The architectural need of wanderers, especially merchants, was for a large, open, fortified space in which to rest overnight. The place of worship was simply a portion of this space—a long hallway, as in Figure 8-4. The Great Mosque at Damascus holds the shrine of the head of Saint John the Baptist; however, it is not in the center of the hall, under the dome, because in a mosque no spot is more holy than another. There is no central focus of attention, unless it is the mihrab, which is centered in the southern wall. The rows of arches constitute a repeated pattern throughout the structure; they emphasize the rootedness of the building and its lack of height. Open space matters here, not dramatic space. Light is less important than openness since prayer is directed not to the sky or the heavens, but to the holy city.

The interior of the mosque appears enormous. When one is seated or kneeling on the prayer rugs, the pillars suggest great vertical space. The lamps (Figure 8-6) hanging from the ceilings on long chains are made of blown and decorated glass; they are filled with oil and lighted with a wick. Their light is particularly warm and soft. If there is such a thing as a "dim religious light," as John Milton called it, it would be cast by one of these lamps, which give the effect of hushed reverence, an effect created by most Islamic mosques.

Figure 8-4
Above: Plan of the Great Mosque at Damascus. (From Titus Burckhardt. *Art of Islam.* London: World of Islam Festival Trust, 1976.)

Figure 8-5
Below: Courtyard and porticos of the Great Mosque in Damascus. (Photo, A. Duncan, Middle East Archives.)

Figure 8-6
Mosque lamp from Syria. A.D. 1286, 10 ⅜ inches high.
(Metropolitan Museum of Art, gift of J. Pierpont
Morgan, 1917.)

PERCEPTION KEY

The Dome of the Rock and the Great Mosque at Damascus

1. What are the primary geometric forms in the layout of the Dome of the Rock
(Figures 8-1, 8-2, and 8-3)? How do they contrast with those of the Great Mosque at
Damascus (Figures 8-4, 8-5, and 8-6)? Does the greater complexity of geometric layout
affect the appearance of the exterior of the more complex building? Why would
complex geometry be important to a temple builder?

2. Which seems more important to the Arab architect—the interior or the exterior
space? Which of these buildings has the most elaborate exterior? Which has the most
elaborate interior?

3. What range of emotional effects do you see achieved in these buildings? Do you
think that the architects were concerned about the emotional effects of the buildings
on viewers or users?

4. How important are decorative elements in Arab architecture? Which of these
buildings pays the greatest attention to decoration? Which has the most successful
decoration? What do you perceive the function of decoration to be in these buildings?

5. What seem to be the most important qualities of Arab architecture? Consider the
questions of use of space, whether the buildings are earth-rooted or sky-oriented, the
attitude toward post-and-lintel or arch construction, the use of decoration, mass, and
size. Is there a clear relation between form and function in these buildings? Using
tracing paper, copy what seem to you to be the most distinctive Arab architectural
shapes.

Figure 8-7
Left: Great Mosque of
al-Mutawakkil, Samarra.
(Photo Researchers, Inc., New
York.)

Figure 8-8
Below left: Minaret of the
mosque at Samarra. (Photo,
E. Boehm, Mainz.)

THE GREAT MOSQUE AT SAMARRA

The ninth-century Great Mosque of al-Mutawakkil, at Samarra (Figure 8-7), is the largest Islamic mosque. Its stark desert setting suggests the pyramid complex at Saqqara; even the minaret (Figure 8-8), with its huge twisting ramps, is evocative of the step pyramid of Imhotep. Its ramps and severe lines also make it resemble Mesopotamian architecture. The color, a yellowish sand tone, blends with the harsh landscape, making it seem as if the mosque had risen from the desert where it stands. The minaret, which is 164 feet high, looks even higher. The walls enclose a space 784 by 512 feet. The interior is ringed by a series of portals marked by thin columns and graceful arches, the basic pattern of the mosque.

THE ALHAMBRA

Not all Arab buildings are in the desert. The Alhambra, in Spain (Figure 8-9), begun in 1230, was built not as a mosque but as a palace for the rulers of Granada. It encloses a space similar to that of the Acropolis, and, like the Acropolis, it has the appearance of a fortification. Inside, the spaces are light, airy, and beautifully sensual—so much so that purists have condemned it as decadent and overdone.

The Alhambra is an architectural puzzle. There is no other structure like it in the Arab world, or anywhere else. Some say that there is mystical significance in the mathematics that underlies its plan (the plan is shown in Figure 8-10); some see the decorations as complex symbols. The grand lifestyle of the rulers of Granada seems to contradict the general puritanism of the Muslims. Since the Christians were reconquering Spain when the Alhambra was built, it is a fortification; but such opulence and splendor in a fortification are unusual.

The detail work in the window of the Queen's Room (Figure 8-11) is all the more astonishing in view of the uncertainties that the Muslim rulers faced when it was being built. The tile work is balanced

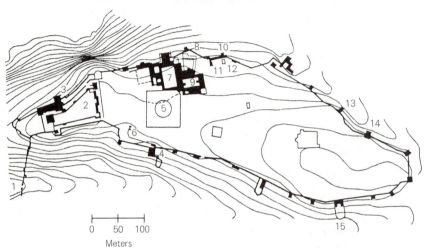

Key
1 Vermilion Towers
2 Alcazaba
3 Gate of Arms
4 Gate of Law
5 Palace of Charles V
6 Puerta del Vino
7 Court of the Myrtles
8 Tower of the Peinador de la Reina
9 Court of the Lions
10 Torre de las Damas
11 Partal
12 Oratory
13 Tower of the Captive
14 Tower of the Infantas
15 Gate of the Seven Heavens

0   50   100
Meters

Figure 8-9
Top: Distant view of the Alhambra. (Photo, Art Resource.)

Figure 8-10
Middle: Plan of the Alhambra. (From Oleg Grabar. *The Alhambra*. Cambridge, Mass.: Harvard University Press, 1978. By permission of Harvard University Press and Penguin Books, Ltd.)

Figure 8-11
Left: Window of the Queen's Room in the Alhambra. (Photo, Ampliaciones y Reproducciones MAS.)

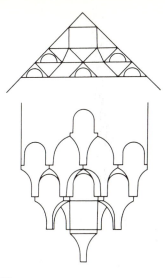

Figure 8-12
Muqarna. (From Oleg Grabar. *The Alhambra.* Cambridge, Mass.: Harvard University Press, 1978. By permission of Harvard University Press and Penguin Books, Ltd.)

Figure 8-13
The Taj Mahal. (Photo, Scala/Art Resource.)

and geometric, with details softened by curves. The side pillars and the decorative emblems above the windows are stylized Islamic script. Many of the decorative carvings in the Alhambra are calligraphy: the script visible in the window of the Queen's Room is poetry, which adds yet another kind of beauty.

Above the central emblem, and below the topmost curve of the arch, are downward-projecting forms, resembling stalactites, which seem layered one on top of the other. They are called "muqarna" (Figure 8-12) and are formed by layering courses of bricks partway over one another. After a layer is formed, the muqarna is gracefully carved to achieve an effect of lightness and motion.

THE TAJ MAHAL

The Taj Mahal (Figure 8-13) holds the body of Mumtāz Mahal, "jewel of the palace," the favorite wife of the great Mogul ruler Shāh Jahān. It was built between 1632 and 1649. Each of its four sides has a large portal arch in the center, and flanking arches repeat the pattern. The building sits on a plinth,

Figure 8-14
Shāh Jahān. (Victoria and Albert Museum.)

Painting:
The Persian Miniature

The Persian tradition of illustrating texts, which was assimilated by Arab artists, may have been the root of the Persian miniature. Many Persian examples, however, are not text illustrations but simply portraits. Some include a text. Some, like that shown in Figure 8-15, illustrate a moment in the life of the Prophet.

The portrait of Muhammad elevated into heaven on his horse, Burak, has Chinese influences. The angels' features are oriental, as are some of the garments. Bright, primary colors are used, with blues, reds, and golds dominating. The Prophet is centered in the composition on his strange, human-headed

Figure 8-15
Miraj Muhammad. c. 1540. 14 ½ by 10 inches. (British Library.)

almost like a sculpture; the four delicate minarets at its corners lean slightly outward so that in case of earthquake, they will not damage the building. The central dome (beneath which the body of Mumtāz Mahal lies) bulges slightly in a pattern that has become the ideal blend of Persian and Indian styles. The striking white marble is inlaid wherever possible with semiprecious stones. The designs of the screens inside the building are generally floral, smooth-flowing, and delicate. It has been said that virtually every form of decoration known to Islam appears in this building.

The construction of the Taj Mahal almost beggared Shāh Jahān (Figure 8-14), whose court was as concerned with beauty and magnificence as any court of the time could be. The Moguls encouraged the arts, and one of their specialities was painted miniature portraits, which they sometimes made of visiting Europeans.

Figure 8-16
Khusraw and Shirin in the Hunting Field. 1530. (Trustees of the British Library.)

horse. Around him are leagues of angels bearing gifts, and he radiates a golden flame that lights his "night visit" like the angelic fires about him. Most of the angels are in motion on a relatively flat physical plane; all the figures are the same size, as if they were all the same distance from the viewer.

The hunters in Figure 8-16 contrast motion and stillness. The hunters are mounted on horses of different colors. A group of onlookers watches from above. Following the conventions of Chinese painting, the higher group is more distant, and the lower group is closer. The hunters in the lowest group are active; they are in pursuit. Those in the upper group are static, enjoying a moment of contemplation. The colors include an unreal light-green wash for the ground under the middle group and lavender around the lower group. The sky is a yellow wash. This is a narrative, and it includes the elements of distance, action, and time. The hunters are pursuing different game with different weapons: the hunter on the right is apparently using a saber to hunt a leopard. The hunter on the left uses his spear to kill a deer. The rabbits, also objects of the chase, scurry out of the way. Just as all the available space is decorated in many miniatures, the space in this painting is filled with action.

Poetry: Persian Lyrics

Persian miniatures and Persian poetry both flourished in the eleventh and twelfth centuries. Sadī (c. 1213–1292), who wrote *Golestān* ("The Rose Garden"), and Omar Khayyám (c. 1048–c. 1141), who wrote the *Rubáiyát* (best known in Edward FitzGerald's translation), are the chief poets of the period. These two works are didactic poetry—their purpose is to teach a lesson.

Sadī's "Reality and Appearance" develops Plato's concept that what we see is not the ultimate reality. His discussion offers a solution to problems of perception in God's all-knowing vision. His subject matter and his conclusions are religious, but his approach is secular:

'Tis light makes colour visible: at night
Red, green, and russet vanish from thy sight,
So to thee light by darkness is made known:
All hid things by their contraries known:
Since God hath none, He, seeing all, denies
Himself eternally to mortal eyes.
From the dark jungle as a tiger bright,
Form from the viewless Spirit leaps to light.
When waves of thought from Wisdom's Sea profound
Arose, they clad themselves in speech and sound.

The lovely forms a fleeting sparkle gave,
Then fell and mingled with the falling wave.
So perish all things fair, to readorn
The Beauteous One whence all fair things were born.

At first the poem seems almost scientific: everything is known by contraries, and without light, dark things cannot be known. Since God has no inherent contraries, however, he cannot reveal himself to people. Sadī likens what we see to "waves of thought from Wisdom's Sea," which leap up into shapes and then perish back into the sea. Sadī's belief, called "Ismailism," was Platonic: all things are an aspect of God's form; they arise from God, exist, and then go back to God.

Omar Khayyám is interested in the world as it seems, the world of the senses. Unlike Sadī, he implies that the most important human questions cannot be answered; therefore, one must be content in living rather than knowing. He has been called the "Persian Bacchus" (Bacchus was the Greek god of wine) because of his praise of the grape as solace. He mentions the Koran, Moses, and Jesus, not irreverently; but he sees these as standing apart from his determination to live a full and rich life. His poetry is for the present, not the future; as he said, "Take the cash and let the credit go." Such a practical merchant's metaphor has its echoes in the Koran.

Nonetheless, Omar Khayyám is complex. Some readers consider him a hedonist intent upon the pleasures of the flesh. But he is said to have given up a chair of mathematics and astronomy at the College of Nishapur to follow a mystical order known as "Sufism." Other important poets of the period were also Sufis. The tradition among Sufis was to use mysterious symbolism and a kind of secret language. Like Taoism, Sufism demanded personal enlightenment and then showed the "way" or "path" to the true life. Some of Omar's images may be symbols, like the images in the Song of Solomon in the Bible. The symbolism of the lover, wine, and bread is religious in the Bible, and it may be so in Omar.

The following brief excerpts are in the form of Rubaiyat stanzas, quatrains in which the first, second, and fourth lines rhyme:

7

Come, fill the Cup, and in the fire of Spring
Your winter-garment of Repentance fling:
    The Bird of Time has but a little way
To flutter—and the Bird is on the Wing.

12

A Book of Verses underneath the Bough,
A Jug of Wine, a Loaf of Bread—and Thou
    Beside me singing in the Wilderness—
Oh, Wilderness were Paradise enow!

13

Some for the Glories of This World; and some
Sigh for the Prophet's Paradise to come;
    Ah, take the Cash, and let the Credit go,
Nor heed the rumble of a Distant Drum!

Omar, at least on the surface, tells us that time is passing quickly: we must snatch what comfort and love we can in this life, trusting that in the next life what will come will come. In questioning the "Prophet's Paradise to come," Omar may be said to be questioning the Koran. In translations other than FitzGerald's he seems to do exactly that. Stanza 3 in the translation for UNESCO, by Paricher Kasra, is as follows:

The Koran, which is called the Holy Word, is read from time to time and not always. [But] around the cup there dwells a verse which is read constantly everywhere.

Omar's concern with understanding the nature of the world is appropriately modern. He sees the questions, but cannot fathom the answers. Life perishes at an alarming rate, and something must be done. One must attempt to understand:

96

Yet, Ah, that Spring should vanish with the Rose!
That Youth's sweet-scented manuscript should close!
    The Nightingale that in the branches sang,
Ah whence, and whither flown again, who knows!

99

Ah Love! could you and I with Him conspire
To grasp this sorry Scheme of Things entire,
    Would not we shatter it to bits—and then
Remould it nearer to the Heart's Desire!

Philosophy: Preservation of Greek Tradition

Arab scholars preserved Greek thought in conquered lands that maintained academies. The dissemination of Greek texts began in the eleventh and twelfth centuries, after the Crusaders returned to Europe

PERCEPTION KEY

 Persian Miniatures and Persian Poetry

1. Is there as much concern for secular, worldly activities in the Persian miniatures shown in Figures 8-15 and 8-16 as there is in the Persian poetry quoted here? Do the miniatures or the poetry seem to take a more detailed look at the way people actually live?

2. Does the imagery in Persian poetry create a strong sense of the visual? Do you "see" the images in a manner that might be reminiscent of the miniatures?

3. How well does Sadī resolve the problem of the importance of sensory experience? Do you find his views satisfying? Do you think that Omar Khayyám would be in agreement with him?

4. Which senses does Omar appeal to most in his poetry? Which images are the most intense, the most successful?

5. Do you feel that Omar is using the images of the lover, wine, and bread in a symbolic fashion, or do you think that he is using them literally and is really making a secular statement? At root, is Omar's work secular or religious?

---

from the holy land, where they had come into contact with Arab soldiers and Islamic culture. To an extent, this interchange set the stage for the Renaissance, which was a flowering of thought made possible largely by the recovery of the great books and great thoughts of the Greeks. Islam, spreading rapidly, had engulfed Cairo, Antioch, and cities in Persia in which Greek schools depended on Greek texts in the fields of medicine, science, and philosophy. They were translated into Arabic and thereby preserved.

Aristotle's *Poetics,* his *Rhetoric,* and his writings on logic were known to Arab scholars who used them in their treatises on religion, and Aristotelian methods were used in the analysis of Koranic texts. One great revolutionary movement in Islam, Ismailism, based much of its approach to religion on Plato's *Republic* and may have been a major force in interpreting Platonic thought. According to Bernard Lewis, Ismailism "might have ushered in a full acceptance of Hellenistic values, heralding a humanist renaissance of the Western type." But in medieval times Ismailism failed to capture the allegiance of all Islam. And the essentially conservative attitudes of its opponents —particularly the Shiite Muslims—directed Islamic thought away from western science and philosophy.

Avicenna, born in Persia in the tenth century, and Averroës, born in Spain in the twelfth century, were celebrated for their advanced views in medicine and philosophy, respectively. Averroës preserved the work of some important Greek philosophers through his translations and commentaries. He asserted that the methods of philosophy, including logic, were pertinent to theology, but he was never wholly accepted by his culture.

Had the Arabs not preserved the great texts of Greek humanism, we might not now have them. They preserved not only the technical manuals and materials related to mathematics and the sciences, but also those relating to aesthetics and ethics. Because of their efforts, western culture eventually "reinherited" the primary sources of its past.

Music

Perhaps because music was a passion with Arab peoples, Muhammad did not specifically condemn it in the Koran. However, later canonic judges implied that it was not to be enjoyed without question. The age-old Mesopotamian tradition of training educated and beautiful dancing girls and female musicians persisted in Arabia.

Arab music was performed using a highly developed system of instruments, including a wide variety of drums called "tabl" (this is the root of the Indian word for drums, "tabla.") Arab kitheras, lyres, psalters, and other harplike instruments were pitched like those of the Greeks, in patterns with four notes. (Some instruments are shown in Figure 8-17.) Arab scales also resemble those of the Greeks. Since the Arabs studied Greek music theory as much as any other Greek learning, such similarities are to be expected.

Indian influences were felt in the preservation of certain kinds of rhythmic patterns and melody patterns for certain kinds of songs. The Indians refer to "ragas" and "talas," melody patterns and rhythmic

Figure 8-17
Arabic musical instruments: kemangeh (bowed stringed instrument), santir (plucked stringed instrument), daraboukkeh (hand drum), zummara arbawija (cane flute). (Metropolitan Museum of Art, Crosby Brown Collection of Musical Instruments, 1889.)

patterns, and the Arabs use the terms "maqamat" and "iqa'at." Some music was notated, but most was improvised. Arab musicians learned the patterns by rote and played many variations, occasionally learning new patterns from captured slaves.

Drums and stringed instruments are not the only sources of music in Arab communities. Various kinds of pipes and flutes are also common. So, too, are high-pitched, middle-pitched, and low-pitched brass instruments. But the most important instrument is the human voice. For that reason, Arab songs almost invariably have a text, often derived from great poems such as those of Sadī, to which the music is obviously secondary. The voice slides and intones in the manner of a wind instrument, as Arab people hear every day in the muezzin's intoned call to prayer, the adhdhan.

One indication of the importance of music to the Arab world is the fact that it took Al-Isfahani fifty years to complete *The Great Book of Songs*, twenty-one volumes long—a history of music to his time, 967. Another indication is the fact that, despite some pronouncements against music, the Koran was soon set to the kind of musical chant that Jewish cantors and others use today. Music was a particular jewel in Arab life.

Summary

Islam began with the Prophet Muhammad's eradication of pagan influence in Arabia. Population growth and religious zeal spread the faith in a series of extraordinary conquests which ranged from Spain to India. The Koran resembles the Bible; it tells the faithful how to live their lives. The Arabs' skill in absorbing native traditions resulted in distinctive styles in architecture and other arts; the Dome of the Rock, for example, absorbs Byzantine styles, and the Tāj Mahal absorbs Indian styles. The Great Mosque at Damascus and the Great Mosque of al-Mutawakkil, in Samarra, are probably the most purely Arab in design. Their huge hall-like spaces, their lack of a central focus, and their soft lighting typify the Islamic atmosphere of worship. Secular architecture—palaces and tombs—tends to be sensual, dramatic, and psychologically distinct from the mosques. Concurrent intellectual developments in Islam in the tenth and twelfth centuries helped, through the efforts of Avicenna and Averroës, pre-serve the Greek texts upon which the Renaissance of the west was based. During these centuries, European nations sent Crusaders to the holy land to attempt to wrest Jerusalem from the Arab invaders. Although their efforts were, finally, in vain, contact with Islam was established, and Europeans took back with them considerable knowledge and learning which later bore fruit. The Islamic attitude toward the visual arts is complicated by injunctions against creating images which might be worshiped as idols. Therefore, much Arab art is decorative and geometric, some of it relying on involved calligraphic techniques. The Persian tradition of illustrating texts was, like so many other foreign traditions, easily absorbed into Arab culture, and the results—the Persian miniature—are impressive and distinct in style. The core of Islam is a commitment to religious principles as revealed through the Prophet. Compared with the limited view of pagandom, which emphasized empty ritual and the propitiation of sometimes terrible gods, the word of Muhammad was enlightened, humanist, and profoundly appealing. A theocentric religion, the Islamic faith puts all emphasis on God and on understanding one's relationship to Allah.

Concepts in Chapter 8

The spread of Islam dates from 622, the year of the hegira, Muhammad's forced exile from Mecca.

The Koran, in which are preserved God's revelations to Muhammad, includes parts of the Old and the New Testaments.

Muhammad overthrew pagan idolaters in Arabia and spread the faith through armed conquest.

The Koran tells the faithful how to conduct their lives.

Arab architecture absorbed native traditions to produce a distinctive style.

The mosque is long, low, and large, with no central focus for the eye.

Arab pointed arches and slender pillars appear on mosques and in secular Arab architecture.

Arab architecture is often decorated with emblems, geometric designs, and stylized calligraphy.

Persian miniatures developed from illustrations of texts.

Perspective and illusionism are unimportant in the Persian miniature.

Persian poetry, like the Persian miniature, is generally secular.

Ismailism, a mystical inward version of Islam, was based largely on interpretations of Plato's *Republic*.

Arab conquests engulfed Greek academies, permitting Arab scholars to absorb and develop classical humanist texts.

Music has a strong appeal in Arab culture.

Greek music theory, instruments, and musical techniques influenced Arab musical styles.

Arab musicians sometimes learned new musical patterns from captured slaves.

Arab music, like Indian music, is patterned improvisation.

Suggested Readings

Arberry, A. J., trans. *The Koran Interpreted*. London: G. Allen, 1955.

———, ed. *Persian Poems*. New York: Dutton, 1954.

Binyon, Laurence, J. V. S. Wilkinson, and Basil Gray. *Persian Miniature Painting*. New York: Dover, 1971.

Blunt, Wilfred. *Splendors of Islam*. New York: Viking, 1976.

Burckhardt, Titus. *Art of Islam: Language and Meaning*. London: World of Islam Festival Trust, 1976.

Du Ry, Carel. *Art of Islam*. New York: Abrams, 1970.

Grabar, Oleg. *The Alhambra*. Cambridge, Mass.: Harvard, 1978.

Grube, Ernest J. *The World of Islam*. New York: McGraw-Hill, 1966.

Kuhnel, Ernst. *Islamic Arts*. London: G. Bell, 1963.

Lewis, Bernard. *The Arabs in History*. New York: Harper & Row, 1966.

Rice, David Talbot. *Islamic Art*. New York: Praeger, 1965.

Said, Edward. *Orientalism*. New York: Knopf, 1980.

Saunders, John J., ed. *The Muslim World on the Eve of Europe's Expansion*. Englewood Cliffs, N.J.: Prentice-Hall, 1966.

PART
FOUR

PART FOUR

KINGDOM OF NORWAY
Oslo

KINGDOM OF SWEDEN

NORTH SEA

York
Worchester

IRELAND
Dublin

WALES
Cardiff

KINGDOM OF ENGLAND
London

Exeter

KINGDOM OF DENMARK

MECKLENBURG

SAXONY Hamburg

Aachen

Brandenburg

FRANCONIA

Worms

Prague

BOHEMIA

Rouen

Paris

Rheims

LORRAINE

Strasbourg

HOLY ROMAN EMPIRE

ATLANTIC OCEAN

KINGDOM OF FRANCE

Clairvaux

SWABIA

KINGDOM OF BURGUNDY

Milan

Piacenza

Venice

Avignon
Arles

Genoa

Bologna
Ravenna

Marseilles

Florence

Bordeux

TOULOUSE

CORSICA

PAPAL STATES

KINGDOM OF LEON

KINGDOM OF NAVARRE

Burgos

ARAGON

CATALONIA

Barcelona

SARDINIA

CASTILE

Madrid

Zaragoza

PORTUGAL

Toledo

Valencia

BALEARIC ISLANDS

CALIPHATE OF CORDOBA

Seville Cordoba

Palermo

MEDITERRANEAN SEA

Granada Cartagena

Ceuta

Tunis

Tangier Oran

CALIPHATE OF CORDOBA

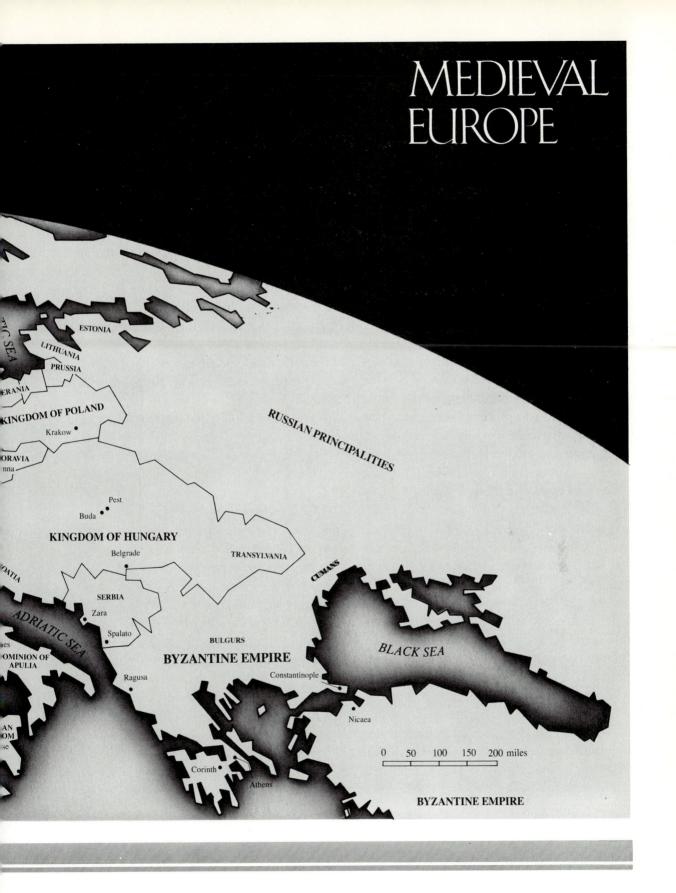

MEDIEVAL EUROPE

ESTONIA

LITHUANIA

PRUSSIA

ERANIA

KINGDOM OF POLAND

Krakow •

ORAVIA

nna

Pest

Buda •

KINGDOM OF HUNGARY

Belgrade •

TRANSYLVANIA

OATIA

RUSSIAN PRINCIPALITIES

CUMANS

SERBIA

Zara •

Spalato •

ADRIATIC SEA

es

OMINION OF
APULIA

Ragusa •

AN
OM
se

BULGURS

BYZANTINE EMPIRE

BLACK SEA

Constantinople •

Nicaea •

0   50   100   150   200 miles

Corinth •

Athens

BYZANTINE EMPIRE

The collapse of the Roman empire in the fifth century after Christ left Europe vulnerable to sudden and rapid change. Germanic tribes, threatened by the eastern Huns, invaded land once held by Rome. In a desperate effort at survival, Constantine moved the capital of the empire to Constantinople, where it endured for almost a millennium. Europe was left to work out its problems alone and to develop Christian ideas and values. Even the Germanic tribes accepted Christianity and, in invading Rome, expressed a desire to accept Roman ways.

By the tenth century, Europe had begun to form into recognizable national regions. The growth of the church demanded high art and significant new architecture. Reliquaries to hold the bones of martyrs and churches to hold the reliquaries seemed to sprout up all over Europe. With Islam in control of trade routes to the east, Europe had to be self-sufficient. The Crusades were partially successful, and the contact with Islam was fruitful in many ways, not the least of which was the recovery of lost Greek texts. Medieval Europe was shaping itself into a feudal society with a hierarchy of social classes based on birth in the secular world and on achievement in the clerical world.

The growth of the arts from 200 to 1400 shows progress in self-confidence and self-awareness. There was little freestanding sculpture, but the sculpture on cathedrals was impressive. Romanesque ideas in church design modified direct borrowings from Roman basilicas; and eleventh-century gothic architecture produced soaring vaulted spaces, a new and revolutionary approach to building.

All artistic activity of the period centered on the power and growth of Christianity. It was a dynamic era in which the Roman achievement changed and developed. The spiritual center of the era was so powerful that the entire world of perception was altered by it. Music was religious; architecture was either religious or military; and the sculpture on churches was religious. Literature was religious: Dante's *Divine Comedy* is a religious vision; and, for all its worldliness, a religious pilgrimage is at the center of Chaucer's *Canterbury Tales*. The period from the conversion of Emperor Constantine at the Milvian Bridge in 312 to the death of Chaucer in 1400 was marked by intense devotion and by growth in religious thought. Nothing like it has been seen in the west since. Even the misnamed dark ages, from the sack of Rome in 410 to the Carolingian Treaty of Verdun in 843, were a busy period during which Germanic tribes were filling the void left by the absence of Roman rule, both absorbing and changing Roman culture.

Brief Chronology

250   Germanic tribes invade Gaul.

312   Sudden conversion of the Roman Emperor Constantine at the Milvian Bridge.

320   Old Saint Peter's built on the Vatican Hill.

324   Constantine establishes Constantinople as the capital of the Roman empire.

354–430   Saint Augustine is bishop of Hippo, in northern Africa.

380   Emperor Theodosius declares Christianity the official state religion of Rome.

404   Ravenna becomes the western capital of the Roman empire.

410   Alaric, king of the Goths, sacks Rome.

432   Saint Patrick arrives in Ireland to convert the Irish to Christianity.

493   Theodoric kills the German chieftain Odoacer to become emperor of the west.

527–565   Rule of Justinian in the east and the flowering of the Byzantine empire.

532–537   The building of Hagia Sophia in Constantinople.

570–580?   The birth of Muhammad.

590–604   Gregorian chant used in churches.

716   Begins the period of Charles Martel's victories; he stopped the Arab invasions into Europe in 735.

800   Charlemagne crowned emperor in Rome by Pope Leo III.

843   Treaty of Verdun splits the empire in the west into three parts: France, Germany, and Lorraine.

910   Founding of monastic orders and building of monasteries.

1000   Viking raids on coast of Europe; settlement in Normandy since 911.

1066   Normans invade England under William the Conqueror.

1096   The Crusades begin; they continue until 1300, capturing Constantinople in 1204.

1150–1200   The composers Léonin and Pérotin.

1163–1235   Gothic Cathedral of Notre Dame, Paris. Chartres Cathedral begun in 1194.

1225–1274   Saint Thomas Aquinas fuses faith with reason.

1265–1321   Dante Alighieri; *The Divine Comedy.*

1309–1376   Papal wars and anarchy in Italy produce a second pope at Avignon, France.

1387   Chaucer began *The Canterbury Tales;* he died in 1400.

CHAPTER 9

EARLY CHRISTIANITY: EXPRESSION OF SPIRITUAL VALUES

The Rise of Christianity

By the year 250 more than one in five Romans were Christian. Christianity spread at first among the poor; it emphasized spiritual values and a gentle god pictured as the good shepherd. Since Orpheus was also portrayed as the good shepherd, the image often disguised, as in Figure 9-1, a believer's faith in times of persecution. After Christians refused to take part in conventional Roman ceremonies, they became threats to the government, which, while tolerant of religions, expected lip service to Roman deities.

The emperor Diocletian, in part maddened over Rome's decay, instituted new persecutions between 303 and 312. Ironically, the martyrs of that period provided an incentive for new church building. The Roman armies were, in the period 240–300, suffering serious defeats. Large migrations of Germanic tribes from the north and the Huns from the east threatened Roman settlements. The worst Roman defeat was at the hands of the revived Persian empire in the year 260, when the emperor Valerian was captured and kept by King Shāpūr I to be used as a living footstool.

The miracle that changed history occurred during the battle at the Milvian Bridge in 312, when Constantine (Figure 9-2) became convinced that his victory was due to the protection of Christ. A vision explained it all to him, and he adopted the faith after the Edict of Milan, which paved the way for Rome to accept Christianity as its official religion. By 330 Constantine was head of both church and state.

Recognizing that threats from Germanic tribes meant that Rome no longer had the strategic position or the cultural energy to serve as capital of the empire, Constantine decided to protect the east because it was a growing source of trade and industry. He moved his seat of government to Constantinople, which he had been building since 324 and which was ready when he moved in 330. A brilliant strategy, the move prolonged the life of the empire for another century, after which it was engulfed by Germanic barbarians.

Architecture

The early churches (Figure 9-3 is an example) followed the form of the Roman basilica, with a long central nave, or hall, and narrow aisles on each side. The Church of the Nativity in Bethlehem has an atrium—a central open space, like those in Roman villas or Islamic mosques—and a nave, in which worshipers gathered. The rotunda at the end of the church protects holy ground: the place where Christ was born. Churches in the holy land could memorialize a site associated with Christ and the apostles; in Rome, most churches memorialized martyrs.

The basilica usually has a nave that is twice the height of the aisles; the high, small windows are designed to admit light only from the north and the south so that no dramatic sunrise or sunset will disturb the services. The interior light is subtle, and nothing outside can distract a worshiper. The window level is called the "clerestory." On the main floor are Roman columns: two rows for the nave and its double story and two more to divide each aisle into two parts. As one enters, the eye is drawn immediately to the rotunda, or apse, which centers attention on the most sacred place in the church. The apse also provides a place from which members of the clergy emerge during services.

THE BASILICA: OLD SAINT PETER'S IN ROME

Old Saint Peter's, built according to plans dating from 324, was begun in 333, after Constantine had moved the capital. Beneath its site, on the Vatican Hill, where Saint Peter was assumed to be buried, is a shrine (Figure 9-4), reconstructed with some guesswork, indicating that in the second century this was known as his burial spot. Constantine ordered construction on a difficult site and on a scale large enough to house thousands of pilgrims. The length of the church was 850 feet; its width was 300 feet.

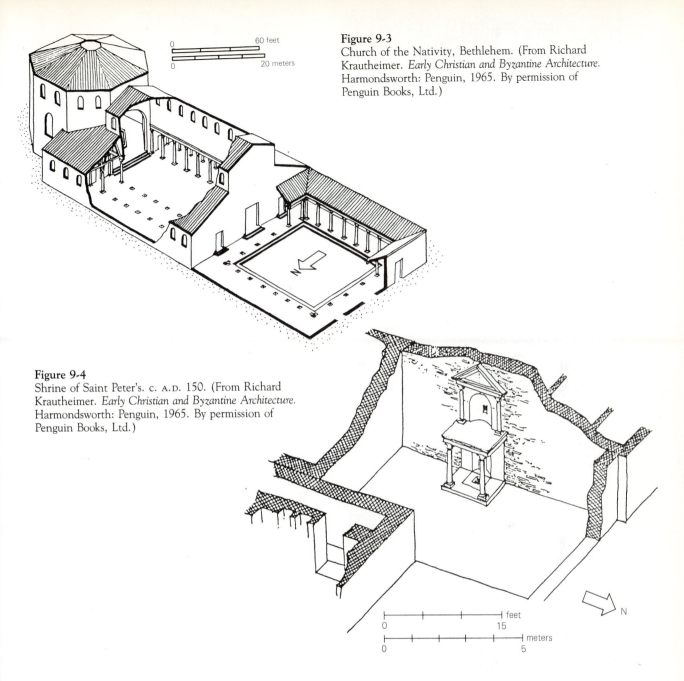

Figure 9-3
Church of the Nativity, Bethlehem. (From Richard Krautheimer. *Early Christian and Byzantine Architecture.* Harmondsworth: Penguin, 1965. By permission of Penguin Books, Ltd.)

Figure 9-4
Shrine of Saint Peter's. c. A.D. 150. (From Richard Krautheimer. *Early Christian and Byzantine Architecture.* Harmondsworth: Penguin, 1965. By permission of Penguin Books, Ltd.)

The building (a reconstruction and floor plan are shown in Figures 9-5 and 9-6) combined the basilica pattern with that of the martyrium, common in the catacombs beneath Rome, which had a walkway in front of an apselike structure so that the faithful could walk past a sacred spot. The transept in Saint Peter's is developed from the martyrium and became a feature in most later churches. Because it was the only church in Rome to house the remains of a martyr, Constantine planned old Saint Peter's on a huge scale. Triangulated wooden trusses permitted a huge space to be spanned. The wall space in the nave above the columns, called the "triforium," was decorated with elaborate visual narratives of the life of Christ.

Old Saint Peter's remained in use until it was replaced by the present building, construction of which began in 1505.

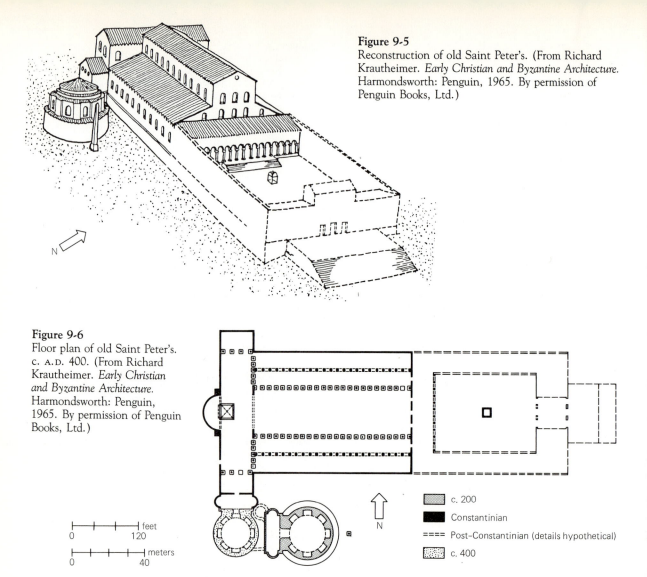

Figure 9-5
Reconstruction of old Saint Peter's. (From Richard Krautheimer. *Early Christian and Byzantine Architecture.* Harmondsworth: Penguin, 1965. By permission of Penguin Books, Ltd.)

N

Figure 9-6
Floor plan of old Saint Peter's. c. A.D. 400. (From Richard Krautheimer. *Early Christian and Byzantine Architecture.* Harmondsworth: Penguin, 1965. By permission of Penguin Books, Ltd.)

```
0        120 feet
0        40 meters
```

N

c. 200

Constantinian

Post-Constantinian (details hypothetical)

c. 400

THE BYZANTINE CHURCH: SAN VITALE

In 395 the emperor Theodosius split the empire in two, appointing his son Honorius administrator of Rome and the western empire. Honorius, threatened by the Visigoths, who sacked Rome in 402, moved the capital to Ravenna. By 476, the generally accepted date of the collapse of the Roman empire, Odoacer, a German tribal leader, controlled Rome entirely and had installed himself as the emperor of Rome. The Germanic people were thoroughly Romanized at this time and thought of themselves as citizens of the empire. In 493 Theodoric, an Ostrogoth trained in

Constantinople, was admitted to Odoacer's private company and killed him with his own hands. Taking over, Theodoric settled in Ravenna and rebuilt the city to his own tastes, which were influenced by the eastern traditions with which he had become familiar in Constantinople.

The empire in the east flourished from 500 to 550, while Justinian ruled. Trade routes to China, India, and elsewhere were relatively open, and the economy was vigorous. Justinian even managed to smuggle silkworms out of China and establish a competitive industry. Constantinople's strategic location permitted it to exploit trade routes and to prosper until the seventh century, when Islamic expansion cut the routes and absorbed the city. Byzantine-style churches, with a dome over an octagonal plan, derived from eastern influence in Constantinople which Justinian helped spread to Ravenna.

Justinian's great achievement in Ravenna is San Vitale, begun in 527, the year after Theodoric's death. Center-planned with dome and apse, it is based on the octagon, with a high interior and small windows spaced widely apart. (A plan is shown in Figure 9-7.) Above its eight piers, two stories up, rises the dome, which covers an unusually large space, compared with the domes of earlier churches. The octagonal shape is numerologically significant: 8 is connected with Christ. The four elements plus Father, Son, and Holy Ghost are 7, the number of humankind. Adding to that the perfect number of God, 1, gives Christ's number: 8, the number of the new beginning. San Vitale is associated with the new beginning because Theodoric was about to persecute orthodox Christians since he preferred his own version of Christianity, Arianism, which preached that Christ was a human whose body did not ascend to heaven: only his soul was saved. Theodoric died before he could institute persecutions, and Justinian, orthodox in faith, brought Ravenna back under his control. San Vitale was a tribute to this.

Saint Vitalis, his sons, and his wife were all martyred in Ravenna. Church doctrine holds that martyrs become one with Christ, and for that reason San Vitale is associated with the Easter liturgy, the renewal. Justinian introduced building techniques that permitted using lighter bricks and less solid concrete in the arches, which meant that no huge drum of masonry (as in the Pantheon) was needed to counter the stresses of the dome of San Vitale. Outside, vertical piers distribute and counterbalance the internal stress, but they are almost unnoticeable. The organic unity of the church—the way each part relates intelligently to every other part—has long been praised as one of its great strengths.

Outside (Figure 9-8), San Vitale is relatively simple, but inside (Figure 9-9) the spaces seem to multiply and grow. The arches are numerous, with graceful repetitions in niches, walls, windows, and piers. The wall surfaces are covered with mosaics as brilliant as any that a church has ever known. The capitals of the piers seem almost to have been done in ivory rather than stone. One scholar has suggested that the church is celebrating the invisible spirit of humankind: the soul. To the early Christians, light was a reminder of the power of godliness, an instrument of faith, and a visible symbol of spirituality. The outer church, visible to everyone, is unimpressive; the inner space, visible to the faithful, is overwhelming.

Ravenna's mosaics are one reason why the interiors of its churches are so radiant. In Color Plate 3, which shows Christ flanked by Saint Vitalis and

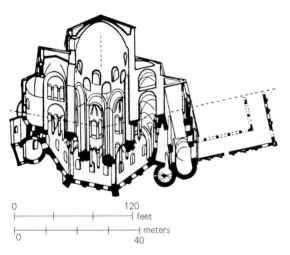

Figure 9-7
Above: San Vitale, Ravenna, reconstruction. (From Richard Krautheimer. *Early Christian and Byzantine Architecture.* Harmondsworth: Penguin, 1965. By permission of Penguin Books, Ltd.)

Figure 9-8
Below: San Vitale, exterior. A.D. 526–547.

Figure 9-9
San Vitale, interior.

angels, the excitement is in the color—the rich, deep blues and reds and the dominant gold. The figure of Christ as creator of the world (pantocrator) is soft and emphasizes humanity. The posture is conventional, but not stiff or geometric. This work is basically two-dimensional, with some effort at shading and modeling to suggest bulk and volume. Christ's face is dominated by the large eyes, but it is still normal, human, and thoughtful. He is not an awesome judge or an uncaring creator.

THE GREAT FUSION: HAGIA SOPHIA

Justinian's other great triumph is Hagia Sophia, in Constantinople, which combines the best characteristics of the basilica and the Byzantine church. The dome, 108 feet wide, is supported by only four colossal piers. (A cross section is shown in Figure 9-10.) Because it is low (rather than high, like the dome in the Tāj Mahal), it gives the impression of being suspended as if by God. Instead of one apse, there are three, and the interior resembles a huge Roman bath. The building is 265 feet long and 228 feet wide, and the dome rises to a height of 182 feet. Originally dedicated to holy wisdom, it is now a mosque, since Constantinople was conquered by Islamic Turks in the early 1400s. The interior spaces are virtually the same as they were in the original design.

Four minarets have been added to the exterior (Figure 9-11), but otherwise Hagia Sophia is much as it was in Justinian's time. The mounting of small

Figure 9-10
(a) Cross section and (b) longitudinal section, Hagia
Sophia. (From W. F. Volbach. *Early Christian Art*. New
York: Abrams, 1961. By permission of Hirmer Verlag
München.)

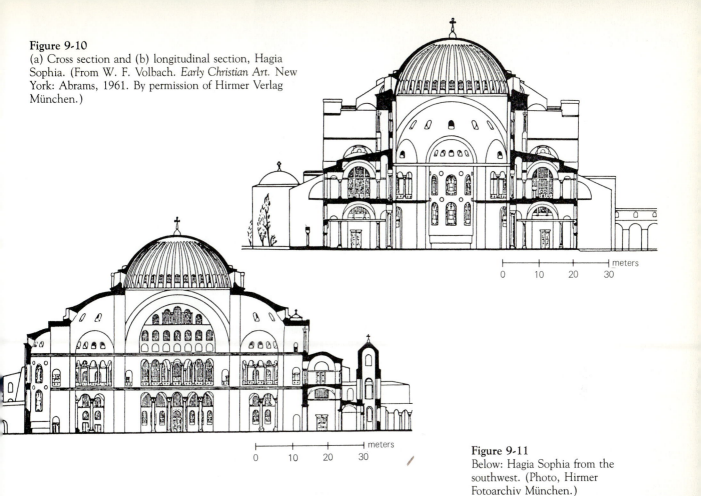

meters

0   10   20   30

meters

0   10   20   30

Figure 9-11
Below: Hagia Sophia from the
southwest. (Photo, Hirmer
Fotoarchiv München.)

Figure 9-12
Hagia Sophia, interior; view of apse, southeast. (Photo, Hirmer Fotoarchiv München.)

domed spaces around the large dome creates a sense of organic unity and grace; outside it seems to hug the ground, while inside (Figure 9-12) it soars. The small windows admit a soft and subtle light. The repetitions of circles throughout the interior are almost without end. The triple apse emphasizes the trinity, and the dramatic suspension of the central dome, as seen in Figure 9-12, is almost magical. The use of light materials and the careful balancing of stresses by the architects—Anthemius and Isidorus, two gifted amateurs—were radical departures from the safer, more massive approaches used by earlier builders.

PERCEPTION KEY

Early Christian Churches

1. Examine the Church of the Nativity (Figure 9-3), San Vitale (Figures 9-7, 9-8, and 9-9), old Saint Peter's (Figures 9-4, 9-5, and 9-6), and Hagia Sophia (Figures 9-10, 9-11, and 9-12). In view of the question of form and function, which of these is most churchlike in appearance? Does the basilica shape suggest churchlike qualities to you? What, as a modern person, do you expect a church to look like?

2. What have these churches contributed to our sense of the appropriate interior form for a church? If possible, find something that each has contributed to the modern concept of a church.

3. How many arches and semicircular lines can you count in Figure 9-9? How many rectangular forms are there? What numerical patterns show up in repeated architectural details? Do the repetitions please you? Do you think that the mood of this interior space is appropriate?

4. The mosaic in Color Plate 3 is an example of the decorated surfaces that one encounters in Byzantine churches. What is the function of such surfaces as far as the worshiper is concerned? Why is the exterior of a Byzantine church not so heavily decorated? Should it be?

5. What building and design techniques in these churches seem most to encourage religious attitudes and to stimulate faith? Which techniques seem least to do this?

The architects took great risks, and the original dome collapsed in an earthquake twenty years after it was built. Now reconstructed, it is both unique and daring; despite its inspiring qualities, it has had few imitators.

ABBEYS AND MONASTERIES: THE RELIGIOUS COMMUNITY OF SAINT GALL

During the ninth century—the Carolingian Renaissance, named for Charlemagne (742–814; see Color Plate 4)—religious institutions like Saint Gall (Figures 9-13 and 9-14) grew and prospered in relative security. Charlemagne's rule brought a measure of political stability to Europe, permitting an earlier institution, the Roman great estate, to develop again. From it an interlocking system of obligation from tenants to the central landowner, or magnate,

stretched to the king himself. Feudal society began in this period. Its great benefit was that everyone had a place in the social hierarchy.

The system had permitted Charles Martel, the grandfather of Charlemagne, to defeat Islamic invaders with well-armed knights on strong, fast horses equipped with stirrups, a novel device that permitted mounted archers to shoot accurately and allowed mounted knights to wield battle-axes and drive their lances with great force. Huge, expensively fed horses (resembling the Persian war-horse) and suits of armor that covered the whole body made it easy for the knights to overwhelm the enemy. Courtly traditions of valor and chivalry originated in Charlemagne's time.

The organization of the church was hierarchical; the pope was at the head, and bishops ruled various geographic regions. Because populations were widely spread apart, the church established abbeys on the

Figure 9-13
Saint Gall: plan for reconstruction, detail. (From J. Hubert, J. Porcher, and W. F. Volbach. *Europe of the Invasions.* New York: Braziller, 1975.)

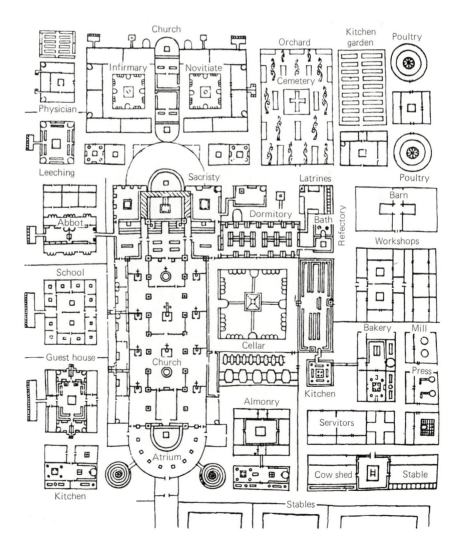

model of the large estates. They included churches, dormitories, cemeteries, schools, hospitals, farms, and other facilities. One of the most ambitious of these is Saint Gall, a Benedictine abbey that dates from the ninth century. It was founded in present-day Switzerland by Saint Gallus, who brought Irish influences from the Irish Saint Columbanus. Saint Gall was an experiment in communal living that focused on the worship of God and the cultivation of a strong spiritual life.

Like many other ideal forms of communities, the abbey had its successes and its failures. Many abbeys were model communities in which life was meaningful and rich; in some, however, inhabitants were interested only in the easy life that the abbey offered. Saint Gall was successful and was in good favor with secular authority; it could, therefore, sometimes act independently of its bishop.

Charlemagne recognized the value of the abbeys for stabilizing a community. Local people often realized that by moving closer to an abbey and observing the monks, they could improve the quality of their lives. Charlemagne paid close attention to the people who controlled specific abbeys, and in some cases he gave control of abbeys in lands he conquered to people whom he knew he could trust.

Excavations of the ruins show that Saint Gall was self-sufficient. (A reconstruction and a model are shown in Figures 9-13 and 9-14.) It maintained a school for children in the surrounding areas and an important library and a scriptorium, a place where books were copied and illuminated. Its library, which has survived, contains important copies of books by Saint Jerome, Saint Augustine, and the more modern Saint Isidore. The range of the library suggests considerable learning and intellectual awareness. This was the age in which abbeys began to be centers of learning and repositories of wisdom.

Figure 9-14
Model of Saint Gall. (Walter Horn and Ernest Born; photo, Raymond Frayne, San Francisco.)

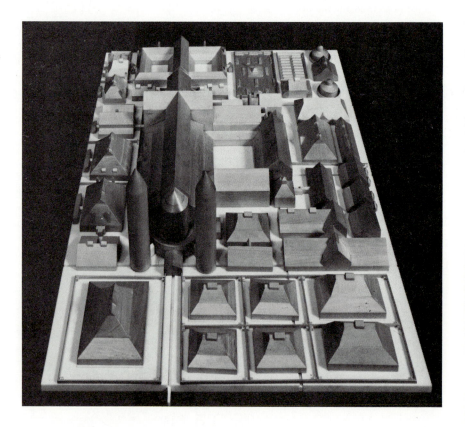

Sculpture

CARVINGS AND RELIEFS

Not a great deal of sculpture survives from this period, and the temptation is to assume that not much was created. But carvings, reliefs, and carved book covers—particularly for illuminated Bibles—survive in abundance and suggest considerable technical achievement. The smaller sculptures which survive (Figures 9-15 and 9-16 are examples) imply that sculpture was for personal use and that the need for large, public sculpture was not great.

Figure 9-15
Saint John the Evangelist. Carolingian, c. 800. Ivory plaque. (Metropolitan Museum of Art, Cloisters Collection.)

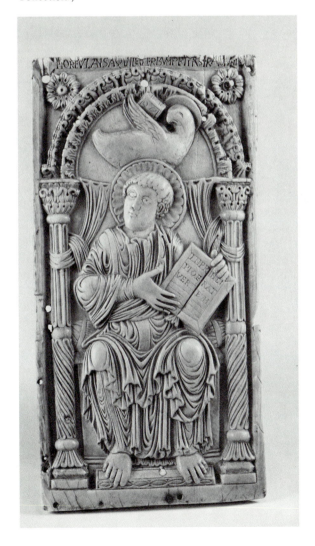

Figure 9-16
Women at the Sepulchre and Ascension of Christ. c. 400. Ivory, 7 ¼ inches high. (Bayerisches Nationalmuseum; photo, Hirmer Fotoarchiv, München.)

The Carolingian ivory plaque of Saint John the Evangelist (Figure 9-15) is typical of much of the relief carving of the period. There is a general disregard for proportions, but a considerable regard for symmetry and balance. For example, the figure of Saint John appears far too large for the pillars and archway around him. However, the attention paid to the folds of his garment and the careful repetitions of knees and feet contribute to an extraordinarily balanced portion of the composition. The use of an architectural framework is among the most common motifs of the period; it is featured in innumerable illustrations and illuminations as well. The symbol of Saint John, the eagle, is almost an amusing afterthought, placed above his head as if it were a dove. The value of this representation is holy and symbolic; it is not meant to be exact or realistic.

Women at the Sepulchre and Ascension of Christ (Figure 9-16), from approximately 400, shows not only visual distortion but also chronological distortion. The proportions are characteristically unreal, and the tomb is too modern, resembling Theodoric's in Ravenna. It is detailed; a tree growing from it symbolizes that here is planted a seed which will thrive. Men and women mourn while Christ, in triumph, accepts the welcome hand of heaven. Several simultaneous events are portrayed, and all the figures are the same size. The panel seems intended to be "read": we start at the lower-right-hand corner, proceed to the left, and then spiral upward to the upper-right-hand corner, paralleling the ascension. The faces of the figures are proportionately too large and are more significant than their bodies, and the simplicity of the clothing implies that people's inner worth is superior to anything external.

Many carvings of the period are narratives. Caskets, or sarcophagi, presented a good opportunity to reiterate the religious truths by which the dead had lived. On the sarcophagus of Junius Bassus in Rome, which dates from 359 (Figure 9-17), the figures are in deep relief; some are almost three-dimensional. Each of the scenes relates a specific biblical tale. The central panel shows the young Christ lecturing in the temple; beneath that is the triumphal entry of Christ into Jerusalem. Next, on the left, are Adam and Eve, who are portrayed as chunky, forceful, and direct. Most groupings contain three figures, with the person in the center balancing the other two. The result is a calm, symmetrical series of scenes, appropriate for the restfulness of the dead.

RELICS AND RELIQUARIES

Reliquaries are containers for pieces of the bodies of martyrs or for objects associated with Christ and the martyrs. Charlemagne paid great attention to relics and their powers. His most carefully preserved relic was the cloak of Saint Martin. The Latin word for "cloak" is "capel"; chapels are so named because Charlemagne took the cloak into every place of worship he visited. Relics were encased in decorated boxes for portability and preservation. Portability was

Figure 9-17
Sarcophagus of Junius Bassus in Saint Peter's, Rome. Marble, 56 ¼ by 95 ½ inches. (Photo, André Held, Lausanne.)

important because there were no stable city centers, and rulers such as Charlemagne moved their courts regularly. The great estates—with millers, farmers, brewers, knights, and other specialists—were large households, but they were not cities and had none of the ferment of Roman or Greek towns. The leaders of the estates were Germanic tribespeople separated from their tribes. Soon they melded with the original Romanized population. All shared a passion for relics and believed in their magical and religious powers.

A reliquary of particular interest, a representation of Charlemagne himself (Color Plate 4), dates from 1350 and survives in fine condition. Inside are portions of Charlemagne's skull. The portrait is highly idealized; there is none of the disproportion of the sculpture of the fourth and fifth centuries. The face is strong, and the neck is powerful; the facial hair and the curling locks suggest strength and manliness. The crown implies loyalty to Christianity, but its small carvings remind us of a Roman past. The mantle about the shoulders is simple, but its surface decoration, the repeated eagle of absolute authority, gives it strength and vitality. The bands of gems are restrained, communicating preciousness appropriate to the contents of the reliquary.

The Monza reliquary (Figure 9-18), designed to hold Saint John's teeth, is made of gold; it is encrusted with gemstones and decorated with metalwork and intricate filigree. The value of the contents, rather than their identity, is suggested by the jewel-covered surface. Some churches sustained themselves largely on the contributions of pilgrims who made special trips to be near such relics.

Although few people could read or write in Charlemagne's time, the gospels had special value. The ornate cover of the Lindau gospels (Figure 9-19) was not unusual, and the covers of many surviving books have been vandalized. The cover of the Lindau gospels shows a distinct Celtic influence, although it was probably made in Salzburg. The interwoven figures on the four quadrants created by the cross include four typically Celtic human figures with huge eyes, ovoid faces, and stylized garments. A Celtic boss of interwoven animals crowns the top and bottom figures.

However, the style of the figures in the four corners is shockingly different. They are the four evangelists—the apostles Matthew, Mark, Luke, and John—with their symbolic animals: the ox, the lion, a man, and the eagle. They are represented with an

Figure 9-18
Reliquary from the cathedral treasury, Monza. Ninth century. 13 ⅜ by 10 ¼ inches. (Photo, SEF/Art Resource.)

Figure 9-19
First cover of the Lindau Gospels. c. 800. (Pierpont Morgan Library.)

Early Christian Sculpture and Reliquaries

1. Consider the relief sculptures shown in Figures 9-15, 9-16, and 9-17. Are they uniformly religious in subject matter? Do you think that they express or interpret religious emotions? Do they seem to be especially emotional?

2. Distortion is often used as a means of interpreting a subject in order to establish content. What are the chief kinds of distortions evident in these sculptures? What kind of content do the distortions help the works establish?

3. Which of the sculptures pays the most attention to formal values of balance, symmetry, and rhythmic repetition of shapes? Does it seem especially satisfying as a result of that attention?

4. What attitudes toward the use of surface do the cover of the Lindau gospels (Figure 9-19) and the Monza reliquary (Figure 9-18) share? What kinds of values are communicated by those attitudes?

5. Color Plate 4, the reliquary of Charlemagne, is much later than the Monza reliquary. What are the most important stylistic differences between the two? Does the reliquary of Charlemagne communicate a religious value to you? Does the Monza reliquary?

---

effort at realistic modeling, which implies that different specialists worked on the cover; they had different intentions and different training, and they achieved different results.

Visual Arts: Illuminated Books

Illuminated books gave visual artists the opportunity to render holy stories imaginatively; they also provided something of interest to the illiterate—and these included most of the powerful and wealthy. Almost all the surviving illuminated books are religious, and many of them are the gospels.

THE BOOK OF KELLS

Illuminated in around 800 in an abbey on the island of Iona, off the Irish coast, the Book of Kells was taken to an inland abbey near Kells, where it was found buried without its covers. One of the great treasures of Irish art, it is on display in the Trinity College library in Dublin, where a page is turned each day.

One of the "evangelist" pages (Figure 9-20) shows the four evangelists, as does the cover of the Lindau gospels. The eagle symbolizes one who can look directly into the sun, seeing God: this is John. The ox symbolizes Christ as a sacrifice for the world: this is Luke. The lion, Mark, is a symbol of Christ triumphant. Matthew's symbol is a man, emphasizing Christ's incarnation. These symbols derived from the vision of Ezekiel in the Bible as well as from the Apocrypha (books excluded from the Jewish and Protestant canons of the Old Testament).

The Book of Kells contains several "evangelist" pages, and each is totally different in detail and design. The page shown in Figure 9-20 is rectangular in form, with a borderlike structure and an evangelist's symbol in each of four openings: Matthew's and Mark's are on top, and Luke's and John's are below. One page divides the space with a huge X; in another there are circular windows in which the symbols are intricately crowded.

Figure 9-20
"Evangelist" page, Gospel of Matthew, Book of Kells, folio 27v. (Trinity College Library, Dublin; Board of Trinity College, Dublin.)

Figure 9-21
"Chi-rho" page, Book of Kells, folio 34r. (Board of Trinity College, Dublin.)

Figure 9-22
Portrait of the evangelist John, Book of Kells, folio 291v. (Board of Trinity College, Dublin.)

Some heavily illuminated pages, such as Figure 9-21, the "chi-rho" page, concentrate on the first letter or word of the gospel. Figure 9-22 shows a portrait of John. The three pages shown in Figures 9-20, 9-21, and 9-22 reveal the immense range of the artists who worked on the book. The stylistic influences range from Byzantine Constantinople to the nearby regions of Charlemagne. Some influences are said to have come from Coptic Egypt. The stylized portraits are Byzantine, while the intricate details, interweaving, and circular whorls are recognizably Celtic. All the spaces are filled; the concealed figures in the design, both animal and human, show a characteristic Celtic playfulness. We do not know the source of the architectonic frame in Figure 9-22; it stabilizes the design completely. Even the "chi-rho" page includes a section of frame in the lower-right-hand corner. Some of these pages took more than a year to complete; they are a testament to the pace of life in ninth-century Ireland as well as a testament to the artists' devotion, their skill, and their love of beauty.

OTHER ILLUMINATED BOOKS

The "evangelist" page from the gospel at Fleury (Figure 9-23) shows Matthew and Mark on the left panel and John and Luke on the right panel in their symbolic representations. Their initials are placed above them. The figures are drawn with less skill than is seen in the Book of Kells, and they resemble figures in Roman wall paintings. The colors are subdued earth tones, and each animal has six wings, as Ezekiel said. Each bears a scroll symbolizing its holy text. The absence of ornamentation is balanced by the double arch with Roman pillars.

The architectural framework of Figure 9-24, a page from the Golden Psalter, shows pillars with Corinthian capitals, perhaps befitting a king like David. A psalter is a book of psalms, and David, represented with musicians and dancers, reminds us that many of the psalms were written by him and that some were sung or accompanied by music and possibly even dance. The four lesser figures mirror one another to help establish balance and symmetry. The values of balance, order, and symmetry are important in all illuminated books.

Figure 9-23
"Evangelist" page, Gospel Book, Fleury, folio 8v, cod. 348. c. 820. 9 ¾ by 7 ⅞ inches. (Burgerbibliothek, Bern.)

Figure 9-24
Saint Gall, Golden Psalter, King David with musicians and dancers, folio 2, cod. 22. Ninth century. 14 ½ by 11 inches. (Stiftsbibliothek, Saint Gall.)

Illuminated Books

1. Examine Figures 9-20 and 9-23, which show two "evangelist" pages. How does the space devoted in each to the evangelist or his symbol compare with the space devoted to design and detail?

2. Compare the use of architectural framework in each "evangelist" page. In which page is it most important? What does it accomplish?

3. Examine Figure 9-22. Does the portrait of John resemble any of the other portraits discussed in this chapter? Does anything in the portrait remind you of his symbol, the eagle? What are the details extending beyond the framework to the top, bottom, left, and right?

4. Which of the illuminated pages is strongest in terms of design?

5. The fundamental values expressed by these illuminated pages are religious. Do you perceive religious values in these works? Which seems to you to be the most obviously religious in content?

Music and Dance

Early Christianity was uncertain about dance. Folk dances done in the fields, particularly circle dances, were based on pagan rituals of fertility. People sometimes danced naked in the fields to guarantee good harvests, and because such dances smacked of orgies, they were condemned by the church. Some processional dancing was associated with rites for the dead and was often done in cemeteries. A secular tradition of dance was tolerated in the eastern empire; Justinian's wife, Theodora, who appears in mosaics in Ravenna, was a ritual dancer before their marriage. The early church fathers, like Saint Jerome and Saint Augustine, were biased against women and feared the stimulation of the flesh implied in dancing. Thus, theoretically there was no place for dance in the church.

However, the power of music to intensify religious feeling made it indispensable. Some branches of the church thrived because they used secular sources for their hymns and songs. The Arian churches, domi-

nated by Germanic tribes, were particularly successful in this regard. Arianism was heretical because it did not consider Christ to be of the same substance as God: Christ was separate; only his soul ascended to heaven, not his body. Since the fourth century, the Arians had developed a hymnody based on popular music that made their appeal profoundly strong. Eventually, orthodox forces condemned the hymns and suppressed Arianism, but only after a great struggle and the loss of many lives.

The temporary success of Arianism had an important result for music. Two eminent churchmen, Saint Ambrose (339–397) and Saint Gregory I (c. 540–604), set out to establish an accepted practice for church music, whose importance was never underestimated. What they established is known as "Gregorian chant."

Since Gregorian chant is still used in services today, we can speak of it with some certainty. It is unaccompanied vocal music with choir and solo parts. In the days of the early Christians, the congregation was broken up into choirs of men, women, and children, which produced a "stereophonic" effect. This is called "antiphony": sounds balanced against one another. Gregorian melodies are simple, but beautiful. They are so characteristically associated with religious services that today they are instantly recognizable as sacred music.

The melodies are slight in range: upward leaps of tones are rarely more than four notes apart, and yet the melody rises to a fairly high note quickly and then descends gradually before rising suddenly again. Because the words are liturgical, they are of great importance and are delivered with stately, slow clarity. Few liberties were taken with the words until the gallican churches in France made it common to "decorate" words by devoting more than one note to a syllable, a practice called "melismatic singing."

Late in the development of Gregorian chant, three possibilities existed for matching notes and words:

Syllabic: one note per syllable

Neumatic: two notes per syllable

Melismatic: many notes per syllable

The melismatic style is ornate and is associated with virtuosity and a curious tension. Boethius said that the greatest music was pure, almost mathematical: the musica mundi (cosmic music), which no one could hear. Church music was thus for the ears of God, and it mattered little how it sounded to humankind. But the effect of the heretical churches on people showed that music could attract believers and help them express their belief.

Gregorian chant had no standard meter; the text often determined such matters. An example in modern notation, shown in Figure 9-25, reveals the use of syllabic, neumatic, and melismatic effects in a simple phrase. Singers would obviously have approached this music eagerly, and yet the melodic range is only an octave, from the low F, on the last note, up to the high F, just before the "-re" of "illuminare."

Figure 9-25
"Arise and shine, Jerusalem." Melisma from the Gradual of the Mass for Epiphany. (From *Liber Usualis Missae et Officii.* Tournai, Belgium: Desclée, 1952. No. 780c.)

Early Christian Music

1. Establish which notes in "Arise and Shine, Jerusalem" (Figure 9-25) are syllabic, which are neumatic, and which are melismatic.

2. Does the importance of the text seem to determine whether it will be treated by syllabic, neumatic, or melismatic techniques?

3. Does melisma occur systematically, or is its use inconsistent? Does such ornamentation interfere with the clarity of meaning of the text?

4. Listen to the passage being sung. Are there perceptible religious qualities in the music? Do melismatic or neumatic techniques help produce a "religious" sound?

5. Listen to a recording of Gregorian chants. Some generally available recordings are *Schola Cantorum of Amsterdam* (Columbia M3X-32329, three disks); *Benedictine Monks, Luxembourg* (Phillips 6580061); and *Guide to Gregorian Chant* (with a dictionary, Vanguard 71217). Describe the melodic qualities in terms of vocal range, range of pitch, and variety. Are all the melodies pretty much alike, or can you distinguish between different chants? Is there a harmonic base, or is the singing generally in unison? How important is harmony relative to melody? Can you distinguish the text, or is it lost in the music? Does the music have perceptible religious qualities? If you feel that you would recognize it as sacred music, why is this so? Does it evoke religious feelings in you?

Religion

SECTS

Sects grew up within Christianity from the first. By the time Christianity had become the official Roman religion, several important sects were competing with the orthodox church for dominance.

The Gnostics broke away in the first and second centuries. They held that only those with special, secret knowledge could understand the meaning of the holy texts. The effect of that was to exclude the ignorant and the illiterate from the inner circle of the church. Moreover, Gnosticism tended to downgrade simple faith in God in favor of specialized knowledge or a rational understanding of church doctrine. The Gnostics produced a Bible which has recently been found and translated. Among its gospels is one according to Mary Magdalene, who claimed to have been the first to see Christ after his resurrection. Another gospel is according to Stephen, representing himself as Christ's twin brother.

The cult of Manichaeanism, which was related to the Roman cult of Mithraism, was also powerful. It preached that God is light, that evil is darkness, and that the fate of the world is in doubt. The struggle is between the forces of light and the forces of dark, and humans must take sides. This belief was heretical because it omitted the will of God and elevated the forces of evil.

SAINT AUGUSTINE

Saint Augustine (354–430), bishop of Hippo in north Africa, was for a time a Manichaean. Manichaeanism produced a belief that is sometimes called "dualism," in which flesh and spirit are considered two separate entities rather than a unity. The problem with dualism was that it led the Manichaeans to elevate spiritual matters and to denigrate flesh and the material world. According to orthodox beliefs, the material world was created by God, and it is good; Plotinus went so far as to say that all matter is God: God is everything and everywhere.

Augustine converted to Christianity when he was in his thirties. Christianity offered him a monistic view (oneness, the opposite of dualism): the flesh and spirit worked together to bring people to God, and love was the basis of the religion. He clarified the nature of God's grace, essential for salvation, pointing out that it was given freely by God, was an act of supreme love, and could not be earned. His emphasis on love as the core of Christianity moved him far from the Manichaeans, whom he spent much time and energy trying to convert. His monism was dependent on Plotinus, who taught that since all creation emanated from God in an act of generosity and love, no part of creation could be bad.

Augustine was a brilliant thinker, a ferocious combatant, and a fearless controversialist. He not only fought the Manichaeans outside the church, but also defended the faith against heresies such as that of Pelagius, who preached that original sin did not exist, that all people are born capable of achieving salvation, and that if an infant dies without being baptized, it will be saved. Augustine defended the view that Adam's sin was visited on all humankind and that people are, without the grace of God, depraved. Evil, according to Augustine, is a result of humankind's freedom of will, and good is a result of God's grace.

Among Augustine's astonishing output of writings is *The City of God*, written between 413 and 426. It establishes the fact that Christianity was replacing the worn-out Roman culture. For Augustine, those who loved God belonged to the "city of God"; those

CONCEPT KEY

Religion—Early Christianity

1. What different attitudes toward the goodness of humankind would be held by (a) a dualist religion that praised the spirit but condemned the flesh; and (b) a monist religion that considered goodness to be an expression of love?

2. Do the sculptures or the visual arts discussed in this chapter emphasize the fleshly, worldly aspect of their subject matter or its spiritual aspects?

3. What might the structure of contemporary Christian churches be like if the Gnostics had gained control of the church? What differences would have resulted if true Christianity had been seen to depend on the possession of esoteric knowledge? What would the priests of such a religion have been like? What kinds of people would have been thought of as most devout or as most important to the faith?

4. How do you feel about the stand that Augustine took regarding the heresy of Pelagius? What difference would it make if Christians believed that Adam's sin was strictly his own and did not affect later generations? What difference would it make if Christians believed that there was no original sin and that people are born without sin, as Pelagius held? Do you think that this would have changed the nature of Christianity?

who loved the world belonged to the "city of the world." The two were not mutually exclusive, but the "city of God" was obviously more important. *The Confessions,* one of the most popular books ever written, dates from about 400; it tells of Augustine's earlier life, his commitment to Manichaeanism, and the details of his conversion and his studies. It stresses his sense of guilt, particularly concerning his sexual feelings, which he made an effort to suppress.

Summary

Christianity rose as the Roman empire fell, but there is no likely causal link. It flourished best when it was protected by Constantine and the power of the empire, whether in Rome or in Constantinople. Christianity was popular with the Germanic tribes and helped Romanize them. The Arianism of the Germanic tribes led to counterthrusts against the orthodox church, particularly when Odoacer, a German tribal leader, commanded Ravenna, the new seat of the western empire. Ravenna was the seat of government and benefited from the building programs of Theodoric and Justinian, who constructed impressive Byzantine churches. As the Germanic tribes settled down, large estates and separate communities marked the beginning of a new era in European life. Feudalism, a hierarchical social structure, and communal agriculture changed life. The abbeys became centers of living and learning where elaborately illustrated and beautifully written books were produced. The emphasis on the power of relics gave artisans the opportunity to work with metal and jewels. Most of the art in this millennium was Christian in inspiration, and it set the stage for the next great age of devotion.

Concepts in Chapter 9

Christianity spread rapidly in Rome up to the fourth century.

Diocletian persecuted Christians early in the fourth century.

Constantine's conversion in 312 set the stage for Christianity to become the official religion of Rome.

The capital of Rome was moved to Constantinople in 330; this created an eastern empire and a western empire.

Germanic tribes engulfed Rome in the fifth century; they were Christian and Romanized.

Early Christian churches were built on the model of the Roman basilica, sometimes employing the transept of the martyrium.

Byzantine churches in Ravenna derived from eastern sources.

The eastern empire flourished until 550, taking advantage of Asian trade routes.

Justinian built the Byzantine church San Vitale, in Ravenna, and was responsible for the fusion of the styles of the basilica and the Byzantine church in Hagia Sophia, in Constantinople.

The great estates in Europe led to the development of a feudal, hierarchical society.

Abbeys, built on the model of the estates, developed as centers of living and learning.

Charles Martel, using new military technology, defeated Islamic invaders in the eighth century.

Charlemagne established political stability in the early ninth century.

Sculpture—in the form of reliefs rather than free-standing works—was virtually all religious during the period of early Christianity.

Sculpture, like the other arts of the period, was unaffected by realism or illusionism.

Lavish reliquaries were created by early Christian artisans; relics of martyrs were supposed to have great powers.

Books were of considerable value to the early Christians and were meticulously illuminated.

The Book of Kells (c. 800) shows a Celtic influence.

Religious music developed Gregorian chants.

Early Christianity was in controversy with cults such as Mithraism and Manichaeanism.

Heresies, such as Arianism, Gnosticism, and the heresy of Pelagius, plagued the early church.

Saint Augustine was a powerful force in clarifying church doctrine and belief.

Suggested Readings

Backes, Magnus, and Regine Dolling. *Art of the Dark Ages.* New York: Abrams, 1969.

Cantor, Norman F. *Medieval History.* 2d ed. London: Macmillan, 1969.

Demus, Otto. *Byzantine Art and the West.* New York: New York University Press, 1970.

Du Bourguet, Pierre. *Early Christian Art.* New York: Morrow, 1971.

Gough, Michael. *The Origins of Christian Art.* New York: Praeger, 1978.

Hubert, J., J. Porcher, and W. F. Volbach. *Europe of the Invasions.* New York: George Braziller, 1975.

Krautheimer, Richard. *Early Christian and Byzantine Architecture.* Harmondsworth, England: Penguin, 1965.

Munz, Peter. *Life in the Age of Charlemagne.* New York: Putnam, 1969.

Pirenne, Henri. *Economic and Social History of Medieval Europe.* New York: Harcourt, Brace, 1936.

Trevor-Roper, Hugh. *The Rise of Christian Europe.* London: Thames and Hudson, 1965.

Volbach, W. F. *Early Christian Art.* New York: Abrams, 1961.

CHAPTER 10

THE GREAT AGE OF DEVOTION: 1000 TO 1400

Cultural Background: Feudal Society

 By the year 900, feudal society was established and functioning. Secular society was as hierarchical as clerical society, with baron, earl, and knight equal in importance to archbishop, bishop, and abbot. The stability of society depended largely on the military power of the knights, and their training and maintenance were the responsibility of the entire social order. The magnates controlled land worked by peasants, who contributed a certain amount of free labor to their lords in return for the privilege of passing on their tenancy to their children. The relationship of lord to peasant, a complex system of interdependency, changed in character from generation to generation.

No peasants were outright slaves. Some were serfs whose labor was not their own; some were able to work their land and produce excess crops to sell at market. By this means they could buy their freedom, which meant that they could keep all their labor and owe none to their lord. However, they would still not own the land they worked. The period up to 1200 saw the establishment of many new villages and the tilling of new land. It was a time of expansion of food supplies and of population.

There was an outburst of religious activity in the year 1000 because that was the millennium, when it was thought that the world would end. The Crusades, an attempt to recover from the Arabs lands that were holy to Christianity, were a huge, international undertaking which involved building fleets and recruiting knights from all the kingdoms. The Crusades also ushered in an era of complex banking and financing that benefited city-states such as Venice, from which several important crusades were launched. A Norman kingdom was established in Jerusalem, but it did not survive after the crusading zeal died down.

Architecture and Sculpture

Virtually no freestanding sculpture survives from this period: all the sculpture decorated churches. The term "romanesque" was coined in the nineteenth century; it refers to a revival of Roman style and Roman techniques in architecture, particularly the use of large, rounded arches and blocky columns. A romanesque church is generally a large, solid, chunky structure. Its distinctive quality lies in its combination of basilica aisles and nave with the northern spire, a conjunction that produced a totally novel effect.

ROMANESQUE SCULPTURE

Romanesque churches are decorated with distinctive sculpture. The half circle (called a "tympanum") over the entrance inspired an appropriate religious emotion in parishioners. The sculpture shown in Figure 10-1, from Autun, in France, is part of the tradition of the apse mosaic of San Vitale (Color Plate 3); Christ's posture and his aureole (halo) are similar here and in the mosaic, but the mood of this sculpture is distinctly different. Christ here is the stern lawgiver. The subject, the last judgment—when sinners go to hell and the saved enter heaven—was the most popular one for tympana over church doors. Stressing the last judgment instead of more

hopeful Christian stories implies fearfulness—a chastening which tends to keep people cautious, in their place, and obedient.

Romanesque sculptured figures are elongated and distorted; the arms and legs are almost always bent, giving them an animal-like quality which may help compensate for the fact that they are seen from below. The Christ in this last judgment is not as personal or appealing as he is in other, earlier works. In Gislebertus's work, the figures at the bottom are people rising from their tombs; the hands reach for only one figure to snatch him upward. The entire work is designed to put people into a "proper" frame of mind when they enter the church to pray. Gislebertus carved his legend: "Let this terror frighten those bound by earthly error."

The apostle in Figure 10-2 is in low relief; it is placed in an architectonic niche with simple thin columns and Roman arch, and the whole resembles an illumination in a book. Like much earlier relief sculpture, the figure is mildly distorted, but to no clear effect. There is no passion in the face, nor any feeling in the stylized drapery. By contrast, the angel in Figure 10-3 is much more dynamic: he does not

Figure 10-1
Gislebertus. *Last Judgment*, Autun. 1130–1140. (Photo, Scala/Art Resource.)

Figure 10-2
Apostle from Saint Sernin, Toulouse. c. 1090. (Photo,
Roger-Viollet, Paris.)

Figure 10-3
Giovanni Pisano (c. 1250–1330). Angel with lion and
ox, symbols of the evangelists Matthew, Mark, and Luke.
Marble plaster, probably from pulpit of the cathedral of
Pisa. (Metropolitan Museum of Art, Rogers Fund, 1921.)

face us straight on but is slightly twisted, and his face
seems to express emotion. This figure, by Giovanni
Pisano (c. 1250–1330), probably comes from a pulpit
pilaster in the cathedral of Pisa. The angel represents
the evangelist Mark; the lion and ox at his feet
represent Matthew and Luke. The group is harmonic,
symmetrical, but not static. Life has been breathed
into the stone: the lines of the garment flow, and the
details of the individual figures impart vitality to the
composition.

THE ROMANESQUE CHURCH

The spire of the romanesque church has little practical use. It can hold a bell to call people to mass or to
communicate in time of trouble, and it can serve as a
watchtower; beyond that, it is not useful. For people
outside the church, it points upward to heaven, to
which all Christians aspire. But inside the church it is
not visible at all. In Byzantine churches, the dome
represented heaven and helped produce a sense of
awe among believers. The spire simply points the

Figure 10-4
Left: Aerial view of Saint Sernin, Toulouse.
c. 1080–1120. (Photo, French Government
Tourist Office.)

Figure 10-5
Below: Interior, Saint Sernin, Toulouse. (Photo,
Jean Roubier, Paris.)

way; yet its appropriateness for church architecture
has rarely been questioned.

Saint Sernin (Figure 10-4), built on the plan of a
cross, served pilgrims heading to Compostela. The
apse rises in two levels, and many rounded chapels
radiate from it. The nave has two levels of roofing,
like the basilica; the transept is wide, and its roof is
low and conservative. The spire rises from the conjunction of nave and transept on an octagonal
pattern resulting from the four main pillars that
support it. The repetitions of the Roman arches—
small, delicate, and symmetrical—are handled with
special directness. This is a sensitive marriage of
styles.

The interior of the nave (Figure 10-5) rises to a
graceful barrel-vaulted ceiling with Roman arches
joined by walls in which the windows are kept small
because of the height of the arches. The architect was
not taking chances with the structure; caution kept
the arched vaults well within their limits. The
spaces, unlike those of a mosque or a Byzantine
church, are not low and wide but dramatically high.
One's eye is pulled toward heaven, just as it would be
outside the church by the spire. The roof vaulting is
of stone, instead of the conventional wood; this

Figure 10-6
Cathedral and campanile, Pisa. 1063–1174.

protected the church from fire and made it appear more permanent.

The cathedral at Pisa and its campanile (the "leaning tower") (Figure 10-6) show the romanesque influence in the astonishing number of repetitions of the rounded Roman arches. Instead of a spire, the cathedral has a small dome at the intersection of transept and nave. The choice of a basilica pattern with two-level roofs on nave and transept meant that no special counterthrusts had to be developed to prevent such a high nave from collapsing. The two side aisles, with their own roofs, counterbalance the central nave. The arches counterbalance one another, as they do in the circular campanile, which leans because its foundations are inadequate.

Despite the dynamic tilt of the campanile, the cathedral, along with its huge baptistry (not illustrated), gives the impression of squat security. The Roman columns help root the building to the ground, and the entirety represents a conservative approach to building. A considerable amount of energy went into the surface decoration, which is extremely rich and varied. The visual power of the cathedral comes from its secure look, its symmetry, and the reassurance provided by its many repeated elements.

Figures 10-7 and 10-8 show an exterior and an interior view of San Miniato, in Florence, Italy.

GOTHIC ARCHITECTURE AND SCULPTURE

Romanesque styles were dominant in the early medieval period. The most dramatic and inspiring style, however, was that of the gothic cathedral, often ascribed to the influence of a single man, the abbot Suger, who built Saint Denis in Paris in the late 1130s. Gothic is a high-risk style; its drama lies in its choice of a high, pointed arch and in its abandonment of the basilica structure. The high nave and the lack of counterbalancing side aisles made the ogival arch—an arch that is not round on top but egg-shaped or pointed—essential. The Islamic arch is of that type, but since the mosque emphasized wide rather than high spaces, nothing like the gothic style was ever attempted by Arab architects. By doing away with the aisles of the basilica, the gothic architect was able to reach directly to the heavens.

Figure 10-7
Above: San Miniato, Florence, exterior. 1013.

Figure 10-8
Right: San Miniato, Florence, interior.

PERCEPTION KEY

Romanesque Architecture

1. Is San Miniato, in Florence (Figures 10-7 and 10-8), in the basilica style?

2. What architectural qualities does it share with romanesque churches? Can it be considered a romanesque structure?

3. The exterior surfaces of San Miniato are black and white marble. Is this a heavily decorated church? What is decorative on the exterior? How does it differ from Saint Sernin?

4. Is the interior of San Miniato (Figure 10-8) more or less romanesque than the exterior?

5. What do you think the interior lighting is like in this church? Can you imagine what the acoustics are like?

Buttressing the arches with heavy outside masonry permitted them to rise to incredible heights; their means of support is invisible inside the church, leaving the worshiper totally involved with the experience of the space and unaware of how it was created. To an early Christian, it must have been a godly experience, like appreciating the universe without seeing the God who created it.

Figure 10-9 shows the distribution of stress from the cross vaulting of the nave roof and the way the vaulting permits long, wide windows between the ribs. The arches are supported by long columns of masonry which lean against them at the point where they begin to curve downward. The narrow aisles below have their own system of cross vaulting,

Figure 10-9
Section of thirteenth-century gothic cathedral. (From James H. Acland. *Medieval Structure: The Gothic Vault.* Toronto: University of Toronto Press, 1972. By permission of University of Toronto Press.)

Figure 10-10
Section of the cathedral at Amiens; high gothic. (From James H. Acland. *Medieval Structure: The Gothic Vault.* Toronto: University of Toronto Press, 1972. By permission of University of Toronto Press.)

although not all gothic cathedrals have such aisles. Individual communities chose various ways of dealing with aisles and the basic plan of the cathedrals. Figure 10-10 shows the double aisle in the cathedral at Reims, which is less than half the height of the nave.

Buttressing made large stained-glass windows possible since the walls bore very little stress. The rose window of Chartres (Color Plate 5) demonstrates the possibilities and shows that the architects chose to maintain a traditional "dim religious light." They controlled it with the beautiful emerald, ruby, and cobalt colors of the stained glass, which establish the mood of the interior space.

The drama of the upward thrust of space is apparent in the interior of Amiens Cathedral (Figure

10-11), whose nave vaulting soars 140 feet above the floor, 40 feet higher than the average gothic vault. The shape of the rounded, riblike columns that form the pillar of each arch is repeated dramatically throughout the interior. The lines of the apse and the repeated arches overhead and on the sidewalls constantly remind us of the power made possible by the gothic arch. These repetitions give the gothic style exceptional unity; the building seems almost of a piece, as if it were sculptured in stone.

The gothic cathedrals were built during a period of intense religious fervor, and they are products of communal love. The skills of masons, architects, sculptors, glassmakers, ironmongers, and many others were needed to make these buildings. The workers, who passed their skills on to their children, were itinerant: when one cathedral was finished, they moved to another community and worked on another building. The cathedrals took an average of fifty to seventy years to build; some took 200 years. Communities sacrificed and scrimped for their cathedrals; it is easy to see why they had to be magnificent.

Gothic architecture has a considerable range, reminding us that descriptive terms, like "gothic,"

Figure 10-11
Above: Amiens Cathedral, interior. Begun 1218. (Photo, Giraudon/Art Resource.)

Figure 10-12
Right: Notre Dame, Paris, south side. 1163–1250. (Photo, Giraudon/Art Resource.)

imply wide possibilities. Notre Dame, in Paris (Figure 10-12), was restored by a modern architect, Viollet-le-Duc, whose drawings and theories have explained much about the style. The windows of Notre Dame are so high that they admit little light, and the interior is impressively dim; it is so wide that it has much of the feeling of a mosque, except that one's eye is drawn instantly to the apse. Six thousand people can worship within it. The acoustics are such that it is used for organ concerts; the organ reverberates with extraordinary power, as if the music were exerting lines of force within the building.

Southern gothic differs from northern: the facade of the cathedral at Milan (Figure 10-13) is dominated by towerlike rising piers, each ending with a spire; the piers shelter large sculptures of saints. Despite the repeated upward-thrusting lines, the facade, with its small windows, has a squat look that is due mainly to its triangular pitch; this facade is not nearly as steep as the facades of most gothic churches.

England's gothic masterpiece, Salisbury Cathedral (Figure 10-14), was connected with a monastic order and served as a church for the monks and for the community. Its long nave has two transepts instead of one. Its buttresses are inconspicuous and close to the walls, and its spire rises over the intersection of the main transept. A chapter house and cloister for the monks are attached to the building. The interior, which is spacious and empty-feeling, is quite dark and can seem gloomy. Yet the setting is impressive, with long, open green lawns creating a unique visual space for anyone who walks onto them from the town and under the medieval arch.

The cathedral at Chartres served no special function other than to accommodate worshipers, and yet it has been compared to a perfect symphony and to great religious music. The west facade (Figure 10-15) is relatively simple, almost severe. The large circular window rests on three Roman-arched windows which sit over the three main entrances; the entrances have slightly ogival arches, like those in the base of the towers. One tower, added in 1506, does not match the original, but that seems not to have bothered the people of Chartres.

Figure 10-13
Milan Cathedral. 1385–1485.

Figure 10-14
Left: Salisbury Cathedral, aerial view. 1220–1258. (Photo, Aerofilms Limited.)

Figure 10-15
Below left: Chartres Cathedral, west facade. 1194–1260.

The sculpture in the royal portal (Figure 10-16) of the west facade is justly famous. In the tympana are, on the left, Christ ascending to heaven; in the center, Christ in glory with the symbols of the evangelists; and on the right, the Virgin and Child, with scenes from the life of Christ. These are more cheerful than the last judgment scenes on the tympana of romanesque churches. The sculptures on the piers below represent kings and queens. Their leanness and length, emphasizing them as architectural details, are "trademarks" of the gothic style.

The figures of the disciples—saints Matthew, Thomas, Philip, Andrew, and Peter—from the south transept, center portal of Chartres (Figure 10-17), show a softening of features almost like what we see in the portrait of Saint Theodore (Figure 10-18). The severity of the narrow vertical space is relieved slightly by the sense of bulk implied beneath the garments. The figures are conceived as a group, and an examination of the rhythm of arms from left to right shows a careful sense of harmony and balance. Each figure bears a symbol appropriate to him (Saint Peter holds a key, which is still the papal symbol), and each glances about him as if communing with a flock; yet each seems psychologically responsive to the others' presence. The figures beneath the feet and the canopies above the heads are all symbolic of the

Figure 10-16
Right: Chartres Cathedral, royal portal. (© Arch. Phot. Paris/SPADEM/VAGA, New York.)

Figure 10-17
Below left: Saints Matthew, Thomas, Philip, Andrew, and Peter. South transept, Chartres; center portal.

Figure 10-18
Below right: Chartres Cathedral, Saint Theodore from the south portal, left door.

special powers and the places of origin of the disciples. This group demonstrates the virtuosity of the artists in using a confined space.

Saint Theodore, a crusader of the later period of Saint Louis, is treated much more realistically (Figure 10-18). The chain mail and the folds of the surcoat are convincing, as is the calm, assured expression on his young face, for which the sculptor appears to have used a living model. Expressing innocence and faith, this later work shows the direction in which sculpture was moving: toward a softer, more realistic style that stressed human emotions and values.

The confidence of the later gothic produced impressive fan vaulting of the kind visible in King's College Chapel (Figure 10-19). The ribwork is not only structural but also exuberantly decorative. Because the windows are not dark stained glass, the interior emphasizes lightness. The architects of King's College Chapel were virtuoso performers who made the stone seem to bend to their will.

Figure 10-19
King's College Chapel, Cambridge. 1446–1515.

PERCEPTION KEY

Gothic Architecture and Sculpture

1. Is the claim that gothic architecture is more daring, more risk-taking, and less conservative than romanesque architecture supported by Figures 10-9 to 10-16?

2. Does the gothic cathedral seem to embody religious values? Does its form express its function as a church? How? Are your answers to these questions based on your cultural background, or is there a basic architectural principle behind the issue of form and function?

3. Do you agree that there are important differences between the last judgment tympanum at Autun (Figure 10-1) and the tympana of the royal portal at Chartres (Figure 10-16)? Make your own comparison, and be sure to take into consideration the frame of mind that these tympana were designed to create.

4. What differences do you see in the representations of Christ (Figure 10-16), of the disciples (Figure 10-17), and of people who lived later, such as Saint Theodore (Figure 10-18)? Are the stylistic decisions regarding realistic representation, symbolic stylization, or impersonal rendering consistent and appropriate?

5. What religious purposes could such decorative exuberance as the fan vaulting in the King's College Chapel (Figure 10-19) or the vertical repetitions on the facade of the Milan Cathedral (Figure 10-13) serve?

Painting and the Visual Arts

GIOTTO

Cimabue (c. 1240– c. 1302) was the first Florentine painter to set the stage for the development of realism in Renaissance painting. But it was Giotto (c. 1267–1337), also a Florentine and Cimabue's student, who made the most striking sylistic inroads. Giotto was a great exponent of fresco painting, in which paint is applied to wet plaster walls—a tricky procedure. Seven hundred years later, his work is as lively and fascinating as when it was first done. His great achievement is the frescoes in the Arena Chapel, in Padua, executed in about 1310. Twelve panels narrate the life of Mary, the life of Christ, and the passion of Christ. Giotto's ability to produce such

narrative works is one of his most distinguishing qualities.

The importance of color and Giotto's conception of the entire composition can best be seen in Color Plate 6, which shows the interior of the chapel facing toward the last judgment. The placement of Mary and Christ in the center of the composition in *The Flight into Egypt* (Figure 10-20) produces a sense of stability. But it has a price: it reduces the tension and the sense of spontaneity associated with the flight. The landscape in the distance is symbolic and spare, suggesting obstacles to be overcome. The guidance of the angel implies tidings about the future. The human figures are unified on the same pictorial plane.

The Raising of Lazarus (Figure 10-21) has no single focal point. Christ stands on the left, and Lazarus, in graveclothes, is on the right. The panel is filled with

Figure 10-20
Giotto. *The Flight into Egypt.*
Arena Chapel, Padua. c. 1305.
(Photo, Alinari/Art Resource.)

Figure 10-21
Giotto. *The Raising of Lazarus,*
Arena Chapel, Padua. c. 1305.
(Photo, Alinari/Art Resource.)

workers, worshipers, and mourners. The most remarkable figure is that of the young man in the
center, whose leaning, attentive posture suggests our
own reaction, were we there. The rhythm of attention that Giotto demands of us is unusual: even the
figures whose bodies are cut off by the framing help us
see how this spills over into life itself.

Giotto's fame in his own day was due to his ability
to paint figures so accurately that they appear three-
dimensional. Known as the finest painter of his time,
he used his reputation to amass wealth and become
influential. He was like many Florentines of the
period: practical, skillful, and unashamed of having
money.

THE LIMBOURG BROTHERS
Illumination reached new heights in the work of the
Limbourg brothers, whose books of hours for Jean,

duke of Berry, have in recent times become modern
best-sellers.

Color Plate 7, from *Les Très Riches Heures du Duc
de Berry* ("The Very Rich Hours of the Duke of
Berry"), is part of an illustrated calendar showing
everyday life in fourteenth-century France. Ordinarily, books of hours, which are guides to prayer,
contain only religious scenes, but this one shows
peasants and the nobility engaged in a variety of
activities during the seasons.

As in Persian miniatures, the highest figures in the
composition in Color Plate 7 (where peasants are
involved in winter activities) are the most distant,
but the action forms a steadily upward-curving arc
that starts on the left, follows the wattled fence, and
continues to the figure and the ass in the upper
center. More important, the figures in the lower left
are larger than the others, which helps create an
illusion of distance.

Painting—Giotto and the Limbourg Brothers

1. Examine the Limbourg brothers' *February* (Color Plate 7). Beginning with the section that first arrests your attention, note the direction in which your eye moves. Diagram this movement using an X for each point of attention; then link the X's. Does this movement imply a narrative? What is the subject matter of this painting?

2. Can it be said that the divine and the human are melded in the work of Giotto? Can you determine which is more important in *The Flight into Egypt* (Figure 10-20)?

3. What qualities do Giotto and the Limbourg brothers share in the works shown here? Consider similarity of subject matter, color, narrative sense, representationalism, illusionism, and concern for human and divine values.

4. Which of Giotto's panels implies more action: *The Flight into Egypt* or *The Raising of Lazarus* (Figure 10-21)? Given the subjects, which ought to be more active?

Literature

The literature of the period from 1100 to 1400 is rich, various, dynamic, and exciting. *El Cid*, a Spanish tale of heroism, was inspired by the wars against the Moorish Islamic invaders. *The Song of Roland* is still widely read, as is Boccaccio's *Decameron*, which is set in a time of plague, when, isolated from the rest of the community, people told stories concentrating on the pleasures of life. Troubadour poetry was also an important development, but the two overwhelming giants of the period were Dante Alighieri in Italy and Geoffrey Chaucer in England.

TROUBADOURS: THE COURTLY TRADITION

Sophisticated European courts encouraged the development of highly refined arts and literature. The courts became the center of political and cultural power where the clergy met with dukes, earls, and knights. Music, dance, and literature read aloud became staple ingredients of court life. The rules of chivalry that guided behavior were only a part of an elaborate system of etiquette that governed people in different stations in life. As the differences between aristocrats and others became more and more ingrained through heredity and custom, styles of behavior became more and more codified.

An art of courtly love grew up around the troubadour, in whose songs one worshiped one's beloved from afar. The troubadours sang their songs in a very high tenor voice; the texts often complained of a lady's indifference. The concept of heartbreak, as well as other concepts of romantic love, dates from this tradition.

Bernard de Ventadour's song (Figure 10-22) shows that each syllable usually has one note; but a small number of short, neumatic episodes are designed to build emotional intensity. The melodic range is slightly more than an octave, and the piece is both lively and plaintive. The text reads:

> When I see the lark fly,
> Joyfully against the sun
> Until, forgetting it must die
> In all the sweetness it has won,
> It falls, I am filled with spite
> For those who dwell in joy apart.
> I marvel, then, that by right
> Longing does not melt my heart.

Figure 10-22
Bernard de Ventadour. "Can vei la lauzeta mover."
c. 1180. Unaccompanied vocal line, in modern notation.
(From Heinrich Besseler. "Die Musik der Mittelalters und
der Renaissance," in *Handbuch der Musikwissenschaft*.
Potsdam, Germany: Akademische Verlagsgesellschaft
Athenaion, 1931, p. 106.)

DANTE ALIGHIERI

The Divine Synthesis

Dante Alighieri (1265–1321; Figure 10-23) was active in the political affairs of his native Florence. His greatest work, *The Divine Comedy*, was composed early in the fourteenth century when he was in exile; it tells of a "journey" that Dante made from hell, through purgatory, and into heaven. Virgil, representing reason and human knowledge, guided him through the lower regions. Beatrice, a symbol of moral beauty and divine revelation, guided him through heaven.

The structure of the poem is governed by numerological considerations: the number 10, the perfect number of God, is squared to get 100, the number of cantos in the poem. The first canto, the introduction, stands alone. Then 33 cantos are devoted to hell, 33 to purgatory, and 33 to heaven; the number 33 is related to the trinity and to the years in Christ's life. The stanzas are three lines long and have a tight rhyme scheme—aba, bcb, cdc, etc.—called "terza rima." These formal strictures give the poem a tense, unified feeling; the difficulties that Dante imposed on himself are virtually unnoticeable. The poem is fluent and natural; it deals with morality, politics, psychology, and the personal behavior of both famous and obscure people. Dante's subject matter is the entirety of life.

Dante began the poem in 1312, setting it on Good Friday, 1300. Unlike Virgil, Dante was never in retirement: he had seen action in war and had been an ambassador in the courts during peacetime. He struggled with older magnates for power, but fell out of favor with his own political party and was exiled in 1302, never to return to Florence.

The Divine Comedy is a great synthesis: Dante walks through the halls of the afterlife talking with poets, politicians, popes, sinners, and saints. Like the cathedral, the poem appealed to everyone. It was written not in Latin, the language of the learned, but in the vernacular, Italian, which gave it a modernity and currency that no Latin poem could possibly have enjoyed.

Figure 10-23
Statue of Dante Alighieri, Florence Cathedral.

Allegory

Yet Dante's allegorical method sometimes gives us problems. The people of the Middle Ages were used to allegorical art, wherein one thing stood consistently for another. Indeed, life was interpreted allegorically. Physical life was to be understood allegorically as a type of the heavenly, spiritual life. The world was an allegory of heaven; and God spoke indirectly in symbols, expecting humankind to be receptive to his messages. All Dante's stories of those in hell, those in purgatory, and those in heaven were meant to instruct us how to live better.

Dante's journey begins:

In the middle of the journey of our life
    I came to my senses in a dark forest,
    for I had lost the straight path.
Oh, how hard it is to tell
    what a dense, wild, and tangled wood this was,
    the thought of which renews my fear! (1:1–16.)

As he climbs a hill, a leopard (lust), a lion (pride), and a she-wolf (greed) challenge him. Dante, an allegory for all mankind, is threatened by the beasts, but Virgil comes to guide him, explaining that climbing the mountain "is the beginning and the source of all joy." Because Virgil is a pagan, he can

take Dante only part of the way; a worthier guide, he tells Dante, will escort him into the realms of light—heaven.

When Dante makes the journey, he is shocked: he had not realized that hell had swallowed up so many people. His pity for them is balanced by his sense that God is just and that they deserved their fate: those who sinned, if justice is a valid concept, suffer, and those who were worthy must be rewarded. *Inferno,* the first part of the poem, is like the tympanum over the entryway of a romanesque church: it narrates the last judgment. The torments of the suffering increase as we move from the outer to the inner circles of hell. Suffering is as much psychological as physical, and sometimes Dante is overcome with grief at the thought of how total it is.

God is truth, love, justice. He appears as a blaring, intense light that Dante cannot look upon directly. Led by Saint Bernard in the last canto of *Paradiso,* Dante has a beatific vision of the true nature of God. He is so overcome that no language can communicate his vision:

For my sight, growing pure, penetrated
    even deeper into the rays
    of the Light which is true in Itself.
From then on my vision was greater
    than our speech which fails at such a sight,
    just as memory is overcome by the excess.
                                        (33:52–57.)

The vision disappears, "yet the sweetness/ caused by it is still distilled within my heart." Dante, true to his feelings about God's universe, ends his poem on a positive note.

Inferno, which is filled with suffering and pain, is the best-known section of the poem, perhaps because we understand sinfulness much better than we do beatitude. Paolo and Francesca, lovers who were killed when Francesca's husband caught them together, are deeply touching. Dante agrees that they must suffer for having been lustful, but he also sees their worth. Since he meets them early in the fifth canto of the poem, Dante is only beginning his moral education: he cannot yet understand how two such good people can be condemned to hell.

As is true of all Dante's sinners, their punishment fits their crime: they are locked together forever, flitting backward and forward in the air. They are victims of their lust and inconstancy. They explain to him that they did not intend to be lustful, but they were

> . . . reading
> about Lancelot, how love constrained him;
> alone we were and without any suspicion.
> Several times that reading made our glances meet
> and changed the color of our faces;
> but one moment alone overcame us. (5:127–132.)

When Lancelot kisses Guenevere in the story, Paolo kissed Francesca, and their affair began. Untrue to the doctrines of courtly love, they acted out their desires. Dante reacts so emotionally to their tale that he faints from grief and must be "brought around" in the next canto.

Dante's reaction shows that his moral education must come slowly, like our own; and as he becomes educated, so do we. Dante introduces us to Charon (the boatman of hell), Achilles, Judas, Paris, Helen of Troy, Virgil, Saint Bernard, Cleopatra, Constantine, and Charlemagne. His own beloved, Beatrice Portinari, a woman he had admired only from afar, in the manner of the troubadours, also figures as his inspiration.

Beatrice allegorically represents divine revelation, while Virgil represents human reason. Virgil guides Dante as far as reason can take him, and Beatrice leads him through the final cantos. Thus, reason and revelation take him into the presence of God. *The Divine Comedy* is as complete a synthesis as had ever been achieved in literature up to that time. It is particularly appropriate to the medieval period because it melds biblical history with political history, faith with reason, and the human with the divine.

GEOFFREY CHAUCER

The brightest and merriest work of the period is *The Canterbury Tales,* by Geoffrey Chaucer (c. 1342–1400; Figure 10-24). His times were lively. England had been invaded by the Norman French in 1066, and a reform of the language had brought English more into the tradition of Romance languages and somewhat out of the tradition of Germanic languages. Chaucer was a major influence in establishing the language; his success was widespread, and his work influenced the way people read and spoke. *The Canterbury Tales* was spoken literature, like Homer's *Iliad* and *Odyssey.* It is written in rhymed couplets,

Figure 10-24
The Ellesmere portrait of Chaucer. (Henry E. Huntington Library and Art Gallery, San Marino, California.)

using the great English five-foot metrical line, the line that was to be modified by Christopher Marlowe in his plays and by William Shakespeare in his. The poem was read aloud by Chaucer at court in London, where he was highly influential.

The Canterbury Tales is an entertainment that tells of a group of pilgrims who are on their way to Canterbury on a religious mission; gathered at the Tabard Inn at Southwark, they are enjoying the good humor of their host, Harry Bailly, and decide that they will tell a round of stories to amuse themselves on their journey. They are each to tell two tales going to Canterbury and two coming back, for a total of 120, but Chaucer did not live long enough to finish all of them.

Chaucer's pilgrims are a cross section of the fourteenth century: a worthy knight, a bawdy miller, the lecherous wife of Bath, a poor Oxford student, a shipman, and a plowman—all secular. From the clergy, he offers us a nun, a nun's priest, a monk, a friar, and a pardoner, among others. The pilgrims range from good, decent people to downright villains. The Prologue reminds us that pilgrimages were seasonal:

As soon as April pierces to the root
The drought of March, and bathes each bud and
   shoot
Through every vein of sap with gentle showers
From whose engendering liquor spring the flowers;
When zephyrs have breathed softly all about
Inspiring every wood and field to sprout,
And in the zodiac the youthful sun
His journey halfway through the
   Ram* has run;   *sign of the zodiac: Aries
When little birds are busy with their song
Who sleep with open eyes the whole night long
Life stirs their hearts and tingles in them so,
Then off as pilgrims people long to go,
And palmers* to set out for distant   *pilgrims
   strands
And foreign shrines renowned in many lands.
And specially in England people ride
To Canterbury from every countryside
To visit there the blessed martyred saint
Who gave them strength when they were sick and faint.
   (Lines 1–18.)

The saint referred to here is the martyred Thomas à Becket (c. 1118–1170), archbishop of Canterbury.

All the characters are described both physically and psychologically, and the stories they tell are tailored to their individual personalities. The knight is an "excellent" man, perfect and worthy. The nun, a prioress, is very fastidious:

She always wiped her upper lip so clean
That in her cup was never to be seen
A hint of grease when she had drunk her share.
   (Lines 117–137.)

The miller, by contrast with the knight and the nun, is a rough-hewn brute:

His mouth would open out
Like a great furnace, and he would sing and shout

His ballads and jokes of harlotries and crimes.
He could steal corn and charge for it three times,
And yet was honest enough, as millers come.
   (Lines 532–550.)

The Canterbury Tales is a collection of forms available to the medieval storyteller: some are direct moral tales; some are fables (animal stories with a moral); and some are fabliaux (bawdy anecdotes, like the Miller's Tale). Some of the stories have classical antecedents, but most were very up to date, which is one reason why Chaucer's peers valued them so highly. The mythical concerns of the ancients were of little interest to Chaucer. His stories are earthy and worldly, and they reflect a growing interest in human concerns. People and what they do—even the less uplifting things—are the central issues, not the meanderings of gods and goddesses.

The entire work is secular, despite the mood of the age. It deals with religion, morals, and the religious life; but it is also characterized by a rollicking sense of the bawdy, the earthy, the smutty, and the farcical. Bawdiness and holiness got along better together in the medieval period than they do in ours. Chaucer's people seem familiar. The wife of Bath, for instance, a woman with an eye for men and with a keen sense of how to dominate them, has had five husbands and knows what she is talking about. She is at once an individual and a type, like most of Chaucer's characters. The poor Oxford scholar ("gladly would he learn and gladly would he teach") is also both an individual and a type. That is one of the strengths and joys of the poem.

A comparison of the structure of the poem with the structure of the Gothic cathedral which the pilgrims visit is possible. For one thing, the characters are both portraits of individuals and types, as are the sculptures on the cathedrals, which bristle with patriarchs, saints, evangelists, crusaders, clerics, and gargoyles. The symmetry achieved by having each character tell two tales going to Canterbury and two tales coming back is like the repetitions of architectonic details in a gothic cathedral. Each tale is analogous to a cathedral arch, and the narrative links that connect one tale with the next are analogous to the cross ribs that tie the arches together. Chaucer was using as his model not necessarily architecture but rather the orderly, systematic architectural habits of mind of the period, which affected many artists in most media.

Medieval Literature

1. The love songs of the troubadours are secular, but how might their doctrine of worshiping the loved one from afar be thought of as allegorical and religious?

2. In the course of Dante's moral education, he goes from fainting at the sight of the suffering in hell to a later acceptance of the fact that those in heaven rejoice in that suffering because they see it as evidence of God's justice. Dante shows us his personal moral development. What changes are implied in that development?

3. From your reading of the excerpts here—and from your other reading in medieval literature—what are the chief concerns of medieval poets? What subject matter does the medieval poet prefer? What techniques does the medieval poet rely on?

4. Judging from the excerpts, how easy or uneasy is the relationship between secular and religious values in *The Canterbury Tales?* The tales are told during a religious pilgrimage; do such pilgrimages seem holy and solemn? What do the tales tell us about such pilgrimages? What do they tell us about everyday life in the medieval period?

5. Read a section of *The Divine Comedy* or *The Canterbury Tales.* What comparisons can you make between them concerning their subject matter, their powers of characterization, their attitudes toward myth, their use of imagery and colorful description, and their approaches to allegory?

Music and Dance

THE DANCE OF DEATH

The fourteenth century was ravaged by the black death, a confluence of three forms of plague—bubonic, pneumonic, and septicemic—carried by a flea whose host was the rat. The plague affected the entire known world of Europe, Africa, and Asia, killing so many millions in so short a time that it is one of the worst catastrophes ever to strike humankind. It began in the Gobi desert and spread by overland and sea trade routes until, in a matter of months, in 1347, it reached Europe on a Genoese freighter. By 1348 it had spread to England, and by 1349 there was hardly a place that it had not scourged. Mortality may have exceeded 50 percent in some places; it was rarely less than 20 percent. The impact of the black death on European culture was complex: food prices rose; labor costs went up; settled habits were radically changed; and population dropped in Europe to levels that stayed low until the sixteenth century. The black death was a constant fact of life in Europe until well after the great fire of London in 1665.

The danse macabre, or dance of death (Figure 10-25), a reaction to the plague, took many forms. The processional form featured dancers who assumed the identities of persons in different walks of life, indicating the indifference of the plague to social rank. The circle, or round dance, was performed with a great deal of gaiety, but eventually a boy or girl would "fall dead" in the center of the group, and members of the opposite sex would kiss the victim back to life; unfortunately, this helped spread the pneumonic form of the disease.

The dance of death was often performed by hysterical people dancing feverishly, and often in cemeteries, as if the dancers intended to communicate with the dead. Its origins seem to have been in Islam: "makabr," an Arabic word, means "churchyard," giving us an appropriate sense of its beginning.

Figure 10-25
Anonymous. *Danse Macabre.* 15th century.
Woodcut. (Photo, Bettman Archive, Inc.)

The church felt that it could make good use of this dance, and so we see many manuscripts containing woodcuts and engravings that show dancers who have joined hands with skeletons (as in modern comic books) and are dancing their way to death. Clerics felt that such illustrations reminded people of their mortality. They were something like the last judgment tympana of romanesque churches.

The black death affected people in widely different ways: some retreated into solemnity and piety; others gave themselves up to wild parties and orgiastic behavior. Survivors of the plague sometimes were employed to take bodies to the mass burial grounds. The morning cry, "Bring out your dead," echoed throughout the world. The connection between the black death and the carrier flea and host rat was never made, and there were no concerted efforts at sanitation until later, when the cities had been re-formed and rebuilt.

ARS ANTIQUA: THE OLD STYLE

Cathedrals may be thought of as empty theaters. In them were conducted elaborate liturgical services that often involved complex music, for which the demand never seemed to cease. Outside the cathedrals folk music flourished, often providing tunes for the troubadours and for the medieval lyrics sung to simple stringed instruments. English melodies of the period still have a contagious merriness; Italian melodies have a high polish and tend to be bright, fully developed, and easy to grasp.

The most important church music was written in Paris, near the Cathedral of Notre Dame. The technique of polyphony—the most significant musical contribution of the age—was developed on the site of the old church of Notre Dame. Most early music is sung in unison—all voices sing the same melody. In polyphonic music, several distinct melodic lines are played or sung at the same time, or several melodies and several texts are sung or played at the same time.

Polyphony was known in Europe, but the Notre Dame school developed its principles. In its simplest form, the organum, a voice sings a melody along with another voice or an instrument, droning one note, in the manner of a bagpipe.

LÉONIN AND PÉROTIN

The two masters of polyphony, Léonin and Pérotin, spanned the late twelfth and early thirteenth centuries and set Gregorian chant to the polyphonic style. The tenor sang "ah," "uh," or "ooh"—a highly effective technique that was quickly and widely imitated. In a short passage from Pérotin's four-part organum on the word "sederunt" from the Gradual of the Mass for Saint Stephen's Day (Figure 10-26), the bottom voice holds one syllable: "se-." The horizontal brackets correspond to the neumes, or ligatures, in the original notation. No melodic line flows fully from any of the four levels of sound, and the voices are all equal in their effect on the listener. Rhythmic passages last for the duration of a breath, and the bottom tone is sustained in the manner of an organ, heightening the emotional tension.

Se -

Figure 10-26
Pérotin. Excerpt from the quadruple organum on the word "sederunt," from the Gradual for Saint Stephen's Day. 1199. (From Richard H. Hoppin, ed. *Anthology of Medieval Music*. New York: Norton, 1978. P. 59.)

ARS NOVA: THE NEW ART

Polyphony turned out to be both a resourceful and an exciting technique whose novelty appealed to many listeners. The melodies of polyphonic music developed into more tuneful songs, resembling those of the earlier troubadours. Several important secular polyphonic forms developed, among them the motet, in which there was usually an instrumental tenor voice.

Guillaume de Machaut (c. 1300–1377) is the most important composer in the French ars nova style. His ballade "Je suis trop bien" (Figure 10-27) gives the tenor voice far more notes than we find in Pérotin. The upper voice carries the text, but in a new way: it is supported by the lower voices, almost in the advanced harmonic fashion that was to come. The ballade, marked for 6/8 time in this modern rendition (meaning that each bar contains six eighth notes), shows that Machaut was more interested in a fixed rhythmic and metric pattern than Pérotin was.

The most popular music of the period was dance music, with a steady, regular structure which sounds lilting, merry, and exciting. It was originally played on pipes, shawms, and percussion instruments. Most music was improvised using simple modes and predictable rhythmic models, but the system of musical notation was improving, and so composers could polish, refine, and preserve their works. The distinction between composer and performer began in this period.

The most popular Italian forms were ballate (from the word meaning "to dance") at court, motets, and madrigals. Motets were vocal music, usually polyphonic; sometimes they were sung in two languages. Madrigals, also vocal music, usually had simple texts for two voices, although they soon became more complex. The madrigal of Lorenzo da Firenze (Figure 10-28) shows some of the playfulness of the form. "Dà" ("give") and "tu" ("you"), like the musical motif, are thrown from voice to voice in a lively fashion.

Figure 10-27
Opposite: Guillaume de Machaut. Ballade, "Je puis trop bien." c. 1340–1370. The text reads: "I can all too well compare my lady / To the image which Pygmalion made. / It was of ivory, so beautiful, without peer, / That he loved it more than Jason did Medea. / Out of his senses, he prayed to it unceasingly, / But the image answered him not. / Thus does she treat me who makes my heart melt, / For I pray to her ever, and she answers me not." (From Archibald T. Davidson and Willi Apel, eds. *Historical Anthology of Music*. Rev. ed. Vol. 1. Cambridge, Mass.: Harvard University Press, 1949. Pp. 48 and 245. Adapted from Friedrich Ludwig, ed. *Guillaume de Machaut, Musikalische Werke*. Vol. 1. Leipzig: Breitkopf und Härtel; Publikationen älterer Musik der deutscher Musikgesellschaft, 1926. Ballade 28, p. 31.)

Je_____ puis__ trop__ bien ma_____
Dy - voi - re fu, tant_____

Contra-
tenor

Tenor

__ da - me com - pa - rer a l'y - ma - ge _____
_____ belle et si_ sans per que plus l'a - ma

que fist Py - ma - li - on. que Me - de - e Ja - zon.

Li_____ folz tou - dis la pri - oit, mais l'y - ma - ge riens ne li re - spon -

doit. Eins - si me fait cel - le_____ qui mon cuer font,

qu'a_____ des_____ la_____ pri et rien ne me re - spont.

Figure 10-28

Lorenzo da Firenze. Madrigal, "Dà, dà a chi avaregia," first part. Fourteenth century. Found in the Squarcialupi Codex, which preserved hundreds of musical works of fourteenth-century Florence. The text reads: "Give, give to those who hoard only for themselves. You, you who have rank, listen to me." (Florence, Bibl. Med. Laur. Pal. 87. From Richard H. Hoppin, ed. *Anthology of Medieval Music.* New York: Norton, 1978, P. 148.)

Medieval Music

1. Listen to a composition by Léonin or Pérotin (Musical Heritage Society MHS 676). Does the music sound religious? Establish the rhythmic patterns, the primary melody, and the droned tones.

2. In the composition you listened to, which is foremost in importance—the music or the text?

3. How does the melodic quality of troubadour music (Musical Heritage Society MHS 675) compare in range, length of melody, and rhythm with the music of Léonin or Pérotin? Is the troubadour melody easier or harder to sing? Is it syllabic? Is it melismatic?

4. Sing Lorenzo's "Dà, dà a chi avaregia" (Figure 10-28) with one other voice. How difficult is it to sing? Is the melodic line simple or complex?

5. Listen to one of the following recordings: *Art of Courtly Love—Machaut and His Age* (Seraphim S-6104, three disks), *Music of the Gothic Era* (Deutsche Grammophon, Archive ARC-2710019, three disks), or *Music of Medieval France* (New York Pro Musica, MCA-2516). How important is a tuneful melody in this music? How steady is the rhythm? Is the rhythm exciting or dull? Can you hear repetitions in different voices? In the same voice? How wide a range does the music have? Can you tell the difference between a religious and a secular piece?

Religion:
The Growth of Scholasticism

Medieval universities were developed to produce educated clerics and to help clerics maintain a strong interest in professions such as medicine and law. The University of Paris was founded in about 1100. Although a university already existed in Bologna and although many more—in Vicenza, in Padua, and elsewhere in Italy—were quick to develop, the one in Paris became the model for the medieval university.

The church depended on teachers like Peter Abelard and Thomas Aquinas. Because of their keen minds and their extensive influence, the teachers of the medieval period were known as "scholastics." Scholasticism has been rightly connected with a revival of interest in the works of Aristotle, whose writings on rhetoric and logic became the basic texts for study in the schools. Aristotle's work had been preserved by the Arab philosopher Averroës, and from the twelfth century it was available for interpretation by Christians.

Saint Augustine had earlier interpreted Plato through the works of Plotinus, establishing the hierarchy of ideas and discounting sensory perception as a path to true knowledge. By way of contrast, Saint Thomas Aquinas (1225–1274) accepted Aristotle, whose theories assigned real value to sensory perception.

Such a view increases the importance of perception and the world of matter. Augustine had established that matter was not despicable, and so it was not impossible for Aquinas to emphasize the value of sensory perception in his *Summa Theologica*, his handbook of religious thought. Modern science can be seen to have stemmed from such a view, since it depends on sensory perception and the gathering of instances of observation, a practice not generally recommended in medieval times because a close examination of the sensory world could lead to the pleasures of the flesh and thus to error.

The symbol of the evangelist Mark can help us understand the prevalent attitudes. The early medieval clergy associated the lion, Mark's symbol, with Christ because they had been taught that the lion was dormant for three days after birth and then was breathed on by its parent, which brought it to life. This was an allegorical truth connecting the king of the beasts with the king of heaven. It was not a literal truth, but it was thought to be. Few people had ever witnessed a lion's birth, and so the belief was rarely questioned. Anyone who questioned it was accused of having faulty senses or of being duped by the devil. Obviously, in an Aristotelian system, repeated observations of actual births would take precedence and blast the earlier concept.

The Aristotelian method was resisted by many traditionalists, in part because their neat numerological symmetries would have had to be scrapped. Humankind as the center of the universe was doomed the moment Aquinas began his work, although it took Galileo, in the seventeenth century, to finally bring the point home. Aquinas was not directly interested in science, but what he did not realize was that once authority in matters of truth was transferred to observation, the old ways had to change.

A connection between Aquinas and gothic architecture has sometimes been made. The great cathedrals were begun a century before Aquinas, and, as Erwin Panofsky has put it, he may have shared a cultural habit of mind with the cathedral builders. The habit of mind that could push the arch to its limits was like the habit of mind that could push daring ideas to their limits: that sensory evidence can produce certainty. The risk involved in building 140-foot-high naves paralleled the risk involved in going against Saint Augustine. Aquinas connected the forces of reason and faith by asserting in his *Summa* that reason reinforces faith. Other members of the clergy did not agree with him and feared that his approach would weaken faith. History has proved them correct; however, Aquinas dared to tell the truth, even though the consequences might be threatening for religion.

Portraying Aquinas as a risk taker may be extreme; but the cathedrals have stood through fire, war, and earthquake for more than 700 years, and so has his thought. The gothic architect, like Aquinas, took a risk to prove that he was right: the structure would stand; it would endure. Aquinas used an architectonic structure. Just as the arch is balanced by a buttress, Aquinas's questions are balanced by answers.

Aquinas's method was to analyze a question and offer an answer, using the best authorities of the past, while always attempting to be logical and consistent in his approach. Question 2 of the first part of his *Summa Theologica* asks "whether the existence of God is self-evident." His immediate answer is, "It seems that the existence of God is self-evident." He then comments on objections to his answer, giving reasons for dispensing with the objections. His method is called "dialectical" because it balances argument with argument and is rigorous:

Obj. 3. Further, the existence of truth is self-evident. For whoever denies the existence of truth grants that truth does not exist. And, if truth does not exist, then the proposition "Truth does not exist" is true. And if there is anything true, there must be truth. But God is truth itself: I am the way, the truth, and the life (John 14. 6). Therefore, "God exists" is self-evident.

On the contrary, No one can think the opposite of what is self-evident, as the Philosopher states concerning the first principles of demonstration. But the opposite of the proposition "God is" can be thought, for, The fool said in his heart, there is no God (Ps.52.1). Therefore, that God exists is not self-evident.

I answer that, A thing can be self-evident in either of two ways. On the one hand, self-evident in itself, though not to us, on the other, self-evident in itself, and to us. . . . Now because we do not know the essence of God, the proposition is not self-evident to us, but needs to be demonstrated by things that are more known to us, though less known in their nature— namely by effects.

The reasoning is this careful and this difficult throughout. The result is that Aquinas unified religion and philosophy and produced a clear-sighted, acute theology. The clarity and brilliance of Aquinas's thought resulted in a powerful document and an almost invincible intellectual force to benefit the church. It did so for centuries, although some contemporary thinkers see his work as the beginning of the triumph of modern secularism.

CONCEPT KEY

Religion and Scholasticism

1. Joining logic and religion is sometimes seen as Aquinas's great accomplishment. Why might logic and religion be incompatible? Does Aquinas seem aware of any such incompatibility?

2. Do you agree with those commentators who feel that reason and religion are already joined in gothic architecture? What would lead people to propose such a view?

3. What are the key ingredients of Aquinas's approach to the proposition that "the existence of God is self-evident"? How does he achieve a balance in the argument?

4. Why would opening up religious questions to argument based on logic be considered dangerous for religion? If religious truths are not based on observation and sensory evidence, what are they based on? What should they be based on?

5. Is Aquinas's argument convincing? If possible, read the entirety of question 2 of the first part, "whether the existence of God is self-evident." What are the most convincing aspects of the argument? What are its least convincing aspects?

Summary

European art and thought, as well as the European economy, grew rapidly from the time of Charlemagne to the end of the fifteenth century. Roman techniques were revived in architecture, and northern influences produced the drama of gothic cathedrals. The dominance of religion was naturally apparent in architecture, but it was also evident in sculpture, painting, and literature. The confidence of the gothic architect matched the confidence of the religious community. Building projects sprouted up throughout Europe; the sheer joy of the vaulting and the excitement of the interiors of the cathedrals suggest a profound religious commitment. The absence of emphasis on the last judgment and its terrors in late gothic cathedrals implies a confidence in Christian mercy.

Set free from Rome, from the Byzantine influence of Constantinople, and from Islam, the Europeans became more self-reliant. With local courts came doctrines of chivalry and the growth of petty kingdoms, from which developed the concepts of nationhood. Courtly music, dance, art, and literature developed a high polish and were in sharp contrast to a still vivid folk tradition. The dance of death reminds us that the second half of the fourteenth century was dominated by the black death, a worldwide scourge that depopulated Europe and laid the groundwork for change, growth, and development, particularly as it weakened the absolute rigidity of social classes and the absolute authority of the clergy and the physicians, both of whom failed to provide the services needed in a time of immense fear and stress. By the end of this period, change was everywhere in the air, setting the stage for one of the greatest periods in any culture: the Renaissance.

Concepts in Chapter 10

The medieval period was an age of expansion, both social and economic.

Medieval architects recovered Roman building techniques to produce what has been called the "romanesque" style.

The romanesque style weds the basilica style with the Norman spire and the Roman arch.

Most medieval sculpture is on churches; little is freestanding.

Scenes from the last judgment generally grace entryway tympana in romanesque churches.

Gothic architecture is based on the ogival arch and counterbalancing buttresses; it is a high-risk architecture of considerable variety.

Stained-glass windows created a solemn light and mood in gothic churches.

Late gothic tympanum sculpture has a hopeful subject matter, often showing Christ as creator.

The sculpture on Chartres illustrates gothic variety and points in the direction of a realistic style, like that of a portrait.

Giotto led painting toward three-dimensional realism.

Illuminated books contain examples of three-dimensional illusionism in painting.

Court life helped refine literature and music.

Troubadour songs contributed to an art of courtly love based on worshiping one's beloved from afar.

Dante's *Divine Comedy* is an allegorical journey through hell, purgatory, and heaven.

Dante's moral education parallels the reader's.

The Divine Comedy is allegorical and is structured according to numerological considerations.

Dante wrote *The Divine Comedy* in Italian, rather than Latin; this gave his poem wide currency.

Chaucer's *Canterbury Tales* is both religious and secular, and it makes use of most of the available medieval narrative forms.

Chaucer chose a symmetrical, balanced form for his moral and instructive tales.

Chaucer emphasized characterization and produced a cross section of innocents and villains, both secular and clerical.

The danse macabre, or dance of death, was a reaction to the ravages of the black death, which, beginning in 1347, killed almost half the population of Europe.

Ars antiqua introduced a droned note that was the beginning of polyphony in church music.

Ars nova developed religious polyphonic music by introducing simultaneously sung and played melodies and texts; secular polyphonic music developed as well.

Thomas Aquinas supplanted Augustine as the major influence on theology.

Scholasticism, which developed in the new universities, was based on the thought of Aristotle, which emphasizes sensory perception as a way of knowing the truth.

Aquinas's *Summa Theologica* is a fusion of reason and faith; it dominated Christian thought for five centuries after it was written.

Suggested Readings

Ackland, James H. *Medieval Structure: The Gothic Vault.* Toronto: University of Toronto Press, 1972.

Gilson, Etienne. *History of Christian Philsophy in the Middle Ages.* New York: Random House, 1955.

Gottfried, Robert. *The Black Death.* New York: Macmillan, Free Press, 1983.

Grodecki, Louis. *Gothic Architecture.* New York: Abrams, 1977.

Heer, Friedrich. *The Medieval World.* Cleveland: World Publishing, 1961.

Hoppin, Richard. *Medieval Music.* New York: Norton, 1977.

Kubach, Hans Erich. *Romanesque Architecture.* New York: Abrams, 1972.

Leff, Gordon. *Medieval Thought.* Baltimore: Penguin, 1958.

Lewis, C. S. *Allegory of Love.* London: Oxford University Press, 1936.

Male, Emile. *The Gothic Image.* New York: Harper, 1958.

Martingale, Andrew. *Giotto: Complete Paintings.* New York: Abrams, 1969.

Orton, C. W. Previte. *The Shorter Cambridge Medieval History.* London: Cambridge, 1952.

Panofsky, Erwin. *Gothic Architecture and Scholasticism.* Cleveland: World Publishing, 1957.

Pirenne, Henri. *Economic and Social History of Medieval Europe.* New York: Harper, 1937, (originally published in 1933).

Runciman, Steven. *A History of the Crusades.* 3 vols. London: Cambridge, 1951–1954.

Tuchman, Barbara. *A Distant Mirror: The Calamitous Fourteenth Century.* New York: Knopf, 1978.

Color Plate 3
Christ with Saint Vitalis, Saint Ecclesius, and angels.
c. 547 A.D. Apse mosaic, San Vitale, Ravenna. (Hirmer
Fotoarchiv, Munich.)

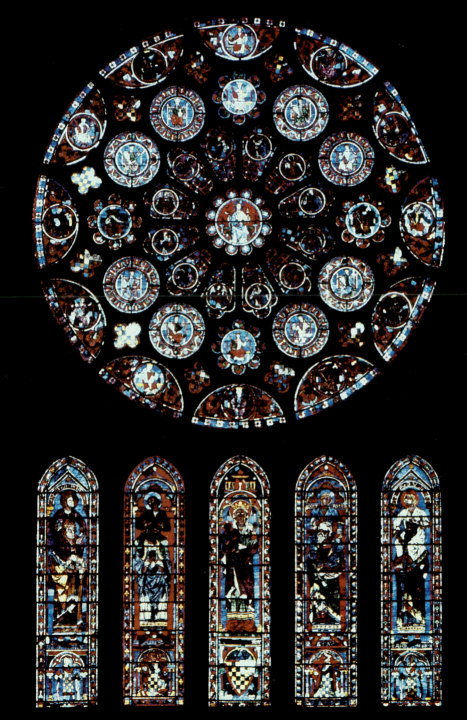

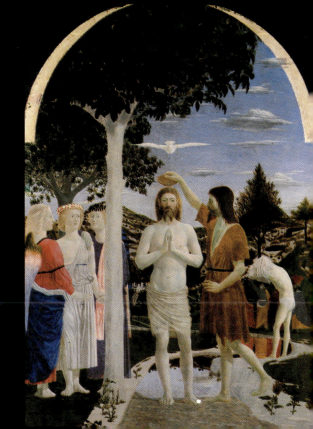

Color Plate 11
Pieter Brueghel. *Landscape with the Fall of Icarus.* c. 1554–1555. Oil on panel, 29 by 44⅛ inches. (Musées Royaux des Beaux-Arts, Brussels.)

Color Plate 12
Leonardo da Vinci. *Madonna of the Rocks.* c. 1485. Oil on panel, transferred to canvas, 78½ by 48 inches. (Louvre, Paris.)

Color Plate 13
Michelangelo Buonarrati. *Creation of Adam.* 1508–1512. Fresco.
Sistine Chapel, Vatican. (Scala/Art Resource.)

Color Plate 14
Raphael. *School of Athens*. Stanza della Segnatura, Vatican. 1509–1511.
Fresco, 25 feet 3 inches long. (Scala/Art Resource.)

Color Plate 19
Guido Reni. *Saint John the Baptist in the Wilderness.*
1640–1642. Oil on canvas, 88½ by 63¼ inches.
(Dulwich Picture Gallery, London.)

Color Plate 20
Michelangelo Merisi da Caravaggio. *Calling of Saint Matthew.*
c. 1597–1598. Oil on canvas, 11 feet 1 inch by 11 feet
5 inches. (Contarelli Chapel, San Luigi dei Francesi, Rome;
Scala/Art Resource.)

Color Plate 21
Nicolas Poussin. *Massacre of the Innocents.* 1630–1631. Oil on canvas,
57⅞ by 67¾ inches. (Musée Condé, Chantilly; Giraudon/Art Resource.)

Color Plate 22
Peter Paul Rubens. *Self-Portrait.* c. 1630. Oil on panel, 24½ by 17¾ inches. (Rubenshuis, Antwerp.)

Color Plate 23
Rembrandt van Rijn. *Self-Portrait Aged Sixty-Three.* 1657. Oil on canvas, 33⅞ by 27¾ inches. (National Gallery, London.)

Color Plate 24
Jean-Honoré Fragonard. *The Swing.* 1766. Oil on canvas, 32⅝ by 26 inches. (Wallace Collection, London.)

Color Plate 25
Antoine-Jean Gros. *Bonaparte at the Battle of Arcola.*
1796. Oil on canvas, 28¼ by 23¼ inches.
(Louvre, Paris.)

Color Plate 26
Théodore Géricault. *Portrait of the Chasseurs
Commanding a Charge.* 1812. Oil on canvas,
115 by 76⅛ inches. (Louvre, Paris.)

Color Plate 27
Francisco Goya. *The Third of May, 1808, at Madrid: The Shooting on Principe Rio Mountain.* 1814. Oil on canvas, 8 feet 8 inches by 11 feet 3⅞ inches. (Prado, Madrid.)

Color Plate 28
William Blake. *Elohim Creating Adam.* 1795. Color print and watercolor, 17 by 21⅛ inches. (Tate Gallery, London.)

Color Plate 29
John Constable. *The Hay Wain.* 1821. Oil on canvas, 51¼ by 73 inches. (National Gallery, London.)

Color Plate 30
J. M. W. Turner. *Rain, Steam, and Speed.* 1844. Oil on canvas, 35¾ by 48 inches. (National Gallery, London.)

Color Plate 31
Camille Corot. *A Farmyard in Fontainebleau.* c. 1860–1865. Oil on canvas, 12½ by 14⅓ inches. (Galerie Robert Schmit, Paris.)

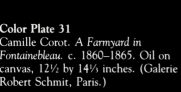

Color Plate 33
Claude Monet. *Impression, Sunrise.* 1872. Oil on canvas, 18⅓ by 25 inches. (Musée de Marmottan, Paris; Georges Routhier, Studio Lourmel; VAGA.)

Color Plate 34
Pierre-Auguste Renoir. *Luncheon of the Boating Party.* 1881. Oil on canvas, 51⅛ by 69¼ inches. (Phillips Collection, National Gallery, Washington.)

Color Plate 35
Paul Cézanne. *Mont Sainte-Victoire.* 1886–1887. Oil on canvas, 23½ by 28½
inches. (Phillips Collection, National Gallery, Washington.)

Color Plate 36
Vincent Van Gogh. *Sunflowers.* 1889. Oil on canvas, 37⅛ by 28¼ inches.
(Rijksmuseum, Amsterdam; Art Resource.)

Color Plate 39
Georges Rouault. *La Sainte Face.* 1933. Oil on paper, 36 by 26 inches. (Centre Pompidou, Paris; VAGA.)

Color Plate 40
Vasily Kandinsky. *Improvisation Number 30 (Warlike Theme).* 1913. Oil on canvas, 43¼ by 43¼ inches. (Art Institute of Chicago.)

Color Plate 41
Pablo Picasso. *Girl before a Mirror*. 1932. Oil on canvas, 64 by 51¼ inches. (Museum of Modern Art, New York; gift of Mrs. Simon Guggenheim.)

Color Plate 42
Giorgio di Chirico. *Mystery and Melancholy of a Street*. 1914. Oil on canvas, 34¾ by 28⅛ inches. (Private collection.)

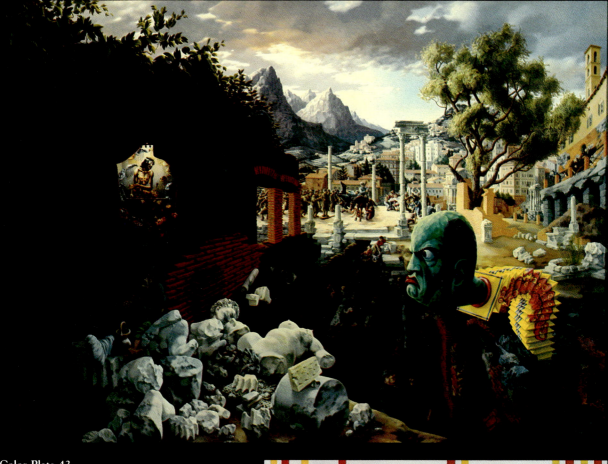

Color Plate 43
Peter Blume. *Eternal City.* 1937. Oil on
composition board, 34 by 47⅞ inches. (Museum of
Modern Art, New York; Mrs. Simon Guggenheim
Fund.)

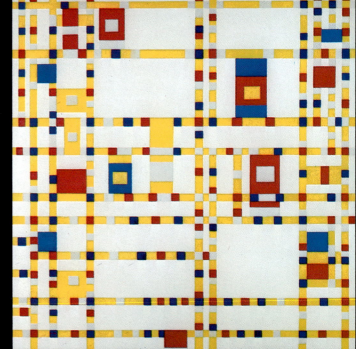

Color Plate 44
Piet Mondrian. *Broadway Boogie-Woogie.* 1943. Oil
on canvas, 50 by 50 inches. (Museum of Modern
Art, New York; given anonymously.)

Color Plate 45
Willem de Kooning. *Woman I.* 1950–1952. Oil on canvas, 75⅞ by 58
inches. (Museum of Modern Art, New York; purchase.)

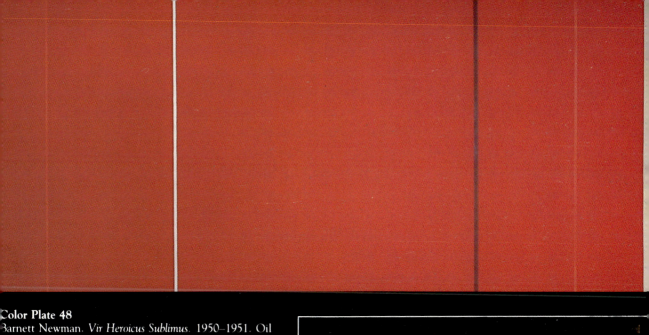

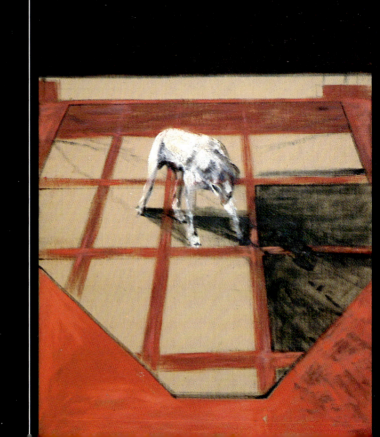

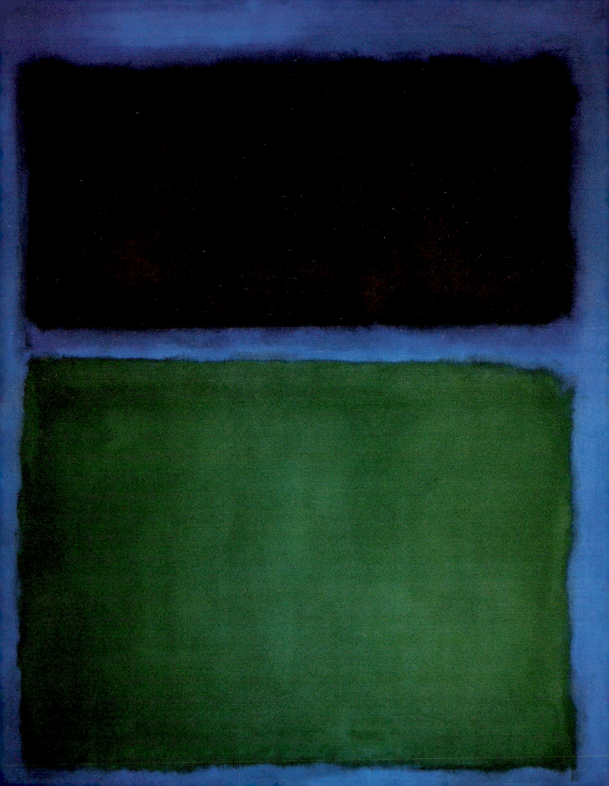

Color Plate 51
Roy Lichtenstein. *Whaam!* 1963.
Acrylic on canvas, 68 by 160
inches. (Tate Gallery, London;
VAGA.)

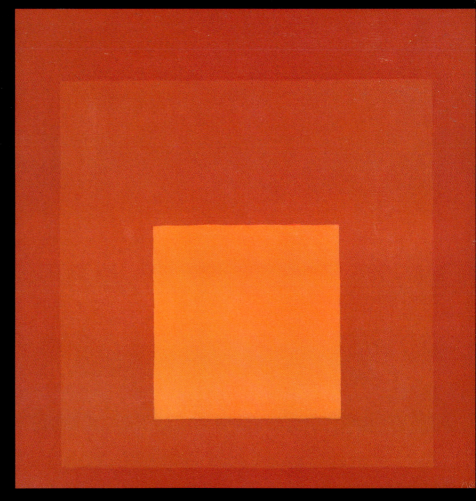

Color Plate 52
Josef Albers. *Homage to the Square: What You Want.* 1969. Oil on masonite,

Color Plate 53
Idelle Weber. *Gutter I.* 1974. Oil on canvas, about 54 by 32 inches. (Yale University Art Gallery; purchased with the aid of funds from the National Endowment for the Arts and the Susan Moore Hilles Matching Fund.)

Color Plate 54
Richard Estes. *Baby Doll Lounge.* 1978. Oil on canvas, 36 by 60 inches. (Courtesy of Mr. and Mrs. H. Christopher Brumder, New York; Allan Stone Gallery.)

PART FIVE

PART
FIVE

RENAISSANCE

REP

DUCHY OF
SAVOY

Bergamo

Milan   Brescia   **DUCHY OF
MILAN**

Piacenza

Turin

**REPUBLIC OF
GENOA**

Cremona

Genoa

Castelfranco

Vicenza

Mantua   Este

**DUCHY OF
MODENA**

Ferrara

Lucca   Modena

LUCCA

Pisa

**DUCHY
FERRA**

**REPUBLIC OF
FLORENCE**

Bologn

Vinci   Florence

Siena   Perugia

**REPUBLIC OF
SIENA**

CORSICA

SARDINIA

TYRRHRENIAN SEA

0   50   100   150   200 miles

THE RENAISSANCE: HUMANISM AND INDIVIDUALISM

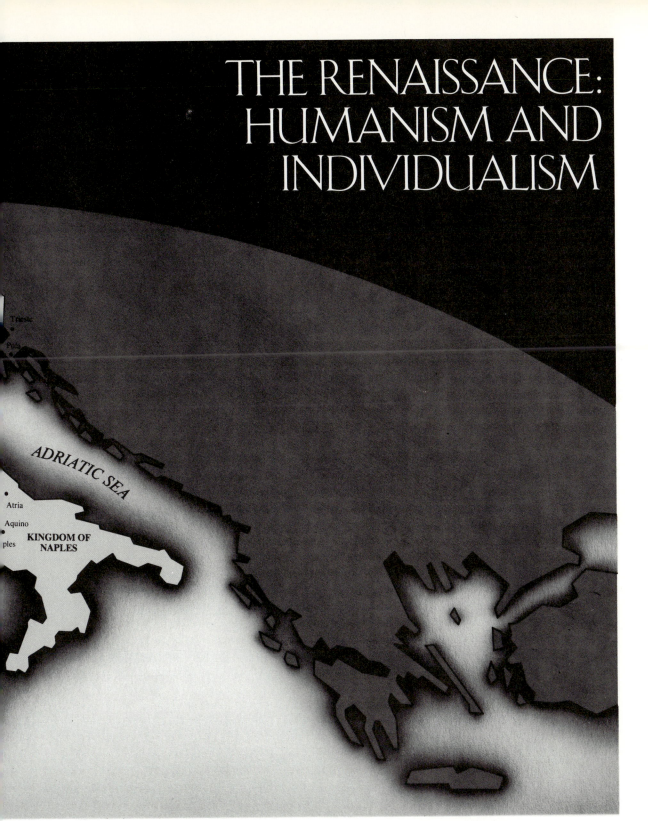

Italian humanism, which was based on an analysis of Greek texts preserved by Arab scholars, developed rapidly in the late fourteenth and early fifteenth centuries. Close ties with Islam helped Italian traders develop their cities into powerful states on the model of the Greek city-states, which were once plentiful in the area near the Mediterranean. Venice, with its protected islands, was particularly powerful, although Florence, as a result of the genius of its banking families, soon became an important rival.

In the north, trading was more difficult, and instead of city-states, powerful, centralized monarchies became the norm, particularly in France, England, Portugal, and Spain, which had only recently expelled the last of the Islamic invaders. When Constantinople finally fell to the Turks in 1453, Italy received a flood of Greek scholars, along with philosophical and scientific texts, which further spurred the development of the Platonic academies that had become the vogue. Ironically, this burst of inspiration also signaled the beginning of the end of Italian dominance, since the Turks would eventually limit Italian influence in the east.

The discovery of America in 1492 turned Europe's attention westward. The new world provided gold, silver, jewels, and other resources for Spain, Portugal, England, the Dutch states, and, to a lesser extent, France. The growing power of these states was based on an influx of wealth from the west, which also provided a haven for Europe's surplus population in the seventeenth century.

The early 1500s witnessed the decline of the authority of the church, largely because the temptations of wealth and power, particularly in Italy, were overwhelming. Dante and Chaucer had complained about corruption in the church; now Erasmus, Rabelais, and others became more vocal. Even Montaigne, who defended the church, could not stem the tide of change. Martin Luther, in 1517, published his Ninety-Five Theses demanding change and thus began the Protestant split in Christianity. This signaled a shift of power northward, a change in church policy (the Catholic church instituted many reforms), and a definite move toward individualism in terms of independence of thought and personal action. Luther's action came at a time when Europeans were shifting their concerns from religious matters to economic and worldly matters: Europe's newfound wealth was virtually intoxicating and produced a headiness and confidence that are often linked to the development of capitalism.

The expansion of political opportunities was paralleled by an expansion of genius in the arts. In a period of little more than 100 years, Leonardo da Vinci, Michelangelo Buonarotti,

Miguel de Cervantes, Francis Bacon, and William Shakespeare flourished. Of this group, Leonardo served the church minimally, Michelangelo served it mightily, and the rest can hardly be said to have served it at all. Shakespeare served neither church nor queen, but attempted to serve a wealthy patron; when that failed, he fell back on the theater. His successes were secular, pointing toward the eventual decline of both the church and the political court.

The Renaissance saw the church and the court grow together. The Papal States waged war to maintain secular power. The great developing nations demanded their own control over religious matters, as witnessed by England's establishment, under Henry VIII in 1534, of its own Protestant church. In the turmoil and excitement of change in the 1400s and 1500s, art, literature, music, architecture, and learning thrived. Almost all the affairs of humankind experienced the excitement of rebirth.

Brief Chronology

1401 Competition for the doors of the baptistry of Florence Cathedral.

1418 Brunelleschi begins the dome of Florence Cathedral.

1425 Early humanist academies established in Mantua and elsewhere in Italy.

c. 1440 Josquin des Prez born: greatest composer of his age.

1452 Ghiberti completes the "Gates of Paradise."

1453 The fall of Constantinople to the Turks; end of the Christian presence in the east.

1469 Beginning of the rule of Lorenzo de' Medici in Florence; period of great high cultural activity. Florentine academies flourishing under the guidance of Marsilio Ficino.

1471 Birth of Albrecht Dürer, German engraver and painter.

1475 Invention of printing with movable type by Johannes Gutenberg.

1485 Botticelli's *Birth of Venus* begun; Leonardo da Vinci's *Last Supper* begun.

1492 Discovery of America by Christopher Columbus, financed by Spain; Spain expels Islamic settlers (Moors) from its territories.

1494 Charles III of France tentatively invades Italy and meets with relatively little resistance. This is sometimes regarded as the beginning of modern military diplomacy.

1498   Savonarola, the great "revivalist" preacher, executed in Florence; end of a period of intense religious enthusiasm.

1509   Desiderius Erasmus' satire on religion and politics, *The Praise of Folly*; Raphael's *School of Athens*.

1512   Michelangelo finishes the Sistine ceiling.

1515   Machiavelli's treatise *The Prince:* advice to rulers on how to keep power, even by resorting to unethical or immoral behavior.

1516   Thomas More's *Utopia*, beginnings of a fantasy-travel literature spurred by explorations.

1517   Martin Luther's Ninety-Five Theses: beginnings of Protestantism and religious reform.

1521   Cortez completes the conquest of Mexico, the destruction of the Aztec and Incan civilizations.

1527   The sack of Rome by Charles V of France, spurring counterattacks by Pope Julius, patron of Michelangelo.

1534   Jesuit order established by Ignatius of Loyola; the Church of England established by Henry VIII; Protestantism spreads in northern Europe.

1545–1546   The Council of Trent reacts to the spread of Protestantism; makes recommendations in arts and other areas for the conduct and aims of the church; begins the Counterreformation.

1550   Giorgio Vasari's *Lives of the Most Eminent Painters, Sculptors, and Architects,* our greatest source of knowledge of the artists of the period.

1552   Last of the first four books of *Gargantua and Pantagruel* published a year before Rabelais's death. Edmund Spenser born, wrote *The Faerie Queene*.

1564   Born: Christopher Marlowe, William Shakespeare, and Galileo Galilei.

1572   Saint Batholomew's Day massacre: a mob-action "religious war" centering in Paris, persecuting Protestant Huguenots.

1579   Palladio's Teatro Olympico, first indoor theater in Europe.

1580   Michel de Montaigne's *Essays*.

1588   England defeats the Spanish armada, securing itself for Protestantism and signaling its ambition for conquest in the new world.

1589   Thoinot Arbeau's *Orchésographie*, important early book on dance.

c. 1596   Shakespeare's *Romeo and Juliet*.

c. 1601   Shakespeare's *Hamlet*.

CHAPTER 11

THE ITALIAN RENAISSANCE: THE RISE OF HUMANISM, 1375 TO 1500

Expansion and Change

 The most exciting developments of the Renaissance were well under way in the medieval period, and we must think in terms of a continuity from one age to the next, rather than an abrupt ending of one and the beginning of the other. The Renaissance church was weakened by internal corruption; secular government became more centralized and powerful; and the economy, which was slowly being strangled in the east, took advantage of the unusual discoveries in the Americas. In addition to these factors we must consider the love of classical learning and the respect for classical values which give the Renaissance its distinctive flavor. All these things (with the exception of the discovery of the Americas) were present in the medieval period, but as seeds. They flowered in the Renaissance.

There were two distinct trends in political developments. In the north, kingdoms began to centralize power and to dominate large geographic masses containing many cities. Italy, however, produced a host of brilliant city-states that competed with one another in politics, art, thought, and finance. The most important of these in the Renaissance was Florence, which produced Donatello, Verrocchio, Leonardo, Michelangelo, Machiavelli, and the great Medici princes. Rome, the Papal State, was also influential and wielded a growing secular power. The papacy had moved to Avignon, France, in the 1300s, but by the 1400s it had returned, differences settled, to Rome. Venice, Milan, and Naples were all mighty trading states and were most dependent on connections with the east through Islam and the lucrative spice trade. Short on resources, the Italian traders demonstrated a financial expertise that made them powerful.

The loss of the eastern Christian empire, whose fate was sealed by the fall of Constantinople in 1453, when it was taken by the Turks, sent survivors of the Greek academies scurrying to Italy, where they tried to continue their traditions. The Turks were much less willing to tolerate Italian domination of trade, and gradually they began choking it off. The Italians maintained contact with Islam, and some scholars, such as Pico della Mirandola, were thoroughly conversant in Arabic. However, the pressures of Islam on European traders led Christopher Columbus, of Genoa, to seek a different route to China and India. Ironically, he found a new world which would turn out to have a greater influence on Europe than he had ever expected. However, it was a world which would ultimately shift power away from Italy.

Architecture and Sculpture

BRUNELLESCHI AND GHIBERTI: THE BAPTISTRY DOORS

The competitive spirit of the Renaissance, as well as its ebullience and its optimism, is obvious in the excitement generated by the competition for the commission to do a series of relief sculptures for the doors of the Florence Cathedral baptistry. The power of mercantile interests, which had grown throughout the Middle Ages everywhere in Europe, is also evident in the fact that the competition was underwritten by the guilds, powerful associations of merchants who traded in the same kinds of goods and who promoted their own well-being by regulating trade and governing admission to their ranks.

The date of the competition, 1401, is often cited as the beginning of the Renaissance explosion in art. The Calimari Wool Finishers Guild, which was rich and influential, set the best artists of the area to work to produce a pair of doors 15 feet high, 8 feet wide, and weighing over 10 tons. Twenty-eight scenes from the life of Christ would be supplemented by panels decorated with representations of the evangelists, the principal fathers of the church, and the heads of prophets, as well as other designs.

The guild demanded that interested sculptors, goldsmiths, and founders submit a trial panel in bronze telling the story of Abraham's sacrifice of his son Isaac. The finalists were Filippo Brunelleschi (1377–1446) and Lorenzo Ghiberti (c. 1378–1455); after some debate, Ghiberti's panel was chosen. Thus the most important artistic commission of the times was given to an artist in his early twenties; Ghiberti would devote most of his life to these and other doors of the baptistry.

The competition panels have been preserved and can be seen in the Bargello museum in Florence.

Figure 11-1
Above: Lorenzo Ghiberti. Competition relief for baptistry doors, Florence. 1401. Gilded bronze, 12 by 17 inches. (Museo Nazionale del Bargello, Firenze; photo, Alinari/Art Resource.)

Figure 11-2
Below: Filippo Brunelleschi. Competition relief for baptistry doors, Florence. 1401. Gilded bronze, 12 by 17 inches. (Museo Nazionale del Bargello, Firenze; photo, Alinari/Art Resource.)

Competition Panels—Brunelleschi and Ghiberti

1. Which of the panels shown in Figures 11-1 and 11-2 places most of the action in the center of the space? What action takes place outside the center? Is centrally placed action more or less dynamic?

2. In which panel is the tension of the moment more arresting? Which makes you more aware that a life is possibly about to be lost? What elements convince you of this?

3. The guild which underwrote the competition specified that the same figures had to appear on each panel. What are they? Which panel shows a greater influence of the Greek male nude?

4. Which panel seems more three-dimensional? Is it also the more realistic or representational panel?

5. Which panel is more horizontally "layered" from bottom to top, in the manner of the Persian miniature? Which panel gives more of an illusion of distance and receding space?

Ghiberti and Brunelleschi were goldsmiths and had considerable experience in casting. Ghiberti's panel (Figure 11-1) was chosen in part because it was cast in one piece; Brunelleschi's (Figure 11-2) consisted of several pieces bolted together. Ghiberti's high finish, careful detailing, and polishing of the surface also impressed the guild.

Comparing these panels helps us understand the new attitude toward style that developed in the Renaissance. The frame, called a "quatrefoil," was determined by preexisting panels on an earlier door. Ghiberti's panel at once seems cleaner and less cluttered. Brunelleschi weights the bottom of his panel with figures that fill the space between the edges of the frame. He shows three levels of action: the lower level, with the ass and the servants; the central level, with the lamb, Isaac, and Abraham; and the upper level, with the angel and some foliage. These levels remain distinct, with the action occurring at the top center of each one; however the absolute center of the panel, where Isaac's torso is placed, is barren of action. The angel, shown in profile from the left, saves Isaac at the last possible moment.

Ghiberti's panel has a three-part organization as well, but a different division of space. By avoiding the horizontal, three-layered approach, he achieves greater unity. The servants and the ass occupy the lower-left-hand corner; a mountainous form swoops up to separate them from Abraham and Isaac, whose bodies echo its curve. The fully modeled nude of Isaac is a masterpiece of classical allusion. Brunelleschi's version of Isaac is more pained, less serene. Finally, the angel above enters not in profile, but at a sharp angle; this gives Ghiberti a chance to show off his skill in foreshortening, which accounts for the apparent visual distortions of the figure coming directly at us.

By avoiding a central composition (no action occurs in the center), Ghiberti leads the eye rapidly from the figures in the lower left to the upper right, while the smooth mountainous rill leads the eye upward again from the lower right to the upper left. The rhythms are subtler in Ghiberti's panel than in Brunelleschi's.

Ghiberti's panel is more avant-garde. Brunelleschi relies on old formulas: the upward motion of action seen in illuminated books, in which distant figures do not diminish in size. Ghiberti's mountainous rill solves that problem: it permits placing the servants and the ass farther from us than Abraham and Isaac; the angel is farther still, and smaller. Ghiberti's version is more dynamic, more dramatic, more realistic, and more daring.

The panels on the north door of the Florence Cathedral baptistry were cast using the lost-wax process; in this process, a wax model is packed in clay, and then molten bronze is poured into the clay, replacing the wax. Each panel is one piece, but they are hollow and therefore were difficult to finish properly. Ghiberti spent twenty years on the north door (Figure 11-3). His contract called for him to do the casting, finishing, carving, chiseling, and polishing with his own hands. When everything was ready, each panel was burnished in gold. The entire door radiates a golden magnificence that testifies to the material ambitions of the Calimari guild. Two of the panels are shown in Figures 11-4 and 11-5.

Figure 11-4
Above: Lorenzo Ghiberti. North door, nativity scene. (Photo, Scala/Art Resource.)

Figure 11-5
Below: Lorenzo Ghiberti. North door, baptism of Christ. (Photo, Alinari/Art Resource.)

Figure 11-3
Below: Lorenzo Ghiberti. North door of the baptistry, Florence. c. 1425. 17 feet high.

The North Door of the Baptistry

1. Which sculptures in Figures 11-4 and 11-5 are most clearly influenced by classical sculpture?

2. How does the modeling of the nude figures compare with that of the figure of Isaac in Ghiberti's competition panel (Figure 11-1)? How does it compare with the modeling in Brunelleschi's panel (Figure 11-2)?

3. Is the expression of human emotion a significant concern in the north door panels? What emotions do you feel are portrayed in these works?

4. Is either of the north door panels shown in Figures 11-4 and 11-5 more heavily weighted in the center than Ghiberti's competition panel? What differences do you see between these three panels?

5. Describe how the eye "reads" the north door panels. Where does it alight first? Where does it move to? Where does it rest?

When he had finished the north door, Ghiberti was commissioned to do the remaining doors (Figure 11-6), which took him twenty-four years. He abandoned the quatrefoil design in favor of a simpler, more open design: ten panels approximately 30 inches square, narrating Old Testament themes. These panels are centralized in composition and have a symmetrical balance that makes them more serene and less dynamic than his competition panel. But the classical nude is more in evidence; the figures are realistic and are carefully modeled. The "new" penchant for including meticulously drawn architectural details in the design helps suggest distance and space. Ghiberti's drama intensifies the value of human action, a quality central to Renaissance thought.

Figure 11-6
Lorenzo Ghiberti. "Gates of Paradise," baptistry, Florence. 1425–1452. 17 feet high. (Photo, Alinari/Art Resource.)

FILIPPO BRUNELLESCHI: ARCHITECT

Brunelleschi, the loser of the Calimari guild competition, took things badly; he and Ghiberti worked on projects together but are said to have been quarrelsome and competitive. Yet after a sojourn in Rome, Brunelleschi returned to triumph as the first important architect of the early Renaissance. By the time the Commission of Works in Florence was ready to begin the final stages of the Florence Cathedral, started in the 1300s, Brunelleschi had developed a reputation for architectural inventiveness.

The Commission of Works held a competition for the commission to do the dome of the cathedral in 1418. The building is a traditional basilica, with a high main aisle and lower side aisles. It has long, narrow gothic windows and gothic buttresses below the dome. The rounded windows of the clerestory, repeated in the drum below the curving section of the dome, are romanesque, like the repeated half-round tribunes beneath the drum. They stand there partly to support what would have been a typical low-round romanesque dome.

Brunelleschi won the competition by avoiding costly scaffolding on the exterior of the dome during construction. This was a revolutionary concept, and so a masonry model was constructed to confirm the workability of Brunelleschi's theories. Because the dome had to be self-supporting while being built, its shape was altered from a romanesque low-round form to a high, pointed form with an oculus (opening) surmounted by a tall lantern, which increased the light inside (Figure 11-7). Its colossal size and novel form make it the focal point of the Florentine landscape (Figure 11-8).

Vasari said:

> How beautiful this building is. . . . It may be confidently affirmed that the ancients never carried their buildings to so vast a height, nor committed themselves to so great a risk as to dare competition with the heavens, which this structure verily appears to do, seeing that it rears itself to such an elevation that the hills around Florence do not appear to equal it.

Brunelleschi cannot be fully understood by observing only his masterful dome. San Spirito was begun "in accordance with his intentions," according to

Figure 11-7
Santa Maria del Fiore, the cathedral of Florence, exterior. 1420 –1436.

Vasari; and while it is obviously more modest than the Florence Cathedral, its proportions reveal Brunelleschi's skill as a mathematician. The front (Figure 11-9), with its three doors and circular window and its gracefully curved facade rising to the upper story, was imitated widely. It helped revive Roman styles, as did the interior (Figure 11-10), with its Roman arches and pillars.

Classical influences dominate the Hospital of the Innocents (Figure 11-11), which Brunelleschi designed in 1419. The regularity of this building is a signal of a new age. The repetitions of the arches create a calming rhythm. The Roman pillars are spaced apart by the exact measure of their height, and therefore the arch, rising half the height of the pillars, surmounts a square space. The round sculpture above each pillar is by Luca Della Robbia (1399 or 1400–1482), who invented a technique for making glazed terra-cotta figures of considerable durability and popularity.

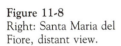

Figure 11-8
Right: Santa Maria del Fiore, distant view.

Figure 11-9
Below: Filippo Brunelleschi. San Spirito, Florence, exterior. Began 1444. (Photo, Alinari/Art Resource.)

Figure 11-10
Left: Filippo Brunelleschi. San Spirito, Florence, interior. (Photo, Alinari/Art Resource.)

Figure 11-11
Below: Filippo Brunelleschi. Hospital of the Innocents, facade. 1419.

DONATELLO: REBIRTH OF SCULPTURE

Sculpture had been attached to churches for so long that the ancient tradition of freestanding sculpture in the round had to be reinvented. Donatello (c. 1386–1466) worked with Ghiberti and traveled to Rome with Brunelleschi. In 1411 he began to create sculpture for the niches in the wall of the church of Orsanmichele, in Florence, and he demonstrated at once an imagination that pointed in new directions.

The move to freestanding sculpture did not come immediately. Donatello's marble *David* (Figure 11-12) was intended to be part of a cathedral, and therefore it had only one proper vantage point: the front. However, it was never installed on the cathedral; instead, it was placed in a public square. David had become the symbol of Florence, and when foreign emissaries visited the city, it was useful for them to see reminders of its reputation. David stands with feet spread apart and body leaning slightly forward—a confident pose. The face is idealized, and the garment, which is smooth and simple, is less important than the body within.

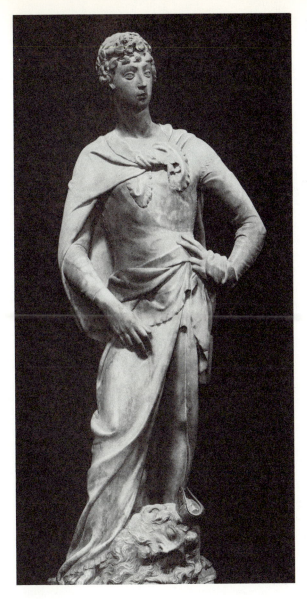

Figure 11-12
Donatello. *David*. 1408. Marble, 75 ½ inches high.
(Museo Nazionale del Bargello, Firenze; photo,
Alinari/Art Resource.)

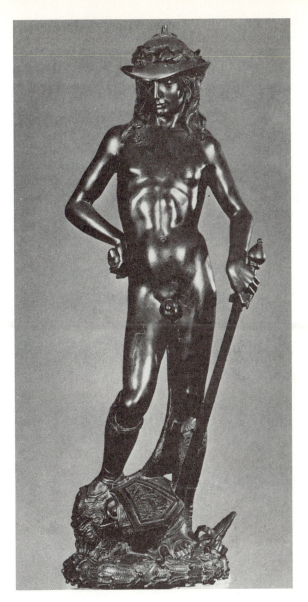

Figure 11-13
Donatello. *David*. 1430–1432. Bronze, 62 ¼ inches
high. (Museo Nazionale del Bargello, Firenze; photo,
Alinari/Art Resource.)

Donatello's bronze *David* (Figure 11-13) is one of the most important sculptures of the Renaissance. Commissioned privately, it ended serving a public purpose. Not only is this the first freestanding sculpture since Roman times, but it is also the first one cast in bronze. The bronze *David* is exceptional because it must be seen from several angles; even from the back it is interesting. David stands with one foot on Goliath's head, beneath which is a triumphal wreath. Yet his face expresses no identifiable emotion, certainly not that of triumph. The body, not yet that of a fully developed athlete, expresses youthful energy. This is a refreshing, immediate young David in the first flush of success.

Medieval sculptors had avoided freestanding pieces for the same reason they had sometimes destroyed ancient Roman statuary when it was found: it suggested the idolatry of the pagans. Once Donatello revived the tradition, dozens of sculptors followed him. This is one example of the way in which classical humanist traditions captured the imagination of Renaissance artists.

Late in his career, in 1455, when he had been away for a decade and had come to be regarded as old-fashioned, Donatello created a wooden statue for the baptistry in Florence: *Mary Magdalene*, one of his most personal pieces (Figure 11-14). The face is neither idealized nor recognizable as a portrait. The surface is textured, almost undulating, and the posture is that of a supplicant. The Magdalene is on the verge of insanity, having endured a solitary journey in the desert. Seeing the work today, set in an evenly lighted area, one senses a vitality pointing to achievements yet to come in sculpture. The statue is 6 feet 2 inches tall. This old, wasted woman, waiting to be rejoined with God, is deliberately not beautiful, and yet she is compelling and powerful.

Figure 11-14
Donatello. *Mary Magdalene*. Florence, baptistry. 1455. Wood, 6 feet 2 inches high.

PERCEPTION KEY

Donatello

1. Read the story of David and Goliath in the Bible (1 Samuel: 17). Does the head of Goliath seem more appropriately formidable in the marble version (Figure 11-12) or the bronze version (Figure 11-13) of the *David?* Which *David* seems more faithful to the Bible story?

2. Does either version make David seem more military? Does either version make him seem more like a mere citizen?

3. How does the later *Mary Magdalene* (Figure 11-14) compare with Donatello's early work? Is it more or less realistic? More or less classical? More or less idealized? Does it have a more or less clear emotional center? Does the *Magdalene* seem more or less personal to you? What qualities support your view? Is the *Magdalene* more natural, more human, than the two sculptures of David?

4. Freestanding sculpture takes a different attitude toward space from that of a work attached to a building. Space is "cut into" by a freestanding work. Which of Donatello's works makes the most use of the space between it and the viewer?

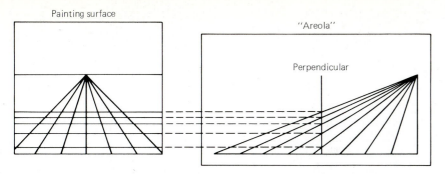

Figure 11-15
Leon Battista Alberti. Perspective chart. (From Leon Battista Alberti. *On Painting and on Sculpture*. London: Phaidon, 1972. Originally published in 1435.)

Painting

ALBERTI AND THE DEVELOPMENT OF PERSPECTIVE

One of the critical discoveries of Renaissance painting was the vanishing-point perspective, a technique that permitted Renaissance painters to create works on a two-dimensional surface that imply a three-dimensional space. Use of the vanishing-point perspective made possible the illusion of deep space and a realism that was new to painting.

Brunelleschi, through his studies of mathematics and Roman architecture, invented the technique. Leon Battista Alberti (1404–1472)—a distinguished architect, poet, painter, playwright, and musician— credited Brunelleschi with having discovered vanishing-point perspective in his book *On Painting* (1435 in Latin; 1436 in Italian), which he translated so that Brunelleschi could read it. Alberti's treatise popularized Brunelleschi's technique, and Renaissance painters developed a number of startling approaches to three-dimensional space. (A perspective chart by Alberti is shown in Figure 11-15).

MASACCIO

Masaccio (Tommaso di Giovanni de Simone Guidi, 1401–1428) knew both Donatello and Brunelleschi, and although he lived to be only twenty-seven, he left works of distinction in Rome and Florence. His fresco in Santa Maria Novella (Figure 11-16) creates the illusion of space receding away from us. Masaccio uses Brunelleschi's technique, in which imaginary lines are drawn to a vanishing point—here, it is just below the feet of Christ, at the eye level of the viewer.

The architecture in the painting helps achieve a sense of real space, as does the modeled roundness of the figures, who are painted as if they were three-dimensional sculptures. The impossible conjunction of modern architecture and the crucifixion of Christ was not bothersome to Masaccio's contemporaries: it was thought to be a reasonable liberty. Another liberty appears in the portraits of the two donors near the Roman pilasters: they are buried in the tomb beneath the fresco.

In 1427 Masaccio painted several frescoes in the Brancacci Chapel in Santa Maria del Carmine, in Florence. Some of the paintings in the tiny chapel are by Masolino and Filippino, but in comparison with these, the six by Masaccio are moving in a new direction. They are narratives of the lives of Adam and Eve, Christ, and in particular Saint Peter. In *The Tribute Money* (Figure 11-17), the vanishing point is at the head of Christ; the narrative is continuous, and there are several focal points. Saint Peter, on the far left, catches the fish that Christ has told him will have a coin in its mouth for the tax collector. In the group of apostles he appears again, at the left of center and pointing to the left, after Christ has told him to catch the fish. To the right he appears again, handing the coin to the tax collector.

Figure 11-16
Left: Masaccio. *Holy Trinity.* Santa Maria Novella, Florence. 1428. Fresco, 21 feet 10 ½ inches by 10 feet 5 inches. (Photo, Alinari/Art Resource.)

Figure 11-17
Below: Masaccio. *The Tribute Money.* Brancacci Chapel, Chiesa del Carmine, Florence. 1427. Fresco. (Photo, Alinari/Art Resource.)

Masaccio

1. Are any of the figures in Masaccio's paintings (Figures 11-16 and 11-17) influenced by the sculptures of Donatello?

2. How does the representation of architectural details within these paintings help achieve a sense of three-dimensional space?

3. Place tracing paper over *The Tribute Money* and draw lines from Christ's head (the vanishing point) to the outer corners of the painting. How do architectural and other angular lines conform with the lines you have drawn?

4. Using the tracing paper, draw in the primary vertical lines of people, trees, and building; then draw the lines of the important angles, such as the outstretched arms of Saint Peter, Christ, and the tax collector. How do these rhythms of line help give the composition a dynamic quality?

5. Masaccio is said to have taken up where Giotto left off (sixty years earlier). What comparisons can you make between the two painters in terms of three-dimensional space, modeling of figures, and realism of representation? Use *The Tribute Money* and Giotto's *Raising of Lazarus* (Figure 10-21) for your comparison.

PIERO DELLA FRANCESCA

Piero della Francesca (c. 1420–1492) knew the work of the great Florentines of the period, although he worked primarily in Urbino and Ferrara. *The Baptism of Christ* (Color Plate 8), painted on a wood panel in about 1450, was probably intended to fit into an existing architectural space in a church in Borgo San Sepulchro, Piero's hometown. Awareness of geometric shape is characteristic of Piero's work: he insisted on mathematical control of space and figures. In *The Baptism of Christ* the colors are pale and delicate, the figures are modeled by light and shadow, and the ambiguity of the source of light adds to the mystery of the painting. Christ stands at the center, forming a line that could divide the work in two; the tree next to him divides the panel into two unequal spaces. To the left and rear are an angel and two figures in classical garb; to the right is Saint John, and behind him is another person about to be baptized. The meandering river is offered as a counterpoint to the rigid vertical divisions.

The smaller *Flagellation of Christ* (Figure 11-18), painted around 1460, is sharply divided into separate spaces; three richly clothed figures appear in the right foreground, while the main action occurs at the left. The smallest figure in the composition is the most important. The architectural divisions of space take on a great importance in the composition, as do the light and dark divisions of the floor and the divisions of the ceiling over Christ: one subject of the painting is the division of visual space, which presents us with an interesting (and modern) conflict. The flagellation of Christ is certainly part of the subject matter of the painting, but the formal elements of the work—the way the architectural lines divide the space and the way the figures are grouped—are so demanding that they are equal in importance to the flagellation. In this painting the tension between the subject and the formal elements leads to basic questions about what Piero is doing: Is form subservient to subject, or is it dominant? Is this a realistic, three-dimensional painting, or is it a two-dimensional iconic representation of an idea?

It appears that the geometric, spatial technique is more important to Piero than the reality of the scene. If it is true that the form of the painting is taking

Figure 11-18
Piero della Francesca. *Flagellation of Christ.* After 1460. 23 by 32 inches. (Galleria Nazionale della Marche, Ducal Palace, Urbino; Soprintendenza per i beni artistici e storici delle Marche, Urbino.)

command, then we can understand why such a horrible scene as the flagellation of Christ is presented with such detachment, such calm. Piero does not want us to become engaged on a superficial emotional level; he wants us to understand the meaning of Christ's suffering intellectually, coolly. He is painting not an event, but an idea; by controlling our emotional responses, he reaches deeper into our intellectual life. The mathematical balance of forms, the careful control, and the balance of colors are all intended to control and focus emotion, not just to stimulate it.

ANTONIO POLLAIUOLO

The *Martyrdom of St. Sebastian* of Antonio Pallaiuolo (c. 1431–1498) (Figure 11-19) places the viewer on the same level as Saint Sebastian. Perspective is apparent not in the architecture, but in the landscape, and the figures in the distance are placed so as to produce the illusion of receding space. The figures in the foreground depend on natural rises in the land to differentiate them, forming an interesting geometric shape beneath Saint Sebastian. The basic triangular form used to organize the composition is apparent in the line drawing shown in Figure 11-20. The effect of such a powerful, basic form can be complex and unpredictable, but here it creates an extraordinary stability for a composition with many diverse elements. The executioners are active, and their faces are interesting; without such a powerful organizing form, they might scatter the focus of the painting. Even the arrows in Saint Sebastian's body help create a triangular shape—the shape of an arrowhead; it is as if the composition were pointing Sebastian toward heaven.

Figure 11-19
Left: Antonio Pollaiuolo. *Martyrdom of Saint Sebastian.* 1475. Tempera on panel, 114 ¾ by 79 ¾ inches. (National Gallery, London.)

Figure 11-20
Above right: Line drawing of Pollaiuolo's *Martyrdom of Saint Sebastian.*

RENAISSANCE PORTRAITS

Portraits such as those shown in Figures 11-21, 11-22, and 11-23 contain no narrative or architectonic details to distract us. We can relate to these faces on a personal level. They show a natural inquisitiveness, as if we, the viewers, were being studied.

All these portraits are strikingly realistic, although there is a distinct austerity to the powerful interpretation of the doge by Giovanni Bellini (1430–1516). There is no setting here (Figure 11-23) beyond the serene azure background, and the only local details are in the intricate workings of the gold and white clothing and in the doge's Venetian cap. He is a man of immense dignity and power; Bellini portrays him as maintaining a distance. The coolness of the colors—

blue, gold, and white—and the impassive expression contribute to the emotional aloofness of the work.

A condottiere (Figure 11-21) is a military figure, an elected official, but not a great leader. The condottiere of Antonello da Messina (c. 1430–1479) is young, handsome, and athletic; he is also clear-eyed, intelligent, and curious. Antonello is known as one of the finest portrait painters of the period; he took a keen interest in examining his sitters closely and projecting their personalities.

The most informal of the portraits shown here is probably the study of an old man and a boy by Domenico Ghirlandajo (1449–1494). The man, who has a diseased nose, has never been identified. The lower part of the painting (Figure 11-22) is domi-

Figure 11-21
Above left: Antoniello da Messina. *The Condottiere.*
1475. Panel painting, about 14 by 15 inches. (Louvre, Paris; photo, Musées Nationaux.)

Figure 11-22
Above right: Domenico Ghirlandajo. *Old Man and Boy.*
c. 1480. Panel painting, 24 by 18 inches. (Louvre, Paris; photo, Musées Nationaux.)

Figure 11-23
Left: Giovanni Bellini. *The Doge Leonardo Loredan.*
c. 1501. Panel painting, 24 ¼ by 17 ¾ inches. (National Gallery, London.)

nated by intense, red clothing; the upper part includes a stylized landscape suggesting a peaceful countryside. The triangular composition formed by the man and the boy is curiously offset by the rectangular window, which has its own triangular structures. The tenderness of the scene is due largely to the fact that the artist has established a relationship between the figures—a grandfather and his grandson.

Renaissance Portraits

1. Which of the portraits shown in Figures 11-21, 11-22, and 11-23 is most realistic? Which seems best to communicate the essence of the sitter?

2. Bellini portrays a doge—the ruler of one of the most powerful states in Italy. Is the doge more commanding than the other figures? Does Bellini make him grand or play down his importance?

3. Which portrait is most informal? Does informality imply more or less realism?

4. Make a simplified line drawing of the portrait that you feel relies most on geometric patterning for its organization. What is the relationship between the form and the emotion portrayed in the face?

5. Which portrait shows the greatest concern for the individual, rather than his office or his social station? Do any of the faces seem "familiar" to you?

SANDRO BOTTICELLI: ALLEGORY OF HUMANISM

Italian humanists—scholars of classical texts who relied on Plato—asserted that Greek and Roman myths were incomplete versions of Christian truths. They resuscitated Pan, and even Venus, by insisting that physical love was an allegory of spiritual love.

Sandro Botticelli (1445–1510) achieved a memorable allegorical synthesis in two great paintings, *Primavera* ("Spring"; Color Plate 9) and *The Birth of Venus* (Figure 11-24). *Primavera,* which was painted for the Medici family, possibly with an eye toward Lorenzo's marriage, is one of the largest secular paintings of the period. Its subject is the eternal spring of Venus's garden of the Hesperides. Venus, modestly draped, is in the center of the composition, radiant against the foliage. The light source is multiple and mysterious; Cupid, like a baby angel above her, is about to shoot his dart. On the left the three graces perform a classical dance; their beauty is chaste, almost intellectual. Holding back the clouds with his hand, Mercury seems ready to make an announcement. Flora, to the right, distributes spring flowers, all painted with great accuracy from nature. One disturbing note is the figure of Chloris, who is about to be raped by Zephyr, the wind god. According to myth, flowers issued from Chloris's mouth in

tribute to her fertility, and Zephyr, regretting his forceful ways, married her and made her a goddess.

The carnal celebration of love, and possibly marriage, would not be clear to anyone who did not know the myth, the subject of the painting. Even the passion of Zephyr is shown only in Chloris's alarmed expression. The detachment of the other figures suggests that all is well; calmness and beauty dominate the scene. The colors are rich; the oranges overhead represent the golden apples of Atalanta, symbols of fertility. The entire emphasis is on fruitfulness, propriety, and a cool kind of divinity.

Conventional emotions are not portrayed in *Primavera,* because it is an allegory of divine activity as it relates to modern Christian life. It takes its inspiration from interpretations of Ovid and other classical authors, relying on commentaries by Marsilio Ficino, whose work aimed to revive Plato. Mercury, a powerful figure in the painting, is famed for spreading the sacred mysteries and is the guiding spirit of texts interpreting the works of classical authors (terms derived from his Greek name, Hermes, include the Hermetic mysteries and hermeneutics, the decipherment of difficult texts). Botticelli used him to signal the mysteries in *Primavera.*

The Birth of Venus is more daring. Venus is nude (although she covers herself chastely with her long hair) in a pose called "contrapposto." Her figure has been traced to classical sources, and the event to classical poetry. Like *Primavera,* this painting is large and was probably intended for a country villa, where the delights of nature, the celebration of fruitfulness, and the pleasures of daily life were a welcome change from the rigors of business and duty in the city.

The Birth of Venus has been described as the most beautiful painting of the Renaissance and as the most radiant painting in European history. The colors are pale and subtle; the line is strong, but not obtrusive. The sense of motion is caught in Zephyr, who clasps Chloris at the left, and in Hour (the attendant), who rushes in with a cloak at the right; both contrast with the ease of Venus, who is at rest. The water wafts the shell ashore; everything beyond the principal figures is simplified. The trees are schematic, and the shore to the right undulates toward the horizon.

Venus's unawareness of the viewer sets her apart from daily life. Ovid's *Metamorphoses* and the Homeric hymns provided Botticelli with the details he needed. Yet Venus's face is human and tender; her body has been described as a hymn to perfection. She

is one of the first Renaissance nudes. *The Birth of Venus* is an allegory of idealized human love, just as *Primavera* is an allegory of idealized divine love.

The scallop shell, like Flora's scattered flowers, is a symbol of the fruitfulness of the world now that Venus is here. It reminds us that nature worships beauty no less than we do. Such a reminder would have been particularly warming to the owner of a country villa, as a reassurance that the lust for beautiful things had a parallel in nature itself.

The space in the painting is relatively shallow. The figures are rounded, but the important space is the surface, the frontal plane. Venus is placed just off-center, to the right of the canvas; this prevents the composition from being static. The curves of her pose echo the curves of the flowery cloak and of Hour's garments. The curves of the scallop shell reinforce the curves of her body. The rigidity of the trees contrasts with Venus's form; their leaves seem to reach out for her, as if to redeem their stiffness. Even the cattails in the lower-left-hand corner bend toward her while Zephyr wafts her ashore.

Figure 11-24
Sandro Botticelli. *Birth of Venus.* 1486. Canvas, 9 feet ¼ inch by 5 feet 6 ¾ inches.
(Galleria degli Uffizi, Firenze; photo, Alinari/Art Resource.)

Botticelli's Primavera and Birth of Venus

1. In classical mythology, Venus was the goddess who could seduce Zeus whenever she wished. Only three divinities, all women, could resist her. She was a symbol of sexual pleasure. How has Botticelli's interpretation (Figure 11-24) kept that aspect of her "history" under control? What has Botticelli done visually to make the myth palatable to Christians?

2. What tensions are apparent in Figure 11-24 as a result of the conflict between Venus's sexuality and Christian modesty and repression of sensuality?

3. Does either Figure 11-24 or Color Plate 9 (*Primavera*) reveal a new attitude toward sensuality, perhaps an acceptance of sensual pleasures? Compare Botticelli's modeling of figures with that of Piero, Masaccio, or any other painter discussed in this chapter. Do any of these painters limit their paintings' sensual pleasures in ways that Botticelli does not?

4. Venus is a neo-Platonic allegory of the gifts of God. All the figures in Botticelli's paintings are mythical; none is human. How, then, can the interpretation of such a myth be said to be humanist?

5. Christian neo-Platonists said that God created the universe by "emanation," an expression of pure love. Are these paintings examples of nature or creation expressed in terms of love?

Venus, allegory of both beauty and fertility, is much like Athena in Periclean Athens. The sculpture on the east pediment of the Parthenon celebrates the birth of Athena in the presence of the gods, while Botticelli celebrates the birth of Venus in the presence of nature. The humanist qualities of the painting center on the celebration of classical myth in human and natural terms. The problem of celebrating such a myth in a Christian context— one in which ancient sculptures of Venus were destroyed— was solved by a combination of scholarship and connoisseurship. The neo-Platonic scholars—in combination with wealthy art lovers and intellectuals, such as the Medici—were able to convince their age that the ancients desired the truths of Christianity so much that their myths echoed them, although imperfectly. Renaissance humanism depended on this concept and flourished as a result of its acceptance.

Literature

THE GROWTH OF HUMANISM

Dante's pattern of scholarship set the stage for the flowering of learning in the Renaissance. However, Dante's age was dominated by Aristotelianism as interpreted by Aquinas. Learning centered on rhetoric and logic and was directed toward theology. Humanism emphasized Plato, particularly as interpreted by Plotinus, a second-century Christian. The neo-Platonists, as they were called, celebrated humankind. Their schools freed up the curriculum and included the study of many classical authors, such as Ovid, Horace, and Cicero, whose works were directed not toward theology, but toward an interest in human behavior. Influenced by these texts, Renaissance humanists developed a moral optimism about human potential that was impossible in the Middle Ages.

THE FLORENTINE ACADEMY:
MARSILIO FICINO AND NEO-PLATONISM

The Florentine academy, based on Plato's model, was the most important of the new humanist academies springing up in Italy. Founded by Cosimo de' Medici, it was headed by Marsilio Ficino (1433–1499), whose translation of Plato from the original Greek was so sound as to remain standard for almost four centuries. His great achievement was his effort to resolve Christianity with Platonism by reinterpreting the works of Plato and Plotinus in his *Theologica Platonica* (1482). Ficino was important for his steadfast Christian faith and his efforts to disseminate information about Plato. However, he was deeply involved with numerology and astrology, and he inadvertently helped introduce concepts of magic into neo-Platonism—concepts that persisted until the twentieth century.

Ficino was a good scholar and was connected with the most powerful family in Florence. He was therefore able to exert considerable influence in clarifying Platonic ideas. He saw the human soul as a Platonic essence above the material world, but nonetheless linked with nature. He helped his followers penetrate to the world of essences, where, he said, the greatest spiritual joy exists.

PICO DELLA MIRANDOLA:
VALUING SCHOLARSHIP

The academy's next brilliant figure was Pico della Mirandola (1463–1494), a student not only of Greek and Latin texts but also of texts in Hebrew and Arabic. When he was twenty he offered to debate in Rome on the axioms of knowledge that he had stated in 900 theses. But no debate took place. He was arrested because thirteen of his theses were considered heretical. Fortunately, he escaped and was taken in by the Florentine academy. His preface to the 900 theses, called "On the Dignity of Man," reveals his immense learning in many languages, and it contains scholarly references that made it a model for humanist writing.

His preface elevated human dignity as high as that of the angels (perhaps a dangerous novelty) and set humankind next to the throne of God. He insisted that all knowledge is one: that the truths of the trinity and the nature of Christ were implicit in Plato and the Hebraic authors. He made classical authors acceptable to the most pious of Christian authorities.

LORENZO DE' MEDICI

A student of Ficino, Lorenzo (1449–1492) was, as scion of Florence's greatest family, its greatest patron. He was a wide-ranging humanist with interests in politics, art, music, and poetry. His poems, which are among the finest of the age, explore classical themes, themes of love, and themes concerning how people live their lives. Some of his poetry seems influenced by Omar Khayyám:

How fair is youth
That flies so fast!
Be happy if you may
All that is to come is uncertain.

Such lines, from his most popular poem, "Carnival Songs," were often set to music.

His sonnets show the influence of Petrarch (Francesco Petrarca; 1304–1374) as well as the progress of both secularism and humanism. His references are frequently classical and rarely religious. Some of his poetry praises the pleasures of the country:

A verdant meadow full of lovely flowers,
A rivulet that bathes the grassy earth,
A little bird who pours love's lament forth,
These win much rather all my deepest ardors.

Along with such a Botticellian effusion is his Petrarchianism in:

I saw my lady by a cool, fresh stream
Among green branches and gay ladies stand;
Since the first hour when I felt love's hot brand
I never saw her face more lovely gleam.

The direction in which Lorenzo pointed was the future. Not only were the classical and Petrarchan aspects of his work prominent in other Italian poetry of the 1400s, but they would continue to appear in French and English poetry until the late 1700s. It was a powerful strain.

MACHIAVELLI: THE VALUE OF POWER

Niccolò Machiavelli (1469–1527) was an aristocrat whose fortunes wavered—like those of most important Florentines—between being accepted by the ruling elite and being threatened with exile. His family was noted for considerable service to the state and for its republican leanings. Machiavelli was a humanist whose studies of the writings of the Romans convinced him that contemporary Italy needed to adopt the values of its forebears. He was particularly concerned by the threat of France and Spain. He longed for a powerful prince who could, through his own strength and cunning, unite all of Italy.

His choice for the job was Lorenzo de' Medici, duke of Urbino and the grandson of Lorenzo the Magnificent. Machiavelli wrote *The Prince* in 1513, and he included a careful dedication to Lorenzo that essentially urged him to take his advice. *The Prince* is a complex document, difficult for the modern age to interpret. Some critics have considered it essentially a satiric comment on the abuses of power, but the general attitude of scholars has been to accept at face value Machiavelli's advice to rule with absolute power, in the manner of the Roman despots. There is no question that he expected Lorenzo to be essentially a worthy ruler, but it is also clear that he expected him to wield power ruthlessly.

We generally view Machiavelli as a cynic who believed that his contemporaries were greedy, corrupt, and too selfish to devote themselves to the noble values that might have saved Italy from becoming the easy prey of other nations. He saw the worst in people rather than the best. Therefore, it was easy for him to advise the prince to trust no one, to appear benevolent even when he was not, and to do anything he had to do in order to maintain power. He also advised the prince that the ends justify the means used to attain them, a political doctrine that is debated even today. Tyrannical governments have generally taken the same view, stating that their harsh, repressive measures are essential for the greater good of the state.

When considering the question whether it is better for a prince to be loved than to be feared, Machiavelli answered:

> I reply that one should like to be both one and the other; but since it is difficult to join them together, it is much safer to be feared than to be loved when one of the two must be lacking. For one can generally say this about men: that they are ungrateful, fickle, simulators and deceivers, avoiders of danger, greedy for gain; and while you work for their good they are completely yours offering you their blood, their property, their lives, and their sons, as I said earlier, when danger is far away; but when it comes nearer to you they turn away. And that prince who bases his power entirely on their words, finding himself stripped of other preparations, comes to ruin; for friendships that are acquired by a price and not by greatness and nobility of character are purchased but are not owned, and at the proper moment they cannot be spent. And men are less hesitant about harming someone who makes himself loved than one who makes himself feared because love is held together by a chain of obligation which since men are a sorry lot, is broken on every occasion in which their own self-interest is concerned; but fear is held together by a dread of punishment which will never abandon you.

Machiavelli's Italy was marked by treachery and deceit, and it may be that his ideas reflected this. Yet his book has been read by modern politicians and has often been applied to modern situations.

Dance and Music

COURT AND COUNTRY DANCE

Renaissance developments in dance included the publication of books on dance and the spread of dance teachers throughout Italy. Dance played an important part in the courts of the time. Because dancing was a social phenomenon, its purpose was often to have fun. The Roman saltarello, which featured a leaping motion expressing joy and excitement, became popular all over Europe, as did, outside the court, the tarantella (named for the tarantula, a spider whose home was Taranto, Italy). A frenzied dance, the tarantella was thought to cure the bite of the spider. Some communities thought that the bite was useful for treating certain diseases, and one way to make the spider bite was to hold it against the body while dancing in a wild frenzy.

BASSE DANCE: COURTLY RITUAL

The best-known dance of the 1400s was the basse dance. Performed by many people, it involved exact steps and exact music. The movements were gliding and stately; the dancers paused to bow to their partners and to change the direction of their movements. The steps were: a reverence (bowing or curtsying), a single (taking one step forward and then drawing the feet together), a double (taking two steps forward and then drawing the feet together), a branle (taking a sideward balance step from left to right), a farewell to one's partner, and a reprise (extending one foot and then drawing it slowly back).

Dances were performed in the cities and in the country, and they served a variety of social purposes. One was to display the gentility of the men and the grace of the women. They may also have been a means of introducing members of the opposite sex, as the dance at the beginning of Shakespeare's *Romeo and Juliet* obviously does. Shakespeare's play is set in the Verona of the late 1500s, but the tradition was still firmly in place.

MUSIC

The Secular Shift

France dominated music in the 1400s, but Italian influences were growing. Most church music was composed for the mass, while much secular music was composed for the purposes of dancing. Since dance was popular, new music was always needed. Music for love poetry was also in demand.

Dance music was marked by a strong, steady rhythm and by melodic lines that accented individual notes for ease of interpretation. The melodies were lively, joyful, uplifting, and gay. Unfortunately, the notation of the day was casual, and melodies were often written down with no indication as to whether they were for voice or an instrument. Apparently, tradition dictated such things, and the tradition has been recorded rather imperfectly.

We do know that music in the period was, like dance, popular among amateurs. Many poets and painters played the lute and sang. Music was an accomplishment of the gracious in this age. There were many professionals as well, who acted not only as household minstrels but also sometimes as heralds at jousts and tournaments and as instrumentalists on the field of battle.

The Development of Homophony: The Frottola

With the growth of secular music came a change from polyphony to homophony. The change was slow, but of great importance. Polyphonic music, which features several melodies and constant musical "motion," had become closely associated with the church. The continual building of melody upon melody, with some voices rising as others fall, gave way to homophony: one melodic line supported by

other voices that play a third, a fifth, or a sixth apart. The differences are considerable; an obvious one is that homophonic music permits much greater emphasis on a sung line of text.

Since modern triadic harmony was only in its infancy, like perspective in painting, some of the earliest work is not as rich in texture as church music. Yet the melodies are exciting, and the potential for harmonic support was great enough for contemporary musicians to express excitement at the prospects.

One of the most important musical products of the 1400s in Italy was the frottola. We do not now listen to frottolas as much as we listen to the ballata (a song accompanied by dancing), the canzona, and the madrigal, which were only just being developed in the period. The frottola was a well-developed form emphasizing one melodic line, usually the cantus (top), and filled in with rich and lingering harmonies. Polyphonic music provided no chance to savor the occasional harmonic chord that might result from the intersection of tunes. But the frottola aimed for rich harmonic moments that are meant to be savored, such as the ending of measure 4 in the frottola by Marchetto Cara (Figure 11-25), in which there is an A in the bass and a C sharp in the cantus. It is rich, surprising, and filled with psychological implications that must be resolved in the succeeding passages.

Marchetto Cara (c. 1465–c. 1525) gives the cantus the main melody and uses the other voices to support it harmonically, either with a single held tone, as in the bass line, or with repeated patterns of notes, as in the tenor line. Note that the text is laid out in full only in the cantus. The translation of the text (an anonymous sonnet) is:

You who hear the sad tears
Of my past and juvenile errors
Be moved to pity by my sorrow
Which makes me sigh with great sadness.
And you happy and unhappy lovers,
Leave all hope of love
And turn your hearts to virtue only,
Leaving behind loving and sweet songs.
Because cruel death will quickly cause
Our fall and disperse fragile hope
And earthly hope passes and does not last.
Virtue gets man used to eternity
Since after death it is closed in the tomb
Where it follows him closely.

Figure 11-25
Marchetto Cara. "Voi che ascoltate." Late fifteenth
century. (From *Collegium Musicum: Yale.* 2d Series.
Madison, Wisconsin: A-R Editions, 1972.)

The Frottola and Fifteenth-Century Italian Music

1. Listen to Cara's frottola (Figure 11-25) played on the piano (it should be playable even by a beginner), or listen to it sung by four voices. Be sure to read the text of the sonnet. How dominant is the cantus melody in comparison with the other vocal lines? Does the music establish a mood which coordinates with the text?

2. Does the music obscure the text or complicate it? What religious and what secular issues are raised? Is this a fusion of the religious and the secular, such as we see in Botticelli?

3. Listen to several short selections of Italian music of the fifteenth century. Some recordings to choose from include *Early and Late Fifteenth-Century Music* (Nonesuch 71010), *Music of the Court of Lorenzo the Magnificent* (MCA 2508), *Music of the Renaissance* (Turnabout 34058), and *A Treasury of Music of the Renaissance* (Elektra EKL-229). Is most of the music you sampled vocal or instrumental? If it is vocal, is the text clearly audible? If you had a text to follow, could you do so? Is the text secular or religious?

4. After listening to some music of the period, consider the following questions:
   a. How many instruments can you hear?
   b. What family of instruments is used in the greatest number?
   c. Is there a duplication of instruments (three or four of any one kind)?
   d. Is the instrumental texture dominated by rhythm, harmony, or melody?
   e. Is the melody lively, jaunty, and bright? Is it sad? Is it dull?
   f. Does the music establish a clear mood?

The piece shown in Figure 11-25 is slow and complex in mood. The text begins by telling us how fine love can be, but it soon reminds us that death cares not for love, but for virtue, which alone accompanies us in the afterlife. The music becomes plaintive, as if suggesting that it is all too sad that virtue, rather than love, must endure. There are feelings of disappointment: why should it be this way? The beauties of this simple, 12-bar composition are subtle and elusive, and the mood of the piece is consonant with the complex moods suggested by the text. Cara naturally praises austere, religious virtue; but he longs for love.

Much of the vocal music of the period is dominated by a secular text that is relatively simple and is well supported by the melodic lines on which it flows.

Melody is naturally dominant in vocal music, and exquisite moments of harmonic suspension and resolution are usually quite evident in sustained harmonic passages. Composers of the period usually enjoyed the newfound pleasures of harmony and made a point of displaying their expertise in creating it.

The rhythmic emphasis of dance music is usually not achieved at the expense of the melody, but the melody is shaped so as to take advantage of the pacing, the accents, and the requirements of the steps. The recorder and percussion instruments were very popular with composers of dance music, whereas the lute was preferred by composers of vocal music. Early Renaissance music was usually played by small groups, with very little duplication of instruments. Therefore, the texture of the music sounds thin in comparison with that of later orchestral music. Nonetheless, the resultant delicacy imparts a sense of grace and lightness and shows the deft touch that is characteristic of the age. The delight in the new musical possibilities is apparent everywhere, even in modern reconstructions. The Renaissance produced new opportunities in all the arts.

Summary

The 1400s in Italy saw new developments in humanist scholarship; a growth in economic and political opportunities, which gave rise to powerful city-states whose wealth became fabulous; and the expansion of secular awareness and optimism concerning the nature of humankind. During the Renaissance there was a revived interest in Greek and Roman culture, in which human concerns were paramount. The human figure, human achievements, and philosophy based on human concerns were all recovered by the humanists' study of the ancients. Neo-Platonism produced art that spoke in allegories and contained deeper meanings than at first met the eye. Learning and intellectuality were reflected in all the arts, including music, in which experiments in homophony were thoughtful and moving. The complexities of the arts flattered intelligent individuals, who were left to make their own discoveries. In portraits we see an interest in the individual personality that seems quite modern. Much of fifteenth-century Italian art, literature, and music seems modern to us, which is perhaps only another way of saying that we respond to it positively; we understand it.

Concepts in Chapter 11

The Italian economy depended on the eastern spice trade, which was being cut off in the late 1400s.

The discovery of America produced opportunities for European expansion.

The eastern Christian empire was lost when Constantinople fell to the Turks in 1453.

Brunelleschi and Ghiberti entered a competition for the commission to make the relief sculptures for the doors of the Florence Cathedral baptistry in 1401; Ghiberti won.

Classical influences appear in Ghiberti's work.

Brunelleschi studied architecture in Rome and revived Roman architectural techniques.

Brunelleschi used new methods of construction for the dome of Florence Cathedral that permitted it to rise to a new height.

Donatello revived the tradition of freestanding sculpture; his *David* is the first cast-bronze freestanding work since classical times.

Vanishing-point perspective, developed by Brunelleschi and Alberti, permitted the illusion of three-dimensional space in painting.

During the Italian Renaissance, painting became more secular and more realistic, and there was a growing interest in portraits.

Some allegorical painting (such as Botticelli's) attempted to fuse classical and Christian themes, in imitation of the humanists.

Humanism was a product of scholarship and of the study of classical texts, led by Marsilio Ficino, Pico della Mirandola, and the Florentine academy.

Literature, like most arts of the period, became more secular. Machiavelli's political handbook, *The Prince,* showed some of the limits of humanism.

Court dances, like the basse dance, became acceptable and popular social activities.

Music became more secular, and the period saw the development of homophony: a single melodic line supported by other voices, as in the frottola.

Suggested Readings

Alberti, Leon Battista. *On Painting* (1435) and *On Sculpture* (1464). London: Phaidon, 1972.

Arbeau, Thoinot (Jehan Tabourot). *Orchesography* (1589). New York: Dover, 1956.

Benevolo, Leonardo. *The Architecture of the Renaissance.* 2 vols. Boulder, Colo.: Westview, 1978.

Blume, Friedrich. *Renaissance and Baroque Music.* New York: Norton, 1967.

Chastel, André. *The Golden Age of the Renaissance: Italy 1460–1500.* London: Thames and Hudson, 1965.

———. *The Myth of the Renaissance 1420–1520.* New York: Skira, 1969.

Gilbert, Creighton. *History of Renaissance Art throughout Europe.* New York: Abrams, 1972.

Goldscheider, Ludwig. *Donatello.* London: Phaidon, 1941.

Hendy, Philip. *Piero della Francesca and the Early Renaissance.* New York: Macmillan, 1968.

Krautheimer, Richard. *Ghiberti's Bronze Doors.* Princeton, N.J.: Princeton, 1971.

Lightbown, Ronald. *Botticelli.* 2 vols. Berkeley: University of California Press, 1978.

Lind, L. R. *Lyric Poetry of the Italian Renaissance.* New Haven, Conn.: Yale, 1954.

Mates, Julian, and Eugene Cantelupe, eds. *Renaissance Culture.* New York: George Braziller, 1966.

Murray, Peter, and Linda Murray. *The Art of the Renaissance.* New York: Oxford University Press, 1963.

O'Kelly, Bernard. *The Renaissance Image of Man and the World.* Columbus: Ohio State University Press, 1966.

Panofsky, Erwin. *Renaissance and Renascences in Western Art.* London: Paladin, 1970.

Prager, Frank D., and Gustina Scaglia. *Brunelleschi.* Cambridge, Mass.: M.I.T., 1970.

Singleton, Charles S., ed. *Art, Science and History in the Renaissance.* Baltimore: Johns Hopkins, 1967.

Vasari, Giorgio. *Lives of the Most Eminent Painters, Sculptors, and Architects* (1550). Mrs. Jonathan Foster, trans.; E. H. Blashfield, E. W. Blashfield, and A. A. Hopkins, eds. New York: Scribner, 1911.

Wind, Edgar. *Pagan Mysteries of the Renaissance.* New York: Barnes & Noble, 1968.

CHAPTER 12

THE RENAISSANCE IN THE NORTH: REFORMATION AND EXPANSION, 1430 TO 1600

Cultural Background

Because travel was common and because Latin, the language of the humanists, had become the language of all educated people in the fifteenth and sixteenth centuries, the literature of any one region was usually influential in others; travelers brought the newest developments from place to place, stimulating growth and change. The political stability of Europe throughout the period was unusual, perhaps in part because of the constant devastation of the black death, which reduced the population, gave new opportunities to the laboring classes, and resulted in a reassessment of old values.

Architecture

THE FRENCH CHATEAUS

Italian influences spread widely throughout the north. The French chateaus, huge houses designed for the central governance of an estate, combined some gothic influences with some influences of Italian revisions of the romanesque style. Although fortified castles were obsolete, the chateaus retained some of the appearance of the fortress.

Under Francis I, a great many chateaus were built in the Loire Valley in France. Most of them served court purposes, and a few were meant to be permanent residences. They were buildings in the country that contained the activity of a city, and they were meant to be viewed and admired.

The style of Chateau de Chambord (Figure 12-1), begun in 1519, is a mixture usually called the "Francis I style." Its four round towers are connected by lighter "screens" with windows in the Italian fashion. The gables on the steep roofs are French—a favorite and persistent detail. The architect was probably Pierre Nepveu, although he has only recently been connected with the chateau at Chambord.

The chateau at Chenonceaux (Figure 12-2) was begun in 1515, but the bridge and gallery extending to the left over the river Cher were added in the 1550s and 1560s by Philibert Delorme (c. 1515–1570) and Jean Boullant (c. 1520–1578). Chenonceaux has a light, bright feeling. The details over the

Figure 12-1
Pierre Nepveu. Chateau de
Chambord. Begun 1519.
(Photo, J. Feuillie/ ©
CNMHS/SPADEM/VAGA, New
York.)

Figure 12-2
Chateau de Chenonceaux.
Begun 1515. (Photo, J. Feuillie/
© CNMHS/SPADEM/VAGA, New
York.)

long vertical windows on the bridge are Italian, as are
the accented rectangles on the second level, which
are used to emphasize the length of the building. The
roofline is busy, like that of the chateau at Chambord, but the arches of the bridge help maintain a
fine, light rhythm, particularly as they reflect in the
Cher. Details are repeated, which creates a rhythmic
balance and a symmetrical extensibility, demonstrating that it, like most chateaus, was designed to please
the eye and to be admired.

Fontainebleau was a medieval hunting castle until
it was redone in the 1520s and 1530s by Gilles le
Breton. The gallery of Francis I (Figure 12-3) was
widely imitated, not only in England and France, but
even in Italy. The designers of the interior (Figure
12-4) were Il Rosso Fiorentino (1494–1540) and
Francesco Primaticcio (1504–1570), both called to
Fontainebleau from Italy by Francis I. The gallery was
used both for large receptions and as a display hall for
military booty from the Italian campaigns. Il Rosso
and Primaticcio reveal a passion for sumptuous detail;
hardly a space is left unadorned. The paintings and
stucco reliefs constitute a sensual spree: decorated
ceilings, elaborate chandeliers, and extraordinary
plaster frames are hallmarks of Fontainebleau.

THE ENGLISH PALACE
AND COUNTRY HOUSE

Hampton Court (Figure 12-5), begun in 1515 as a
residence for Cardinal Wolsey, stands as a fine example of Tudor style, while still maintaining medieval
details associated with a fortress. But this is a ceremonial fortress in which towers and other details have
become slim, light, and primarily decorative. The
corner towers are not massive; the central towers are
graceful. The main gate is a delicate, curved portal;
the machicolations on the roofline are visual repeti-

Figure 12-3
Above: Fontainebleau, gallery of Francis I, exterior. c. 1540. (Photo, J. Feuillie/ © CNMHS/SPADEM/VAGA, New York.)

Figure 12-4
Left: Fontainebleau, gallery of Francis I, interior. c. 1540. (Photo, J. Feuillie/ © CNMHS/SPADEM/VAGA, New York.)

Figure 12-5
Hampton Court, front entrance. 1515.

tions rather than functional defenses. The windows are almost generous.

Hampton Court became a favorite residence for English monarchs. Eventually, Cardinal Wolsey gave the estate to Henry VIII in 1526 as a way of appeasing him. It has remained a royal residence to this day. Its location, directly on the Thames and only 15 miles from the heart of London, made it a convenient retreat for royalty.

Longleat House (Figure 12-6) was built between 1554 and 1568 for Sir John Thynne from drawings by an unknown designer. The master mason, Robert Smythson, may have been responsible for many design features. The tradition at the time was to provide drawings and sometimes materials to a master mason, who then carried out the work using his own design motifs. Longleat is unusually modern in appearance. It is a rectangular structure, with three levels and no steep roof, and its vertical lines are emphasized by bay windows: four along the front and three along the side. The bays are decorated with pilasters: Doric, Ionic, and Corinthian.

Wollaton Hall (Figure 12-7), built between 1580 and 1588 by Robert Smythson as a home for Sir Francis Willoughby, maintains the vertical emphases, but it also retains more of the flavor of a fortress, particularly in the prominence of its corner turrets. The long vertical windows resemble those at Longleat. Italian influences, probably introduced through handbooks on architecture that had recently been published, can be seen in the balustrade along the roofline, the highly decorated tower crests, and the wreathed medallions on the towers. It is a vigorous building; its proportions are like those of a fortress, there are echoes of Gothic in the mock buttresses on the towers.

Figure 12-6
Left: Longleat House, Wiltshire. 1554–1568. (Royal Commission on Historical Monuments, England.)

Figure 12-7
Below: Wollaton Hall, Nottinghamshire. 1580–1588. (Royal Commission on Historical Monuments, England.)

Northern Renaissance Architecture

1. Establish what you think is the function of each of the buildings shown in Figures 12-1 through 12-7. In which building do you think that form best follows function?

2. Each of these buildings is, to some extent, a residence. Which seems most like a home? Since "home" is a subjective concept, it is essential to attempt to define the word in architectural terms. Which building seems least like a home?

3. Most of these buildings achieve balance through symmetry and visual rhythm created by repetitions of architectural details. Establish the symmetrical details of one of these buildings. How is symmetry achieved in this building? What kinds of elements are repeated? What is the effect of the repetitions?

4. These buildings are secular in function. What design elements differentiate them from buildings that have a religious function? Would you ever mistake one of the buildings discussed in this chapter for a church? Compare these buildings with the structures shown in Figures 11-7 through 11-10 or with the Gothic churches shown in Chapter 10.

5. Most of the architecture shown in this chapter was designed for members of the nobility. What qualities did they value most in their buildings?

The Visual Arts

Painting in the north tended to develop some of the traditions established in illuminated manuscripts. Great attention to detail and three-dimensional realism gave northern painting an international reputation. Some critics maintain that there is a gloomy cast to some northern painting, largely because there is an unusually intellectual cast to the subject matter. But there is also a fascinating interest on the part of northern painters in the everyday doings of ordinary people. The range of interest of the northern painters reflects an increasingly secular society, even though most official paintings were commissioned by the church and had religious subjects.

JAN VAN EYCK

The miniatures of the Limbourg brothers (Color Plate 7) established a tradition that continued, particularly among Flemish and Dutch painters. It represented an older, international style that was eventu-

ally outmoded by painters such as Jan van Eyck (c. 1385–1441), whose signed work begins in 1430. He earned a reputation for representing reality so perfectly as to be the envy of painters throughout Europe. His fame extended to Italy, where he was praised for his painstaking attention to detail and—mistakenly, by Vasari—for having invented oil painting. He often used a combination of tempera and oil, and his work has a special liveliness because of his use of oil techniques: he was a brilliant colorist. One of his major technical achievements was aerial perspective: using brighter colors for figures closer to us, and darker colors for those more distant.

Van Eyck may have done illuminations for the Duke of Berry, and in his paintings he seems to transfer the illuminator's skills to the larger medium. He is said to have used a single hair from a brush to paint figures so tiny that he may have needed a magnifying glass to execute them. His themes are generally religious, but his treatment of bulk and space shows that he did not shrink from materialistic pleasures as perceived through the senses. His works,

Figure 12-8
Hubert and Jan van Eyck. The Ghent Altarpiece. Cathedral of Saint Bavon, Ghent.
Completed 1432. Oil on panels, 11 feet 5 ¾ inches by 15 feet 1 ½ inches
when fully open. (Photo, Scala/Art Resource.)

which are vibrant and rich in color and texture, show
an enormous respect for the world as it is. Divine
figures—such as Mary, who was a poor, simple
woman—are portrayed wearing the most opulent
clothing because if they did not have them in real
life, they *deserved* them.

The gigantic Ghent Altarpiece (Figure 12-8) presents us with a mystery. An inscription on the frame
says that it was begun by Hubert and finished by Jan
van Eyck, and some people have therefore assumed
that Jan had an older brother, Hubert, who died in
1426. The evidence for this is very slim. Hubert may
have been another artist from Maaseyck, van Eyck's
hometown, but we are not sure. The work is primarily by van Eyck, but x-ray studies show that the design
was altered and that another hand may have been at
work here. Visual references to the religious styles of
an earlier time may indicate that the project was
begun by Hubert and then partially modified to
express some of van Eyck's more characteristic attitudes toward religion and modern life. It was a huge
project, spanning the years from 1425 to 1432. It is

more than 11 feet high and 15 feet wide when open; twelve scenes are visible when the wings are open, and another eight when they are closed.

The upper central portion of the work is dominated by God, who is represented much as he is in Byzantine apse mosaics or gothic tympana, such as those at Chartres. God is clothed in red and wears a papal tiara. Below, in another panel, the dove (symbol of the holy spirit) hovers over an altar on which is a lamb, symbol of Christ's sacrifice. The largest scene, showing the adoration of the lamb, is curious for its awkward perspective, something rarely seen in van Eyck's work. Despite the power of the figures and the rhythms of their representation, the scene is indebted to an earlier visual conception: the contemporary world of the Ghent burgher is not well represented here. Adam and Eve oppress us with a sense of their sin; they are presented feeling shame and contrition, rather than imparting a sense of joy in the gift of life.

The Madonna of the Chancellor Rolin (Figure 12-9) is a much smaller, more typical work showing some of the connection between Northern Renaissance painters and the miniaturists and illuminators. The chancellor, Nicholas Rolin, is portrayed with the Madonna and Child, who blesses him. Their eyes do not meet; van Eyck portrays the world of nature (Rolin's) and the world of grace (that of the Madonna and Child) separately, emphasizing the separateness with vacant glances. Rolin was alive when the work was done, in about 1433 or 1434. He later gave the painting, an oil, to the church at Autun, where his son became bishop in 1437. The inclusion of the donor—the person who commissioned the work—in a scene with the Madonna is conventional in this age. We might imagine this as portraying Rolin's reward for having lived an exemplary life.

The setting is palatial, befitting the mother of God. The architectural details are generally romanesque, and three arches symbolize the trinity. The

Figure 12-9
Jan van Eyck. *Madonna of Chancellor Rolin.*
c. 1433–1434. Oil on panel, 26 by 24 ⅜ inches. (Louvre, Paris; photo, Musées Nationaux.)

city visible through the archways has been the subject of much debate. It teems with life: people are leaning out of windows, walking along the streets, and rowing boats in the river. It may represent Maastricht, Lyons, Brussels, Utrecht, or Prague. The sense of reality is so strong that people have proposed all these as its site.

The painting is filled with detail. The eye roams over the surface, observing the tiny angel hovering with a highlighted crown; the richness of the Madonna's cloak and hair; the intense detail in the landscape, which bustles with activity; the garden with the full-blown lily (a symbol of virginity) and the peacock (a symbol of Christ); and the richly detailed marble floor. One is almost overwhelmed. However, part of van Eyck's genius is that none of the detail detracts from the central balance and harmony of the composition. The eye moves smoothly from Rolin to Christ, and then to the Madonna. Despite the space between them, they cohere, and the painting does not fragment into a group of smaller paintings.

The portrait of the Arnolfini (Color Plate 10) is listed at the entrance to the National Gallery in London as among its twenty most important masterpieces. Because it is signed and dated 1434, it has been treated as a legal document, a marriage license. The two figures are held together in space not only by their joined hands but also by the "link" of the dog at their feet and by the mirror and the chandelier, which "close" the space at and above their heads. The eye moves naturally from Giovanni's face, through the chandelier, to Giovanna's face, down her furred sleeve, through the dog, and back up through Giovanni's raised hand. This oval shape brings together the disparate elements of the composition and emphasizes the unity of marriage.

Erwin Panofsky has explored the symbols in the painting. The dog implies faith and fidelity; the fruit on the shelf beneath the window symbolizes fertility. Because their shoes are set aside, the couple are considered to be standing in a holy place. The whisk broom on the bedstead implies that all unholy spirits have been swept away. Above it is carved Saint Margaret, patroness of marriage. The single candle lighted in the chandelier implies the presence of the holy spirit. The tiny round representations on the frame of the mirror are some of the stations of the cross, perhaps implying the trials of marriage. The turbaned man in the mirror is van Eyck, showing us the scene through his eyes.

PERCEPTION KEY

Van Eyck, *Portrait of the Arnolfini*

1. Refer to Color Plate 10, the portrait of the Arnolfini. Van Eyck seems to have painted this as a record of the marriage of Giovanni Arnolfini and Giovanna Cenami, who were his friends in Bruges. He signed it beneath the chandelier as evidence that he had witnessed the event. What details suggest that this is a wedding scene?

2. What devices does van Eyck use to bring the two figures together in the visual space? What design elements or details connect them?

3. What is the source of light? Are the colors harmonious? Do any colors surprise you or seem not to "fit" the needs of the painting?

4. A marriage is a religious sacrament; what are the religious elements in this painting? Does this seem to be a holy moment?

5. There are a great many detailed objects in the room. Which seem to have the greatest importance? Can you see their relevance to the marriage? What do the details of the setting tell you about the background of this couple?

The color is impressive: the lightest tones are in the green of the bride's gown, gathered up not because she is pregnant, but because she wishes to be. Her husband, in darker browns, looms large but permits her to glow radiantly in contrast. The deep reds help integrate the spaces in the room, while reminding us of the comforts and delights of the marriage bed. The painting fuses religious and secular values, emphasizing the rich, costly fabrics as well as the holiness of the moment.

The painting celebrates the piety, worthiness, and seriousness of the merchant class to which the Arnolfini belong and which van Eyck does not shun. The merchant class was on the rise throughout Europe, and this masterpiece is one of the earliest to recognize it. The northern mercantile class was extremely pious and conservative, at once anxious to enjoy its newfound comforts while still emphasizing its holiness and its attention to religious and community duties. One reason why the stations of the cross are so small in the painting may be to deemphasize the unpleasant aspects of religion; only a century earlier, they might have been the most important element of the composition.

LATER NORTHERN PAINTERS

The three paintings shown in Figures 12-10, 12-11, and 12-12 fall within a generation of one another; Petrus Christus (c. 1420–1472 or 1473) was in Bruges in 1444 and may have been van Eyck's student. His work shows some evidence of van Eyck's influence, including a fascination with objects and details and a delight in reflections.

The earliest of the paintings, the Mérode Altarpiece (Figure 12-10) by Robert Campin (c. 1378–1444), also shows the influence of van Eyck, particularly of the Ghent Altarpiece. The donors, portrayed on the left, are evidence of the growing tradition of honoring the wealthy classes who could afford such gifts. On the right is Saint Joseph making a mousetrap. (Medieval tradition held that Christ was the bait, and the world a trap, for the devil.) The central panel—more formal, more idealized, and less realistic

Figure 12-10
Robert Campin. Mérode Altarpiece. 1425–1426. Panel painting; center panel is 25 ¼ by 24 ⅞ inches. (Metropolitan Museum of Art, purchase, Cloisters Collection.)

Figure 12-11
Petrus Christus. *Saint Eligius as a Goldsmith.* 1449. Oil on wood, 39 by 33 ½ inches. (Metropolitan Museum of Art, Robert Lehman Collection, 1975.)

—is on the theme of the annunciation, the moment when the angel informed Mary that she would bear the son of God. The perspective is somewhat unnatural; the table is tilted so that we can see the symbols, among them the lily, of the Virgin. The same is true of Joseph's workbench. Campin provided an altarpiece in the style that the donor (or receiver) thought appropriate for the annunciation.

Charles Cuttler has called Christus' portrait of Saint Eligius (Figure 12-11) "the first genre painting in northern art." Genre paintings depict the ordinary events of daily life, and since they were to become a staple of northern painting in the sixteenth century, this work is a milestone. Saint Eligius is shown as a goldsmith in his shop; behind him stand a couple, and the woman is reaching for the ring he has just weighed. The scene is rendered as we might see it if we, like the people reflected in the bubble mirror at

the lower right, were peering into the window of the shop at this moment. We have the feeling of being a witness, as we do with van Eyck's portrait of the Arnolfini, except that these people seem less aware that they are being watched. It has been speculated that this, too, is a record of a wedding, but that has never been confirmed.

All the details in the painting are portrayed so distinctly that we are convinced that they have meaning. Eligius (588–659), the patron saint of goldsmiths, eventually rejected the things of this world, and in his role as a wealthy man dealing with precious metals, he is a powerful argument in favor of piety.

The Avignon Pietà (Figure 12-12), long considered a work by an unknown artist but now attributed to Enguerrand Charonton (fl. 1444–1466), was painted sometime between 1455 and 1460. It is

Figure 12-12
Enguerrand Charonton.
The Avignon Pietà.
c. 1460. Panel painting,
63 ¾ by 85 ⅞ inches.
(Louvre, Paris; photo,
Musées Nationaux.)

COMPARISON KEY

Three Northern Paintings

1. In which of the paintings shown in Figures 12-10, 12-11, and 12-12 is the portrayal of space most realistic? In which painting is the perspective most natural? In which is it most unnatural?

2. Which of the paintings seems most influenced by the style of van Eyck? What stylistic details does the painter seem to have borrowed from him?

3. What evidence is there of a growing interest in humanism in these works? Which of the paintings is most concerned with the events of everyday life?

4. All these paintings are religious in subject matter. Which of them *appears* most religious? What formal decisions has the artist made to intensify the religiousness of the subject? Which painting gives the greatest insight into its subject?

5. Which of these compositions achieves the greatest visual stability? Which seems most unstable? Is the visual stability or instability put to good use in terms of interpreting the subject?

tempera on a wood panel, done in very subdued colors. The figures are presented linearly, and the artist has taken great care with the faces and their modeling. The details of the clothing are generally simple. The donor to the left is treated in the general manner of the time, looking off, as Chancellor Rolin does, to the other world. The fascinating power of Christ, who is lying at an impossible angle on Mary's lap, makes the painting oddly disconcerting and unstable. The sharp angularity of Christ's body is used to intensify the emotion that is expressed only by Mary Magadalene, to the right. The faces of the Virgin and the evangelist are deeply calm and reassured. The three saints form a stable triangle; the disconcerting angularity of Christ disturbs that stability and adds a psychological dimension to the scene.

HIERONYMUS BOSCH

Optimism was the prevailing spirit of the age, but there were moments of uncertainty. Hieronymus Bosch (c. 1450–1516), a Dutch painter, remains an enigma; little is known of him, and less of his intentions. We do not know whether he was being sarcastic or comic or whether he was simply portraying a northern pessimism of the sort that caught the imagination of several artists. *The Garden of Earthly Delights* (c. 1500; Figure 12-13) teems with grotesque invention, much of it so openly sexual and orgiastic that some people have suggested that Bosch's real interest was pornography in the guise of pious disapproval. One speculation is that the many tiny set pieces illustrate proverbial sayings, most of which are lost to us.

The left panel shows the creation of Eve; the right, the torments of hell. The earth, in the central panel, is filled with innumerable grotesqueries that offer a cautionary note regarding our optimism over the growth of humanism. People are revealed not in a glowing fashion, filled with potential and grandeur, but tormented, perverse, and degraded. Bosch's work has never lost its fascination. Some of the images may be drawn from dreams or nightmares and seem to allude to popular dream books of the period. The dark

Figure 12-13
Hieronymous Bosch. *The Garden of Earthly Delights.* c. 1505–1510. Panel painting; wings are 86 ⅝ by 38 ¼ inches, center is 86 ⅝ by 76 ¾ inches. (Museo del Prado, Madrid.)

side of contemporary psychology is evident in Bosch and stands as a useful corrective as we contemplate the coming period of the Reformation, when the church began to split on doctrinal grounds and Europe was split into different religious camps. Bosch's vision is not far from that of Calvin, whose writings emphasize human depravity.

PIETER BRUEGHEL

Pieter Brueghel (c. 1525 or 1530–1569) virtually chronicles the lives of peasants in his paintings. But an interesting twist is the way in which he also shows an awareness of classical myths, as he does, for instance, in his most famous painting, *Landscape with the Fall of Icarus* (Color Plate 11).

Landscape with the Fall of Icarus is a witty painting. It includes a number of related landscapes: the nearby field plowed by a well-dressed peasant, the lower pasture, the distant white cliffs. Commerce is portrayed in the ships, whose sails are in full, busy billow. But the actual fall of Icarus can hardly be seen. In the sea, Icarus's struggling legs are barely visible. His death, the core of a significant myth, goes unnoticed by all those in the scene. The irony of the sun's rising while Icarus falls suggests that the world of work and trade often remains ignorant of the importance of serious events.

In this northern dawn, the color seems unreal. The sharply contrasting red doublet of the peasant in the foreground suggests that he is well-off, comfortable, and perhaps even self-important. The red arrests our attention, making it all the more difficult to find, in the dominant sea-green and earth tones, the figure of Icarus. The psychological realism is reinforced by the colors, which help us realize that the significance of such events is usually lost on the mass of people.

The distortion of the perspective in this painting helps link our awareness to that of the peasant behind the plow. For a moment, we seem to share his perspective, seeing the world as he sees it. The world of the sixteenth century is busy, productive, and active. Icarus is anachronistic in this scene, since he fell thousands of years earlier; it is as if Brueghel were saying that if something as momentous as this happened in his age, the general busyness of the people would render it invisible.

PERCEPTION KEY

Brueghel, *Landscape with the Fall of Icarus*

1. What are the dominant colors in *Landscape with the Fall of Icarus* (Color Plate 11)? What color area is most in contrast to those colors? What is the effect of this contrast?

2. How many different landscapes are in the painting? What activities are going on in these landscapes?

3. What is the point of view of the painting? Is a single point of view dominant?

4. Where is Icarus? What is he doing? (Note: Icarus was the son of Daedalus in Greek myth. Both attached wings to themselves so that they could fly, but Icarus, because he was vain, flew so close to the sun that the wax holding the wings to his body melted, and he fell. The myth is an ancient warning against aspiring beyond one's station in life.)

5. What comment does the painting make on the myth of Icarus?

Technology

The invention of printing with movable type in the 1450s by Johannes Gutenberg (c. 1400–1468) signaled the development of new kinds of presses that made it possible to begin dissemination of high-quality woodcuts and other kinds of prints to a large audience of people who could afford prints but not paintings.

Woodcuts had been available earlier, but they were relatively crude. The woodcut process leaves a line of wood in relief that absorbs ink and transfers it to paper. Engraving, widely used in the sixteenth century, is the opposite process. A metal plate is cut into with a burin, which removes a portion of the metal equivalent to the line desired. Then the plate is inked, the excess ink is removed, and paper is pressed against the plate to receive the ink held by the grooves. Great detail can be achieved by the engraving process.

Albrecht Dürer: The Value of Craft

There were innumerable fine printmakers in the north in the fifteenth and early sixteenth centuries, but none more famous than Albrecht Dürer (1471–1528), who was born in Nuremberg. He was a superb painter, but he became internationally known for his prints. The world, as he viewed it, was so filled with detail that the true artist could not ignore it. He sought to portray the world he saw. As he said, "Every form brought before our vision falls upon it as upon a mirror." Therefore, the artist is like a mirror, representing the world with the clarity and precision of nature.

Dürer was also a learned man, committed to understanding theory. He followed the advice of the Roman architect Vitruvius, who conceived the body in a circular space, with head, arms, and legs all ending on the perimeter of the circle. For his figures, Dürer used an exact system of ratios and proportions which he hoped would produce the effect of beauty. Dürer, then, can be thought of as a humanist, since he returned to classical texts, while treating, in most cases, religious themes.

Figure 12-14 shows an engraving by Dürer (*Adam and Eve*); Figure 12-15 shows one of his woodcuts (*The Fall of Man*). There are substantial differences

Figure 12-14
Albrecht Dürer. *Adam and Eve*. 1504. Engraving, 9 ⅞ by 7 ⅝ inches. (Fonds Albertina, Wien.)

between the engraving and the later woodcut. The engraving accurately represents the body, and there are echoes of classical sculpture. The modeling is subtly handled in an effort to convince us of the three-dimensionality and bulk of the figures. Because of the darkness behind them and the extraordinary detail of the animals and the vegetation, the nude bodies almost seem to radiate light. They dominate the composition and are linked visually by the tree and by their arms and the serpent's head. The engraving may be portraying the moment just after the eating of the apple, since Adam and Eve have covered their loins with leaves; yet none of their splendor has worn off.

The woodcut solves the problem of unity by entwining Adam and Eve in each other's arms. Totally nude, they contemplate the apple, and Eve tempts Adam to eat. The woodcut, with its heavier, blunter lines, seems aimed at a more dramatic

moment—the instant before Adam raises his arm to take the apple and complete the fall of humankind. There is an irony here: we are asked to appreciate the beauty of the woodcut, while reflecting on the horror of the moment that it portrays. The mild instability of the composition results because Adam and Eve no longer each dominate half of the space. They are intertwined the way the vegetation is intertwined. Eve's arm encircles Adam the way the serpent encircles the tree.

The engraving asks us to be awed by the beauty of humankind; the woodcut asks us to be saddened by the loss of that beauty. In each case the profusion of detail—the teeming world of nature—reminds us that the outcome of this moment involved everything and everyone. Paradise was lost, and the world was gained. Nothing, not even vegetation, escaped the effects of Adam and Eve's decision.

Figure 12-15
Albrecht Dürer. *The Fall of Man*. c. 1511. Woodcut. 5 by 3 ¾ inches. (Fonds Albertina, Wien.)

COMPARISON KEY

Dürer, Adam and Eve and The Fall of Man

1. In which of the prints shown in Figures 12-14 and 12-15 are the figures of Adam and Eve most idealized? Does either have the frankness of van Eyck's portrayal in the Ghent Altarpiece (Figure 12-8)?

2. Which print most calls our attention to the act of eating the apple?

3. Which print seems most interested in the psychology of the moment? Can either print be said to be dramatic?

4. What differences can you see between the technique used in the woodcut and the technique used in the engraving? Which is more detailed? Which is more forceful in line? Does one show nature in a warmer, more positive light than the other?

5. What elements in these works might be thought of as emphasizing the human qualities of Adam and Eve? Are they positive or negative qualities?

Literature

Northern literature was exceptionally vigorous in the sixteenth century. It reflected the intensity of intellectual concerns regarding humanism that marked the age, particularly as it went through the stress of the fragmentation of the church into Catholic and Protestant. In France, François Rabelais (c. 1483–1553) and Michel de Montaigne (1533–1592) absorbed the flavor of humanism and produced a literature of lasting value. Rabelais's work is broad, amusing satire intended to make people laugh at—but not lament—the human condition. It is essentially optimistic, although at times it employs the grotesque plentitude of Hieronymus Bosch. Montaigne is famous for his essays on human behavior. His work takes important concepts and explores them in incisive, brief studies which began the vogue of the short, intense essay.

In England, the sixteenth century saw a flowering of Italian influence, particularly in the sonnet and in elaborate, classically attuned narrative poems. Theater began to develop in the last decades of the sixteenth century, producing numerous geniuses, among them Christopher Marlowe (1564–1593), whose plays were among the most popular of his day. His world, like that of most of the playwrights of his time, was essentially secular, but he often turned his eye toward the implications of human actions in light of religious belief.

FRANÇOIS RABELAIS: THE VALUE OF FREE WILL

Northern literature expressed confidence in the ability of human beings to manage their affairs. Concepts such as fate and the will of God were never totally forgotten, but they were held in abeyance. Human will was what literary people examined; it drove their characters, guided the dramatic action, and shaped the dramatic moment. The triumph of human will implied gaining control of the world, both in terms of human behavior and in terms of the world of nature and science. Human learning was of great importance because of its implications for controlling events.

Rabelais's masterpiece, *Gargantua and Pantagruel*—published in five parts, between 1532 and 1564—is the story of a family of giants whose appetites for life, love, and learning are so huge that they could be those of the entire human race. The book is lusty and often offensive, but never scabrous. Its ultimate intent is to ask us to treat with dignity all that is human.

Classical texts are cited frequently in its pages, indicating Rabelais's connection with humanism. The first book gives advice on education in the sciences and mathematics, since such an education fitted the new person of the Renaissance.

Gargantua tells his son, Pantagruel, how much better modern education is:

> My father Grandgousier, of blessed memory, made every effort that I might achieve mental, moral and technical excellence. The fruit of my studies and labors matched, indeed surpassed, his dearest wish. But you can realize that conditions were not as favorable to learning as they are today. Nor had I such gifted teachers as you. We were still in the dark ages; we still walked in the shadow of the dark clouds of ignorance; we suffered the calamitous consequences of the destruction of good literature by the Goths. Now, by God's grace, light and dignity have been restored to letters, and I have lived to see it. Indeed, I have watched such a revolution in learning that I, not erroneously reputed in my manhood the leading scholar of the century, would find it difficult to enter the bottom class in a grammar school.

In one episode in *Gargantua and Pantagruel*, Gargantua founds a new religious order to which he gives his estate, Thélème. The name means "free will"; the order contains both men and women, but only beautiful women and handsome men. The monks and nuns can wear any clothing they like, and their outfits are often described in marvelous terms. Thélème includes tennis courts, playing fields, and shooting ranges, and the residents also enjoy falconry and hunting.

Gargantua is guided by the view that people are good and can govern well without outside restraints. In Chapter 57 of Book 1, Rabelais tells us how those at Thélème lived:

> Their whole life was ordered not by law, statute or rule, but according to their free will and pleasure. They arose when they pleased. They ate, drank, worked and slept when the spirit moved them. No one awoke them, forced food or drink upon them or made them do anything else. Gargantua's plan called for perfect liberty. The only rule of the house was: DO AS THOU WILT because men that are free, of gentle birth, well-bred and at home in civilized company possess a natural instinct that inclines them to virtue and saves them from vice.

Such a view of humankind would be revolutionary in any age. Of course, Rabelais predicated his view on class structure: not everyone had the breeding or background to qualify for such unrestricted progress. Rabelais recognized the emergent classes, who, while not the nobility, were bred into privilege and a position of honor. During the Renaissance, new families were added to the nobility as a reward for distinguished service in military and domestic affairs. Even the clergy could pass opportunity on to their families. Rabelais reflected the growing optimism of the emergent classes, who were changing European culture.

MICHEL DE MONTAIGNE: HUMANISM AND SKEPTICISM

Like Rabelais, Montaigne was a humanist. His *Essays* (1580) include discussions of Seneca, Plutarch, Cicero, Julius Caesar, and Greek philosophers. He quotes liberally from innumerable classical authors. In the humanist tradition, he also includes references to modern authors, demonstrating an immense learning. The *Essays* represent a new kind of literature—one that anatomizes human culture by examining its details closely. The titles include: "Of Idleness," "Of the Education of Our Children," "Of Friendship," "Of Names," "Of Virtue," and "Of Experience." In the process of writing about such topics, Montaigne reveals much about himself and the values of his age, which centered on the human condition and on human knowledge. Very few of his essays deal with religious topics, and none of them treat religion uncritically.

Montaigne's essays study human behavior with an eye toward helping readers clarify their own values. His essay on friendship, a favorite Renaissance topic, presses beyond casual connections between people:

What we ordinarily call friends and friendships are nothing but acquaintanceships and familiarities formed by some chance or convenience, by means of which our souls are bound to each other. In the friendship I speak of, our souls mingle and blend with each other so completely that they efface the seam that joined them, and cannot find it again. If you press me to tell why I loved him, I feel that this cannot be expressed, except by answering: Because it was he, because it was I.

Montaigne always invites us to examine a topic along with him and to question our own assumptions

as well as his. His examination of values knew few bounds, since his mind was inquiring and wide-ranging. One of the most important subjects that he examined was the validity of human knowledge, which was of great interest in an age that had revived Platonism. "Apology for Raymond Sebond" focuses on Sebond's book *Natural Theology*, which tried to show that human knowledge, unaided by faith, could "read" the truth about God in his works —nature. Montaigne demonstrates that human knowledge is faulty because it depends on the senses, which are fallible and uncertain. Montaigne strikes out against the vanity of those who think that everything can be known or who forsake everything for knowledge. Human behavior, he points out, varies from culture to culture, which demonstrates that no certainty can be achieved through reason or knowledge. Therefore, one must have faith in things as they are.

All knowledge, Montaigne says, rests on faith. He became known as a "fideist," one who is willing to take the knowledge of God on faith alone. Such a view places religious knowledge off to one side, while making questions of science and human behavior the chief concerns of those who are interested in learning. Inadvertently, Montaigne secularized the search for knowledge. In his age, geniuses like Thomas Aquinas, who devoted their intellectual research to religion, gave way to geniuses such as Johannes Kepler (1571–1630), the astronomer and mathematician who helped establish the fact that the earth revolves around the sun, and not the reverse.

Montaigne was an enthusiastic student of human nature. His efforts were widely imitated. Francis Bacon (1561–1626) was inspired to write his own series of essays, and, like Montaigne, he was indifferent to religion. A man of the world, he was concerned, as his age was concerned, with secular matters. One of Montaigne's legacies was the splitting of faith and knowledge into separate spheres; this set the stage for the development of secular science, the achievement of the next century.

CHRISTOPHER MARLOWE: THE LIMITS OF KNOWLEDGE

Christopher Marlowe, one of the greatest of the English playwrights during the reign of Elizabeth I, wrote plays for only six years. He was educated at Cambridge and may have been a foreign agent for the government. A roisterer, he was killed in a tavern during a fight over a bill when he was twenty-nine. His interests were so openly secular that he was accused of being an atheist, a very serious charge in the late 1500s.

The Tragicall History of Doctor Faustus (1592–1593), probably written with a collaborator, is the story of a brilliant theologian who was educated at the University of Wittenberg (where Martin Luther and Hamlet studied). Faustus is a symbol of his age: he is adventurous, daring, self-confident, and possessed of an insatiable thirst for knowledge. When he finds that he has studied everything that can be known, he turns to the occult and magic, two areas of study that were of particular fascination to northern thinkers.

Faustus is so given over to his quest that he is willing to become the ultimate revolutionary—to contest with the highest authority, God. Faustus sells his soul to the devil, Mephistopheles, in return for a guarantee of unlimited knowledge.

One of the ironies of the play is that when Faustus becomes possessed of knowledge and power, he can do very little with it. He plays tricks on the authorities and surveys the world, but nothing positive or important results from his power. He demands that Helen of Troy be brought to him, and when he sees her, he says:

> Was this the face that launched a thousand ships
> And burnt the topless towers of Ilium?
> Sweet Helen, make me immortal with a kiss.
> (Act 5, Scene 1, line 98.)

Helen, who had long fascinated classical writers, is seen as a demon by Faustus; his involvement with her condemns his soul forever. Thus, the illusion of beauty captivates him.

Marlowe struck a chord that was popular in his age. The transition to the Renaissance was not made without uncertainty and pain, and the more conservative among the populace looked upon those who carried out scientific experiments and who quested for knowledge as potentially dangerous. The world of

---

PERCEPTION KEY

 Rabelais, Montaigne, and Marlowe

Reading: For this perception key, read Book 1 of *Gargantua and Pantagruel*; Montaigne's "Of Experience," "Of Friendship," and "Apology for Raymond Sebond"; or Marlowe's *Tragicall History of Doctor Faustus*.

1. Rabelais: Are the characters or the circumstances in *Gargantua and Pantagruel* realistic? Are the ideas and concerns humanist? Is there any noticeable awareness of classical tradition or the tradition of scholarship? How positive is the book's view of religion?

2. Montaigne: What are the primary concerns of the essays that you read? Are they consistent with our discussion of humanism? What is Montaigne's position on the question of human knowledge? Is he generally optimistic about the fate of humankind, or is he pessimistic? Does he show a serious interest in religion in his essays? Is he irreligious?

3. Marlowe: Do you find Faustus an attractive character? Is he three-dimensional and psychologically believable? To what extent is he a symbol of his era? Does he treat classical learning positively? How clear is Marlowe's commitment to Renaissance progress? Is Faustus a warning to the Renaissance?

science was new and exciting, but it was also threatening to a people whose faith had always centered on heaven and God. Turning to the earth and to humankind was an unsettling and fearful experience. The play ends with this warning:

Cut is the branch that might have grown full straight,
And burned is Apollo's laurel bough
That sometimes grew within this learned man.
Faustus is gone: regard his hellish fall,
Whose fiendful fortune may exhort the wise
Only to wonder at unlawful things
Whose deepness doth entice such forward wits
To practice more than heavenly power permits.

The seriousness of the warning does not detract from Faustus' appeal as a character. He has daring, flair, and zeal; he is one who risks everything, and although he fails, he does so with such energy that he is vastly more memorable than a timidly pious hero.

The Protestant Reformation

By the sixteenth century, the church had become a powerful political organization; its authority in secular matters extended directly from Rome and the Papal States. The pope carried on international diplomacy and even waged war against French invaders who were attempting to take command of Naples, Milan, and other territories.

MARTIN LUTHER

When Martin Luther (1483–1546; Figure 12-16) nailed his Ninety-Five Theses to the door of the church in Wittenberg in 1517, he began a revolution which no one in his day could have foreseen. The son of a miner, Luther went to the university at Erfurt, where his parents expected him to study law. He might have done so; however, one evening, during a terrifying electrical storm, he prayed to Saint Anne and vowed to give his life to the church if he was saved. After the storm, he shocked his parents by joining an order of monks. He continued his education, devoting himself entirely to the most demanding of theological subjects, and became a doctor of theology in Wittenberg in 1512.

Eventually, Luther developed the concept of "justification by faith," by which he meant that above all, God demands the faith of his flock. Faith is what

Figure 12-16
Lucas Cranach. *Martin Luther*. Oil on canvas. (City of Bristol Museum and Art Library.)

determines salvation, not perfection of duty or action. Luther felt that the Bible taught this.

The church's practice of selling indulgences was the chief target of Luther's attack. An indulgence is a lessening of the time spent in purgatory (that is, of the penalties incurred by sin). Sinners were thought to have to endure penance on earth and in purgatory until they were pure enough to enter heaven. The church relied on what it called a "treasury of good works" to help sinners "balance their books" with God. At first, good works, such as acts of charity and pilgrimages to distant holy places, were required for indulgences to be granted. But in Luther's time, indulgences could be bought for cash.

Luther felt that this practice in either form perverted the meaning of Christianity because it shifted the emphasis away from justification by faith and toward justification by good deeds. When Luther posted his theses, he began a public debate on the issues. The pope, outraged, sent his legate to Wittenberg to force Luther to recant. Luther was excommunicated by the church after his famous declaration, "Here I stand," which meant that he stood firm on the principles he found in the Bible. He would listen to no other authority, including the pope.

Luther would have been severely chastised, perhaps killed, if he had not had the support of the secular authorities in Saxony. The result of his stand is that the church was split into a northern Protestant church and the church of Rome. The primary split came in regard to church governance. An immense shift took place as a result of Luther's view that the Bible was the ultimate authority and that the individual must act in accordance with personal faith and understanding. The individual became, through justification by faith, the final authority on religious matters. The authority of the church community—pope, bishop, and priest—was lessened.

In his book *On Christian Liberty*, Luther said, "If you were nothing but good works from the soles of your feet to the crown of your head, you would not be worshipping God; [that is done not] by works, but only by faith of heart." The distinction between works and faith is critical, since it shifts the emphasis to the individual; this ties in with the general spirit of the Renaissance, when an interest in biography developed (in the work of Montaigne and others) and when there was a growing psychological interest in character in drama and in painted portraits. In the same vein, Luther centered on the spiritual inwardness of the individual. He proclaimed that we would see a "spiritual, inward, new man" who would contrast with the "fleshly, outward, old man." Luther's views led to a profound spiritual revolution whose center was the heart of the faithful. In a sense, his views paralleled those of Rabelais's Gargantua, who established the monastery of Thélème: the new spiritual person no longer needed the absolute weight of absolute authority—particularly when it went against the conscience and seemed wrong.

OTHER REFORMERS: ERASMUS, ZWINGLI, AND CALVIN

Luther founded a church which still bears his name. But without the presence of many other dissatisfied clerics clamoring for reform, his actions would have gone for nothing. The time was right for his break with the church, and many others followed him.

The Dutch Christian humanist Desiderius Erasmus (c. 1466–1536) had set the stage for reform in his widely read book *The Praise of Folly* (1509), which was written in Cambridge in the house of Sir Thomas More (1478–1535; himself the author of a satire on explorations and discoveries, *Utopia*). In his work Erasmus observed that the entire world was in the grip of folly and that folly was the true demigod of the politicians, the clergy, and the professionals. His criticism of the church was so keen and so accurate that it was said, almost in his own time, that "Erasmus laid the egg that Luther hatched." He did not, however, abandon his church; he remained a Catholic despite the schism occurring around him.

The Swiss humanist Huldrych Zwingli (1484–1531) took another direction. He believed that God would be impressed not by outward appearances, but only by inward holiness; thus his church had no decorations—no paintings, no carvings.

Zwingli was a scholar. He did not have the political impact of Luther and did not found a religion. However, his most famous student, John Calvin (1509–1564), was to help shape the development of Protestantism in France, England, and eventually America. Calvin was neither as extreme as Zwingli nor as conservative as Luther. He stood between them, anxious to avoid the excesses of the Roman church but also eager to preach a doctrine based on the inwardness of the religious experience. Calvin's view of humankind, however, was rather dark. He laid heavy stress on human depravity, caused by the fall of Adam, and on the teaching that only a few people would be among the chosen who would enter the kingdom of heaven. The "conscience is my guide" school of religious thought developed from Calvinism, which was popular in Holland, Flanders, Belgium, and England.

THE REFORMATION IN ENGLAND

England was a special case. Reformation came there not only because of a deep spiritual commitment, but also for political reasons. As can be seen in Figure 12-17, the celebrated northern painter Hans Holbein (c. 1497–1543) offers us a special insight into the character of Henry VIII (1509–1547), who declared himself head of the English church in 1534 when,

after a long period of negotiation, he was unable to get the pope to approve an annulment of his marriage to Catherine of Aragon, who had given him no male heir. When he married Anne Boleyn (mother of Elizabeth I), his archbishop, Cranmer, annulled his marriage to Catherine and took over as the spiritual head of the church.

Henry quickly abolished the monasteries in England and gave the land to favorites. And although much of value was lost in the destruction of the monasteries, some good was done. The monasteries were no longer the rich cultural havens they had been during the Middle Ages but had degenerated. Distributing the wealth of the monasteries to influential persons helped establish Henry's control over the country. The reform of the English church, despite

Figure 12-17
Left: Hans Holbein. *Henry VIII.* 1539–1540. Oil on canvas, 34 ¾ by 29 ½ inches. (Galleria Corsini, Rome; photo, Alinari/Art Resource.)

CONCEPT KEY

The Reformation and the Crisis in Values

1. Luther praised an inner vision—a spiritual commitment that could not be legislated by an institution. How did his view become an expression of individualism and differ from the view of the established church?

2. How could Luther's actions—breaking away from the Roman church and establishing his own—have serious consequences for the future of politics as a whole? How might centering authority for one's actions on one's conscience undermine the authority of an institution?

3. If the "conscience is my guide" variety of religion is to be followed, what might be required of those who are religious?

4. The Reformation was in some measure a result of spiritual and theoretical differences and in some measure a result of political differences. Is it possible to see these differences expressed in the art and literature of the age? Can one tell which was of greater importance to the Reformation by examining the arts?

the fact that many zealous Protestants urged greater change, was not as complete as most reformers wished. The Puritans who settled in America in 1620 had left England a generation earlier for Holland because they considered the English church too Roman. It still depended on the hierarchy of king, bishop, and priest. Radical reform came for the Puritans only on American soil.

Music

NORTHERN MUSIC

The great musicians of the late fifteenth and early sixteenth centuries were from France, Flanders, Belgium, and the Netherlands. Northern music was still dominated by great religious composers, such as Guillaume Dufay (c. 1400–1474), Jean Okeghem (c. 1410–1495), and Josquin des Prez (c. 1440–1521). Secular songs set to a lute or some other stringed instrument were popular in most northern communities. They tended to be smooth, lyric pieces characterized by rich melody and appealing vocal coloration. Polyphonic religious pieces such as motets, sung in Latin, were also popular. The motets of Okeghem and Josquin are justly famous for their melodic inventiveness and their rich sonorities. Sound itself pleased both composers and listeners, just as rich surfaces and colorations in architecture and painting pleased architects and painters and those who viewed their work. The complex polyphony of the earlier age gave way to a subtler form in which a dominant melodic line was constantly heard.

The harmonic structures in Renaissance music are based on the consonance of thirds and sixths; there are occasional dissonances, but rarely on the strong beats unless the dissonance is a suspension—a harmony that quickly resolves into the consonance of a third, a sixth, or an octave. Most northern Renaissance music is a careful blend of voices concentrating on mellifluousness, sonority, richness, and pleasing sounds. The use of cadences—chord progressions that signal a conclusion—was becoming more and more common, and composers explored ways of making cadences more pronounced and more varied.

Luther recognized that music was a key ingredient in the mass, but instead of emphasizing the huge musical mass, such as those by Okeghem and Josquin, Luther emphasized the hymn—a simple structure, with effective melodic and harmonic qualities, that appealed to Protestant churchgoers. Luther himself wrote a number of powerful and lasting hymns, among them "A Mighty Fortress Is Our God," which is still sung.

The great masses now included many instruments as well as voices. Vielles and the newer viols were much in evidence, as were horns, recorders, and shawms. The organ eventually became a favorite among Protestants; later, the possession of a portable organ was sometimes thought to be the equivalent of a profession of Protestant faith. The harmonic richness, particularly after 1530, of instrumentation in the mass and other religious choral music was an indispensable prelude to the much later development of symphonic music.

JOSQUIN DES PREZ: TOUCHING THE EMOTIONS

When Igor Stravinsky was dying, he wished to listen to the music of two composers. One of them was himself. The other was Josquin des Prez. Although Josquin had been born in Hainault, he spent most of his creative life in Italy, serving the Sforza family in Milan. He moved among the nobility, who admired him and commissioned him to compose works, and his reputation was so great that 100 years later he was still referred to as a perfect composer. His motets are filled with variety and imagination, but the great challenge in his time was the music for the mass, which usually had five parts:

Kyrie: Lord Have Mercy

Gloria in Excelsis Deo: Glory to God on High

Credo: I Believe

Sanctus (with Benedictus): Holy, Holy, Holy, Blessed

Agnus Dei: O Lamb of God

Josquin's masses are deeply moving. Music historians, such as Howard Mayer Brown, credit him with being "the first composer fully aware that music can be the art that most directly touches human sensibilities." He touched those sensibilities by concentrating on the character and quality of sound. He built structures of sonority that flow and rise in magnificent stages, creating gentle tensions and then releasing them in slow, long arcs of melody that shift from voice to voice. Rarely do the four voices sing the same words in his masses; rather, one voice begins while another is in the middle of a phrase. Melodies join one another the way all the parts of his musical structure do: with no trace of junctures. Missa "Pange Lingua" (mass on the text, "Now my tongue the mystery telling") and Missa "l'Homme Armé" (mass of "The Armed Man," or Saint Michael, who is usually shown in armor) are built from smooth risings and fallings of music whose beauty is intense and spiritual.

Josquin's harmonies depend on English song techniques and the development of triadic harmony. The triad, based on two intervals of thirds (C-E-G, for instance), becomes a lush, sensual, and extraordinarily pleasing source of musical complexity and invention. On it is built much of the harmonic experiment of later ages. The old-fashioned cantus firmus style—in which the tenor held a long, sustained note—gave way to a style in which each voice shares the job of providing stability and harmonic tension.

Josquin preferred the polyphony of contrapuntal canons—something like the rounds that children sing in "Row, row, row your boat"—or other forms that permit the repetition of melodic material; these gave him the opportunity to develop full harmonic patterns and strong cadences. His method is often called "imitative polyphony," by which is meant that one voice enters imitating the pattern of the preceding voice, thus integrating the melodic material in a complex and fascinating manner. The method creates a characteristic texture which must be described as sensually rich and pleasing, while still recognizably

spiritual. A cantus firmus (a melody that is repeated in the tenor voice) acts as a skeleton for Josquin's Missa "l'Homme Armé." A folk tune (reproduced in Figure 12-18), it ends with a strong sense of finality (at bar 9) where the tenor ends "doubter" on G; then rises solidly to D, a fifth above, three times; only to end again on G. This pattern, known in modern terminology as the "V-I cadence," will produce a strong sense of finality in any key. The use of a popular folk tune in a mass is a technique of Renaissance humanism. It helped the average churchgoer establish an immediate relationship with the music, instead of maintaining an impersonal distance.

Josquin sometimes used the tune directly in a given voice, and at other times he borrowed patterns from it and spread them through the voices so that no one could possibly hear the entire tune. Instead, anyone who read the music would have the satisfaction of knowing that the original tune was there as a substructure.

The Gloria (Figure 12-19) of his Missa "l'Homme Armé Sexti Toni" (his second mass on the theme, written in the sixth of the old church modes, beginning on F) reveals some of his technique. He does not use the folk tune directly, but we know that he mined it for materal, which he then "buried" again.

The upper voice begins, the altus voice is heard next, and then the tenor and bass enter at measure 25. This produces a strong contrast because it is simply a pattern of five descending notes: C held for three measures and then C, B flat, A, G, and F. It is the folk tune transposed a tone lower. The descent in the folk tune is A to D, which is repeated in reverse

Figure 12-18

"L'Homme Armé." A translation of the text is: "Oh, the man, the man at arms / Fills the world with dread alarms. / Everywhere I hear them wail, / 'Find, if you would breast the gale, / A good stout coat of mail.' / Oh, the man, the man at arms / Fills the world with dread alarms." (From Gustave Reese. *Music in the Renaissance.* Rev. ed. New York: Norton, 1959. P. 73.)

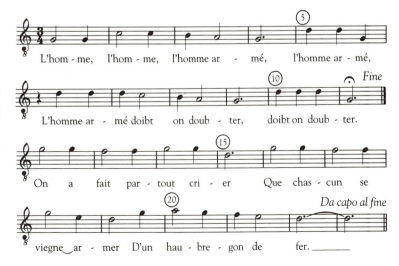

Figure 12-19
Josquin des Prez. Gloria from Missa "L'Homme Armé,"
measures 21 to 30. (From Albert Smijers, ed. *Josquin des
Prés*, Opera Omnia. Rev. ed. Vol. 1. Amsterdam:
Alsbach, 1957. Fascicle V, P. 112.)

Northern Renaissance Music

For this listening key, listen to at least a section of one of the following records (or to a recording of music by one of the following composers): Josquin des Prez, *Missa l'Homme Armé* (Vanguard HM-3); Josquin des Prez, *Missa Pange Lingua* (MCA 2507 or Musical Heritage Society MHS 1000); *Motets* (Turnabout 34437); Guillaume Dufay, *Missa l'Homme Armé* (Lyrichord 7150); *Missa Sine Nomine* (Lyrichord 7234); or Jean Okeghem, *The Motets to the Virgin* (Musical Heritage Society MHS 1306).

1. Establish the pacing of the music. Is it regular, like dance music, with a beat and accents?

2. Which voices are most prominent? Are you aware of more male voices or more female voices? Do the voices sing in unison at any time, or are they usually singing harmony or polyphony? Are musical instruments used in addition to voices? Can you identify their families: Horns? Strings? Percussion?

3. Do different voices sing different texts "against" one another? Can you identify sections in which a group of voices begins a melodic line which, after a few moments, is picked up by another group of voices and then, after a time, is picked up by yet another group? What is the effect of hearing the melody passed back and forth in this fashion?

4. Is the harmonic texture evident? Do the voices support one another with a full and rich sound? Can you hear the cadences as a piece reaches its ending? How much variation is there in the volume of the voices?

5. In a mass, can you tell when the Kyrie ends and the Gloria begins? These are usually the first two sections of the mass. Can you detect the beginning and ending of the Credo, the Sanctus-Benedictus (they are sometimes separate), and the Agnus Dei? Is a different mood established in different sections of the mass? What musical devices are used to change the mood?

here: D to A, not a full cadence. The last notes of the lower voice rise from C to F, which is a weaker cadence than the descent from C to F.

These complexities actually delight the ear. They also delighted the ears of composers who studied Josquin's works to see what they could learn from them. Josquin was able to answer the intellectual needs of the music while also respecting the emotional demands of the composition. His attention to detail must be seen as a concomitant of the age, akin to van Eyck's concern for detail. Nothing was too insignificant to concern God; therefore, the artist must respect all details.

Summary

One consequence of the development of humanism in the northern countries was the gradual separation of religious and secular matters. Just as everyday life grew more and more secular, so did art. Religious forces were still powerful, but religion was becoming political and worldly. The Reformation was both spiritual and political; it separated a northern Protestant church from the southern Catholic church. The architecture of the period was largely secular; a profusion of great houses were built for the growing nobility. Italian influences reached northward, but they were absorbed into what became an idiosyncratic style. Religion was still the subject of much visual art of the period, but there was a growing interest in the portrait—in the individual—and in the details of worldly objects. Some works remained strongly symbolic or allegorical, and realistic detail was used for the purpose of adding meaning to a scene. In other works, realism was used to probe into the psychological dimension of the circumstances or the individuals represented. The literature of the north was especially vigorous; it centered on the anxieties accompanying the growth of humanism, which brought an acute awareness of the writings of the classical authors. Humanism also resulted in highly developed scholarship, which involved wide reading of both ancient and modern texts and a considerable regard for learning in general. The Reformation grew out of humanist learning, which had brought with it a developing optimism. The emphasis on the inward spirituality of the individual was part of a growing religious revival in the north, which may seem paradoxical in an age characterized by secular expansion. Yet it was simply a sign of the degree to which religious and secular matters had grown apart from one another.

Concepts in Chapter 12

Growth in the economies of the northern countries led to the absorption of numerous influences from Italian humanism.

The black death seriously affected northern economic and social structures; it resulted in depopulation and led to greater opportunities for workers.

Architectural developments in the north focused on large houses for landowners; they were used as provincial courts and as focuses for aristocratic activity.

English country houses, such as Longleat House and Wollaton Hall, show a strong northern influence in their design, merged with Italian motifs.

Northern painting, particularly the work of Jan van Eyck, gained a reputation for realism and extraordinary attention to detail.

Allegory and symbolism were common in the work of van Eyck and other northern painters.

Most northern painting was commissioned by the clergy or by wealthy donors, whose portraits appear with the Madonna or various saints.

Northern portraits set a standard for accuracy and for sensitivity to the personality of the sitter; this was a result of the strong influence of humanism.

The widespread growth of printing processes created a market for woodcuts and engravings which painters such as Dürer were quick to exploit.

Humanism affected literature, particularly the work of Rabelais, whose *Gargantua and Pantagruel* satirized his age and its institutions.

Rabelais's optimism, which led him to suggest reform of religious communities, is expressed in his fictional Thélème, the creation of Gargantua.

One of the great concerns of humanist literary figures was education, which was stressed by both Rabelais and Montaigne.

Allusions to classical authors and texts are common in the work of northern writers, which suggests the extent to which humanism affected their work.

Humanists inadvertently created a split between religious knowledge (theology) and human knowledge (science).

Christopher Marlowe's *Tragicall History of Dr. Faustus* reveals the anxieties of the age regarding the fact that human knowledge may have "gone too far."

In 1517, Martin Luther nailed his Ninety-Five Theses to the door of the church at Wittenberg, thus beginning the Protestant Reformation.

Luther's argument with church doctrine centered on justification by faith, as opposed to justification by works; the former is a matter of conscience, and the latter is a matter of church governance.

Other reformers, such as Zwingli and Calvin, joined with Luther in breaking with the Roman church.

As a result of a dispute regarding a divorce, Henry VIII was responsible for England's break with the Roman church in 1534.

The music of Josquin des Prez deemphasized traditional polyphony and emphasized melodic content; this helped him center on the effect of music on human sensibilities.

In music, stronger forms of cadence were developed; these stronger cadences made possible a sense of "completion" that listeners later came to anticipate in music.

Suggested Readings

Brown, Howard Mayer. *Music in the Renaissance.* Englewood Cliffs, N.J.: Prentice-Hall, 1976.

Cantor, Norman F. *Renaissance, Reformation, and Absolutism: 1450–1650.* New York: Thomas Y. Crowell, 1972.

Cuttler, Charles D. *Northern Painting from Pucelle to Brueghel.* New York: Holt, 1968.

Grout, Donald. *A History of Western Music.* New York: Norton, 1973.

Leymarie, Jean. *Dutch Painting.* New York: Skira, 1956.

Munrow, David. *Instruments of the Middle Ages and Renaissance.* Angel EMI Recording SLS 988 with ninety-seven-page booklet. London: Oxford, 1976.

Murray, Peter. *Renaissance Architecture.* New York: Abrams, 1971.

Panofsky, Erwin. *Early Netherlandish Painting.* 2 vols. Cambridge, Mass.: Harvard, 1953.

van Puyvelde, Leo. *Hubert and Jan van Eyck.* New York: Scribner, 1956.

Weinstein, Donald. *The Renaissance and the Reformation.* New York: Free Press, 1965.

White, Christopher. *Dürer: The Artist and His Drawings.* New York: Watson-Guptill, 1971.

CHAPTER 13

THE AGE OF GENIUS: 1475 TO 1600

Cultural Background

 The economic and intellectual expansion caused by the discovery of America and the spread of humanism produced an age of genius and adventure. The balance of power in Europe shifted westward and northward as Spain, Portugal, France, and England exploited their holdings in the new world. As Italian cities began to feel the strain of economic decline, certain signs of hysteria and fear surfaced. The invasion of Italy by Charles III of France in 1495 (at the invitation of Ludovico the Moor, who regretted it almost immediately) created an opportunity for the evangelical priest Girolamo Savanarola (1452–1498) to convert Florence into a puritanical stronghold in which transgressions against church law were dealt with severely. His governance of Florence under the eyes of the French was marked by a revival of religious zeal in excess of anything that Florence had ever known. He had convinced the Florentines that the French presence was a result of Florentine immorality. After only four years, Florence found Savanarola intolerable and had him hanged and burned.

In the new world, the church was preoccupied with converting the Indians, whose populations were decimated by Spanish conquistadors and European diseases. The wholesale destruction of the Aztec, Mayan, and Incan empires was undertaken by a handful of men who were thorough and overwhelming.

Achievements in science were considerable, particularly in the area of astronomy. Accurate observation, a hallmark of modern science, became the vogue. Leonardo da Vinci studied human anatomy and military engineering. Since the church taught that God had put human beings at the center of his creation, the views of Copernicus (1473–1543) were unwelcome. He described the earth as off to one side of a central sun, thus placing it on the same level with the other planets. Copernicus was proved right, and the resistance of the church ultimately weakened its authority in other matters. Science and the arts thrived, and the achievements of scientists and artists were known to people in almost all walks of life.

Architecture

DONATO BRAMANTE

The influence of Brunelleschi was dominant in Italy for a century after his death. One of the architects who absorbed his ideas and continued developing the tradition he had established was Donato Bramante (1444–1514), whose tempietto at San Pietro in Montorio, in Rome (Figure 13-1), is considered an epitome of Renaissance work. It is a round church built on the spot of Saint Peter's martyrdom. Its proportions and lines have been admired and imitated widely. Pope Julius II, a great patron of the arts, employed Bramante to tear down the 1100-year-old basilica of Saint Peter's and replace it with a Renaissance church. Bramante did the early planning (Figure 13-2) and the piers that were to support the dome (these can be seen in Figure 13-3); then he died. Michelangelo was appointed to continue the work in the 1540s. His most important contribution to the completion of the plan was the dome.

Figure 13-1
Right: Donato Bramante. Tempietto, Rome. (Photo, Barbara Malter.)

Figure 13-2
Below left: Plan of Saint Peter's. (From Creighton Gilbert. *History of Renaissance Art.* New York: Abrams, 1972.)

Figure 13-3
Below right: Interior of Saint Peter's. (Photo, Alinari/Art Resource.)

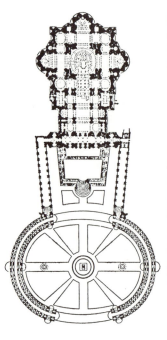

Bramante planned a church in the form of a cross set in a square. The dome would then be commanding from any angle. When Michelangelo built the dome, he thought Bramante's plan would be carried out; however, Carlo Maderna (1556–1629) and others finished the church much later and added a nave and side aisles as well as an elaborate facade, all of which obstructed the view of the dome from every side but the rear (Figure 13-4)—which is the only direction from which one can see Michelangelo's work today.

ANDREA PALLADIO: THE PROPORTIONS OF CLASSICAL ORDER

Palladio (1508–1580), who had been a stonemason, studied buildings in Rome and illustrated an architectural handbook on Vitruvius before writing his *Four Books on Architecture*. Villa Rotunda (Figure 13-5), in his native Vicenza, imitates a Greek temple. It is square with four identical porches. Later architects have admired this building for the same reasons they admire Bramante's tempietto: its flawless proportions

Figure 13-4
Above: Michelangelo, dome of Saint Peter's, seen from the rear of the building. 1546–1564. (Photo, Alinari/Art Resource.)

Figure 13-5
Right: Andrea Palladio. Villa Rotunda, Vicenza. Begun 1550. (Photo, Alinari/Art Resource.)

Figure 13-6
Above: Andrea Palladio.
San Giorgio Maggiore,
Venice. 1556.

Figure 13-7
Right: Andrea Palladio.
Teatro Olympico,
Vicenza. Begun 1579.
(Photo, Alinari/Art
Resource.)

and the sense of perfection that it imparts. In this building, Palladio demonstrated a formula for achieving a classical look in modern times.

That look is also apparent in San Giorgio Maggiore, in Venice (Figure 13-6). One sees the church from a distance, across from the Piazza San Marco. It rises marvelously from the water, gleaming white against the sky. It is innovative in that it adapts the Greek temple front to the basilica design, thereby merging Greek and Roman architectural styles and achieving a special kind of classicism. The lower roofs, over the aisles, parallel the main roof, which creates the illusion of a Greek pediment interrupted by another

Greek pediment in front of it. Palladio experimented with the design and varied it in several ways, always maintaining the pleasing proportions for which he is noted.

Late in his life Palladio built the Teatro Olympico (Figure 13-7), the first indoor theater of the Renaissance. The London Palladium imitates it almost exactly. Vitruvius inspired the design; and the scaena —the wall in Figure 13-7—was built according to his directions. The openings in the scaena were made specially to fool the audience into thinking that there was a colossal amount of space where there was really very little. Actors who entered the audience's space could be seen coming from a great distance, which made processional ceremonies more dignified. The building became the model for the modern theater and helped spread Palladio's reputation throughout Europe. He became the most influential architect of his time.

Painting

The brilliance of painting in the period was such that it presents us with an embarrassment of riches: Giorgione, Raphael, Titian, and Tintoretto. In another age any one of these might have been the most influential painter of his generation. But they are all eclipsed by two towering figures, who were rivals in their own day: Leonardo da Vinci and Michelangelo Buonarroti.

LEONARDO

Leonardo (1452–1519) was the illegitimate son of a barmaid and a Florentine notary. He was taken into his father's house and was apprenticed at an early age to one of the most important workshops in Florence, that of Andrea del Verrocchio. As a youngster, he came into contact with artists of the first order, such as Pollaiuolo and Botticelli. Apparently, he showed such talent that Verrocchio, according to legend, quickly assigned all the chores of painting to him. Leonardo was not a well-educated man: he could not read classical languages, and so he shared in the excitement of the humanist authors only through translations. However, what he did excel at was observation. As his tirelessly prepared notebooks show, very few people of his time could have noted more carefully and more exactly what they saw.

The Renaissance delight in high finish is apparent in *The Madonna of the Rocks*, painted in 1485 (Color Plate 12). A triangle underlies the figures of the Virgin, Christ, Saint John, and Elizabeth, Mary's cousin. The pyramidal arrangement is dynamic, not static. If one draws a triangle over the painting, one sees that its sides project beyond the borders of the painting, and yet the eye naturally comes to rest on the face of the Virgin. The background—with the dramatic, oddly shaped rocks and the mysterious lighting and mist—is a tour de force. These elements have no simple geometric organization.

Geometry also underlies the organization of Leonardo's *Last Supper* (Figure 13-8). Christ sits at the center of the table, and his head, his arms, and the edge of the table closest to him form a triangle. Behind him are three windows, symbolic of the three-part nature of God. The figures on one side of the table are gesturing to one another agitatedly; some are leaning and pointing toward the center of the composition, themselves forming a pyramidal trinitarian grouping. The moment is dramatic: Christ has just revealed that one of the disciples will betray him.

Using tracing paper, you may wish to try your own version of the drawing in Figure 13-9. The lines of perspective in the room radiate from Christ's face. His arms, which point to the bread and wine (symbols of the eucharist), are part of a solid triangle that centers and stabilizes the composition. The patterns in the ceiling also radiate toward Christ's face. Above his head is a semicircular pediment over the central window; one of the few curves in the composition, it suggests a halo. Beneath the table is another curve, which is actually in the wall of the refectory (dining hall) at Santa Maria delle Grazie, in Milan, whose order commissioned the fresco. More such lines of force and even more geometric patterns can be discovered by examining the painting carefully and analyzing the groupings of the apostles. The orderliness of the painting is part of its power. The formal elements operate on us on a subliminal level, centering our emotional attention on Christ, who is a serene figure in a turbulent emotional vortex. The dramatic moment shown here is like that portrayed on the east pediment of the Parthenon, where the "shock waves" produced by the birth of Athena radiate from the center of the composition through the gods seated to the left and right.

Leonardo's fresco technique has unfortunately hastened the deterioration of the *Last Supper*. He did not want to use the traditional watercolors, and so he used oil on top of dried plaster. The humidity in the refectory began to damage the painting only fifty years after it was finished. Many efforts at restoration —some less successful than others—have been made (another is now in progress), and the entire refectory, except for this wall, collapsed during a bombing in World War II. Nonetheless, the *Last Supper* is still among the most powerful works of art in western culture.

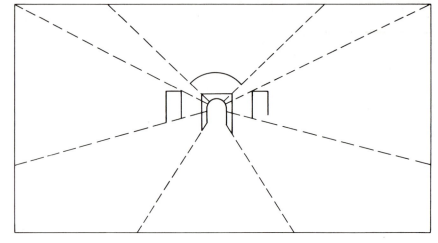

Figure 13-8
Above: Leonardo. *The Last Supper.* Santa Maria della Grazie, Milan. 1495–1497. Fresco, oil and tempera on plaster. (Photo, Scala/Art Resource.)

Figure 13-9
Right: Perspective drawing of Leonardo's *Last Supper.*

The *Last Supper* is, like most of the work of the period, religious in subject matter. The technique is realistic, cautious, and scientific. But Leonardo's *Mona Lisa* (Figure 13-10) is a secular painting. It may have been commissioned by the husband of the woman in the painting, or it may have been done solely because the woman fascinated the artist. We do not know. One of the few things we do know about the *Mona Lisa* is that Leonardo took it with him wherever he traveled. When he died at Cloux, in France, it was found among his possessions; that is

why it is now in the Louvre, in Paris. In its own time it was thought to be a miraculous piece of work: Vasari talks about its freshness of color and the remarkable degree to which it resembles the sitter. Its realism was one of its most highly praised qualities.

Today, however, it is praised for its mysterious quality. It may be realistic, but we see it as a suggestive portrait. The expression on the face is totally enigmatic and virtually baffling. The painting is so encrusted with varnish and dirt that Kenneth Clark has called it a "submarine goddess." In the

great hall of the Louvre, where it attracts excited crowds, it seems pitifully small, and the glass that covers it makes it difficult to see; yet going to see the *Mona Lisa* has become an aesthetic pilgrimage.

Mona Lisa's posture creates a basic triangle, much like that of Christ in the *Last Supper*. Her form is calming, secure, and solid. However, the position of the body is quite unusual. The pose now seems natural to us because it has been so widely imitated, but it would be difficult to find it in an earlier painting. The unsettling quality of this pose is counterpointed by the triangular solidity of the form. It has often been observed that the landscapes visible behind the head are unconnected: one is icy and mountainous, and the other is rocky and watery. The road to the right and the bridge to the left help achieve aerial perspective, an unusual effect in a portrait with a landscape background.

Figure 13-10
Left: Leonardo. *Mona Lisa.* 1503–1506. Oil on panel, 30 ¼ by 21 inches. (Louvre, Paris; photo, Musées Nationaux.)

PERCEPTION KEY

Leonardo, Mona Lisa

1. What is the most prominent geometric form underlying the composition of the *Mona Lisa* (Figure 13-10)?

2. Establish the position in which Mona Lisa sits. Can you assume this position? Have you seen an earlier portrait in which a woman sits in this position?

3. Does the background show evidence of the use of vanishing-point perspective? Is the landscape on the left clearly related to the landscape on the right?

4. Would you mistake this for a religious painting? Does the *Mona Lisa* look like any portrait of the Madonna that we have examined? Is it clear that the painting is secular?

5. Describe the emotional qualities of the painting. Does it reveal Leonardo's response to his sitter? Does he look upon her approvingly or disapprovingly? Do you detect a warmth toward her or a distant coolness? Do you feel an emotional response to this painting? Why are people so fascinated by it?

Figure 13-11
Leonardo. *Saint John the Baptist*. 1513–1516. Oil on panel, 27 ½ by 22 ½ inches. (Louvre, Paris; photo, Musées Nationaux.)

Figure 13-12
Leonardo. *Self-Portrait*. c. 1512–1514. Red chalk drawing, 13 ⅛ by 8 ⅜ inches. (Turin Royal Library; photo, G. Rampazzi, Turin.)

Another painting that Leonardo possessed when he died is *Saint John the Baptist* (Figure 13-11), a haunting figure with an enigmatic expression. Saint John's luminosity is part of the subject matter of the painting; it reminds us that he identified Christ as the messiah. Leonardo had used both the unsettling smile and the upward gesture of the arm and hand before, but he had never isolated them so totally as in this painting. He was old and partially paralyzed when he painted this work; thus the anatomy is not as accurate as that in earlier pieces. Yet the painting has a striking mystical simplicity and also an unforgettable form: Saint John is an angel, and a messenger from God.

Leonardo himself was almost as enigmatic as the people in some of his portraits. He was not conventionally religious, and he wrote little about his spiritual commitments; even Platonic theories and humanist debates seem to have been outside his sphere of interest. He was a practical man whose capacity for studying nature is revealed in the innumerable studies of water that he did in his later years. Such a commitment to examining the material world may have made him antagonistic to Platonism. The famous self-portrait shown in Figure 13-12, which was done when he was in his sixties, shows that he could turn his talents to the meticulous study of his own character.

MICHELANGELO

Michelangelo (1475–1564) lived in interesting times. He was born in Arezzo to parents of modest means but was soon brought to Florence. His father did not want him to be an apprentice in an artist's workshop, despite his skill in sculpture and his lack of interest in school. He therefore apprenticed himself, before he was fifteen, to the workshop of Ghirlandajo, studied the great works in the Medici gardens, and was soon regarded as a member of the Medici household.

Through the Medici, he seems to have come under the influence of neo-Platonism, which helped fuse classical values with the message of Christianity. It pointed toward God and showed that flesh could aspire to spirit. Michelangelo was, however, also a keen observer of the world. He is said to have been a student of anatomy and to have dissected corpses in the Hospital of the Innocents, in Florence. The somewhat bitter rivalry between Leonardo and Michelangelo may have been due to Michelangelo's philosophical and religious position. It may also have been due to the fact that they were both geniuses. At the end of his career, Leonardo watched as Michelangelo, who was at the beginning of his, was hailed as a genius.

During much of his career, Michelangelo was in the service of the warrior pope, Julius II, who led the Papal States in pushing the French out of Italy. He undertook the painting of the ceiling of the Sistine Chapel (Figure 13-14) for Pope Julius. By integrating classical, Hebrew, and Christian motifs, Michelangelo reinforced the Platonic view that all myth is one. Michelangelo was not indifferent to such a philosophical position. His views were so strong that he probably argued successfully with Pope Julius for the right to decorate the ceiling as he chose. Michelangelo developed a reputation for "teribilità" (dread force of will) which matched that of Julius, who was known for the same quality.

PERCEPTION KEY

Michelangelo's Sistine Chapel Ceiling

1. What are the chief geometric forms visible in the patterning of the Sistine Chapel ceiling (Figures 13-13 and 13-14)? Which act primarily as frames? How many different "scenes" can you detect? What seems to be implied by the orderliness of the structure? Is the composition dynamic or static?

2. Which figures are the most visible? Why are they as prominent as they are? Are they part of a narrative, or are they to be viewed individually?

3. Are the figures that you can see influenced by classical sculpture or classical idealization of the human figure? The narratives and the images which Michelangelo portrays are from the Old Testament; is that evident from a visual examination of the Sistine ceiling?

4. How should we look at the Sistine ceiling? Is one vantage point obviously best?

5. The central panel represents the creation of Eve. Why should that panel play such an important role in the composition? The panel below depicts the creation of Adam, and the panel above shows the fall of Adam and Eve, with the serpent wound around the tree of the knowledge of good and evil. Why are these events portrayed so prominently?

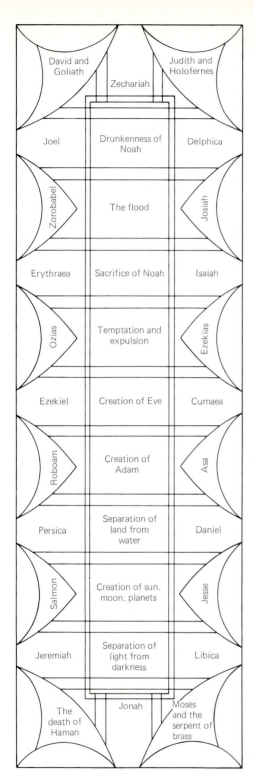

David and Goliath | Zechariah | Judith and Holofernes

Joel | Drunkenness of Noah | Delphica

Zorobabel | The flood | Josiah

Erythraea | Sacrifice of Noah | Isaiah

Ozias | Temptation and expulsion | Ezekias

Ezekiel | Creation of Eve | Cumaea

Roboam | Creation of Adam | Asa

Persica | Separation of land from water | Daniel

Salmon | Creation of sun. moon. planets | Jesse

Jeremiah | Separation of light from darkness | Libica

The death of Haman | Jonah | Moses and the serpent of brass

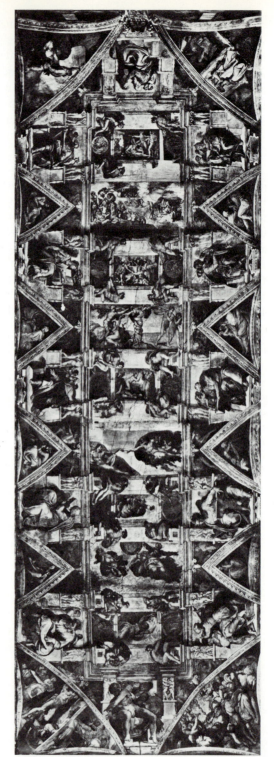

The rationale for the design of the Sistine ceiling (Figures 13-13 and 13-14) has never been adequately explained. Some experts believe that an official theologian was assigned to discuss the project with Michelangelo; others believe that Michelangelo knew the traditions well enough to use Old Testament themes in an apposite fashion, relying on their typological representations of New Testament events. The *Creation of Eve*, for instance, the center panel in the composition, has been understood as a symbolic creation of the church as well as of the Virgin Mary. The figure of Adam, in the adjacent panel, has been interpreted as a type of Christ, as have the figures of Noah, Jonah, and others.

Neo-Platonic orderliness is evident in numbers: the influence of Plotinus's *Enneads* (treatises arranged into groups of nine) can be seen in the division of the space of the barrel vault into nine convenient sections. There are nine prophets and sybils on the left side of the ceiling and nine on the right. The central sections include nine scenes from Genesis. At the ends of the ceiling are six panels depicting nine main characters. The numbers 1, 3, and 9 were critical to the neo-Platonists because they helped establish a mathematical understanding of universal truth. The number of God the creator was 1; 3 stood for the trinity; and 9 was the perfect number of God. Three panels are devoted to the creation of the universe, three to the creation of Adam and Eve, and three to the story of Noah. Three panels treat separation: light from darkness, land from water, and Adam and Eve from the garden. Three treat the activities of humankind. All, in one sense or another, treat separation, since creation is the separation of the created from the rest of the world. The dual theme of creation and separation underscores the begetting and separation from God of Christ. The neo-Platonic ideal of the "ultimate one" is easily realized by the ceiling.

The ceiling is 65 feet above the floor, and there is

no single right way to view its panels. As viewers, we stand on the level of this world, in a place which celebrates the mass, and look upward into infinity—to the world of the pagan sybils and the Hebrew prophets who sensed the coming of Christ. Then we peer into the earliest moment of creation, seeing both the world of God and the world of humankind integrated on one surface, mimicking the neo-Platonic ideal of unity.

The unity is part of a neo-Platonic theory that the division between flesh and spirit is a mystery which we must struggle to understand. As we look up, we stand where the spirit of God presents itself by miracle in the flesh during every mass. This is where spirit and flesh must be fused.

The profusion of nudes in the composition testifies to the integrity of flesh and spirit: the perfection of the body is a metaphor for the perfection of the soul. The perfect body of Adam, in the scene of his creation (Color Plate 13), reminds us of the perfection of the body of Christ. Adam's body seems influenced by the sculptures of the Parthenon—although Michelangelo never saw those works. Adam, whose name means "ground," is neither on the ground nor off it; he is being elevated by the infusion of spirit from the finger of God.

The profusion of trees and wood in the composition reminds us that the pope for whom the chapel is named, Sixtus IV, was a member of the della Rovere family, as was Julius II. Rovere means "oak tree," a fact which explains the representations of acorns and oak leaves. But there are other levels on which the references must be taken, references that include the tree of life, the tree of the knowledge of good and evil, and the tree on which Christ was crucified. Renaissance painting is filled with puns. Thorough study of the ceiling will uncover many more such patterns of repetition that were designed to intensify the harmony of the composition. Plotinus felt that the universal harmony of all creation was part of the expression of the perfection of God, and Michelangelo made his ceiling—like the sky, God's ceiling—express a harmonic relationship of parts.

Figure 13-15 shows one of the most dynamic aspects of the painting of the chapel—the *Last Judgment*, which covers the wall behind the altar. Here there are no painted architectural details between the scenes and no marble frames to separate one narrative moment from the next, as in the ceiling paintings. Dante broke his narrative into

Figure 13-15
Michelangelo. *The Last Judgment.* Sistine Chapel, facing the altar. (Photo, Alinari/Art Resource.)

manageable units—the cantos; the ceiling divisions do the same. But the *Last Judgment* is quite different and suggests the baroque fluidity of the next generation. It is a smoothly flowing scene with God at the center, accepting the saved. One detail shows Michelangelo himself—a body with no skeleton, like a limp cloth—being lifted to heaven. This is not the pessimistic view of the romanesque tympanum at Autun. But it has a protean dynamism that is at least as frightening as the orderliness of the ceiling is reassuring.

RAPHAEL

Raphael Sanzio (1483–1520) was younger than Leonardo and Michelangelo, and he built on their achievements. He modeled figures sculpturally, as Michelangelo did, while maintaining the effects of light and color associated with Leonardo. He was noted for the accuracy of his portraits and for his ability to reveal as much of the essence of the sitter as any painter of the age.

Pope Leo X with Cardinals Giulio de' Medici and Luigi

Figure 13-16
Raphael. *Pope Leo X with Cardinals Giulio de' Medici and Luigi de' Rossi.* c. 1517. Panel painting, 60 ½ by 47 inches. (Galeria degli Uffizi, Firenze; photo, Scala/Art Resource.)

de' Rossi (Figure 13-16) tells an interesting story. Pope Leo X was originally Giovanni de' Medici, and Cardinal Giulio de' Medici was his cousin. Leo succeeded Pope Julius in the papacy, and he was as interested in personal indulgence and gain as Julius had been interested in self-sacrifice and in ridding Italy of foreigners. The painting may have been done in 1517, the year Luther posted his theses on the church door in Wittenberg—in which case it would reveal visually some of Luther's complaints about the church. Leo is shown examining a magnificent illuminated manuscript, which symbolizes his love of collecting and his delight in ownership. This portrait reveals the involvement of the church in secular politics as well as the predilection of high church officials for self-indulgence and the pursuit of worldly pleasures.

Raphael is quite frank in this portrait, as he is in other portraits of secular patrons. The faces are hardly idealized; instead, we feel that they must reveal their sitters all too cruelly. The darkness of the room and of the clothing contrasts with and isolates the faces, and Leo's and Rossi's hands and arms create a sharp diagonal line of force. The triangular shape produced by the cape and head of Leo should stabilize the composition, but the rhythm of the other two heads immediately unsettles it. In no sense does this painting give us a feeling of spiritual simplicity or spiritual reassurance. Instead, Raphael has provided an insight that could have come from Dante's own complaints about church governance.

Raphael's huge fresco in the Vatican Palace, *The School of Athens* (Color Plate 14), portrays the greatest philosophers of Greece on the walls of the palace most central to the Roman church. The painting was commissioned by Pope Julius II; it is part of a group in the Stanza della Segnatura, which Raphael completed with relative ease and without the anxieties and arguments associated with Michelangelo's nearby Sistine ceiling.

Raphael took advantage of the tympanum-shaped space available to him; he echoes its half-round curve in the multiple receding Roman arches that lead the eye to the two central figures. With the aid of the arches, the two central figures also seem to radiate back through the painting. Just as philosophy stems from these figures, lines of force radiate from them. Every figure overlaps or touches another, which implies continuing influence and development.

The action seems to be the discourse between Plato and Aristotle, which is overheard by those near them. Plato holds a copy of his *Timaeus* and points toward heaven, the source of his ideas. Aristotle holds a copy of his *Nicomachean Ethics* and points toward the people, for whom his theories are conceived. Other figures are engaging in private discourse, writing, or simply thinking. In the foreground, two groups of philosophers are at work. The group on the left, which includes Pythagoras and Heraclitus, discusses rules of proportion. On the right, Ptolemy and Euclid consider astronomical problems. The colossal statues by the arch are representations of Apollo and Minerva, who look on approvingly.

The architecture in the painting has long been a problem. It is difficult to determine what kind of building these figures are in. The Roman arches are anachronistic, although such details rarely bothered a

Raphael, The School of Athens

1. What is the action of *The School of Athens* (Color Plate 14)? The bearded figure in the center is Plato, talking with Aristotle. The other figures are philosophers and students. Is this a narrative painting?

2. Examine the painting in terms of stability, balance, centrality of composition, high finish, three-dimensional modeling, and realism.

3. What geometric principles of organization does Raphael use to integrate so many diverse figures? Does the architectonic form of the semicircle, a feature of the wall, help or hinder the organization?

4. Considering that Plato is said to have taught his students in an olive grove, why has Raphael imagined such an imposing setting?

5. How does this painting compare with the Sistine ceiling in terms of the handling of classical ideas? Compare the works in terms of symmetry, balance, and the reverence shown for classical figures. Which seems to be the more "classical" composition?

Renaissance audience. (Throughout the Renaissance, history was only beginning to develop as a discipline. Most people learned about history from plays and other literature.) Raphael's decision to put most of the philosophers on the topmost step, in a line, helps produce a sense of calm integration. The arches caress the figures. The perspective, with the usual marble patterning in the floor, helps integrate the figures on the lower steps, who are, with a notable break in the center, also in a straight line. The perspective, which is emphasized by the architecture and the floor patterning, forces the eye constantly back to the center of the painting as a way of reminding us of the sources of humanism.

TWO SECULAR PAINTERS: GIORGIONE AND TITIAN

Secular painting became more daring during the Renaissance. Two important Italian painters — Giorgione and Titian—are noted for their lasting achievements in secular painting. Their work pointed in new directions and tended to influence painters centuries later. Giorgione (c. 1477–1511), a Venetian, worked in the typical tradition of clarity,

distinctness, and strong color that was characteristic of the Bellinis and other important painters of that city. Titian (1488 or 1490–1576) was one of his students.

Both the *Sleeping Venus* (Color Plate 15), by Giorgione, and the *Concert Champêtre* (Figure 13-17), by Titian, are important Renaissance paintings. For one thing, they both portray nude women not as goddesses (except perhaps in name), but as real people. Venus is shown nude in a landscape that is not clearly connected with her (it was painted by Titian). This is the first of a long line of such "Venuses." We do not see Venus as we do in Botticelli's paintings. We are prepared to believe that a real model posed for the painter and that we see a study of her. The value of the beauty of the human form—the form of a lovely woman—is the true subject of the painting. The title is like a smokescreen.

Titian's *Concert Champêtre*, formerly attributed to Giorgione, is even more bold, since there is no pretense of a classical god or goddess, or even a specific scene from classical or biblical lore. It is a portrait of two musicians and their undraped female companions. For us the circumstances may be unusual, but the musicians seem hardly ruffled. The

Figure 13-17
Titian. *Concert Champêtre*. c. 1508–1510. Oil on canvas, 43 by 54 inches.
(Louvre, Paris; photo, Musées Nationaux.)

women, too, take the circumstances for granted. This painting seems not to have shocked the Venetians, but its capacity to shock modern viewers is not to be underestimated. Both paintings take on considerable importance because they opened the way for portrayals of the nude for its own sake, without embarrassment, and in completely secular circumstances.

Titian was naturally influenced by his teacher. He was impressed by Giorgione's use of color; in fact, one of Titian's own hallmarks is the use of a lush red which often bears his name. He was a successful portrait painter, as *Portrait of a Man* (Color Plate 16)—possibly a study of the epic poet Ariosto—demonstrates. This is a simple, direct work. No background landscape or townscape competes with

the person for our attention. The man's dress is sumptuous; the oversized puffed sleeve is a rich, commanding blue. His expression arrests us. He is examining us as carefully as we are examining him. Titian may have imagined a conversation between this portrait and its audience. We are challenged and appraised by this gentleman, and in turn his challenging glance reveals something about his personality. He commands our respect because he seems so demanding himself. Titian has concentrated everything on the expression on his face, and we are convinced that a personality exists behind it. Moreover, we are convinced that we understand something about that personality, because the expression is so modern.

FOUR MANNERISTS:
PONTORMO, PARMIGIANINO,
TINTORETTO, AND EL GRECO

Vasari used the term "maniera" to describe a new style that we now call "mannerism." Mannerist works call attention to their own artfulness, are apparently self-conscious, are sometimes very odd, and usually demand a psychological readjustment on the part of the viewer. The mannerists seemed determined to work against the principles of calmness, proper proportion, stability, symmetry, and centrality of composition—all of which dominated the painting of the Renaissance masters. They experimented with unusual lighting, distortions, foreshortening, and psychologically unsettling situations.

At the time when the mannerists were active, the church was involved in the Counterreformation, the purpose of which was to oppose the spread of Lutheranism. The arts were a powerful weapon in clarifying the relationship of the church to the community and in holding the community firm in the faith. However, mannerism was an embarrassment to the church because it seemed to propagandize not churchly values but artistic values. The artist and the craft of painting were always at the center of mannerist works, whatever their subject matter.

Pontormo and Parmigianino

Color Plate 17 shows *Deposition*, by Pontormo (1494–1559), and Figure 13-18 shows *Madonna della Collo Longo* ("Madonna of the Long Neck"), by Parmigianino (1503–1540). These paintings are among the chief works of the mannerists. They achieve a precarious ambiguity in almost every sense. Without guidance, it would be very difficult for us to be sure whether their subject is religious or secular. Parmigianino's painting is less obviously religious, since there are no familiar clues that one might associate with the Madonna and Child. Pontormo's painting, despite the ambiguous clothing, depends on the familiar posture of the dead Christ to acquaint us with its subject. In comparison, the way in which the Child lies on the Madonna's lap in Parmigianino's painting is almost a foreshadowing of Christ's eventual descent from the cross.

In neither painting is there a clear underlying or organizing geometry to hold the figures together. In both, we could trace a circular form linking the faces of the figures, but in both cases the circle would be severely distorted. Within each painting we can see familiar pyramidal forms, most obviously in the body of Parmigianino's Madonna. But Parmigianino disrupts the stability of the pyramid with the powerful

---

PERCEPTION KEY

Pontormo and Parmigianino

1. What is the subject matter of each of the works shown in Color Plate 17 and Figure 13-18? Are these works clearly religious or secular?

2. What underlying geometric forms help integrate the figures or stabilize their relationships? Do any formal elements produce instability?

3. Does either painting aim more for symmetrical balance? Which painting is more dependent on centrality of composition?

4. Is space treated realistically in these paintings? Is the viewer clearly aware of the space taken up by the figures and of their relationship to their setting?

5. To what extent does each painting depend on distortion for its effect? Does the distortion alienate you from the painting, or does it intrigue you?

Figure 13-18
Parmigianino. *Madonna della Collo Longo*. 1535. Oil on wood, 85 by 52 inches. (Gallerie Pitti Firenze; photo, Scala/Art Resource.)

down on the figures carrying him, who themselves look off into the space that we inhabit as viewers.

Pontormo's colors are pale, and the light from the upper right seems to wash some of them out entirely. Parmigianino's colors are subdued but are deep and rich, and yet the source of light is quite uncertain. Chiaroscuro, the dramatic juxtaposition of light and dark elements in a painting, is evident in this work; Parmigianino uses a very dark background, against which the important elements are brightly portrayed and emotionally contrasted. Chiaroscuro was to become even more popular later.

The physical distortions in Parmigianino's painting are partly responsible for its name. The Madonna has an unusually long neck, as well as unusually long fingers, both of which may have been intended to give her an aristocratic appearance. The Child is much too big to fit on her lap; his position suggests that he may tumble off at any moment, and this produces a curious form of psychological instability. The expressions on the faces of the children to the left are not clear, but they seem to be aware of the space outside the painting. The prophet in the lower-right-hand corner is an enigma; his outstretched hand holds a scroll, but he turns his head away from it. His space is thoroughly mysterious. The lush draperies in the upper left are equally mysterious, and their rich coloration emphasizes a sensuality that is already intensified in the painting. For many viewers it is an inappropriate sensuality, considering the subject matter.

Tintoretto

Venetian mannerism combined with a revival of profound religious feeling spurred by the Counterreformation. Tintoretto (c. 1518–1594) had a special gift for using light, color, and visual organization to produce high drama. His asymmetrical works often depend on a "tunnel" effect of light and dark, with unusual and unexpected diagonal lines of force.

His *Presentation of the Virgin* (Figure 13-19) shows a link with Pontormo and Parmigianino. The tunnel effect is achieved by the upward-swirling arc of light at the right. The figure pointing to the Virgin leads the eye upward; the Virgin stands below an obelisk which competes with her for our attention. The effect is strange and unexpected. The contrast between light and dark, chiaroscuro, intensifies the

light-colored leg of the water-bearer on the left and with the totally ambiguous Doric column on the right.

Neither painting has action at its center. Pontormo's Christ is asymmetrically placed to the left; Parmigianino weights his figures heavily to the left, leaving much of the canvas devoid of interest. The mannerist tendency to crowd figures together is apparent in both paintings, and both paintings present the figures in an ambiguous space and location. The figures in Pontormo's painting seem to be floating; even the weight of Christ does not appear to bear

Figure 13-19
Tintoretto. *Presentation of the Virgin.* c. 1551. Oil on canvas, 169 ⅞ by 189 inches. (Santa Maria del Orto, Venice; photo Alinari/Art Resource.)

Figure 13-20
Tintoretto. *Last Supper.* San Giorgio Maggiore, Venice. 1592–1594. Oil on canvas, 12 feet by 18 feet 8 inches. (Photo, Scala/Art Resource.)

drama and models the major figures, such as the woman and child in the foreground. There is none of Botticelli's overall, even lighting in the works of the mannerists.

Mannerist ambiguities abound in this work. The obelisk competes with the Virgin; the rounded steps of the temple seem to have no sure direction. The relationships of the figures with one another are unclear. The circumstances of the painting are left to the imagination of the viewer. Yet it is a dynamic composition, with power and vigor.

Late in his life, Tintoretto maintained his interest in chiaroscuro, strong diagonals, and tunnel effects. In the *Last Supper* (Figure 13-20), which shows his power at its greatest, there is a distinct mannerist concern for wrenching line and dramatic light.

COMPARISON KEY

Leonardo's Last Supper and Tintoretto's Last Supper

1. In which of the paintings shown in Figures 13-8 and 13-20 is centrality of composition more important? In which painting are balance and symmetry more important? In which painting is an underlying geometry the organizational principle?

2. Which painting has a greater sense of depth and perspective?

3. Which painting has even lighting? What effect does the lighting have on the way your eye "reads" the main part of the action?

4. Which painting calls more attention to its technique and style? Does the attention that we pay to the style of a painting distract us from its subject matter? Is the more stylized painting also more realistic?

5. Which painting would have a greater impact on a person who does not know the story of the last supper? Why?

El Greco

A younger painter in Spain, El Greco (1541–1614), put distortion and other mannerist techniques to distinctive use. El Greco saw that other painters did as they wished; and, even in an age when painters worked for wealthy and powerful patrons, he was able to answer to his own demands and develop a distinctive style. His elongated figures suggest that he was influenced by Gothic sculpture, but there has been no convincing explanation of his predilection for distortion.

In his *Resurrection* (Color Plate 18), elongated bodies abound. As in many paintings of the period, the upper half is separate from the lower, despite the effect of the rising white pennon and the rising white figures, which help hold the halves together. The falling military figures, including the inexplicable nude in the foreground, contrast with Christ's rising. The colors are strangely rich and harmonic, but with a touch of unreality. They are used for effect, not for purity of representation. The greenish-black tones of the background set off the deep reds, greens, and blues of the garments, which contrast with the flesh tones and the whites. Instead of realistic representa-

tion, we have a distinctive palette which we associate with El Greco.

One achievement of the Renaissance was to establish a painter's palette as a hallmark of style. El Greco's works are instantly identifiable by their muted colors. Extremes of tones are avoided, and El Greco attempts to match colors in terms of their relative intensity and their relative "weightedness" in different parts of a painting. In the *Resurrection*, for instance, the large blue area on the right helps balance the reds on the left. The more intense red at the top left of the canvas and the white pennon at the top right draw the eye upward to Christ and help give a sense of weight to the top of the painting. The single figure of Christ, along with the areas of color in the clothes, balances the tangle of figures below. Christ dominates them, as he should.

In the *Resurrection*, El Greco helps us experience the event. He is often described as a mystical painter. The term "mystical" implies an emphasis on spiritual values—that is, on what lies behind the realities of perception. Saint Ignatius formulated a series of meditations whose purpose, on one level, was to help the believer intensify the experience of religion.

Meditating on the *Resurrection,* for instance, would bring the experience into the emotional and intellectual awareness of the believer. The work of El Greco is frequently linked with that of Ignatius, since his paintings reach beyond the literal level of action and into the emotional significance of the event. They ask the viewer to participate in the event, not as one who might have been there as a passive observer, but as one whose heart and mind are affected by what is observed. The end result of the distortions of anatomy, the treatment of light, the balance of colors, and the organization of forms is to build an emotional tension appropriate to the subject.

Sculpture: The Genius of Michelangelo

Naturally, the Renaissance produced many good sculptors, but one, Michelangelo, was so overwhelming a presence that his work dominated sculpture for several generations. His sculpture is marked, in its early stages, by realism and ease. He was legendary for spending months in the quarries of Carrara searching for marble from which to carve his great pieces. (Political turmoil in Florence was such that even Michelangelo's position was often threatened. Factions in Florence opposed the Medici, and at one point, in 1530, Michelangelo escaped assassination only because the pope personally prevented it.)

His earliest work of genius, begun when he was twenty-three, is the *Pietà* (Figure 13-21), which was carved in Rome and now stands in Saint Peter's, protected by a bulletproof screen. It is regarded today as one of the greatest pieces of sculpture ever made; in its own day it was considered a model of perfection. Michelangelo completed the work when he was twenty-five, and it was the only piece that he ever signed: his signature is on the strap that crosses the breast of the Virgin.

The underlying pyramidal form of the *Pietà* accounts for some of its extraordinary three-dimensionality. We feel that there is essentially one position from which it should be viewed: from the front, where the triangular form is accented by the expressive left hand of the Virgin and the flowing of her garments on the right. The triangle implies the trinity, and it may be connected with the simple physical requirements imposed by the marble. It also

Figure 13-21
Michelangelo. *Pietà.* Saint Peter's, Rome. 1498 or 1499–1500. Marble, 68 ½ inches high. (Photo, Alinari/Art Resource.)

implies the reassurance of the Christian godhead and the ideals of resurrection.

In showing the nude perfection of Christ, Michelangelo began his lifelong essay on the theme of the human figure and the perfection that it implies. He was inspired by the humanism of the Medici and the Florentine academy as well as by a deep commitment to the principles of Christianity. His was a fusion of those ideals in stone. He made many studies of classical nudes in the Medici gardens and elsewhere, and for him, the human figure was a symbol of the perfection possible in heaven. Vasari and others were ecstatic over the illusion of reality achieved in the body of Christ, which imparts the sense of real muscle and real bone.

The Virgin's face expresses neither anguish nor assurance, but rather calm acceptance. Her face is indeed young, and when challenged on this point, Michelangelo said simply that virgins age more slowly

Michelangelo, The Pietà

1. The Virgin and Christ in the *Pietà* (Figure 13-21) form a geometric shape. What does the choice of a geometric organization achieve in terms of stability and integration of the two figures?

2. Does the body of Christ look lifeless to you? Does it look realistic?

3. In Michelangelo's day, people complained because the Virgin looked too young to be Christ's mother. Does this seem true to you? Would it be a problem for a modern viewer?

4. In later years the complaint arose that the figures were too cool and impersonal—that no deep religious feeling was expressed in the work. Do you agree with that judgment? What feelings do you associate with it?

5. The mannerists engaged the psychology of the viewer by playing with the viewer's relationship with the work—usually breaking down the distance between painting and viewer. What kind of psychological distance is maintained by the *Pietà*? What is implied by the fact that neither figure notices us? Is that in any way unsettling?

than married women. No one has taken this seriously. In the *Pietà*, he may have been idealizing the Virgin, or, more subtly, he may have made Christ seem older because theologically he precedes her as her savior and the savior of humankind. She may symbolize the church itself.

The *Pietà* has become a sentimental talisman to popularizers of culture, but despite this it has a distinct emotional coolness that should prevent any trivialization of its statement. The passion connected with Christ's death is not overtly expressed; it is deep within the stone itself, deep in the recognition that comes only upon reflection that the religious values which Michelangelo wishes to express are not superficial. They are implied in the essence of this moment—the loss of the son whose loss saves all. Michelangelo's is a language of perfection: traditional signs of grief or loss would have made the work less touching, less impressive, and less memorable.

In Florence, Michelangelo carved the famous *David* (Figure 13-22) from a single piece of marble over 14 feet long. It had already been worked on by several sculptors who were also apparently intent on creating a David. The raw piece of marble was popularly referred to as the "white giant," and by the time Michelangelo got the commission, it had been begun rather badly by the sculptor Duccio. Vasari believed that Michelangelo returned to Florence essentially to accept this commission, although a shift in political leadership in Florence, and the appointment of a gonfaloniere (a hereditary leader) friendly to Michelangelo, may have had a hand in his decision. Political turmoil—the French invasion and the efforts of Julius II to stem its tide—made the *David* a symbolic declaration of independence for Florence.

Michelangelo's is an older, much larger David than Donatello's, and he stands in preparative repose, in a moment of contemplation and thoughtfulness. He is filled with potential. Unlike the *Pietà*, which is stable, David's pose creates a sense of instability, as if it might change at any instant. There is no underlying geometric form to achieve stasis; the huge right hand bearing the stone shot is curved in anticipation and filled with energy. The muscles are only temporarily relaxed. The bend of the torso

Figure 13-22
Michelangelo. *David.* Accademia, Florence. 1501.
Marble, 14 feet 3 inches high.

implies the torsion preceding rapid motion. The angle of the left elbow is almost like an arrow, while the left knee implies the flexion needed to spring forward. All this is melded with keen-eyed observation of the face: the brows are knit, alert, intent, and careful. It was such a perfect figure for the city that it

was placed, after much debate, in front of the building where foreign emissaries paid their calls on the government. Vasari said, "Anyone who has seen Michelangelo's David has no need to see anything else by any other sculptor, living or dead."

David made Michelangelo the premier sculptor of his time. Pope Julius II saw in Michelangelo the sculptor for his tomb (Figure 13-23), which was planned to be freestanding near Saint Peter's. The critic and historian Howard Hibbard called it "the greatest sculptural commission of modern times." It was, however, an agony. Michelangelo spent eight months in Carrara searching for marble, but the blocks were lost in shipment. In addition, the pope failed to make payment. Michelangelo's letters to his father from 1506 to 1511 often complain about the money Julius owed him. In 1510 he wrote, sending 100 ducats as a loan to a relative: "I have no money. I have had to wring my very heart strings to send what I am sending you now, and I do not feel justified in asking for any more, for I have no assistants working under me, and I alone am doing but little."

Figure 13-23
Michelangelo, Raffaello de Montelupo, and Boscoli. Tomb of Julius II. Saint Peter in Chains, Rome. *Moses*, 1513. (Photo, Alinari/Art Resource.)

Ultimately, the project became a wall tomb in the church of Saint Peter in Chains, in Rome, where it can be seen only dimly in the darkness of a considerable space, as Figure 13-23 suggests. A mixture of styles, its greatest figure, the "horned" Moses, is the work of Michelangelo. Most of the rest of the figures were done by lesser sculptors. The figure of Moses has the real power; he sits like a god, like one with a vision of the truth. The connection between Julius II and Moses is implied in their mutual relationship with God, in their leading their people out of bondage, and in their positions as interpreters of the laws of God. Michelangelo was genuinely moved by Julius's greatness, and the tomb, over a period of forty years, became a work of conscience.

Two other works of conscience—also tombs—celebrate the Medici brothers, the dukes Giuliano and Lorenzo, whose deaths marked the end of the Medici line, and consequently the end of a great era in Florentine history. In each work the casket is placed beneath a heroic-sized portrait. Giuliano (Figure 13-24) adopts the pose of a Roman general; Lorenzo (Figure 13-25), also in armor, that of a Roman warrior. Each was an officer in the Roman church, and each is carefully idealized.

The mannerist qualities of the works are apparent

Figure 13-24
Above: Michelangelo. Tomb of Giuliano de' Medici. Medici Chapel, Florence. 1519–1534.

Figure 13-25
Right: Michelangelo. Tomb of Lorenzo de' Medici, Medici Chapel, Florence. 1519–1534.

Michelangelo's Sculpture

1. What are the most important architectural details observable in the tomb of Julius II (Figure 13-23)? Do they seem stylistically compatible with the sculptured figures? Do you feel that the tomb should be discussed more properly as a work of sculpture or as a work of architecture?

2. Is architecture more or less important in the tombs of the Medici (Figures 13-24 and 13-25) than in the tomb of Julius II? What stylistic differences can you detect?

3. Judging from the tombs, what is Michelangelo's position on the importance of balance, symmetry, centrality of composition, and repetition of form (visual rhythms)?

4. Is it reasonable to suppose that Michelangelo competed directly with the ancient Greek and Roman sculptors in his portrayal of the nude? Consider that while Michelangelo was constructing the tomb of Julius, the Laocoön group (Figure 4-20) was discovered in a vineyard and was brought to the Vatican for him to study. What influences of classical sculpture can you detect in his work?

5. Michelangelo's subject matter in his sculpture is both religious and secular. Which do you feel he handles more successfully? Is there evidence of religious concerns in his secular works or of secular concerns in his religious works? Can you detect the fusion of Christianity and humanism promoted by the Medici?

---

in the postures of the figures (compare them with the posture of Parmigianino's Madonna in Figure 13-18). Beneath each brother and surmounting his casket are symbolic representations of time. Giuliano's casket is surmounted on the left with Night, who is accompanied by such symbols of darkness as the moon and an owl. On the right is Day, whose face, like the sun, cannot be looked upon. Night seems to be reclining into sleep, while Day seems to be rising from rest. These symbols remind us not only of the value of time but also of the dying and revival of the sun. Lorenzo's tomb is surmounted by Dusk and Dawn, figures whose intermediary position in time implies an ambiguity, but also a control over time that is as absolute as the duke's control over Florence had been.

The representations of the times of day on the tombs may also be representations of river gods, as their reclining posture, which has appeared in art since preclassical times, implies. The rivers represent the flowing of power and influence into the corners of the earth, commemorating the works of the Medici.

Among Michelangelo's most interesting works are the unfinished figures of slaves, which were intended for the tomb of Julius. Several that are finished are now in the Louvre, while those which we now call "captive"—because they are not freed of the marble —stand in the academy in Florence, near the *David*. The detail of the *Awakening Slave* (Figure 13-26) shows some of Michelangelo's carving technique. But it shows something else, too. The high finish which characterizes his work is only one stage in the

Figure 13-26
Michelangelo. *The Awakening Slave*, detail. c. 1520.
Marble, unfinished.

creative process. The unfinished state of the *Awakening Slave* shows that this stage too has rare power. Our modern age is more capable of appreciating an unfinished work since the concept of high finish is not as important in the twentieth century as it was in the Renaissance. We find that an unfinished piece has more than one vantage point from which to view it. The sense of dynamics of the *Awakening Slave* is intensified, if only because we are never sure precisely where we should stand to see it best. Moreover, we cannot resist marveling at the way the figure seems to emerge from the stone with a life of its own. Seeing it is like observing creation.

Literature:
The Genius of Shakespeare

William Shakespeare (1564–1616), born and raised in Stratford-upon-Avon, eventually journeyed to London looking for preferment. Although we do know something of his life, we are ignorant concerning some basic things. For instance, we know little about his education. He was probably educated in a grammar school in Stratford-upon-Avon, where he would have studied grammar, rhetoric, and the Latin classics. Beyond that we know nothing of his early life. Some scholars believe that he went to Oxford or Cambridge and probably attended one of the Inns of Court in London (the equivalent of a law school). However, most think that he was probably self-educated; considering his immense knowledge in so many fields, this is an astonishing possibility.

THE SONNETS

In London Shakespeare began writing verse to please a patron. His sonnets and other poems were in the forms acceptable to readers of the time. For a while he hoped to secure the patronage of the Earl of Southampton, to whom many of his sonnets are addressed. The "dark lady" of Sonnets 127 to 152 has never been identified, despite extensive literary detective work. The sonnets—there are 154 in the edition published by Thomas Thorpe in 1609—represent a momentous achievement in the form.

Sonnet sequences were popular in the late sixteenth century, with important contributions made by Thomas Wyatt, Sir Philip Sidney, and Edmund Spenser. But when Shakespeare's sonnets were written, sometime between 1592 and 1597—and certainly when they were published (without his approval)—the vogue for sonnet sequences was over in England. Hence, they remained curiosities in their own time, to be taken up by excited readers only later.

With only three exceptions, the form of Shakespeare's sonnets is three quatrains and a couplet ending, rhyming abab, cdcd, efef, gg. Each quatrain tends to be self-contained, expressing a thought or meditating upon a question, while the ending couplet tends to be conclusive and final, like a cadence in music. Moreover, in the early sonnets Shakespeare praises a young man—possibly his patron—rather than a woman, such as Petrarch's Laura. Later, he praises a quite unideal dark lady who arouses in him sometimes shameful feelings of lust.

To appreciate the sonnets and Shakespeare's ability to deal with extraordinary subject matter in only fourteen lines, consider Sonnet 73:

That time of year thou may'st in me behold
When yellow leaves, or none, or few, do hang
Upon those boughs which shake against the cold—
Bare ruin'd choirs where late the sweet birds sang.
In me thou see'st the twilight of such day
As after sunset fadeth in the West,
Which by and by black night doth take away,
Death's second self, that seals up all in rest.
In me thou see'st the glowing of such fire
That on the ashes of his youth doth lie,
As the death-bed whereon it must expire,
Consumed with that which it was nourish'd by.
   This thou perceiv'st, which makes thy love more strong
   To love that well which thou must leave ere long.

The central meaning of the poem is embedded in metaphors, and, as in most of the sonnets, the metaphors are part of an emotional and sinuous language that is designed to penetrate our defenses and reside in our unconscious. Three different metaphors, grouped in sections of four lines each, make a point that is summarized in the final couplet.

The first metaphor, a comparison of the aging poet to winter, is intensified by an image of scant leaves on the boughs of trees, a reference to the poet's thinning hair. The boughs, the "choirs" where the birds sang, are like the poet's head, where he sings. Then, moving from the season to the day itself, the second quatrain points out that the poet is in his "twilight." He is aging, as the day ages. The theme of death is introduced with the metaphor of night, "that seals up all in rest." The most powerful metaphor, the comparison of the poet's life to a glowing fire, is saved for last. The fire consumes its fuel, just as life consumes youth. The bed of the fire becomes a "death-bed," and the theme of death appears once more.

PERCEPTION KEY

Shakespeare, Sonnet 73

1. The ideas in Sonnet 73 are "compartmentalized" in groups of lines. Identify each group and establish what it contains. Is the poem "choppy"? Do its elements fail to cohere once you have perceived each of its sections?

2. The choirs in a church and the boughs in a tree are high in the air. They are metaphors for parts of the poet's body. Are they appropriate metaphors? Do you feel that they are powerful in the sense of intensifying your emotional response to the ideas expressed?

3. The poet compares himself to the day and the setting sun. He also compares himself to a glowing fire. What does the fire consume for fuel? Is the comparison surprising and effective?

4. The poem contains a number of repetitions, such as the repetition of lines of the same length. (It is written in iambic pentameter, a line consisting of five metrical feet made up of one unstressed syllable followed by one stressed syllable.) Repetition is also evident in the constant rhyme, and words and phrases are repeated as well. What is the function of these repetitions? Are they effective?

5. Shakespeare emphasizes perception in lines 1, 5, 10, and 13. What words does he use to call our attention to it, and what does he expect the person addressed to perceive? As a result of that perception, what should this person be aware of?

The couplet introduces no new metaphors, but draws the conclusion implied by those already developed: since we must die, we must learn to value life. The metaphors make this abstract observation more concrete and meaningful. As we read the poem, we participate in its steady buildup of image and metaphor because they speak a language of feeling; they intensify the intellectual message.

THE PLAYS

Shakespeare turned to the stage as a way of making a living when his bid for patronage was confounded. He had hoped that the Earl of Southampton would support him, but Southampton chose another writer, John Florio, who had translated Montaigne's *Essays* into English. No one knows whether Shakespeare's background was in any way related to the theater; but in any case, beginning a theatrical career must have been a desperate move for him. The stage was a place for entertainment, not for literature. Still, there were great writers and actors working in Elizabethan times; Shakespeare began as an actor, went on to write for a theater company, then became its owner, and finally retired to spend his last years quietly in Stratford.

Of his thirty-seven plays, only one, *The Tempest*, is entirely original. All the others are derived from histories, documents, stories, and earlier plays by other writers —and Shakespeare even got the idea for *The Tempest* from a shipwreck that had taken place off the coast of Bermuda. Shakespeare was busy preparing plays for his company, and the luxury of inventing new material must have been denied him. Yet there is no question that he made everything he "borrowed" his own by improving it immeasurably.

The Comedies

The ten comedies —which include *The Taming of the Shrew, A Midsummer Night's Dream, The Merry Wives of Windsor, Much Ado about Nothing,* and *Twelfth Night; or What You will*—were inspired by classical authors and abound in mistaken identity and multiple confusions, as well as improbable circumstances and resultant efforts at solution. The farcical confusion of *The Comedy of Errors,* which is based on Plautus's *Menaechmi,* involves the arrival of "lost" twins from Syracuse in the town of Ephesus. It depends on broad humor and preposterous slapstick. Shakespeare adds the details of identical servants and identical clothing to make the confusion all the more intense. At the other extreme is *Measure for Measure,* a highly serious play centered on the mishandling of power by Angelo in the absence of the true duke, Vincentio. The play's title comes from Christ's sermon on the mount: "Judge not, that ye be not judged. For with what judgment ye judge, ye shall be judged: and with what measure ye mete, it shall be measured unto you again." Because of its religious imagery, it has been interpreted as a Christian play, although certain distortions result from such an interpretation.

The hallmark of the comedies is wit and brilliant wordplay. In the formidable scene from *The Taming of the Shrew* in which Katharina and Petruchio meet, they prove by their wit that they are a match for each other.

> *Kath.* Asses are made to bear, and so are you.
> *Pet.* Women are made to bear, and so are you.
> *Kath.* No such jade as you, if me you mean.
> *Pet.* Alas, good Kate, I will not burthen thee,
> For knowing thee to be but young and light.
> *Kath.* Too light for such a swain as thee to catch,
> And yet as heavy as my weight should be.
> *Pet.* Should be! should—buzz!
> *Kath.*   Well ta'en, and like a buzzard.
> *Pet.* O slow-wing'd turtle,* shall a buzzard   *dove*
> take thee?
> *Kath.* Ay, for a turtle, as he takes a buzzard.
> *Pet.* Come, come, you wasp, i' faith you are too angry.
> *Kath.* If I be waspish, best beware my sting.
> *Pet.* My remedy is then to pluck it out.
> *Kath.* Ay, if the fool could find it where it lies.
> *Pet.* Who knows not where a wasp does wear his sting?
> In his tail.
> *Kath.* In his tongue.
> *Pet.*   Whose tongue?
> *Kath.* Yours, if you talk of tales, and so farewell.
> (Act 2, Scene 1, lines 199–217.)

The imagery of birds and flying insects devolves into a barnyard imagery of cocks and hens, and soon into physical abuse when Kate slaps Petruchio. But finally Petruchio talks her down and tells her:

> Thou must be married to no man but me:
> For I am he am born to tame you, Kate,
> And bring you from a wild Kate to a Kate
> Conformable as other household Kates.

She, astonished at him, complains to her father that he wishes to wed her "to one half lunatic." The complexity of the situation is typical of the comedies. At the end of the play we do not know whether Kate is really tamed or whether she is pretending. She eventually obeys Petruchio, but in such a way as to remind us of her lively spirit, evident in their earliest exchanges.

The Histories

In Shakespeare's time, history was transmitted largely by literature. Shakespeare's history plays focus on the English kings and the problems inherent in their succession. The three parts of *Henry VI* and the two parts of *Henry V* were individual, but related, plays. *The Life of King Henry V* takes up where *Henry IV* leaves off, following its hero, Prince Hal, into his own reign. The evil that kings sometimes do is studied closely in *The Tragedy of King Richard III*, which has left most English-speaking people with the image of a humpbacked, dwarfish figure who ruthlessly murders everyone who might stand between him and the throne.

The histories have much of the range of the comedies and the tragedies. Murder, death, fate, and flaws of character pursue some figures, while others are obviously comic. In the two parts of *Henry IV* appears one of the greatest of Shakespeare's characters, Sir John Falstaff, a huge tun of a man and a braggart who hangs out with petty criminals and highwaymen in Mistress Quickly's Boar's Head Tavern. He is Hal's boon companion, during an apparently profligate youth filled with drinking and lowlife associations, while Hal is waiting to take his place as King Henry V. But when Hal becomes King Henry, his character changes, and he rids himself of his former associates with a brush of his hand. When Falstaff tries to be familiar with him, calling him "King Hal" and "sweet boy," he is totally rebuffed:

I know thee not, old man, fall to thy prayers. . . .
Reply not to me with a fool-born jest,
Presume not that I am the thing I was,
For God doth know, so shall the world perceive,
That I have turn'd away from my former self.

The histories deal with numerous problems of interpretation of real events, and Shakespeare was daring in treating them. Most of his audience would have relied on his plays for their knowledge of the people and events described. Since most of the histories involve struggles for the crown, there was a tendency to give a nod of approval to those who survived the struggles. One play, *Richard II*, was thought to carry an underlying political message approving of rebellion, and it was taken by some as a tacit approval of the rebellion led by the Earl of Essex against his former intimate, Elizabeth I, in 1601. The Earl of Southampton was involved in the uprising, and on February 7, the night before they set out for Whitehall, the rebels arranged for a special performance at the Globe Theater by Lord Chamberlain's men, who had not played it in years (it was probably written in 1595). When they faltered in their lines, the rebels supplied them from memory. Even Queen Elizabeth, at the celebrated trial of Essex, said, "I am Richard II; know ye not that . . . this tragedy was played forty times in open streets and houses." She exaggerated, but she knew that a slight was intended: Richard, for his crimes, had been deposed, slain, and replaced by Henry IV.

The Tragedies

The greatest of the tragedies—*Romeo and Juliet, Julius Caesar, Hamlet, Othello, King Lear, Macbeth,* and *Antony and Cleopatra*—are played continually all over the world in virtually all cultures. They read the human condition with such accuracy and reproduce it with such fidelity that local customs, styles, and even languages give way to their majesty. They are studies of the most profound human passion, and they demonstrate a psychological depth and awareness that help us understand why mannerist painters took such a strong interest in their relationship with their audience. Like Titian's *Portrait of a Man*, Shakespeare's characters are like real people; indeed, they have a dimension, like that of Hamlet, which proves them psychologically much richer and more complex than most real people.

The range of emotions portrayed in the tragedies is vast. Love and the hatred that sometimes besets families are centermost in *Romeo and Juliet.* Jealousy and anger at being undervalued are at the center of *Othello.* Consider the role of ambition in *Julius Caesar,* the agonies of middle-aged love in *Antony and Cleopatra,* the vanity and anger of King Lear, the

Figure 13-27
Royal Shakespeare Company production of *Hamlet.*
(Photo, Donald Cooper, London.)

ambition of Lord and Lady Macbeth, and the complex and rich emotions of Hamlet, who is beset by the agonies associated with his father's death, his mother's remarriage, and his uncle's ascent to the throne. All the primary characters in the tragedies are richly and skillfully modeled; these are among the most profoundly realized literary characters in all drama.

Hamlet (Figure 13-27) contains some of the most memorable lines of dialogue in the English language. Like most of the tragedies, it is a balance of serious—in some cases, dark—moments, contrasted with periods of comic relief. After Ophelia has killed herself, two clowns, who are digging her grave, argue over the question whether, as a suicide, she deserves a Christian burial.

Since she was drowned, one clown decides the matter simply:

> Here lies the water; good. Here stands the man; good. If the man go to this water and drown himself, it is, will he, nill he, he goes, mark you that. But if the water come to him and drown him, he drowns not himself; argal, he that is not guilty of his own death shortens not his own life. (Act 5, Scene 1, lines 15–20.)

Such a mixture of simplemindedness and shrewd reasoning takes on a darkly comic cast.

Soliloquies appear often in the tragedies. The characters are usually found, like Kate and Petruchio, in interchange with each other, but we never know how seriously to take them because everything they say is designed to have an effect on another person. Only when the character soliloquizes can we be sure of the sentiments of the speaker. Some of the greatest of Shakespeare's soliloquies are in *Hamlet*. One of them is world-famous: Hamlet's contemplation of suicide as a means of ending the psychic pain that wears him down in the court of Denmark:

> To be, or not to be, that is the question:
> Whether 'tis nobler in the mind to suffer
> The slings and arrows of outrageous fortune,
> Or to take arms against a sea of troubles,
> And by opposing, end them. To die, to sleep—
> No more, and by a sleep to say we end
> The heart-ache and the thousand natural shocks
> That flesh is heir to; 'tis a consummation
> Devoutly to be wish'd. To die, to sleep—
> To sleep, perchance to dream—ay, there's the rub,
> For in that sleep of death what dreams may come,
> When we have shuffled off this mortal coil,
> Must give us pause; there's the respect
> That makes calamity of so long life:
> For who would bear the whips and scorns of time,
> Th'oppressor's wrong, the proud man's contumely,
> The pangs of despis'd love, the law's delay,
> The insolence of office, and the spurns
> That patient merit of th'unworthy takes
> When he himself might his quietus make
> With a bare bodkin.*   *dagger*
> (Act 3, Scene 1, lines 55–75.)

Hamlet makes his suffering plain. Life is painful, but there is the equally painful fear that the life which waits for him "after death, / The undiscover'd country, from whose bourn / No traveller returns," is possibly more agonizing than this one. Ironically, he has already seen his father's ghost and realizes that death is by no means an undiscovered country and that by returning from it, his father has given him good reason not to commit suicide.

In many ways *Hamlet* epitomizes the thrust of the Renaissance. Its subjects include courtliness and a willingness to kill for power. The refinement of the court of Denmark is notable, particularly in contrast with the more barbaric armies of Fortinbras, from Norway, which march past on their way to brawl with the equally brutal "sledded Polaks." Humanist interests show up in the deep psychological probing of Hamlet, who worries about the ambiguous position in which his father's ghost has put him in relation to his mother and his love for her. There is no nearby theologian who can solve Hamlet's problems, nor is there a pious catechism that will help him decide

what action to take. He is adrift in the universe, with only himself and his beliefs and values to guide him.

The Renaissance discovery of both good and evil in the heart of humankind is as apparent in *Hamlet* as in any artifact of the age. Claudius has murdered his brother, old Hamlet, (an action he regrets only later), and has married Gertrude, Hamlet's mother, after an embarrassingly short period of mourning. Claudius prays for forgiveness, but he is not sincere, and he knows it. He is glad that he has done what he has done, and he tries to have Rosencranz and Guildenstern murder young Hamlet when he becomes a threat. Hamlet murders Polonius by mistake —he thought the old man was Claudius. He regrets his rash action and fears that he will lose his immortal soul. Further, one of the issues raised by Montaigne —the question of the reliability of human knowledge —is at the core of the play. Hamlet at first suspects that his father was killed, then hears the ghost tell

PERCEPTION KEY

Shakespeare

1. Examine one of the later sonnets (Sonnets 127 to 152) concerning the dark lady. Does each quatrain contain a complete thought? Is that thought treated fully in the final couplet? What is the subject matter of the poem?

2. Read *Hamlet* carefully. Why does Hamlet decide that his father has been murdered? Considering the Renaissance concerns for the validity of knowledge obtained through the five senses, do you feel that Hamlet has enough "proof" to act upon?

3. What, in the final scenes, does Hamlet really know? If Hamlet were to have followed the law rather than seek revenge, how should he have behaved? What is the religious and moral position in which he finds himself?

4. Do the references to classical figures in *Hamlet* equal or outnumber the references to Christian religious figures or circumstances? Is there anything religious about the ghost of old Hamlet?

5. If *Hamlet* is a humanist drama, is it optimistic or pessimistic concerning the capacities of humankind to live fully? Remember that tragedies contain nothing that is inherently pessimistic; rather, they examine the darker sides of human experience. Does such an examination as *Hamlet* leave us feeling ambiguous about our place in the world?

him so, and then tests his powers of observation against Horatio and others before he believes that he has even seen a ghost. He devises the "Mousetrap," a play that will expose Claudius. Recalling that Christ was regarded as a mousetrap to catch the devil (see Robert Campin's Mérode Altarpiece, Figure 12-10), we see that Hamlet's theological training is useful.

The final scenes of the play, in which both the guilty and the innocent die together, remind us of the risks involved in human action. There can be no certainty, but there is an art to living with uncertainty. Hamlet knows that once a course is charted, there is no turning back. Once he believes that his father's ghost is good and is not a devil conjured up to make him lose his soul, there is only one direction in which he can go. It is not fate, but a form of Christian inevitability. The complexity of the play is so great that we can study it only by reading it very carefully.

The Romances

Some of Shakespeare's last plays are difficult to describe. *Pericles, Cymbeline, The Winter's Tale,* and *The Tempest* are not, strictly speaking, comedies, histories, or tragedies. An indeterminate term, "romances," has been invented for them.

The romances are filled with extraordinary poetry, often in the form of songs, which are sung independently of the plays. One of the most memorable is Ariel's song in *The Tempest:*

> Full fadom five thy father lies,
>   Of his bones are coral made:
> Those are pearls that were his eyes:
>   Nothing of him that doth fade,
> But doth suffer a sea-change
> Into something rich and strange.
> Sea-nymphs hourly ring his knell:
>   Burthen [within]. Ding-dong.
> Hark now I hear them—ding-dong bell.
>   (Act 1, Scene 2, lines 397–405.)

The mystery and musicality of these lines have attracted all lovers of literature. And the transformation implied in the "sea-change" has had a power similar to that associated with Botticelli's Venus, wafting in on her scallop shell. Hardly an intellectual strain of Renaissance thought or ambition escapes the pen of Shakespeare. As James Joyce put it in *Ulysses,* "After God, Shakespeare created most."

Summary

The flowering of genius in the sixteenth century came at a time of declining economic power in Italy and developing economic power in the northern countries. The Reformation, which resulted in the breaking away of Protestant religions, signaled a new age, including a Counterreformation led by the Roman church. The advent of Protestantism weakened the authority and absolute power of the church, as well as the authority of other institutions. The artists of the period were still concerned largely with religious subjects, particularly in Italy, where papal authority was strong. But more and more, the major painters and sculptors turned to secular subjects. Leonardo's work shows a reverence for religious themes, but the *Mona Lisa* is a completely secular work. Michelangelo was more concerned with the confluence of Christian and neo-Platonic thought, as mediated by the Medicis, and most of his art is religious, with a strong classical influence. In the mannerists we see a growing interest in secular themes. Giorgione, Titian, and others point in new directions. The development of portraiture demonstrates a humanist concern as well as a growing interest in private commissions. In Shakespeare's work, we find little formal religion, although religious figures and religious issues are often present. Shakespeare's concerns were total: his subject matter was human nature. He knew that the proper study of humankind is human beings, and his work takes humanism as far as it was able to go in his age. *Hamlet*—with its focus on the uncertainty of human knowledge, on anxieties concerning an afterlife, and on struggles for power—is in some ways the epitome of the drama of the age. Hamlet's anxieties are close enough to our own to be totally recognizable and familiar.

Concepts in Chapter 13

Expansion in the northern countries produced the French invasion of Italy, which upset Europe's balance of influence and signaled political change.

Italian domination of eastern trade dwindled in this period, and yet the arts developed in unequaled grandeur.

Andrea Palladio discovered a coherent architectural vocabulary with which to modify classical proportion.

Leonardo da Vinci, a prototypical Renaissance man, was concerned with painting, military engineering, music, and most of the sciences.

Leonardo used an underlying geometric stability to give his paintings unusual power and rational organization.

Leonardo's style is realistic, almost scientific; his scientific observations influenced his painting.

Michelangelo was influenced by the humanism of the Medici and by neo-Platonism, which fused classical and Christian values.

Pope Julius II, who repelled the invading French, was also Italy's greatest patron of the arts during the Renaissance.

Michelangelo's Sistine ceiling reveals a neo-Platonic orderliness.

Michelangelo's sculpture shows a concern for classical nudes: the *David*, thought to be a marvel of perfection, competes directly with the work of the sculptors of antiquity.

Raphael's *School of Athens*, in the Vatican Palace, shows the extent to which Greek philosophical thought had become acceptable to the hierarchy of the Roman church.

Secular painting, following Giorgione and others, began to flourish during the Renaissance; the secular portrait was particularly powerful.

Mannerist painters developed an unsettling self-conscious psychological style.

Mannerist effects depend on asymmetry, imbalance, and ambiguity.

Shakespeare wrote serious sonnets at a time when the sonnet had lost some of its popularity.

Shakespeare's comedies, histories, tragedies, and romances dominated the Elizabethan stage.

Classical influences, as well as influences from popular literature, are prominent in Shakespeare's plays.

Hamlet is an embodiment of Renaissance anxieties: concern for power, worry over religion, and uncertainty about human beings' position in the world and the value of human knowledge.

Suggested Readings

Ackerman, James S. *The Architecture of Michelangelo*. 2 vols. New York: Viking, 1961.

Bradbrook, M. C. *Shakespeare: The Poet in His World*. New York: Columbia University Press, 1978.

Brinton, Crane. *The Shaping of the Modern Mind*. Englewood Cliffs, N.J.: Prentice-Hall, 1953.

Chastel, André. *The Crisis of the Renaissance 1520–1600*. New York: Skira, 1968.

Clark, Kenneth. *Leonardo da Vinci*. 2d ed. London: Cambridge, 1952.

de Tolnay, Charles. *Michelangelo*. 5 vols. Princeton, N.J.: Princeton, 1968.

Dickens, A. G. *Reformation and Society in Sixteenth-Century Europe*. London: Thames and Hudson, 1966.

Gilmore, Myron P. *The World of Humanism 1453–1517*. New York: Harper & Row, 1952.

Hartt, Frederick. *History of Italian Renaissance Art*. 2d ed. New York: Prentice-Hall–Abrams, 1979.

———. *Michelangelo*. New York: Abrams, 1964.

Hibbard, Howard. *Michelangelo: Painter, Sculptor, Architect*. New York: Vendome, 1974.

Murray, Linda. *The High Renaissance and Mannerism*. New York: Oxford University Press, 1977.

Murray, Peter. *Architecture of the Renaissance*. New York: Abrams, 1971.

Pevsner, Nikolaus. *Studies in Art, Architecture, and Design*. New York: Walker, 1968.

Pope-Hennessy, John. *Italian High Renaissance and Baroque Sculpture*. New York: Phaidon Publishers, 1963.

Schoenbaum, Samuel. *William Shakespeare: A Compact Documentary Life*. New York: Oxford University Press, 1971.

Shakespeare, William. *The Riverside Shakespeare*. G. Blakemore Evans, ed. Boston: Houghton Mifflin, 1974.

Shearman, John. *Mannerism*. Harmondsworth, England: Penguin, 1967.

Wasserman, Jack. *Leonardo*. New York: Abrams, 1975.

Wolfflin, Heinrich. *Classic Art: An Introduction to the Italian Renaissance*. New York: Phaidon Publishers, 1953.

PART SIX

KINGDOM OF
GREAT
BRITAIN

SCOTLAND

Edinburgh
Glasgow
York
Newark
Cambridge
Oxford London
ENGLAND

Dublin
IRELAND

KINGDOM OF
DENMARK
AND
NORWAY

UNITED P
Amsterdam

Ostend
Aachen

AUSTRIAN
NETHERLANDS
Rheims

Strasburg

Brest

Nantes

Rouen

Versailles Paris
Orleans

Tours

Geneva

KINGDOM OF
FRANCE

Turin

RE

ATLANTIC OCEAN

Limoges

Bordeaux

Avignon

Marseille

Valladolid

Barcelona

Oporto

KINGDOM OF
SPAIN

Madrid

KINGDOM OF
PORTUGAL

Toledo

Valencia

MAJORCA

Lisbon

Cartegena

MEDITERRANEAN SEA

Granada

Seville

Cadiz

0   100   200 miles

Gibraltar

BARBARY STATES

THE SEVENTEENTH AND EIGHTEENTH CENTURIES

Uppsala
FINLAND
Christiana
Goteborg
Stockholm
Kalmar
Karlskrona
BALTIC SEA
Revel
Saint Petersburg
RUSSIA
Narva ESTONIA
Memel Riga LIVONIA
Smolensk Novgorod
Moscow
Stralsund
Konigsberg
nburg Potsdam Berlin BRANDENBURG
LITHUANIA Vilna
SAXONY
Posen
KINGDOM OF
POLAND
Minsk
HOLY
ROMAN
EMPIRE
BOHEMIA
SILESIA
Warsaw
Lubin
Kiev
Munich Vienna Prague Breslau
BAVARIA SALZBURG AUSTRIA
Krakow
TYROL
Venice Trieste
KINGDOM OF
HUNGARY
MANTUA
Buda Pest
MODENA
Florence
DALMATIA
BOSNIA
Belgrade
TRANSYLVANIA MOLDAVIA
BESSARABIA
LUCCA
TUSCANY
PAPAL
STATES
Rome
MONTENEGRO
Bucharest
WALLACHIA
SERBIA
Sofia
BULGARIA
BLACK SEA
Naples
OTTOMAN EMPIRE
Constantinople
KINGDOM
OF
NAPLES
Brindisi
Otranto
ALBANIA
Palermo SICILY
Syracuse
Athens
CRETE

Ages of Monarchy and Revolution: 1605 to 1789

The period from the death of Elizabeth I in England to the French Revolution and the death of Louis XVI spans almost 200 years, encompassing virtually all of the seventeenth and eighteenth centuries. These are the centuries in which demands for greater personal freedoms, more democratic political institutions, and even greater participation by the laity in church affairs became common. In many ways they resemble our own century: they were characterized by political unrest, constant examination of religious institutions, fear of world conflagration as a result of the jockeying of nations, and constant intellectual turmoil and uncertainty. When we say that these centuries are the beginning of modern times, we mean that people experienced the same kinds of anxieties, agitations, fears, and hopes that we do. Our anxieties over political forms of government, over the power of the church in our daily lives, and over the balance of power between great political blocs, as well as our uncertainties concerning new discoveries in science and their ultimate meaning for us—all these are feelings that we share with the people of this epoch.

The Political Balance of Power

One of the most important concepts to arise during the seventeenth century was that of the political balance of power among nations. The concept of balance of power was virtually inevitable, given the fact that so many strong nations—such as France, Spain, Portugal, England, Sweden, Holland, and eventually Russia— emerged as a result of the political lessons of the Renaissance. No one of these nations was absolutely powerful, and therefore alliances were essential to guarantee national influence. The power of Italian city-states—such

as Genoa, Tuscany, Venice, the Papal States, and other trading cities—was drawing to an end by the seventeenth century. Europe looked to consolidated nations for its leadership. Nations constantly waged wars in order to solidify their boundaries and extend their influence on world trade. The colonization of the new world had brought such wealth to the old world that monarchs could conceive of themselves and their nations on a grand scale sometimes echoing that of Rome.

The older political concept of the city-state persisted in Italy and Germany (in the form of principalities) and doomed both to become the prey of the larger, more solidified nations. France became a dominant political power in Europe, with England and Holland not far behind. Their power came from their strategic geographic advantages for controlling trade. Spain's decay, from the golden age of the sixteenth century, was steady and slow, despite its power in the Americas. Spain was still controlled largely by the church and was in the grip of the Inquisition. Therefore, newer democratic institutions did not arise there as they did elsewhere in Europe. The drain on the Spanish economy, caused by the demands of the overseas colonies, was such that the nation did not have the economic strength to compete with France, England, and Holland. Yet it waged war throughout the latter part of the seventeenth century—primarily with France—in a hopeless effort to regain its lost power.

The Holy Roman Empire existed, but in name only. The Hapsburgs controlled the empire, but—through Austria—were generally distracted by the constant threat of invasion by the Turks, whose Ottoman empire stretched from Turkey to Greece and up through Yugoslavia almost to Vienna (which was attacked in 1683 by the Turks). As a result of the almost constant waging of war among nations, control of trade shifted, and nations became more clearly established, with relatively stable boundaries. In some cases excessive expenses began to lessen the ambition of kings who had begun to think of themselves as immortal and unlimited in power.

The Changing Monarchy

The nature of monarchy in the seventeenth century shifted from the Elizabethan concept of a head of state ruling with a large council to that of the autocratic government, in England, of the Stuarts: James I and Charles I. The concept of the "divine right of kings," the theory that God had chosen the monarch to rule in his stead, had led King James and his son King Charles I of England to ignore the growing power of the mercantile middle classes. These classes seized power in the 1640s, ultimately beheading Charles I and ruling until 1660 in a Commonwealth and Protectorate. This was the first political "earthquake" in modern European history. It signaled the fact that an economically emancipated middle class could demand and secure its rights and that the king and the nobles could not withstand their force.

With Louis XIV, the French monarchy had become virtually absolute. Louis divested himself of advisers, after the departure of Mazarin and Richelieu, and managed the government alone. He was despotic, autocratic, and extraordinary both in his charm and in the mystique he created about himself. During the latter part of the seventeenth century, Louis XIV had isolated himself and his court in Versailles, and so he had no real concept of the needs or sufferings of the people. He had been warned by his advisers in the 1690s, but he paid no attention. He was more concerned with controlling the troublesome nobles. The general poverty and misery of the ordinary French people were in sharp contrast with the glitter, glamour, and immense wealth of those who flocked to the court to surround Louis and share his passion for grandeur.

The day of reckoning came for the French monarchy in the eighteenth century, when the French people rose up against King Louis XVI in 1789. The bloodiness of that revolution, and its general violence, made it quite unlike the English revolutions of the seventeenth century, which were generally restricted to restraining the king, and were not attacks on an entire social class.

The Development of the Middle Class

In part because of changes in agriculture and crop planning and in part because of changes in industrial techniques that helped England become a major trading power, the English were able to create a class that rivaled the nobility in power and influence. As this new moneyed class grew, the nobility shrank in importance. The new middle class was particularly powerful because it derived its strength from forms of Protestantism that considered economic success a result of God's blessings. Simply having a lot of cash in a time when others had little was enough to make the new middle class feel that it deserved a large voice in the governance of the nation. When revolution came to England, this new class led the fight against the traditional powers of an arbitrary king. And it won.

The structure of government in France was, by contrast with that in England, oppressive. A moneyed middle class was slower to develop. The nobles were weakened deliberately because they had risen against Louis XIV when he was a child in the care of Cardinal Mazarin. One of his strategies was to sell peerages, thereby cheapening the value and power of nobility. He did little, however, to help create an influential middle class such as existed in England. The French Revolution was fueled largely by the desires of those who, under another system, might have become conservative landholders and businesspeople. Instead, by the time the eighteenth century was about to end, those very people clamored for—and got—the blood of the ruling class, while England and the rest of Europe looked on in horror.

The American Revolution, beginning in 1776, was fought in some measure by landed gentry who saw a distant parliament and king taxing them in a punitive fashion. King George III, like some of the later Georgian kings, seems not to have understood the meaning of the English revolution of the 1640s or of the Bill of Rights of the late 1680s. George learned his lessons in struggles with shrewd prime ministers and influential politicians. One cost of those lessons was the loss of the American colonies. But at least England experienced no revolution of the sort that ravaged France.

Religion

The Middle Ages saw the rise of the church to its position of greatest power; Renaissance individualism saw the beginning of its decline; the seventeenth century saw the church cease to be a power of the first magnitude; the eighteenth century saw a new attitude toward religion altogether.

The fact that an upsurge in personal religious commitment occurred when religion was losing its political power seems paradoxical. However, it is not. Protestantism weakened the power of the institution of the church, but it preached that the real church was within the breast of every human. The Catholic Council of Trent, which ended in 1563, had concluded that the Catholic church had to win back the souls it had lost by means of a Counterreformation, which stressed a spiritual revival. The Council of Trent affected art deeply by insisting that religious art should move people toward the faith. Thus an art which touched the emotions developed in Italy and elsewhere. It was an art of intense emotional experience, an art that eventually became the baroque: eccentric, individualistic, theatrical, grand, and intensely involving.

The zeal of the Council of Trent and the energy of the Protestant reformers eventually ran their course in the seventeenth and eighteenth centuries. Whereas early in the seventeenth century most poetry was on religious themes, by the end of the eighteenth century such themes were, by comparison, almost absent. Most paintings were commissioned by religious authorities early in the seventeenth century, while secular commissions predominated in the eighteenth century. Scenes of the deposition and pietà were supplanted by scenes of military victories, portraits, scenes of everyday life, and landscapes. Religion never ceased to be important in the life of Europe during these centuries; however, it became more personal, less political, and less the center of intellectual and philosophical dispute.

Science

Religion had a formidable opponent which, as the seventeenth-century English poet John Donne said, "called all into doubt." Scientific inquiry was born—at least in its modern form—in the seventeenth century. Francis Bacon, an English statesman and philosopher, was

largely responsible in the period 1590–1620 for laying the groundwork for an inquiry into nature in which experiment and hypothesis were the twin tools of investigation. Rather than relying on the doctrines or authority of any institution (such as the church), Bacon urged people to open their minds and to see things as they really are. He pioneered the inductive method: reasoning from observation and experiment, an intellectual approach that doomed all authoritarian institutions.

Galileo, an Italian scientist, came into conflict with the church in the 1630s. He had proved that the earth goes around the sun, thereby attacking the church's concept of humankind as the center of God's universe. Had he been less abrasive, and had the pope been less personally threatened by the discovery, Galileo might have made his discoveries unchallenged. The church had a good record for absorbing such discoveries without shame—as it had done when Columbus demonstrated that the world is not flat. But the church felt threatened by Galileo and ultimately forced him to recant. It would be the last such "victory" for the church. By the end of the eighteenth century the march of science had transformed the world, providing inventions that revolutionized the production of steel and iron, of clothing and textiles, and of objects used in everyday life. Science transformed travel, produced new forms of energy, and pointed toward a future that promised a "brave new world" of human progress. The very concept of progress as a good thing developed in the late eighteenth century as a legacy of the inquiries of the early seventeenth century.

Science, perhaps more than any other gift of the seventeenth century, is what makes us see how modern the period was. Science taught people to value the mind's capacity to understand what it perceives. It made them ready to consider questions of human rights—questions asked by Thomas Paine during the American Revolution and then the French Revolution. The "rights of man" became an issue because industrialization and changes in agronomy had begun to create more people who had a claim to the dignity often reserved for their "betters." Many of them had to leave Europe and seek a living in the Americas. But most important, by the end of the eighteenth century it was clear that these people had a dignity and worth which prosperity had made possible. The French effort to suppress the people failed; the revolution preached democracy: liberty, fraternity, and equality. The eighteenth century began to spread that philosophy throughout Europe. The modern world still aspires to it. The revolutions in thought and society that began in the seventeenth century and flourished in the eighteenth century are still in progress in the twentieth century.

Brief Chronology

1603–1625 Reign of King James I in England.

1610–1643 Rule of Louis XIII in France.

1620 Mayflower lands the pilgrims in Massachusetts; Francis Bacon publishes *Novum Organum,* a philosophical treatise describing the need for a new intellectual method to produce true science.

1643–1715 Reign of Louis XIV. The growth of a French court distant from the populace; the almost mythic dimension of a monarch who has nearly absolute power.

1641–1649 English civil wars; they end with the beheading of Charles I.

1648 French Royal Academy founded; supports, but also governs, the arts.

1660 Commonwealth rule ends in England; Charles II returns from the continent to rule; Parliament has close control of government.

1661–1682 Building of Versailles in France. The court, 15 miles from Paris, symbolically and genuinely separates Louis and government from the people.

1682–1699 Hungary recaptured from the Turks; last Turkish siege of Vienna.

1688 Bloodless revolution in England: James II flees; William of Orange is king; 1689, English Bill of Rights.

1689–1725 Rule of Peter the Great in Russia; growth of European influence in eastern nations.

1701–1714 War of the Spanish Succession; Louis XIV loses influence and power during this war.

1714 George I, elector of Hanover, and first of the Georgian kings, succeeds to the British throne.

1740–1780 Maria Theresa, Hapsburg empress of Austria, is effectively monarch of the Holy Roman Empire.

1740–1786 Frederick the Great is emperor of Prussia; Prussia becomes a military power.

1740–1748 War of the Austrian Succession; Spain controls parts of Italy.

1755–1762 Seven Years' War: England against France; Russian victories over Prussia.

1772–1795 Series of Russian partitions of Poland.

1774–1792 Reign of Louis XVI.

1776 America declares independence; beginning of the American Revolution.

1789 Beginning of the French Revolution.

CHAPTER 14

THE SEVENTEENTH CENTURY: A NEW SYNTHESIS

Cultural Background

The seventeenth century inherited the advances in thought made possible by science, humanism, the Reformation of the church, and the loosening of religious restraints. Northern monarchies put pressure on Italy, which was a weak collection of independent trading cities. Northern artistic innovations revealed how economic changes could affect leadership in the arts. The early parts of this discussion reveal Italian dominance in most arts, but the later parts show clearly what the age knew: that the center of art was shifting northward toward Paris.

However, Paris was only one center that benefited from the power of monarchy and the strength of centralized government. London, as well, saw its share of innovation and achievement in architecture and literature. Painting in the low countries became especially distinguished, and several of the most accomplished painters of the century were from Flanders and Holland.

The rise of the middle classes is reflected in the art of the period, as are the efforts of the aristocrats to maintain their powers. The struggle between the older classical and the new baroque styles for dominance in painting can be thought of as mirroring the tension between classes. The older, aristocratic classes were steeped in conservatism of the kind best represented by classical values. Meanwhile, the newer, expanding middle classes were marked by energy and risk taking as well as by a willingness to experiment with new emotional approaches to high-intensity arts. Baroque styles cannot be explained by simple social stress or social change, but their energies are symptomatic of the excitement of the age, which sought a new synthesis between the more static traditions of classicism and the dynamic distortions of mannerism, whose oddities had become unacceptable. Baroque styles borrow from both forces. In the arts they reflect the struggles toward a new political synthesis, in the form of alliances between nations, whose shifting patterns were characteristic of the flux evident everywhere in the age.

Architecture

ITALY: CLASSICAL PROBLEMS AND BAROQUE SOLUTIONS

The remodeling of Saint Peter's, in Rome, had been going on since 1505, when Donato Bramante (1444–1514) was engaged by Pope Julius II to build a new church on the site of the badly deteriorating old basilica. Bramante's tempietto (Figure 13-1) was a model of classical style, and the church he designed (his plan is shown in Figure 14-1) was equally classical and carefully balanced. After confronting many structural problems, other architects added to the original plans, and Julius commissioned Michelangelo to build the dome in Brunelleschi's style in order to carry out Bramante's plan of placing the Pantheon dome on Constantine's basilica. Gian Lorenzo Bernini, the dominant sculptor of the century, was finally engaged to finish the project. However, since the remodeling went on for so many years, a large number of other architects had a hand in shaping it. The most significant of those is probably Carlo Maderna (1556–1629), who completed the facade (Figure 14-2) between 1606 and 1612.

The facade has a great flaw: it obscures Michelangelo's dome, which can now be seen best only from the rear. This was caused in part by the lengthening of the nave of the church by the addition of three bays. Maderna's huge but nonfunctional Corinthian columns and pilasters are spread symmetrically across the facade, with an arch on the right and the left; the details of windows and portals give the impression of a three-story building.

The classical features, the central pediment, and the Corinthian columns are essentially lost because of the spread of the facade. Instead of a clean, balanced, classical facade, Maderna's design is busily dominated by ornamentation. The decorative exuberance on the roofline of the facade is not classical, but rather a baroque enjoyment of ornament for its own sake. Maderna's facade has effectively undone the original classical intentions of Bramante and Michelangelo.

Today, one is struck by the huge open space in front of the facade, where Bernini in 1667 extended two huge colonnades that open in the shape of a keyhole (Peter's symbol is crossed keys). Many describe the result as representing the arms of mother church reaching out for her flock. The entire concept, with its oval spaces reminiscent of a forum and its Tuscan columns, which end with abrupt temple-front pediments, is emphatically Roman, reminding us that the church has inherited the authority of the empire that tried to quash it. Yet it is hardly classical

Figure 14-1
Donato Bramante. Plan (below) and perspective study (right) of Saint Peter's, Rome. 1506. 544 feet square. (Anonymous drawing, ink and pencil, Gabinetto dei Disegni, Uffizi, Firenze. Photo, Alinari/Art Resource.)

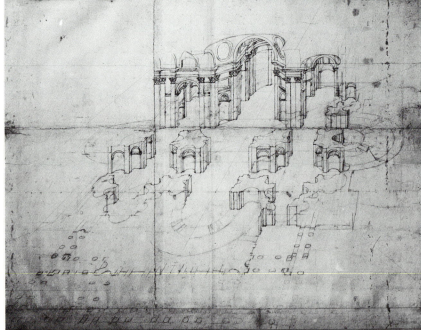

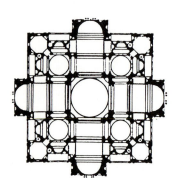

Figure 14-2
Above: Carlo Maderna. Facade of Saint Peter's.
1606–1612.

Figure 14-3
Right: Gian Lorenzo Bernini. Baldachino, Saint Peter's.
1623–1633. Bronze, 85 feet high. (Photo, Alinari/Art
Resource.)

and static: its careful angles and curves produce a new emotional awareness that may best be described as an aspect of baroque expression.

Bernini's baldachino (Figure 14-3) covers the altar inside the church. Its twisted columns (designed to resemble those in the original temple in Jerusalem) support an ornately decorated canopy. Its height, 85 feet, makes it the focal point of the space beneath the dome. It resembles architectural details found in mannerist paintings, which were a powerful artistic influence in Rome in the 1620s. Bernini avoided a classical solution in favor of absorbing the oriental influences of the serpentine columns in a gracefully curved canopy. Such curves and such ornamental detail became a hallmark of later baroque architecture.

Francesco Borromini (1599–1667) set the standard for many later churches when he designed Sant' Agnese (Figure 14-4) in Piazza Navona, Rome, built

from 1653 to 1657, and then finished by others in 1666. Its balanced, rounded towers are separated by a larger but not overwhelming dome. This pattern influenced later architects, such as Christopher Wren, in England.

The facade of Sant' Agnese is rhythmic with gothic towers softened by rounded corners that echo the lantern atop the dome. This synthesis caught the imagination of Europe as far east as Russia. In the facade we see the same Roman main portal, with attached pillars and a triangular pediment over the door, that we see in Saint Peter's. The pilasters on the main level are echoed in the towers and the dome. The various horizontal details move across the entire facade, and the symmetrical patterns of Maderna's facade for Saint Peter's are here too: everything on the left of the facade is repeated on the right. Even the ingenious treatment of the surfaces—in which the center and wings of the facade are closer

Figure 14-4
Francesco Borromini. Facade of Sant'
Agnese, Piazza Navona, Rome.
1653–1657, completed in 1666.
(Photo, Alinari/Art Resource.)

COMPARISON KEY

Francesco Borromini, Facade of Sant' Agnese, and Carlo Maderna, Facade of Saint Peter's

1. What classical details do the facades of Sant' Agnese (Figure 14-4) and Saint Peter's (Figure 14-2) share? Consider the treatment of pediment and columns and the balance of apparent stories. Can either facade be described as essentially simple in design?

2. How important is symmetry for Borromini? What specific elements are symmetrically placed? Consider vertical details, such as columns, as well as openings on the surface of the facade.

3. Are the proportions of one facade more pleasing to you? Which architect seems to have taken the most care with proportion?

4. Sant' Agnese has two gothic towers that balance the central dome. Saint Peter's was intended to have such towers. Do you feel that its facade would be more or less classical if the towers had been added? Would the towers have improved the facade?

5. Architectural critics have complained that the proportion of vertical to horizontal lines in the facade of Saint Peter's is inappropriate, that the facade is much too horizontal, and that the columns and pilasters, which are 87 feet high, look dwarfed. Can such criticisms be made of Borromini's facade? What would cause critics to make such a judgment of either facade?

to us than the body—is symmetrically handled. This recession of portions of the surface of a facade became a passion among some seventeenth-century architects. The scale of Sant' Agnese is not even close to that of Saint Peter's, but both respect symmetry and balance.

ENGLISH DEVELOPMENTS: NORTHERN SYNTHESIS

The influence of Palladio spread rapidly during the seventeenth century, as it had in the sixteenth. The proportions of the banqueting hall at Whitehall, (Figure 14-5), the work of Inigo Jones (1573–1652), have been much admired. The attached pillars—Doric below and Corinthian above—with pilasters at the corners are adapted from Palladio. The details over the windows, alternating pediments and half circles on the first and second floors, are borrowed from Italian styles of the period. The interior of the hall consists of one main room in which some of the great Stuart masques—musical and dance entertainments performed for and by aristocrats took place. In its ceiling is a painting by Rubens of the apotheosis of James I. It is appropriate in a room in which so many masques were performed, since one of the most popular themes of the masques was the elevation of a mortal into the world of the gods.

When the great fire of 1666 burned down virtually all of London, the task of rebuilding the churches fell largely to Christopher Wren (1632–1723), whose masterpiece is Saint Paul's Cathedral (Figure 14-6). Old Saint Paul's had been a huge wooden structure that dominated the London skyline. Plans for remodeling it had begun when the fire struck. Wren's church is immense, although not as large as Saint Peter's. The symmetrical facade shows Borromini's influence, with two towers flanking the large dome, whose lantern echoes the tower designs. The dome is encircled with Corinthian columns that repeat the stately paired columns of the facade. Each side tower features a dramatic spiral stairway which most visitors never see. What they see inside (Figure 14-7) is an elaborate decoration (actually done in the nineteenth century). Wren's original design for the baldachin—similar to Bernini's—was executed in recent times; it now stands over the altar.

London's relatively tight spaces make it difficult to appreciate the exterior of Saint Paul's. Most visitors are impressed by its interior (Figure 14-7), which is filled with memorabilia of the empire and of the nation's wars. The exterior is interesting because of several illusions that it creates. For instance, the dome is actually three domes, one inside another. The dome that supports the lantern is exactly the same shape that one would get by hanging a chain

Figure 14-5
Inigo Jones. Banqueting hall, Whitehall, London. 1619–1620.

Figure 14-6
Christopher Wren. Saint Paul's Cathedral, London.
1675–1712. (Photo, A. F. Kersting.)

Figure 14-7
Christopher Wren. Saint Paul's Cathedral, interior.

Figure 14-8
Christopher Wren.
Fountain courtyard,
Hampton Court.

from its ends (but inverted, of course)—which makes it an unusually powerful structure. The outside, visible dome is decorative in function. That is true, as well, of the upper-level walls of the nave: they simply hide the buttressing, and yet they look very impressive.

On the facade, the raising of the pediment to the second story helps give it greater emphasis and importance in the design. The double-story columns also help emphasize the verticality of the facade. They are not specifically faithful to classical designs, but they help the facade balance its dome and towers and continue its upward thrust. Compared with Saint Peter's, the emphasis is vertical.

Wren's affection for symmetry is evident in his Fountain Courtyard in Hampton Court (Figure 14-8), which he remodeled and added to in the latter part of the century. We see first a level of repeated arches with no columns or pilasters; then there is a level of long, narrow windows with triangular pediments. Above those is a level of square motifs, topped by a level of square windows, and then a level of balusters reminiscent of Jones. The result is pleasing, calming, and reassuring. Wren achieves an almost musical harmony based on the repetition of motifs that remain pleasing without becoming dull.

FRENCH ARCHITECTURE

In part because of the extraordinary personality of the monarch, Louis XIV, the Sun King (1638–1715; Figure 14-9), French architecture began to serve aristocratic purposes on a scale that no other country could have imagined. Louis, a model of the absolute monarch, ruled (from 1661) as if he had been endowed with divine right from God.

During Louis's reign, the principal geniuses of French architecture were François Mansart (1598–1666), a builder of country houses and the inventor of the mansard roof; Louis le Vau (1612–1670); Claude Perrault (1613–1688); and the grandnephew of Mansart, Jules Hardouin-Mansart (1646–1708). Their great, collective achievement was to move the Italian Renaissance and baroque styles toward a modern classicism, epitomized by the east facade of the Louvre (Figure 14-10), the work of Claude Perrault, built from 1667 to 1670.

Louis XIV personally supervised the project, as he did virtually all projects in France. He had asked

Figure 14-9
Hyacinthe Rigaud. *Portrait of Louis XIV.* 1701. Oil on canvas. 9 feet 2 inches by 7 feet 10 ¾ inches. (Louvre, Paris. Photo, Musées Nationaux.)

Bernini to come to Paris to submit designs for the building, but Bernini seems to have been so contemptuous of the existing French construction that Louis rejected his designs and sent him home. Claude Perrault then submitted a design unlike that of any building seen in Italy to that time. It has since become a model for classical grandeur.

It appears to have only one story, with the ground floor acting as a pedestal for the main level and with a pavilion on each end connected by a string of paired Corinthian columns. The central pediment is a modification of the pediment of the Parthenon. The effect of the building is similar to that which would be achieved by opening the left and right columned sides of the Parthenon and placing them level with

Figure 14-10
Left: Claude Perrault. East
facade of the Louvre.
1667–1670.

Figure 14-11
Below: Louis le Vau and Jules
Hardouin-Mansart. Palace of
Versailles, garden view.
1669–1685.

the east or west pediment. This facade differs from Wren's Fountain Courtyard in terms of rhythm and harmony. Unlike the courtyard, it has the effect of unity and power. As Louis's residence, it was an expression of the extraordinary power vested in the French monarchy, and, in a revision of Roman classicism, it imparted tradition, authority, and permanence to Louis's government.

Louis le Vau and Jules Hardouin-Mansart worked on the most colossal architectural project of the era, the palace of Versailles (Figure 14-11). Versailles was a city in itself. Its cost has been blamed for bankrupt-

ing the nation. The palace became Louis's seat of government (which the Louvre might have become), and everything in it revolved around him and the sun. At *levée*, sunrise, servants performed prescribed rituals while Louis rose from his bed. Rituals were performed at sunset as well. Versailles is still intact and is one of the wonders of the world; splendid gardens and vistas, strewn with classical statuary copied from originals in Rome and elsewhere, seem to extend for miles. The interior of the palace, in which there is a wealth of detail—virtually every surface is covered with exuberant baroque decoration

Seventeenth-Century English and French Architecture

1. The fusion of Renaissance and classical architectural forms depends in part on symmetry. How is symmetry expressed in French architecture of the period? Is it expressed differently in English architecture? Consider the treatment of entrances, windows, domes, and spires.

2. The buildings of the period were rhetorical: they were meant to be seen and marveled at. Any rhetorical architecture is expressive of a given purpose. Which of the English and French buildings shown in Figures 14-5 through 14-11 are most expressive of political purposes? Which are most expressive of religious purposes?

3. The buildings of the period depend on repetitions of important elements, such as pillars, pilasters, and pediments. What is the effect of such repetitions? Is there a difference between horizontal and vertical repetitions? Do English and French architects handle repetitions in a similar fashion?

4. What are the architectural differences between religious buildings and secular buildings in terms of the emphasis on vertical and horizontal elements?

5. What qualities of the east facade of the Louvre (Figure 14-10) helped impart a sense of empire, permanence, and absoluteness to the government of Louis XIV? How can such architecture express political values and political purposes? Do other buildings illustrated in this chapter express such purposes?

—relates to Louis's concerns, his life, and his rituals. The Hall of Mirrors, for example, opens onto his bedroom, and each morning he beheld seventeen windows admitting sunlight reflected in seventeen mirrors.

Sculpture: Bernini, Father of the Baroque

Many sculptors worked in Europe in the seventeenth century, but one, Gian Lorenzo Bernini (1598-1680), dominated the field so totally that he was still a primary influence two centuries later. His technique was commanding, and his skill in working marble surfaces had no peer. He was so at ease with the material that it is sometimes difficult to believe, even when one is standing close, that one is looking at stone. This is particularly true of works such as *Apollo and Daphne* (Figure 14-12). Bernini's skill was so great that he began work for Cardinal Barberini—later the pope—in Rome when he was in his early twenties.

One walks around *Apollo and Daphne* because it demands many perspectives. For this work Bernini turned to the Greek myth in which the lusty Apollo attempts to rape Daphne, the daughter of a river god; Daphne escapes his advances and protects her virtue by being changed into a laurel. In the sculpture, her toes are already taking root, her fingers have begun to turn into branches, her hair is developing into leaves, and the lower part of her body is starting to be covered with bark. The surface of this piece is vibrant

Figure 14-12
Gian Lorenzo Bernini. *Apollo and Daphne.* 1622–1625. Marble, 8 feet high. (Galleria Borghese, Rome; photo, Scala/Art Resource.)

Figure 14-13
Gian Lorenzo Bernini. *Ecstasy of Saint Teresa.* Santa Maria della Vittoria, Rome. 1645–1652. Marble, 11 feet 6 inches high. (Photo, Alinari/Art Resource.)

with light. The skin of the two figures seems lifelike, and the sense of motion is impressive. The realism achieved in this work is so startling that we are left almost breathless. Only later does it occur to us that Bernini has metamorphosed marble into apparent life (or is it the reverse?). The baroque qualities of illusion, perfection, and wit are all present in this sculpture. Its sensuous richness and literary allusion to Ovid's *Metamorphoses* are also baroque qualities which Bernini, thought by some to be the inventor of baroque style, imparts to most of his work.

In *Ecstasy of Saint Teresa* (Figure 14-13), Bernini represents Teresa in the most dramatic moment described in her journals: when the angel of the Lord came to her in a vision and pierced her heart ecstatically with his arrow. The sexual allegory is religious: Christ marries his church, and allegorically his angel ravishes the saint.

Saint Teresa appears on a proscenium behind the altar (Figure 14-14), and each sidewall contains a theater box from which members of the Cornaro family lean out, marveling at the vision of the saint in her ecstatic union with God. In actuality, they cannot "see" her, since she is visible only from the front, where the viewer must stand. The baroque melding of media is explicitly evident here in the combination of architecture in the design of the chapel, sculpture in the design of the statuary, painting in the decoration of the surfaces, and drama in the representation of the theatrical setting. Such an intermingling of art forms is considered an epitome of baroque style. If Bernini was not its inventor, he was among its most skillful practitioners.

Figure 14-14
Gian Lorenzo Bernini.
View of Cornaro Chapel,
Santa Maria della
Vittoria. 1645–1652.
(Photo, Barbara Malter,
Rome.)

Painting

ITALIAN CLASSICISM AND ITALIAN BAROQUE

At the end of the sixteenth century, mannerism was the dominant force in Italian painting. Anatomical distortions, eccentric uses of color, and psychological disjunctions similar to those in Parmigianino's *Madonna della Colla Longa* (Figure 13-18) were the rage. The chief complaint about mannerism was that, in the hands of painters less gifted then Parmigianino, Pontormo, and El Greco, it broke down into a weak, decadent parody of itself.

Two styles sought to restore painting to a position of vitality and importance. The classical style looked back to Renaissance clarity, harmony, proportion, balance, and realism—a sharp contrast with mannerism, which was unbalanced, eccentric, artificial, and unreal. Led by Annibale Carracci, classicism emphasized observation of nature, beginning with Michelangelo's muscular fusion of classical ideals and Christian values as expressed in his Sistine ceiling.

Baroque style also insisted on direct observation of nature, but it was a lush, sometimes eccentric, and very sensual style pioneered by Caravaggio. His idiosyncratic use of lighting and his reliance on living models imparted an unusual realism to his work, which dominated the later seventeenth and early eighteenth centuries. It did not have a strong ethical center, like classicism, despite the fact that late practitioners of the style were themselves often pious and serious in their concerns.

Carracci and Classicism

Heroic themes attracted Annibale Carracci (1560–1609) and his followers, who rendered them consistent with Christian values by emphasizing moral courage. *The Choice of Hercules* (Figure 14-15) portrays a moment of heroic decision, but it is a moral decision, not a military one. Hercules must choose between Vice, on our right, and Virtue, on our left. Virtue and Vice are portrayed as women. In comparison with the human figures, Carracci's landscape is of little account. The muscular, three-dimensional figures are Michelangelesque Renaissance ideals. Yet they are not so idealized that the connection between

Figure 14-15
Annibale Carracci. *The Choice of Hercules.* 1595–1597. Oil on canvas, 65 ¾ by 93 ¼ inches. (Galleria Nazionali di Capodimonte, Napoli; photo, Alinari/Art Resource.)

Hercules and ourselves is lost, since one of the points of the painting is to convince us that we, too, have a moral choice and should emulate Hercules in choosing Virtue.

Carracci places all the figures on the same flat horizontal plane; visual connectedness is maintained by having both groups form an approximation of the letter "N." Hercules's left leg begins a diagonal that is carried out in Virtue's upraised arm, pointing to the reward of the difficult way (the winding path). That same leg almost touches Vice's foot, as the diagonal in an "N" does. Near Vice are her theatrical masks of

PERCEPTION KEY

Carracci, The Choice of Hercules

1. How important are the values of balance and symmetry in *The Choice of Hercules* (Figure 14-15)? Is the composition balanced and symmetrical?

2. What is the focal point in the painting? Where does your eye rest? Does it rest on the most important part of the painting?

3. Is the lighting even over most of the surface, or is it, like Tintoretto's, highly selective? How "deep" is the space?

4. What structural devices are used to integrate the figures in this painting? Do the figures relate clearly to one another?

5. What are the most evident classical qualities of the painting? If you did not know the narrative, would you be aware that an ethical question is being resolved in this work?

deception. But by making Virtue and Hercules seem to touch each other, Carracci reveals his choice.

Hercules's choice between good and evil was read as an allegory of the moral choices of those in high places, such as monarchs, who could see themselves as having power and responsibilities similar to those of Hercules.

Guido Reni: A Follower of Carracci

Carracci's interpretation of classicism attracted a number of followers. Among them was the remarkable Guido Reni (1575–1642), who, like Carracci, was from Bologna. His work was held in such esteem that was known as "the divine Guido." He was intrigued by the work of Raphael, and he developed a style which had the simplicity, clarity, and directness associated with Carracci but softened Carracci's sometimes severely idealized figures.

Color Plate 19 shows Saint John the Baptist as an appealing young man, handsome, well developed, and obviously sensual. Yet there is no hint of anything but a spiritual intent in the painting. No specifically fleshy or coy personal expression interferes with our sense of inward strength and meditating seriousness. The figure forms a sharp angle pointing to the right. An unstable triangle is formed by the body as a whole, yet the instability is minor, calling our attention to the fact that John is about to speak, to announce the coming of the Messiah.

Caravaggio: The Beginnings of Baroque

The baroque synthesis in painting fused the psychological energies of mannerism with the realism and force of classicism. In painting, it began with the work of Michelangelo Merisi (1573–1610), known as Caravaggio, who was often in trouble with the law and at odds with his friends. His genius was great, but his capacity for staying within the limits of the social constraints of his day was small. He eventually murdered a man during an argument over a tennis match.

His criminal life provided him with models for his paintings, even for scenes from the Bible. People who commissioned works from Caravaggio often rejected them because they recognized the faces of rogues on the bodies of saints. Everyday life excited him; what he saw he put directly onto canvas. He was not interested in moral allegory or in the classical taste for clarity, balance, and idealization of physical form. Instead of allegory he provided a close study of the real surfaces of life. He believed that artists should paint from nature and use real people.

The Calling of Saint Matthew (Color Plate 20) is based on the book of Matthew: "As he went on from there, Jesus saw a man called Matthew sitting in the tax collector's office, and said to him, 'Follow me.' He rose and followed him" (IX Matthew: 9–13). The painting was shocking because the people in the scene are so ordinary-looking. If one were not told what is happening—that Christ is summoning Saint

PERCEPTION KEY

Caravaggio, Calling of Saint Matthew

1. In Color Plate 20, which figure is Christ? Which is Saint Matthew?

2. Are any of the figures idealized, or are they all represented realistically?

3. What is the source of light? Is it possible to tell whether this is an indoor or an outdoor scene?

4. Does the painting urge us to do anything? Is there a moral to the dramatic scene that Caravaggio portrays?

5. Do any qualities in the painting tell us that this is a religious work? Do you feel that the painting either represents or evokes any religious emotions?

Matthew to be his apostle—one would not know the subject of the painting. Even Christ is difficult to recognize. Caravaggio's contemporaries were shocked because he transformed his cronies into holy personages. No one considered that, since Christ often associated with unsavory people, these portrayals might be appropriate.

The most striking quality of this painting is its use of light. We cannot tell its source, although it may be coming from the right, over Christ's head. We recognize Christ partly by the halo (only a thin line) and partly by his right arm, which alludes to Michelangelo's *Creation* in the Sistine ceiling (Color Plate 13). The incoming radiance strikes him first. Matthew's rhetorical gesture, as if he is asking, "Do you mean me?" identifies him. The light is mysterious, rich, and selective: it does not strike everyone equally. The figure to the right of Matthew seems unaware of what is happening, though the light bathes him as

well. The figures to the left of him are busy counting money—Christ is of no importance to them.

There is little in this painting to identify it as religious. Yet that is part of Caravaggio's point. Rather than idealize Christ and set him apart from the human experience, Caravaggio places him in ordinary surroundings. Christianity was the religion of the poor as well as the rich—it was to touch everyone's life. Instead of placing the religious experience on a high, unreachable plane, Caravaggio shows us that it is within the grasp of even the meanest of us. This implies a revival of early Christian ideals.

In *Doubting Thomas* (Figure 14-16), Caravaggio also uses light mysteriously to emphasize the body of Christ, the forehead and left shoulder of Thomas, and the face of the figure in the background. The heads are knit together in a lozenge shape, with the focal point, Christ's wound, well to the left of center. The figures are intensely realistic, but without the

Figure 14-16
Michelangelo Merisi da Caravaggio. *Doubting Thomas.* c. 1601. Oil on canvas, 42 ⅛ by 57 ½ inches; now lost. (Staatliche Schlosser und Garten Potsdam Sanssouci.)

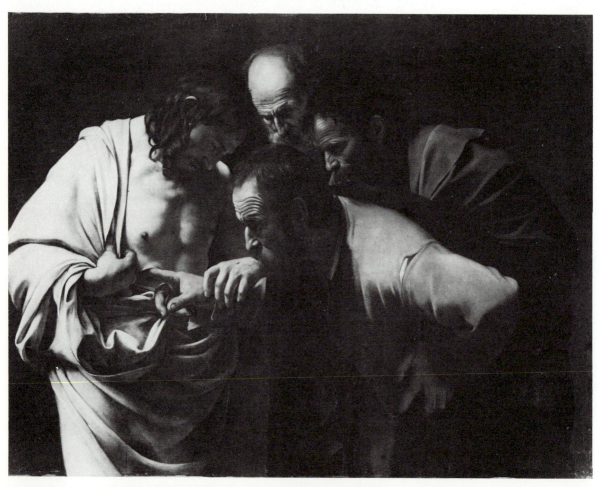

classical idealization of Carracci. These could be people called in from the street, which is why such paintings baffled their original owners.

SPAIN: VELÁSQUEZ

The Spanish painter Diego Velásquez (1599–1660) applied Caravaggio's style to secular subjects. In his portrayal of the poet Góngora, he uses harsh sidelight and catches an inexplicable emotional expression (Figure 14-17). We cannot help wondering what Góngora is thinking as he studies us with his powerful gaze.

The famous *Maids of Honor* (Figure 14-18) depends on numerous ambiguities for its power. The five-year-old princess looks toward us as she is offered a drink by a lady-in-waiting. One dwarf stands thoughtfully on the right, while another dwarf play-

Figure 14-18
Diego Velàsquez. *The Maids of Honor.* 1656. Oil on canvas, 10 feet 5 inches by 9 feet ½ inch. (Museo del Prado, Madrid.)

Figure 14-17
Diego Velàsquez. *Luis de Góngora y Argote.* 1622. 19 ¾ by 15 ¾ inches. (Museum of Fine Arts, Boston; purchase, Maria Antoinette Evans Fund.)

fully pokes a dog. Velásquez steps back from the canvas. The mirror in the background reflects the king and queen; a nobleman is seen departing at the end of the room.

Velásquez plays with the relationship between life outside the painting and the scene that we behold, in which we become the viewed. Indeed, we see things from the point of view of those who are being painted, as if we were sitting for a portrait. The ambiguity of our relationship to the space and our point of view toward it is part of the subject matter of the painting. We experience a similar ambiguity in *Portrait of Góngora* and in other paintings by Velásquez. In his *Maids of Honor,* he avoids mannerist uncertainty by emphasizing the ordinariness of the household scene. So much is going on, and there are so many nuances of psychological interrelationships between the figures we see and ourselves, that we are riveted by the subtleties of expression. The rectangle and the pyramid integrate the elements of the painting. The shape of the little princess is a pyramid, and other figures group or lean toward the center of the painting to form more pyramids. In the background are the more secure, stabilizing rectangles—mostly paintings.

Velásquez avoids stiff, mathematical linear perspective. Instead, he gives us a camera's view. The softness of the forms and the absence of lines demarking the figures from one another show us that Velásquez was a forerunner of modern painters: light, not line, distinguishes each figure. Modern ambiguities of space, lighting, point of view, and action characterize the work.

This may be, like van Eyck's portrait of the Arnolfini (Color Plate 10), a painting that witnesses something. Apparently, Velásquez had expected to be raised to the nobility, since by 1656 he was a painter of very great importance, but his lowly trade made it difficult for him to be accepted by the nobility. This painting may have been designed to show his honored place in the royal household. The point of view alone demonstrates that he was accepted "in the eyes" of the king and queen. If this is what the painting was to accomplish, it is an effective piece of rhetorical persuasion, because it worked. After his death, the cross of Santiago was added to his chest (in the painting) in recognition of his station: he died a nobleman.

FRENCH CLASSICISM: POUSSIN AND SCHOLARLY REALISM

In France, Nicolas Poussin (1594–1665) took Carracci's influence in a new direction. He painted classical subjects (as in Figure 14-19) in a manner that was not in imitation of classical paintings, not an attempt to update classical events or persons, and not an attempt to produce idealized scenes as an inspiration for action. Rather, he wished to produce imaginative, scholarly reconstructions of classical events. This involved considerable research and a commitment to authenticity.

Figure 14-19
Nicolas Poussin. *Rape of the Sabine Women.* c. 1637. 60 ⅞ by 82 ⅝ inches. (Metropolitan Museum of Art, Harris Brisbane Dick Fund, 1946.)

Poussin's paintings often depend on narratives which must be "read" intellectually for a thorough appreciation. He established the classical ideal as cool, intellectual, and Apollonian: he concentrated more on thought than on feeling and more on control than on abandon. But Poussin did not slight the other side of Roman life, that of the carefree, sensuous Dionysian revelry. He painted a series on Bacchus, the Greek god of wine, and the bacchanalia, wild celebrations of the gods, often mentioned in classical literature.

The Massacre of the Innocents (Color Plate 21) is filled with movement whose rhythms are expressed in the arms and legs. Light models the figures clearly, while selectively focusing on the faces and arms of the imploring mother and child. The narrative is Herod's killing of all newborn children to prevent Christ's mission on earth. The background is a Roman setting, with grieving mothers and their dead children. The powerful pyramidal structure of the central three figures was a favorite of Poussin.

A similar grouping is at the right of *Rape of the Sabine Women* (Figure 14-19), where a Sabine man holds back a Roman soldier. The story is that of a Roman settlement which needed women in order to survive. When the nearby Sabines refused to send the Romans their young women, the Roman leader, Romulus, invited all the Sabines to a feast, which ended with the Romans carrying off the women. They spared the Sabine men and children, and eventually peace was restored—negotiated by the Sabine women.

Poussin reveals a capacity to integrate masses of action and rhythms of motion. Romulus stands above, to the left, with his cloak raised to signal the instant at which the Romans took the Sabine women. The clarity with which the figures are modeled and the selectivity of the light help make this a forceful painting. Poussin treated his subject heroically because he admired the Romans for doing what was necessary to ensure their survival.

FLANDERS: RUBENS—BAROQUE SCHOLARSHIP

Peter Paul Rubens (1577–1640) traveled extensively —to study works of the masters when he was young, and then later to execute commissions. He studied the ancients with as much intensity as Poussin, but with completely different results. Whereas Poussin

invested his work with a deep sense of calm, clarity, and precision, Rubens represented dynamic motion, rich sensuality, and intense—if fleeting—emotion. Poussin, as Bernini once said, painted with his head, which is to say that he was intellectual and sometimes detached. But for Rubens the intellect was not enough: we must feel as well as understand the scene before us.

Fluent in many languages and widely read in ancient and modern literature, Rubens remains one of the most learned and scholarly painters of any age. Most of his life centered on Antwerp, despite his travels. His work was usually on a gigantic scale; large portions of his great canvases were executed by his students and assistants. For Rubens the conception of the painting was primary; others could carry it out under his direction, while he provided the finishing details. Poussin, by contrast, would not permit assistants to work on his canvases and was satisfied with fewer and smaller paintings.

The Descent from the Cross (Figure 14-20), an early painting, is the central panel—the side panels treat

Figure 14-20
Peter Paul Rubens. *Descent from the Cross.* Cathedral of Our Lady, Antwerp. 1612. Central panel from a triptych, 13 feet 9 inches by 10 feet 2 inches (Photo, Scala/Art Resource.)

Rubens, Carracci, Caravaggio, and Poussin

1. Rubens knew the work of Carracci and Caravaggio and made numerous copies of their paintings when he could. What influence of either painter is apparent in the examples of Rubens's work shown in Figure 14-20 and Color Plate 22?

2. Poussin studied the classics with great thoroughness. Rubens was equally thorough. Both made drawings of the same classical works. What differences are apparent in their treatment of the human figure? Does Rubens idealize the human figure as much as Poussin does in Figure 14-19 and Color Plate 21?

3. Does the evidence of the paintings support the contention that besides understanding his subject matter intellectually, as Poussin did, Rubens also understood it emotionally?

4. Is Rubens's self-portrait (Color Plate 22) indebted to classical values as understood by Poussin? Does Rubens treat himself heroically?

5. Moral values were of great importance to classical painters. Which of the paintings shown in Figures 14-19 and 14-20 and Color Plates 21 and 22 seems most centrally concerned with imparting moral values? Is Rubens more or less concerned with moral values than Poussin?

related subjects— of a huge altarpiece. It contains the characteristic swirling motion that we associate with Rubens's large works, and yet it portrays a moment when Christ slumps and the world's energy also slumps. The action swirls downward from the upper right. Christ's graveclothes cut across the darkness of the canvas. Saint John—wearing a rich, red robe—holds him, and we virtually feel his weight. And while it is a weight of sorrow, the expressions on the faces are more those of care and faith. Even the face of the Madonna, as she reaches to touch Christ, expresses resignation as well as pain. Each figure is integrated into the composition by touching another figure; most overlap. The lighting is selective, and yet everyone is visible. Rubens takes the emotional energy of this moment as his subject matter.

Rubens's control of color and his skill at modeling are evident in his *Self-Portrait* (Color Plate 22). This is not the splashy Rubens, but the thoughtful and meditative Rubens. About fifty years old, he looks as if he is waiting for someone to finish speaking so that he can respond. He reveals a deep self-awareness and honesty. The painting is almost photographic in its accuracy, and the color of the flesh has a luminosity and clarity that mark Rubens's best work. The tilt of the head must have been characteristic of Rubens; it is engaging and disarming.

THE NETHERLANDS: VERMEER AND REMBRANDT

Holland, a land of wealthy mercantile burghers, had a relatively democratic government, unlike the hereditary monarchies found elsewhere in Europe. Holland's influence depended on its access to the sea, its skill in trading, and its use of Italian banking techniques.

Figure 14-21
Jan Vermeer. *The Artist in His Studio,* or *Allegory of the Art of Painting.* c. 1665. Oil on canvas, 52 by 44 inches. (Kunsthistorisches Museum, Vienna.)

Vermeer

Jan Vermeer (1632–1675) painted interiors which convey a realistic sense of light and space without strain or stiffness. He may have used the camera obscura to study certain scenes, or he may have used it as an aid to planning his canvases, but his coloration seems to capture the atmosphere of a scene as it must have been. *The Artist in His Studio* (Figure 14-21), like Velásquez' *Maids of Honor* (Figure 14-18), puts us in the privileged position of watching a painter at work in his studio. The sense of privilege comes in part from the drapery at the left of the painting, which has been drawn aside to give us a special view. The artist has sketched in his subject, a woman representing Clio, in classical tradition the muse of history. He works from the top down, beginning with the laurel wreath on her head. Some people feel that this painting was made to give a sense of how Vermeer worked.

The realistic details of the room, the sense of receding space achieved by the use of perspective, and the natural point of view are typical of Vermeer, but there is also an allegorical representation in the muse, in the map of Holland—which appears often in Vermeer's paintings—and perhaps in the tile floor, alluding to Renaissance perspectivists. The fact that in Vermeer's time Holland became a world power, changing the course of history, is part of the painting's content.

Rembrandt

The influence of Caravaggio is easy to detect in Rembrandt van Rijn (1606–1669), whose genius was expressed in his individual grasp of lighting, space, and color and in his unusual sense of plasticity in the portrait. His best-known subjects are self-portraits; portraits of his wife, his son, and his mistress; and stories from the Bible, particularly the Old Testament. But Rembrandt was also a master of the group portrait, as can be seen in his complex painting depicting an anatomy lesson and in his equally complex group portraits of businessmen. Early in his career his highly lucrative commissions made him rich, but he mismanaged his money and by the mid-1640s was in deep financial trouble. By the 1650s he had recovered, but his mood had changed dramatically, as had his style. Rembrandt expressed his deepest feelings about his subjects while trying to meet the demands of his commissions.

The Blinding of Samson (Figure 14-22), a dramatic and baroque painting, is a mass of action. The powerful sidelight coming from the left, which makes it seem as if the action is taking place in a cave, sensitizes us to the significance of Samson's blinding. Rembrandt moves beyond the style of Caravaggio and uses his own distinctive approach to lighting. The figure on the left with a pike is almost silhouetted. The expression on Delilah's face is animated as she races into the light holding a lock of hair. The soldiers are intent as they gouge out Samson's eyes. None of the clothing is biblical (the original story appears in Judges). Rembrandt has taken liberties with such details—unlike Poussin, but quite like Caravaggio. This dramatic scene, filled with anxiety and action, is a high point in the development of baroque painting.

Rembrandt's *Descent from the Cross* (Figure 14-23), an earlier work, demonstrates how he focused on a subject to find its dramatic and emotional center.

Figure 14-22
Top of page: Rembrandt van Rijn. *The Blinding of Samson.* 1636. Oil on canvas. 93 by 119 inches. (Stadelisches Kunstinstitut, Frankfurt; photo, Ursula Edelmann.)

Figure 14-23
Left: Rembrandt van Rijn. *Descent from the Cross.* 1633. Oil on wood. 35 ½ by 22 inches. (Alte Pinakothek, Munich.)

Rembrandt, Descent from the Cross, and Rubens, Descent from the Cross

1. Compare Figure 14-23 and 14-20 in terms of use of dramatic lighting. Which seems more indebted to Caravaggio?

2. Which painting has a more "tormented" composition? Which is less stable and more dynamic?

3. Is one painting more realistic than the other? Is realism an important artistic goal in these paintings? How can one tell?

4. Does one painting involve the viewer more completely on an emotional level? Is either painting explicitly intellectual in its treatment of the subject matter?

5. Does one painting portray the suffering of Christ more successfully? If so, how? Does size or scale affect that success?

The Descent from the Cross by Rubens (Figure 14-20) is in many ways more baroque and unstable than Rembrandt's treatment; in the Rubens, the swirling of the figures is so intense as to prevent the eye from perceiving the group in a formal way. By contrast, Rembrandt has moved the scene away from us, almost as if it were on a modern stage, and the main figures, along with the striking white graveclothes, form a pyramid. This geometric structure unifies the figures and settles them at the same time. Rubens concentrates on "tormented" emotional values; each figure reaches toward Christ in a way that, in comparison with Rembrandt's version, looks stagy.

True, Rubens's sense of drama is powerful, and his organization is dynamic. But Rembrandt concentrates on the more natural flow of the figures. His people are less distinct from one another (in the Rubens, they are almost separate portraits), and the focus, in part because of the "divine spotlighting" of a single ray of light, is more clearly on Christ. The grief portrayed in the Rubens is agitated; in the Rembrandt it is calm, perhaps deeper in a sense. Both these works are masterpieces, but they approach the portrayal of a deeply emotional moment quite differently.

Self-Portrait Aged Sixty-Three (1669; Color Plate 23), one of many self-portraits, relies on a softened chiaroscuro: the light falls softly on the face and on the hands; the background drops out, but not abruptly. The face is that of an older man—thoughtful, resigned, and at rest. Rembrandt has made no attempt to hide his wrinkles or to disguise the weight of care that is clear in his expression. He is frank and truthful even when representing himself. If there is disappointment in the face, it is an honest emotion. Rubens's self-portrait (Color Plate 22) reveals much more dynamism and more youthful ambition; the self-portrait of the older Rembrandt, who had only eleven more years to live when it was painted, shows the strain of financial ruin and slow recovery. The honesty of this portrayal is a mark of genius.

The Night Watch (Figure 14-24) is misnamed because of a very dark varnish that covered it until the 1940s. It should be titled *The Company of Captain Frans Cocq.* It is a group portrait of a company of civil guards under the command of Cocq and his lieutenant, Willem van Ruytenburch (in light garb).

This painting was successful. The fact that some members of the company are partially obscured by the action did not cause the work to be condemned, as

Figure 14-24
Rembrandt van Rijn. *The Night Watch*. 1642. Oil on canvas. 12 feet 2 inches by 14 feet 7 inches. (© Rijksmuseum-Stichting, Amsterdam.)

has been suggested. In this painting Rembrandt solved the problem of the group portrait in such a dynamic way that few after him could ever again sit or stand their subjects in a static line or a static grouping. Rembrandt shows Cocq and his men in motion: their lances are askew, their muskets are out of order, and they all project a sense of the vitality of their mission. The canvas is gigantic and was originally even larger. In this group portrait Rembrandt captures the personality of the entire company.

Literature and Theater

THEATER IN FRANCE:
MOLIÈRE AND THE COMEDY OF MANNERS

France produced a popular drama in the works of a genius whose comedies are still performed all over the world, Jean-Baptiste Poquelin, known as Molière (1622–1673). Molière was an actor, born in Paris; he and his company were always beset by problems, from threats from the Inquisition and church authorities to withdrawals of plays by prominent writers. Molière's great successes were *Tartuffe* (1664), *The Misanthrope* (1666), *The Miser* (1668), *The Bourgeois Gentleman* (1670), and *The Imaginary Invalid* (1673). Instead of using myth, he introduced material from everyday life; the situations in his plays are realistic and suggestive of the circumstances of the lives of the audience of his day. We call his most successful plays "comedies of manners." The manners are those of his audience.

Despite his avoidance of classical subject matter, Molière must be seen in light of an environment that praised classicism and approved of little that broke with it. Molière had studied the classics and had been nurtured on Aristotle. Although he studied with the philosopher Gassendi, whose views differed from those of Aristotle, Molière's theories of drama remained classical; in his introduction to *Tartuffe*, he says that Roman plays were the models of comedy that he used to achieve his own purposes. Tartuffe, a hypocrite, was modeled on many people whom Molière knew, and because the play revealed so much, it was forced off the stage.

Molière and Classical Comedy

1. For this perception key, read *Tartuffe, The Misanthrope,* or *The Miser.* Begin by identifying the "type characters." A type character has personality traits that are predictably associated with a certain kind of person. (In classical drama, the braggart warrior is the most obvious type character; in modern literature, the dumb blonde and the evil landlord have become types.) Begin with the title character and establish the extent to which he is a type.

2. Classical comedy rarely makes fun of humankind; rather it makes fun of individuals or classes of people. Is this true of Molière?

3. Classical comedies often rely on improbable circumstances for their comic premise. Is this also true of Molière? What improbable circumstances produced comic results in the play that you read?

4. What is the ultimate purpose of Molière's comedy? Does it, in keeping with the high-mindedness of Poussin, contribute to the betterment or reform of society?

5. Are there any baroque ambiguities in the play that you read? Is it clear how you are to value each of the characters and their actions, or does Molière make it difficult for you to know what his own attitudes toward the characters are?

POETRY: THE ENGLISH METAPHYSICAL POETS

Metaphysical poetry is in some ways the literary equivalent of mannerism; it depends on distortion, exuberant imagery, tortured metaphor, and psychological turns that upset the reader's expectations. This is especially true of early-seventeenth-century poets, such as John Donne (1572–1631) and Richard Crashaw (c. 1613–1649), some of whose work still mystifies and shocks the modern sensibility.

John Donne

Donne's work is prized for its directness, its vitality, and its complexity. He used a recondite vocabulary, and his metaphors grew into twisted conceits: knotty concepts that have to be carefully worked out by the reader. An intellectual poet, he valued wit and complex, imaginative situations. He also lived an exciting life: he was a warrior, a statesman, and a dashing romantic before settling down to become dean of Saint Paul's and a great churchman.

Donne was known for the colloquial beginnings of his poems, usually a direct address, such as "Death, be not proud," a poem in which he speaks to Death as if it were a person, telling it to be more humble, since its powers are limited. In trying to coax his mistress into bed, he declares, "Come, Madam, come! All rest my powers defy! / Until I labor, I in labor lie." The witty conceit of the male lover being in labor, likening him to a woman about to deliver a child, is typically metaphysical. One of Donne's most amusing addresses to his mistress begins with, "For God's sake hold your tongue, and let me love."

Some of his technique is apparent in one of his "Holy Sonnets":

Batter my heart, three-personed God; for You
As yet but knock, breathe, shine, and seek to mend;
That I may rise, and stand, o'erthrow me, and bend
Your force, to break, blow, burn, and make me new.
I, like an usurped town to another due,
Labor to admit You, but oh! to no end;
Reason, Your viceroy in me, me should defend,

John Donne, "Batter My Heart, Three-Personed God"

1. The direct address of the first line makes it seem as if Donne is giving orders to God. Why does such an approach to God seem unusual? Would such an approach be shocking to a pious reader?

2. Donne compares himself (in a conceit) to a town usurped by an enemy. He compares God to a beseiging army. What does he want God to do? Who is the enemy that has usurped Donne?

3. If Donne thinks of himself as enthralled to another (the enemy), how can he say "I . . . Labor to admit You"? Is he somehow free while being enthralled? Why is reason God's "viceroy"? How should it help Donne belong to God?

4. The word "ravish," in the last line, implies a rape. Does it seem appropriate for Donne to request that God rape him to free him from the enemy to whom he is "betrothed"? Why is such sexual language used in a religious poem?

5. Consider Donne's use—or lack of use—of classical devices such as allusions to classical gods or goddesses; clarity and simplicity; balance and symmetry; humanist themes; and moral purposes.

But is captived and proves weak or untrue.
Yet dearly I love You, and would be loved fain,
But am betrothed unto Your enemy.
Divorce me, untie, or break that knot again,
Take me to You, imprison me, for I
Except You enthrall me, never shall be free;
Nor ever chaste, except You ravish me.

Donne tried to shock his audience into paying attention, as the mannerist painters did. The first part of the poem sets up an unusual conceit: Donne as a city under seige by God, who, as yet, has made no real effort to break down Donne's resistance. The problem seems to be that Donne's reason, his rational mind, has been made captive; it "proves weak or untrue," which reminds us of the controversies about knowledge in the works of Montaigne, Bacon, and later Descartes. Donne separates himself—the true person—from his reason, which he identifies as a kind of police officer that would guide him to God if it were not captive.

However, because his reason is captive, he has betrothed himself—meaning that he is virtually married—to the enemy, the devil, or at least worldly concerns. Because he is "married," Donne must plead for a divorce, which the church does not permit except in the most extraordinary circumstances. The irony of the conceit becomes clear when we realize that he has set things upside down simply because an imprisoned reason has made him do what he did not wish to do. The only way to undo this is to end the marriage which binds him to the material world. Asking God to rape him is shocking because it makes Donne's readers realize that they, too, may be married to Mammon and materialism.

Donne upsets his readers' expectations in order to penetrate to their deeper levels of feeling. By playing against ordinary expectations and by using unusual metaphors (Donne for a beseiged city, and God for an anxious bridegroom), Donne gives the attentive reader new delights. He stirs deep religious feelings and avoids the older clichés of religious thought.

Richard Crashaw

Crashaw was born Protestant and turned Catholic. During the English civil war, he was on the side of King Charles and had to flee England, finally arriving in Rome, where he made a slender living in the service of the church. Most of his poems are religious, and many seem to have been inspired by Ignatian meditation on a specific religious person or event.

Bernini's sculpture of Saint Teresa (Figure 14-13) was not unveiled until after Crashaw's death, but he may have seen it in progress. Crashaw wrote two poems on Saint Teresa. One, "A Hymn to the Name and Honor of the Admirable Saint Teresa," depicts the saint in the same ecstasy that attracted Bernini. Like Donne, Crashaw uses sexual imagery when he talks about giving oneself up to the raptures of God:

> Thou art love's victim; and must die
> A death more mystical and high.

Into Love's arms thou shalt let fall
A still-surviving funeral.
His is the dart must make the death
Whose stroke shall taste thy hallow'd breath.

Crashaw uses a seventeenth-century pun: "die" as a colloquial term for orgasm:

> O how oft shalt thou complain
> Of a sweet and subtle pain.
> Of intolerable joys;
> Of a death in which who dies
> Loves his death, and dies again,
> And would forever so be slain,
> And lives and dies; and knows not why
> To live, But that he thus may never leave to die.
>   How kindly will thy gentle heart
> Kiss the sweetly-killing dart!
> And close in his embraces keep
> Those delicious wounds, that weep
> Balsam to heal themselves with.

PERCEPTION KEY

Crashaw and Bernini

1. Is Bernini's sculpture of Saint Teresa (see Figure 14-13) as frankly sensual and sexual as Crashaw's depiction of her? What kinds of ecstasy does each artist treat?

2. Do Crashaw and Bernini make an effort to be shocking in their treatment of the saint? Is Bernini's extreme realism matched in the intensity of Crashaw's imagery?

3. Do the mannerist elements in Crashaw's lines make you regard Bernini's work as still possessing a mannerist quality? Consider Crashaw's "Sweet . . . pain," "Loves his death," "Sweetly-killing," and "delicious wounds" as examples of mannerist disjunction— efforts to shock a reader into a new awareness.

4. Sex and death were metaphorically related in the seventeenth century, when it was held that each sexual union involved a little death. Is that metaphor treated equally in each of these works? Does Bernini seem to have relied on his audience's knowledge of that conceit?

5. In another poem on Saint Teresa, Crashaw upbraids a painter for a drawing of the scene that Bernini depicts; he complains that the angel is more female in appearance than the saint, and he urges the painter to reverse the figures and make the angel Saint Teresa, and Saint Teresa the angel. Do you think that the figures in Bernini's sculpture should be reversed?

John Milton

Milton (1608–1674) was the last and the greatest of the European baroque poets. He was a new kind of man: he had no profession, and yet he was not an aristocrat. His father supported him when Milton made it known that he wanted to be a poet. When the civil war broke out in 1642, he was in Italy, traveling and meeting writers, scientists (even Galileo), and humanists, such as the members of the Florentine academy. When he returned to England, he joined with Cromwell and became Latin secretary to the Puritan government. For eleven years most of his creative energy went into writing pamphlets that defended the decision to behead King Charles I and govern England as a Commonwealth. He went blind while in the service of his government.

Despite Milton's blindness, *Paradise Lost* (completed in 1665 and published in 1667; revised in 1672) is powerfully visual and lush, like the paintings of Rubens. Milton uses the imagery of Revelation to describe Satan, who is in the form of a dragon on a fiery lake, lifting himself up to the land's more solid fire:

> Forthwith upright he rears from off the Pool
> His mighty stature; on each hand the flames
> Driv'n backward slope their pointing spires, and roll'd
> In billows, leave i' th'midst a horrid Vale.
> Then with expanded wings he steers his flight
> Aloft, incumbent on the dusky Air
> That felt unusual weight, till on dry Land
> He 'lights, if it were Land that ever burn'd
> With solid, as the Lake with liquid fire. (1: 221–229.)

The ironic detail of the air feeling "unusual weight" reveals that the world is for the first time experiencing Satan—the embodiment of sin and the grievous weight that pulls people into hell—as he moves from his prison. This is the first step toward the goal of conquering mankind and turning God's wrath against his creation, and Milton makes us feel the seriousness of that moment through intense and careful description.

In some places *Paradise Lost* resembles science fiction. It describes flying through the vast reaches of hell and chaos as well as soaring through the magnificence of heaven toward earth. There was no existing literature of interstellar travel, such as we have now, and Milton had few models to rely on. Yet he gives a convincing and substantial portrayal of the agonies of hell (he had Dante to help him) and of the vastness of empty space that separates the worlds of angels and humankind.

Milton is most eloquent when writing about the terrors of hell. In the following passage, which describes the devils as they wander through their new "home," Milton reveals the resources of sonority (making the sounds as rich as the description), a technique for which Italian poets were noted:

> Through many a dark and dreary Vale
> They pass'd, and many a Region dolorous,
> O'er many a Frozen, many a Fiery Alp,
> Rocks, Caves, Lakes, Fens, Bogs, Dens, and shades of
>   death,
> A Universe of death, which God by curse
> Created evil, for evil only good,
> Where all life dies, death lives, and nature breeds,
> Perverse. (2: 618–625.)

Milton's experiences in government must have convinced him that evil still dominated the affairs of the world. His own age witnessed the victory of the middle classes over the king and his nobles and had seen the establishment of a government based on the reform of a "corrupt" church. Milton had lived for eleven years in a new "Eden," Cromwell's Commonwealth; yet the forces of good, the forces of enlightenment (from his point of view), had lost it all because they had lost the will to retain it. In 1660 Charles II was placed on the throne without a shot being fired. The worldly paradise that Milton had hoped for, worked for, and risked his life for had been lost. The gaiety of the Restoration period was marked by dissipation, licentiousness, and high living—the very opposite of the Puritan ideals. Milton risked a horrible execution by defending the Commonwealth up to the eve of Charles's return. Tradition has it that a poet, Sir William Davenant, intervened and saved him on the grounds that his genius should not be lost to the nation.

Paradise Lost is not a pessimistic poem. It is a great example of Christian humanism. The poem ends with the archangel Michael forcing the reluctant Adam and Eve to leave through the eastern gate of Eden and go out into the world. Milton held that all this adversity was part of God's plan, that it was important to express one's faith through optimism, and that humankind would triumph with God. Therefore, his description of Adam and Eve as they pick their way gingerly through a new territory must be seen as a portrait of a couple accepting the greatest challenge that the human race has known:

> High in Front advanc't,
> The brandisht Sword of God before them blaz'd
> Fierce as a Comet; which with torrid heat,
> And vapour as the Libyan Air adust,
> Began to parch that temperate Clime; whereat
> In either hand the hast'ning Angel caught
> Our ling'ring Parents, and to th'Eastern Gate
> Led them direct, and down the Cliff as fast
> To the subjected Plain; then disappear'd.
> They looking back, all th'Eastern side beheld
> Of Paradise, so late their happy seat,
> Wav'd over by that flaming Brand, the Gate
> With dreadful Faces throng'd and fiery Arms:
> Some natural tears they dropp'd, but wip'd them soon;
> The World was all before them, where to choose
> Their place of rest, and Providence their guide:
> They hand in hand with wand'ring steps and slow,
> Through Eden took their solitary way. (12: 632–649.)

No English poet attempted such a major religious poem after Milton, and yet almost every great poet who followed him looked to him for his mastery of language, his expansiveness of imagery, and his conceptual power. He dominated his age and ages to come. His achievement resembles Dante's, coming as it does at the end of a great era of thought. Dante's poem was written at the end of the great age of religion, and Milton's at the end of a period of humanism, when Europe stood on the brink of great discoveries in science and when the myth of the fall of humankind was destined to be ignored rather than understood. Milton's genius was expansive: his achievement was a fitting end to an era.

Music

THE EARLY BAROQUE

Because our current use of the term "baroque" derives from nineteenth-century art history, and because it has been adapted from painting to music, it must be understood in a somewhat different way from that in which we have used it earlier. The stylistic polarities between the French Lully and the Italian Monteverdi approximate the classicism of Carracci and the baroque innovations of the Caravaggists. Definite changes and stylistic challenges occurred between 1600 and 1750. Thus, the baroque style in music is in reality many styles, and the term refers especially to achievements made after the Renaissance. It was shaped, in part, by the energies of the Catholic Counterreformation, when it was seen that Luther's relatively simple but stirring hymns had a profound effect on Protestant worshipers and that the power of music to stir deep emotions could be used to help bring people back to the church.

The power of music to stir the emotions had been recognized in the late Renaissance, but in the 1600s one of the chief intentions of the baroque composer was to devise a means by which to stir the emotional life of the listener. A theory of the "affections," or the emotions, had been growing in Europe. It considered that the relative proportions of the four humors in the body determined health and temperament: the choleric person was easily angered; the sanguine person was energetic and vigorous; the phlegmatic person was slow and lumbering; and the melancholic person was intellectual and introverted. Certain kinds of music, because of their effect on the humors, could sustain a mood over a long period of time.

Claude Palisca has said: "If there is any common thread that unites the great variety of music that we call baroque, then, it is an underlying faith in music's power, indeed its obligation, to move the affections." To an extent, this links musical developments in the period with the efforts of the mannerist and baroque artists, whose motives were to produce and control an emotional response to their subject matter.

QUALITIES OF BAROQUE MUSIC

Baroque style does not imply a structure into which composers had to shape their musical ideas. Some musical genres associated with the baroque are the madrigal, a song using a text in the vernacular language; the canzona, a short instrumental composition deriving from the French chanson, or song; the concerto, a work in which a solo instrument or instruments are contrasted with the orchestra and in which there are extremes of conflict and musical resolution; the cantata, an extended vocal composition; the oratorio, an extended vocal composition with soloists, chorus, and orchestra, usually on a text from the Bible; and the opera, a dramatic instrumental and vocal composition developed in this period, usually on a secular or classical subject. Like the fugue, which grew in popularity during the eighteenth century, none of these is a form. They are musical procedures which are governed by certain rules, but they do not determine the shape of a composition.

The shape of a baroque composition was determined by its expressive needs. Thus, one can never be sure what a composition of the period sounds like simply by knowing what kind it is. The subject matter of the composers of the period can best be described as the expression of human emotion, often implied by the texts with which they worked. The composers' concerns were linked with making the music conform to the words of the texts.

In most baroque music composed after the middle of the century, rhythm is very pronounced. Early baroque works are almost exclusively homophonic; that is, a single melodic line is often accompanied by a basso continuo, a chordal filler. Homophony was often used when there was a text to be sung; it was easier to evoke an appropriate mood for a given text if only one melodic line was heard. Later in the seventeenth century, however, there was a growing preference for polyphonic musical textures, particularly in orchestral compositions. Polyphony, with clearly marked melodies, gave the later composers ample opportunities to exploit their musical ideas.

The orchestra, usually consisting of not more than forty musicians, employed a rich range of textures and timbres, from the improved and brilliant violin family, whose range was extraordinary, to the dazzling brasses, which delighted Venetian composers particularly. Vocal music was enlivened by contrasts of solo and choral parts, and the invention of opera gave it an infusion of aesthetic energy as a result of dramatic texts which became available.

Energy, brightness, and development of contrast —in pitch, in instrumentation, and in dynamics— are all qualities of baroque music, which is sometimes described as filling all its musical "spaces" with action and color. Sudden changes from quiet to loud were not characteristic of earlier music, nor were the general techniques of contrast, which delighted the baroque composers. Baroque music became intense, emotional, and sensual, exploring new ways of stirring its audience.

CLAUDIO MONTEVERDI

The Success of Modern Music

Monteverdi (1567–1643) explored most of the resources of early baroque music. His madrigals, published in eight books, use a wide variety of texts whose dramatic demands are impressive. His religious music, such as his settings for the mass and his *Selva Morale e Spirituale* ("Moral and Spiritual Pieces"), of 1640, are rich and expressive. The *Selva* are fascinating because they explore a wide range of religious emotion. Monteverdi knew his audience and knew how to move it. The *Selva Morale e Spirituale* were composed for Saint Mark's, in Venice, where Monteverdi was chapelmaster from 1621 until his death. They are a collection of spiritual madrigals, vespers, parts of the mass (such as the Credo), psalms, and hymns, all using religious texts as the subject matter. The pieces are composed for groups of as few as two and as many as seven voices with chorus and continuo. Violins, organ, and the orchestra are also sometimes used in these wide-ranging works. Monteverdi made this collection to reveal his power as a spiritual composer, just as he assembled the best of his secular work in the eighth book of madrigals in 1638.

Monteverdi published the *Vespers of the Blessed Virgin* in 1610, demonstrating that he could not only write powerful small compositions but also conceive an overall structure, or architecture, with which to unify them. Designed to be sung and played through the vigil and the feast of the Virgin, they explore a number of modern techniques, particularly the homophony that Monteverdi felt best supported a work of complex emotional significance.

During the late sixteenth and early seventeenth centuries, a great controversy arose among musical theorists. Theory was essential because of the role of music in religious ceremony. Mishandled, music could distort religious values or introduce secular ones. Therefore, it was of the utmost importance that music be composed and performed correctly. Changes were inevitable, but as in science, all changes had to be approved by the authorities before they could be accepted. The controversy was between the old music and the new music: the "first practice" and the "second practice."

Both practices agreed on many things. The basic rules of harmony, rooted in the triad, and the basic approach to melody were part of both. To an extent, they shared the view that the rules of rhetoric applied to music as well as to language. Therefore, such techniques as repetition of phrases and passages, imitation of sounds (birds, cannons, and bells, for example), and other ingenious effects designed to appeal to an audience on an emotional level were present in both. The emphasis on rhetoric in music of the period is evidence of the commitment of musicians to move their audience not only intellectually but also emotionally.

The practices differed in terms of the relative importance of words and music. Some musicians called the first practice the "old style," and the second practice the "new." Monteverdi was adept at both styles, choosing the first practice for his secular pieces and later religious works. He actually cited Plato in defense of the second practice, in which the words are dominant and the music is designed to fit them. He claimed that the technique was used by

. . . loftier spirits with a better understanding of true art. [Plato] understands the one that turns on the perfections of the melody, that is, the one that considers harmony not commanding, but commanded, and makes the words mistress of the harmony.

The practical result of Monteverdi's declaration—and his musical observances—was to move music toward a modern style. The treble voice begins to be the primary voice in madrigals and motets; the basso continuo provides a chordal filler. The middle voice or voices provide the third melodic line, which is particularly effective in harmonic moments based on the triadic chord. The result is that the fabric of the music is almost gossamer—translucent voices on a solid foundation of the bass line, soaring, retiring, and elevating again. In the reverberant transepts of stony Saint Mark's and other great cathedrals, it must have been an overwhelming experience.

Along with the second practice, Monteverdi claimed to have discovered how to portray emotions that music had failed to express before:

I have reflected that the principal passions or affections of our mind are three, namely, anger, moderation, and humility or supplication; so the best philosophers declare, and the very nature of our voice indicates this in having high, low, and middle registers. The art of music also points clearly to these three in its terms "agitated," "soft," and "moderate."

Plato's *Republic* suggested to Monteverdi that constant repetition of a phrase or note (ostinato) would produce the agitation that he associated with anger and war. In 1638 he published his eighth book, *Madrigals of Love and War,* in which he demonstrated how constantly repeated passages could create emotions associated with war. The "Battle of Tancred and Clorinda," from the eighth book, was a landmark. It included stage directions and directions for playing. Its first audiences were usually reduced to tears by the emotions that the music stirred in them. Today, the effects are not so strong, because we are used to the techniques; their novelty has worn off.

Orfeo and the Beginnings of Opera

Monteverdi did not write the first opera, but his *Orfeo* (1607), the story of Orpheus and Eurydice, was the first great operatic "hit." (A modern performance is shown in Figure 14-25 and the aria "Possente Spirto" in Figure 14-26.) A number of preconditions

Figure 14-25
Claudio Monteverdi. Apollo descends in Act 5 of *Orfeo;* an outdoor performance at Ipswich, Massachusetts, Castle Hill Festival, 1978.

had led to the development of opera. One of the most important of these was the Florentine stile rappresentativo—recitative style. In recitative, words are half recited and half spoken to the music, in such a way that they are totally dominant.

Monteverdi's success derived from his ability to weld the narrative line to the musical line, as when the music descends into the deep bass as Orpheus descends into Hades. But even more important, he was successful in using almost forty instruments as well as voices. In *Orfeo,* madrigals and canzone tell the story of the prince of singers, Orpheus, whose wife, Eurydice, is killed by a snake in a harmless-looking meadow. Eurydice is taken to the underworld for Pluto's court, and Orpheus, profoundly grieved, pleads with the gods to allow him to descend to the underworld to secure her release. The gods agree to this, and in the underworld he is carried across the river Styx by Charon, the boatman who transports human souls to Hades. There, Orpheus sings so beautifully that Pluto releases Eurydice on the condition that Orpheus ascend first and not look back at her until they reach the world. Orpheus, unable to restrain his desire to see her, turns and looks, and she is lost to him forever.

The myth of Orpheus figured in many operas. It is a moving tale of love and loss that features a beautiful singer. Monteverdi's version would have pleased the Christian humanists: Orpheus is rewarded in Act 5 when Apollo —the greatest singer among the gods— takes pity on him and elevates him to heaven and eternal bliss. Since Orpheus has been linked with

Figure 14-26
Claudio Monteverdi. "Possente Spirto," measures 27–53, from *Orfeo,* Act 3. 1607. The cornett (not a relative of the modern cornet) was a wooden instrument with a cup-shaped mouthpiece, popular in orchestras of Monteverdi's time. (From Edward R. Lerner, ed. *Study Scores of Musical Styles.* New York: McGraw-Hill, 1968. Pp. 146 –147.)

LISTENING KEY

Monteverdi and Baroque Music

1. Listen to a recording of madrigals. Is the subject matter of the text likely to move the listener on an emotional level? How many voices are there? One? Three? Can you hear a distinct melody? Do the instruments compete with the voices?

2. Monteverdi wrote at a time when professional musicians rather than amateurs would have been expected to play his compositions. Does the music sound more complex or more difficult than earlier music?

3. In Figure 14-26, the music from "Possente Spirito," does Monteverdi create musical symmetry? Which passages might be thought of as asymmetrical? Which are symmetrical? (Remember that symmetry in music is based on the repetition of similar elements.)

4. Listen to one of Monteverdi's religious pieces (from *Selva Morale e Spirituale, Vespers of the Blessed Virgin,* or another liturgical piece). What techniques does Monteverdi use to make his music sound religious? Can music sound religious?

5. Does Monteverdi's reliance on a classical subject in *Orfeo* imply that he is absorbing classical values? Listening to *Orfeo,* are you aware of classical values that are in any way comparable to those of Carracci?

Christ from the earliest days of the church, we can see how Monteverdi's audience understood the fusion of pagan and Christian values.

"Possente Spirto" ("All-Powerful Spirit"), Orpheus's aria to Charon, is in six stanzas, each of which uses approximately the same musical material. This is the second stanza:

> I do not live, no, for since my dear spouse is deprived of life, the heart is no more with me, and without heart how can it be that I live?

The voice, as we see in Figure 14-26, alternates with two cornetts, while the bass line is a series of sustained harmonies that do not interfere with the melodic motion. Such extremes of contrast resemble Caravaggio's chiaroscuro and the baroque energy of Bernini.

JEAN-BAPTISTE LULLY: MUSIC AT VERSAILLES

The dominant figure in French music in the second half of the seventeenth century was Jean-Baptiste Lully (1632-1687), who was born in Florence but was brought to France as a young boy. He was part of the orchestra of the French court, served as music master to the royal family in 1662, and became a friend of Molière. Thus, his work was often regarded with high seriousness, and it was known by his own term, "lyrical tragedy."

Lully was exceptionally accomplished as a writer of ballet, and since Louis XIV was a ballet lover, Lully was naturally favored. Lully was able to take the Italian opera and enrich it with a fuller orchestration and with a greater range of tone color than Monteverdi liked. He also found ways to integrate recitative

Figure 14-27
Jean-Baptiste Lully.
Alceste. A performance
in Louis le Vau's marble
court at Versailles in
1674. (Engraving by
Lepautre; Metropolitan
Museum of Art, Harris
Brisbane Dick Fund,
1930.)

(a text half recited to music by a solo voice) with the arias and choral portions of the opera. The method is homophonic, with harmonic support coming from the entire range of the orchestra, not simply a basso continuo.

Lully's rhythmic genius is considerable, and it is particularly evident in one of his most amusing scenes—in *Isis*, an opera in which the characters are classical, not Egyptian. Called the "Shivering Chorus," it uses a vocal trio singing in a broken rhythm that imitates shivering. Not only is it amusing and effective; it was also powerful enough for the English composer Henry Purcell (c. 1659–1695) to borrow it for use in his opera *King Arthur*.

Lully's melodies serve to move the text forward and to keep the action smooth. The harmonies are enriched by Lully's skillful orchestration. The settings and performances of his operas were naturally rich and expensive; but Figure 14-27, which shows a performance in Louis le Vau's marble court at Versailles, suggests that the costuming was impressive while the staging was more simple.

Lully's classicism dominated French opera and determined its shape for the age. Lully was in a position of almost absolute authority, and he used it to secure the advances that he had made. He wrote the operas, the ballets, the interludes, and the overtures. He trained the orchestra. He was in charge of the ballet. No detail in the operation of the French opera was outside his control. The result was a highly charged, disciplined, and successful musical reign. His subject matter, usually a classical text, guaranteed his acceptance into the Poussinesque orbit preferred by the French aristocracy. Lully was a composer for royalty.

Science and Philosophy

The church, depending on the scholastics, made Aristotle its primary authority. Aristotle based his views on sensory perception and the deductive process: drawing a conclusion from a set of premises. By the seventeenth century, deduction had come to mean reliance on authorities who hand down fundamental principles of belief, which then become the basis of all reasoning. Aristotle's complex logic was taught to every student. Since it was deductive, it relied on basic truths, and these were now truths handed down by the church. Many such "truths" were false. For instance, when Galileo proved that the earth is not the center of the solar system, the church declared that he was wrong and in 1633 forced him to recant or face death. Until the power of Aristotle and the scholastics was broken, there could be little progress in science.

FRANCIS BACON

Bacon (1561–1626) was not the first to fight against Aristotle, although he was among the most persistent and careful of those who did. Before him, in sixteenth-century France, Petrus Ramus and Michel de Montaigne had both attacked Aristotelian thought. Ramus offered a new logic based on direct observation; Montaigne went on to demonstrate that nothing can be totally known, and therefore the general customs of humankind must be accepted as truth. Bacon, a prominent politician in the court of Elizabeth and then James I, began his literary career in imitation of Montaigne by writing a series of essays exploring morality, politics, and the social graces. A popular book, expanded many times before his death, Bacon's *Essays* took a practical stance: a principle would be tested by action and then accepted or discarded.

But his *Novum Organum* (1620), written after his forced retirement from the chancellorship of England (he was in disgrace for having taken a bribe), contained a much more important body of work. It was a new kind of logic designed to replace Aristotle's *Organon* (his writings on logic and theories of knowledge) and undo Aristotle's grip on current thought. Few of Bacon's contemporaries saw the full implications of *Novum Organum;* in it lay the seeds of induction: reasoning which depends on collecting evidence from direct observation and then deriving reasonable hypotheses to explain the phenomena under study. Bacon called himself the "priest of the senses" and vowed to do away with the "cobwebs of learning." One advance which he expected to see in science—which, he lamented, was terribly slow—was the production of new tools by which the senses could be extended. By "new tools" he meant telescopes and microscopes, which did indeed prove to be the means by which the seventeenth century developed modern science.

In clearing away the cobwebs of learning, Bacon identified four impediments to understanding. He called these "idols" because they captured the imagination and distracted people from the true way. The "idol of the tribe" is the tendency of humans to see themselves as more important in the universe than they actually are. The "idol of the cave" is the distortion that each of us brings to a problem because of past experiences and prejudices. The "idol of the marketplace" is the sloppiness of language and termi-

nology which we pick up in commerce with other people; it distorts reality. The "idol of the theater" is the dogmas and theories that we derive from prominent thinkers; these also distort our perceptions. Bacon's important contribution was to show that sensory perception is crucial to scientific inquiry, but not enough in itself. It must be accompanied by the brushing away of the idols that distort perception.

RENÉ DESCARTES

Some scholars consider Descartes (1596–1650) the first modern philosopher. He wrestled with many of the same problems as Bacon. One crucial difference, however, was his faith in mathematics. In the England of Bacon's day it was almost impossible to study mathematics seriously. The first English edition of Euclid's *Elements* was not published until 1572, when Bacon was in school. Its impact was enormous. On the continent, geometry began to take on great importance because the uncertainties that accompany sensory perception were clearly not relevant to geometry. A triangle or a circle or a square is a real thing even if one does not see it. Bacon, untrained, did not realize the implications of mathematics, even though he often set up his thoughts as if they were axioms from which he proceeded to proofs.

Descartes looked for an answer to the question how we can know anything by trying to find questions that could be as clearly posed and understood as mathematical problems. His *Discourse on Method* (1637) brought Bacon's concepts up to date. Descartes determined that nothing he could inquire into could be free of doubt. He was able to question every "reality" that he perceived, except one: the fact that he was engaged in the act of thinking about reality. He finally concluded that he knew he thought; if that was true, then he knew he existed. *Cogito, ergo sum,* for which he is famous, means "I think, therefore I am"; it became a cornerstone of modern philosophy. From that Descartes built a solid edifice which permitted him to make observations of matter in motion—something that fascinated all thinkers of the century.

Analytic geometry was essential for the creation of calculus, which was invented independently by Sir Isaac Newton (1642–1727) and Gottfried Wilhelm Leibniz (1646–1716). Newton used calculus, the mathematics of moving bodies, to formulate his theories of gravitation and laws of motion, which dominated physics through the early part of the twentieth century. The Bacon-Descartes-Newton connection resulted in the developing concept of the universe as a perfectly functioning machine. As its elements became more and more explainable, it took on the "logic" of the complex timepiece. The mechanistic theories that derived from this line of inquiry were accepted eagerly, but in the next century.

THOMAS HOBBES

The views of Thomas Hobbes (1588–1679), like those of Bacon and Descartes, were anti-Aristotelian. Hobbes was deeply influenced by both writers, especially Bacon, for whom he acted as secretary. Like Descartes, he was entranced by geometry and began to see it as a model for clear thought. His most important work is *Leviathan* (1651), a study of social institutions in which he concludes that the social contract is entered into by all people for their own good. They give up a small amount of freedom for greater security and the advantages of culture. But Hobbes also saw that they invested their monarchs with powers over themselves to such an extent that the monarchs ruled in their stead. That is to say, a monarch acted as the people would act; therefore, the people owed complete obedience to the ruler. Laws were absolute because they proceeded from the people; justice did not exist outside the law: it was defined as the proper application of the law.

Hobbes's views are somewhat in line with modern forms of tyranny; they were singularly out of favor in England in his own time, since the Puritans had only recently beheaded Charles I. *Leviathan* was a logical treatise which tried to apply principles of clear, scientific thought to social matters. In this respect it was remarkably successful, even if it was unappreciated in its earliest editions.

Two important consequences emerged from the development of thought in this period. One was not obvious: Descartes, in his theorizing, established the mind as separate from the body. His view is called "dualism," and its implications are serious. In his system the mind becomes separate from the physical world, while the body becomes a mechanism of quite another order. Even the connection between body and mind becomes tenuous, almost questionable at times.

The second consequence is more obvious: scientific method developed as a tool that would bring about even more changes in later ages. Bacon thought that the gathering of facts, experiments, and observations would produce logical hypotheses. But he was wrong. Descartes refined the view to suggest that one should begin with a probable hypothesis, and then test and modify it by experiment. This is the method that scientists everywhere use today; it enables them to combine the techniques of both deductive and inductive reasoning. It took the entire seventeenth and much of the eighteenth centuries for Europe to reach that point, but when it did, the swift progress of modern science was inevitable.

Summary

The seventeenth century was a period of growth and power politics in Europe. The balance of power between France and its neighbors—England, Holland, Spain, and the Holy Roman Empire—was always delicate. The Italian city-states suffered from fragmentation, invasion, and a weakened economy. Italian artists, as usual, were spread throughout Europe, and adaptations in France of Italian designs helped create a French classicism that impressed the rest of the world. The easy interaction of all the arts became a hallmark of the new baroque style. The two primary stylistic expressions of the age were the classicism of Carracci and his followers—which depended on the developments and achievements of Michelangelo's painting—and the newer baroque developments pioneered by Caravaggio.

Art had begun a pattern of secularization, as had the society in general. The church was losing its power, despite the threats of the Inquisition, the achievements of the Counterreformation, and the contributions of Bernini and Monteverdi. Spiritual matters were still of great importance, however, as we can see from the churches of Wren and from the great religious poetry of Donne, Crashaw, and Milton. Part of the secular vigor was the result of developments in philosophy and of inquiries into scientific matters. In particular, the loss of the power of Aristotelian logic—in the form standardized by the scholastics in the universities—created a new kind of intellectual inquiry. The revolution in mathematics and physics, due to the work of Bacon, Descartes, and Newton (to name the most important), was to place humans more in command of their environment, the goal that Bacon set for science. As that goal was approached, the church—in part for political rather than spiritual reasons—began to lose its control over opinion and the arts.

The worldliness of the seventeenth century was partly the result of successes in trade, expanding markets, and a bustling economy that made more people wealthy. The new merchant classes in Europe sought to govern themselves and threatened the stability of the social order. Much painting of the period reflected the world in which people actually lived, employing a new attitude toward realism which eventually swept all before it. Along with the new realism came a new attitude toward classicism and historical accuracy in the work of Poussin and others. To an extent, this was a working out of the forces of humanism, which had been active since the thirteenth century. The seventeenth century began with a slightly antique odor; when it ended, it pointed in the direction of what Shakespeare, in *The Tempest*, called a "brave new world."

Concepts in Chapter 14

The strengthened monarchies of France and England fostered these countries' growth and influence in the arts in the seventeenth century.

Italian influences, while still very powerful, were slowly giving way to northern dominance.

Seventeenth-century architecture was dominated by the influence of Palladio, but new syntheses with northern styles were evident in the work of Jones and Wren.

The grandeur of French architecture was largely the result of meeting the demands of Louis XIV, the Sun King.

Versailles was a symbol of the remoteness and indifference of the French government.

Bernini was the dominant figure in sculpture; his fusion of the effects of several artistic media became a hallmark of baroque styles.

Stylistic changes in painting occurred first in Italy and later in the northern countries.

Two styles vied for dominance in the early part of the seventeenth century: classicism (based on Michelangelo's muscular idealizations, in the work of Carracci) and baroque (which was best expressed by Caravaggio).

Classicism had always had a moral center and concerned itself with moral choices, particularly in its attempts to influence those in power.

The baroque was more sensual, more realistic, less idealized, and more concerned with giving pleasure than earlier styles; instruction was not its primary intent.

Followers of Caravaggio, such as Velásquez, began playing with the implied relationship between the viewer and the canvas.

Followers of Carracci, such as Poussin, often did much research in classical subjects to achieve their effects.

To some extent, Rubens managed to fuse both the classical and the baroque styles, while essentially moving on to a new, personal style.

The influence of Caravaggio is clear in paintings by Rembrandt, interpreting stories from the Old Testament and other biblical subjects.

The genius of Molière was expressed in the socially aware comedy of manners.

English metaphysical poets, such as Donne and Crashaw, were often intent on shocking the sensibilities of their readers; their works have been linked with baroque and mannerist paintings.

Milton, the Christian humanist poet, wrote *Paradise Lost* as a culminating statement of the myth of the lost paradise; it was a rear-guard action in the sense that it professed a deep religious faith in an age which had, by mid-century, begun to turn emphatically away from religion.

Baroque music was dominated by a number of important Italian composers, in particular Monteverdi, whose *Orfeo* was one of the first and most important operas.

Opera was also popular in France, where such composers as Lully performed their works for the delight of Louis and his aristocratic court.

Science and philosophy, led by Bacon, Descartes, and Hobbes, turned more and more toward secular matters and questions concerning human knowledge.

The seventeenth century was a prosperous age, dominated by a political balance of power in Europe that permitted limited wars and fostered a growing secularism and material success.

Suggested Readings

Baudouin, Frans. *Peter Paul Rubens.* New York: Abrams, 1977.

Bazin, Germain. *The Baroque.* New York: Norton, 1978.

Blume, Friedrich. *Renaissance and Baroque Music.* New York: Norton 1967.

Blunt, Anthony. *Art and Architecture in France, 1500–1700.* Baltimore: Penguin, 1958.

Bukofzer, Manfred F. *Music in the Baroque Era.* New York: Norton, 1947.

Friedlaender, Walter. *Nicolas Poussin.* New York: Abrams, 1964.

Held, Julius S., and Donald Posner. *17th and 18th Century Art.* Englewood Cliffs, N.J.: Prentice-Hall, 1972.

Kitson, Michael. *The Age of the Baroque.* New York: McGraw-Hill, 1967.

Martin, John Rupert. *Baroque.* New York: Harper & Row, 1977.

Munz, Ludwig. *Rembrandt.* New York: Abrams, 1954.

Palisca, Claude. *Baroque Music.* Englewood Cliffs, N.J.: Prentice-Hall, 1968.

Pope-Hennessy, John. *Italian High Renaissance and Baroque Sculpture.* London: Phaidon, 1963.

Sewter, A. C. *Baroque and Rococo.* New York: Harcourt Brace Jovanovich, 1972.

Sypher, Wylie. *Four Stages of Renaissance Style.* New York: Doubleday, 1955.

Willey, Basil. *Seventeenth-Century Background.* New York: Doubleday, 1954 (originally published in 1934).

Wittkower, Rudolf. *Bernini.* London: Phaidon, 1966.
———. *Studies in the Italian Baroque.* Boulder, Colo.: Westview, 1975.

Wölfflin, Heinrich. *Renaissance and Baroque.* Kathrin Simon, trans. Ithaca, N.Y.: Cornell, 1966 (originally published in 1888).

CHAPTER 15

THE DECLINE OF THE ARISTOCRACY: 1700 TO 1798

Cultural Background

The eighteenth century is called the "age of reason" partly because intellectual advances, building on the work of Bacon and Hobbes, changed attitudes toward society, politics, and religion. As usual, the complexities of rapid social change appear to be paradoxical—at least on the surface. For instance, one paradox is that while religion submitted to reason among the educated and wealthy, the majority of impoverished workers, affected by John Wesley's teachings of Methodism, became all the more passionate and emotional in their faith.

THE PRIVILEGED ARISTOCRATS: A TASTE FOR THE ROCOCO

Social critics warned of self-destruction as a result of the dissipation of the aristocrats. In the second half of the century France reacted with a high-minded neoclassical style. England and other nations also concentrated on social reform and adopted methods of classical satire in literature, the chief means of reforming manners. Neoclassicism was more than a style; it was a movement influenced by Rome (as earlier classicism had been influenced by Greece). Neoclassical values were associated with Roman society in the imperial age: the values of personal effort, honor, self-sacrifice, and concern for the state. Such values contrasted with the rococo celebration of pleasure and the soft eroticism of the dissolute aristocrats. Eventually neoclassicism won out. The century ended with the French Revolution, a violent social "corrective" that bore out the worst prophecies of those who had worried that the aristocrats were destroying themselves with their extraordinary self-indulgence.

THE DEATH OF LOUIS XIV: WAR AND POVERTY

The costly War of the Spanish Succession (1701–1714) reduced France's role in European politics. When the great Louis XIV died in 1715, there followed a nine-year regency, during which the duke of Orleans—a gambler, drinker, and good fellow—readied Louis XV (1710–1773), who was temperamentally unsuited to rule, for the throne. His court was moved from Paris to the remote pavilions of Versailles, where he governed ineffectually for seventeen years. His grandson, the ill-fated Louis XVI (1754–1793), was weak, vacillating, and indecisive. It has been said that even when the French Revolution was under way in 1789, Louis XVI could have survived, perhaps even have been its leader, if he had only known how to take action.

Proposals for reform were ignored. France in the eighteenth century has been described as virtually medieval or feudal. The people suffered terrible periods of economic hardship brought on by wars, overpopulation, the wastefulness of the aristocrats, and antiquated methods of agriculture and industry.

Italy, controlled by foreign nations, was not much better off. Its great city-states were shadows of their former selves, despite the fact that some, like Venice, still showed a spark of vitality in their arts. Germany was fragmented but had ambitions to emulate the grandeur of France. The state of Brandenburg-Prussia was developing into a first-class war machine which would tip the balance of power toward the Germans. Late in the century, Russia also became involved in European politics—again imitating French grandeur —an involvement that began a more important shift of political power eastward. Fortunately for the English, their revolution of the 1640s had made it impossible for an absolute monarch to hold sway against a strong Parliament. The solidification of parliamentary power in 1688–1689, when William of Orange brought stability to the throne, led to a period of peace and growth. Many English institutions began to reform—with the church and the courts leading the way. But other serious problems challenged English society and threatened the rest of Europe.

THE AGRICULTURAL REVOLUTION

Since Europe was still overwhelmingly agricultural, England's agricultural revolution, which began with the enclosure acts, affected the continent. The growth of landlordism and the accumulation of large farming estates in the hands of a few wealthy farmers meant that many people remained dependent on a few. Medieval tradition had established open fields around towns as common property. Everyone could graze a cow or a few sheep or goats at no cost. But the creation of large farms made experimentation with breeding and crop choices a vogue. Early in the century common lands were enclosed, and certain portions were assigned to individuals who used them to breed better strains of animals: heavier, healthier, and more valuable. The ordinary people without grazing privileges were dispossessed and unable to support themselves. Everywhere in England, masses of people eventually grew dependent on charity.

Charity came in the form of the workhouse. Each parish was responsible for feeding and housing its destitute. But eventually there were so many of them that some parishes rebelled, and the workhouse became a commonplace of English life. Enterprising people employed inmates of workhouses for little better than slave wages. Children worked as soon as they could walk. Everyone worked from sunup to sundown.

THE INDUSTRIAL REVOLUTION

The agricultural revolution improved crops and livestock, but at a terrible human cost. In turn, it made possible the industrial revolution—the application of seventeenth-century science and theories to practical machines and operations. With factories developing throughout England, and with abundant cheap labor, industrialists created empires. Coal and iron, England's most plentiful resources, fueled the expansion of its industry and manufacturing. Inventions refined the processes. The spinning jenny made it possible to manufacture cheap cloth, the pride of England's trade. The steam engine powered machines. Throughout the century, English goods— which were cheaply manufactured, widely available, and in endless supply—began to dominate world trade. Huge fortunes were made. London was noisy, filthy, poverty-stricken, and dangerous; but it still lured those who were forced from the land. The cunning, and the lucky, could make a fortune. By contrast, in France and elsewhere in Europe, the opportunity to move rapidly out of poverty was almost unheard of.

Thus the rich proliferated in England; and because they sometimes emerged from the armies of the poor, they were not always totally severed from, or indifferent to, the poor and their sufferings. Despite the general hardship, the upper classes were filled with optimism and a bubbling enthusiasm for life.

RELIGION

The very poor had religion. John Wesley traveled 224,000 miles and preached 40,000 sermons, and he gave the average workhouse laborer—who was caught up in a round of suffering, poverty, and meaningless work—something to live for. Wesley promised salvation and love to people who were so poor and so uneducated that many of them had never heard of Christ. His movement was part of a growth of moral concern and interest in moral issues that is everywhere reflected in English literature and European arts of the latter half of the eighteenth century. Eventually, neoclassicism came to emphasize high moral purpose and a commitment to human values and republican reforms. Meanwhile, however, Wesley's Methodist message was soothing to those whose pains were not only great, but obviously also permanent.

The desperation of the poor produced criminality. In the middle of the century, the privileged could not travel alone in London after dark, and often they were attacked and robbed in broad daylight. Highwaymen had been common for some time, but marauders in towns like London were rare before the eighteenth century. Armed convoys of the rich moved from one end of London to another in their carriages. Even the great Samuel Johnson reports beating off three robbers one night while on his way home from his club. Poverty had made large sections of London a sinkhole for prostitution, bearbaiting, and other grim forms of violence.

Architecture

ROCOCO ARCHITECTURE: FRANCE AND GERMANY

Architecture generally reflected the influence of Palladian classicism as interpreted by the work of Inigo Jones and Christopher Wren in England and Jules Hardouin-Mansart and others in France. But experimentation in the rococo furthered baroque ornamentation, freedom of form, and dynamic energy. Rococo architecture produced fantastic forms which demanded considerable imagination. Many of the most interesting examples of the rococo are outside France and England. And the most interesting are interiors, rather than exteriors. In the case of

some buildings, such as the Hôtel de Soubise, in Paris, the exterior is simple and classical, while the interior is an explosion of rococo energy.

Figures 15-1, 15-2, and 15-3 reveal a taste for overwhelming ornamentation. Every contour in the Hall of Mirrors (Figure 15-3) and the Princess' Salon (Figure 15-2) is emphasized with gold trim. Every open space is either occupied by a mirror or outlined and framed as if awaiting a decoration. In the Hotel de Soubise, the upper spaces between mirrors and openings are filled with paintings, and decorative treatments occupy the upper spaces in the Hall of Mirrors. Both rooms are done in white and gold. Such interiors reveal immense wealth and served people who thought no detail too unimportant for their entertainment.

Figure 15-1
Simpert Kramer, Johan Michael Fischer, and others. Abbey Church, Ottobueren, Bavaria. 1737–1767. (Photo, Hirmer Fotoarchiv München.)

This is true, too, of the Abbey Church (Figure 15-1) whose surfaces are roiling with holy activity. The sumptuous carvings and the paintings rival one another for realism. There is no place for the eye to relax: everything is in motion; the activity is ceaseless. Yet the Abbey Church is brilliant, the light is stunning, and the achievement is remarkable. The fusion of architecture, painting, and sculpture is brought to its conclusion in the rococo.

Figure 15-2
Left: Germain Boffrand. Princess's Salon, Hôtel de Soubise, Paris. 1735–1740. (Photo, Conway Library, Courtauld Institute of Art.)

Figure 15-3
Below: Francois Cuvillies. Hall of Mirrors, Amalienburg, Schloss Nymphenburg, Munich. 1734–1739. (Verwaltung der staatlichen Schlösser, Gärten und Seen Museumsabteilung, Munich.)

NEOCLASSICAL ARCHITECTURE

England

The eighteenth century witnessed active research into Roman ruins. Pompeii and Herculaneum were excavated from 1738 to the end of the century, giving people their first view of the life of the ancients. Books carefully reproduced genuine Roman art and architecture, inspiring many contemporary architects, such as Sir John Soane in England.

The ingenuity of the design of Saint Martin-in-the-Fields, in London (Figure 15-4), built by James Gibbs (1682–1754) between 1722 and 1726, is lost on most of us because it was copied so widely in colonial America. Gibbs built a conventional structure with a single central spire; then he added a Greek portico with Corinthian columns, as well as pilasters and Corinthian columns on the front of the building itself. The gracefulness of the treatment is obvious, and the fact that it has been widely copied is a testament to its effectiveness. The spire has pilasters with Ionic trim on two levels, but they are not clearly visible. The Italianate treatment of the highest level suggests Borromini.

Gibbs's Radcliffe Camera (Figure 15-5), the first building at Oxford designed explicitly to be a library, is psychologically striking because one expects to see a dome on top of a building rather than set on the ground. It rises abruptly from the earth, and in its surroundings it comes as a surprise, since it is tucked into groups of buildings which obscure it from the level of the walkways. The influences of Wren and Michelangelo are plain. The double columns remind us of Wren, the balustrade of Inigo Jones, and the whole of Bramante's tempietto (Figure 13-1).

A trend in the latter part of the eighteenth century toward city planning is evidenced in the Royal Crescent, in Bath, a town popular as a resort for members of "society" in England throughout the century. The crescent (Figure 15-6), which is the work of John Wood the Younger (d. 1782), is a semicircle of attached houses resembling the colon-

Figure 15-4
James Gibbs. Saint Martin-in-the-Fields, London. 1721–1726.

Figure 15-5
James Gibbs. Radcliffe Camera, Oxford. 1739–1749.

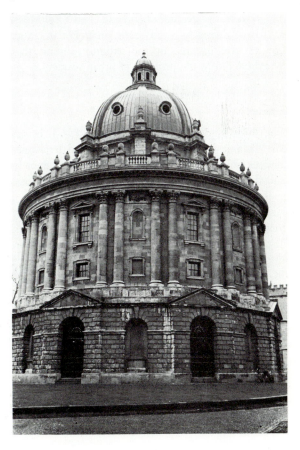

Figure 15-6
Left: John Wood the
Younger. Royal Crescent,
Bath. 1767–1775. (Royal
Commission on
Historical Monuments,
England.)

nade of Bernini in front of Saint Peter's, in Rome.
The facade of the crescent is punctuated by a procession of Ionic columns, which gives it an ordered
regularity. The curve of the crescent, along with the
columns and the window treatments between them,
creates a unifying effect. The crescent faces west;
there is a fine view of the hillside beyond, and at
sunset it is bathed in a warm glow, as the great
cathedrals are. Its orderliness, calmness, and purity of
design were imitated in London and elsewhere. Much
of late-eighteenth- and early-nineteenth-century
London was inspired by the striking solution that
Wood offered to the problem of urban residences.

France

The Petit Trianon at Versailles (Figure 15-7), begun
for Madame de Pompadour and designed by Ange-
Jacques Gabriel in 1762, shows the direct influence of
Palladio. It was carefully placed in a setting with long
walkways, beautiful plantings, and a circular pool
visible in the distance. The building is perfectly
proportioned, with fine Corinthian columns, a high
first level, and balustrades across the roofline—as in
Inigo Jones's banqueting hall at Whitehall (Figure
14-5). The effect is one of correctness of proportion,
harmony with the surroundings, and repose.

The Panthéon in Paris (Figure 15-8), the work of
Jacques-Germain Soufflot (1713–1780), is built on a
gigantic scale, with tall Corinthian columns supporting a Greek portico over the entrance. The huge
set-back dome is derived from the dome of Saint

Figure 15-7
Below: Ange-Jacques Gabriel. Petit Trianon, Versailles.
1762–1768. (Photo, Roger-Viollet, Paris.)

Figure 15-8
Above: Jacques-Germain Soufflot. Panthéon
(Sainte-Geneviève), Paris, exterior. 1755–1795.

Figure 15-9
Below: Soufflot. Panthéon, interior.

Paul's, in London. The interior is simple, almost austere. The exterior is also simple, with large expanses of blank brick walls. The lighting inside the church (a view of the interior is shown in Figure 15-9) is strong and direct and relieves any gloom that might be expected from such a severe design.

The United States

Neoclassical architecture was as appealing in America as in Europe. One of the best-known examples is Thomas Jefferson's home at Monticello (Figure 15-10). Like Gibbs, Jefferson placed a Greek portico over the front entrance to his house. The detail of the dome is not particularly Greek, and yet it does not disturb the design, which is pleasing, simple, and effective. It was taken as evidence of high-mindedness and worthwhile ambition, both qualities that Jefferson prized.

Figure 15-10
Below: Thomas Jefferson. Monticello, Charlottesville, Virginia. 1770 –1784. (Photo, Thomas Jefferson Memorial Foundation.)

Eighteenth-Century Architecture

1. What qualities distinguish a rococo building from a neoclassical building? Consider the questions of ornamentation and structural elements and the moods they create.

2. Rococo is perhaps most obvious in interiors; neoclassicism is perhaps most obvious in exteriors. Which kinds of buildings (religious, public, domestic, or aristocratic) impress most with their exteriors? Which impress most with their interiors? For what kinds of buildings does the neoclassical style seem most appropriate? For what kinds of buildings does the rococo style seem most appropriate?

3. What social or humanist values seem to be implied in Wood's Royal Crescent (Figure 15-6) and his approach to urban planning?

4. Visit a building that is influenced by either the rococo or the neoclassical style. Describe it by establishing which style is dominant. Considering its function, is the style appropriate? Was the building designed to be more impressive on the inside or on the outside? What kind of impression does it make, and for whom is the impression intended?

5. The eighteenth century is considered the age of reason. Which architectural style, rococo or neoclassical, would make the stronger appeal to reason? Which of the buildings shown in Figures 15-1 through 15-10 seems to be most clearly the product of reason and rational planning? Is it also devoid of emotional value? Does heavy ornamentation imply an appeal to reason?

Sculpture

Eighteenth-century sculpture is undistinguished. For one thing, it was apparently impossible to shake off the influence of Bernini; for another, few great commissions were awarded, so that most of what was done is on a small scale. The sculpture of Clodion (Claude Michel; 1738–1814) is typical of much work of the age. In his *Satyr and Bacchante* (Figure 15-11), he uses the opportunity afforded by an erotic classical reference to produce an openly erotic work. The piece celebrates flesh and sexuality. The bacchante, a woman, holds the drinking cup that she has just emptied, and she clings to her satyr in delight. The work is small, delicate, and vibrant.

Jean-Antoine Houdon (1741–1828) did larger pieces—portraits—which ranged from the natural to the idealized. He worked in a classical mode, in-

formed by the astonishing realism of Bernini, and was gifted with an ease that was the envy of other sculptors. He portrays Voltaire (Figure 15-12) seated, wearing a voluminous robe and a stocking cap. We cannot call this statue forceful, but it is natural. Voltaire is in repose, but the tension in his body gives the figure vitality. The classical robes imply that he is the equal of the classical philosophers. This is as much a tribute to the age as to Voltaire, since Houdon is saying that a modern philosopher is on a par with the ancients.

Antonio Canova (1757–1822), a proper heir to Bernini, was valued most for his portraits. He produced a cool, disengaged portrait of Napoleon's sister, Pauline Borghese (Figure 15-13), in the early part of the nineteenth century, near the end of his career. She asked to be portrayed nude—but in a classically chaste pose—just as her famous brother

Figure 15-11
Above left: Clodion. *Satyr and Bacchante.*
c. 1775. Terra-cotta, 23 inches high.
(Metropolitan Museum of Art, bequest of
Benjamin Altman, 1913.)

Figure 15-12
Above right: Jean-Antoine Houdon. *Voltaire.*
1781. Terra-cotta model for marble, 47 inches
high. (Musée Fabre, Montpellier, France;
photo, Claude O'Sughrue, Montpellier.)

Figure 15-13
Right: Antonio Canova. *Pauline Borghese as
Venus.* 1808. Marble, life-size. (Borghese
Gallery, Rome.)

Eighteenth-Century Sculpture

1. Are the sculptures shown in Figures 15-11, 15-12, and 15-13 primarily rococo or neoclassical in spirit? Determine the style of each sculpture.

2. Judging from these examples, what is the relationship between neoclassicism and realism? Is the rococo style realistic?

3. What kinds of values do these works seem to project? Is any of these sculptures "heroic"? Is any socially conscious? Is the influence of Michelangelo evident? How much respect do the sculptors reveal for their materials? Do they make us aware of the special properties of their stone?

4. Bernini's influence is present in all eighteenth-century sculpture. Refer to the discussion of Bernini in Chapter 14. What differences are apparent between his work and that of the eighteenth-century sculptors? What are the obvious similarities?

had been. The work is so idealized that there was no suggestion of any erotic intention. It looks positively chaste in comparison with the paintings of the early part of the century. It is a commanding but distant work: Pauline Borghese reclines on marble that looks like cushions. The pose, echoing that seen in Etruscan funerary sculpture, inspired dozens of imitations.

Painting

ROCOCO: VISUAL HEDONISM

Watteau and the Fêtes Galantes

Jean-Antoine Watteau (1684–1721) learned his craft under the influence of Flemish painting. His early experience included time spent with wandering commedia dell'arte actors, who often appear side by side with patrician figures in his landscapes and his depictions of celebrations. His paintings, as Edward Lucie-Smith has said, "have no set 'subject'; their purpose is simply to convey a mood." It is the mood which the age adopted and made its own.

The Departure for the Island of Cythera (Figure 15-14) portrays an aristocratic party about to leave for the island, which is sacred to Venus—the herm of Venus stands sublimely on the right, balancing the decorated barge on the far left. The serpentine line of

the figures is as lyrical and subtle a portrayal of people in a landscape as the age was to see. The work is an example of a subgenre of painting which expresses the spirit of the age: paintings depicting the "fêtes galantes," elegant entertainments which often involved processions and incorporated themes from mythology. This painting naturally alludes to the delights of the goddess of love. Since this group is leaving for a day in the land of Venus, we can expect that their celebrations will include languorous love-making and appropriate dalliance, particularly since the courtiers are grouped into couples, with an occasional child as a clear allusion to Cupid.

Watteau was, like his society, fascinated by music and dance. His *Plaisirs du Bal* (Figure 15-15) portrays the delights of music and dance. People in Watteau's society gathered whenever and wherever they could for a celebration. Where there were celebrations, there was music and dance. In *Les Plaisirs du Bal,* two groups of figures are listening to a small chamber orchestra. One couple performs a delicate minuet, the dance that characterizes the formal elegance of the age, and two other couples seem to be about to dance. The setting is outdoors, and the figures are protected by an arcade—a sensual, decorated piece of architecture that mimics a stage setting. The rhythms implied in the movement from right to left are subtle and graceful: a visual approximation of music.

Figure 15-14
Above: Jean-Antoine
Watteau. *The Departure
for the Island of Cythera.*
1717. Oil on canvas, 50
by 75 ½ inches. (Louvre,
Paris; photo, Musées
Nationaux.)

Figure 15-15
Left: Jean-Antoine
Watteau. *Les Plaisirs du
Bal.* 1717–1719. Oil on
canvas. (London,
Dulwich College.)

Because *The Mezzetin Playing the Guitar* (Figure 15-16) shows one person rather than a gathering, it is touching, and perhaps sentimental. Dressed in the costume usually used in the commedia dell'arte, the figure seems to be genuinely theatrical rather than an aristocrat who is dressing up. The setting, as in many of Watteau's paintings, is outdoors, and yet the figure does not seem to be part of nature—he is simply in it. Behind him stands a classical statue of a woman, perhaps implying that he is serenading a woman. The atmosphere of the painting is serene (befitting a serenade), and nothing distracts us from the mezzetin and the deep, romantic concentration of his upward gaze. The centrality of composition, balance, and harmony of the painting help focus our attention and complement the scene that it portrays.

Figure 15-16
Jean-Antoine Watteau. *The Mezzetin Playing the Guitar.* 1718–1719. Oil on canvas, 21 ¼ by 17 inches. (Metropolitan Museum of Art, Munsey Fund, 1934.)

PERCEPTION KEY

Watteau

1. What seem to be the chief concerns of the people represented in Figures 15-14, 15-15, and 15-16? What kind of life might they lead?

2. These paintings seem to have rhythms and harmonies that are implied by the positioning of the figures and the structural elements. What contrasts and similarities can you see between them?

3. Edward Lucie-Smith has said that these paintings have no set subject, but rather present a mood. What moods are obvious? How has Watteau created them?

4. Are these paintings realistic? Do they show an indebtedness to any of the painters discussed in Chapter 14?

5. What formal qualities help project the values of pleasure and enjoyment expressed in these works? What do the people in the painting seem most to enjoy?

6. Watteau probably did not title his painting. *The Departure for the Island of Cythera* is sometimes called *The Departure from the Island of Cythera.* Is it possible to tell from the painting whether these people have experienced or are about to experience the pleasures of Venus?

The visual rhythms in *The Departure for the Island of Cythera* lie in the grouping of the figures. Carracci and Poussin might place their figures in a line, as in a tableau, in imitation of classical reliefs; but Watteau has solved the problem of grouping figures in a more ingenious way—he has created a dance. Some of the figures adopt a dance position, while others seem to be preparing to dance. This establishes a romantic mood appropriate to the subject matter: leaving for the world of Venus, which is the world of romantic love.

Les Plaisirs du Bal portrays a leisurely, delicate, and elegant way of life. The rich clothing, the architecture, and the lush natural setting all balance one another. The erotic sculptures near the arches lend a decadent note to the scene, but they are hardly discordant. The music would have been light, elegant, and harmonically rich. The painting is, indeed, visually musical—its elements balance one another harmonically, with visual repetition and thematic development. The eye can wander from corner to corner of the piece without tiring, gathering—as it wanders—appropriate rewards of richness and visual discovery.

These paintings appeal much more to our imagination than to our sense of reality. They ask a suspension, a relief from the tensions of the everyday world. Yet, by their very insistence that we leave the real world behind, they establish a welcome, pleasing mood which must have softened the occasional roughness of eighteenth-century life. The people in the paintings lead a life of pleasure. Their activities are entertainments rather than business; Watteau's work must have provided a pleasantly romantic escapism for the age.

Fragonard and Greuze

Jean-Honoré Fragonard (1732–1806) lived through the demise of the so-called "ancien régime," the old style of government, and into the next age. He experimented with neoclassicism, a style which became dominant in the latter part of the eighteenth century, and established himself as a serious painter, in favor with high-minded aristocrats anxious for reform.

Fragonard's *Swing* (shown in Color Plate 24) is less academic and serious than his neoclassical work, and yet it reveals the age in a way that matches the

insights of Watteau. The subject is a gentleman, in the lower left, enjoying a view (up the skirt) of his mistress on her swing. Ironically, and by the request of the man who commissioned the painting, the woman is being pushed by the local minister. She gaily tosses her shoe toward her lover as she is about to swing backward. The setting is fantastic: nature is portrayed as it ought to be, rather than as it is. The statues balance the composition and suggest romance, but the mood of this piece is one of naughtiness. The swing is symbolic, suggesting that romantic love is fickle and that erotic play is sanctioned by society.

Jean-Baptiste Greuze (1725–1805) enjoyed an enormous success by avoiding the aristocratic penchant for romantic eroticism that pleased Watteau and others. He joined those who felt that art could stimulate social reform and inculcate positive social values in a decadent society. Greuze's work has a pronounced moral basis that appeals to high-mindedness. When Greuze showed paintings like *A Father's Curse* (Figure 15-17), his future was assured. He was followed by a school of imitators who made morally uplifting statements. People in the latter part of the eighteenth century became aware of the threat of depravity inherent in the lush eroticism of the earlier decades, and Greuze's influence in painting was similar to John Wesley's influence in religion.

Greuze's figures could have been drawn from the contemporary stage. They assume the exaggerated poses, like those in a tableau, that were popular on the eighteenth-century French stage. We still use the term "histrionic" to describe postures like that of the son in *A Father's Curse*, whose right arm is extended in a final gesture and whose mother does her best to hold him; such postures imply that the action is overdone, obvious, and unrealistic. These figures exhibit the passion we tend to associate with acting rather than with real life.

Greuze's contemporaries saw him as a powerful intellectual and moral force, whose aim was to uplift the sights of all people. *A Father's Curse* shows a father rebuking his son, who is ready to go off with an evil-looking ruffian. The father, who is infirm, is both angry and pleading. The son is about to abandon his impoverished family, in which there are several other children (we can see four in the painting), for a life of dissipation.

Figure 15-17
Jean-Baptiste Greuze. A *Father's Curse*. 1775. Oil on canvas, 51 ⅛ by 63 ¾ inches. (Louvre, Paris; photo, Musées Nationaux.)

Neoclassicism: David

Jacques-Louis David (1748–1825) spanned the eighteenth and nineteenth centuries and embodied neoclassical ideals before and during the French Revolution. His most famous early work is *The Oath of the Horatii* (Figure 15-18). Its subject matter is the oath made by the three Horatii brothers to fight to the death against the three Curiatii brothers as a way of settling a war between Rome and Alba. One of the Horatii survived. He returned home to find his sister, who had been betrothed to one of the Curiatii, weeping for her beloved. Taking this as an insult to his own honor, he slew her. Ultimately, he was imprisoned for losing his temper; but he was later released in testament to his honor and his victory over Alba.

David chose the moment when the oath was taken—when, not knowing the outcome of their efforts, the Horatii vowed to give all for the state. They stand as an antidote for the indolent, fleshly dissipations portrayed by Watteau and Fragonard. They have committed themselves to the classical virtues of self-control, discipline, self-sacrifice, and respect for the state. David was hailed as a prophet and praised for his high-mindedness and nobility. His paintings became the rallying point for those who felt that the dissipations of the aristocrats would bring ruin (as in fact they did) to society. The neoclassical style praised conservatism; it looked back to a better time and condemned current morals and current styles in art. Because rococo was virtually worn out as a style by the 1780s, the triumph of neoclassicism was almost guaranteed.

David was acutely aware of Watteau's *Departure for the Island of Cythera*; his students used to throw chunks of bread at it to show their contempt. David's *Oath of the Horatii* is crisp and clear. Every figure is virtually chiseled, in tribute to the achievement of classical sculpture and to the achievement of Poussin in the seventeenth century. Watteau's figures are soft, mellow, and almost vague by comparison. There is no sense of focus in Watteau's painting, no sense of a principal group of characters. The David clearly focuses on the three swords—symbols of civic responsibility—and on the moment of declaration of faith and allegiance to the state. Watteau's painting, on the other hand, alludes to the softer pleasures of Venus and sexuality, pleasures which are self-indulgent, personal, and by comparison frivolous.

Figure 15-18
Jacques-Louis David. *The Oath of the Horatii.* 1784. Oil on canvas, 10 feet 10 inches by 14 feet. (Louvre, Paris; photo, Musées Nationaux.)

COMPARISON KEY

The Departure for the Island of Cythera and The Oath of the Horatii

1. One clear difference between the paintings shown in Figures 15-14 and 15-18 is in the arrangement of the figures. Which painting has the more integrated grouping? Which painting makes clearer distinctions between the groups of figures, in terms of their position and their function?

2. One painting is set in the outdoors; the other is set in a house. What contribution does the setting of each painting make to its mood?

3. In which painting is the central action of the figures more clearly established? Remember that in the eighteenth century the moment celebrated in each painting would have been clear to everyone.

4. Which of these paintings can be said to be more clearly influenced by the stage?

5. Which painting is simpler, more direct, and more economical in its presentation of figures and action? Which is more lush, more complex, and more seductive in its softness and sensuality?

The sinuous line of figures in Watteau's painting contrasts with the clear, straight line of figures in the David. Watteau's figures seem to blend from one end of the canvas to the other (even the Cupids, rising in the air near the barge seem to be a natural continuation of the action). David's figures fall into distinct groups. The three brothers form one group. Their arms are outstretched in the salute which Hitler (who liked this painting) adopted for his army in the twentieth century. The father, who holds the swords, is a separate figure and dominates the center of the canvas.

The women at the right in David's painting allude to the sadness which must ensue from the oath. David reveals that there will be suffering which must and can be endured. By contrast, the Watteau could admit to no such emotions. We cannot imagine the painters of the fêtes galantes portraying grief, which is the neoclassical concomitant of self-sacrifice.

The natural world of Watteau is vague, shifting, pleasant, and sensual. By contrast, the stone of the house of the Horatii is hard and unyielding. It demands seriousness and commitment. The arches and pillars are Roman, symbolizing chastity, honor, and seriousness. But this background is also simple, direct, and uncomplicated. So, too, is the message of the painting. One must be willing to sacrifice for the privilege of living in the greatest society in history. Rome was great because the Romans were great. David is suggesting that by emulating the Romans, the French people of his time might be able to make France great. His message was heard by the designers of the French Revolution.

PAINTING IN ENGLAND: HOGARTH, WRIGHT, GAINSBOROUGH, AND REYNOLDS

Aristocratic dominance was not the same in England as in France. Greuze's approach had been foreshadowed by the work of William Hogarth (1697–1764), who likened his work to a morality play. He made up for his figures' lack of motion by executing sequences of paintings, each portraying a scene in the rise, fall, or progress of a central character. His paintings, which were reproduced in cheap prints, were so successful that they influenced the reform of English society. His sequences —The Election, which portrays corruption in politics; The Rake's Progress, which chronicles the destruction of a worthy young man;

and Marriage à la Mode, which depicts the fate of a couple who marry for the wrong reasons—all aim to teach a moral lesson.

Figure 15-19, the third scene from The Rake's Progress, shows us the rake at the end of his "progress," being attended by women on whose faces are the black patches used to hide syphilitic pustules. His fate is sealed, and his path is the path to ruin. Such social commentary made Hogarth popular, and his popularity in turn made him effective. The novelist Henry Fielding and the poet and lexicographer Samuel Johnson approved of his work and joined him, in their own work, in trying to improve contemporary morals.

Joseph Wright of Derby (1734–1797) has been recognized as one of the most important painters of the century, and yet his work is not well known. An Experiment on a Bird in the Air Pump (Figure 15-20) has as its subject an experiment of the sort that was the rage among gentlemen of the time. Air is being pumped from a glass bell, in which a bird seems to have struggled and then given up the ghost. The reactions of the people around the table are extremely varied. A young girl looks on with scientific interest. An older girl cannot look at all. A young woman is more interested in the young man to her right, who looks on with fascination. At the right, an older man meditates deeply on the experience. The scientist himself controls not only the experiment but also the composition of the painting. The source of light is mysterious, but Wright uses it brilliantly. The human responses are intense, deep, and moving. Science has become significant in people's lives. There are few ages in which such a scene could be represented. The technique is impeccable; the composition is dynamic, rhythmic, and coherent. And though Wright was not a major painter, he shows that painting had a place in English life, even in the provinces.

The later geniuses of English painting, Sir Joshua Reynolds (1723–1792) and Thomas Gainsborough (1727–1788), were not as intent on uplifting the morals of their age as Hogarth or as interested in visual experiment as Wright. Unlike Fragonard and Watteau, they did not attempt to portray their subjects—usually people of wealth and position—in erotic or otherwise compromising circumstances. The subjects of their painting seem to be worthy, noble, decent people bent on worthwhile goals.

Reynolds's Discourses, one of the most important

Figure 15-19
Left: William Hogarth. *The Orgy,* from *The Rake's Progress.* c. 1734. Oil on canvas, 24½ by 29½ inches. (Trustees of Sir John Soane's Museum, London.)

Figure 15-20
Below: Joseph Wright of Derby. *An Experiment on a Bird in the Air Pump.* c. 1767–1768. Oil on canvas. 72 by 96 inches. (Tate Gallery, London.)

Figure 15-21
Joshua Reynolds. *Mrs. Siddons as the Tragic Muse.* 1784. Oil on canvas, 93 by 57 ½ inches. (Henry E. Huntington Library and Art Gallery, San Marino, California.)

Figure 15-22
Thomas Gainsborough. *Mrs. Siddons.* 1785. Oil on canvas, 49 ½ by 39 inches. (National Gallery, London.)

theoretical documents of the time, underscores his commitment to the Royal Academy and his concern for high standards of performance. His greatest rival was Thomas Gainsborough, whose portraits made him famous throughout Europe. The differences between them are apparent in their portraits of Mrs. Siddons (Figures 15-21 and 15-22), who was not an aristocrat but one of the most famous actresses of the age.

The assumption has been that Reynolds—a theoretical, academic painter—was vastly less gifted than Gainsborough, who was less well educated and less socially adept than his rival. These paintings may not reveal such a difference in skill, although the apparent allusion in Reynolds's portrait to the seated prophets in Michelangelo's Sistine ceiling may indicate his need to rely on earlier models. However, the skill with which Reynolds portrays the self-possessed yet relaxed actress is such that we can hardly fault the painting.

The Gainsborough may be more original. Few earlier portraits strike a note anything like this direct, forceful presentation. The tilt of the hat at a sharp angle from the plane of the canvas and the strong, determined face are all arresting. Reynolds's dramatic portrayal, which includes fantastic creatures from classical divinity, is more attentive to Mrs. Siddons's work as an actress. Yet the presence revealed in the Gainsborough is so profound as to suggest that he was trying to portray that quality in her which we now call "charisma," the personal force that made her dominate the stage in her time.

Reynolds and Gainsborough

1. Which of the portraits of Mrs. Siddons shown in Figures 15-21 and 15-22 seems to have been influenced by the work of earlier painters? Do you see allusions to other famous paintings?

2. One of these painters is said to have had enormous talent and great originality, while the other is said to have made the most of a limited talent. Can you tell which is which?

3. Mrs. Siddons is known to have been a great actress. Which painting is more obviously concerned with her work as an actress? Is that painting also the more dramatic of the two?

4. Which painting seems to reveal more of the essence of the woman herself? Is either painting concerned with revealing her personality?

5. Is either painting neoclassical? Is either influenced by Watteau or Fragonard?

Literature and the Enlightenment

While John Wesley was traveling across the land delivering sermons at the rate of 1000 a year, northern European intellectuals and politicians were moving in an entirely different direction. Sir Isaac Newton (1642–1727) discovered the laws of motion, and these produced descriptions of the universe in the metaphor of a machine, thus permitting an analysis of humankind in mechanical terms. Julien la Mettrie (1709–1751) wrote *Man the Machine* (1747), in which he declared that "Man is a machine so compounded that it is at first impossible to form a clear idea of it, and consequently to define it." He recommended a careful analysis of physiology as a means of understanding the metaphysical nature of humankind.

The result of such thinking (and it was popular long before la Mettrie) was a modern form of humanism, unlike the humanism of the Renaissance. It truly had the study of humankind as its center—not just the study of ancient writings and thought. Therefore, the eighteenth century saw an enormous surge of interest in social matters, particularly analyses of modes of government. Some of these analyses attacked the concept of the monarchy as it then existed; others led to different concepts, such as that of the benevolent despot, modeled to some extent on Catherine the Great of Russia, who reigned from 1762 to 1796 and was well aware of the intellectual currents in France.

The French scholar Denis Diderot (1713–1784) produced his twenty-eight-volume *Encyclopedia* between 1751 and 1776. The people associated with the project, called "les philosophes" (the philosophers), controlled the intellectual life of France, and their product, the *Encyclopedia*, was designed to clarify the range of human knowledge. Jean Le Rond d'Alembert (1717–1783), a brilliant young mathematician, wrote the *Preliminary Discourse to the Encyclopedia of Diderot* (1751), in which he credits Francis Bacon with having clarified the divisions and limits of human knowledge. Bacon's system, adopted by the philosopher, established the categories of understanding as memory (including history), reason, and imagination. Bacon had also included faith, but since it was beyond the limits of understanding, d'Alembert ignored it. So did the philosophes. Thus, the achievement of the *Encyclopedia* was to secularize knowledge once and for all.

The debates of the century did not center on the conflict between reason and faith. That conflict had been raised in the seventeenth century and would be raised again in the nineteenth century. The eighteenth century focused on the conflict which lies totally within humankind: the conflict between reason and passion. These polarities are part of human nature and became the grand subject of the writers and philosophers of the century. The literature of the period had become genuinely humanist. Its concerns were human concerns —the concerns not of God and ultimate faith, but of humanity and the structure of society.

JONATHAN SWIFT

"Savage Indignation"

His epitaph cites his "savage indignation," but readers of Jonathan Swift (1667–1745) would hardly need an epitaph to know how savage he was in his criticism of his fellow beings. Yet beneath his brutality is his intent, in his satire, to improve people by pointing out their foibles.

In 1704 Swift published two works that established patterns of debate which continued throughout the century. *A Tale of a Tub* satirizes varieties of religious worship by belittling the distinctions between Christian sects. *The Battle of the Books* debates the question whether the ancients were wiser and more learned than the thinkers of Swift's day. The Renaissance held that, except for the revelations of Christianity, the ancients — especially Plato and Aristotle—were far superior to contemporary philosophers. But by 1704 the attacks of Francis Bacon and others on Aristotle had made their effect, and Swift could postulate a real debate. Diderot's *Encyclopedia,* by adapting Bacon's system of knowledge, favored eighteenth-century thinkers. The debate spread from philosophy to the arts and did not subside easily.

Swift used satire to treat social injustice. In *A Modest Proposal* he suggested that the Irish fatten their children to be killed and sold to the English as holiday roasts. This plan would control population, turn a liability into a source of profit, and help feed England. Some readers have taken him seriously; but Swift, who was Irish, was protesting against the way the English bled his country. He hoped to awaken them to their misdeeds.

Gulliver's Travels

Gulliver's Travels is often treated as a children's book, but it was written in earnest for adults and contains many satirical attacks. One, an attack on the petty quarrels of religious factions, pits the Bigendians against the Littlendians in a vicious war. The Bigendians have always opened their soft-boiled eggs on the big end. The Littlendians have always cracked the little end. Only one way, each group points out, can be the right way. Such a satire reduces serious religious battles to silliness.

The most disturbing aspect of *Gulliver's Travels* appears in the last section, when Gulliver discovers the Houyhnhnms, a race of reasonable, high-minded, gentle horses who have learned to isolate and control the Yahoos, detestable creatures who are driven by passion and dark appetites—and who are physically like humans.

No one has ever satisfactorily clarified Swift's intentions in this section. On the one hand the Yahoos are models for the lowest and most destructive human drives; but on the other hand the Houyhnhnms lead dull lives and experience no normal human passion. In this dramatic debate between reason and passion, Swift seems to be telling us that Gulliver, with all his faults, is the mean between two undesirable poles. Yet his vision of human nature, in an age that generally extolled its virtues, is dark, uncertain, and foreboding.

ALEXANDER POPE: "WHATEVER IS, IS RIGHT"

Alexander Pope (1688–1744) was a gifted, sickly child. A Catholic, he was unable to attend an English university, and therefore his knowledge of Greek and Latin—the tools by which most learning was made accessible—was sketchy. Because of his poor health, he developed a deformation which made him appear dwarfish and humpbacked. Yet he was eventually to become a socially accepted literary figure, and he was quite attractive to the women of his circle. His success in literature was financial as well as artistic. Until the eighteenth century, writers were supported by patrons or made a living in the commercial theater. But Pope, a serious poet, depended on a fundamentally urban audience of subscribers—people who were offered books and purchased them in advance of publication. His translations of Homer's *Odyssey* and *Iliad* earned him (even after expenses were paid to the translators who aided him) some 8000 pounds: enough to make him rich.

Pope indulged in satire, as befitted the age, and later devoted himself to serious philosophical poetry. But he also produced a masterpiece of poetry that can be described as a literary equivalent of the rococo. *The Rape of the Lock,* written in 1712 (before his translations of Homer), is a mock epic satirizing the conventions of heroes and heroines, mighty battles, and the machinery of the gods. It is based on a real incident: Lord Petre snipped off a lock of the hair of Lady Arabella Fermor, who took offense. Their families—prominent Catholics—had a falling-out. Pope was urged to write a poem to help patch up the quarrel. It was a great success and was published at the suggestion of Lady Arabella.

The Rape of the Lock has all the elements of the Homeric epic: heroes, battles, gods and goddesses who take the part of one combatant or the other, and wonderful set pieces that allude to incidents in Homer's work. The rococo qualities are achieved by the transformation of the rugged Homeric figures into delicate beaux and belles—genteel social figures.

One of the most wonderful moments in the poem—and possibly one of its most rococo moments—is when the heroine, Belinda, who is seated at her toilet (her makeup table), is portrayed as a priestess sitting before an altar on which are displayed objects used in a religious ritual:

> And now, unveiled, the toilet stands displayed,
> Each silver case in mystic order laid.
> First, robed in white, the nymph intent adores,
> With head uncovered, the cosmetic powers.
> A heavenly image in the glass appears;
> To that she bends, to that her eyes she rears.
> The inferior priestess, at her altar's side,
> Trembling begins the sacred rites of Pride.
> Unnumbered treasures ope at once, and here
> The various offerings of the world appear;
> From each she nicely culls with curious toil,
> And decks the goddess with the glittering spoil.
> This casket India's glowing gems unlocks,
> And all Arabia breathes from yonder box.

Pope's late, incomplete work, *An Essay on Man* (1733–1734), is in the form of letters to close friends, and so its tone is consistent, easy, and familiar. Yet it

CONCEPT KEY

Alexander Pope

For this concept key, read *An Essay on Man* and *The Rape of the Lock.*

1. In what sense can *An Essay on Man* be said to approve of learning?

2. The last line —"Whatever IS, is RIGHT"—offers an insight into Pope's politics. Would he be seen as a conservative or a liberal?

3. In another of his letters in *An Essay on Man* Pope says, "Know then thyself, presume not God to scan; / The proper study of mankind is Man." How do these lines fit in with the development of thought in this period?

4. If the lines quoted from *The Rape of the Lock* can be called rococo, is it also possible to describe the lines quoted from *An Essay on Man* as neoclassical?

5. Pope, like Swift, does not address aristocrats; but he does address people of substance—landowners, politicians, merchants, and professionals. Judging from his poetry, what values were important to his audience?

expresses what Pope felt was the sum of his wisdom concerning ethics. His intention was to follow in John Milton's footsteps: he wished to "vindicate the ways of God to man"—Milton's intention in *Paradise Lost* was to "justify the ways of God to man." In his *Essay on Man*, Pope does not need to refer to the devil, Christ, or the angels. Basically he appeals to humankind to look closely at God's works and understand their nature. As he explains to his friend Lord Bolingbroke:

> All Nature is but art, unknown to thee;
> All chance, direction, which thou canst not see;
> All discord, harmony not understood;
> All partial evil, universal good:
> And, spite of pride, in erring reason's spite,
> One truth is clear: Whatever IS, is RIGHT.

Pope's couplets, his constant references in dramatic verse to gods and goddesses (but without the seriousness of the seventeenth century), and his careful translations of Homer's epics reveal him as neoclassical. He could play with the decorative, light, and pleasant tones of the rococo, but his seriousness places him in the mainstream of neoclassicism. Even the lines telling us that "The proper study of mankind is Man" turn our attention, as Bacon did, away from theological issues and toward the issues which are central to humanism, the heart of neoclassicism.

In assuring us that "Whatever IS, is RIGHT," Pope is saying that if we were able to understand the universe and the workings of the world, then we would see that everything is as it should be. Pope's political optimism is conditioned by the fact that, born in the year of the bloodless revolution, his was a stable political environment—such optimism would not have been seen in France and elsewhere. Pope felt sure that the institutions he knew were suitable, successful, and appropriate.

VOLTAIRE

"Whatever Is, Is Wrong"

François-Marie Arouet, known as Voltaire (1694–1778), began as an optimistic philosopher. He was trained as a Jesuit, broke with the church, and became one of "les philosophes" who contributed to Diderot's *Encyclopedia*. The crisis of his life occurred when the great Lisbon earthquake struck on All Soul's Day, 1755; it destroyed the city, first with fire and then with a tidal wave. The ironies of that event were stunning. The churches were crowded with the faithful. In many cases, when the first tremors did not destroy the churches, priests called people who were running hysterically about in the open to come into the protection of the cathedrals, only to have them collapse on everyone. When it seemed that the rains would put out the fires, the tidal wave brought destruction. Since Lisbon was thought of as one of Europe's most pious cities, no justice could be served by such a catastrophe. Voltaire was never to be the same again.

Candide

Candide, or Optimism, is a funny, sad, but serious work meant to ridicule those who, like Dr. Pangloss and his student, Candide, believe that this is the best of all possible worlds. Candide travels through the old world, the new world, and the orient. Nothing he sees justifies his optimism, which is based on the deluded philosophy of Dr. Pangloss. He comes upon one horror after another. He is impressed into the Bulgarian army; his beloved Cunégonde is captured by pirates; he is left penniless and wretched. When the book ends, the characters are so much the worse for wear that they cannot change their ways or reconsider their ideas. Candide says that "we must cultivate our garden," by which he seems to mean that we cannot speculate on the nature of the world; we cannot decide whether to be optimistic or pessimistic. By cultivating our garden, we emulate Adam and Eve: we limit ourselves to the world before us; beyond that we can know or do nothing.

Dr. Pangloss says, on the last page of the book:

> "All events are linked together in the best of all possible worlds; for, after all, if you had not been driven from a fine castle by being kicked in the backside for the love of Miss Cunégonde, if you hadn't been sent before the Inquisition, if you hadn't traveled across America on foot, if you hadn't given a good sword thrust to the baron, if you hadn't lost all your sheep from the good land of Eldorado, you wouldn't be sitting here eating candied citron and pistachios."
>
> "That is very well put," said Candide, "but we must cultivate our garden."

Voltaire

1. What connection can be made between Dr. Pangloss's faith that this is "the best of all possible worlds" and Alexander Pope's statement, "Whatever IS, is RIGHT"?

2. Can Candide's final decision, to cultivate his garden, be interpreted as optimistic or pessimistic? Is it neutral?

3. Is the idea that this is the best of all possible worlds religious or secular? Is it in any sense neoclassical? Is it a moral concept?

4. Does Candide, in following the teachings of Dr. Pangloss, show a satisfactory regard for reason? Is reason a satisfactory guide?

Pope's views are those of Dr. Pangloss, at least to a certain extent. Yet Dr. Pangloss does not have Pope's shrewdness. Candide is an innocent who is taken advantage of again and again. Swift's Gulliver, by contrast, is worldly-wise. While not an optimist, neither is he a pessimist. He remains between these extremes. Candide is like Gulliver in that, by insisting on cultivating his garden, he renounces only a part of his optimism. He does not condemn the world, although he retires from it into his own backyard, whose scope is known to him and where he can avoid those who would take advantage of him. Voltaire does not provide Candide with experience to replace his innocence. Even Dr. Pangloss persists with his bad advice. *Candide* portrays an amoral world in which people are almost casual victims. In one way, *Candide* shows that whatever is, is wrong, since whatever Candide approaches is virtually certain to harm him. This may reflect a moral concern, and yet the moral issues center on innocence and the ways in which the world will take advantage of it.

SAMUEL JOHNSON

Candide had a counterpart in England: Samuel Johnson's novel *Rasselas, Prince of Abyssinia*, written in 1759. Johnson (1709–1784), who compiled the first dictionary of the English language in 1755, wrote *Rasselas* in little over a week to pay for his mother's funeral. (Voltaire, incidentally, is said to have written *Candide* in three days.) When Johnson wrote *Rasselas*, he was already well known; but for professional writers, even successful ones, making a living was precarious. Johnson developed the theme of the "vanity of human wishes"; the phrase is the title of one of his poems. He was a famous talker, a famous moralist, and a translator of the classics.

Rasselas, a prince of Abyssinia, sets out to explore the world with his trusted teacher, Imlac. The book begins with an enjoinder to the reader:

Ye who listen with credulity to the whispers of fancy, and pursue with eagerness the phantoms of hope . . . attend to the history of Rasselas, prince of Abyssinia.

Rasselas's homeland is the Happy Valley; it is a paradise, and yet it does not satisfy him. Rasselas has a "new species of affliction," restlessness:

"If you had seen the miseries of the world you would know how to value your present state." "Now," said the prince, "you have given me something to desire. I shall long to see the miseries of the world, since the sight of them is necessary to happiness."

In seeking happiness, Rasselas is confounded. He learns that "Human life is everywhere a state in which much is to be endured, and little to be enjoyed." He meets sages whose wisdom is understood less as it is heard more; he is told to live according to nature, but he is not told what that means. None of what he learns is useful to him. Consequently, the novel ends with Rasselas, his princess, and Imlac deciding to return home. Like Candide, who wishes to tend his garden, "the prince desired a little kingdom, in which he might administer justice in his own person." But since he cannot return to the Happy Valley, which he left, his future is uncertain. Johnson and Voltaire, unknown to each other, seem to have been trying to say similar things.

Music of the Late Baroque

Musicologists consider baroque styles to persist into the middle of the eighteenth century. Baroque music in the first half of the eighteenth century developed a strong sense of "keyness," which is to say that composers experimented with establishing a piece in a given key and then introducing contrasting sections in related keys as a means of adding variety and maintaining interest. Exploration of keys implied a new attitude toward harmony, and it was during this period that some of the most interesting treatises on harmony were written. One result of experiments with keys was the development of a sense of "arrival," the feeling that we have reached "home" at the end of a given portion of the music. The use of cadence, which shapes our sense of arrival, affects our response to music by teaching us to anticipate moments of rest after periods of development and excitement.

VIVALDI

Antonio Vivaldi (1678–1741), of Venice, was justly famous for his concertos, which offered a basis for larger symphonic works. *The Four Seasons* (Opus 8, 1725) is one of a number of experimental program pieces which describe musically an event or a series of events. The program of the four concertos in this composition is seasonal change. Each concerto interprets a sonnet, which may have been written by Vivaldi, with accompanying suggestions for musical treatment; and each concerto has its own melody.

In the first concerto, "Spring," after an introductory melody, the strings imitate lightning and thunder, the song of birds in the trees, the bark of a shepherd's dog, and the murmuring of breezes—and

all this is done while an appropriate musical mood is established and developed.

"Summer" begins with a drooping rhythm that makes us aware of a dramatic change—the enervation and torpidity of the summer months. The cuckoo and turtledove sing, and the final passages are dominated by the buzzing of summer insects.

"Autumn" begins with a violin imitating a drunken peasant: "With song and dance, the peasants mark / The happy harvest time, / Drink deep from the cup of Bacchus / And end their joy in slumber." Eventually, the music seems to subside in a sleepy falling-away. Then the "Autumn" melody continues. An autumn hunt follows: "The chase is on. / The tiring and bewildered beast / Assailed by dogs and the din of guns / Falls fatigued, and wounded, dies."

"Winter" describes "cruel winds," "and our teeth chatter from the cold." (Lully's "Shivering Trio" was similarly inspired.) High-pitched violin passages suggest ice skating, strong winds, and intense cold. The entire orchestra "shivers and shudders."

The structures of the four concertos are much the same. Each consists of three movements, all featuring the violin as the solo instrument, with various groupings of other instruments, viola and continuo, and the entire orchestra. The music is definitely homophonic, although there are also complex textures that indicate Vivaldi's interest in counterpoint. Both the viola and other lower-register instruments provide a rich harmonic structure throughout. The first movement of each concerto is fast; the second is slower and in the same key as the first, or a related key. The last movement is fast. The two fast movements usually follow the pattern:

Ritornello (home key)
Solo
Ritornello (distant key)
Solo
Ritornello (home key)

This flexible structure offers contrast and an opportunity for experimentation in tempo and in tone coloration. The return of familiar musical material after interludes of development or variation produces a sense of "rightness," unity, and coherence. Vivaldi's concerto form is important because from it developed the later classical sonata form.

Vivaldi, The Four Seasons

Listen to *The Four Seasons.* Many recordings are available, among them Seraphim S-60144, Columbia MS-6744, and Odyssey 3260132.

1. Identify the musical passages which interpret the events described in the quotations from the sonnets. Does knowing what these events are make the musical experience richer? If so, why?

2. Identify each of the melodies in the four concertos. If possible, listen to them one after another. Are there qualities within the melodies that suggest the seasons to you? Does each concerto convey a specific mood?

3. Is this composition basically homophonic or polyphonic? Are you aware of elements of harmony? Are the melodies distinct and clear?

4. Establish the basic structure of each concerto. Do all the concertos follow the same structure?

5. Despite the programmatic nature of the music, would it still be enjoyable to someone who knew nothing of its narrative? Does knowing the narrative diminish or enhance your response to the music?

BACH

The Range of Bach's Music

A religious rather than a secular composer, Johann Sebastian Bach (1685–1750) centered his career in Germany, particularly in Weimar, Köthen, and Leipzig. A devout Lutheran, he wrote about 200 church cantatas — songs for chorus and soloists — usually on sacred texts and usually in German, to be sung in church as part of the services. Most were composed in Leipzig; among the most famous are Cantata Number 4, "Christ Lay in Death's Dark Prison," and Cantata Number 80, "A Mighty Fortress Is Our God." An orchestra accompanied the singers, although it was clear that the text was of consummate importance.

The church cantatas are rich musical experiences that use techniques derived from contemporary concertos as well as from opera. Bach is noted for his brilliant use of soloists, chorus, and orchestra to create a full musical texture. He frequently balances soloists with orchestral and choral sections in a manner that gives the piece great interest. Among the operatic devices he used is the da capo aria, in which part A consists of ritornello–solo–ritornello in the home key; B is a contrasting section in a related key; and then A is repeated from the beginning. This structure, like the poetic couplet, proved to be flexible, contained, and effective.

Bach's responsibilities as a composer involved the production of a huge volume of music, and he often transformed or "cannibalized" his own or other people's works. Therefore, some of the music of the secular cantatas—such as "Phoebus and Pan," Cantata Number 201; the "Wedding Cantata"; and the "Coffee Cantata"—derives from church music. Many of these use melodies which are singable and easily remembered. All use musical techniques of contrast: loudness and softness, instrumental groupings, and modes of interpreting the text which are musical equivalents of chiaroscuro in painting.

Bach wrote no operas; but his *Passion According to St. John* (1724) and *Passion According to St. Matthew*

(1729) sometimes pit soloist against chorus and orchestra in operatic ways. Some of the text (derived from the gospels) is sung with contrasting free poetic passages sung in recitative.

Bach also wrote a very important body of music not intended for the church. *The Art of Fugue* (1748–1749) is a progressively more complex study of the possibilities of writing fugues; it is an unfinished work, but it is exhaustive in its treatment. *The Musical Offering* (1747) takes a theme by Frederick the Great of Prussia and varies it in delightful ways. *The Goldberg Variations* (1742) is also a theme-and-variations composition of great subtlety. All these pieces are intellectual, theoretical experiments—examples of the way Bach exhausted the permutations and combinations of a theme and unfolded its possibilities. *The Well-Tempered Clavier* (Part 1, Köthen, 1722; Part 2, Leipzig, 1744) is, like the pieces mentioned above, an exhaustive "study"; it is analytic, experimental, and challenging. It consists of two sets of twenty-four preludes and fugues (one of Bach's favorite devices) in all the major and minor keys. They are remarkable for their intellectuality and their inventiveness.

The Brandenburg Concertos

Speaking about key-based compositions in the abstract is unsatisfactory. In preparation for this discussion of the Brandenburg Concertos, listen to a recording (Nonesuch HB-73006, Angel S-3787, or Telefunken 2635043). The Brandenburg Concertos are six concerti grossi, works in which the orchestra plays in contrast with various instruments or groups of instruments—in the second concerto, flute, oboe, trumpet, and violin—at different times. They were written between 1710 and about 1721, and in different places: Mühlhausen, Weimar, and Köthen. They were dedicated to the margrave of Brandenburg, an ardent lover of music who had admired Bach's work.

Figure 15-23 shows the opening motif from Brandenburg Concerto Number 2. This concerto imparts

a sense of delight and joyousness. The rhythm is energetic. Bach opens with a five-note pattern. The first note is F, the tonic of the home key; then the music moves to C, A, B flat, and C, followed by a pattern that alternates C and F in a pattern of eighth notes. The expectation which we feel—the sense of incompleteness established by the opening pattern of F–C–A–B flat–C—is resolved only when we hear the F, the home note of the F major scale. When one studies the score and observes these relationships, one becomes aware of the ingenuity that Bach brings to this simple pattern.

Experimentation with the key relationships is continued in the first movement in interesting ways. The first key Bach uses is F major, but he then moves to C major and back to F in a pattern which we might anticipate from the opening notes, F and C. Then, however, he experiments with a dark-sounding but fascinating passage in D minor. He moves to a passage in F; then to B flat; then to C minor and G minor as a means of contrast; then to A minor; and finally back home to F. The result is that, even if we know nothing about the keys, we hear a statement of thematic material and then its development, which is perceptible even to someone who knows little about music. It causes us to want to hear the original material again as a means of establishing "closure" of the piece. Bach makes us long for the cadences, particularly the final cadence in F major.

Bach explores the key of F major thoroughly. In the first movement of the concerto, he uses a ritornello pattern—the ritornello is a "refrain" which appears in F major at measures 1, 46, and 103. Preceding its reappearances are key modulations: D minor to C major before measure 46 and B flat to A major before measure 103.

Bach's Influence

Bach's genius was not limited to the ingenuity of the Brandenburg Concertos. His musical inventions spread rapidly after his death, particularly through

Figure 15-23
J. S. Bach. Brandenburg Concerto Number 2, opening motif. 1721.

Bach, Brandenburg Concerto Number 2

1. Which instruments are you aware of when you first hear the composition? List those which you hear.

2. The first section is intensely rhythmic. Can you describe the rhythms? Are they dancelike? Are they restful? Are they restless?

3. The concerto opens with the thematic motif in the violins shown in Figure 15-23. Can you hear it repeated later in the piece?

4. The thematic motif is restated in different keys, either a tone higher or a tone lower. Can you hear these "different" restatements? Which instruments make the restatements?

5. Each movement of the concerto is marked for a contrasting tempo. Movement 1 is fairly fast, movement 2 is moderately slow, and movement 3 is fast. This is one means of achieving variation and contrast. Is the contrast distinct and effective? What other means of achieving contrast does Bach use?

---

the work of his sons, whose fame in their own time obscured his. He lived and worked in Germany, hardly known except to those who had been affected by his music. His work centered on stirring a deep spiritual response in his audience, in essence paralleling the ambitions of the social reformers in other countries. When Bach died, others were taking his experiments and molding them into different shapes and forms, and achieving different results.

Classicism in Music

HAYDN

The second half of the eighteenth century was dominated by a new spirit that grew out of the old. Franz Joseph Haydn (1732–1809) wrote 104 symphonies; more than eighty concertos, oratorios, and keyboard pieces; and many more compositions.

His refinement of sonata form represents his most important achievement. The four-movement symphony, borrowed from the baroque concerto, consists of a fast movement, a slow movement, a dance

movement, and a final fast movement. Sonata form, or "sonata allegro form," is usually used in first movements, which are often marked "allegro." It can be represented as follows:

A. *Exposition*
First subject; second subject
Tonic key; dominant key

B. *Development*
Material in various keys, often reshaped
Many keys

A. *Recapitulation*
First subject; second subject
Tonic key

Sonata form is dependable, clear, and—in the opinion of composers of the period—a kind of logic applied to music. The musical material is treated coherently and intellectually, producing a degree of expectation against which the composer can work. Haydn was able to weave this structure carefully through all his symphonies, maintaining complexity and interest by beginning with melodic material in the major key, then working with secondary material in the dominant of that key, and then shaping and reshaping that material in the development section. After the development, the same melodic subjects are heard in a new way in the recapitulation.

ROCOCO MUSIC

Connections have been made between the paintings of Watteau and Fragonard and the music of the early classical and late baroque composers. Some of the works of Georg Phillip Telemann (1681–1767), Carl Philipp Emanuel Bach (1714–1788), and even Haydn have been seen as delicate, refined music which was produced to delight the aristocrats who also enjoyed the delicacies of rococo architecture and rococo painting. Even the touches of imitation—the songs of birds, the susurrus of leaves in the wind, the tinkling of water in streams—in many compositions were considered rococo.

Rococo music is criticized as frivolous, lighthearted, and empty. But it led the way for the classical composers, who experimented with a much more open texture than that which appealed to the baroque. The music of the classical composers emphasizes the single voice of a given instrument much more than even Bach's Brandenburg Concertos. There is much polyphony in Bach; in Haydn's work, homophony provides a powerful harmonic base for the thematic material. Some of Haydn's themes are based on folk tunes. And because the texture of much of his work is more open than that of baroque music, his experiments with keys and with harmonies are more apparent.

The third movement of Haydn's symphonies is a dance movement, in many cases a minuet. The minuet was the chief dance of the age—stately and cool, yet exuberant and orderly (Figure 15-24). It was not confined to the aristocrats, although it was never a dance of the people at large. Its inclusion in a symphony is a pleasant contrast.

MOZART

The great musical genius of the eighteenth century was Wolfgang Amadeus Mozart (1756–1791), a child prodigy whose father, also a musician and composer,

Figure 15-24
A minuet: Jean Baptiste Joseph Pater. *The Dance in a Pavillion.* No date. Oil on canvas. (Cleveland Museum of Art, gift of Commodore Louis D. Beaumont.)

was quick to exploit his son's talents. Mozart was writing music by the time he was six. He finished his first full-length opera at the age of twelve. During his short life he wrote a prodigious amount of music. His symphonies, concertos, and other works all represent supreme achievements.

Mozart and Opera

Mozart's love of Italian opera influenced all the music that he wrote; in particular, it shaped his lyric, melodic style. His greatest operas—*The Marriage of Figaro* (1786; a performance is shown in Figure 15-25), *Don Giovanni* (1787), *Cosi fan tutte* (1790), and *The Magic Flute* (1791)—are among the most important works of the century. The music is superb; the texts are on interesting subjects, both moral and political; and the demands they make of vocalists set them apart. They are among the only operas dating from this period that are still regularly performed.

Figure 15-25
A performance of Mozart's
Marriage of Figaro at Covent
Garden. (Covent Garden;
photo, Reg Wilson, London.)

Conventions of Mozart's Music

Mozart's compositions, particularly his concertos,
tend to follow a clear and established pattern, just as
Haydn's symphonies do. Most of his concertos begin
with a statement of the thematic subject in the home
key (the tonic). The orchestra and the solo instrument introduce the subject again, along with a
second subject, and then move to the dominant key,
in which the previous material is "reshaped" musically. There are clear cadences to establish the shape of
the melodic material as well as its keys. After the
development of this material, there is a recapitulation in which the original subjects return, as if giving
us a chance to see how much has been changed. In
the concertos, Mozart includes a cadenza—a short,
technically brilliant passage that allows the solo
instrumentalist to display virtuosity. On occasion,
the instrumentalist is permitted to improvise the
cadenza, rather than play what is written. Shortly
after this passage, the entire orchestra returns to the
tonic key and makes use of much of the original
thematic material. A movement such as this is
usually a first movement, in sonata form. Movements
modeled on a dance form do not have such symme-

try. The last movement imparts a sense of rounded-
ness and finality.

Referring to such a composition as "classical" is
justified—or partly justified—not because the music
has antecedents in the ancient world, but because it
has the values that we associate with classical art.
That is, it is symmetrical, balanced, clear, and
thoughtful. We have the feeling that reason, not
passion, dominated the response to most of the
instrumental music not only of Mozart but of Haydn
as well.

Opera is by nature more emotional than instrumental music, if only because it offers us the spectacle
of people in action on a stage. But there are other
reasons for thinking of Mozart's operas as being full of
feeling, significant, and unusual. *The Marriage of
Figaro,* which is based on a play by Beaumarchais,
contains social commentary. It is the story of Figaro,
an ordinary person, who wishes to marry Susanna, a
serving woman in the household of a petty count.
The count expects to enjoy the sexual favors of the
bride in the medieval tradition called the "droit du
seigneur" (right of the master). However, *The Marriage of Figaro* is subversive: it shows that Figaro's

pride and honor are as important as the count's. Tradition, when it is a bad tradition, can be changed. We find ourselves moved by the music, which portrays Figaro's sufferings at the thought of having to share his beloved with the count. Figaro's is a social victory, and for those who saw the opera in Mozart's day, it was a reaffirmation of their own intermediary position. They were neither nobles nor peasants; they were beginning to conceive of themselves as democrats.

Symphony Number 41 in C Major, "Jupiter"

No one knows who named Mozart's last symphony, and it is not clear why the name seemed appropriate. Jupiter was the great Roman god (equivalent to the Greek Zeus) who had many liaisons with goddesses and mortals. His will was fate, and some critics liken the opening passage of the symphony (Figure 15-26), with its triplet group (G–A–E) leading to the tonic, C—the home key of the symphony—to the lightning stroke of Jupiter.

The four movements of the symphony are marked:

1. Allegro vivace—fast and lively
2. Andante cantabile—flowing and songlike
3. Menuetto: allegro; trio—dancelike and moderately fast
4. Finale: allegro molto —very fast

Typically, the structure of the classical symphony is as follows. The first movement is fast, in sonata-allegro form. The slow introduction (where one is present; the "Jupiter" begins immediately with the allegro) is followed by the exposition (A), the musical subjects. The development section (B) changes and metamorphoses the thematic material, often by exploring it in different keys, putting it in new relationships with harmonic material, and working with it in different instrumentation. The recapitulation (A) restates the original thematic material in the home (or tonic) key, bringing the movement to a powerful cadential conclusion.

The second movement is usually slow and lyrical, with thematic material that could be sung. We often hear distinct tunes in this movement.

The third movement usually begins with a dance form: AABABA, with sections repeated exactly (A and BA). Not all recordings of a given symphony include all the repeats, and so in some the pattern may not be followed exactly. The middle section, or trio (so named because in earlier times it was customarily scored for only three instruments) follows the pattern CCDCDC. Then the movement ends with an ABA treatment.

The fourth movement is usually very fast and dynamic. Often it is in sonata form (ABA), and sometimes it is in rondo form (ABACADABA, in which A repeats after a contrasting passage. In Mozart's "Jupiter" Symphony, it is a fugue, with several different thematic motifs. Usually the movement ends with a strong coda that brings the symphony to a powerful cadential conclusion in the tonic key.

Figure 15-27 shows the second subject from the first movement of Mozart's Symphony Number 41. This movement contrasts thematic material stated by the orchestra with that stated by the strings. When that material is developed—as it is in several related keys—we begin to see the potential that lay hidden in it when we first heard it. In the middle portion of the movement, we almost lose touch with the original thematic material and are pleasantly surprised when it returns, intact, even more interesting for its transformation.

Because the key of the symphony, C major, is the basic key of the piano (the white keys are in the scale

Figure 15-26
W. A. Mozart. Symphony Number 41 in C Major, K. 551, "Jupiter," opening notes. 1788.

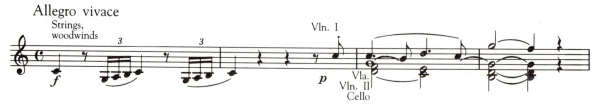

Mozart's Symphony Number 41 in C Major, "Jupiter"

1. For this listening key, listen to a recording of the symphony (Philips 6570 087, Seraphim S-60367, or Columbia M-31825). Identify the exposition, the development, and the recapitulation in the first movement. These are marked by dynamic changes, cadences (points of arrival), and changes in keys.

2. How many different melodies can you detect in the second movement? Is it a songlike movement? How effective is the contrast of the slow final section of the movement?

3. Is the third movement an adequate contrast to the first two? How different is the thematic material from that of earlier sections? Are there contrasts within the movement?

4. What identifies the finale as being, in fact, final? Are the thematic materials from the earlier parts of the symphony audible in this movement? How often does the movement reach a cadence? Are some cadences more powerful than others? Does the ending leave you with a sense of conclusion and a feeling of satisfaction?

Figure 15-27
Mozart. Symphony Number 41, second subject from the first movement.

of C major), one would think that this key would already have been thoroughly explored. Yet Mozart constantly finds colorations in the development and treatment of the melodic material that surprise and delight us.

As a guide to listening, it is possible to identify the important sections of the first movement by using a clock. While not all recordings are identical in timing, most are close enough. The first theme of the movement is stated immediately by the orchestra, and the second theme enters after approximately 35 seconds. After another 40 seconds, another thematic passage intervenes for 50 seconds, after which the exposition ends and the development begins. Mozart often begins the development early without a major cadence. The deepest, most cerebral section of the development passage—when the thematic material is most imaginatively altered and transformed— comes approximately 4½ minutes into the movement. A major cadence with the entire orchestra, approximately 6 minutes into the movement, signals a change and the beginning of the recapitulation. The most intense, momentous cadence—the final one— occurs approximately 8¾ minutes into the movement, bringing it to a close. The cadences function as moments of release, arrival, climax, and musical fulfillment. They are the emotional and musical signposts of the symphony.

The songlike second movement, in F major, presents us with three themes that almost seem to be one. Their unfolding is an interesting relief from the dynamic force of the first movement, which uses the full resources of the orchestra and aims for an intensity that is absent in the second movement. The long, slow final passages of the movement are an interesting, meditative contrast to the power of the first movement. In the same sense, the third movement, in E major, adds the interest of a dance tempo. The key of E major is curious, since it has been hinted at earlier, and when it is given its chance, it seems refreshing and novel. The trio is in the key of C major again, and our expectations of hearing some of the original musical material in its home key are partially fulfilled.

The last movement is both witty and brilliant. It is primarily in the key of C major, with contrasting keys. It is in sonata form (ABA), but it ends with its four thematic motifs in a complex fugue that in many ways is a look over the shoulder at the great fugues of Bach and other baroque masters. Mozart is borrowing a distinctive technique of the earlier period, while introducing gigantic cadences that can be achieved only by the entire orchestra. Most baroque fugues are composed for keyboard instruments and sometimes played by small ensembles. But Mozart had at his disposal a fairly large orchestra of perhaps forty musicians, and the effect of the entire orchestra's using fugal material is unusual.

Mozart died three years after completing the "Jupiter" Symphony. He was only thirty-five years old. He had been capable of sitting down and writing music the way others can sit down to write a letter. He could copy out a piece he had composed in his head and hold a conversation with friends at the same time. Rarely, if ever, has there been such a genius. Yet it is a puzzling fact that he was never given the secure kind of support that marked Bach's career. No patron ever took Mozart under his wing and made it possible for him to write without financial or emotional worry. His biographers say that the sheer weight of worry may have been the most important cause of his early death. The popular musical stage could not support the free-lance composer. Even operas, at which Mozart excelled, could not sustain him financially. When Mozart died, he had so little money that he was buried in an unmarked pauper's grave. His remains have never been recovered. The age, which was undergoing a transition regarding the ability of a composer to earn an independent living, is largely to blame for this. But Mozart's sometimes abrasive personality and his overwhelming genius (which gave rise to envy among lesser composers) may have combined to make his circumstances impossible. Nonetheless, few ages have produced such a genius.

Summary

The eighteenth century was a period of political turmoil and intellectual ferment. The revolutions in politics, which resulted in the independence of the United States and the revamping of government in England, were matched by revolution in industry and in agriculture which displaced many thousands of people. The industrial revolution changed the way people worked and lived, as well as their entire sense of themselves. It changed trade patterns, it made many costly items cheap and readily available, and—although it caused much pain and anguish among the poor—it helped spur on the economic democratization of Europe. Remnants of the rococo were everywhere in the arts in the early part of the century. But the powerful movement that swept all before it was neoclassicism, which brought with it the penchant for reason, orderliness, balance, harmony, restraint, calm, and moral purpose that marked the century. Neoclassicism became the dominant style in all the arts, although it often meant something slightly different in each of them. Society was moved deeply by the philosophes in France, the English philosophers, and thinkers in Germany, all of whom felt that humankind could best realize its potential through the exercise of reason. The age believed that reasonable action could make all things possible. Reason could help people understand the world, the stars, and the nature of things. It was also sufficient for understanding God and religion. The arts were expected to reflect this optimism; those artists who did not feel the enthusiasm of the period produced satirical works that at least continued the focus and attention on the values of thought and its dominance in all affairs.

Concepts in Chapter 15

Scientific advances made during the seventeenth century gave the eighteenth century confidence in the ability of reason to solve social problems.

Economic successes in the new world created a moneyed population that enjoyed the sensual pleasures of the rococo style.

Rococo was a hedonistic style concentrating on sensual pleasures and often tending toward the trivial.

Neoclassicism, in reaction to the rococo, looked to Roman values for inspiration.

The agricultural revolution in England resulted in better strains of crops and livestock, but at a cost: the poor lost their grazing privileges on common land.

The industrial revolution in England put the dispossessed poor to work in workhouses and factories.

A religious revival in the form of John Wesley's Methodism swept northern Europe; it appealed primarily to the poor.

Rococo architecture is characterized by sumptuous interiors, and classical architecture by distinctive exteriors.

Sculpture was not distinguished in this period; sculptors could not shake off the influence of Bernini and did not have the advantages of important commissions.

Rococo painting portrayed a leisurely society at play, often centering on the pleasures of dance, music, and erotic pastimes.

Neoclassical painting championed the Roman republican ideals of self-sacrifice and honor as a way of countering the lush sensuality of rococo painting.

Neoclassical styles eventually came to dominate in the century.

Hogarth and other painters aimed at social commentary in an effort to reform the age.

The philosophes helped Diderot create the *Encyclopedia* in France in mid-century.

Swift, Pope, and other English satirists consciously aimed at changing social values.

Voltaire and Johnson, who did not know each other, countered the prevailing optimism with *Candide* (Voltaire) and *Rasselas* (Johnson).

Early-eighteenth-century music is considered baroque.

Vivaldi and Bach developed musical forms that helped shape later, classical music.

Bach wrote no operas, but his church cantatas and his great *Passion According to St. John* and *Passion According to St. Matthew* were landmark vocal works.

Bach's theme-and-variations compositions were important instrumental works.

Bach and other late baroque composers made important contributions to the development of strongly key-centered compositions; Bach's experiments in key relationships were basic to the music of later composers.

Developments in music later in the century included the classicism of Haydn and Mozart.

Mozart was the most significant classical composer of

symphonies, concertos, chamber music, and operas of the period.

Classical music upheld the values of order, clarity, balance, and high-mindedness associated with neoclassicism.

Suggested Readings

Behrens, C. B. A. *The Ancien Régime.* London: Thames and Hudson, 1967.

Biancolli, Louis. *The Mozart Handbook.* Cleveland: World Publishing, 1954.

Gay, Peter. *The Enlightenment: An Interpretation.* 2 vols. New York: Knopf, 1966, 1969.

————. *The Enlightenment: A Comprehensive Anthology.* New York: Knopf, 1973.

Hayes, John. *Gainsborough.* London: Phaidon, 1975.

Held, Julius, and Donald Posner. *17th and 18th Century Art.* Englewood Cliffs, N.J.: Prentice-Hall, 1972.

Holt, Elizabeth. *A Documentary History of Art.* Vol. 2. New York: Doubleday, 1958.

Honour, Hugh. *Neo-classicism.* Harmondsworth, England: Penguin, 1979.

Lucie-Smith, Edward. *Concise History of French Art.* London: Oxford, 1971.

Mitford, Nancy. *The Sun King: Louis XIV at Versailles.* New York: Harper & Row, 1966.

Paulson, Ronald. *The Art of Hogarth.* London: Phaidon, 1975.

Plumb, J. H. *England in the Eighteenth Century.* Harmondsworth, England: Penguin, 1950.

Rosen, Charles. *The Classical Style: Haydn, Mozart, Beethoven.* New York: Viking, 1971.

Rosenblum, Robert. *Transformations in Late Eighteenth Century Art.* Princeton, N.J.: Princeton, 1970.

Rude, George, ed. *The Eighteenth Century: 1715–1815.* London: Free Press, 1965.

Scheider, Isidor, ed. *The Enlightenment.* New York: George Braziller, 1965.

Summerson, John. *Architecture in Britain: 1530–1830.* Baltimore: Penguin, 1958 (revised edition published in 1969).

————. *Heavenly Mansions.* New York: Norton, 1963.

Sunderland, John, and Ettore Camesasca. *The Complete Paintings of Watteau.* New York: Abrams, 1971.

PART
SEVEN

PART SEVEN

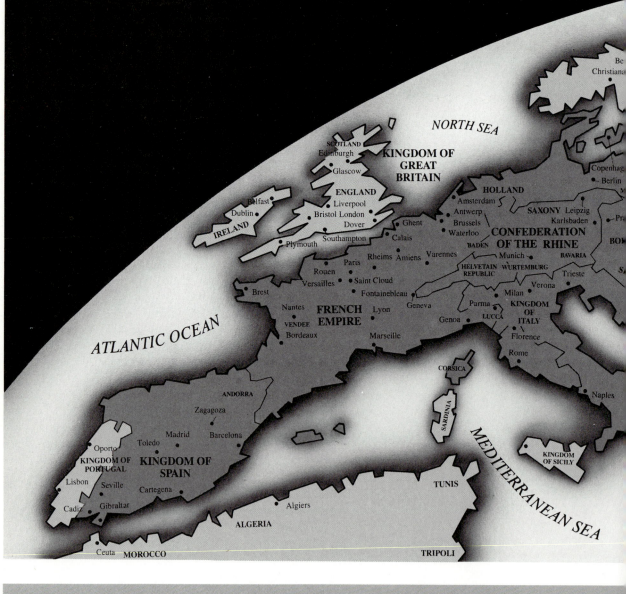

THE NINETEENTH CENTURY

EUROPE IN NAPOLEON'S TIME 1812

KINGDOM OF
DEN
olm

FINLAND

Saint
Petersburg

ESTONIA

BALTIC SEA

KOURLAND

Riga LIVONIA Novgorad

Moscow

DANZIG

Konigsburg Tilsit

Borodino

Friedland

Vilna Vitebsk Smolensk

KINGDOM OF
PRUSSIA Eylau

Kiev

RUSSIAN
EMPIRE

Warsaw GRAND DUCHY
OF WARSAW
Krakow

GALACIA

VIA

MOLDAVIA

BESSARABIA

AUSTRIAN
Pest EMPIRE
Buda

Odessa

TRANSYLVANIA

CRIMEA

AVONIA

Belgrade Bucharest

SERBIA

BLACK SEA

IA

WALLACHIA

MONTE-
NEGRO

BULGARIA Sofia

OTTOMAN EMPIRE Constantinople

ALBANIA

Athens

OTTOMAN EMPIRE

CRETE

CYPRUS

SYRIA

0   100   200   300 miles

The nineteenth century was a time of enormous innovations in life in Europe, Africa, the Americas, and Asia. We are still reeling from changes that took most people in their own age by surprise. Intellectual movements began early in the century, developed, matured, and then gave way to yet newer movements, beginning a cycle of change of the sort that we, in the twentieth century, have become used to. One of the problems of the age was learning how to adjust to rapid changes in thought and style. Later in the century, advances in science were such that basic concepts, ancient ideas, and some religious views were shaken to the core. The arts were responsive to these changes and explored avenues which were unimagined at the beginning of the period.

The era began in 1789 with the French Revolution, an unheralded uprising of the poor and the common people against the rich nobility, who had lived an exclusive, unconcerned life of ease and grace. The violence of the revolution—the bloodshed and the brutal treatment of the upper classes—frightened many people who otherwise would have been sympathetic to the new movement toward republicanism and equality. Nations, such as England, which had already had their own revolutions were cast into a political conservatism—a form of backlash that had consequences for more than a generation. William Wordsworth and other romantic poets whose themes had been the nobility of the human spirit and the equality of humankind were at once fascinated by the turmoil and fearful of it.

The rise of Napoleon as the leader of the French people and the development of a modern army that was immensely powerful and skillfully organized eventually threw Europe into a major cataclysm. Until 1814 the century was threatened with a form of tyranny in Napoleon's zeal to "liberate" Europe. Wars in Spain, Italy, Austria, Russia, and Egypt demonstrated Napoleon's strength. Only a major alliance of powers—England, Austria, Prussia, and Russia—was able to bring Napoleon to his knees. But part of the price of this victory was the upsetting of certain long-standing balances of power and the introduction of Russia into European politics in a way that had never before been envisaged. That introduction produced ambitions in Russian leaders which some political observers insist are still being acted on in our own century.

The explosion of romanticism—an artistic movement that was truly universal, embracing artists and writers in Russia, the Germanies, Italy, England, France, and the Americas—began in the 1790s. It was marked by a faith in the potential of humankind, a belief in the equality of the spirit, and a yearning for the liberating power of the imagination, even when it contradicted the censorious, controlling power of reason. Romantic poetry was socially aware, concerned with the fate of humanity, anxious to search within for the inmost soul, and often ecstatic in the face of the beauties of nature. Deep feeling was its hallmark. And if that depth of feeling arose from sometimes odd sources—contemplation of the terrible, as in some gothic horror tales; or the awareness of fearful nightmares; or even an interest in people who were pathetic and crazed—the romantics were still anxious to respond. Feeling was first.

In part because of egalitarian attitudes, most painting developed a commitment to romantic realism. The neoclassical idealizations were no longer needed except in France, where neoclassicism was dominant because of the thrust first toward republicanism and then toward imperial designs. Republicanism produced a zeal for grandeur, which retarded the romantic energies that had been inherent in the potential for freedom and independence represented by the revolution. Although realism was slow to develop in France, it burst forth after a period of simmering. In England and elsewhere, artists explored the beauties of genuine locales and genuine people.

The second half of the century was marked by more revolutions—the wave of uprisings of 1848, which shook Europe and demonstrated that the new moneyed classes were not going to permit themselves to be dominated by a wastrel nobility. Even if they had to go to the barricades and fight, they were intent on reform and change. The struggles of Germany to become a unified nation gave rise to war with France in 1871. European nations began the extensive practice of establishing colonies in Africa, Asia, and the Americas in the 1880s. New technologies had produced machines with extraordinary capabilities, but the raw materials needed to be dominant in world markets were not available in quantity in Europe.

The realist painters were shocked by the development of photography in the 1840s. Their work immediately showed signs of its influence, and many important painters, such as Edgar

Degas and Thomas Eakins, used the camera in order to study subjects for their paintings. Photography rapidly distinguished itself from painting; after an early period when it imitated many painterly effects, it moved toward self-discovery.

The most important developments in painting were the growth of realism into a democratic art form and the advent of impressionism, which also depended in part on certain developments in photography. Impressionism established the importance of the sensibility of the painter, since it was always the painter's own impression which would appear on the canvas. The placing of primary importance on the manner in which a subject was represented, rather than on the subject itself, signaled a shift in values and a brand-new attitude toward painting. Painting ceased to be a mirror of nature or a lens by which nature was idealized. The postimpressionists—among them Gauguin, Van Gogh, and Cézanne—were even more intent on directing our attention to the canvas than the earlier impressionists, such as Renoir, Degas, Manet, and Monet.

Poetry and philosophy moved further in the direction of inward examination. Nietzsche's philosophy of will and idea, a development of the earlier romantic idealism of Immanuel Kant, caught the imagination of many thinkers near the end of the century. Darwin's theories changed their attitude toward nature and toward their place in it. One of the popular consequences of Darwin's thought was the weakening of the absolute concept of good and evil. If survival depends on fitness, and if nature selects for the fittest, then the concept of good and evil seems a useful human invention, but still only an invention. The social applications of Darwin's theories, which had gained rapid acceptance among younger scientists, were almost inevitable, and Nietzsche was not the only person to postulate that there was such a thing as spiritual selection of a kind of superhuman for whom the ordinary standards of the average person would be like imprisonment, an injustice which nature itself would not tolerate.

The century ended with uncertainty and fear on the one hand—and prosperity, peace, enormous technological promise, and astonishing potential on the other. A taste for the decadent was apparent in the poetry of Baudelaire, whose *Flowers of Evil* shocked readers in mid-century. Music was dominated by the mythicizing Wagner, whose *Ring of the Nibelung*

explored new avenues in operatic experiences. His theories of harmony began a revolution in tonality that was continued into the early twentieth century. Taking a cue from Nietzsche, Wagner constructed his series of operas in part as a way of reviving pagan Germanic values and demonstrating the strength of indigenous northern European myth. Nietzsche, whose relations with Wagner were stormy, agreed that the Greek and Roman values had given way under the discoveries of science, the revolutions in politics, and the manifestos of the communists. He feared that rapid technological changes might cause a breakdown in European civilization and produce an era of bloodshed and war on a scale never before imagined.

Brief Chronology

July 14, 1789   The fall of the Bastille in Paris. August 27, the Declaration of the Rights of Man and Citizen.

April 1792   France declares war on Austria.

January 1793   Louis XVI is executed. In February, France declares war on Great Britain. In August the levée en masse, a general army draft, makes the French army the most powerful in Europe.

1798   Wordsworth and Coleridge publish *Lyrical Ballads*.

1803–1805   Beethoven composes *Fidelio*.

1804   Napoleon crowns himself emperor, dashing hopes for true republicanism in France. Beethoven rededicates his Third Symphony as the "Eroica" in disappointment over Napoleon's act.

1806–1812   The period of Napoleon's greatest power.

1814   Napoleon returns from Elba and is defeated at Waterloo; he is banished to Saint Helena.

1821–1822   Greek war of independence from the Turks. Faraday develops the electric dynamo.

1830   The Bourbon monarchs in France are overthrown. Louis-Philippe, the Citizen King, becomes a constitutional monarch.

1832   Important social and labor reforms in England. Goethe publishes *Faust*, Part 2.

1839   Daguerre demonstrates photography in Paris. The painter Paul Delaroche says, "From today painting is dead."

1848   Marx publishes *The Communist Manifesto*. In Europe there is a wave of revolution, quite independent of Marx. Louis-Philippe's government is overthrown.

1851   Great London Exposition; Crystal Palace is built.

1853   Louis-Napoléon, after a coup d'état, reigns as Napoléon III. Admiral Perry negotiates treaty beginning contact of Japan with western powers.

1853–1857   The Crimean war: England and France against Russia.

1853–1874   Wagner composes *The Ring of the Nibelung*.

1859   Darwin publishes *On the Origin of Species by Means of Natural Selection*.

1860–1870   Italy is unified.

1861–1865   The American Civil War.

1866   Alfred Nobel invents dynamite.

1869   The Suez Canal in Egypt opens.

1870–1871   The Franco-Prussian war. France loses to a developing Germany. Bismarck is made chancellor of a new unified Germany.

1874   First impressionist show is held at photographer Nadar's studio.

1875   Russia and Turkey at war.

1876   Alexander Graham Bell patents the telephone.

1877   Thomas Edison patents the phonograph.

1879   Edison invents the first practical electric light bulb.

1885   The internal combustion engine propels the first car.

1894–1895   Japan and China at war.

1895   Marconi develops the telegraph. X-rays are discovered.

1898   The Curies discover radium and radioactivity.

1899–1902   The Boer war in South Africa.

CHAPTER 16

THE ROMANTIC TEMPER: 1789 TO 1848

Cultural Background

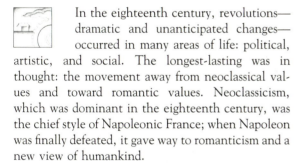 In the eighteenth century, revolutions—dramatic and unanticipated changes—occurred in many areas of life: political, artistic, and social. The longest-lasting was in thought: the movement away from neoclassical values and toward romantic values. Neoclassicism, which was dominant in the eighteenth century, was the chief style of Napoleonic France; when Napoleon was finally defeated, it gave way to romanticism and a new view of humankind.

THE FRENCH REVOLUTION

The assistance given by France to the colonies during the American Revolution was so costly that Louis XVI had to reestablish the Estates-General, a parliamentary organization composed of the three estates of French life: the clergy, the aristocrats, and the bourgeoisie. In 1790, this body established a constitutional monarchy which Louis at first accepted and then rejected. When it became clear that no progress

in government was possible with Louis XVI, his life was forfeit.

The storming of the Bastille (July 14, 1789) was a symbolic act: it began the French Revolution. Once the Estates-General secured the constitutional monarchy, the nobles forsook their feudal rights to the land (thus making peasants landowners). The model of the American Revolution inspired those in France who were anxious to press for reform and revolution. Other European nations had been, in turn, eager to see that the French king was treated well and that no harm came to him.

NAPOLEON

In the disorder of the revolution following the death of the king, several forms of government came and went. France had been declared a republic in September 1792, shortly before Louis XVI was executed, and the new model was built directly on Roman lines, which created an atmosphere even more sympathetic to neoclassicism.

In August 1793 the French government, threatened by war with several neighbors, invented the levée en masse; this was the first universal draft of citizens to form a national army. Whoever controlled the army would control France. Napoleon was chosen consul— on the model of republican Rome—in 1799. His term was extended to ten years, and then to life. After a succession of stunning military victories in 1804, he was made emperor. Until that moment, he had appeared to be a great hero, spreading a doctrine of liberty, fraternity, and equality to the nations of Europe. But when he accepted a hereditary emperorship, it was feared that he could become a tyrant.

Europe was dominated by a France stronger than it had ever been. Its army was powerful because it battled smaller mercenary groups who had no stake in the nations for whom they fought. Napoleon usually outnumbered his adversaries with an army that supported itself on the spoils of conquest. Soon England, Austria, Russia, and Sweden leagued themselves against France and Spain. The battles of Trafalgar at sea and Austerlitz on land were decisive enough to show that France was not invincible. Yet Napoleon continued. Having won in Italy, Egypt, and Austria, he pressed on to Russia in the bitter campaigns of 1812 and 1813. Eventually, at Leipzig, in 1813, he was decisively beaten and stripped of power. He was exiled to Elba, where it was thought that he could do little harm. But he escaped in 1814, raised a new army from among his followers, and fought again for the celebrated "hundred days." Then Arthur Wellesley, duke of Wellington, an Irish general, defeated Napoleon at Waterloo, the last and most famous of the huge battles fought in this period.

NEOCLASSICISM VERSUS ROMANTICISM

Neoclassicism culminated in the painting of Jacques-Louis David. His *Oath of the Horatii* (Figure 15-18) had, only five years before the revolution, established him as the most important French painter of the period. Neoclassical adherence to Roman values supposedly stimulated the best, most nationalistic, and most republican sentiments.

On the other hand, romanticism, which was growing in Germany and England, opposed neoclassicism. It grew outside France during the Napoleonic years and was connected at first with cults of sensibility that stressed deep feelings and the emotional life. Romanticism promoted individual rights and the dignity of humankind, democracy, natural and unstructured religion, the imagination, and freedom from constraint.

THE IMPORTANCE OF THE IMAGINATION

According to James Engell, the imagination was the key to the growth and eventual triumph of romanticism. Engell sees the imagination as linking the world of nature and the world of humans as well as the worlds of matter and spirit. Samuel Taylor Coleridge, a romantic poet and philosopher, wrote eloquently, treating the imagination as a hint of the power of divinity. The imagination was instrumental in perceiving the emotional content of works of art. Coleridge saw it as the primary creative faculty of the mind: "the living power and prime agent of all human perception," as he said in *Biographia Literaria* (1817). The godlike qualities of the imagination, he said, repeated "in the finite mind . . . the eternal act of creation in the infinite I AM." The liberation of the imagination was a shaping force in romantic art.

THOUGHT AND EMOTION

A characteristic of romantic style, particularly in poetry and music, is the elevation of feeling over analytic thought. The debate over the relative values of reason and passion—thought and emotion—had raged in the middle of the eighteenth century. Indirectly, it helped the romantics by calling attention to the values of deep feeling. If passion was undesirable because it was reckless and uncontrolled, it was also attractive because it offered a way of knowing and of understanding human experience that sometimes transcended the limits of rational thought and rigid logic. Deep feeling, it was understood, could be a positive human virtue, an avenue to understanding the nature of the divinity and the potential for goodness in the human breast.

Painting

THE DEVELOPMENT OF ROMANTIC STYLE

Jacques-Louis David

David (1748 – 1825) was lionized after exhibiting *The Oath of the Horatii* (1784; Figure 15-18). The later romantic painter Delacroix called him the "father of

French painting." During the revolution, which *The Oath* had helped stimulate, David had access to revolutionary circles. But one of his greatest paintings—some say his very greatest—is in a style that departs from Roman neoclassicism: *The Death of Marat* (Figure 16-1) resembles earlier painting depicting the death of Christ.

The French poet Charles Baudelaire thought *Marat* poignant and revealing, which shows that even David used painting to reveal emotion. Marat had been David's friend. An official during the revolution, he was murdered by a distraught woman, Charlotte Corday, who gained an audience with him by means of the letter that lies before him in the painting. He was in his bathtub because of a painful skin disease. David said of the painting, which was based on his examination of the corpse and on his visit to Marat the day before he died:

> I found him in a striking pose. Next to him was a block of wood, on which were paper and ink. Out of the bathtub his hand wrote down his last thoughts for the good of the people. . . . I thought it would be interesting to show him in the attitude in which I had discovered him.

The Death of Marat is neoclassical in its simplicity, its directness, and its clarity. Marat is idealized by a

Figure 16-1
Jacques-Louis David. *The Death of Marat.* 1793. Oil on canvas, 63 ¾ by 49 ¼ inches. (Musées Royaux des Beaux-Arts de Belgique; photo, A.C.L., Brussels.)

PERCEPTION KEY

Jacques-Louis David, *The Death of Marat*

1. Does *The Death of Marat* (Figure 16-1) have as clear a political message as *The Oath of the Horatii* (Figure 15-18)?

2. How intense is the emotional content of the painting? Is David more interested in presenting an emotional situation than in evoking a response from the viewer?

3. Since it is generally agreed that David is a neoclassical painter, we expect to see classical values —in style or theme or both—in his work. Are they apparent in this painting?

4. Would you say that David is more influenced by Carracci or by Caravaggio in this painting? (See Chapter 15.) What are some of your reasons?

5. What is the effect of having such a plain background take up so much space?

visual connection with the pietà—Michelangelo's, for example (Figure 13-21). The strong, cool vertical lines of the white sheet and the plain wooden box, balanced by the equally strong horizontal lines of the bathtub and its cover, suggest control, balance, and solidity. Yet the pathos in the face and pose urges us to experience the sense of loss that David expresses. The critic Linda Nochlin has said that this painting announces a shift away from the traditional pietà, which stresses the rewards of heaven. David, she suggests, stresses the "reward . . . of earthly immortality." She sees Marat as a "martyr to the new religion of reason."

Transition to the Romantic: Gros, Charlet, and Géricault

David's influence on his students and followers prevented an abandonment of neoclassical principles. One student, Antoine-Jean Gros (1771–1835), found it so difficult to move away from the path that David had laid out for him that he committed suicide when his *Hercules and Diomedes*, on a classical theme, was disregarded in the Salon of 1835. Delacroix lamented the loss of Gros, whose command of color was notable. In his exhilarating portrait *Bonaparte at the Battle of Arcola* (1796; color Plate 25), he uses colors sparingly, but they are intense and vibrant. The glow of the youthful Napoleon contrasts with the dark tunic, in which no details — except spots of gold and red—are shown. The thrust of the arm suggests imminent movement, and all seems in readiness for Napoleon's leap into destiny. Gros had the power of the romantics, command of their color, and their enthusiasm, but he also possessed the ability for detail and clarity that we associate with neoclassical painters.

A student of Gros, Nicolas-Toussaint Charlet (1792–1845), showed *The Retreat from Russia* (Figure 16-2) in the Salon of 1836; the painting portrays the defeated French army wandering through the ghastly Russian snows and cold amid the wreckage of war. Napoleon had saved himself; the great generals had left the front. The army marches forlornly—defeated, as Charlet's canvas implies, by the grimness of the weather and the landscape.

Théodore Géricault (1791–1824) is too great a painter to think of only as a transitional figure between neoclassicism and romanticism. He died tragically young. Like Gros, he was a powerful colorist. He often included dynamic studies of horses in his paintings; he was a daring and foolhardy horseman, and in fact his death resulted from a riding accident. Like others of his generation, he had been trained to the standards of the French Academy, although not in the workshop of David. His inclination was toward the dramatic, intense, colorful canvas, and he felt that there had to be a way to express the intensities of contemporary life while respecting the classical painters whom the Academy admired. Neither he nor any other artist of his time solved that problem.

Géricault became famous at the age of twenty-one with the *Portrait of the Chasseurs Commanding a*

Figure 16-2
Nicolas-Toussaint Charlet. *The Retreat from Russia.* Undated. Oil on canvas, 43 by 82 ½ inches. (Musée des Beaux-Arts, Lyons.)

Figure 16-3
Théodore Géricault. *The Raft of the Medusa.* 1819. Oil on canvas, 193 ¼ by 218 ⅞ inches. (Louvre, Paris; photo, Musées Nationaux.)

Charge (Color Plate 26), which he showed in the Salon of 1812. Almost 10 feet high, it began from an observation of a high-spirited cart horse fighting against its traces—something Géricault witnessed on September 13. To qualify for that year's Salon, paintings had to be submitted by October 12. Within that span of time, Géricault did his sketches and finished his work. Such urgency, inspiration, and bravado are almost romantic trademarks. The painting's romantic energy is visible in the powerful diagonal line of action, the total instability created by the rearing of the horse, and the emotional stirrings of battle.

Géricault's capacity for criticism is apparent in *The Raft of the Medusa* (1819; Figure 16-3). The subject of the painting is an event that was well known to Parisians: the sinking of the *Medusa*, which was captained by an inexperienced man favored by the government. The boat was carrying settlers on their way to Senegal in Africa in 1816 when it sank. The sailors manned the lifeboats, and 150 people, including one woman, were placed on a hastily prepared raft which was to be towed by the lifeboats to shore. But the sailors soon cut away from the raft, since it was impeding their own progress. Set adrift, the raft wandered for fifteen horrible days, during which there were mutiny and cannibalism. Only fifteen people survived. The two who came to Géricault

with the story appear by the mast of the raft. Géricault portrays the moment of the first, futile sighting of the *Argus*, a ship that at first passed them by but then returned to save them.

The painting—in its diagonal instability, in its choice of a scene from a contemporary historical event, and in its search for the peak of visual and emotional intensity—is obviously romantic in style. But the nudes in the foreground are neoclassical elements and show the influence of Michelangelo. The fact that the bodies do not show the effects of two weeks of starvation and thirst is evidence of Géricault's indebtedness to classicism. His indebtedness to Caravaggio shows up in the chiaroscuro lighting and the remarkable realism. This painting did not make Géricault an overnight sensation, although to our eyes (it hangs now in the Louvre) it is impressive. In fact, the indifference of the critics led him to take the painting—which was so huge that he had to hire a special studio in which to paint it—to England, where it was put on display for a fee.

Eugène Delacroix: The Genius of Romanticism

Eugène Delacroix (1798–1863) displayed his first Salon piece, *Dante and Virgil in Hell* (Figure 16-4), in 1822. The literary subject matter, the use of color, and the tribute to Dante, the poet of the divine

Figure 16-4
Above: Eugène Delacroix.
Dante and Virgil in Hell. 1822.
Oil on canvas, 74 ⅜ by 96 ⅞
inches. (Louvre, Paris; photo,
Musées Nationaux.)

Figure 16-5
Right: Eugène Delacroix.
Liberty Leading the People. 1830.
Oil on canvas, 102 ⅜ by 128
inches. (Louvre, Paris; photo,
Musées Nationaux.)

Eugène Delacroix

1. Establish the range of subject matter in Delacroix's paintings (such as Figures 16-4 and 16-5). Contrast it with that of any painter discussed in Chapter 15.

2. Are any explicitly neoclassical qualities apparent in any of Delacroix's paintings? Consider subject matter, treatment of background architecture, clarity of line, and balance of composition. Does the presence of Virgil in Figure 16-4 make the painting neoclassical?

3. Does Delacroix clarify an emotional content? Do the paintings still evoke an emotional response from the viewer?

4. What role does the imagination play in the paintings shown in Figures 16-4 and 16-5? Contrast the literalness of the scenes with their symbolic qualities.

5. Enumerate the romantic qualities apparent in these paintings. Refer to the works by Gros, Charlet, and Géricault (Color Plates 25 and 26 and Figures 16-2 and 16-3) and enumerate their romantic qualities. This should help you begin an inventory of romantic qualities in painting.

imagination, mark it as a romantic painting. Not everyone who saw the painting in the Salon admired it. Guérin, Delacroix's teacher, was disturbed, suggesting that it looked like a "daub." It does not have neoclassical clarity and regularity. The dark canvas depicts the underworld with full, intense, rich colors.

A later painting by Delacroix, *Liberty Leading the People* (Figure 16-5), caused a disturbance. It shows the allegorical figure of Liberty as a half-draped woman wearing the traditional Phrygian cap of liberty and holding a gun in one hand and the tricolor in the other. It is strikingly realistic; Delacroix, the young man in the painting wearing an opera hat, was present on the barricades in July 1830. Allegory helps achieve universality in the painting: Liberty is not a woman; she is an abstract force.

Revolutions had rocked Europe since the turn of the century. The wave of revolutions in the period 1820–1830 touched Lisbon, Cádiz, Madrid, Paris, Naples, Brussels, Warsaw, and Saint Petersburg. In France, the revolution of July 27–29, 1830, opposed the installation of Charles X as king of France. The allies had imposed a Bourbon king in a constitutional

monarchy that worked fairly well. But the French were resistant to the further imposition of an unpopular ruler. In a short-lived riot in which 2000 people were killed, Charles was turned out and a popular (but not better) figure, Louis-Philippe, was installed in what was called the "July Monarchy." *Liberty Leading the People* shows the lower classes moving France toward freedom.

Francisco Goya

The influence of the French enlightenment and the French Academy reached into Spain. Francisco José de Goya y Lucientes (1746–1828) was trained in Saragossa and Madrid; he traveled to Italy but was not impressed enough to stay. He is often described as an intense and pure romantic, and while he found the rigors of the Academy constricting, he certainly did his best to become acceptable to it. He became its president in Madrid, despite uncongenial competitions favoring subjects such as Hannibal crossing the Alps. He never succeeded in any of those competitions, although he often tried.

Figure 16-6
Above: Francisco Goya. *Naked Maja.* 1800. Oil on canvas, 37 ⅜ by 74 ¾ inches. (Prado, Madrid.)

Figure 16-7
Opposite: Francisco Goya. *The Sleep of Reason Produces Monsters.* 1796–1798. Etching with aquatint, 7 by 4 ¾ inches. (Museum of Fine Arts, Boston, bequest of William Babcock.)

The two primary influences in Spanish painting in Goya's day were the baroque-rococo style of the Venetian Giovanni Battista Tiepolo (1696–1770 and the neoclassical style of the German Anton Raphael Mengs (1728–1779), both of whom lived and worked in Spain. Mengs, partly because he outlived Tiepolo and partly because he saw correctly the dominant style of the enlightenment, was the force with which Goya had to deal. Goya tried to paint according to the prevailing standards, but found it impossible. When he was in his mid-twenties, he left Madrid and returned to Saragossa, where he became successful working for the local religious authorities —painting frescoes and executing designs for tapestries to please his commissioners.

But Madrid was where he had to be tested. His brother-in-law, Francisco Bayeu, was his competitor in Saragossa, and Goya could not live in his shadow. Back in Madrid, and finally as a member of the Academy, Goya spent the decade of his thirties courting the king and aristocratic society. One of his patrons was the duchess of Alba, who was at first very generous to him, and with whom he may have had a love affair. His many portraits of her have a richness and a spontaneity that mark his great work. She may be the woman shown in his *Naked Maja* (Figure 16-6). (Goya also painted a clothed version, but that did not stop the Inquisition from examining him.) However, the term "maja" refers to a sporting group of lowlifes who invigorated the streets of Madrid at this time and to whom Goya had been attracted; and the woman in this painting may be one of them, rather than the duchess of Alba. Goya never told anyone her true identity, including the Inquisition.

After Charles III died, Goya realized his ambition to become chief painter to the king. The years of peace that Charles III had somehow managed to secure for Spain were to give way to the horrors of war, which Goya was to confront when he was in his fifties. His portrait of Charles IV and the royal family is almost abusive in what it reveals about the odd-looking, pompous, and vain people who were to help bring Spain to ruin. It is the only painting that Goya was asked to do of the royal family.

El sueño de la razon produce monstruos.

While painting the royal family, Goya was also at work on a series of etchings called *Los Caprichos*, a landmark of social satire, which began as a humorous series. "Caprichos" means "caprices" or "whims." The original frontispiece for the collection (Figure 16-7) shows a portrait of Goya sleeping, while monsters loom in the background. Goya had adhered to the principles of the French enlightenment—the superiority of reason, the potential of humankind to do good, and the triumph of science—and felt that reason had to keep the imagination under control. The imagination dominates this etching, which is not realistic, clear, balanced, or classical. It is meant to stir the emotions.

The magnificent canvas *The Third of May, 1808* (Color Plate 27), memorializes the events that followed the uprising against the French troops stationed in Madrid. They were not to have been an occupying army, because Spain was supposed to be France's ally. But the kind of ally that France proved to be is established in the painting. This uprising was the beginning of the most brutal civil war of the nineteenth century. The term "guerrilla" was coined during this war, and the brutalities visited upon the Spanish and the French alike defy description. Goya, although he managed not to be involved in these horrors, recorded them in his series of etchings on the

PERCEPTION KEY

Francisco Goya, The Third of May, 1808

1. Comment on the use of light and color in *The Third of May* (Color Plate 27). Which figures are represented by light, bright colors? Which figures are highlighted by the brightness of the chiaroscuro technique? What is the source of light?

2. How are the two groups of men contrasted? What does the orderliness of the firing squad tell us emotionally? What are the implications of such orderliness?

3. Why is the town in the background? Does the distant skyline have an emotional value?

4. The painting is not realistic. We sense that the position of the soldiers is distorted and that the gestures of the men who are about to die are exaggerated. If this painting were more realistic, would it achieve a stronger emotional effect?

5. What is the effect of combining past, present, and future time in this painting?

miseries of war; and *The Third of May* remains one of the most powerful works on the theme of war's inhumanity ever painted. The compression of time is one of Goya's great achievements here. We see the anonymous firing squad mechanically shooting defenseless men, some of whom are protesting their innocence. That is present time. The dead of past time lie unburied. The future victims can barely stand to look at what is to be their fate; they are helpless and virtually cooperate in their own death. All these things reveal the meaning of war.

Starkly realistic paintings may evoke an emotion regarding the particular event portrayed, but they do not necessarily comment on the event. In a painting such as Goya's *Third of May*, on the other hand, the nonrealistic technique does make a comment: it intensifies the general significance of the event at the expense of specific significance. We do not know, for example, who the man in the white shirt is. The specifics are not important. What is important is the awful efficiency of the killers and the horror and terror of those who are about to die.

The artificial light—coming from the squarish lantern in front of the firing squad—illuminates the innocent people, while it tends almost to silhouette the killers, making them all the more sinister and anonymous. The lighting may be derived from Caravaggio, but its application is essentially nonrealistic. The fact that the shootings occur at night—that the killings must go on and on—demonstrates all the more horribly how depraved humankind has become. It is horrifying that the killers are Spain's "allies." The city in the background stands as ironic comment: civilization exists there (a church steeple is visible), but to no avail. Here on the outskirts of Madrid, Spaniards must die brutally, as if in a wilderness. This huge, imposing canvas has been an inspiration for modern painters, who have seen more such slaughter than even Goya might have expected.

PAINTING IN ENGLAND

Despite the influence of Joshua Reynolds, the British Royal Academy did not dominate painting, as the French Academy did in France—although Constable (who had to wait much too long to become a member) said that without it painters would have been thought of as mere tradespeople. The Academy did approve certain subject matter: classical themes with classical figures, nudes drawn from approved models, and historical incidents. The academic style demanded a high finish, careful detail, and appropriate colors. Conventional painters were preferred, and the truly original painter suffered.

In England, the absence of a powerful political force such as Napoleon helped produce a diversity and ease that French painting lacked. English romantic poetry was so forceful that it radiated throughout Europe, inspiring many paintings on literary subjects that emphasized the imagination and nature. The romantic message in England was combined with a love for monuments of the past—particularly gothic ruins—and a delight in nature untamed. The age of reason had considered that nature ought to be regulated by human design. Now English painters such as Constable and Turner revealed nature without the overlay of reason. Constable specialized in the calmness of scenes he had lived with all his life. Turner eventually applied his genius to the most turbulent of natural phenomena—storms.

William Blake

The distinction of being prominent as both a romantic poet and a romantic painter belongs to William Blake (1757–1827). He believed that painting should reveal what lies beneath the surface of apprehension. Feeling was what mattered—not slickness or technique. As part of his early training he drew sculpture in gothic cathedrals, and this gave him a love of a style that stood in strong opposition to neoclassicism. Thus, Blake was both a visionary, depending on pure imagination, and a primitive, looking to earlier styles for his inspiration. Many painters in Europe sought alternatives to the rigidity and intellectuality of neoclassicism. One alternative was to look beyond Michelangelo to the softer, more naturalistic Raphael. Another was to look even further to the gothic.

Neoclassicism and the baroque both tend toward realism; for Blake, this was a form of tyranny over the imagination. Numerous contemporary painters represented nightmares and dreams as a way of breaking the stringencies of realism. But Blake's visionary art—whether of imagined scenes, recorded visions, or images from Milton or Dante—always attempted to penetrate into the life of feeling. He was, as Anthony Blunt has said, an antirationalist "with a preference for those forms of art which most directly emphasize spiritual content."

The gothic penchants for filling all the available space and elongating the human figure are evident in one of Blake's most powerful early works, *Elohim Creating Adam* (Color Plate 28). "Elohim" is the Hebrew word for "God the creator" or "God the justice giver." Blake's concern with the Bible was great; his faith in God was mystical, intense, and unorthodox.

The design of this work is dominated by the rising sun beaming joyful blazons of red and blue light beneath a heavy layer of clouds. The spaces are filled with design. Blake has combined the joy of creation with the sorrow of the fall of humankind. Such a twinned vision is reechoed in the serpent tangled about Adam's leg, alluding to the temptation by Satan (in the form of a serpent) in the Garden of Eden. Elohim seems to be both flying and standing still. His beard is wafted back over his body; his garment is borne upon the wind. His hand on Adam's head reminds us of the touch of a violinist. The parallel lines of the arms and bodies stress a unity with God and are in contrast to the twining of the serpent's coils. The beginnings of life (symbolized by the rising sun) and the unity of God and humans at the creation are emphasized by the parallel forms. The future is expressed in the lowering clouds (fate overhead) and the devilish serpent below.

Blake fitted the figures into the space created by the sun, using the horizon as a base for the composition, because he wanted the work to have the greatest possible emotional impact on the viewer. His distortions and his symbolic suggestions force us to consider the implications of the design rather than concentrate on its literalness. Yet there are—as modern commentators have noted—literal qualities of color and design in this work as well. Blake's colors are always beautiful on a sensual level. The age of reason, which downgraded sensuality at the same time it downgraded passion, was, for Blake, a denial of human nature. Blake adhered to his greatest inspiration, John Milton, in his demand that art be simple, sensuous, and passionate. *Elohim Creating Adam* is an invitation to respond to the most important moment in the Bible, the moment which "contains" all that is to come.

Paradise Lost inspired Blake and the romantic poets. Milton soared through earth, heaven, and hell with dramatic ease. He treated the basic myths, which the contemporary world of industry, work, politics, and revolution had lost sight of. The rise of materialism had already begun, in the march of science and industry, to obliterate the spiritual nature of humankind. Blake looked to Milton for spiritual leadership and guidance.

Raphael Warns Adam and Eve (Figure 16-8) is virtually monochromatic, although it has a slightly golden coloration, with tinges of red in the fruit and in the wings of Raphael, the genial archangel. The scene illustrates the moment in *Paradise Lost* (Book 5, lines 377–385) when the archangel Raphael dines with Adam and Eve and warns them that Satan may be in the garden, ready to tempt them. He points to the tree of the knowledge of good and evil, already entwined by a serpent, as he reminds them of the prohibition against eating its fruit. Blake emphasizes the gothic qualities of the scene. The flowers create a gothic arch that encloses the composition, and Raphael's wings create yet another gothic arch. The linear verticals in the benches of both Adam and Raphael are more gothic touches, as is the intertwined foliage,

Figure 16-8
William Blake. *Raphael Warns Adam and Eve*. 1808. Pen and watercolor, 19 5/16 by 15 5/8 inches. (Museum of Fine Arts, Boston; subscription of 1890.)

reminiscent of the decorations on gothic manuscripts. The lines are essentially vertical, like most gothic lines, and the figures are quite unlike the classical forms favored by David, or even Delacroix.

The romantic period in the arts was the first to put forth the standard of novelty as opposed to the standard of mastering past techniques. Blake had done an apprenticeship and could draw in any contemporary academic style, but he rejected such work for philosophical reasons and became a romantic figure: singular, spurned, but steadfast in a heroic devotion to principle. Milton had provided Blake a model in his own life and in his works. Blake's *Milton* is considered his most important illuminated book, and for good reason.

John Constable

The great painter of English landscapes was quite unlike William Blake. John Constable (1776–1837) had few of Blake's predilections for the world of the spirit. He was interested in the world of humans and nature and in catching its shifting qualities by representing an exact sense of place.

Today, when Constable is a favorite for posters and calendars, it is difficult for us to think of him as controversial. Yet year after year he was denied membership in the Royal Academy while now-forgotten second-raters marched past him. Fortunately, he had the means to support himself. He started painting relatively late; at an age when Géricault and Turner were dazzling their audiences, Constable was wondering whether painting was a calling he should pursue.

Constable was not politically suave. Like Blake and Turner, he could be caustic. But he managed to secure a few good friends, to study at the Royal Academy schools, and to become a full-fledged member of the Academy six years before he died. He loved landscape—what he called the "natural painting"—although he might have made a good living at portraits or Academy set pieces: historical, allegorical, moralistic, or "picturesque" paintings. He realized that he had problems when he said, "My art flatters nobody by *petiteness*, it is without either *fal de lal* or *fiddle de dee*; how then can I hope to be popular?"

Constable's method was to sketch in the open air, very rapidly, in very small scale. For his largest canvases (on the order of 4 by 6 feet), he would work up a full-sized sketch in oils in his studio to see how the proportions and colors worked. The finished painting followed.

One painting not done in his studio, but painted totally in the outdoors, is *Boat-Building near Flatford Mill* (Figure 16-9). It portrays a canal boat of the sort

Figure 16-9
John Constable. *Boat Building Near Flatford Mill*. 1815. Oil on canvas, 20 by 14 ½ inches. (Victoria and Albert Museum.)

that Constable frequently saw on the river Stour, which meandered past his father's mills, the familiar scenes of his childhood. This particular painting was never sold, but (like Leonardo's *Mona Lisa*) stayed with him throughout his life. The composition is simple and direct. The boat is centered at a slight diagonal, and trees weight the canvas to the right. The colors are very light; the sky is a softly tinted blue, and the grass and earth in the foreground are also pale in tone. (The age preferred very dark canvases.) Like a good portrait, it communicates the spiritual nature of the subject: the concentration of those who are building the boat, which stands for the work that is done along the canals and for honest labor in a fruitful country where individual effort is rewarded.

Constable's most famous painting has been overexposed in calendars and greeting cards. *The Hay Wain* (Color Plate 29) portrays workers cooling off the hot metal bands that rim the wheels of their hay wain (cart). To the left is the cottage of Willy Lott, a colorful local character who lived to be eighty and who never spent more than four days away from home. Constable sketched and painted Willy Lott's cottage frequently. The colors are subdued but natural, the atmosphere is typical of the area, and the light is characterized by Constable's "whitewash" technique: placing specks of white in color areas to brighten them. A figure to the right of the dog has been painted out to simplify the composition (it remains in the completed sketch). It is surprising to learn that Constable could not sell the painting for 150 guineas.

Joseph Mallord William Turner

Constable's rival in England was a year younger and was accepted by the Academy decades earlier. Turner (1775–1851) had little education, but he possessed strong intelligence and immense talent. An experimenter, he was concerned especially with color theory. Both Newton and Goethe proposed theories of color; Turner propounded Goethe's because it was based on pigments and their behavior. As it happens, Newton was right and Goethe was wrong; but Turner's interest in color theory is important because some of his paintings that we most value today are studies in color sensation.

It must be said immediately that Turner did many paintings for himself which were never shown or sold, and among these are some that are most praised today. The paintings that made his reputation in his own time were more conventional Academy pieces: classical scenes, historical and genre paintings, and some pieces that compete directly with works of the old masters. Turner was cocky, determined, and very successful. His large fortune was earned through the mass production of etchings of his work. Thus, he was not only successful in the Academy but also generally popular. Unlike Constable, Turner traveled extensively—to Rome, Naples, and Venice—for inspiration. He was not always the darling of the Academy, however; like other revolutionaries, he paid a price when he veered from the traditional paths.

Turner's "competition" with certain old masters is of particular interest. *Dido Building Cathage* (Figure 16-10), for example, was in direct competition with the work of Claude Gellée, known as Claude Lorrain (1600–1682). The composition derives from Claude's *Seaport: The Embarkation of the Queen of Sheba* (Figure 16-11). Turner gave his *Dido* to the British nation on condition that it always be hung next to Claude's painting as evidence of his own superior skill.

Like Poussin, Claude was an important shaper of the neoclassical style. His painting emphasizes the clear lines of classical architecture in the Corinthian column on the left and in the Palladian building on the right. Compared with Turner's, Claude's buildings are much weightier and impart more of a sense of classicism and orderliness. The stone embankment in the foreground emphasizes the degree to which the unruly water has been tamed.

Turner's painting has no restraining foreground; the trees looming on the right are distinctly romantic because they suggest the power of untamed nature. Turner's light on the water—he was much involved with water—is commanding and dramatic. We cannot be sure what is happening in the painting. The figures are pressed to the left of the canvas, with Dido near the water. The atmosphere seems to be natural and genuine; the distant buildings are in a haze. In Claude's painting, distance is suggested by reducing the size of objects, and the atmosphere is clear and essentially unimportant. Claude's painting is calm and static; everything is under control. The figures

Figure 16-10
J. M. W. Turner. *Dido Building Carthage.* 1815. Oil on canvas, 61 ¼ by 91 ¼ inches. (National Gallery, London.)

Figure 16-11
Claude Lorrain. *Seaport: The Embarkation of the Queen of Sheba.* 1648. Oil on canvas, 58 ½ by 76 ¼ inches. (National Gallery, London.)

are spread across the canvas in careful balance. By contrast, Turner's painting is more daring, more risk-taking. In Dido's effort we sense a hint of the danger that is to come: the ultimate destruction of Carthage by the forces of classicism—Rome itself.

As a man, Turner had some peculiarities: among them his pathological secretiveness (he sometimes used a pseudonym), his bitter tongue, and his egoism.

But for an almost uneducated person, he was well-read; he was deeply moved by poetry and had written a poem, "The Fallacy of Hope." Although he never married, he had two children by his mistress, Sarah Danby, and was known for his generosity toward children. To match his ego, he had a prodigious talent, and he was regarded as a genuine virtuoso. By the time he began the experimental work that drew

COMPARISON KEY

Claude and Turner

1. Is the subject matter of either Turner's *Dido Building Carthage* (Figure 16-10) or Claude's *Seaport* so distinct that the titles are not interchangeable?

2. Is either painting more strictly classical in style? Consider the elements of clarity, balance, architecture, and use of light.

3. What are the romantic qualities of each work? In which painting is the action more static? In which is it more dramatic?

4. Compare the paintings in terms of the relative importance of natural forms and artificial forms. In which painting is the presence of humans more significant?

5. Do you think that Turner was right in insisting that these paintings be hung next to each other? What do you feel is achieved by hanging them side by side? Do you think that the National Gallery was right in accepting the painting on this condition?

---

critical attack, he was selling extensively to the new moneyed class of industrialists, who bought his work eagerly at his own gallery in London.

Snowstorm: Steamboat Off a Harbour's Mouth (Figure 16-12) originated when Turner, like the legendary Ulysses, had himself lashed to a mast and for four hours witnessed a violent snowstorm, fearing that he might be killed at any moment. The result is a painting which—unless we were told otherwise—we would consider to have no subject at all.

A similar experience resulted in *Rain, Steam, and Speed* (Color Plate 30). A woman reported seeing Turner put his head out the window of a speeding train during a storm. After nine minutes, he withdrew his head, closed his eyes, and considered his vision.

Figure 16-12
J. M. W. Turner. *Snowstorm: Steamboat Off a Harbour's Mouth.* 1842. Oil on canvas, 36 by 48 inches. (Tate Gallery, London.)

Turner's vision in both paintings is a partial blur. He used his experiences as pretexts for experiments in coloration, and because he did this so often, many people place his works among the first modern paintings—paintings in which the sensation of color is experienced directly, not modulated by a classical drama, a landscape, or a historical event. Color itself is the subject matter of such paintings. Most of Turner's contemporaries saw them as mere daubs, the products of a charlatan fooling the public. But Turner was committed to painting sensation more directly than anyone had done previously.

PAINTING IN GERMANY

Caspar David Friedrich (1774–1840) is probably the best known of the German painters of his day. His style is clear, realistic, and detailed. Yet it is not neoclassical. It examines the emotional values of a scene or dramatic setting. He painted landscapes, often including mysterious figures looking out on the morning sunlight or the evening sea and evoking a strong mood. A member of the Dresden Academy (in 1816), he was a deeply committed romantic.

Friedrich's most famous painting portrays, like the work of so many French and English painters, a disaster. *Arctic Shipwreck* (Figure 16-13) conveys a sense of the desolation of the far north, as well as a sense of the colossal power of nature. The forces of the ocean are apparent in the waves of Turner and other painters, but Friedrich depicts them as solid, and thus even more sinister. As a portrayal of an anonymous terror— emphasizing the cold indifference of nature—Friedrich's icy pyramid crushing a ship within its monstrous slabs is overwhelming. The realistic technique is typical of Friedrich, although realism was not his only goal. He was interested in the emotional responses that his visions could induce.

Throughout Europe, and very quickly in the Americas, painters reacted to neoclassicism by evolving a variety of approaches to perception and the imagination and by reassessing nature and our relation to it. Natural forces and sensation became primary subjects; the academic set pieces, on classical and standard subjects, were still produced, but not by the most significant painters of the period. Innovation in painting expressed the new spirit of the times, a new expansiveness of thought and feeling.

Figure 16-13
Caspar David Friedrich. *Arctic Shipwreck.* 1824. Oil on canvas, 38 ½ by 51 ⅛ inches. (Kunsthalle, Hamburg; photo, Ralph Kleinhempel.)

Figure 16-14
Benjamin Latrobe.
Catholic Cathedral,
Baltimore, interior.
(Photo, Holmes I.
Mettee, Baltimore.)

Architecture

The romantic delight in revival of older styles was evident in architecture. The period 1800–1850 saw new techniques—particularly the use of cast iron for internal support—which were later to revolutionize architecture. But before that the revival of Greek, Roman, gothic, and other styles preoccupied architects who were building not primarily churches, but secular structures used for government, education, the arts, or public entertainment.

There is no separate romantic style in architecture, but a widely recognized term, "romantic classicism," is useful for describing the architectural achievement of the age. Indeed, there is a sense in which the ambitions of the classical style (regularity, strength, and even moral stalwartness) merged with romantic ambitions (emotional involvement, nostalgia, imagination, and daring). As Figures 16-14 and 16-15 show, there is as much variability in the styles of architecture of this period as there is in the styles of painting. Architecture made demands of its viewers and expressed the values of both the architect and the society.

The power of the Roman Pantheon shows up in the interior design by Benjamin Latrobe (1764–1820) for the Catholic cathedral in Baltimore, begun in 1805. The exterior of the cathedral has been altered from Latrobe's original design, which resembles Soufflot's Panthéon in Paris (Figure 15-8). The interior (Figure 16-14) is hemispheric; there is an oculus at the center, and modified Roman arches support the dome. The modification of the arch, apparent above the altar, is a refreshing and original touch.

Figure 16-15
Charles Barry and A. Welby Pugin. Houses of Parliament. Begun 1836.

The destruction of the original Houses of Parliament by fire gave Sir Charles Barry (1795–1860) and Augustus Welby Pugin (1812–1852) the opportunity to fuse gothic with classical styles. Westminster Hall had survived the fire, so that their design had to integrate smoothly with a well-known building. Barry and Pugin's elegant solution created a landmark known today around the world (Figure 16-15). Gothic values are evident in the spires, the corner towers, and the towers breaking the regularity of the extensive walls. But the regularity of classical repetitions is also apparent in the treatment of the windows and in the horizontal lines that separate the several stories. There are no buttresses, which authentic gothic would have needed, and neither are there columns or classical orders (such as Doric or Corinthian). Yet the fusion is successful.

The structure does not point to republican sentiments, as a building in the Roman style might do. This is fitting for a nation in which the monarchy is still revered. The pure gothic would have been inappropriate as well, connoting values associated with the universities of Oxford and Cambridge or with the church. The success of the building has to do with the fact that it refers to the gothic but is not tied to absolute religious values. The design modifications (romantic gothicism) retain the sense of righteousness that we associate with the church while absorbing the values of the law, which perhaps are also implied in religious justice. The Houses of Parliament clarify the values of religious authority and legal authority.

Barry and Pugin's original charge was to design new Houses of Parliament in a national style. Gothic and Elizabethan were the styles considered national. In choosing gothic—in which the arch is relegated to an unimportant decorative function, in which the regular vertical lines dominate, and in which a classical layout and regularity tie all the decorative features together—Barry and Pugin created an evocation of a national design which even today seems perfect to many people. It did not, however, survive in other buildings or become widely influential.

A much more amusing and flamboyant approach to the fusion of styles is evident in a work by John Nash (1752–1835): the exotic Royal Pavilion in Brighton (1815–1817; Figure 16-16). A fusion of Islamic and Indian architecture, it is technologically important because it has interior cast-iron column supports, which made it economical and simple to build. Yet it has frequently been described as a piece of confectionary, a kind of architectural amusement meant to delight but hardly to instruct the eye. Such buildings would not influence architecture. They demonstrated only what could be done, not what should be done, and they expressed an interest on the part of the public in exotic architectural ideas. Given the romantic infatuation with Islam and the Turkish-controlled lands of Greece, it may well have been inevitable that something like Nash's building would appeal to the English. Certainly, countless English poems and novels were set in the near east, which fed an appetite for unusual environments, cultures, and practices.

Figure 16-16
John Nash. Royal Pavilion, Brighton. 1815–1817. (Photo, A. F. Kerstin, London.)

Figure 16-17
Henri Labrouste. Library of Sainte-Geneviève, Paris. 1843–1850. (Caisse Nationale des Monuments Historiques, Paris; photo, J. Feuillie/ © CNMHS/SPADEM/VAGA, New York.)

Two interesting buildings in Paris offer a useful contrast. The first, by Henri Labrouste (1801–1875), is the library of Sainte-Geneviève (1843–1850; Figure 16-17), in which James Joyce once studied. The second, by Charles Garnier (1825–1898), is the Paris Opera (1861–1874; Figure 16-18).

Nash's Royal Pavilion is a fantasy. Many designs of the period were. The fusion of gothic and classical forms is a fantasy, like the revival of ancient styles. Fantasy is a relative of the imagination, and it does for romantic architecture what the imagination does for romantic poetry. Labrouste's somber facade for the library is hardly an expression of fantasy. However, the interior of the building depends on slender iron posts which almost seem to be made of gossamer,

in contrast to the massive interior that we might expect from looking at the outside. The building is low, solid, and marked by repeated Roman arches. The detailing is simple; the appeal is to the mind and not to the senses. Though not severe, it is clear, undisturbed, and practical.

None of this is true of Garnier's Paris Opera, which is as lavish as we would expect the sets for its productions to be. There is a touch of fantasy in the paired columns, derived from the Louvre, which are built on a solid base of arches that might have been borrowed from Labrouste. The surfaces of the opera are encrusted with sculpture and decoration, which was intended to suggest richness and lavishness but which has caused it to be considered both overdone

Figure 16-18
Charles Garnier. Opera, Paris. 1825–1898. (Photo, J. Feuillie/ © CNMHS/SPADEM/VAGA, New York.)

Henri Labrouste and Charles Garnier

1. Is either the library of Sainte-Geneviève (Figure 16-17) or the Paris Opera (Figure 16-18) more obviously neoclassical?

2. Which forms are repeated in each building? Which building has more variety in the repetitions?

3. Which building is more heavily decorated? Which is more explicitly interested in its emotional effect? What kinds of emotional effects do you feel are evoked by each building?

4. One of these buildings has been described as "overdone and vulgar." Which would it be? Is this a reasonable description?

5. One building is a library; one is an opera house. In what ways is the design of each building appropriate to its function?

---

and vulgar. The charge of vulgarity is due to the fact that the taste of the rising industrialists of the 1850s ordinarily expressed itself in the most flashy, the most lavish, and the most obviously expensive manner. Restraint, a classical virtue, could hardly be recommended to those adventurers who had made their fortunes quickly and wanted to demonstrate their wealth to the rest of the world. On the other hand, the values associated with the library are those of toil, scholarship, history, and patience. The intensely sensual experience of the opera, not to mention the social importance of being seen there, naturally resulted in a building whose decoration is on an appropriate scale.

Literature

Edgar Allan Poe in America, Victor-Marie Hugo in France, Aleksandr Pushkin in Russia, and many lesser writers in other nations defended romantic credos and the romantic spirit. The most influential poets, however, were those in Germany and England; others rapidly followed their lead.

We see the strongest expression of romanticism in Blake, Wordsworth, Coleridge, Shelley, and Byron. In Germany, Goethe shaped the values of romanticism—an international, widespread, and

powerful drive to elevate the imagination and explore the human estate—by probing into its deepest emotional and psychological reaches. The romantics measured themselves against the best writers of the past, risked madness, and explored, as Goya did in *Los Caprichos,* the darker recesses of the mind and of feeling. They began a revolution, and the age of reason was their target.

A trend toward democratization is one of the clearest romantic qualities of the period. A certain "reverse snobbery" is apparent in the work of Wordsworth and Coleridge, who felt that common people were fitter subjects for poetry than the more socially elevated. Poets often described a world dominated by social revolution but frightened by the tyrannies of Napoleonic conquest.

Constable's affection for landscape had its counterpart in literature: a profound respect for nature which was so strong that some romantic poetry seems to be "nature poetry." Wordsworth, in his "Lines Composed a Few Miles above Tintern Abbey," examined his responses to nature over a period of years. Both Wordsworth and Constable thought of the landscape as a suitable subject for serious work. Wordsworth thought that maintaining a connection with nature was essential to spiritual growth. And, unlike the writers of the age of reason, he did not want to show that reason is superior to nature.

Rather, he demonstrated that no matter how strongly we are guided by reason, we are always intimately involved with the powers of nature, even those which are stormy, passionate, and dark.

THE ENGLISH ROMANTIC POETS

William Blake

Blake (1757–1827), who usually illustrated his work, was among the first true romantic poets. *Songs of Innocence* (1789) and *Songs of Experience* (1794) seem close to children's rhymes. Their meter is simple and lilting, and yet the sentiments are anything but simple. These poems attempt to show the soft, human side of people, as well as the terrible and frightening side. Blake's subject matter is moral innocence and moral experience. His inspiration was Milton's *Paradise Lost*, in which the innocence of Adam and Eve is converted into sin. Blake is not a simple poet.

No brief discussion can touch on all the qualities of Blake's work, but its range is demonstrated in two poems from *Songs of Innocence* and *Songs of Experience* which contrast with each other: "The Lamb" a song of innocence, and "The Tyger," a song of experience.

The Lamb
  Little Lamb, who made thee?
  Dost thou know who made thee?
Gave thee life & bid thee feed,
By the stream & o'er the mead;
Gave thee clothing of delight,
Softest clothing wooly bright;
Gave thee such a tender voice,
Making all the vales rejoice!
  Little Lamb who made thee?
  Dost thou know who made thee?

  Little Lamb I'll tell thee,
  Little Lamb I'll tell thee!
He is called by thy name,
For he calls himself a Lamb:
He is meek & he is mild,
He became a little child:
I a child & thou a lamb,
We are called by his name.
  Little Lamb God bless thee.
  Little Lamb God bless thee.

The Tyger
Tyger! Tyger! burning bright
In the forests of the night,
What immortal hand or eye
Could frame thy fearful symmetry?

PERCEPTION KEY

"The Lamb" and "The Tyger"

1. In what ways are "The Lamb" and "The Tyger" a study of opposites? Consider the rhyme, the rhythm, the stanza pattern, and the subject matter.

2. What within "The Lamb" alludes to or suggests innocence? What within "The Tyger" suggests experience?

3. What aspects of nature are explored in these poems? Do they make one feel fearful of nature or reassured by it?

4. If these poems are symbolic, as many people suggest, what might the symbolic meanings be? What does the lamb usually represent symbolically? What qualities of the tiger might be construed as symbolic in the context of the lamb?

5. What aspects of human nature are explored in each poem? Can these poems be thought of as psychological?

In what distant deeps or skies
Burnt the fire of thine eyes?
On what wings dare he aspire?
What the hand, dare seize the fire?

And what shoulder, & what art,
Could twist the sinews of thy heart?
And when thy heart began to beat,
What dread hand? & what dread feet?

What the hammer? what the chain?
In what furnace was thy brain?
What the anvil? what dread grasp
Dare its deadly terrors clasp?

When the stars threw down their spears,
And water'd heaven with their tears,
Did he smile his work to see?
Did he who made the Lamb make thee?

Tyger! Tyger! burning bright
In the forests of the night,
What immortal hand or eye
Dare frame thy fearful symmetry?

These poems represent the core of Blake's *Songs of Innocence* and *Songs of Experience*. The lamb symbolizes Christ, as it has since the early days of the church. Blake helps us feel the innocence of the lamb by making the poem seem like a children's rhyme. The rhythm is comforting, solacing, and reassuring. The image of Christ makes us feel threatened neither by nature nor by the world. But the contrary image of the predatory tiger does not represent the devil. Rather, it represents the forces of nature that are savage, brutal, and terrifying. The poems ask the question: Should nature be thought of as benevolent, the creation of a merciful god, or as threatening, perhaps the creation of a god of wrath?

Much of the body of Blake's work—*The Marriage of Heaven and Hell, The Book of Thel, Milton,* and *America: A Prophecy*—is inspired and visionary, the way his painting is visionary. Blake respected myth, but instead of using Greek and Roman sources, he created a native myth. His character Albion, an ancient name for England, dominates much of his poetry. Liberty and the release of human energy also find expression in his work. As he said, "The same law for the lion and the ox is tyranny." The implications of such a statement were clear to the romantic poets who sang of independence and the individual.

Blake's connection with the poets of the age of reason is evident in *The Marriage of Heaven and Hell* (1790–1793), an illustrated book that includes "The

Proverbs of Hell," an inversion of Proverbs in the Bible. They show that Blake believed that the tyranny of social conventions produced psychological repression. Emotions had to be expressed, or they would fester and destroy the individual. He was sympathetic with many views developed later by Freud. Some of his proverbs are:

The road of excess leads to the palace of wisdom.
Prudence is a rich ugly old maid courted by Incapacity.
He who desires but acts not, breeds pestilence.
A fool sees not the same tree the wise man sees.
Prisons are built with the stones of Law, Brothels with bricks of Religion.
The tygers of wrath are wiser than the horses of instruction.

These proverbs oppose the axioms of the eighteenth-century poets. But Blake's talent in this form shows that for him, poetry had some of the same functions as it did for Pope: to instruct people and inspire them to improve.

Wordsworth and Coleridge: Preface to Lyrical Ballads

The fullest bloom of English romanticism begins with the collaboration of William Wordsworth (1770–1850) and Samuel Taylor Coleridge (1772–1834). Their *Lyrical Ballads* was published in 1798; the Preface was added in 1800. The ballad form, a folk idiom, derived its energy from the people and was not considered elevated enough for most poetic thought. This work, then, was inspired, democratic, and revolutionary. It includes one poem of immortal value by each man: Wordsworth's "Lines Composed a Few Miles above Tintern Abbey" and Coleridge's "Rime of the Ancient Mariner."

In the Preface, which was revised in 1802, Wordsworth tells us that he and Coleridge experimented with poems that used "the real language of men in a state of vivid sensation." He wanted to

. . . give a full account of the present state of the public taste in this country, and to determine how far this taste is healthy or depraved; which, again, could not be determined, without pointing out, in what manner language and the human mind act and re-act on each other, and without retracing the revolutions, not of literature alone, but likewise of society itself.

The heart of the theory is in Wordsworth's summary of his purposes:

The principal object, then, which I proposed to myself in these poems was to choose incidents and situations from common life, and to relate or describe them, throughout, as far as was possible, in a selection of language really used by men; and, at the same time, to throw over them a certain coloring of imagination, whereby ordinary things should be presented to the mind in an unusual way. . . . Low and rustic life was generally chosen, because in that condition, the essential passions of the heart find a better soil in which they can attain their maturity . . . and speak a plainer and more emphatic language.

From that time on, older poetic diction would sound stilted.

William Wordsworth

Wordsworth's "Ruined Cottage," "Michael," and "Lucy" are all in the spirit of his declarations in the Preface. "Tintern Abbey" celebrates a joyfulness in nature, but Wordsworth adds interesting complications. The poet addresses himself to his sister, Dorothy, with whom he is walking in a locale familiar to him from a solitary walk that he took there some five years earlier. He realizes that his heart has often been stirred by memories of this rural environment, that this place has reached into his inner being, and that by contemplating nature, "We see into the life of things." He also realizes that he was closer to nature when he was younger. Now he sees that youthful zeal in his sister, and he celebrates their sharing of the experience. He declares himself "a worshiper of Nature . . . unwearied in that service."

Samuel Taylor Coleridge

Coleridge agreed with Wordsworth's view of the mission of poetry, although the two had different opinions regarding the expression of the philosophy of romanticism. Coleridge's "Rime of the Ancient Mariner," from *Lyrical Ballads,* provided a full-length ballad for the collection and introduced the theme of living with respect for all nature's creatures.

His summary of the poem is

How a Ship, having first sailed to the Equator, was driven by storms to the cold Country towards the South Pole; how the Ancient Mariner cruelly and in contempt of the laws of hospitality killed a Seabird and how he was followed by many and strange Judgements: and in what manner he came back to his own country.

Coleridge's image of the mariner with an albatross—the murdered seabird—tied around his neck has become part of our language. The adventures on a cursed sea are harrowing, humiliating, and in some ways inhuman. The mariner, haunted by spirits, sees the vision of death in life and proceeds on his journey until he is on the verge of madness. When his horror is over, he is condemned to wander, telling his story to one of every three people he meets. As he tells the wedding guest before he lets him go:

"He prayeth well, who loveth well
Both man and bird and beast.
He prayeth best, who loveth best
All things both great and small;
For the dear God who loveth us,
He made and loveth all."

Coleridge, like Wordsworth, traveled extensively. He was influenced by German literature and German idealist philosophy. His most influential work is *Biographia Literaria,* finished in 1815 but not published until 1817. In it he attempted a critique of the concepts of poetic language that Wordsworth had developed in his Preface. Coleridge disagreed concerning the similarity between the language of poetry and the language of ordinary discourse, except in certain kinds of poetry. He quarreled with the word "real" in Wordsworth's defense of "language taken . . . from the mouths of men in real life." Coleridge clearly disagreed with Wordsworth on this point, but not so fully as to disparage his views.

Coleridge distinguished between fancy and the imagination. Fancy was a mechanical mental faculty that joined together disparate elements to form new concoctions. He called it a "mode of memory emancipated from the order of time and space . . . it must receive all its materials ready made from the law of association." But the imagination, a far grander faculty, he associated with Milton. It was, as he said, "the living power and prime agent of perception." It was vaster and more creative than fancy, a divine force linked to God himself.

Wordsworth and Coleridge

1. Read Wordsworth's "Ode: Intimations of Immortality from Recollections of Early Childhood" and Coleridge's "Dejection: An Ode." Compare the use of language. Which poem is more formal? Which poem is more concerned with the language of everyday life? In which does the thought seem more profound? Which is more philosophical? Which is lighter-hearted? Does either poem have qualities which you feel are not romantic?

2. Do Wordsworth and Coleridge seem concerned with nature? Is there a sense of nature's being both threatening and comforting, as in Blake's poems on the tiger and the lamb?

3. Wordsworth and Coleridge are autobiographical in much of their poetry. What might the implications of autobiographical poetry be for establishing the character of romantic verse?

Lord Byron

The most international poet of the age, George Gordon, known as Lord Byron (1788–1824), was educated at Cambridge, where he took a master's degree before setting forth on a tour of the continent. *Childe Harold's Pilgrimage,* published in 1812, made him renowned almost overnight. (He said, "I awoke one morning and found myself famous.") The poem is a "romaunt," or romance. The taste for romances— adventure stories that often included knights and damsels in distress and mythic battles with evil tyrants—was so widespread in the late eighteenth century that the term "romantic" was derived from them. *Childe Harold* made Byron not only famous but also independently wealthy. Its regular nine-line stanzas and archaic diction give it an antique feeling. Byron played masterfully on the romantic nostalgia for the antique. (Another poet of the antique, Thomas Chatterton, 1752–1770, achieved fame by writing an imitation of Chaucerian verse. Unfortunately, he tried to pass off his work as original, and when his "forgery" was found out, he killed himself. He may have been the most gifted preromantic poet. He died at the age of nineteen.)

Childe Harold was a knight-to-be (which is what "childe" means). In defiance of Wordsworth, the poem adopts many archaisms as a way of distancing the language from everyday speech. Lines such as "Childe Harold was he hight," meaning "He was called Childe Harold," mark the early passages of the poem. But later, the style becomes simpler, more direct, and more passionate. Byron's technical facility with difficult forms is apparent in the following stanza from Canto 3:

> Tis to create, and in creating live
> A being more intense, that we endow
> With form our fancy, gaining as we give
> The life we image, even as I do now.
> What am I? Nothing: but not so art thou,
> Soul of my thought: with whom I traverse earth,
> Invisible but gazing, as I glow
> Mixed with thy spirit, blended with thy birth,
> And feeling still with thee in my crushed feelings'
>   dearth.

Byron's subject is his imagination and its product, Childe Harold. As a young person who is struggling, traveling, seeing the world, and opening himself up to deep feelings, and a wide range of human contact, Childe Harold projects Byron's own experience. The poem is a self-portrait, but it is a portrait of the striving and emotion that lie within. Byron's hero strives without ceasing. He is an adventurer for whom the world is rich, ever-changing, and thrilling.

Byron created heroic figures loosely modeled on himself. Childe Harold is young, striving, energetic, intense, and attractive; he has charisma. The most intense Byronic hero is a man of middle age: Manfred. Byron was inspired to write *Manfred,* a closet drama, when in 1816 he heard a friend read a free translation of Goethe's *Faust,* a modern version of Marlowe's play, which Byron did not know.

The poem begins with Manfred brooding over an unrevealed sin, possibly incest with his sister Astarte, who has committed suicide. People have assumed from this that Byron was working out his own sense of guilt over his incestuous relationship with his sister (who was alive at the time). Manfred is a human version of Milton's Satan: his aspirations are unlimited, and he risks all for intellectual passions. When he is besieged by devilish spirits during a night of terror, he does not yield. He holds firm to his own views and refuses to be in league with the spirits. He eventually dies of exhaustion, but as he dies, he says:

> "What I have done is done; I bear within
> A torture which could nothing gain from thine:
> The mind which is immortal makes itself
> Requital for its good or evil thoughts. . . .
> *Thou* didst not tempt me, and thou couldst not tempt
>   me;
> I have not been thy dupe nor am thy prey—

> But was my own destroyer, and will be
> My own hereafter.—Back, ye baffled fiends!
> The hand of death is on me—but not yours!"

Thus, Manfred places his humanity on a level with that of the immortal power of the devil. His death is a triumph of the will on the part of a hero who can cope with the gods on an equal footing.

John Keats

John Keats (1795–1821) died of tuberculosis at the age of twenty-six. He was never able to write a major book-length poem, and yet his odes stand as the most masterful in English poetry. His three greatest—"Ode to a Nightingale," "Ode on a Grecian Urn," and "To Autumn"—were all written in a single year, 1819; their subject is impermanence. Life, as Keats well knew from watching his family die and from struggling with his own illness, is fleeting. His knowledge that he would die before he could produce a large body of work led him to ask for this inscription on his tombstone: "Here lies one whose name is writ on water."

Fortunately, he achieved more than he realized. In his rhapsody on a Grecian urn (a composite of several he had seen) he celebrates the fact that the people represented on it would not die, would not change.

PERCEPTION KEY

Byron and Keats

1. Would Byron agree with Keats's view of the Grecian urn as a symbol of perfection or of beauty?

2. What do the fourth and fifth lines of "Ode on a Grecian Urn" say about Keats's respect for the urn and what it stands for? Is there uncertainty in his tone?

3. In some printed versions of the poem the last two lines are in quotation marks, indicating that they are "spoken" by the urn. How does this change the message of the urn?

4. What does it mean to insist that "Beauty is truth, truth beauty"?

5. Since this is a Grecian urn, the poem has classical roots. If possible, read the entire ode. In what sense is the poem classical or influenced by a classical view? In what sense is it romantic?

The urn would always exist as a symbol of beauty and inspiration. The famous last stanza reveals his ambivalence as he regards its "cold" beauty:

> O Attic shape! Fair attitude! with Brede   *pattern
> Of marble men and maidens overwrought,
> With forest branches and the trodden weed;
>   Thou, silent form, dost tease us out of thought
> As doth eternity: Cold Pastoral!
>   When old age shall this generation waste,
>   Thou shalt remain, in midst of other woe
> Than ours, a friend to man, to whom thou say'st,
>   "Beauty is truth, truth beauty,"—that is all
>   Ye know on earth, and all ye need to know.

ROMANTIC POETRY IN GERMANY

Johann Wolfgang von Goethe

Goethe (1749–1832), the foremost intellectual of his time, lived much of his life in Weimar, the center of German romanticism. His studies had introduced him to alchemy and other occult sciences that found their way into *Faust*. But Goethe was not only a literary figure. His scientific writing fills fourteen volumes, and he made permanent contributions to physics.

Goethe's literary achievements were startling from the first. He came under the influence of Johann Gottfried von Herder (1744–1803), a writer whose work contributed to the sturm and drang—storm and stress—literary movement, which was related to the Byronic hero and derived its name from a play of that title by Friedrich Maximilian von Klinger (1752–1831). Sturm und drang was marked by profound emotional energy: great heights and great depths of passion as well as striking restlessness. Goethe's first dramatic success, *Götz von Berlichingen* (1773), a play invoking German mythical sources, and *The Sorrows of Young Werther,* a cult novel which Napoleon carried with him to war, fueled the movement. Young people throughout Europe were moved by the story of Werther's growth to manhood and by his intense, unrequited love. Werther's suicide was imitated widely by both men and women, and the novel was banned in many communities. Because the book was personal and was a contribution to the romantic affection for the self-portrait, Goethe was shocked by the degree to which readers saw it as a portrait of themselves.

Goethe's Faust

Faust (Part 1, 1808; Part 2, 1832), like Byron's *Manfred,* places its hero in a world in which materialism is not a worthwhile goal in life. We might interpret the play as looking backward to a time when it was not thought unusual that people would traffic with devils, and for this reason we can see it as nostalgic, in the same way that much romantic art is nostalgic. But it is forward-looking too, since it concentrates on probing into the inward Faust—the psychological Faust—and what it finds is a moral uncertainty, a darkness of spirit, that is as frightening as that of Manfred. The romantic willingness to search into the depths of human psychology indicated a desire to go beyond the implications of terms such as "optimism" and "pessimism." For the romantics, Goethe signaled a willingness to look at people as they truly are, even at the risk of seeing a frightening vision.

Like Marlowe's Dr. Faustus, Goethe's Faust is larger than life—a romantic figure who dares all, risks all, and experiences all. He lives life at such an extreme pitch that his daring redeems him. He is a model, in some ways, for the romantic temper, which insinuated itself into the lives of many romantic artists.

Early Romantic Music

Because the classical style in music extended into the second decade of the nineteenth century, establishing historical limits for romantic music presents difficulties. The period 1800–1914 will constitute its range for us. Ludwig van Beethoven bridges both styles and was the major force of the earlier one. In addition to Beethoven, we will consider Franz Peter Schubert and Frédéric-François Chopin.

INSTRUMENTAL MUSIC

As a result of the excitement generated by the intense sonorities of newly improved instruments and larger orchestras, new concert spaces were built, some of which were theaters, and new audiences flocked to them. Furthermore, the development of the pianoforte permitted Beethoven, Schubert, and

Chopin to create piano works rivaling those for orchestra. The audience for music went far beyond the limits of the aristocracy of Haydn and Mozart's time, and that fact freed composers to create for themselves rather than for patrons. Musicologists point out that Haydn wore the livery of a servant for most of his musical life, whereas Beethoven could openly insult the aristocracy and still be in overwhelming demand.

OPERA AND OTHER VOCAL MUSIC

The chief vocal music of the period was opera, particularly the French "rescue" opera, which involved melodramatic heroism, excitement, and plenty of action. Beethoven's one opera, *Fidelio*, is among the best of the genre. *Lucia di Lammermoor*, by Gaetano Donizetti (1797–1848), based on Sir Walter Scott's novel *The Bride of Lammermoor*, may also be considered to be in this category. Donizetti was only one of many successful Italian opera composers of the period. Masses were also still being written; one of the greatest examples of the form is Beethoven's Missa "Solemnis." But the most distinctive vocal music of the age was the lied, or art song: an interpretation of text by a singer and a pianist. Schubert was the best-known composer of art songs, and some of Beethoven's work in the genre is especially beautiful.

QUALITIES OF ROMANTIC MUSIC

Romantic music differs from classical music in several basic and profound ways. First, the value of sound itself is emphasized far more than in classical compositions. In late romantic music, oceans of sound sometimes transport the listener; in the late symphonies of Beethoven, complex and huge sonorities of the entire orchestra combine to achieve such an effect. Further, the desire to affect the emotions of the listener is so great that in some instances formal demands are abandoned. The romantic composers have been described as probing into their own emotional lives in order to move their audiences. This is the first age in which people spoke seriously about composers' "expressing themselves."

Apart from an intense interest in the sensa of sound, the music of the early nineteenth century displays an affection for the "singing," extended melodic line. In some commentaries, romantic music

is described as little more than melody with accompaniment. This means that the polyphonic forms of earlier ages, including the resourceful fugue (a favorite device of Beethoven, who liked it in final movements), are rarely in evidence. Instead, the themes of many symphonies of the period are "singable" melodies. The first theme is usually extended and emotionally powerful. Contrasting themes are quiet, sonorous, and limited. Such contrasts are not maintained rigidly, but they are often present in important works. The concentration on melody meant that the resources of harmony were developed extensively, and much that is distinctive in the music of the age is evident in daring harmonic relationships, shifting tonal centers, and a reluctance to permit the musical line to come to rest in cadences of the sort evident in Mozart's work (see the discussion of the "Jupiter" Symphony in Chapter 15).

PROGRAM MUSIC

Some music of the classical period alludes to events or places, but such allusions are relatively short. Romantic music often describes events musically, as the "storm" in Beethoven's "Pastoral" Symphony does. Mendelssohn's *Fingal's Cave* overture and his *Midsummer Night's Dream* are typical of romantic program music based on literary themes. Shakespeare was the literary figure who most inspired romantic composers. Often a geographic location—such as the Hebrides—inspired an intense, emotional work. But the program favored by the romantics was the mapping out of the interior of the soul, by which is meant the exploration of the inner life of the emotions. Composers who used such programs depended in part on Jean-Jacques Rousseau's *Confessions*, which suggests that if one can know oneself fully and honestly, one can know humankind, because what one person is capable of, all humanity is capable of. The stormy inner life of Beethoven, for example, is accessible to us because we can recognize in his music shapes that are cognate with our own expressions of emotion.

LUDWIG VAN BEETHOVEN

The personal agony of Beethoven (1770–1827) began when, at the age of twenty-nine, he began to lose his hearing. Eventually, he became completely deaf. His hearing loss caused him to avoid society, which made him deeply unhappy. In a letter written in 1801 he says: "You would hardly believe how lonely and sad my life has been for the last two years. My bad hearing haunted me like a ghost and I fled from mankind, must have seemed a misanthropist and yet am so far from being one." Beethoven was keenly aware of the implications of deafness for a composer, and some of his writings indicate that he considered suicide at times.

Beethoven's Early Period

One of Beethoven's earliest biographers established three periods of development in his musical life. The first, 1794 to 1800, is marked by an indebtedness to Haydn and Mozart. The works are formally accurate, clear, and intelligible to any audience familiar with eighteenth-century music. The first two symphonies belong to this period. Although early, they have the fullness, power, dark tone color, and structural details of his later work.

Beethoven built his symphonies from melodic material that sometimes looks as if it consisted of scraps. Yet his capacity to explore a melody was so extraordinary, and his ability to "mine" a musical motif for its hidden content was so inexhaustible, that he was able to construct amazing and delightful works. His attention to dynamics—the loudness and softness of given passages—is reflected in his concern for powerful orchestral sound. His most popular early composition was the Septet in E flat major for Strings and Winds, Opus 20. It was such a crowd pleaser that it was requested wherever he went, and he grew to dislike it.

The first two piano concertos, the first six string quartets, and numerous minor works date from this period. Each of them is quite recognizable as deriving from the works of earlier composers, but each has a touch of the later Beethoven. One of his most characteristic techniques is that of rising to a powerful full-volume sound and then softening it instantly. Another is the inclusion of details and material which seem to have been invented on the spot (Beethoven was a famous improviser on the piano) and woven into the musical fabric. The effect is always pleasing, but often unexpected.

Beethoven's Second Period

The years 1801 to 1814 saw Beethoven in Vienna—the city was then at the height of its musical glory but

Figure 16-19
Ludwig van Beethoven. Symphony Number 5 in C Minor, Opus 67, opening theme. 1807.

was also shelled and occupied by Napoleon (for whom Beethoven had earlier felt admiration). Vienna was thus unsettled, but there was still a great demand for concerts and for compositions to be played at them. Beethoven was unusual in that he could support himself well by composing: so many publishers vied for his works that he once said that when it came to fees, he asked and they paid. This made it possible for him to compose only what he wished to. His independence of spirit is a quality that has become associated with romanticism, and though Beethoven is a transitional figure, his fiery nature, his reaching deep within himself, and his expression of profound emotions all mark him as romantic.

The great compositions of the second period include the Third Symphony ("Eroica") through the Sixth Symphony ("Pastoral"), especially the brilliant Fifth Symphony in C minor, Opus 67, with its famous motif, shown in Figure 16-19, which Beethoven described as "fate knocking at the door." (The ingenuity with which that motif is stated and varied by different families of instruments is extraordinary.) Other important works from this period are the Concerto in D major for Violin; the Fourth Piano Concerto and the Fifth Piano Concerto ("Emperor"); the piano sonatas Number 14 ("Moonlight"), Number 21 ("Waldstein"), and Number 23 ("Appassionata"); the Opus 59 quartets ("Rasoumovsky"); and his one opera, *Fidelio*.

Symphony Number 3 in E flat Major, Opus 55, "Eroica"

The Third Symphony, subtitled "Eroica" ("Heroic"), is said to have been Beethoven's own favorite among his symphonies. According to legend, Beethoven, believing that Napoleon shared his ideas of liberty and freedom, intended to dedicate the "Eroica" to him. But when the symphony was finished in 1804, Napoleon had crowned himself emperor. This undemocratic gesture is said to have caused Beethoven to declare that Napoleon was nothing but an ordinary, ambitious sovereign, and he tore up the dedication.

Perhaps the story is true; Beethoven did erase Napoleon's name from the title page, although later his attitude toward Napoleon was ambiguous. The Third Symphony, nonetheless, is properly heroic. For one thing, it is immense. Even Mozart's "Jupiter" Symphony is small in scale by comparison. Moreover, the "Eroica" contains suggestions of military material, particularly in the second movement, which is a funeral march. The symphony is not programmatic, but is pure music—which is to say that it is a formal structure whose effect arises from the organization of its material, not from any narrative or association with outside references. It strives to interpret a wide range of emotions. Among them, particularly in the first and last movements, are those associated with triumph and victory over complications. The musical complications are associated with the established key of the symphony and episodes in contrasting keys which create and resolve tension in highly imaginative ways by unfolding the hidden resources of the basic material. The movement from key to key and the resolution of key-based tensions are among Beethoven's greatest achievements.

In preparation for the following discussion, listen to the entire symphony; then listen to it again as each movement is described. First, notice that the symphony is daunting in its length. Gone are the Haydn-esque clarity of sound, the lightness, and the straightforward treatment of lyric themes or motifs. Instead, we have a new instrumentation: a dominance of the dark, low-register cellos and contrabasses; a deep power in the brasses and horns; and a liquid contrast in the flutes and reeds. The rhythms are intense; the pace is exhausting. The melodic material is in many ways quite simple; much of it is built on basic triadic chords. The contrasts are dramatic and the development is always surprising. Beethoven uses the resources of all the families of instruments: horn, woodwind, string, and percussion. The musical material builds to huge crescendos and then suddenly drops to softness, and in those periods of softness the music builds very slowly, as if renewing its vigor, until it grows to even greater volume and energy. The cadences are sometimes withheld to build more tension, but when they are heard they are strong, full, and complete.

The first movement is marked allegro con brio — fast and spiritedly. It is long and energetic, a hallmark of romantic music. The movement begins with two full chords (see Figure 16-20) in the basic key of the symphony. Then at the third measure the main theme of the movement is introduced (see Figure 16-21). We hear the theme first in the low register in the cellos. A new theme, the first of several transitional subjects, enters at bar 45 (Figure 16-22), a descending pattern of three notes that moves from instrument to instrument almost as if it were being chased.

Allegro con brio

Vln. I

Figure 16-20
Left: Beethoven. Symphony Number 3 in E flat Major, Opus 55, "Eroica," opening chord. 1803.

Figure 16-21
Below: Beethoven. Symphony Number 3, main theme from first movement.

Cello

Figure 16-22
Right: Beethoven. Symphony Number 3, transitional theme from first-movement exposition.

Figure 16-23
Beethoven. Symphony Number 3, theme from second movement.

Figure 16-24
Beethoven. Symphony Number 3, theme from fourth movement.

The two subjects are distinct from each other. The first is sustained and lengthy—almost songlike—while the second is brief and fragmentary. Yet they complement each other and offer unusual resources for development. The development section has several quiet passages that suggest mysterious, tremulous changes in the material. The recapitulation, which begins at bar 398, abruptly shifts to a restatement of the first theme in a new key by the horns at bar 408; it continues until bar 556, leading into a totally unanticipated second development section which gives way to a long, slow, quiet passage just before the final coda, itself a passage of incredible power and rushing energy.

The second movement is marked marcia funebre, adagio assai—"funeral march, very slow." The main theme (Figure 16-23) is plaintive and slow and is marked (in the third complete bar) by a kind of "snap" rhythm, typical of Beethoven: the beat is subdivided so that an accented short note precedes an unaccented long note. At approximately bar 214 the movement quietly picks up, and it ends not with a sense of unrelieved sadness but rather with a sense that there will be change. The unstable ending makes us anticipate the next movement.

The third movement is marked scherzo, allegro vivace—"fast and lively." Literally a joke in sprightly dance time, it is a welcome contrast to the preceding funeral march. The choice of a scherzo instead of a slow, stately dance in this movement was another of Beethoven's innovations. Near the end of the movement passages in the horns sound like fanfares, and

its final section is so solidly in E flat major that it virtually sounds like a repeat of earlier material.

The fourth movement, allegro molto ("very fast"), does not begin with the theme that will eventually dominate it. After a brief opening flourish, the music drops to near-silence as the strings play the opening theme (Figure 16-24) pizzicato (that is, plucked rather than bowed). When the main theme does enter at bar 76, played by the oboe and clarinet, we discover that the original pizzicato theme is the bass line accompanying it, played here by the cellos, basses, horns, and bassoons. Beethoven has introduced and developed the opening theme so imaginatively that it may seem difficult at bar 76 to say which is the main theme and which the accompaniment.

At bar 117 the first violins introduce what turns out to be an elaborate fugue with the simple theme of Figure 16-24 as the principal subject. After the fugue, at bar 348, an andante ("rather slow") section begins; here the main theme of the movement dominates. The simplicity of this melodic line contrasts with the marches, dance rhythms, funereal passages, and fugues of the rest of the work. The andante rises to a climax in which the main theme is played fortissimo by several of the dark-sounding instruments: horns, clarinets, bassoons, cellos, and basses.

The slow passage is followed immediately by the concluding presto ("quite fast"). At first, groups of instruments enter one after another with fragments of themes, as if contending for supremacy. The rhythm becomes more intense and insistent until the movement ends on its huge, final cadence.

Beethoven's Symphony Number 3 in E Flat Major, Opus 55, "Eroica"

Some available recordings are Columbia M-31822, RCA AGL1-1525, RL32052, and CBS MY37222.

1. Listen to the first theme of the first movement (see also Figure 16-21). Establish its pattern and then listen for the pattern in later passages. How often is it repeated? Do you find yourself welcoming its repetitions?

2. How effective is the second movement as a contrast to the first? In what ways, specifically, does there seem to be a contrast between them? Consider melodies, rhythms, tempo, tone color, and instruments.

3. Why does Beethoven use a funeral march in the second movement? Does the first movement imply the death of the hero (or anyone else)? Do you think that the funeral march is for the dead hero?

4. Does the scherzo seem musically related to the first and second movements?

5. Listen to the movements of the symphony out of order. Does any order other than the right one make you feel that the work is complete, coherent, and satisfying? Have someone play the beginning of one movement. How long did it take you to recognize the movement? What is most recognizable about it?

6. The final movement is filled with energy and unusual fugal passages. Does this movement bring the symphony to a satisfactory close for you? Explore some of your expectations and the disjunction between what you expected and what you receive. Donald Grout says that the symphony "stands as an immortal expression in music of heroic greatness." Do you perceive that expression of heroism?

Beethoven's Third Period

1815, a difficult year for Beethoven, marks the beginning of his third and last period of development. The Napoleonic wars were over, and the Congress of Vienna had determined the nature of the peace. Musical tastes had changed. The politicians needed relief, as did the war-weary Viennese. Therefore, light music of various kinds was in demand. Very little of Beethoven's music was popular. Moreover, his hearing was so bad that he had to give up performing. His personal life was racked by a legal fight for guardianship of his nephew, Karl.

The music of the third period is often rather dark in tone color, highly personal, and difficult to follow. Yet it is music of the very highest quality. Nothing like it had ever been written before, and while the music of the second period dominates the concert stage today, it is the music of the third period that many lovers of Beethoven thrill to most. The great Symphony Number 9 in D minor, Opus 125 ("Choral")—gigantic in size and with a final movement that incorporates solo voices and chorus singing the romantic poet Schiller's "Ode to Joy"—became the inspiration for symphonies of the late nineteenth and early twentieth centuries. It is a sublime piece of music with an unprecedented symphonic dimension. To this period also belongs Missa "Solemnis" in D major, Opus 123. The last piano sonatas (Opuses 101, 106, 109, 110, and 111, which are dark, difficult, and thrilling); the great last string quartets

(Opuses 127, 130, 131, 132, and 135); and the Great Fugue (Opus 133) all would have established any composer as a genius.

Astonishingly, Beethoven was totally deaf when he composed these works. Legend has it that after the first performance of the Ninth Symphony, Beethoven, who was on the stage facing the orchestra, had to be turned around to see the crowd applauding; he had feared that the work was a failure. Beethoven composed with his "inner ear." His last works demand much of the listener. The music is emotional and intense, and in it Beethoven works out advanced problems and musical implications.

FRANZ PETER SCHUBERT

Schubert did not live long enough for his work to be divided into periods. He was born in 1797 and died of typhoid fever in 1828. He composed symphonies, pieces for piano, masses, operatic pieces, chamber works, and over 600 songs.

Unwise about money, Schubert lived a bohemian existence, which gave him an "artistic" aura that still persists in the mind of the public. He was in the center of Viennese intellectual life, and among his friends were artists and poets with whom he often spent an evening in a "Schubertiad"—he played only his music, and his friends danced to his waltzes. Schubert's music is immediate and emotional. Unlike Beethoven, he composed quickly and almost effortlessly.

Schubert is said to have read Goethe's ballad "The Erlking" and to have produced his song of that name immediately. (Such stories about romantic artists are common, but often the evidence of false starts, ruined drafts, and partial sketches contradicts them.) "The Erlking" describes a distraught father riding through a storm with his ailing son in his arms. The boy hears not only his father's voice but also that of the Erlking—the symbol of death. The father, galloping relentlessly through the night, fights to save his son, but in the end the child is dead—taken from his father's arms by the Erlking.

The tension in the narrative derives from the dialogue, with the main characters (all portrayed by a single vocalist) singing alternate stanzas. The child wants to remain with his father, while the Erlking tries to entice him away to the world of the supernatural with promises of flowers, games, and many wondrous things. Tension is achieved by intensifying the piano part and letting it dominate the voice. The powerful, insistent triplets (Figure 16-25) represent the galloping horse and establish a feeling of urgency. The child's lines are sung in a higher key at each entry, so that the emotional intensity keeps increasing. The Erlking sings softly in calming, sonorous tones, usually in a major key and often in an appealing melodic strain designed to lure the boy to the world of the supernatural. The frantic father races onward trying to save his child. At the end, the father reaches his destination, "but the boy was dead in his arms." Even the power of the father's love was insufficient to save his child from the other world.

"The Erlking" is through-composed, meaning that Schubert wrote different music for each stanza, instead of repeating the same music for each one—as would be done in a strophic song. Through-composing can generate a wide variety of emotional effects without regard for repeats. Meanwhile, the rhythm, which presses on and on, maintains the intensity.

Figure 16-25
Franz Schubert. "The Erlking," first three measures, showing triplet rhythm in the piano part. 1815.

FRÉDÉRIC CHOPIN

Like Keats, Chopin (1810–1849) died young of tuberculosis, a disease that had made him frail. He was born in Warsaw, but spent most of his life in exile in Paris. His social circle consisted primarily of writers, musicians, and intellectuals who were themselves prominent romantics. Fortunately, Chopin did not have to earn a living as a performer, although his infrequent public performances made him legendary. He did most of his playing in intimate circumstances, those of the salon, before a small number of friends. On these occasions—which resembled the "Schubertiads"— Chopin reigned supreme.

Most of his work is for piano. There are volumes of études, preludes, waltzes, mazurkas, polonaises, ballades, and nocturnes, as well as concertos and sonatas. It is difficult to give titles to his pieces; one, the so-called "revolutionary étude" (Number 12), may have been written in protest against the Russian invasion of Warsaw in 1831. Yet Chopin's works are often described as tone poems. A tone poem is an effort to achieve in music what a poet achieves in words and ideas. In the case of Mendelssohn and others, the subject is a scene, landscape, event, or emotion, which is usually revealed in the title. In the case of Chopin, the subject is the emotion described, expressed, or excited by the musical structure. A tone poem, like poetry, interprets an emotional state or mood.

Chopin's music is sonorous, lyrical, passionate, and sensuous. Its appeal is not intellectual, but emotional. His nocturnes are appropriate, he felt, to the evening; his preludes seem to anticipate action; his waltzes are filled with romantic exuberance; his mazurkas have an unusual verve. All are filled with a romantic affection for life.

Chopin's Prelude in A major is reprinted in its entirety in Figure 16-26. It is simple, direct, and beautiful. Its effect, for such a short piece, is almost

Figure 16-26
Frédéric Chopin. Prelude in A Major, Opus 28, Number 7. 1839.

miraculous. The melody begins with E and rises immediately to C sharp, thus creating a feeling of anticipation. The final chord is the home chord for the key, A, and provides a satisfactory resting place. The melodic material is simple enough: a cluster of tones reaching through two measures and ending with a single chord repeated three times. The repeated chords are candidates for a full cadence or conclusion. Our ear rejects them, but only after having savored each one, until we reach the final conclusive and pleasurable chord. The last 7 bars build anticipation which is so emotionally complete that the work does not need more than its 17 bars to make it whole.

Chopin had a profound love affair, lasting nine years, with Georges Sand—the pen name of Amandine-Aurore-Lucile Dudevant, a feminist who believed in free love and who dressed in men's clothing to emphasize her independence of convention. Chopin's life was as romantic as his music, which was written to move other romantics—those interested in art and the inner life of the emotions. It reveals the emotional life of his circle of friends, who were among the most interesting people of the age.

Dance

THE WALTZ

The waltz, an "intoxicating" novelty in which couples danced closely and intimately, supplanted the formal, distant minuet of the eighteenth century. Because the waltz was exuberant, was danced to lush and sensuous music, and brought young people into close physical contact, it was often condemned and sometimes even prohibited. It was the most popular dance of the period, and its romantic, sexual nature emphasized the value of emotion, which was both stirred and expressed by the art of the age.

THEATER DANCE: MARIE TAGLIONI AND LA SYLPHIDE

Theater dance was in a decline until the 1820s. Ballet as we think of it today did not exist until Filippo Taglioni (1777–1871) choreographed *La Sylphide* for his daughter, the celebrated and idolized Marie Taglioni (1804–1884; Figure 16-27). *La Sylphide,* choreographed to music written by Chopin, was first performed on March 12, 1832, at the Paris Opera. It is a thoroughly romantic story, quite in

Figure 16-27
Marie Taglioni. (Collection, Stravinsky-Diaghilev Foundation, New York.)

keeping with romantic poetry. James, the hero, is a Scot; he is about to be married to his cousin, Effie, the woman he "should" marry. While he sleeps by his fireplace the night before his wedding, the sylphide appears to him and they kiss. He realizes that he loves the sylphide, not Effie, and he longs for what he cannot have. The story of the ballet thus has close connections with the romantic ambition to achieve the ideal. The power of the imagination is evident in the fact that the sylphide is apparent only to James. Reality and its limits are revealed when a witch gives him a rose-colored scarf that will make the sylphide's wings drop off. James believes that when this happens, the sylphide, unable to escape, will be his. He follows the sylphide into the forest and wraps her in the scarf, and her wings do indeed drop off, but as a result she loses her essential nature and dies.

Marie Taglioni was well known before *La Sylphide* was performed, but afterward she became a legend. Romantic music was dominated by virtuoso performers who were sometimes thought to be possessed. Taglioni was the first of a long line of brilliant ballerinas who qualified as virtuosos. We know relatively little about the way she danced. Illustrations show her hovering slightly above the stage; her movement was always described as "airy," like that of the sylphide herself.

Taglioni invented the technique of dancing "en pointe" in *La Sylphide*: she had the tips of her ballet slippers stuffed with cotton so that she could balance on her toes and give the illusion of gliding or floating across the stage. Today many passages for women in formal ballets are performed en pointe. Another innovation from *La Sylphide* is Taglioni's light, short-skirted white garment, which has become the modern ballet tutu. It suggested airiness, lightness, and motion, while permitting the body to be observed and giving the dancer a heavenly quality.

Philosophy

There were several important developments in philosophy in Germany, France, and England during this period. German idealism, which flourished most fully in the writings of Immanuel Kant (1724–1804), has had innumerable followers and modifiers, including Georg Wilhelm Friedrich Hegel (1770–1831) and Arthur Schopenhauer (1788–1860). Positivism, which affected a number of later movements, was developed in France by Auguste Comte (1798–1857). All these schools of thought affected romantic artists and thus the age.

IMMANUEL KANT AND IDEALISM

Kant's life was a model of machinelike regularity. He was so dependable on his afternoon walks in Königsberg that the local citizens could set their watches by him. Yet he created an intellectual revolution. A professor of physics, he respected the achievements of contemporary scientists, who depended on an analysis of cause and effect to describe and understand natural phenomena.

Kant examined reason to see whether it was possible to have the same kind of knowledge about God, truth, and the good that scientists had about natural phenomena. He began by postulating that although our knowledge begins with experience, it is not limited to experience. Thus, the experience of

witnessing an event may permit us to know about causation. Kant proposed that two kinds of knowledge are possible: phenomenal, which depends on perception, and noumenal, which depends on thought. In some cases intuition—a favorite term of later romantics—assists thought by helping us grasp ideas which go beyond the realm of the phenomenal.

Like Plato, Kant realized that the world we perceive is not the real world, because sensory perceptions tell us about experience and are in the mind, not in the objects we experience. Hence, he predicated the concept of the "thing in itself," or the thing as it really is beneath the veneer of perception. If things do exist "really" beyond the limits of perception, then their reality makes true knowledge possible. Kant insisted that the mind cooperates with the world of experience, so that what is known is dependent on the knower—the mind itself. Basic concepts that govern knowledge, such as quantity, quality, relation, and form, are in the mind. Thus the world is in some sense a product of the mind, and therefore Kant can be considered an idealist, one whose thought establishes the importance of the mind. His thought is sometimes called "transcendental" because it presses us beyond the world of experience. His concepts of the self, the cosmos, and God are all transcendental in that they give us knowledge that is the product of pure reason, since we have no means of experiencing these three critical ideas.

Kant pointed out four antinomies, or arguments that can be equally well defended and attacked:

1. The cosmos is limited in space or time; or it is limitless.

2. The world is composed of simple parts; or there are no simple parts in the world.

3. There is freedom of will; or, because everything operates according to the laws of natural causation, there is no freedom of will.

4. There exists an absolute being as the first cause of the world; or there exists no absolute being.

The most important of these concerns the proof of the existence of God. Kant insisted that the medieval and traditional proofs of the existence of God were essentially empty exercises because the theoretical reason we apply to phenomena, matters of sense, cannot apply to any of the antinomies. Yet if God's existence cannot be proved, neither can it be disproved.

Kant's moral views, then, arose from thought rather than from any external tradition or churchly imperative. Duty was for him a value that not only should take precedence in the life of the individual but also would increase the possibility of the individual's happiness. Kant's famous categorical imperative applies to the way people ought to act: "Act only on that maxim whereby thou canst at the same time will that it should become a universal law." Thus individual behavior should reflect the way people ought to act in a society, and truly rational beings should act in such a way that their behavior could form the basis of a "universal law of nature." Kant said that good behavior is consistent with happiness, and while it may not have been absolutely essential for him to postulate the existence of God in order to promote moral behavior, he felt that the path of reason leads directly to the concept of God.

G. W. F. HEGEL

Hegel was born in Stuttgart and became a professor at the University of Jena. He inherited the system of Kant's thought and began to modify it in several important ways. Instead of honoring Kant's antinomies, he asserted that Kant was wrong and that "everything that is is knowable." Hegel felt that Kant's views about "things in themselves" were wrong; things can be known, and we do not need such artificial constructs. Ultimately, he declared that reality is rational and that what is known is what is real. Hegel postulated an absolute mind that knows everything, since he realized that human minds do not create the world and that much in the world is unknown to us. Therefore, if knowing and being are one and the same, reality must be included in the concept of an absolute idea. Appearance, then, becomes reality because appearance is nothing but our idea of what is; for the absolute mind it must, then, be absolute reality.

An advantage of this system is that it does not need to postulate, as Plato did, any ideas that exist only in heaven. Rather, what we see is the true nature of things. Hegel's views simplify much of what we think about the world, but they also increase the extent to which the material world gains importance in thought. True, Hegel still gives authority to the absolute idea, and his views are idealistic in that importance is placed on the value of the mind and of its ideas. But since the mind has ideas that are

generated by the world of matter, that world, too, takes on increased importance.

One of the longest-lasting innovations of Hegel's thought is his dialecticalism. Unlike Kant, Hegel realized that it was a distinct advantage to admit that any proposition implicitly contains its opposite. He felt that every *thesis* has its *antithesis* and that by examining both, one can abstract their inherent truths to produce a *synthesis*, which will in turn become the *thesis* for the next round of reasoning. From Hegel, Karl Marx developed his dialectical materialism, the philosophical cornerstone of Russian communism. Hegel was able to see certain historical concepts in terms of his triadic thought. For instance, he felt that Asian culture had no concept of freedom, except for its rulers; that classical culture had made some citizens free; but that the German system made everyone free. Such nationalistic philosophizing implies a sense of progress in history, which is a fundamentally optimistic, modern idea. Hegel's dialecticalism recognized the implications of progress in all human endeavors, and from his time on, progress was a positive value.

COMTE AND THE RELIGION OF HUMANITY

In a separate development in France, Auguste Comte advanced the idea of positivism, a philosophy that abandoned the thought of ever knowing the truth about the "essential" nature of things. It also declared that the universe has no special ends or goals of its own and that what we can know consists essentially in our understanding of the relationships between the things that we can perceive. Newton, for instance, could codify his laws of gravity and motion by means of close observation. Yet he neither knew, nor needed to know, the essential nature of gravity.

Comte, like Hegel, saw history as progressing in three stages. The first was theological, in which gods or a god explained why the world is as it is. The second was metaphysical, in which the concept of divinity was replaced by abstract forces like Hegel's absolute mind; these forces still retained a relationship with the concept of divinity. The final stage is positivist, in which the world is explained in terms of scientific observation and in which any attempt to go beyond what we can actually observe is abandoned.

Comte attempted to formulate the science of sociology. One implication of his views is that observation can be extended beyond physics and chemistry to human affairs. Thus, laws, social structures, and the state itself all became of interest to Comte.

He postulated a "religion of humanity" in which the human spirit was the divine force in the universe. As Frank Baumer says, "Collective humanity became the new god. He called it the Great Being . . . 'whose existence admits of no demonstration, or comparison with anything real.'"

Summary

The political and social revolutions of the romantic period sparked all the arts. The conservative forces of neoclassicism, clustered about Napoleon, blazoned forth the values of stability, republican government, orderliness, self-sacrifice to the state, honor, and nobility. But those values, even as we see them in the later work of Jacques-Louis David and others, were already showing signs of romanticism, which grew more rapidly outside France (beyond Napoleon's reach) in Spain, Germany, and England. The literature of the English romantics began with William Blake and flowered in Wordsworth and Coleridge's *Lyrical Ballads*. The values of individualism, the pursuit of the ideal, the love of nature and its untamable forces, and the democratization of language and society were all expressed clearly in the poetry, novels, and drama of the age. Architecture revealed the romantic delight in appropriating older styles in a series of revivals of gothicism and other indigenous styles, culminating in a taste for the ruined castle. In music, self-expression and the power of the self-willed composer dominated. Romantic music is sensuous, secular, ambitious, and emotional —all qualities that were present in other arts and in the conduct of life. The philosophy of the period was appropriately idealistic and yet practical—the kind of philosophy that would benefit an age coping with a new wealthy middle class with a great ambition to reshape the world of its forebears. Positivism happily limited the scope of human ambitions and constructed a religion of humanity. Romanticism was a force that elevated the individual, renovated the sensual in art, rewarded independence and even eccentricity, and venerated spiritual heroism, social democracy, and virtuosity of all kinds. It was an age not only of revolution but also of spiritual exuberance.

Concepts in Chapter 16

The romantic period began at about the time of the French Revolution.

Neoclassicism in France retarded the development of the more democratic and liberal romantic styles in art.

Romanticism became important early in England and Germany but had to wait for the defeat of Napoleon in France.

Early in the century, Europe was dominated by Napoleon's war of "liberation."

Romanticism celebrated equality and human values; the liberation of the imagination was a chief shaping force in the arts of the day.

Romanticism elevated the emotions over analytic thought.

The romantics were fascinated by Greek classical values, which they interpreted as distinct from neoclassical Roman imperial values.

The French Academy, which controlled much of the taste in painting, was imitated by academies in other nations; its ambition was to find a modern expression for classical values.

English painting reflected romantic changes even before the beginning of the century.

Blake, Constable, Reynolds, and Turner were leaders in English romantic painting.

The architecture of the period was largely revivalist in style: romantic classicism, romantic gothicism, and romantic orientalism.

Newly rich industrialists in England constituted a new audience for the arts.

Wordsworth and Coleridge championed the imagination in poetry; they insisted on a simple, more natural language, close to everyday speech.

Byron, depending on a developing nostalgia for ancient times and exotic lands, became famous for his epic travel poetry.

Manfred became the type of the Byronic hero: brooding, inward, and deeply suffering.

Developments in German romantic literature and philosophy were stimulated by Goethe.

The period of romantic styles in music can generally be said to have lasted from 1800 to 1914 and to have begun with the work of Beethoven.

Romantic music aimed at evoking emotional response through the sensuousness of sound; sometimes formal constraints were abandoned in favor of emotional effect.

Beethoven depended on an imaginative approach to thematic material and the resources of "keyness."

Beethoven exploited contrast and drama in his symphonies.

Beethoven's musical life can be divided into three periods: early (1794 to 1800), middle (1801 to 1814), and late (1815 to 1827).

Classical ballet had its beginning with Marie Taglioni and *La Sylphide*.

Kant proposed a modern form of idealism in which the materials of perception were seen as worthy and important contributions to knowledge.

Hegel's dialecticalism was based on the premise that things can be known and that the truth arises from a conflict of opposites.

Comte's positivism insisted that we can know only those things which we can experience; it was based on scientific progress and became a widespread philosophy.

Suggested Readings

Aiken, Henry D. *The Age of Ideology*. New York: New American Library, 1956.

Baumer, Franklin L. *Intellectual Movements in Modern European History*. London: Macmillan, 1965.

Berger, Klaus. *Gericault and His Work*. W. Ames, trans. Lawrence: University of Kansas Press, 1955.

Blunt, Anthony. *The Art of William Blake*. New York: Columbia, 1959.

Brion, Marcel. *Art of the Romantic Era*. New York: Praeger, 1966.

Clare, Charles. *J. M. W. Turner*. London: Phoenix House, 1951.

Clark, Kenneth. *The Gothic Revival*. New York: Humanities Press, 1970 (originally published in 1928).

Einstein, Alfred. *Music in the Romantic Era*. New York: Norton, 1947.

Eitner, Lorenz. *Neoclassicism and Romanticism, 1750–1850*. 2 vols. Englewood Cliffs, N.J.: Prentice-Hall, 1970.

Engell, James. *The Creative Imagination*. Cambridge, Mass.: Harvard, 1981.

Forbes, Elliot, ed. *Thayer's Life of Beethoven*. 2 vols. Princeton, N.J.: Princeton University Press, 1969.

Frankl, P. *Gothic*. Princeton, N.J.: Princeton, 1960.

Fraser, John Lloyd. *John Constable*. London: Hutchinson, 1976.

Friedlaender, Walter. *David to Delacroix*. Cambridge, Mass.: Harvard, 1952.

Gassier, Pierre. *Goya*. James Emmons, trans. New York: Skira, 1955.

Gaunt, William. *The Restless Century*. London: Phaidon, 1972.

Gautier, Maximilien. *Delacroix*. London: Oldbourne, 1964.

Honour, Hugh. *Neoclassicism*. Harmondsworth, England: Penguin, 1968.

Knight, Frida. *Beethoven and the Age of Revolution*. New York: International Publishers, 1973.

Kolodin, Irving. *The Interior Beethoven*. New York: Knopf, 1975.

Leymarie, Jean. *French Painting: The Nineteenth Century*. New York: Skira, 1970.

Longyear, Rey. *Nineteenth-Century Romanticism in Music*. Englewood Cliffs, N.J.: Prentice-Hall, 1973.

Meeks, Carroll L. V. *Italian Architecture: 1750–1914*. New Haven, Conn.: Yale, 1966.

Migel, Parmenia. *The Ballerinas*. New York: Macmillan, 1972.

Praz, Mario. *The Romantic Agony*. New York: Oxford University Press, 1950.

Starobinski, Jean. *The Invention of Liberty: 1700–1789*. New York: Skira, 1964.

Taylor, Basil. *John Constable*. London: Phaidon, 1973.

Tovey, Donald. *Essays in Musical Analysis*. 6 vols. London: Oxford University Press, 1935–1937.

———. *Beethoven*. London: Oxford University Press, 1963.

Vaughan, William. *Romantic Art*. London: Thames and Hudson, 1978.

Wildenstein, Georges. *The Paintings of J. A. D. Ingres*. London: Phaidon, 1954.

Willey, Basil. *Nineteenth-Century Studies*. London: Cambridge, 1981.

CHAPTER 17

REALISM AND REFORM: 1848 TO 1900

Cultural Background

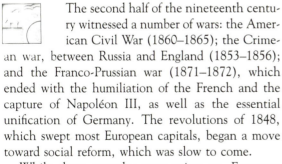

The second half of the nineteenth century witnessed a number of wars: the American Civil War (1860–1865); the Crimean war, between Russia and England (1853–1856); and the Franco-Prussian war (1871–1872), which ended with the humiliation of the French and the capture of Napoléon III, as well as the essential unification of Germany. The revolutions of 1848, which swept most European capitals, began a move toward social reform, which was slow to come.

While these struggles were going on, European and American science and industry produced wealth and power. It was a period of materialism, characterized by the expansion of colonial interests in Africa, Asia, and South America. In 1854 Admiral Perry obtained a treaty that opened Japan—where he had discovered an ordered, talented society—to trade with western powers. Perry left the emperor a brass cannon with a brass chain and a ceremonial carriage. When he returned a year later, twenty such cannons were arrayed to greeted him. Each was a perfect replica of the original, right down to a reproduction of the dedicatory plaque honoring the emperor.

Progress was celebrated at expositions and world's fairs. Industry produced marvels: railroads that linked nations; balloons that permitted aerial photography, daring escapes, and novel celebrations; and machines that could weave, manufacture, and sort products of all kinds. Supplanted skilled artisans sometimes attacked the machines which had taken their jobs. But not only did they eventually give in to the machine; some people came virtually to worship it. Engineering feats such as the suspension bridge, the subway in London, the Eiffel Tower, and the iron and glass buildings of the expositions produced a feeling of awe and of confidence in the power of science and industry. These influences found their way into the arts, which interpreted them and gave them back to the community for contemplation.

Painting and Photography

REALISM: REFLECTING THE WORLD AS IT IS

The most important influence of industry on painting was the development of photography. When the acclaimed academic history painter Paul Delaroche saw the official demonstration of the daguerreotype in Paris in 1839, he declared, "From now painting is dead." He was wrong, and later he wrote approvingly of the new science after painters began using photographs in place of live models, real buildings, and actual landscapes.

By mid-century, the realist movement insisted not on accuracy of portrayal or detailed representation, but on the doctrine that the painter is like the scientist, who studies only what can be perceived. Constable, who was sympathetic to the realists, thought that careful observation of a landscape contributed to scientific understanding. The realists insisted that even the most detailed and "photographic" history painting was unreal. It could not portray a scene witnessed by the painter, and was thus invalid as a realist composition. Representations of events from mythology were scorned for the same reason, as were idealizations of form. There was also an emphasis on seeing beyond the surface to the implications of the scene portrayed. Meaning, in other words, was integral to the realist vision; there were often social "messages" in realist works.

Realism can be understood only by examining works that led to its development and works that express it. Champfleury (Jules-François-Félix Fleury-Husson), a friend of the realist painter Gustave Courbet, made this complaint in a letter to the novelist George Sand: "All who bring forth new ideas are called *realists*. We will certainly see realist doctors, realist chemists, realist factory owners, realist historians. Courbet is a realist; I am a realist—because the critics say it, I let them." Nature and reality were correlated, and Courbet, in addressing a group of students, said: "Beauty is in nature, and in reality is encountered under the most diverse forms. As soon as it is found it belongs to art. . . ."

Jean-Baptiste-Camille Corot

Corot (1796–1875) linked the romantic painters with the realists. He was associated with the Barbizon school, a group who painted in the forest of Fontainebleau, outside Paris. Painters before Corot had worked outdoors—but, like Constable, they made sketches which they brought back to their studios to be developed into finished works. The pleinairists, as these painters were known, insisted that direct observation of light and color in the outdoors was necessary in order to do their work.

Corot was influenced by photography, both by being photographed and by using photographic techniques in his etchings, producing clichés-verres, copies on photographic glass plates. He also possessed a

PERCEPTION KEY

Camille Corot, Farmyard in Fontainebleau

1. What is the subject matter of *A Farmyard in Fontainebleau* (Color Plate 31)? What are its chief visual elements? What is the action?

2. To what degree is the scene idealized? Does the light seem to be natural? Is the coloration natural?

3. How does this painting compare with Constable's *Boat-Building near Flatford Mill* (Figure 16-9)? Is it as effective in evoking a sense of time and place?

4. The realists were accused of having ugliness in their work. Is this painting ugly?

large collection of photographs which were found in his studio after his death. The whereabouts of these photographs is no longer known, but it is reasonable to surmise that a number of them were landscapes that he used as memory aids in his work.

Color Plate 31 shows Corot's painting *A Farmyard in Fontainebleau.* This painting is in the realist vein. It seems to be a rapidly executed slice of life and to reflect the pressure of working directly from life. Only the briefest of brushstrokes indicate branches on the pollarded tree (the third from the right). The shadows on the cottage wall appear to have been painted with speed, but also with accuracy of color and definition. The figures are economically painted with unmodeled planes of color, and like the other elements in the work they are distinguished by considerable ease and vitality. The central figure, a child, plays a whistle while a turkey approaches him. The barn itself is simple; only a portion of it appears in the painting, suggesting the way a building might be cut off in a photograph. The flat planes of color, a trademark of Corot's earliest work (which influenced the later impressionists), are relieved by suggestions of texture and gradations of color. The foreground, which is rendered in rapid, broad strokes, indicates speed in observation of the scene. The composition is balanced, and the figures have their own sense of natural, unaffected harmony which suggests that they are at peace with nature. They stand in contrast with most other portrayals of city dwellers from the same period.

Honoré Daumier

Daumier (1808–1879) was a realist who pointed the way toward impressionism. Jean Leymarie has described him as having "the temperament of a Romantic and the approach of a Realist." A republican and a satirist, he was the son of an artist and grew up in the company of artists in Marseilles. He is known for his lithographs of Parisian lawyers, doctors, and politicians, particularly those who frequented the Palais Royal in Paris, where Daumier spent much time during his late youth. His skill and speed were striking, and in the late 1840s and 1850s his work appeared in newspapers regularly. His lithographs number in the thousands. His style was easy, skillful, and— despite his satiric purposes—gentle.

Rue Transnonain (Figure 17-1) records a riot in 1834 in a working-class district of Paris. Troops searching for a sniper went into a building on Rue Transnonain and killed everyone inside. Daumier, called in to draw the scene—almost as a photojournalist would be called in today—records everything without comment. The dead man is still in his nightshirt, hardly out of bed. His body creates a sharp diagonal in the composition. Daumier has made this man heroic without idealizing him. He is a martyr: defenseless and only partly awake, he has thrown himself across the body of the dead child lying beneath him. The presence of other bodies in the room only reminds us of the crowded conditions in which this man lived.

Figure 17-1
Honoré Daumier. *Rue Transnonain.* 1834. Lithograph, 11 ⅞ by 17 ½ inches. (Philadelphia Museum of Art, bequest of Fiske and Marie Kimball.)

The poet Charles Baudelaire, who considered Daumier a "great moralist," said:

> Over the deplorable massacres in the rue Transnonain, Daumier showed his true greatness; his print has become rather rare, for it was confiscated and destroyed. It is not precisely caricature—it is history, reality, both trivial and terrible.

Some of Daumier's few paintings have been hailed as forerunners of the works of the impressionists—particularly the striking series he did on Don Quixote and Sancho Panza. All of them show a great pleasure in color. Daumier did principally black-and-white lithographs, but he obviously relished the chance to work with color. *The Washerwoman* (Figure 17-2) is dominated not by line, but by color. The washerwoman and her child have physical bulk, like pieces of sculpture, while the buildings across the Seine are

Figure 17-2
Honoré Daumier. *The Washerwoman.* 1861. Oil on canvas, 19 ½ by 13 inches. (Louvre, Paris; photo, Musées Nationaux.)

PERCEPTION KEY

Daumier

1. One critic has called the series to which *Rue Transnonain* (Figure 17-1) belongs "vengeful." To what extent is an explicit emotion expressed in this lithograph? Does the lithograph express vengeance?

2. What can we tell about life in this room? Witnesses said that Daumier's lithograph is a record of what one might have seen. Is it a journalistic work? If so, what does it mean to call it "journalistic"? Does that demean its value as a work of art?

3. Almost thirty years separate *The Washerwoman* (Figure 17-2) from *Rue Transnonain*. What stylistic differences can you detect in these works? Consider the dominance of the principal figure in each scene as compared with physical objects. Consider, too, the different approaches to line and to the representation of the human body.

4. Which of these works is more realistic? Which is more romantic? List the qualities that make each work realistic or romantic.

5. What do you think Baudelaire had in mind when he said that *Rue Transnonain* was both "trivial and terrible"?

flat and ghostly. The laundry is piled up, ready for drying, and the woman attends to the child, who trudges up the stairs in the same posture as her mother. Daumier's laborers are possessed of dignity, but they are not sentimental. They are informed with a power expressed through sculptural bulk; yet the faces are not distinguished. Daumier has generalized them in order to give us an impression of their nature and a sense of their involvement in their work and their commitment to one another.

Gustave Courbet

Courbet (1819–1877), the most committed of the realists, was born in Ornans, a small town in the east of France. He went to Paris to study law, but he abandoned it for painting, and as part of his training he copied works of the masters—particularly Spanish painters, such as Velásquez—in the Louvre. One of his paintings was accepted by the Salon of 1842, when he was only twenty-three, but he was frequently rejected after that because of his novel style. After the revolution of 1848 and the introduction of the Second Republic, however, tastes in art expanded, and his work was exhibited in the Salon of 1849.

His gigantic painting *Burial at Ornans* (Figure 17-3) was shown at the Salon of 1850–1851, where it was greeted with scorn by people who could not accept the fact that the common citizens of Ornans could be portrayed in the manner that had once been reserved for royal families and noble gatherings. In terms of composition, the painting has often been compared to the great Spanish paintings that Courbet copied.

Despite the adverse criticism it received, the importance of *Burial at Ornans* could not be overlooked. On the surface, the painting portrays the common people of Ornans attending a typical ceremony. The women are separated, by tradition, from the men; the members of the clergy enjoy a place of prominence. The painting reveals the local people as they were, and their "ugliness" offended Parisian critics. But it is also an effort to paint a religious subject in an era when religious painting was considered a thing of the past. The crucifix dominates the upper part of the canvas. The group shares a reverent, communal moment. This painting shows religion in action, and the open grave in the foreground reminds us of the "final things" that are the true province of religion.

Figure 17-3
Gustave Courbet. *Burial at Ornans.* 1849. Oil on canvas, 10 feet 3 inches by 21 feet 9 ⅜ inches. (Louvre, Paris; photo, Musées Nationaux.)

Figure 17-4
Gustave Courbet. *The Painter's Studio.* 1855. Oil on canvas, 11 feet 10 inches by 19 feet 7 ¾ inches. (Louvre, Paris; photo, Musées Nationaux.)

One of the most mysterious paintings of the age was also begun in Ornans: Courbet's *Painter's Studio: A Real Allegory Summing Up Seven Years of My Artistic Life* (Figure 17-4). The title alone was overwhelming and puzzling. Courbet's friend Champfleury, who is in the painting and who was sent an explanatory letter concerning it, felt that "An *allegory* cannot be *real*, any more than a *reality* can become *allegorical*." He preferred *Burial at Ornans. The Painter's Studio*, like *Burial at Ornans*, is colossal; it portrays more than thirty life-size figures. It was rejected from the important exhibition of 1855, and as a result Courbet built a special gallery—Realism—in which he showed forty of his works, including this one. The venture was financially disastrous, but it made him even more famous than he had been. (At the same time, for somewhat different purposes, the French Photographic Society held its first major salon to promote the cause of photography as art.)

Courbet, in the letter to Champfleury, described *The Painter's Studio* as follows.

It's the moral and physical history of my studio, part 1: all the people who serve my cause, sustain me in my ideal and support my activity; people who live on life, those who live on death; society at its best, its worst and its average. . . . it's the whole world coming to me to be painted. . . . On the right are all the . . . friends, fellow-workers and art lovers. On the left is the other world of commonplace life: the masses, wretchedness, poverty, wealth, the exploited and the exploiters, people who live on death.

Between these groups appear Courbet applying a ceremonial dab of paint to a finished landscape, an admiring young boy, and a model who was once praised as the finest nude in painting. Hélène Toussaint's recent analysis of *The Painter's Studio* shows that either Courbet's letter was a screen to disguise his true motives, or he may have shifted his intentions in the work. Toussaint has demonstrated that the figures who are the "world of commonplace life" are portraits of very important people, such as the leaders of national groups fighting in the uprisings of

Courbet

1. What are the differences in treatment of the people in *Burial at Ornans* (Figure 17-3) and Daumier's *Washerwoman* (Figure 17-2)? Which work is more emotionally demanding? Which is emotionally more clear?

2. What are the chief realistic qualities of *Burial at Ornans?* How would you define realism if you had only this painting to depend on?

3. What are some of the differences in the portrayal of people in *The Painter's Studio* (Figure 17-4) and *Burial at Ornans?* Is either group less anonymous? Is either less real? Are the emotional demands of the paintings at all similar?

4. Is *Burial at Ornans* a religious painting? Compare it with any other religious painting discussed in Chapters 11 through 16. What makes it religious? What differentiates it from paintings whose chief purpose is to serve a religious purpose?

5. *The Painter's Studio* has Courbet at its center. Can it be said that *Burial at Ornans* also has him at its center? Is Courbet egotistical? How does he compare with romantic poets and artists? Should a definition of realism include the artist's self-centeredness?

1848—the first of the seven years that this allegory covers. Thus, the sense in which this is a "real" allegory is plain: it points to the events of the real world in which the painter has been living and to the social influences under which he has developed.

Toussaint has identified the first of the six standing men at the left as Achilles-Marcus Fould, a Jewish financier (Courbet said that the figure was modeled on a Jew he had seen in London, but there is no record of his ever having been in London). The second man is Louis-François Veuillot, a Catholic journalist; the third is a soldier and republican, Lazare-Nicolas-Marguerite Carnot; the man with the cross straps and rifle is Giuseppe Garibaldi, the fighter who helped unify Italy; the man next to him is Lajos Kossuth, the Hungarian fighter for independence; and finally, the man in the white hat is Thaddeus Kosciusko, the Polish revolutionary.

Other recognizable figures are Napoléon III, the first seated man at the left. The woman at the right in the flowered shawl is probably Apollonie Sabatier, a good friend; the woman in the doorway wearing white and in a loving embrace is a likeness of Juliette,

Courbet's sister. Champfleury sits in front of her, and the poet Baudelaire is shown reading. These identifications have been worked out carefully, although they are still controversial. Perhaps the most amazing of the identifications is that of the nude model. In an ordinary allegory, she would be thought of as a muse. Actually, she is the subject of a photograph by Vallou de Villeneuve (Figure 17-5) which Courbet owned and mentioned in a letter connected with this painting. Villeneuve's photographs were used by many artists when models were not available.

All this identification helps us understand what Courbet's age did not understand—the manner in which the painting can be thought of as a "real" allegory. The reality of the people assembled here, their influence not only on Courbet's life but also on the world in general, and the special influence of the reality of the photograph on painting—all these things are enriching to a painting that has long been thought of as a curiosity, even as "figures . . . simply assembled by chance." What Courbet has done here is to create a new kind of painting, one in which the conventional mythical or religious allegorical signifi-

Figure 17-5
Vallou de Villeneuve. Photograph of a nude.
(Bibliothèque Nationale, Paris, acquired 1854.)

cances have been replaced by social and personal significances. The allegory is real in that it concerns the real life of a real person: the painter, who is no longer serving a patron or an institution. He and his work are serving him and his artistic life. Perhaps this is the deepest meaning of realism as Courbet understood it.

Two American Realists: Homer and Eakins

American painters of the period were dominated by European techniques and achievements. Winslow Homer (1836–1910) and Thomas Eakins (1844–1916) studied in Europe. Homer had been an illustrator for *Harper's Weekly* and had developed an illustrative style. Eakins was in the tradition of French academic painters, although he avoided the academic conventionality of the 1850s and 1860s. He spent the years 1869 and 1870 studying the works of Velásquez and Ribera in Spain. He also developed a passion for photography and used photographs in his work.

Most painters of the 1860s, 1870s, and 1880s used photographs to some extent in their work. But Eakins's use of photographs—sometimes he literally copied poses from them—made his work distinctive and powerful. Homer relied more on the newly popular prints of the Japanese woodblock artist Hokusai. The bright, flat colors of the Japanese prints had affected most western artists by mid-century, as had their choice of subject matter: ordinary moments in daily life. Homer's early work was limited by his illustrative technique, but in the 1860s he developed a new sense of coloration and a freer brushstroke.

The result of his powerful new style can be seen in *Carnival* (Color Plate 32). It shows a group of blacks making a brilliantly colored costume for a carnival. The figures are grouped linearly. The primary figures working on the costume are centered, while a group of children, anticipating the excitement, are clustered in a knot on the right. A single child watches uncertainly on the left. The painting is marked by bright highlights and dark shadow areas. The background, reduced in color intensity, is almost blurred, as might happen in a photograph, and thus it does not compete with the deep concentration of the figures. To the modern eye, the appeal is in the coloration and in the rhythm of the carefully grouped figures and their absorption in the activity.

Dr. Samuel David Gross often lectured at Jefferson Medical College, where Thomas Eakins studied anatomy and did many of his sketches. In the painting shown in Figure 17-6, Eakins centers on the professor, who has turned away from the operation to explain a point to his students. The patient's blood is still on his hand and his scalpel. His assistants attend to their duties—Eakins is at the right of center, looking down. The mother of the patient (or so she has been indentified), at the left of the canvas, shows her grief and offers a contrast to the scientific detachment. In the background, dim and distant, are medical students in the theater, learning their profession. The dark clothing permits the powerful contrast of the patient's blood and his skin. Eakins is indebted to Rembrandt in this painting and also to the photograph, as is apparent in the intense highlights, the receding shadows, the selective focus, and the blurring of the instruments at the lower left.

Figure 17-6
Thomas Eakins. *The Gross Clinic.* 1875. Oil on canvas, 96 by 78 inches. (Thomas Jefferson University Medical College, Philadelphia.)

THE IMPRESSIONISTS: THE VALUE OF PERSONAL VISION AND SPONTANEITY

Edouard Manet

Manet (1832–1883) changed painting. He was aligned with the realists and with Courbet, but he pointed in the direction of the impressionists. His work redirected attention from the subject matter of a painting to the paint itself. In 1895, a fellow painter, Maurice Denis, said: "Remember that a picture—before being a war horse, a nude woman, or an anecdote—is essentially a plane surface covered with colors assembled in a certain order."

Most painters wanted viewers to forget the paint and imagine themselves as witnesses of an event. In contrast, Manet applied paint to his canvases in such a way that it was impossible for a viewer to see them without being aware of the sensual values of colors, hues, and intensities. It is said that Manet painted with an improvisational zeal so intense that his models sometimes became frightened of his ferocity.

The most important event anticipating the impressionists was the Salon des Refusés—the "salon of the refused"— of May 1, 1863. Members could show what they wished at the Academy, but those who were not yet members had to submit their works to a jury. In 1863, Manet and about 2000 other artists

COMPARISON KEY

Homer and Eakins

1. What are the distinguishing features of the style of realism practiced in Homer's *Carnival* (Color Plate 32) and Eakins's *Gross Clinic* (Figure 17-6)? Is it radically different from that of Courbet?

2. Which of these paintings makes a stronger emotional appeal to the viewer? What is the source of that appeal? Is it in the subject matter or in the formal presentation?

3. Which seems fresher, more independent of European influence? Why?

4. Are both these paintings portraits? If not, why not? If only one is a portrait, what are the implications of that fact for realism? Is a portrait more realistic than a work that is not a portrait?

5. To what degree do these paintings reveal a social awareness on the part of the painters? Is it different from Courbet's? Is it in any sense typically American?

Figure 17-7
Édouard Manet. *Luncheon on the Grass.* 1863. Oil on canvas, 6 feet 9 ⅛ inches by 8 feet 10 ¼ inches. (Musée d'Orsay, Galerie du Jeu de Paume, Paris; photo, Musées Nationaux.)

were excluded. Napoléon III decided to hold a special salon to show their work. It marked the first major break of the "official" world of art with the avant-garde, those who were ahead of their times.

Manet's *Luncheon on the Grass* (Figure 17-7) offended almost everyone who came to the Salon. It portrays two well-dressed young Parisian men casually picnicking with a totally naked, unashamed woman, while another woman, partially clothed, bathes in the background. In this painting, classical mythology seems to be mixed indiscriminately with contemporary life. The people are obviously moderns, even though the woman bathing in the stream resembles a river nymph; the man at the right, whose hand is raised, is modeled on a water spirit who has figured in the arts since—at least—the time of the sculpture on the east pediment of the Parthenon (see Figure 4-15); and the other two figures in the foreground are drawn from traditional sources in the history of art. The audience failed to see the traditional references. What they saw was a "shameless hussy," not a classical nude.

The figures in the foreground are grouped in a traditional way, but their space is flattened, and the space between them and the woman bathing in the background is mysterious. The "grass" between the figures in the foreground and the woman bathing is a color blur; like many of the color areas around the edges of the painting, it is not clearly defined. The most detailed and distinct areas of the painting are the faces of the figures, particularly the face of the nude woman. The space is so oddly handled that it may be true, as some historians have suggested, that Manet was beginning to break down the traditional attitudes toward Renaissance perspective. That quality alone, even without the introduction of a strikingly realistic nude, would have been enough to unsettle most viewers at the Salon.

Manet often declared that he was trying to be himself when he painted and that it was puzzling to him to be ridiculed for work that he felt was honest and serious. Fortunately, he was part of a circle of artists who reinforced one another. The impressionists, as a group, were usually ridiculed by the establishment, and their mutual support was essential to the survival of the movement.

Figure 17-8
Édouard Manet. *The Execution of the Emperor Maximilian.* 1867. Oil on canvas, 8 feet 3 ¼ inches by 12 feet ⅛ inch. (Stadtliche Kunsthalle, Mannheim.)

A painting of Manet's that met with particular derision was *The Execution of the Emperor Maximilian* (Figure 17-8). Maximilian, an Austrian archduke, proclaimed himself emperor of Mexico. French troops kept him in control until an American protest caused Napoléon III to back down and abandon him; he was captured by a republican army of Mexico and shot. His wife, when she heard the news, went mad. Paris was impassioned about the event, and people were disturbed by the coolness of Manet's treatment. His firing squad is a collection of symmetries: with their ballooning trousers and their heads all cocked in unison, they are almost like dancers striking a pose. Maximilian, with the hat, watches impassively, almost without feeling.

Even though the painting was based on Goya's *Third of May* (Color Plate 27) and on documents and reports of witnesses, it seems unrealistic. The members of the firing squad seem almost not to be firing at their victims. Their distance from them is ambiguous. The ground on which they stand and the wall against which they are silhouetted are both vague and

ill-defined. One is left with an unusual mixture of feelings about the event, in part because of the uneasiness generated by the surfaces of the painting itself.

Claude Monet

Monet (1840–1926) capitalized on the changes implied in Manet's style. Like Manet, Degas, and Renoir, Monet frequented the Café Guerbois, which was popular with the impressionists. In the tradition of Corot, he painted most of his work in the outdoors. His *Impression, Sunrise* (Color Plate 33) earned the impressionists their name—given in derision by a critic who was reading through the catalog of the group show put on in the photographer Nadar's studio in April 1874.

The delicacy of colors in the scene of Le Havre harbor shown in Color Plate 33 is explicitly impressionistic. Monet thought of himself as painting the spontaneity of light, and to do so he had to work with speed and intensity. As Henry James pointed out, the impressionists "send detail to the dogs and concentrate on the general expression." In this painting Monet concentrates on the lavender tones of the sunset and on the incandescent ball of the sun and its reflection in dabs of orange on the water. The impressionists' propensity for using violet and lavender was so great that contemporary journalists charged them with "violettomania." Karl Huysmans said:

> Suffice it to say that the eye of most of them had turned monomaniacal; this one saw parrot blue in all of nature; that one saw violet; earth, sky, water, flesh, everything in his work was tinged with lilac and deep purple.

Monet followed a recently published theory which insisted that colors interact, that adjacent colors affect and intensify one another. The theory suggested that in painting or weaving, it was better to place different colors next to each other and let the eye mix them, rather than mix them together on the palette. The enthusiastic acceptance of this concept by most of the impressionists was one source of ridicule. Their dabs of color made their paintings look unfinished, like the large oil sketches of Constable or even of Manet. The impressionists were accused of being hasty and sloppy, when in fact they were working carefully to give the most accurate rendering of a moment in light. Monet never abandoned this ambition: he spent the last twenty-seven years of his life painting water lilies, whose surfaces are always changing.

Edgar Degas

Degas (1834–1917), a regular at the Café Guerbois, is said to have owned one of the first Kodak cameras in Paris. He often cut off figures arbitrarily in his paintings, as a camera does. His ballet scenes frequently reveal a photographic approach. Experiments with photographing horses in motion resulted in Eadweard Muybridge's publication of photographs showing that all four hooves leave the ground when a horse is galloping. Degas drew from Muybridge's photographs and used them as guides for his paintings of horses.

Figure 17-9 shows a photograph by Adolphe-Eugène Disdéri (1819–1890?) of the Prince and Princess de Metternich; Figure 17-10 shows a portrait by Degas of the princess.

Disdéri and Degas

1. How has Degas relied on the photograph by Disdéri (Figure 17-9) for his portrait of the Princess de Metternich (Figure 17-10)? What has he added or subtracted? Do his changes represent important interpretations of the subject matter?

2. Is either of these representations more realistic than the other?

3. Is Degas less of an artist because of his reliance on a photograph?

4. What is the effect of the blurring in the painting?

Degas's portrait is haunting. The Princess de Metternich's posture is odd: the absence of the prince leaves her little reason to assume such a pose; Degas does not even provide her with a left arm. He selects more carefully than Disdéri did; Disdéri's purpose was simply to make a clear head-to-foot record of what the couple looked like. Degas wished to produce an interpretation and evoke an emotion, and his close-up is much more effective. His blurring of the eyes and the mouth is difficult to understand as a technique: it almost seems that he smudged the canvas. But the results are marvelous. The blurring adds to the woman's mysteriousness and creates a dynamic sense that the photograph lacks entirely. One has the impression that the princess has been snatched away momentarily from some activity.

Degas loved the ballet. He made studies in oil, pastel, and pencil of performances and rehearsals. In *The Rehearsal* (Figure 17-11) the figures are arranged with a certain casualness, as they might be in a photograph. The dancers are absorbed in their immediate tasks. There is even some awkwardness in the arms of the dancers relaxing at the left and in those of the dancers performing at the right of center. The scene has an absorbing quality, and we feel like casual observers watching from a box such as the one we see across the stage. The cutting off of the figures is what we would expect to see in a photograph, as is the contrast of light and dark, but Degas makes his paints and canvas respond even more instantly to the light than the camera of 1874 could do indoors under these conditions.

Figure 17-9
Opposite, top: Disdéri. Photograph of Prince and Princess de Metternich. c. 1860. (Bibliothèque Nationale, Paris.)

Figure 17-10
Opposite, bottom: Edgar Degas. *Portrait of the Princess de Metternich.* c. 1862. Oil on canvas, 16 by 11 ⅜ inches. (National Gallery, London.)

Figure 17-11
Right: Edgar Degas. *The Rehearsal.* 1874. Oil on canvas, 26 by 32 ¼ inches. (Musée d'Orsay, Galerie du Jeu de Paume, Paris; photo, Musées Nationaux.)

Pierre-Auguste Renoir

Renoir (1841–1919) was among the most lush of the impressionists. His canvases radiate light; his nudes seem alive in their flesh; and his portrayals of outdoor parties, boating picnics, and other diversions of the sort that attracted young Parisians of his day are manifestations of sensual delight. *Luncheon of the Boating Party* (Color Plate 34) is radiant with life, youth, and a wonderful zest. It was shown in the seventh impressionist show in 1882. The camera's way of seeing—its ability to capture an instant in time, its framing of a scene, and its "candidness"—is part of the painting's spontaneity. Renoir portrays a summer day by the water; his people, shaded by their awning, are shown in lively conversation. The woman with the dog is Aline Charigot, who later became his wife.

Renoir often painted in Argenteuil with Monet. *Monet Painting in His Garden* (Figure 17-12) uses the technique of impasto, in which the paint is heaped up on the canvas so that it stands out from the surface, although Renoir was not concerned with producing a three-dimensional illusion in this painting. The layering of paint intensifies the lushness of the vision.

Figure 17-12
Pierre Auguste Renoir. *Monet Painting in His Garden at Argenteuil.* 1873. Oil on canvas, 18 ⅜ by 23 ½ inches. (Wadsworth Atheneum, Hartford, bequest of Anne Parrish Titzell.)

The fence stands out from the roses clustered behind it (in a black-and-white reproduction the roses are almost invisible, but they are actually brilliant spots of color against the bushes above the fence). The houses are distant and flat; perspective is not Renoir's concern here. An important aspect of the subject is Renoir's delight in what he sees.

Berthe Morisot

Women did not enjoy the pleasure of the conversations at the Café Guerbois, because it was not yet considered seemly for them to be in such company. But Berthe Morisot (1841–1895) was close to Manet and other impressionists; she married Manet's brother, Eugène. In *The Harbour at Lorient* (Figure 17-13) she captures a lively sense of light and color. Morisot's sister, Edma, perched on the wall and wearing a striking white dress, is balanced on the opposite shore by the white building. The muted earth tones of the wall balance the mild blues of the water and the sky. In the painting Morisot uses a sharply contrasting color—white—in order to shift the visual focus suddenly to one side of the canvas.

Morisot was a favorite subject of Manet, who painted several strikingly beautiful portraits of her before her marriage to his brother. After she was married, he never painted her again.

THE POSTIMPRESSIONISTS: VALUE OF FORM; INTENSITY OF SURFACE

By 1886 the last group show of the impressionists had been held. The next generation of painters had much in common with them: a love of color, a concern for making the painted surface the most important aspect of the painting (as opposed to the illusion of three dimensions), and an unceasing interest in experimentation, which made their work more and more personal.

Figure 17-13
Berthe Morisot. *The Harbour at Lorient.* 1869. Oil on canvas, 17 ¼ by 29 inches. (National Gallery, Washington, Alisa Mellon Bruce Collection.)

Paul Cézanne: A Personal Vision

Cézanne (1839–1906), the son of a banker, was freer than most of the impressionists to paint as he wished. He showed with them in their first group exhibition in 1874, and then again in 1877, but not at all after that. Except in 1882, none of his work was shown in the official Salon. It was, by the 1880s, too radically different to be received with any widespread approval. His work moves more and more away from the kind of reality portrayed by the camera. It is as if he had realized that painting, if it were to grow, would have to give over to the realists (who still painted) and to the photographers that which they did best: reproducing exact detail. Painting was to have a new role, analysis of form and structure.

Color Plate 35, *Mont Sainte-Victoire,* is one of many studies of this mountain. Cézanne seems to have been influenced by Hiroshige's great color woodblock prints of Fujiyama, which appeared in a book that had just become available. Hiroshige made 100 prints of Fujiyama. Japanese prints—which had been used as wrapping paper for porcelain imported into Paris in the late 1850s—had shown the impressionists that they could use flat color and flat perspective to advantage. Cézanne is not using such a technique in this painting, but he shows the fascina-

tion of the Japanese with repeating a visual experiment—each time slightly differently, as if paying homage to the subject matter.

The mountain is framed by the pine trees to the left and above. The forms of the buildings, the aqueduct to the right, and the flat lozenge shapes of the fields draw the eye to the summit of the mountain. The colors are strong, intensely conceived, and driven onto the canvas with a palette knife, leaving sharp, distinct ridges that catch the light and produce unusual dynamics. Cézanne does not just represent the mountain for us; he presents it to us. The experience of the mountain as he has conceived it—his analysis of its simplest shapes and its formal powers—is the subject of the painting. Cézanne's is a personal interpretation which reduces the reality to a surface, or a series of surfaces, which has yielded to his vision and on which he has produced a personal order. The muted but lively colors offer little contrast and no focal point of the kind we see in the paintings of the impressionists. Instead, the color seems to expand and accent Cézanne's analytic approach, in which he reduces the landscape to shapes and simple forms.

Figure 17-14 shows Cézanne's *Bathers* ("Les Grandes Baigneuses"). This painting is a dramatic break with much of the past— except Cézanne's own

Figure 17-14
Paul Cézanne. *Bathers.*
1898–1905. Oil on canvas, 82 by 98 inches. (Philadelphia Museum of Art; purchased: W. P. Wilstach Collection.)

Cézanne, Bathers

1. What is the relationship of *Bathers* (Figure 17-14) to the works of the realists? Does it continue in the direction of Courbet, or does it move in a new direction?

2. Would this painting have caused the same kind of scandal as Manet's *Luncheon on the Grass* (Figure 17-7)?

3. In what ways does the painting analyze forms or shapes? Is it possible to see that analysis as a part of the painting's subject matter?

4. Is this an emotional painting? That is, does it invite emotional involvement, emotional response and reaction, or sentimental attachment?

5. This painting has been described as an important move toward abstraction in the visual arts. If this view is correct, what does abstraction mean for painting?

---

past. It is not an effort to shock an audience, as Manet's *Luncheon on the Grass* had done. These bathers are not naked women; they are nudes. Instead of realism we have an analysis of form and shape—a melding of the forms of the women with the forms of the trees, which lean inward, creating a triangle whose apex is outside the canvas. The figures are forms manipulated for the purposes of the composition; their shapes have been abstracted from nature —they are not represented naturalistically—and yet Cézanne links them with nature by fusing them with the shapes of the trees, the clouds, and the water. He has not invited us to gawk at them, to feel a romantic nostalgia, or to become emotionally involved with the scene.

The average viewer of Cézanne's day found the painting ugly. But that was part of the point: Cézanne had begun to free painting from the responsibility of being superficially beautiful (or "pretty"). The beauty of the painting is in the deeper formal harmonies that reside on the painted surface. Our emotional responses to the painting are complicated by the fact that we must respond to a painted surface, not to the illusion of reality. The impressionists had been moving us in that direction, but their subject matter was so constantly engaging, so positive in

outlook, and so sensually rewarding that it is difficult to see the degree to which their work implied a deeper revolution. Cézanne makes that finally clear to us, revealing that painting was moving in a direction which led inexorably to Picasso (who was influenced by the forms in this painting and who painted his own bathers) and toward the abstract expressionism of the twentieth century.

Georges Seurat: The Science of Divisionism

Pointillism is the name often given to a technique of applying paint in small dots from the end of a brush, developed by Seurat (1859–1891). He called it "divisionism" because he wished to emphasize the fact that the colors were divided from one another. Seurat's method was neither casual nor unstudied. He understood virtually all there was to know in his time about the ways in which colors work and interact with one another. He realized that a dot of red will leave a trace of its complementary color, green, in the eye of the beholder. A dot of another color next to it will do the same, and so on. Thus, his works were carefully— even painstakingly— constructed to achieve highly specific effects.

A Sunday Afternoon on the Grande Jatte (Figure

Figure 17-15
Georges Seurat. *A Sunday Afternoon on the Grande Jatte.* 1884–1886. Oil on canvas, 81 by 120 ⅜ inches.
(Art Institute of Chicago, Helen Birch Bartlett Memorial Collection.)

17-15) angered and irritated critics who saw it in the impressionist show of 1886. They felt that it was "Egyptian" in character, which is to say stiff, formal, rigid, and profoundly stylized.

Perhaps the critics would have been more accurate if they had complained about its Greek look. Seurat said that he was interested in the processional qualities which the Greeks were able to achieve in the frieze on the Parthenon. *The Grande Jatte* shows people in the modern equivalent of a procession, a promenade. The figures appear to us either in full face or in profile, which accounts for the formality and the "ancient" quality of the painting. If the fluidity of Monet's *Impression, Sunrise* (Color Plate 33) represents one way of dealing with the spontaneity of experience, Seurat's painting represents another.

Seurat fills the canvas with visual echoes: the bustle of the woman in the right foreground is echoed in that of the woman fishing at the left; the posture of the seated girl at the right of center, looking at a bunch of flowers, is repeated in that of the woman seated at the left with two men; the parasols and trees echo one another. These formal repetitions highlight the painting's abstract qualities and intensify its order and completeness. The perspective, which is intense, specific, and almost mathematical, is achieved by line, not by the vagueness of atmosphere and distance that is typical of the impressionists. The freshness of the light and the natural intensities of the shadow are something of a surprise; they are a direct legacy of the impressionists. *The Grande Jatte* is Seurat's last major painting of an outdoor scene; his important work done after 1886 explores the world of artificial light.

Figure 17-16
Paul Gauguin. *Ia Orana Maria—Ave Maria.* 1891. 44 ¾ by 34 ½ inches. (Metropolitan Museum of Art, bequest of Samuel A. Lewisohn, 1951.)

Paul Gauguin: Abandoning Description

Gauguin (1848–1903) was a tortured man, as was his friend Vincent Van Gogh. He was a successful stockbroker until he was thirty-five, when his passion for painting finally became so great that he gave up his career to paint full time—which meant that he led a life of poverty. He spent time in several exotic places: Peru while he was working as a stockbroker; the south of France when he began to paint; and then finally Tahiti, where he went after seeing a brochure. Tahiti was not only beautiful; it was also inexpensive. It was exotic enough so that Gauguin could pursue his greatest interest—not representing and describing his impressions of the world, but expressing the significance, as he understood it, of what he saw.

Gauguin knew the impressionists, and he was aware of his differences with them. He was not content to paint the world of perception. *Ia Orana Maria—Ave Maria* (Figure 17-16) is in a symbolist religious vein. The women praying to the Virgin are based on a photograph Gauguin saw of a temple frieze in Cambodia. Many of his Tahitian paintings are religious, but many of them also explore the symbolism of animals, such as the fox, the Indian symbol of perversity. The imaginative design and color of his works influenced later painters.

Vincent Van Gogh: The Expression of Self

Van Gogh (1853–1890) had one of the most intense personal struggles in the history of art. He was born into a family which included three art dealers; but his own father was a Calvinist preacher. He tried preaching and tried working for one of his relatives as an art dealer. He met with little success in either field and began to paint and draw in earnest, even though he seemed to have little unusual skill. Although he was self-taught, he got advice and help from several painters. He particularly liked Delacroix, especially his dynamic use of color. It is said that his lips trembled with emotion when he spoke of him. In Antwerp in 1885, Van Gogh spent some time studying the work of Rubens, an experience which helped him broaden his range of color.

His search for himself led him into a maze of insanity. He and Gauguin lived together at Arles in 1888 and began immediately to discuss and argue about aesthetics. Once, in a rage, Van Gogh attacked Gauguin, and then mutilated himself by cutting his left ear. Both men regretted the event, and Van Gogh voluntarily entered an asylum at Saint-Rémy in the hope that he could recover. The precise nature of his sickness is unknown; and while the work he did in the last two years of his life is intense, angular, and almost violently dynamic, it is not a product of his insanity. He painted only in those periods when he was healthy.

Two paintings done in the last year of his life— *Starry Night* (Figure 17-17) and *Sunflowers* (Color Plate 36)—are especially powerful. They show Van Gogh's work at its strongest, pointing to the later developments of the expressionists. The impressionists were concerned with recording their impression of a subject; the expressionists were concerned with expressing themselves through an interpretation of a subject. Van Gogh painted *Starry Night* and *Sunflowers* with an almost nightmarish energy: his colors are intense, and his line is dynamic and fused with the shapes he represents.

Figure 17-17
Vincent Van Gogh. *Starry Night.* June 1889. Oil on canvas, 29 by 36 ¼ inches.
(Collection, Museum of Modern Art, New York, Lillie P. Bliss Bequest.)

PERCEPTION KEY

Van Gogh, Starry Night and Sunflowers

1. How significant a role does visual perspective play in the paintings shown in Figure 17-17 and Color Plate 36? If perspective is not important, what is?

2. What are the dominant formal patterns and echoes in each of these works? What is their effect?

3. Is either of the paintings more realistic than the other? Is realism an apparent concern in either painting?

4. If these are expressionistic paintings, what do they express?

5. Do these paintings retain the impressionists' delight in spontaneity? Do they have the freshness of impressionist paintings?

Both paintings have a sense of dynamic motion. The cypress in the foreground of *Starry Night,* like the echoed shape of the steeple in the center, implies the aspiration of both nature and humankind, through religion, to the heavens. The heavens seem troubled and active, rather than calm and passive. The painting is filled with instability and anxiety; the only stable points are the triangles and rectangles of the church. Everything else is in restless motion.

Sunflowers is hardly as troubled a painting, nor is it as dynamic. Yet it is not a lyric or passive reproduction of a flower arrangement. The angular leaves are exaggerated and bristling, almost unfriendly. The sunflowers are painted in a thick impasto that makes light falling on the painting vivify the colors. Van Gogh intended *Sunflowers* as a decoration for his room in the house at Arles, and he may well have painted it from memory rather than from nature.

Both paintings reveal the truth, and since for Van Gogh the truth was a personal vision, these paintings are highly personal in their technique and concerns. Classical perspective is abandoned. In *Sunflowers* the table, the wall, and the vase are all schematically rendered so as not to interfere with the true subject—the immediate, sensual experience of the flowers and their significance. There is no need for perspective in these paintings. It would add nothing; it would only distract a viewer by implying a kind of reality and truth that are not Van Gogh's concern.

PHOTOGRAPHY: THINGS AS THEY ARE

The Camera and Its Influence

The camera had been known since the early Renaissance, but there had been no way to make its images permanent. Joseph-Nicéphore Niepce (1765–1833) found a way to do this in 1826, but the further work of Louis-Jacques-Mandé Daguerre (1789–1851) was required for a practical process to be worked out. Daguerre made a public demonstration of the daguerreotype process in 1839, and the French government bought the rights, making it possible for individuals to use the process commercially.

At first, photography was called the "pencil" or "mirror" of nature because, through chemistry, a natural process, nature was made to imitate and reproduce itself. The earliest photographers were influenced by painting and its conventions, and some painting had already begun to approach the photographic in technique and style. The extent to which photographs affected the work of artists such as Delacroix, Monet, and Degas is not surprising, since painting from photographs became common by the end of the century.

Three Early Photographers

Julia Margaret Cameron (1815–1879) was one of the most enthusiastic and successful amateur photographers in England during the period. She traveled to exotic countries, such as India and Sri Lanka, where her husband was a prominent civil servant. In England, she became friends with Sir John Herschel, whose research into optics and chemistry forwarded the development of photography. Cameron photographed him as well as a number of other friends, many of whom were, like Alfred, Lord Tennyson, quite famous. She did her most important work in the 1860s, when she posed her models for as long as four minutes for an exposure.

Her niece, Mrs. Duckworth, a widow (Figure 17-18), married Leslie Stephen. She was the mother of the noted twentieth-century novelist Virginia Woolf. The pose that Cameron usually preferred was this severe profile, in which the clothing and background are reduced to the essentials. Cameron tried to make a photograph reveal the inner as well as the outer truth of a sitter. She sometimes struggled to achieve an effective, almost dramatic light in an effort to reveal the innermost person. As she said, a photograph well taken is "almost the embodiment of a prayer."

Nadar (Gaspar-Félix Tournachon, 1820–1910), a professional photographer and friend of the impressionists, was skilled in many fields: aeronautics (he was a balloonist), the visual arts, and poetry. The first impressionist show, in 1874, was held in his studio. Once he became known, he photographed most of the important people in Paris. His subjects included Courbet, Manet, Millet, Daumier, Alexandre Dumas père and Alexandre Dumas fils (father and son), Delacroix, Corot, Gustave Flaubert, Émile Zola, and countless others.

Charles-Pierre Baudelaire (1821–1867), a friend of Nadar and the impressionists, was antipathetic toward photography. He thought it could not achieve the purposes of art, such as the revelation of character, which one might expect in a painted portrait. Fortunately, Baudelaire posed for the photograph

Figure 17-18
Julia Margaret Cameron. *Mrs. Duckworth.* April 1867.
Photograph. (National Portrait Gallery, London.)

Figure 17-19
Nadar (Felix Tournachon). *Portrait of Charles Baudelaire.*
c. 1855. Photograph. (Bibliothèque Nationale, Paris.)

shown in Figure 17-19 (and others), perhaps in the belief that nothing of himself would be revealed. Baudelaire presents himself with a bohemian dash befitting a young man who had already wasted a good part of a fortune on lowlife excitement. Despite his follies, he stares almost disdainfully at the camera, not only unashamed of his unpopular ways but also intent on maintaining them.

Figure 17-20
Peter Henry Emerson. *Pond in Winter.* 1888. Platinum print. (George Eastman House.)

Three Early Photographers

1. Which of the photographs shown in Figures 17-18, 17-19, and 17-20 is most like a painting? What qualities make it seem so? Is any of these photographs explicitly unrelated to painting in terms of subject matter or formal organization?

2. Was Baudelaire correct in assuming that the photograph is unable to reveal the inner nature of the sitter? Why would it be less likely than a painting to reveal the character of the sitter?

3. Do these photographs do anything that a painting cannot do? If not, why were artists in the latter half of the nineteenth century so excited about photography?

4. Which of these photographs has the most interesting formal organization? Which has the most original formal organization? If you have chosen different photographs in answer to these questions, does that mean that originality is not as interesting as certain other qualities in a photograph?

Peter Henry Emerson (1856–1936), a graduate of Cambridge, had many theories about the relationship of photography to art. He saw that a photograph can do many things that a painting does, and he set out to demonstrate this in his work. He was committed to showing that science and art come together in photography. He tended to concentrate on a particular locale, photographing carefully and presenting his work in portfolio form in limited editions.

Pond in Winter (Figure 17-20) was originally the first plate in his book *Pictures from Life in Field and Fen* (1888). The composition is balanced and delicate, with a figure in uninterrupted silhouette acting as the focal point. The pond is represented by the rhythmic curves of both its near and far banks. Nothing explicit is happening in this photograph, which is not true of most of Emerson's views of country life. We must respond to the organization of the elements in the composition: the balance of small and large trees; the counterpoint of water, land, and sky; the isolation of the human figures; and the atmosphere created by the photographic rendering of weather. Emerson laid the foundations for the later development of documentary photography, which had as its purpose the discovery of form and order in things as they are.

Sculpture: Rodin—New Directions, New Values

Auguste Rodin (1840–1917) was the first sculptor since Bernini to offer a new vision of what sculpture can be and do. Rodin saw himself as a bridge between the past and the present. His early struggles were immense. He knew by age twenty that he would be a sculptor, but he spent the next twenty years of his life in poverty, trying to discover himself in his art. His earliest works were not well received by the artistic establishment, and they were often harshly rejected. But he believed in himself and continued to struggle. In the Salon of 1877 he showed a male nude inspired by Michelangelo; it was not a success with the critics, but the public found it powerful and expressive. Eventually, he began receiving commissions for important works.

The Kiss (Figure 17-21) shows Rodin's affection for Michelangelo and his respect for the stone from which his figures emerge. As in *The Awakening Slave* (see Figure 13-26), the rough, uncut stone is an integral part of the composition—a technique that was foreign to Bernini and his followers. Rodin

Figure 17-21
Auguste Rodin. *The Kiss.* 1886. Marble, heroic size.
(Musée Rodin, Paris.)

Figure 17-22
Auguste Rodin. *The Gates of Hell.* 1880–1917. Bronze,
18 feet high by 12 feet wide by 33 inches deep. (Rodin
Museum, Philadelphia; gift of Jules E. Mastbaum.)

originally composed the sculpture in clay; then he
had it cut by professional stonecutters, watching all
the time for expressive qualities in the uncut portions
of the block. As they appeared, he retained them.
The result is an eloquent pattern of contrasts: the
smoothness of human skin and the roughness of
stone; the passion of the figures and the impassivity of
the material from which they are modeled; the
softness and fluidity of the flesh and the harder—yet
still fluid—rhythms of the stone as it yields up its
human treasure. The eloquence of the counterpoint
of flesh and stone is compelling.

Without question, Rodin's most important commission, and one of the most important works of art
of the last quarter of the nineteenth century, is his

unfinished *Gates of Hell* (Figure 17-22). It was commissioned in 1880 by the French government as a
portal for a building that was to be a museum of
decorative arts. In fact, the museum was never built,
and Rodin returned the government's money at the
turn of the century. But from 1880 to the end of his
life he worked on the gigantic gates, refining their
design and developing pieces and groups as separate
works. (The gates were largely completed in 1887.)

Rodin began with the realization that he was
working in the same tradition as Ghiberti in his *Gates
of Paradise* (see Figure 11-6), for the baptistry in
Florence. That was a religious tradition, not a secular
one, and as a means of bridging the gap between the
religious and the secular, Rodin chose Dante, whose

Divine Comedy had bridged the gap between the classical world of Virgil and Dante's own Christian world. Rodin saw this as a chance to link the Christian values of the past with the generally secular values of his own time.

There never was a clear, formal structure for the design. Rodin began imagining panels, like Ghiberti's, representing separate episodes, but soon he found that his imagination was spilling over and that he was seeing the spaces filled in a much more open and fluid manner. Figures of lovers lost in lust, individuals suffering anguish and pain, and people in a bewildering variety of emotional states appear, jutting out from a background of flames. On top of the door are the three shades, spirits who are reluctant to keep their appointment in hell. Directly beneath them is the famous *Thinker*. *The Thinker* was originally to have been Dante; but as the work progressed, Rodin realized that it was a metaphor for the creator in general. As Rodin said, "The fertile thought slowly elaborates within his brain. He is no longer dreamer, he is creator."

The Thinker became the headstone for Rodin's grave and, in a sense, his epitaph. He may be meditating on the human condition. The figures in Rodin's hell are clearly tormented people whose passions dominate them completely; the Thinker's rational silence, then, may offer a calm counterpoint to the passionate, twisted, and agonized poses of those he surveys. This is best observed in the detail in Figure 17-23, showing the position from which *The Thinker* is viewed: from below. Seen this way, the contrast between him and the other figures is almost painfully evident.

The Thinker derives from classical torsos, particularly as interpreted by Michelangelo. By crossing the right elbow over to the left knee, Rodin achieved a powerful torsion that seems expressive of anguish or psychological tension.

When the town of Calais asked Rodin to provide a public monument for its main square, Rodin decided on a work depicting the six worthy men who in 1347 had offered their lives to King Edward III of England in exchange for his lifting an eleven-month siege of the city. *The Burghers of Calais* (Figure 17-24) was so original that the commissioners hardly knew what to make of it. The six men are in tormented, almost accidental, postures. There is no clear visual center to the composition; rather, one is encouraged to perceive the continuously dynamic relationships of

Figure 17-23
Rodin. *The Gates of Hell,* detail. (Rodin Museum, Philadelphia; gift of Jules E. Mastbaum.)

the figures. Rodin intended the composition to be at ground level so that people could walk around it and participate directly with the movements of the burghers. That in itself was such a revolutionary concept that Rodin had been dead for almost ten years before the commissioners acceded to his wishes. This informal and spontaneous approach to monumental sculpture may be said to be influenced by, and perhaps part of, the impressionists' concept of art.

Even more impressionistic in feeling is a later work, *Balzac* (Figure 17-25), a portrait of the French writer whose *Human Comedy* was widely regarded as a work of genius. Rodin's *Balzac* is a figure of impressive bulk and power. Rodin has simplified the forms, almost to the point of making them abstract. The commissioners of this work were also baffled, as the commissioners of *The Burghers of Calais* had been. They knew it was Balzac—Rodin had worked carefully to produce a good likeness, even going so far as to use as a model a workman whose resemblance to Balzac was striking. Yet they refused to put the work in its intended position until 1939.

Figure 17-24
Above: Rodin. *The Burghers of Calais.* 1884–1886. Bronze, 82 ½ by 95 by 78 inches. (Hirshhorn Museum and Sculpture Garden, Smithsonian Institution, Washington.)

Figure 17-25
Left: Rodin. *Balzac.* 1893–1897. Bronze, 9 feet 3 inches high. (Collection, Museum of Modern Art, New York, in memory of Curt Valentin.)

In *Balzac,* Rodin has carefully analyzed form, choosing a stance in which the man leans back, as if surveying his own vast achievement. Rodin is said to have imagined Balzac, wrapped in his cloak, haunted by a sense of the living presence of his characters. Critics have looked on this work as foretelling the direction that sculpture would take—toward a poetry of mass and bulk rather than toward a simple reinterpretation of observable reality.

Rodin

1. What qualities in Rodin's sculpture link him to the realists in painting? What qualities link him to the impressionists? Is his style clearly either more realistic or more impressionistic?

2. Compare Rodin's *Thinker* (Figure 17-23) with Michelangelo's figures on the Medici tombs (Figure 13-24 and 13-25). What qualities of *The Thinker* reveal the influence of Michelangelo? Consider the questions of realism and of idealization of the human figure; consider, too, the originality of the pose.

3. Are any of Rodin's works so realistic that they could be disturbing to a contemporary audience? Why would *The Burghers of Calais* (Figure 17-24) be problematic for the people of the town that commissioned it? Why would they resist placing this work in their public square?

4. What are some of the emotional responses evoked by *Balzac* (Figure 17-25)? Is it an emotionally charged piece? Which of Rodin's works reproduced here (or other works, if you know them) demands the strongest emotional response?

5. If Rodin can be considered the first truly important sculptor since Bernini, what qualities differentiate their work? What qualities does their work share?

Architecture: Responding to a New Age

The Crystal Palace (Figure 17-26), by Joseph Paxton (1801–1865), was erected to house the exhibits at the great London Exposition of 1851; it was intended to be Prince Albert's answer to the Paris Exposition of 1849. The building was originally to have been constructed of iron and brick, but innumerable problems made that plan inadvisable. The commissioners of the exposition then heard of Paxton, who had built an enormous iron and glass greenhouse to hold a gigantic water lily recently discovered in Guiana. The lily, named after Queen Victoria, had leaves that measured 5 feet across and was strong enough to support Paxton's little daughter. In building the greenhouse, he studied the structure of the leaves, imitated their ribbing in iron, and then placed glass panes between the ribs to produce a light, airy, strong structure.

Glass was not a generally accepted building material in 1850—for one thing, because it had been heavily taxed until 1844. With new machinery, however, the cast-iron ribbing needed for use with glass could be produced cheaply; and prefabrication of the ribbing meant that construction and glazing could be carried out with amazing speed and efficiency. When the commissioners saw Paxton's drawing, and when they considered the cheapness of construction, they gave him the job, along with an almost impossible deadline. Yet the main building was complete in five months, and in nine months the entire job was finished. The building covered almost 19 acres and enclosed 30 million cubic feet of space.

The Crystal Palace was a brilliant success, inspiring imitations in Europe and America. During the course of the exposition, 6 million people visited some 14,000 exhibitions of world art, manufacturing, machinery, and other achievements. John Ruskin called the building an "oversize greenhouse," but Queen Victoria's reaction was one of the most

Figure 17-26
Joseph Paxton. Crystal Palace, Hyde Park. 1851. 1848 feet long by 408 feet wide; height of transept: 108 feet. (Royal Commission on Historical Monuments, England.)

telling. She said: "One felt—as so many did whom I have since spoken to—filled with devotion, more so than by any service I have ever heard." Her sense of religious awe was shared, as she herself noted, by many of her acquaintances. Even the London *Times* declared that there was a "sense of mystery" about the building. These reactions indicated the degree to which the age had become secular. The emotions generally reserved for a religious experience had been transferred to the new "religion" of industrial progress. The Crystal Palace supplied the awe that the great cathedrals had provided in the Middle Ages.

It was sold to Paxton at the end of the exposition; then it was moved and reconstructed—with changes that made it even larger and grander—in Sydenham, within sight of London. Until a spectacular fire destroyed it in 1936, it stood there as a testament to the achievement of new building materials, principles of prefabrication, and the efficiency of modern machinery. It influenced the way modern buildings would be constructed: out of ribbing and skin.

Literature: The New Romanticism and Secular Realism

Literature in the second half of the nineteenth century continued many of the trends of romanticism. The major writers extended the achievement of the romantics by stressing the qualities of the individ-

ual, as in the work of Walt Whitman (1819–1892), whose *Song of Myself* celebrates his own personality; and of Emily Dickinson (1830–1886), another American poet whose work is distinctively introspective. English poets, such as Alfred, Lord Tennyson (1809–1892), and Robert Browning (1812–1889), may be said to have continued certain romantic traditions in terms of their exploration of deep personal feelings, examination of values, and experimentation in verse forms.

But at the same time these writers were at work, a new vision, paralleling that of the realist painters, was emerging in the work of Charles-Pierre Baudelaire (1821–1867) and Gustave Flaubert (1821–1880) in France, Fyodor Dostoyevski (1821–1881) in Russia, and Henrik Ibsen (1828–1906) in Norway. These writers, along with many followers in Europe and the Americas, crafted a movement toward sometimes brutal realism in literature. They are usually described as realists or naturalists, thoroughly objective—virtually scientific—in their detached observation of the human condition. They attempted to look equally upon the squalid and the divine and inspired in human experience. The result was a literature of striking power and honesty which offended the general public and the official authorities enough to cause bans and condemnations.

WALT WHITMAN: POET OF SPONTANEITY

Whitman made numerous changes in, and additions to, *Leaves of Grass* between its first appearance in

1855 and his death in 1892. Its most striking quality is its proselike style; Whitman takes the advice of Wordsworth and Coleridge to its logical conclusion, producing a poetic language that is even closer to the way people speak than that of the English romantics. He begins his great poem, "Song of Myself," from *Leaves of Grass,* with the simple lines, "I celebrate myself, and sing myself, / And what I assume you shall assume, / For every atom belonging to me as good belongs to you." The style is casual and easygoing, virtually emulating the impressionists' spontaneity. "Sweet spontaneous me," a catchphrase of Whitman, urged his readers to be themselves, to take off their clothes and swim in the rivers, to love their fellow beings as themselves, and to treat women with the same respect as they treat men.

Whitman's connection with the romantics and their love of nature is illustrated in these lines:

> I think I could turn and live with animals, they are so placid and self-contain'd,
> I stand and look at them long and long.
> They do not sweat and whine about their condition,
> They do not lie awake in the dark and weep for their sins,
> They do not make me sick discussing their duty to God,
> Not one is dissatisfied, not one is demented with the mania of owning things,
> Not one kneels to another, nor to his kind that lived thousands of years ago,
> Not one is respectable or unhappy over the whole earth. (Stanza 32.)

Whitman's willingness to speak directly and to repeat himself when he needs to and his avoidance of rhyme make his poetry seem almost accidental, as if he was convinced that whatever he spoke or thought was by its own nature poetry.

At first glance, Whitman seems to have abandoned poetic technique, but that is not so. It is true that he does away with rhyme and with conventional stanza forms, but he substitutes a consistent voice which shapes the length of the lines, and he relies on a poetic device that is much older than rhyme: repetition. The technique of anaphora, the repetition of a word or phrase at the beginning of successive lines, informs this hymn to the earth:

> Smile O voluptuous cool-breath'd earth:
> Earth of the slumbering and liquid trees!

Earth of departed sunset— earth of the mountains misty-topt!
Earth of the vitreous pour of the full moon just tinged with blue!
Earth of shine and dark mottling the tide of the river!
Earth of the limpid gray of clouds brighter and clearer for my sake!
Far-swooping elbow'd earth—rich apple-blossom'd earth!
Smile, for your lover comes.

It may be outrageous for Whitman to posture as the lover of the earth—that would place him on a par with Zeus. Yet he did possess a godlike exuberance and energy. His poetry came from him as if from the mouth of a prophet.

CHARLES BAUDELAIRE: VALUING EVIL

Quite a different approach to poetry was taken by Baudelaire, who was dissolute, squandered his inheritance, used opium, and was most unsteady in his relationships. He contracted (or possibly inherited) syphilis and had a long and turbulent relationship with the black actress Jeanne Duval. Yet when he made his way to Paris, after his parents had sent him on a long sea voyage, he met some of the most important people in the literary and artistic circles of his day. He translated the American writer Edgar Allan Poe, and by 1843 he had begun the first of the poems that were to be published as *Les Fleurs du Mal* ("The Flowers of Evil").

The title was suggested to him by a friend when some of the poems were published in 1855. The poems frankly admired the darker side of life— prostitution, casual sex, homosexuality, and other passions that respectable society of the day tried to ignore. Baudelaire treated these subjects as if they were flowers to be examined and savored. His title is openly ironic, but his method is very serious. Because of the queasiness of his society, Baudelaire had available to him an enormous range of subject matter that had rarely been dealt with by a recent poet.

However, the official world of Paris was not pleased with his work. In 1857 the public prosecutor confiscated the entire first edition of *Les Fleurs du Mal* and fined Baudelaire. Eventually, the book was published, but only after the removal of six particularly offensive poems which speak quite openly about sex and sexual perversions. Other poems speak approvingly of death, describing in graphic detail rotting

Whitman and Baudelaire

1. As an aid to considering the questions in this comparison key, read a few verses from Whitman's *Leaves of Grass* and Baudelaire's *Fleurs du Mal.* Is there a perceptible difference in the energy of the lines of these poets? Is one poet more vital than the other?

2. How do these poets differ in their views on humanity? Does either poet seem to have a more essentially positive view of the value of humankind? Is Whitman's praise of animals, quoted in the text, an indication that he devalues humanity?

3. Is either poet more objective or less prejudiced in his approach to his subject matter? Could either one be said to be "scientific" in his poetry?

4. Baudelaire, in the original French, usually relies on a four-line stanza with an abab rhyme pattern. Whitman avoids such traditional patterns. Is either poet's approach inappropriate to his subject matter?

5. Is either poet more or less a realist? What is the significance of their choosing titles relating to the world of vegetation? What is the significance of their avoiding narrative and extensive description in their work?

---

corpses and their "perfume." The general public was disgusted by Baudelaire's subject matter, but he lavished on his poetry a remarkable talent for rhyme and a careful control of word sound—what he called his "secret architecture." The first poem of the collection addresses the reader, accusing him (the reader is addressed as male) of being not only a hypocrite but also a likeness of the poet, his twin.

One of the censored poems, "The Metamorphoses of the Vampire," is about a liaison with a prostitute: "The woman, meanwhile, writhing like a snake / across hot coals and hiking up her breasts / over her corset-stays, began to speak / as if her mouth had steeped each word in musk." She is quite business-like, yet she is appealing to the speaker. Once the liaison has been completed, her metamorphosis is revealed:

> When she had sucked the marrow from my bones,
> and I leaned toward her listlessly
> to return her loving kisses, all I saw
> was a kind of slimy wineskin brimming with pus!
> I closed my eyes in a spasm of cold fear,
> and when I opened them to the light of day,

> beside me, instead of that potent mannequin
> who seemed to have drunk so deeply of my blood,
> there trembled the wreckage of a skeleton
> which grated with the cry of a weathervane
> or a rusty signboard hanging from a pole,
> battered by the wind on winter nights.

GUSTAVE FLAUBERT: CREATING THE MODERN NOVEL

In 1857, the same year Baudelaire's *Fleurs du Mal* was confiscated, Gustave Flaubert's *Madame Bovary* was condemned for indecency. Baudelaire, who recognized Flaubert's genius, took comfort in this shared distinction. But the two writers had offended public taste in different ways.

The public was, for one thing, dismayed and confused by the protagonist of Flaubert's book. Emma Bovary was a countrywoman who married her father's doctor and began to aspire to the bourgeois comforts of the local professionals and merchants. She found her husband boring; gave in to a seducer, Rodolphe, who lost interest in her; and eventually ignored her own child to take on a childish lover, Léon. She also piled up debts, and she ended as a suicide, poisoning herself with arsenic.

For another thing, it was not clear to Flaubert's readers where he stood. He did not interrupt his narrative, as was the style of novelists of the time, to explain how his audience should react. Nor did he include a character to speak for him, to clarify the moral implications of the action. Despite Emma's terribly limited nature, her ignorance, her silly ambitions, her baseless dreams of grandeur, her deceit, and her terrible end, the readers were not at all sure what they should make of her. The novel was not a moral tale. It was, instead, a portrayal of a life as it had been led. Flaubert had seemed to emphasize fate in Emma's life, as if to suggest that such a person in such a small town in such a time would inevitably end up as she did. But this did not redeem the book in the eyes of the authorities, who recoiled at scenes revealing Emma's lust and her cavortings with illicit lovers.

Flaubert, who was a patient, slow worker, presented in *Madame Bovary* a portrait of French society that pleased no one. The local priest is unable to understand Emma's spiritual quandary. Religion itself is portrayed as thin, sentimental, and extraneous to the lives of the novel's characters. Emma's husband, Charles, at her insistence, performs a hideous operation on a victim of clubfoot early in the novel, demonstrating not only his vanity and pride, but also his ignorance and incompetence. Homais, the "intellectual" and "up-to-date" pharmacist, is both stupid and stiflingly proud.

Flaubert invented the modern novel, a novel of observation of characters whose lives are revealed as they are rather than as they should be. Flaubert omitted the commentator, producing a view of his characters and their circumstances that was very close to perfect objectivity. However, he was not indifferent or wholly detached in his views. He satirized his society, parodied its vanities, and exposed its weaknesses.

Madame Bovary has both a story and a striking character, but it has much more. Flaubert once remarked, "A novel's story or adventure doesn't matter to me in the least. . . . When I am working on a novel my thought is that I am rendering a coloration, a nuance." Like Baudelaire, Flaubert had music in mind, the music of Richard Wagner, who constructed his operas using the technique of the leitmotif, a musical figure or theme associated with a

force, value, or significance that is repeated throughout the opera. Flaubert uses clothing—particularly hats, shoes, and other details of Emma's dress —with great care, investing such references with meaning. Other details also have a larger significance: for example, there is the inexorable drone of a turning lathe; Emma hears it when she is first contemplating suicide, and it becomes a symbol of destiny shaping lives. Even the clubfoot (there are, in fact, several limping characters) is a reminder of Oedipus (whose name means "clubfoot"), who could do nothing to escape his destiny. The repetition of events, locales, details, and even speeches resembles repetition in music and adds a dimension to the novel which was unheard-of before.

When Emma dies, we cannot help being moved by her predicament. Flaubert may have observed her with great objectivity, but certainly not with indifference. The identification of Flaubert with Madame Bovary was made very early by Baudelaire, who noted how masculine and willful she was. But Flaubert is also said to have identified himself with her in the famous expression: "Madame Bovary, c'est moi." It is perhaps this implicit sympathy that caused the first readers to be concerned about the way in which they should understand Emma Bovary and the meaning of her story.

HENRIK IBSEN: A DRAMA OF NEW VALUES

If Flaubert created a new novel, Ibsen created a new and modern drama. The late nineteenth century was not distinguished for its theater. Most of the dramas performed in Europe and America were turgid, sentimental, artificial, and melodramatic. In some ways it was an escapist drama.

Ibsen focused on issues of the sort that Flaubert developed in his novels. In *A Doll's House* (1879), he treated the question of women's equality in the stifling middle-class society of his native Norway, which was a model of European middle-class values. Audiences had long delighted in seeing their own values praised in the theater. Now, Ibsen showed that life in Nora's neat, protected world has a fearful cost: she is not allowed to grow up. Early in the play, Nora behaves like a child. She wheedles, whines, and acts stupidly to please her essentially dull husband. The play is about the gradual education she receives from a woman friend whose husband has left her. The differences between them are immense, and when Nora sees that the only way she can ever be her own person is by leaving her protected environment, she goes. As she leaves, she slams the door on her shocked husband. The reverberation of that slammed door was heard, as some contemporaries remarked, throughout Europe.

One of Ibsen's best-known plays, *Hedda Gabler* (1890; Figure 17-27), treats a powerful woman who rejects the man she loves because he is impoverished and who marries another man on the strength of his prospects of becoming a professor and earning a comfortable living. After the wedding tour, she returns to a house that she feels is inadequate to her station. She is pregnant; she is aware that her husband is a thorough bore without an ounce of spirit; and she learns that Eilert Lövborg, the lover she rejected, has written a brilliant book which may give him the professorship that her husband, Tesman, thought he had been guaranteed.

Figure 17-27
Glenda Jackson in Henrik Ibsen's *Hedda Gabler.* (Photo, Gerry Goodstein, New York.)

Hedda's complexity is the primary reason the play works so well. She is detestable on one level: she thinks of no one but herself; she treats her family and friends callously; she finds the missing manuscript of Lövborg's second book, which is more important than the first, and allows him to believe that it is permanently lost; she belittles her husband; and she gives Lövborg the gun with which, in despair over his book, he shoots himself in the groin, dying horribly. And finally, she commits suicide. Yet there is nobility in her. She is General Gabler's daughter and she can ride and shoot like a man. The tragedy she experiences is the fact that she is a woman and must realize her destiny through men. And the men she knows are vastly less interesting and less accomplished than she.

Hedda's situation at the end of the play is intolerable. With Lövborg dead, Tesman is planning to reconstruct the lost manuscript from the notes in the possession of Thea Elvsted, who had the courage to leave her husband and help Lövborg rebuild his life. Judge Brack, who has been hoping for some time to make Hedda his mistress, is offered by the stupid Tesman as company for her during the long evenings he expects to spend on his research. She wants none of it. She kills herself the way her father, or any other military man, might.

Ibsen's realism and his honesty are directly responsible for the kind of drama we have enjoyed in the twentieth century. His settings were the very drawing rooms his audience had come from, and his focus was on the kinds of lives they led there. Thus, the insights his audience was likely to derive were insights into themselves.

Music
WAGNER: THE VALUE OF MYTH IN THE NEW AGE

The Leitmotif

Richard Wagner (1813–1883) connected music and myth, influencing Flaubert, James Joyce (1882–1941), and many others through his use of the leitmotif, a musical expression which builds and repeats throughout a work and which acts as an emotional intensifier as well as a structural link. When a character first appears in the cycle of operas known as *The Ring of the Nibelung*, a specific leitmotif

Rhein - gold!   Rhein - gold!

Figure 17-28
Richard Wagner. Rhinemaidens' song from *The Rhine Gold*, one of the leitmotifs representing the gold. 1857.

is heard, and later when the character reappears in a different circumstance, the leitmotif also reappears, fusing certain emotional and musical associations in the listener's mind. Novelists achieved a similar effect with repeated events or objects—such as the lathe and the recurrent descriptions of clothing in *Madame Bovary.*

The Rhine Gold leitmotif (Figure 17-28), in the first opera of the *Ring* cycle, shimmers as the unstable first chord is resolved into C major. Even playing it on the piano reveals its power and Wagner's ability to associate a musical idea with the text of a drama.

The Ring Cycle: An Effort to Interpret the Age

The Ring of the Nibelung, which Wagner worked on intermittently from 1848 to 1874, was conceived on the same scale as Dante's *Divine Comedy,* and for some of the same reasons. Like Blake, Wagner ignored Greek myth and worked directly with indigenous myths, Celtic and Germanic, which he reworked to suit his needs.

The *Ring* is a cycle of four "music dramas": *The Rhine Gold* (1854), *The Valkyrie* (1856), *Siegfried* (1871), and *The Twilight of the Gods* (1874). It tells the story of the quest for the ring fashioned from gold lying at the bottom of the Rhine. Whoever possesses the ring controls the world.

The first of the four operas, *The Rhine Gold,* is a prologue in one act. It begins with Alberich, a misshapen dwarf, contemplating the Rhine maidens, who guard a hoard of gold at the bottom of the Rhine, as they sport beneath the water. This underwater scene is dominated by mistiness and the undulation of the river. Alberich is taunted by the maidens, who sense that he is in love with them. He spots the gold and determines to have it, even though its cost is the renunciation of love, and while the

shocked Rhine maidens look on, he steals it. From the gold, his brother, Mime, makes him a magic ring.

Meanwhile, Wotan, chief of the gods, has had Valhalla built by the unsavory giants Fafner and Fasolt, who have been promised Freia, goddess of youth and love, as their reward. But Wotan goes back on his word, pretending that he made no such promise. The giants' anger is such that Wotan realizes that he must give them something, but not Freia. Loge, the god of fire, suggests another reward—the ring made from the gold from the Rhine—and eventually he and Wotan steal it from Alberich.

On one level, Wagner seems to be protesting the materialism of his own age, its quest for gold and power, and its inability to behave honorably. Wotan has the power to do as he wishes, but he does not respect his own laws—which have become the source of his power. The giants Fafner and Fasolt built Valhalla in good faith, and though we find it hard to sympathize with them, we know that Wotan has behaved badly. He was wrong to have promised them Freia in the first place.

Scene 3 of *The Rhine Gold,* in which Wotan and Loge find Alberich, is one of the most powerful in the cycle. They descend into an underworld where Alberich, because he has the power of the ring, forces all the gnomes to work for him. The music is dominated by anvils—actual tuned anvils—that are struck continuously. The industrial model is difficult to ignore. Wotan deceives Alberich and steals the ring. But even the chief of the gods cannot be excused for theft. Alberich curses the ring: "May he who has it not covet it with rage; and may he who has it retain it with fear."

At first Wotan will not give the ring to the giants. But Erda, the most ancient divinity, intervenes, foretelling the end of Valhalla, and Wotan relents. The curse begins almost immediately, when Fafner murders Fasolt in combat over the ring. Fafner then becomes a dragon in order to protect his treasure. When Wotan and the gods turn to enter Valhalla, it is shrouded in storm clouds. Wotan hears the Rhine maidens crying for their lost gold, but he does not help them. His march into Valhalla is triumphant, but it is a false sense of security that he feels in his new home. Wotan knows that in the future a race of human heroes will bring about the downfall of the gods and undo the wrong that he has done.

In *The Valkyrie,* a powerful race of human warriors has been created; the most worthy of them are wafted by the Valkyries, Wotan's warlike daughters, into Valhalla when they die. There they become immortal heroes. As the opera opens, there is a storm; Siegmund and Sieglinde, noble twins who have been separated since youth, meet but do not recognize each other. When Hunding, Sieglinde's husband, arrives on the scene, he challenges Siegmund to combat in the morning. After Hunding leaves, Siegmund recognizes his sister and falls deeply in love with her, and in their union they conceive Siegfried. Meanwhile, Siegmund has retrieved the hero's sword, Nothung, from the ash tree in which it has been lodged and has determined to use it to fight Hunding. The beautiful passages that Sieglinde sings, praising Siegmund as the spring that has come to her in the winter of her marriage, are among the most lyric in the cycle.

At first, Wotan instructs his daughter Brünnhilde to make Siegmund the victor, but Fricka, Wotan's wife, demands that the marriage vows be held sacred. Siegmund must die. Wotan relents and gives new instructions to Brünnhilde, but she disobeys, thinking that she is doing his secret bidding. In a rage, Wotan shatters Siegmund's sword with the spear on which his laws are engraved, and Siegmund dies. As punishment, Brünnhilde is made a mortal, asleep on a mountain peak and protected by a ring of fire through which only the purest warrior can pass.

The Valkyrie contains one of the most famous leitmotifs of the cycle, in "The Ride of the Valkyries" (Figure 17-29). The leitmotif is especially prominent in the first scene of the final act, in which the eight Valkyries are seen (and heard) wafting their heroes to Valhalla, over a brilliantly scored orchestral accompaniment. (Elsewhere in the cycle, the "Valkyrie" motif is used to represent Brünnhilde.)

In the concluding part of Act 3, Scene 1, Brünnhilde directs Sieglinde to a forest refuge, assuring her that she is to give birth to a great hero. As Sieglinde dies, in the opera Siegfried, she gives the child over to

Alberich's brother, Mime, who had made the Rhine gold into the ring for Alberich.

Siegfried is almost a relief from the struggles of the earlier operas in the Ring cycle. Siegfried grows up communing with nature, but he senses that he has a human mission and demands to know of the outside world. In an intensely realistic scene, he begins to reforge the pieces of his father's sword, Nothung, which Mime could not do. When Mime realizes that Siegfried is successfully reforging Nothung, he devises a scheme. He will send Siegfried to kill Fafner and then poison him and make off with the ring and the Tarnhelm, the helmet that permits its wearer to assume any shape. But his plan does not work. When Siegfried kills Fafner and tastes the dragon's blood on his tongue, he becomes able to understand the language of birds, who warn him of Mime's scheme. He also learns about Brünnhilde, sleeping in her ring of fire. She can be rescued only by a hero who has no fear. In the course of his journey to find her, Siegfried splits even Wotan's spear with Nothung: this is the first of the race of heroes who will displace the gods themselves. At the end of the opera Siegfried and Brünnhilde realize that their fate is to destroy Valhalla. In a passionate duet, they sing of their love and of their willingness to face their fate together.

The Twilight of the Gods is the final opera in the cycle. The pattern of fate is becoming clear. In the first scene the three fates spin the thread which they have spun since time began. It suddenly breaks, and they go to the goddess Erda for instructions.

Siegfried leaves the magic ring with Brünnhilde, as a sign of his devotion, and goes to face his next challenge. At the court of Gunther and his sister Gutrune, Siegfried meets a betrayer—Hagen, the bastard son of Alberich. Hagen concocts a potion that makes Siegfried forget his love for Brünnhilde and fall in love with Gutrune. Hagen demands that Siegfried bring Brünnhilde to the court to be Gunther's bride, which, completely deceived, he does. Brünnhilde schemes with Hagen to have Siegfried killed during an upcoming hunting feast, since she knows that only in death will they be rejoined.

At the feast, Siegfried tells of his adventures in the "Rhine Journey," a beautiful lyric passage that is filled with motifs drawn from all his earlier appearances. When Siegfried finishes, Hagen plunges his spear into his back. The potion has just begun to wear off, and Siegfried calls for Brünnhilde. His funeral dirge is impressive and elegant.

Figure 17-29
Wagner. The Valkyrie, "Ride of the Valkyries," leitmotif.

Wagner's Ring of the Nibelung

The *Ring* cycle is a complex, enormous work of art. Careful preparation—which means reading the libretto and being able to understand the action at any given moment—is necessary before listening. Some of the following questions specify listening to only a few passages; others treat general issues. Recordings of the operas in the cycle are plentiful. Two complete recordings are Deutsche Grammophon 2720051 (Herbert von Karajan) and London RING s (Georg Solti).

1. Listen to Scene 3 in *The Rhine Gold*, in which Wotan and Loge enter the dark regions where Alberich's gnomes are working. Does the music interpret the scene accurately? What emotions seem appropriate to the music?

2. Listen to the opening of *The Valkyrie* or to "The Ride of the Valkyries." What images are conjured by the music? How do you imagine the Valkyries? Can you make any judgment regarding their moral nature? What emotions does the music stir in you? Are others affected by it in the same way?

3. The opening of *Siegfried* is different from the rest of the cycle. What kind of contrast do you perceive in the music? What is different about the tempo, the melodic lines, the harmony, the volume of sound, and the tonal colors? Is this music explicitly descriptive? What emotions might one associate with the music?

4. Listen to the last several minutes of *The Twilight of the Gods*, when not only are Siegfried and Brünnhilde purified by fire, but also the gods themselves are consumed by flames, along with their beloved Valhalla. How does the music communicate the seriousness of these events? Consider dynamics, tempo, musical colorations, orchestral volume, and melodic line.

5. Consider the *Ring* cycle as a whole. Is Siegfried an appropriate modern hero? What criticism is being made of modern European industrialism or modern European capitalism? What message might the narrative have concerning the fate of religion in the late nineteenth century? Why would Wagner choose Celtic mythology—stories of gnomes, sea maidens, and ancient gods and heroes—for a work such as this?

The curse of the ring is still active. Hagen kills Gunther during a quarrel, and when Hagen tries to remove the ring from Brünnhilde's finger, the hand of Siegfried is raised in warning. Brünnhilde builds a huge funeral pyre for the body and, giving a triumphant call, rides to join Siegfried in death, saying:

Those who efface the fault of the gods are predestined to suffering and death. Let one sacrifice end the curse. Let the Ring be purified by fire, the waters dissolve it forever. The end of the gods is at hand. But though I leave the world masterless, I give it this precious treasure. In joy or in suffering, happiness can alone come from love.

The fire is extinguished by the overflowing waters of the Rhine, and the Rhine maidens finally recover their treasure. But above them, the glow of Valhalla in flames illuminates the sky. The end of the gods is at hand. From this moment on, free will, not the will of the gods, will direct events. The fearless hero has been victorious; love alone can triumph over death.

DEBUSSY: THE IMPRESSIONIST MUSICAL PALETTE

Debussy's Music

Impressionism and other experiments with color had an effect on music. Claude Debussy (1862–1918) used tone clusters in a style reminiscent of pointillism. His solo piano works such as "Clair de Lune" ("Moonlight"; c. 1905), "Gardens in the Rain" (1903), "The Happy Isle" (1904), and "Image: Reflections in the Water" (1905) reveal, by their titles alone, their impressionistic qualities. They attempt to produce a musical impression of a subject which exists outside the work. Such pieces excite emotional states experienced by the composer in relation to a subject, which is usually identified in the title. For Debussy, the idea was always of uppermost importance. He established programs for his music and often wrote about them in his letters, discussing his inspiration and his intentions.

La Mer: A Symphony of the Sea

Debussy once told a friend that he had almost become a seaman. His experience of the sea was actually quite limited; but his impressions of it were intense—his imagination was even more valuable to him than experience. Reality, he once pointed out, had a way of deadening the emotional value of an idea, or at least its value for musical composition.

The first section, titled "From Dawn to Noon on the Sea," opens with the low strings. Then violins play a very tentative passage, with muted trumpets building (one minute, fifteen seconds—the timing is, of course, approximate) and then lowering in volume. The flutes (2:05) seem to shimmer, and the music raises and lowers in intensity. Then a mix of instruments (3:15) leads to a tremolo of the strings (3:45) that suggests change, a dark before the brightness, which (4:15) comes with a passage in the violins. A crescendo, which suggests splashing (5:05), eventually gives way to a quiet passage in which (5:45) a simple theme is stated in the muted trumpets. All the thematic material is brief, such as that beginning in the strings and woodwinds (6:25). A swelling passage (7:20) crescendos (7:30) in a conclusion dominated by timpani and horns.

The second section (8:10) is called "Play of the Waves." Flutes play in sharply accented patterns, followed by accented trumpet and string passages

---

LISTENING KEY

La Mer

1. Without consulting program notes or referring to the description in the text, try to establish the program or subject matter of this composition. Its title, *La Mer* ("The Sea"), is a beginning. What does this work appear to reveal about the sea?

2. Which families of instruments are you most aware of in the opening passages of the composition?

3. Are you most aware of melody, harmony, or rhythm in *La Mer*? Could you sing any of the opening passages of the composition?

4. Does the music create an impression of the sea for you? Would it do so if you did not know the title of the work? List the specific qualities or characteristics of the sea that you feel Debussy evokes in *La Mer*.

5. After considering the description in the text, write a short (about 150 words) verbal impression of each of the sections of the composition. Do other people have similar impressions?

(8:45). Bells (9:10) suggest glints on the waves. The oboe (9:30) continues the theme, interrupted by a trumpet accent and catches of melody from the flutes. The rhythm and swell of the volume suggest the motion of the waves. This is a purposely vague interlude (the French word for "wave" is "vague"). The section ends in a dynamic crescendo of strings followed by undertones of horns and muted percussion, such as the bells and flutes (14:30).

The third section, "Dialogue of the Wind and the Sea," begins with an ominous fragmented pattern played by the strings. Thematic material heard earlier is introduced and restated by the trumpets (15:15). The strings, which are bright and tentative (16:00), suggest expectation and uncertainty. The brash horn passages (16:45) deftly imply glints and spray and then suggest crashing sea swells (17:30). Quiet passages offer a contrast, usually dominated by the strings. Strings also build tension (18:30) and anticipation, answered by the woodwinds (18:45), which build a sustained melodic passage that rises and mixes with the horns, falls (20:15), and transforms itself into more anticipation (20:30), repeating thematic material heard earlier. The dynamics of the horns and strings build to a coda (22:15), which ends in a resounding crescendo concluded by the timpani.

Debussy understood that he was opening new doors for composers and that his work incorporated a theory which could change music. In *La Mer*, he evokes images of the sea by making the instruments and melodic material congruent with our imaginative sense of the sea. Despite the fact that other composers had tried to do the same, his achievement is singular. He persisted in his impressionistic efforts much more than any composer before him.

Dance

CLASSICAL BALLET

The second half of the nineteenth century saw the development of classical ballet, much as it exists today. Paris was the center of dance, and most of the important dancers came from Italy. But in Russia, the French choreographer Marius Petipa (1819–1910) composed more than thirty major ballets and adapted almost 100 more during his forty-year career. In the latter part of his reign he had a collaborator, Lev Ivanovich Ivanov (1834–1901), whose work is apparent in many of the important scenes of *Swan Lake*.

Figure 17-30
Margot Fonteyn and Rudolf Nureyev in *Swan Lake.*
(Dance Collection, New York Public Library.)

SWAN LAKE: ENCHANTMENT AND THE VALUE OF DEVOTION

The music for the ballet *Swan Lake* was composed by Pyotr Ilich Tchaikovsky (1840–1893) between 1871 and 1877. Its first performance in Moscow was a failure. But when Petipa and Ivanov teamed their efforts for its first complete performance in 1895, it was a resounding success, and it has been popular ever since. (Figure 17-30 shows a performance by Margot Fonteyn and Rudolf Nureyev.)

The pretext, or narrative, concerns Siegfried, a handsome young prince whose mother has determined that he must marry. Rothbart, a magician, has meanwhile surrounded himself with a bevy of women whom he has changed into swans (in some versions of the myth the Valkyries are swan maidens). When the ballet opens, Siegfried sees the swans in flight and determines to go hunting. In Act 2, Rothbart is tending his flock of swans, who regain their womanly shape only at night. Odette, the white swan, is the most beautiful of them, and she leads the others in a dance based on an interpretation of swan gestures. At first, Siegfried's hunters want to shoot the swans, but he holds them back. In a duet, he discovers that Odette is enchanted but that he can free her if he remains true to her. She warns him that Rothbart will do everything he can to trick him, but Siegfried vows to be faithful.

At the ball that Siegfried's mother has given for him, Petipa shows off a number of regional folk dances. Women from numerous lands have come to perform for Siegfried, and each does her native dance for him. But the dancing is interrupted by the appearance of Odile, the black swan. She is really Rothbart's daughter, and he has made her look exactly like Odette. When she dances, she captures Siegfried's heart. He has no suspicion that she is not Odette until, after he has committed himself to her, she disappears and he knows he has been duped. He rushes off to find the real Odette.

Act 4 ends in one of several ways. In one version there is a happy ending. Odette forgives Siegfried, who wafts her to a mountaintop to prevent Rothbart from drowning them in a storm he has conjured up. In a more ambiguous version, Siegfried finds Odette dancing mournfully in the midst of the other swans. He can do nothing to break the spell she is in, and he watches as she plunges into the lake. Then, in an act of self-sacrifice, he plunges in after her. The lake disappears, and we see them moving away together in the distance, indicating that Rothbart's spell was broken by love after death.

The power of *Swan Lake* to hold our attention today is largely the result of the extraordinary opportunities for expressive dance that Petipa and Ivanov's choreography affords. The significance of the myth is not comparable to what we find in Wagner, despite the fact that both Siegfrieds must sacrifice themselves and both are beguiled by a magician. Over the years, the role of Siegfried has attracted the best dancers of each generation, as has been true of the role of Odette and Odile, which today is usually danced by the same ballerina.

Science and Philosophy

DARWIN: THE SURVIVAL OF THE FITTEST

Charles Darwin (1809–1882) began college intending to be a physician, but soon he transferred from Edinburgh to Cambridge to prepare for the clergy. He never lost his interest in science, and when he was given a chance to sail on the *Beagle,* which was making a scientific expedition to South America that would last five years, he eagerly accepted. It was on this famous voyage that Darwin began to collect evidence of species that showed a striking range of variations from the norms expected in Europe. The result of his observations and thoughts was the formulation of the theory of evolution.

The idea of evolution itself was not completely novel. Diderot had proposed something of the sort, which he called "transformism," in his *Encyclopedia* in the 1750s. The basic problem with any theory of evolution was simply that species were thought to be immutable; they did not change. The geologic record, showing extinct mastodons, mammoths, and hundreds of other beings, challenged the theory of special creation, based on the Mosaic books of the Old Testament. But some contemporary scientists explained that God had simply created certain animals which he permitted to become extinct and then replaced with new animals.

Darwin's contribution was the concept of "natural selection." Humans had been altering plant and animal species for thousands of years. The cultivation of stronger varieties of grain as well as the breeding of superior dogs, horses, and domestic animals showed that species could be altered. The question was: How could this happen in nature? Darwin proposed that variations are always occurring in nature in a random fashion and that some are useful and some are not. Those which best take advantage of the peculiarities of the environment will survive. Those which do not will perish. As he said in *On the Origin of Species by Means of Natural Selection* (1859):

> Can it be thought improbable, seeing that variations useful to man have undoubtedly occurred that other variations useful in some way to each being in the great and complex battle of life, should occur in the course of many successive generations? If such do occur, can we doubt (remembering that many more individuals are born than can possibly survive) that individuals having

any advantage, however slight, over others, would have the best chance of surviving and procreating their kind? On the other hand, we may feel sure that any variation in the least degree injurious would be rigidly destroyed. This preservation of favorable individual differences and variations, and the destruction of those which are injurious, I have called Natural Selection, or the Survival of the Fittest.

Darwin's research was corroborated by another scientist, Alfred Russel Wallace (1823–1913), who propounded the same theory at precisely the same time (thus forcing Darwin to publish *Origin of Species* earlier than he might otherwise have done). It is not surprising, therefore, that the scientific community (except for some older scientists whose views clashed explicitly with it) generally accepted the theory of evolution as Darwin proposed it. Moreover, the theory began almost immediately to affect the way people thought about life, particularly about such things as history, sociology, warfare, and colonialism.

Darwin described life in nature as a battle for survival. Therefore, it was not long before social theorists—who found the idea convenient—began to think of nations as individuals who had to keep "in shape" by waging war, thereby perfecting civilization. The theory, which was easily abused, became widespread by the end of the century.

Like Galileo, Darwin removed humankind from the center of the intellectual universe postulated by earlier ages. If people evolved from lower beings, the animal nature of humankind might take precedence over its angelic nature. In *The Descent of Man and Selection in Relation to Sex* (1871), Darwin discussed these implications. His opponents meanwhile argued that humans did not undergo evolution and that even if the concept of the "survival of the fittest" applied to nature, it did not apply to people.

The view of nature which results from Darwin's theory is the opposite of that of Wordsworth and the other romantics. Religious and other thinkers who saw the world as designed by God in every detail were challenged by wastefulness, disharmony, random variation, and selection of species by brutal means: the war for survival. Instead of a great "guiding mind" with which humankind could participate in nature, Darwin's views left a system guided by chance and ruled by brute force and an indifferent environment. But the unity of humans and nature, a concept popular with the romantics, was not incompatible with Darwin; it was his opponents who saw humanity and nature as two separate realms.

Because Darwin's age was secular in the extreme, his views found considerable acceptance. Thomas Henry Huxley (1825–1895) was an ardent supporter of Darwin and began a trend toward agnosticism in religious matters. Agnostics assumed that knowledge of the nature of God is not possible. Agnosticism was meant to contrast with the views of the early Christian gnostics, who felt that they knew God and that they understood all there was to know about life after death. Agnosticism grew in popularity in Europe, particularly in England and Germany, during the remainder of the century.

MARX: DIALECTICAL MATERIALISM AND THE EVOLUTION OF ECONOMICS

Most of the powerful thinkers in the last part of the nineteenth century were more influential in the next generation than in their own time. Karl Marx (1818–1883) is an example.

The Communist Manifesto was published in February 1848, only months before the wave of revolutions spread across Europe. It did not, however, have any direct influence on these revolutions. Its purpose was strictly to explain what communism meant for those who struggled to achieve it in Europe. His life's work, *Capital,* published in part in 1867, is his most influential theoretical piece. It was not until after Marx's death that it was published in its full form by his friend and long-time collaborator, Friedrich Engels (1820–1895).

Marx's thought was based in part on the dialecticalism of Hegel. Marx saw progress as a process of action and reaction. He posited that a thesis, or positive force, is opposed by an antithesis, or negative force; the conflict between them yields a synthesis, which in turn becomes the thesis for yet another antithesis, and so on. His view was that progress was a union of opposites, a negation of negations. He saw revolution as antithetical to the established order; out of it would grow the synthesis of the proletariat, which would in turn yield to the classless society.

Marx's views, as well as those of Engels, grew in some measure from their observation of the general misery of the common worker in Europe at the time of the industrial revolution. Workers toiled for a pittance while their industrial overlords grew rich. The inequities in the economic scheme of things made the hardest-working people the poorest. The unwillingness of the rich to propose relief or legislation to help the poor worsened the situation until late in the century. Marx's theories spoke directly to these inequities and this kind of social injustice.

Marx had no room for religion in his scheme. He declared that religion was the "opium of the people" and focused entirely on the material world of experience. Communism was an inevitable stage in the evolution of civilization, he declared, taking an essentially scientific attitude toward social events. Today his views guide the attitudes of a third of the world's population.

NIETZSCHE: THE WILL TO POWER

Like Marx, Friedrich Nietzsche (1844–1900) was ahead of his time. He was a German philosopher whose undergraduate work at the universities of Bonn and Leipzig was so astonishing that he was given a professorship in classical philology at Basel in 1869, before he had even graduated. In only ten years, however, his health forced him to withdraw from the university. By 1888 he was declared insane.

Nietzsche read Darwin and was, for a time, a devotee of Wagner. When he was still an undergraduate, he read a work by the German pessimist philosopher Arthur Schopenhauer (1788–1860), *The World as Will and Idea*. And though he was a theology major, he began to abandon his beliefs in Christianity. His parents were distressed, but he persisted. His own writings are derived essentially from Schopenhauer and are characterized by brilliant negation of most of the values held by those before him. Yet this negation was his way of trying to reach a more profound understanding and a deeper truth.

The Will to Power (1895–1901) taught that the Judeo-Christian system of values, based on humility, pacifism, and the negation of pleasures, was quite wrong. These values went against people's basic instincts: the will to dominate and to possess and use power. The connection with Darwin is not strong, although Nietzsche thought that the truly unusual person, the "superman," whose ethical views were superior to those of the mass—what he called "slave values"—must be permitted to exist. The "superman" had the imagination and the excellence of character that made it impossible for him to be like

the masses and to be less than he was. Among the aphorisms Nietzsche wrote on this subject was, "I am writing for a race of men which does not yet exist: for the lords of the earth."

One of Nietzsche's longest-lasting insights, developed in a book written early in his career, *The Birth of Tragedy from the Spirit of Music* (1872), was inspired by his interest in Wagner. He found the deeply passionate nature of Wagner's music extremely moving. His analysis led him to conceive of two great forces in the human psyche. One was the Apollonian—the high-minded, rational, dispassionate thoughtfulness associated with the Greek god of music, Apollo. He stands for the individual, for self-control, and for order. The other was the Dionysian, which was associated with the Greek god of drunkenness and dark passion, Dionysus. He stands for loss of control, lust, loss of individual identity, and mob action. He is passion, the opposite of reason.

Nietzsche's searches into music and other arts resulted partly from his conviction that aesthetic or artistic values were among the only ones that could be substituted for conventional religious values. Nietzsche declared that "God is dead," and he feared that when people became aware of that fact they would behave irrationally. He predicted a breakdown in values, a new brutalization, and a frightening world in which no new values would replace the old ones. He predicted an era of brutal warfare and destruction. His predictions have been in much too large measure fulfilled. His age, which at the turn of the century congratulated itself on its comfort, its achievements, and its general peacefulness, was on the brink of massive wars and unending ideological struggle.

Summary

The last half of the nineteenth century was marked by increasing secularization, as advances in technology and science produced a faith in progress and in the advancement of humankind. Artistic movements enjoyed relatively short life spans. Realism emphasized sometimes unappealing details in paintings, novels, and plays. Realism dealt with things as they were, without sentimentality. Impressionism was also interested in things as they were, but the impressionists used a different approach. Intrigued by the spontaneous and even the accidental, Monet,

Manet, Degas, Rodin, and others portrayed their impressions of the world of experience. Their work was characterized by immediacy and was often very personal. For almost twenty years, western painting was influenced by the work of the impressionists, who were in turn influenced by the newly discovered Japanese prints, characterized by bulkless figures, flat but brilliant colors, and a distinctive approach to perspective. The most important musical influence of the last half of the nineteenth century, Wagner's *Ring of the Nibelung,* is relatable neither to realism nor to impressionism. It represents an extraordinary excursion into indigenous myth and perhaps universal symbolism. It is an analysis of materialism and the lust for power, and it demonstrates that only heroic sacrifice and love can undo the evil that materialism and the lust for power create. The century ended with a peaceful calm, at least in comparison with the Napoleonic wars that began it. But the century had begun with a general belief in traditional religious values, reinforced by romantic idealism. The findings of Darwin and others shattered those views, and the pundits of industrialism tried to substitute a faith in the progress of technology; they were helped in their efforts by the excitement generated by the Crystal Palace and the London Exhibition of 1851, which so awed Queen Victoria. The century ended with Darwin shattering romantic views of nature, with Marx's "spectre of communism" haunting Europe, and with Nietzsche's ominous warning that God was dead and that it would not be long before the world found this out.

Concepts in Chapter 17

The second half of the nineteenth century witnessed the slow beginning of a pattern of social reform.

Artistic styles in many media became sharply realistic.

European and American industry produced extraordinary wealth, leading to extensive colonization in Africa and Asia.

Realism in painting was linked to scientific perception—seeing things as they are.

The work of the realist painters often included social messages.

The painters of the Barbizon school worked outdoors.

Photography influenced painting from 1839 until the end of the century.

Social criticism was implicit in the work of painters like Daumier.

Courbet's realism shocked Paris; his *Burial at Ornans* treated common people with the seriousness usually reserved for the nobility.

American realist painters were influenced by developments in Europe.

The impressionists emphasized personal vision—the "impression" of the painter.

Manet's work called attention to the nature of the paint itself.

Monet took great delight in the sensa of painting; his *Impression: Sunrise* gave the impressionists their name.

Degas, like many other painters, made use of photography.

Cézanne's analytic approach to painting produced a new style that forced people to look at the canvas, not the illusion of what was represented.

Van Gogh and other painters of the period were expressionistic in their attitude; they were concerned with expressing personal feelings, rather than with portraying their impressions of a scene.

Early photographers were indebted to painting, while struggling for their own artistic identity.

The work of Rodin, the most important sculptor of the age, was both impressionistic and realistic.

Paxton's Crystal Palace reflected a new era in architecture marked by the use of iron, glass, and prefabrication.

Literature in France, England, and America carried on romantic trends.

Whitman and Baudelaire were diametrically opposed in terms of their attitudes toward humankind.

Flaubert, whose work is marked by the use of such formal devices as repetition and symbolism, created the modern novel; his realism caused his work to be suppressed.

Emma Bovary is presented objectively; Flaubert provides no clues as to how she should be judged.

Ibsen treated unpleasant subject matter in his plays; he created a realist drama.

Wagner employed the leitmotif, a musical figure that is repeated at crucial moments throughout a composition, creating a sense of organic unity.

Wagner's *Ring* cycle, consisting of four operas, depends on Germanic myth of Celtic origins; it celebrates the destruction of the gods and the redemption of the world through love.

Much of Debussy's impressionistic music is programmatic: the music interprets a specific subject derived from outside itself.

Classical ballet developed in Russia in the works of Ivanov; *Swan Lake* derives from Celtic myth and is reminisiscent of portions of the *Ring* cycle.

Darwin's theory of evolution shocked those whose worldview was people-centered.

Marx's theories implied a natural evolution of civilization resulting in communism.

Nietzsche's theories elevated human will as a force in the universe; Nietzsche postulated a morally superior "superman" for whom the society would have to make way.

Nietzsche feared that the twentieth century would be racked by war and dissension as a result of the death of the idea of God.

Suggested Readings

Adhemar, Jean. *Honoré Daumier.* Tisné: New York, 1954.

Barzun, Jacques. *Darwin, Marx, and Wagner.* New York: Columbia, 1953.

Baudelaire, Charles. *Les Fleurs du Mal.* Richard Howard, trans. Boston: David Godine, 1982.

Baumer, Franklin L., ed. *Intellectual Movements in Modern European History.* London: Macmillan, 1965. (Acton on Marx; Lovejoy on Darwin.)

Beaver, Patrick. *The Crystal Palace.* London: Hugh Evelyn, 1970.

Bellony-Rewald, Alice. *Lost World of the Impressionists.* Greenwich, Conn.: New York Graphic Society, 1976.

Boudaille, Georges. *Gustave Courbet: Painter in Protest.* Greenwich, Conn.: New York Graphic Society, 1970.

Bouret, Jean. *The Barbizon School.* Greenwich, Conn.: New York Graphic Society, 1972.

Champa, Kermit S. *Studies in Early Impressionism.* New Haven, Conn.: Yale, 1973.

Einstein, Alfred. *Music in the Romantic Era.* New York: Norton, 1948.

Elsen, Albert. *Rodin.* New York: Museum of Modern Art, 1963.

Hanson, Anne Coffin. *Manet and the Modern Tradition.* New Haven, Conn.: Yale, 1977.

Holt, Elizabeth Gilmore. *From the Classicists to the Impressionists: Art and Architecture in the Nineteenth Century.* Garden City, N.Y.: Doubleday, 1966.

Johns, Elizabeth. *Thomas Eakins.* Princeton, N.J.: Princeton University Press, 1984.

Kelder, Diane. *Great Masters of French Impressionism.* New York: Crown, 1978.

Leymarie, Jean. *Impressionism.* J. Emmons, trans. 2 vols. New York: Skira, 1955.

Licht, Fred. *Sculpture—Nineteenth and Twentieth Centuries.* Greenwich, Conn.: New York Graphic Society, 1967.

Newhall, Beaumont. *The History of Photography from 1839 to the Present.* Rev. ed. New York: Museum of Modern Art, 1982.

Newman, Ernest. *The Life of Richard Wagner.* 4 vols. New York: Knopf, 1933–1946.

———. *The Wagner Operas.* New York: Knopf, 1949.

Nochlin, Linda. *Gustave Courbet: A Study of Style and Society.* New York: Garland, 1976.

———. *Realism.* Harmondsworth, England: Penguin, 1971.

Rewald, John. *The History of Impressionism.* 4th ed. New York: Museum of Modern Art, 1973.

———. *Post-Impressionism from Van Gogh to Gauguin.* 2d ed. New York: Museum of Modern Art, 1962.

Schapiro, Meyer. *Paul Cézanne.* 3d ed. New York: Abrams, 1965.

Strunk, Oliver. *Source Readings in Music History: The Romantic Era.* New York: Norton, 1965.

Sutton, Denys. *Triumphant Satyr: The World of Auguste Rodin.* London: Country Life, 1966.

Turner, Peter, and Richard Wood. *P. H. Emerson.* Boston: David Godine, 1974.

PART
EIGHT

PART EIGHT

THE WORLD IN 1914

CANADA

UNITED STATES

UNITED
KINGDOM

ATLANTIC OCEAN

PACIFIC OCEAN

0   500   1000 1500 2000 miles

British   French   Belgian   Dutch   Portuguese

THE TWENTIETH CENTURY

CHINA

JAPAN

INDIA

PACIFIC OCEAN

DUTCH EAST INDIES

INDIAN OCEAN

SOUTH AFRICA

panish Danish Italian German United States

Total War and Uneasy Peace: 1903 to the Present

The twentieth century was expected to usher in an era of lasting peace and scientific progress. The as yet unheard-of achievements of flight and the almost unimagined adventures in space of *Sputnik* and the Voyagers would have convinced the nineteenth century that a golden age was coming. However, Nietzsche had long warned that the new age might bring disaster in the form of war, unparalleled cruelty, and materialism. He feared that progress would erode the values which had traditionally bound people together and given their lives meaning. Nietzsche foresaw an age in which meaning would be lost, and thus people would be lost, paving the way for tragedy.

It is still difficult to explain precisely what happened. The century began with the Boer war. Tensions in central Europe grew; Germany, longing for expansion, demanded its "rightful place" in Europe's economy and power structure. Other nations were blinded by patriotism, assuming that the wars they risked were traditional in nature. They did not learn from the experience of the American Civil War; instead, they planned strategies on the basis of their studies of Napoleon's campaigns, believing that war would be fought as it always had been.

World War I (1914–1918) proved everyone wrong. At first, and typically, lightly clad men marched bravely into fire from machine guns, sacrificing themselves for reasons that few people could understand. But the bloodletting became so intolerable that people reacted by not following their leaders. The breakdown in authority which characterizes modern times began in response to the slaughter in Europe—in which a single engagement sometimes took 100,000 lives. The casualties on both sides numbered in the millions. (By comparison, the entire Vietnamese war took 58,000 American lives.)

The war became a defensive stalemate, a war of attrition, fought in trenches with artillery and bombs. Russia withdrew after the Bolshevik revolution and the creation of Soviet communism; and although the United States, in a patriotic flurry, sent enough fresh troops to tip the balance and bring the war to an end, nothing was really settled.

The 1920s were a decade of uneasy jubilation. In the United States, prohibition of alcoholic beverages was forced on the entire nation, making everyone who drank a criminal.

Organized crime became big business and remains so. The jazz age saw the first rebellion of youth, with young people turning against the moral standards of their parents.

The great depression brought a loss of faith in democratic capitalism and turned many people to communism or—as in Germany, Italy, and Spain—to fascism. The 1930s saw the rise of Mussolini and Hitler. Germany blamed the Jews for inflation and economic uncertainty; and Hitler rebuilt German armies and based a new national pride on the anti-Semitism of the middle classes. Manipulating the mass media as no one had ever done before, Hitler created a state capable of greater terror and horror than had ever been experienced in history. Fascism was defeated in World War II (1939–1945)—a war significant for having been one in which the victors understood why they were fighting.

Victory was ambiguous, however; with it came the realization that the two forces left, capitalism and communism, could not easily coexist. Russia achieved its long-held dream of dominance in eastern Europe. The United States was the only undamaged western nation capable of leadership; but it had used the atom bomb against the Japanese at Hiroshima and Nagasaki, and this eventually contributed to the erosion of its moral leadership. The United Nations' "peace action" in Korea (1950–1953), America's first limited war, pitted the United States against China, which had become communist at the end of its civil war in 1949. The Vietnamese war (1963–1975) was extremely unpopular in the United States, leading to colossal protests and social upheavals. The United States also suffered its worst modern race riots and rebellions during those years. Drugs—some brought in through Vietnam and some distributed by organized crime—became epidemic. With the resignation, in disgrace, of President Nixon and Vice President Agnew, the failure of moral leadership became almost total.

After the end of the Vietnamese war, stability returned to the United States—which meant that it returned to its western allies as well. But the mid-1970s saw an international economic recession comparable in magnitude to the great depression of the 1930s. The mid-1980s have seen the beginning of a worldwide economic recovery.

Such changes, cataclysmic by the standards of other ages, have produced a remarkably resilient population. Change is the only "constant" that modern people have come to expect.

Art and the Irrational

In the arts several important intellectual trends have produced changes which are as total, as uncompromising, and as unexpected as those in political life. The writings of Sigmund Freud influenced the arts of the entire century. Freud's theory was that the mind has a powerful irrational content, the subconscious, which must be fully integrated with its rational counterpart, the conscious, if health is to be maintained. Nietzsche's study of Greek culture and music in *The Birth of Tragedy from the Spirit of Music* (1872) had foreshadowed this view. Freud demonstrated that the subconscious communicates in dreams, when it is not censored by the conscious mind. Surrealism, an art movement that has persisted throughout the century, is based in large measure on Freud's views. Surrealist painting, literature, dance, and film—which all have a dreamlike, mysterious quality—aim at portraying the inner realities, the kinds of deep meanings that Nietzsche saw in the great Greek tragedies.

Freud's theories offered a way to explore the irrational. World War I shook artists' faith in reason, which had produced destruction and stupidity. The dadaists chose to attack reason by espousing unreason. Their art was a tissue of illogic and whimsy—and a flagrant attack on the comfortable middle-class mores and values that had brought us to the maelstrom of death in 1914. Naturally, the middle classes could not understand this meaninglessness, and a schism between artists and the public—a typical situation in the twentieth century—began.

The surrealists also attacked middle-class logic and values. Their attack on reason and logic was conducted through an analysis of dreams and the subconscious. The films of Luis Buñuel, Ingmar Bergman, and Federico Fellini were particularly influential in the second half of the century in forwarding surrealist goals. The exploration of mythic values became an adjunct of Freudian and Jungian theories: myths were the cultural repository of suppressed emotion, just as dreams were our personal repository of guilt. By examining myth we gain insight into the deepest of human understandings.

Existentialist philosophers helped Europe find a reason to continue in the face of the destruction of its cities, its economies, its youth, and its values. By defying the medieval theory that we are essentially what we are no matter what we do, existentialism gave a new value to the concept of existence. Action comes first. We are what we do, and we should be careful of everything we do, since every action shapes us as human beings.

The existentialist view is that life is devoid of meaning until we give it meaning. Our actions create meaning. The church is not responsible for giving meaning to our lives, nor is the state responsible for making us feel part of a great patriotic or world movement. Those values led to death and war. Instead, the individual must face the terror of the absurd (a form of illogic) and wrench a meaning from existence. Jean-Paul Sartre and Albert Camus were among the most influential writers in the existentialist mode. They gave a sense of hope to artists around the world.

The abstract expressionists, whose nonobjective "gestures" on canvas did not produce conventional portraits or realistic representations, were deeply existentialist. They defined themselves in their art every time they worked. Their work was personal, painful, and a form of agony linked with existentialist suffering. They were completely successful in the 1950s and early 1960s, when the first wave of pop art began to challenge their authority.

Some of the artists of the 1950s and the 1960s looked to eastern religions, such as Japanese Zen Buddhism and Indian Hinduism, which preached a faith in irrationality that contradicted the conventional western faith in logic and reason. John Cage, Jack Kerouac, Allen Ginsberg, the Beatles, and many others found that eastern religions, sometimes in combination with drugs, produced the liberation which they considered they needed to create their work.

The attack on rationality and logic has not yet ended. The threat of nuclear destruction has not disappeared, and the arguments for maintaining stockpiles of weapons and pouring national wealth into weaponry instead of human projects are based on strict logic and reason. Even the most exacting realist artists of the new superrealist school tend to remove the logical function from their work. Their paintings and photographs are incredibly detailed, but they often have no apparent "reason" behind them. What they mean is obscure to a conventional middle-class audience. The values that artists have espoused and explored in the twentieth century remain separate from the mainstream of the culture. In this sense, art in our times is largely subversive—an attempt to reform the culture and help it understand itself. Culture almost died in 1914, and then again in 1939; the world still reels from the sounds of cannons and bombs.

Brief Chronology

1903   The Wright brothers make their first flight.

1904   Publication of Sigmund Freud's *Psychopathology of Everyday Life.*

1905   Alfred Stieglitz opens his Photo-Secessionist gallery, known as "291," in New York; the fauves show their work in Paris; Einstein formulates the theory of relativity; the Russo-Japanese war ends in defeat of the Russians.

1907   Picasso and Braque begin developing cubism.

1909   Henry Ford builds cars on an assembly line.

1910   The futurist manifesto.

1911   The Chinese revolution establishes a republic.

1912–1913   War in the Balkans sets the stage for World War I; the New York Armory Show.

1914   World War I begins.

1916   Dadaism founded in the Café Voltaire, Zurich.

1917   The United States enters World War I; the October revolution in Russia establishes the Bolshevik (communist) government under Lenin.

1918   World War I ends.

1919   The League of Nations founded.

1920   First regular radio station broadcasts.

1922   Fascists seize government in Italy; inflation destroys the German economy; James Joyce's *Ulysses* and T.S. Eliot's *Waste Land* are published.

1923   The French occupy the Ruhr because Germany reneges on reparations.

1924   The first surrealist manifesto.

1929   The Wall Street crash: beginning of the great depression.

1933   January 30, Hitler becomes chancellor of Germany.

1936   Civil war in Spain, lasting until 1939.

1937 Guernica bombed.

1938 Germany absorbs Austria.

1939 August: Germany and Russia sign nonaggression pact; Germany invades Poland in September; Britain and France declare war on Germany; first television station begins regular broadcasts.

1940 May: the British expeditionary force is evacuated from Dunkirk.

1941 December 7: the Japanese attack Pearl Harbor, Hawaii; the United States declares war on Japan and on the European axis.

1944 The first computer technology is developed.

1945 May 8: the war in Europe ends; August 6 and 7, atom bombs are dropped on Hiroshima and Nagasaki; the war ends September 2— casualties: 15 million military personnel and approximately the same number of civilians; United Nations Charter signed.

1947 The Marshall Plan begins rebuilding Europe.

1948 Israeli independence after the Arab war.

1949 Chinese communists under Mao Tse-tung win the civil war; Russia explodes its first atom bomb.

1950–1953 The Korean war, a United Nations peacekeeping effort, but fought primarily by United States forces against North Korean and Chinese communists.

1957 *Sputnik,* first satellite in space, launched.

1961 First manned space flight by Russian astronauts.

1963–1974 The Vietnamese war.

1967 The Israeli-Arab six-day war.

1969 The United States places first astronaut on the moon.

1974 *Skylab,* an orbiting space laboratory, launched.

1980 Successful launching of the space shuttle *Columbia.*

1983 First artificial heart transplant performed.

CHAPTER 18

GENERATIONS OF WAR AND THE CRISIS IN VALUES: 1900 TO 1945

Historical Background

COLONIZATION: THE DOMINANCE OF POWER

 The period 1880–1914 saw the greatest colonial expansion in modern times. Europe used its technology to dominate Asia and Africa and, to a lesser extent, South America. Raw materials, which Europe lacked, were in abundance in these lands, and thus the key to continued growth and economic expansion lay in securing colonies. The process was somewhat Darwinian: the technologically more advanced nations simply appropriated the resources and lands of those which were less advanced.

WORLD WAR I: THE DESTRUCTION OF VALUES

The general gloom that marked much of the art of the 1890s in Europe centered on psychological isolation. But Nietzsche's prophecies of the destruction of civilization were not only psychological, but also communal and technological. By the turn of the century Sigmund Freud had made his observations about the existence in the mind of an unconscious that is capable of strange behavior. Freud did not discover the death wish until he studied shell-shocked victims of the First World War, but in retrospect it seemed that the entire European culture had begun, in 1914, to act out a self-destructive psychological drama. Many people refused to serve in the armed forces, and some moved to neutral nations, such as Switzerland. Others, still clinging to the heroic military values that had obtained since the time of the Greeks, marched valiantly off to battle to the tune of simpleminded patriotic hit songs.

Instead of ending quickly with a determined offensive, the war became a defensive stalemate. Artillery, barbed wire, and machine guns had made defense an advantageous strategy. Trenches were dug, and the war became a murderous nightmare, with losses in the major battles sometimes exceeding half a million men. The stalemate persisted until the United States entered the war in April 1917. Eventually, Germany and Austria were forced to surrender.

THE RUSSIAN REVOLUTION

In March 1917, the antiquated, inefficient Russian czarist government collapsed. From then on, Russia was out of the war. The Germans permitted the revolutionary Vladimir Ilich Lenin (1870–1924) to cross Germany in a sealed railroad car to lead the revolution of October 1917, in which the communists began to put into action some of the theories of Karl Marx, whom Lenin regarded as the most prophetic voice of the previous century.

THE PEACE THAT FAILED

The war ended on November 11, 1918. But the aftermath of peace was almost as frightening as the war itself. In Russia, there was civil war in the 1920s, with the Red armies victorious over the White armies. In Germany, even though it had been undamaged by war, conditions were appalling. France, which had been a battleground, demanded extensive reparations from Germany and Austria. Since France had had to pay reparations in 1815 and 1871, it was determined to be repaid now. The United States had loaned enormous sums to Great Britain and France, and it, too, demanded repayment. The drain on the German and Austrian economies was overwhelming, producing a financial crisis that peaked in 1923; the United States dollar, which had been worth about 4 German marks in 1914, cost 800 million marks in 1923. Inflation wiped out life savings and destroyed all the security that the German middle classes had built during generations of work.

In the face of inflation, Britain decided not to demand further repayments, and France, too, agreed to change its attitude. But the United States held that not paying a debt was dishonorable. Most of the reparations that had been collected had gone to the United States in any event, and when Germany defaulted, the French army moved to occupy parts of nearby industrial Germany.

DEPRESSION:
THE REACTIONARY MIDDLE CLASSES

The result of all this inflation and financial breakdown was a form of chaos for which the middle classes blamed bankers, Jews, intermediaries, and socialists. The stage was set for the rise in Italy of Benito Mussolini and in Germany of Adolf Hitler, two shrewd politicians who knew how to play on the sympathies of the middle class, which had swept them into power. They became heads of government legally, but both used private armies of storm troopers to intimidate the population. They always supported nationalism and patriotic values, and they offered law and order to their people; but the price was tyranny. They were efficient (Mussolini, it was said, made the trains run on time) and ruthless—those who did not agree with them were forced to submit for the "greater good" of the whole, or else they were murdered or imprisoned in concentration camps.

The great depression, which struck in October 1929, made it all but impossible for the United States, Great Britain, and France to monitor what was happening in Italy and Germany. The Treaty of Versailles had restricted the military power of Germany, but Hitler's private armies made such restrictions meaningless. The great experiment of the League of Nations at Locarno, Switzerland, failed when the United States withdrew its support, despite the fact that the League had been a dream of President Woodrow Wilson. The United States still wanted to remain apart from European affairs.

WORLD WAR II

Hitler wanted to reunite all German-speaking districts with Germany. The other western nations were slow to take action against him because they saw fascism as an alternative to communism. That is, communism was considered more of a threat to the capitalist nations than fascism. When the Spanish civil war raged in the late 1930s, the fascists fought the republicans, who were aligned with the communists. (It was during the Spanish civil war that the Germans bombed a Basque village, Guernica, as an experiment, and Pablo Picasso, the century's greatest artist, memorialized the event in a painting.) The powers that could have prevented World War II stood by and watched.

When the war finally came, it was designed, like the previous one, as an offensive war. The French had built the Maginot Line, a series of fortifications designed to be a concrete buffer against Germany, but the line ended at Belgium—and in any event Hitler was determined never to fight a trench war. His "blitzkrieg"—lightning war—was made possible by armored columns that could travel at high speeds and by Stuka dive-bombers, which guaranteed air superiority. The Second World War was totally different from the First World War because of armor and air power.

France was defeated in a little over two weeks; the Maginot Line had been skirted at Belgium. The English were stranded at Dunkirk, where only a miraculous civilian and military effort saved the better part of the expeditionary force. Air power figured in the Japanese bombing of Pearl Harbor. In northern Africa, Marshal Rommel and General Patton demonstrated the power of highly mobile armored columns and tanks. The submarine had changed naval warfare in the First World War, and it remained supreme in the Second World War. But all this new technology was outmoded entirely in 1945, when the atom bomb leveled first Hiroshima and then Nagasaki. Terrifying as the first war had been, the second was an even more "total" war, with upward of 30 million victims.

Painting

THE FAUVES: EXPRESSING PAINTERLY VALUES

The twentieth century is filled with art movements, the first of which was that of the fauves, a nickname derived from a critic's comment suggesting that painters such as Henri Matisse (1869–1954), Georges Rouault (1871–1958), Maurice de Vlaminck (1876–1958), and André Derain (1880–1954) painted with the abandon of "wild beasts." Fauvism, whose adherents were a much more tightly knit group than the impressionists, lasted about five years, from 1905 to 1910. As an offshoot of the expressionists, the fauves were concerned with the value of color, line, and distortion.

Henri Matisse

Henri Matisse, the leader of the group, exhibited with other fauves at the Autumn Salon of 1905. His gigantic celebration of dance (Color plates 37 and 38) offers a glimpse into the new aesthetic.

Matisse's subject matter is dance, treated as it might be on a Greek vase. The scale of the paintings — each is over 12 feet long—adds enormous vitality to the images. Matisse, however, like a vase painter, is concerned with decorative values; this is evident in the flat colors, the rhythmic line of the dancers, and the uniform covering of the entire surface. These are techniques used in Japanese ukiyo-e prints, depicting scenes from everyday life, which were circulated in Europe beginning in the 1850s. The result is unexpected freshness and a sense of exuberance.

In these paintings Matisse is representing emotion —a response to the *idea* of dance—and the rhythmic

---

COMPARISON KEY

 # Matisse

1. What is the subject matter of Color Plates 37 and 38? Are they realistic or impressionistic?

2. Comment on the colors—their range and their variation. Are they realistic? Are the people modeled and sculptural in the manner of, say, Caravaggio? Is there any chiaroscuro here? Is there volume? Do the paintings create an illusion of a scene?

3. What kinds of emotions are suggested by the paintings?

4. How do these paintings differ from each other?

5. What is the respective importance of line, color, volume, space, and perspective in the paintings?

form and the eternal harmony implied in the circle dance. In both versions, the circle is broken momentarily where the hands of the lowest figure and the next figure to the left do not join; yet the rhythmic curves of the legs and arms—more fluid and full in the second version—suggest that the circle will not remain broken. The figures reach for one another. The first version seems more spontaneous, but the second seems more intense. The blue and green backgrounds are flatter and less textural in the second version, and we detect a greater security in the force of the line, which is more schematic and less concerned with depicting anatomy than with serving a unifying purpose.

Georges Rouault

Georges Rouault was only briefly a fauve, and his connection with the movement shows how close it is to the general mode of expressionism. *The Holy Face* (Color Plate 39) is a later work. Rouault uses heavy black lines, filling the spaces between them with intense, luminous color; he learned this technique from his work as assistant to a restorer of stained-glass windows in France. *The Holy Face* is less rigid than some of his other compositions, but the beading of color on the borders and the suggestion of a frame within the painting reinforce the window pattern. The face, however, is reminiscent of the veil of Veronica, a familiar medieval representation (like the shroud of Turin). Much of Rouault's work is religious, setting him apart among the fauves. Yet this painting, with its elongated gothic distortion, is intensely expressionistic. The eyes are enormous, like those in primitive Christian paintings. The long lines of the nose and hair; the overlaying of the colors, through which other colors show; and the excitement of the colors themselves—dominated by the white of the veil—all contribute to a personal vision on Rouault's part. It is the expression of a spiritual concern that dominates his work.

ABSTRACT ART

Wassily Kandinsky: Exploring the Subconscious

A new interest in psychology was stimulated by the work of Sigmund Freud, whose *Psychopathology of Everyday Life* (1904) asserted that our actions are controlled by our will, even when we are unaware of it. Freud's techniques of psychotherapy depended on the use of free association—rapid responses in which the censorship of the conscious mind is avoided. By free-associating, one comes into contact with the reservoir of emotion and understanding in the subconscious. This theory insisted that everything has meaning, even the slightest gesture.

Freud influenced Wassily Kandinsky (1866–1944), who in 1896 left Russia and a career as a professor of law to begin painting in Munich. His early work is close to that of the fauves in dynamics, but it has a childlike, dreamlike quality that made official art organizations reluctant to accept it for shows. Like Gauguin, Kandinsky paid attention to the sensual qualities of colors and patterns of colors. Often, his subject matter is not clear; and it gradually became subservient to the purposes of form and color. His book *Concerning the Spiritual in Art* (1912) reveals that his views had taken a new direction by the year 1910. He returned home late one night and saw one of his own paintings upside down. He did not recognize it, and yet it seemed to him to have great power. That experience resulted in new ways of thinking and painting. Kandinsky began to feel that all colors, all forms, and all combinations had meaning, even though different "readings" of his works might be proffered at different times. His view was that since the intrusions of physics into the atom had destroyed our concept of the material reality of the world, the ultimate reality must be that of the spirit.

Kandinsky is credited with having made the first abstract painting. Yet he warned against losing sight of representative subject matter. His fear was that painting would become decoration rather than an interpretation of nature and experience. His own work took several forms. He began his "compositions" with a plan and a clear idea in mind. His "improvisations" were more spontaneous. The brush and the color were extensions of the subconscious, and Kandinsky almost refused to control his motions. The results are a thoroughgoing break with the past as it had been dominated by the classical realism of the Renaissance.

As early as 1913, many of Kandinsky's improvisations had a recognizable subject. In *Improvisation No. 30* (Color Plate 40), cannons at the lower right spew red-tinged explosions, toppling a church directly in front of them. People below the church scream through blood-red mouths. City buildings fall directly above the cannons, suggesting that destruction is uniform for both the destroyer and the destroyed. The forms and shapes seem to have a life of their own. Lines of troops are suggested near the cannons, and the sky is an unnatural reddish orange. Some of the forms are childlike and innocent in their implication. Everything is askew; there are no stabilizing horizontal and vertical lines. We are set on our heads by the disorder of the canvas; yet it is exciting, expressive, and, given its date, terrifying in its prophecy.

The critic Roger Fry commented on this painting and others by Kandinsky in 1913, saying, "They are pure visual music." Kandinsky himself wrote:

> The presence of the cannons in the picture could probably be explained by the constant war talk that had been going on throughout the year. But I did not intend to give a representation of war; to do so would have required different pictorial means; besides, such tasks did not interest me—at least not just now. This entire description is chiefly an analysis of the picture which I have painted rather subconsciously in a state of strong inner tension.

Kazimir Malevich and the Supremacy of Feeling

Malevich (1878–1935) was a one-man movement. He began suprematism in 1913 when he painted a black square on a black background. Suprematism insisted that emotional reactions to shapes and forms were the only concern of art. Emotional reactions to representations of things or events were inferior: aesthetic emotion was supreme. Like Kandinsky, Malevich had little regard for the world of perception, but he had great regard for the value of his own emotions. If Descartes could place all authority in his awareness of his own thought, then Malevich was able to place authority in feeling. That, he knew, was real; it was important. His most famous series of paintings consists of studies of white squares on a white background. In these works the visual field is reduced literally to the brushstroke.

Suprematist Composition, Black Trapezium and Red Square (Figure 18-1) developed from the simple square that dominated his first efforts. Malevich concentrated on a supremacy of feeling or perception in art by representing basic forms which could not be interpreted as anything other than form. Form is elemental; in a pure representation such as Malevich's, it excites feelings of a highly focused kind. Malevich experimented with aesthetic emotions, not the emotions connected with the events of daily life.

Figure 18-1
Kazimir Malevich. *Suprematist Composition, Black Trapezium and Red Square.* After 1915. 39 ¾ by 24 ⅜ inches. (Stedelijk Museum, Amsterdam.)

The Value of Significant Form

Looking at Malevich's work now may not suggest the interest that it excited in its time. But Kandinsky and Malevich were the originators of a new wave in modern art which is still going on: abstract art. The English critics and aestheticians Roger Fry (1866–1934) and Clive Bell (1881–1964) were extreme in their claims for formalism, asserting that only art which achieved "significant form" was of real interest. Significant form was the organization of elements in a visual medium in such a way as to excite aesthetic emotions rather than emotions connected with other areas of life. Form, not representation, took precedence. Both Fry and Bell were deeply impressed by nonwestern art and were attracted to Malevich's work.

But Malevich's painting could quickly deteriorate into decoration, lacking an expressive content and rewarding perception alone. The fact that many of his designs were used on such things as plates, cups and saucers, and bookbindings demonstrates their limitations. Yet he was a pioneer, leading the way in twentieth-century art.

CUBISM: THE HIERARCHY OF AESTHETIC VALUES

Cubism developed from a recognition of one aspect of the achievement of Cézanne and was guided by a specific figure, the one acknowledged genius of the century: Pablo Picasso (1881–1973). Numerous painters experimented with the approach, but only one other figure, Georges Braque (1882–1963), brought power and genius to cubism.

Cubism was developed through shared efforts. Like Malevich, the cubists evoked emotions related to art rather than to everyday experience. In this, both suprematism and cubism avoided sentimentality, banality, and emotional clichés. Cubism retained a degree of representation, however limited, and concentrated on multiple perspectives and analysis and resynthesis of form. The theories of Albert Einstein (1879–1955) may also have affected cubism, since they were popularly interpreted as replacing absolute values with relative values. By changing the apparent absolute relationships of the parts of objects, the cubists established a new relativism which, in the end, affected all values, particularly those held by the hierarchical establishment early in the century.

The Impact of Nonwestern Art

Part of the inspiration for this new art came from contact with African sculpture and the wooden masks of the peoples of Oceania. Between 1900 and 1906 African masks were shown in galleries in Paris. They were originally regarded as products of inept artists. The European prejudice for Renaissance realism was absolutely dominant, and it took an act of revaluation to bring the real genius of African art to the attention of Europeans. It is apparent, particularly in the realism achieved by certain Benin sculptures

Figure 18-2
Benin head. Bronze, about 11 inches high. (By permission of the Trustees of the British Museum.)

(Figure 18-2, for example), that African artists had the technical ability not only to produce realistic likenesses but also to cast them in bronze flawlessly.

The stylization of facial form for emotional effect in African masks and sculptures attracted collectors and artists. By 1907, Picasso was seeing African and New Caledonian sculptures, some of which appear in snapshots taken of him in 1908. Figures 18-3, 18-4, and 18-5 show some sculptures that are typical of what people were seeing.

Figure 18-3
Above: Babangi mask from the French Congo. Wood, 14 inches high. (Collection, Museum of Modern Art, New York; given anonymously.)

Figure 18-4
Above: African sculpture. Wood, about 20 inches high. (Reproduced by permission of the University Museum, University of Pennsylvania.)

Figure 18-5
Left: African mask. Wood, about 9 inches high. (Yale University Art Gallery, Director's Discretionary Fund.)

Pablo Picasso

The effect of such sculpture on Picasso is apparent in *Les Demoiselles d'Avignon* (Figure 18-6), which he began in May 1907 and reworked later that year, during the period when he is said to have had a "revelation" about African art.

On one level the women in the painting allude to Cézanne's *Bathers* (Figure 17-14), but the irony is that these women are prostitutes from the brothel on D'Avignon street in Barcelona, which was well known to Picasso and his friends.

Figure 18-6
Pablo Picasso. *Les Demoiselles d'Avignon.*
1907. Oil on canvas, 96 by 92 inches.
(Collection, Museum of Modern Art,
New York, Lillie P. Bliss Bequest.)

PERCEPTION KEY

Picasso, Les Demoiselles d'Avignon

1. What are the principal modes of distortion apparent in *Les Demoiselles d'Avignon* (Figure 18-6)? Consider the distortions of faces, bodies, objects, and space.

2. Is it possible to tell where these people are? Are they immediately recognizable as women?

3. Is the influence of African masks apparent in all the women?

4. Is a clear emotional statement being made in the painting? Is the emotional expression explicit?

5. Is there significant form in this painting? How important are the formal elements in relation to the subject matter, the prostitutes? Is form dominant? Is the painting beautiful?

In many ways *Les Demoiselles d'Avignon* is a brutal representation of a traditional scene. The distortions of form force us to look at it differently from the way we would examine a realist, impressionist, or fauvist painting. We can think of this work as expressionistic because it distorts for the purpose of expressing feeling, but the expression is not reducible to a single range of emotion. Even though we know what the subject matter is—which would not be true of a viewer who lacked the proper background—we are still not aware of a simple emotional statement.

The positioning of the figures—not all of which are immediately recognizable as women—on the canvas is compelling and memorable. The composition seems inevitable to us now and constitutes a kind of visual "discovery." The two central figures have the huge almond eyes and the profile nose in a full-face view that we find in a number of Picasso's paintings of this period. The other three faces show the influence of African masks; in the face at the upper right there are signs of scar patterning. The study of African masks contributed to the process of fragmentation and rebuilding of spatial structures that grew into cubism.

Ma Jolie (Figure 18-7), painted in Paris in 1911 and 1912, is a study of a woman playing a stringed instrument—a zither or possibly a guitar; it typifies the cubist approach in that the forms are fragmented into geometric suggestions, which are then rearranged to fit the needs of the design.

In *Ma Jolie* there are forms associated with the instrument itself: fragments of the strings, angles of the body, and even a treble clef. The repetition of similar forms, angular planes, lines, and occasional curves is suggestive of the repetition of notes in a musical composition. Roger Fry said that some abstract painting was like music, and most cubist works of this late, analytic variety resemble music in the use of patterning, repetition, and rhythms of lines. Cubism demonstrated that its audience had the ability to respond to nuances of form, color, balance, and line, much as it would have been able to respond to a passage in a string quartet. It is not accidental that so many of the best-known cubist works had music as part of their subject matter.

Girl Before a Mirror (Color Plate 41) was inspired by Marie-Thérèse Walter, Picasso's model and mistress and the mother of his daughter Maya. In this painting Picasso has used strong black lines, almost with the force of Rouault, to delineate almost every

Figure 18-7
Picasso. *Ma Jolie* (Woman with a Zither or Guitar). 1911–1912. Oil on canvas, 39 ⅜ by 24 ¾ inches. (Collection, Museum of Modern Art, New York, Lillie P. Bliss Bequest.)

aspect of the figure and her environment. The wallpaper changes in color from section to section. The figure is fragmented into fruitlike shapes, and the face, breasts, body, and womb are analyzed into the traditional shapes associated with fertility. The interaction of the figure with her image is realized by the arm that reaches to the reflection, which offers no clear clue as to how she sees herself. Both expressions are enigmatic. The colors are stark, but not violent. They interact and reflect in intense rhythms, just as the forms do. The painting takes the risk of breaking down into separable images—usually a fatal flaw in such works. But here the balance holds. The logic of the reflection and the device of the hands caressing the mirror integrate the two visions.

Figure 18-8
Picasso. *Guernica.* May 1–June 4, 1937. Oil on canvas, 11 feet 5 ½ inches by 25 feet 5 ¾ inches.
(Museo del Prado, Madrid.)

PERCEPTION KEY

Picasso

1. Compare the representations of woman in *Les Demoiselles d'Avignon* (Figure 18-6) with those in *Girl Before a Mirror* (Color Plate 41). How do the paintings differ in terms of emotional attitudes toward women? How do they differ in terms of distortion of the figures? Does either painting condemn or praise women?

2. Consider Picasso's *Guernica* (Figure 18-8) in relation to Kandinsky's *Improvisation No. 30* (Color Plate 40). They treat a similar subject matter, and both use powerful distortions and disintegrations of form. What are the primary differences in their approach to color, form, line, space, modeling, and illusion? Is either painting more "modern" in your view?

3. *Guernica* is said to have a clear relationship with earlier cubist works. What do you see in the painting that verifies this judgment?

4. Can it be said that Picasso's ambition is similar to Kandinsky's: to represent things as they really are, rather than as they appear to be? Which painting best represents things as they really are?

Picasso's most ambitious painting of the 1930s is also his most famous: *Guernica* (Figure 18-8), which he painted for the Spanish pavilion at the Paris International Exposition in 1937. Picasso called this "the worst time of my life"; in 1935 his marriage to his wife Olga was breaking up, and Marie-Thérèse became pregnant. He had been painting and drawing bullfights and the minotaur, the half man, half bull who symbolized irrational, savage qualities.

Spain was in the throes of civil war in 1937 when the republican government requested a painting for the pavilion. A few months after the request, German bombers, called in by the fascist forces of Generalissimo Franco, bombed a Basque village, Guernica, as a demonstration of the effectiveness of aerial bombardment. The destruction was overwhelming; in Picasso's interpretation, people reach heavenward and are rained upon by destruction. Figures are dismembered. The bull at the left suggests the minotaur, while the horse in the center suggests the destruction of innocence. Figures coalesce into a pyramidal shape, rising to the light held by the human hand and to the light provided by the new technology of electricity. Both are of no avail. The rendering in black, gray, and white is as leveling as the destruction of overhead bombing.

Georges Braque

Braque and Picasso worked so closely together that their works of the years 1911 and 1912 are sometimes indistinguishable. Braque, like Picasso, often chose a musical subject, as in *The Portuguese* (Figure 18-9), a study of a guitarist. The painting has been linked with *Ma Jolie* and other works by Picasso of the period. In both, the dominant movement is upward in a form that is wider at the base than at the top, suggesting a seated human figure.

Both paintings add a conceptual demand to the usual perceptual demand of design. Because of the titles—and other readily available information—we know what the basic subjects of these paintings are. Without the titles or other information, we could hardly be expected to "see" in them any given subject. Even knowing as much as we do, we hardly "perceive" the subjects of these paintings; rather, we "conceive" or imagine them. This is not new. Many realistic paintings present us with the same problem —often the title tells us what the exact subject is, which we would otherwise not know. The difference

Figure 18-9
Georges Braque. *The Portuguese.* 1911. Oil on canvas, 46 ⅛ by 32 inches. (Oeffentliche Kunstsammlung, Kunstmuseum, Basel, Switzerland.)

is, however, that with Courbet, for example, we can tell a landscape from a portrait. Cubist paintings rarely offer the same distinguishing percepts.

FUTURISM AND DADA: REACTION TO THE MACHINE CULTURE

The movements just before, during, and after the First World War proliferated, flowered in a burst of experimental energy, and then dispersed, only to be caught up in the next movement. Futurism, which was begun by an Italian poet, Emilio Filippo Marinetti (1876–1944), attracted a number of Italian painters and writers between 1909 and 1916, when Umberto Boccioni (1882–1916), a driving force of the movement and a brilliant sculptor, died in a riding accident. Like the adherents of so many artistic movements of the period, the futurists produced a manifesto; in it they explained why the art of the past had to be disregarded and why only an art of the future could serve humanity. One of their declarations was that "a clean-sweep should be made of all stale and threadbare subject-matter in order to express the vortex of modern life—a life of steel, fever, pride, and headlong speed."

The dadaists began as a small group of artists in Zurich protesting the First World War. The word "dada" was chosen while these artists were making plans for a cabaret entertainment; it may be connected with the Slavic "da," meaning "yes." Dadaism was not a style, but an approach—an irreverent approach —to art. It was countercultural: Marcel Duchamp (1887–1968) drew a moustache and goatee on a print of the *Mona Lisa;* Kurt Schwitters (1887–1948) created merz art, using the ragtag ends of found materials. If culture led to war, then culture be damned. If the bourgeois middle class brought the world to war, then art should scandalize and berate it, not entertain and pander to it.

The photographs of Eadweard Muybridge showing the frame-by-frame motion of horses, doves, and people had produced a visual catalog of kinetic gestures. And when the dadaist painter Marcel Duchamp began to experiment with multiple kinetic gestures on the same canvas, he produced one of the most controversial paintings of the decade before the war, *Nude Descending a Staircase* (1912; Figure 18-10); it was shown in New York in 1913 at the famous Armory Show, at which were exhibited over 1100 works by modern painters. It is a futuristic painting, relying on photographic studies, and it created a furor in the press. Duchamp said: "I knew that it would break forever the enslaving chains of naturalism."

In the painting a figure descends what appears to be a flight of stairs; the motion is portrayed as it might appear in a photograph of a slow-moving subject made with an open lens. Yet the audience of 1913 found this work enigmatic, insulting, and degenerate: a welcome reaction as far as Duchamp was concerned.

The dadaists came from Romania, France, Germany, Holland, and even Sweden. Tristan Tzara (1896–1963), from Romania, was a writer, editor of the *Dada Review,* and propagandist for the group. He kept in touch with Marinetti and the futurists, as well as with other avant-garde groups in Europe. Du-

Figure 18-10
Marcel Duchamp. *Nude Descending a Staircase, Number 2.* 1912. Oil on canvas, 58 by 35 inches. (Philadelphia Museum of Art, Louise and Walter Arensberg Collection.)

champ is certainly the most famous of the dadaists, while Kurt Schwitters is among the most important.

Schwitters created merz art from found objects. The term "merz" comes from a detail in a collage that Schwitters cut from the word "Kommerz." It is thus related to commerce and to the world of finance, and it insulted those for whom the war was being fought.

Schwitters's early *Merz 19* (Figure 18-11) is a collection of randomly gathered bits of paper that may have come from the floor of a tram, a wastebin, or a dump. Candy wrappers, cigarette papers, tickets,

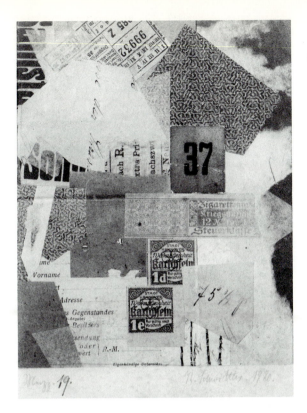

Figure 18-11
Kurt Schwitters. *Merz 19.* 1920. Collage, 7 ¼ by 5 ⅞ inches. (Yale University Art Gallery, Gift of Collection Société Anonyme.)

and notes appear in a totally novel context. Schwitters forces us to look at these things in a new way and to see them as being as much a part of the medium of painting as a brushstroke, a geometric form, or a portion of anatomy. They are artistic counters, his medium of expression, and the artist has a right to order them as much as any other visual element. Schwitters said: "The materials are not to be used logically in their objective relationships but only within the logic of the work of art."

SURREALISM: STRIKING OUT FOR THE DARK INTERIOR

The work of the Italian Giorgio De Chirico (1888–1978) quickly took on a haunting, dreamlike quality that suggests the nightmare. Freud's view of dreams was that they reveal the deepest truths about ourselves. In De Chirico's paintings, the realities of external appearance gave way to the realities of internal experience.

De Chirico's landscape in Color Plate 42 is filled with dream symbols. The circle, the arched doorways and windows, and the strange "container," which is both cavelike and mobile, suggest feminine sexuality, while the red-tipped tower at the left suggests a phallus. The shadow of a male figure, perhaps that of a public statue, looms across the street. Freud treated all dreams as symbolic, insisting that most symbols in dreams were sexual. This painting taps the power of that theory. The innocence of the child playing with a hoop is like the innocence of all people before Freud in regard to the symbolic content of their dreams.

Surrealism has not ended: it spans the entire century. Some observers see it as predating the twentieth century. André Breton composed a manifesto of surrealism which attempted a definition:

> Surrealism, n. Pure psychic automatism. . . . Thought's dictation, free from any control by the reason. . . . Surrealism rests on a belief in the superior reality of certain forms of association hitherto neglected, in the omnipotence of the dream, in the disinterested play of thought.

Not all surrealists adhered to this statement, nor were all painters working in the surrealist vein necessarily part of the movement.

One of the most influential painters linked with surrealism is Marc Chagall (1887–1985), who was born in a remote province of Russia. He has said that he paints images that "obsess" him, but that he can attach no specific meanings to them.

In *Self-Portrait with Seven Fingers* (Figure 18-12) we see a familiar image on the easel: a headless milkmaid drifting over the roofs of the town on her way to a cow, which is also in the sky. The Eiffel Tower implies that the artist is in Paris, but the cloud issuing from his head suggests that images of Russia and the tiny village where he was born still obsess his imagination. The seven fingers on his left hand have baffled viewers for years. They may express Chagall's own recognition that he was unusual—a kind of freak. The formal organization is obviously cubistic; the subject is analyzed by means of planes and color zones. Chagall's self-portrait is whimsical, brilliantly colorful, and—like much of his work—amusing.

Figure 18-12
Marc Chagall. *Self-Portrait with Seven Fingers.* 1912. Oil on canvas, 42 by 50 ½ inches. (Stedelijk Museum, Amsterdam; © ADAGP, Paris, 1986.)

Joan Miró (b. 1893), like Picasso, was born in Barcelona. In 1919 he went to Paris, where the most experimental of the modernists in painting shocked him so much that he became an almost reactionary realist. But eventually he absorbed the novelties that were going on around him and associated with the surrealists. André Breton once described him as the "most Surrealist of us all."

His most distinctive works are characterized by unusually plastic forms that have an organic quality but few counterparts in nature. Some of the forms in *Painting, 1933* (Figure 18-13) are recognizable, although that is unusual. One figure has a curious face and what seem to be breasts; another has dripping hair. Some forms are childlike. We must free-associate and take them for what they appear to be: dynamic and fluid shapes. Miró spent years exploring what seem to be icons or counters in a mysterious dream language that suggests total fluidity of interior space, a symbolic world with no restrictions.

Persistence of Memory (Figure 18-14), by Salvador Dalí (b. 1904), has been parodied in advertisements, in other paintings, and in comic books and media of all kinds. The limp watches suggest a timelessness that has distorted time itself—or at least the tangible, material symbols of time. The fleshy form in the

Figure 18-13
Joan Miró. *Painting, 1933.* Oil on canvas, 51 ¼ by 63 ½ inches. (Wadsworth Atheneum, Hartford; Ella Gallup Sumner and Mary Catlin Sumner Collection.)

Figure 18-14
Salvador Dalí. *The Persistence of Memory.* 1931. Oil on canvas, 9½ by 13 inches. (Collection, Museum of Modern Art, New York; given anonymously.)

center of the canvas is vaguely humanoid and is also limp, as if to suggest its perishability. The smaller watch at the left seems to be under attack by ants, as if it, too, could perish. The landscape is barren, but in the distance are rocky cliffs, symbols of archaeological timelessness and eternity. The structures at the left also have a timeless quality, although human beings have made them, not nature. None of the watches tell the same time, implying that Dalí had a knowledge of Einstein's theory of relativity. The painting applies the relativity of time to a wide variety of forms: manufactured, natural, and human.

SOCIAL AWARENESS

Despite all the aesthetic formalism of the era, there was also considerable activity among painters concerned with social issues. Picasso's *Guernica* is one example of a painting with social concerns as part of its subject matter. The murals of Jose Clemente Orozco (1883–1949) in Mexico and in the United States are another. The American painter Peter

Blume (b. 1906) painted *The Eternal City* (Color Plate 43) in 1937, when Italy endured both fascism and war in Ethiopia. He used techniques of expressionism and surrealism, particularly in its symbolic form, to express a personal view of a political situation soon to erupt into total war.

Blume assumes an understanding of history: the Roman forum is in the distance and the Colosseum in the foreground. In the lower left foreground lies the wreckage, first of classical statuary, and then of a woman, poor, crippled, begging. To the far left two pious middle-class women pray before a lighted reliquary with an image of Christ. In the middle distance, soldiers gather and dissidents are beaten. In the caves of the Colosseum people gather. One couple looks up at the bilious green jack-in-the-box Mussolini, whose sneer governs all. Blume's allusion is to the assassination of the tyrant Julius Caesar. However, in his painting there is no modern Brutus. The citizenry either offers faint approval or remains uninvolved. There is no modern tyrant slayer to save Europe from the fate of fascism.

Surrealism

1. In some cases, surrealism attempts to portray a reality that is more real than the normal reality that we know. Which of the paintings shown in Color Plates 42 and 43 and Figures 18-12, 18-13, and 18-14 seems more real than the world as we ordinarily perceive it?

2. Which of these paintings seems most concerned with the interior realities of psychology and the dream state? How can one tell when a painter is alluding to the interior psychological world?

3. Do these paintings establish the reality of our interior life? Since all experience is in fact interior (as Kant and others in the nineteenth century demonstrated), is it possible that a surrealist painting is truly more *real* than a painting that portrays only the outward appearances of things?

4. The interior dream world speaks to us in symbolic language, as Freud explained. Which of these paintings seems to have the most clear symbolic content? Can you discuss that content?

5. Is it possible that surrealism is simply a variant of symbolism of the kind that we encounter in many art forms? If so, would that change our approach to it?

Photography: A Search for New Values

STIEGLITZ AND THE PHOTO-SECESSION

Alfred Stieglitz (1864–1946), who had been awarded prizes by the English photographer Peter Henry Emerson, created a group of his own, the Photo-Secession, in 1902; it was modeled on similar German art organizations and was designed to take photography out of the shadow of painting. Stieglitz seceded from the union of art, protesting against the sentimentality of soft-focus, impressionistic photographs that seemed staged and artificial.

Stieglitz had a serious interest in contemporary painting and sculpture rather than in the work of the late nineteenth century. His movement eventually flowered into "straight photography," characterized usually by sharp focus and unsentimental images, many of which are not traditionally beautiful to the viewer or flattering to the subject.

In 1903, Stieglitz said:

This protest, this secession from the spirit of the doctrinaire, of the compromiser, at length found its expression in the foundation of the Photo-Secession. Its aim is loosely to hold together those Americans devoted to pictorial photography in their endeavor to compel its recognition, not as the handmaiden of art, but as a distinctive medium of individual expression.

Later, in 1921, he wrote: "Photography is my passion. The search for Truth my obsession."

The photograph that most clearly displays what Stieglitz hoped to achieve in his work is probably *The Steerage* (Figure 18-15), a view of immigrants returning to Europe on the ship *Kaiser Wilhelm II*. They are huddled together in the steerage, the cheapest class. Stieglitz was a more privileged traveler, whose view of these passengers was from a distance. When he saw the sharp diagonal of the gangplank, the angle of the smokestack at the left, and the sharper angle of the ladder at the right, he thought that he was observing

Figure 18-15
Alfred Stieglitz. *The Steerage.* 1907. Photograph.
(Collection, Museum of Modern Art, New York; gift of
Alfred Stieglitz.)

pure form. He paid close attention to the straw hat in the upper center and to the white shawl in the lower center, but he also took care to balance numerous other design elements in the composition. What he captured in the making of this photograph was not just a huddled group of people, but a musical relationship of forms.

PHOTOGRAPHY AND SOCIAL AWARENESS

The social awareness of photographers has been strong from the start; one of the most serious early photographers, Lewis Hine (1874–1940), was an American professor of sociology. His photographs of children working in mills and other environments follow Stieglitz's ideals. *Carolina Cotton Mill* (Figure 18-16) shows a small child minding a spinning machine in a textile mill. It is an unsentimental look at child labor, which offended few in 1908. Hine concentrates on form: he balances the receding parallel lines of the machine at the left with the windows at the right and places the child directly in the center, in focus; the child in the distance falls naturally out of focus. This straightforward, apparently unselfconscious approach to photography became dominant, particularly in America throughout the great depression, when a number of photographers recorded the human damage caused by economic collapse.

Figure 18-16
Lewis Hine. *Carolina Cotton Mill.* 1908. Photograph. (Collection, Museum of Modern Art, New York, Lillie P. Bliss Bequest.)

Figure 18-17
Dorothea Lange. *Migrant Mother.* 1936. Photograph.
(Reproduction from Collections of the Library of
Congress.)

Dorothea Lange photographed a migrant mother
in 1936 in Nipomo, California. While driving home
after a long series of "shoots," she caught sight of a
sign: "Pea pickers." She drove on, but soon turned
back; at the camp she found the family that she
portrays in *Migrant Mother* (Figure 18-17). She stayed
with them only ten minutes, during which she
produced a series of classic images.

The technique is straightforward. We draw our
own conclusions about the people (the woman portrayed complained bitterly forty years later that she
never made a nickel from this often-reproduced
photograph). Facts are what we see. We know that
the photograph was taken of migrant farmers in
California, and we may well be struck by the irony of
their suffering so obviously in the land of plenty. But
beyond that, the photograph is filled with careful
formal touches: the mother looks ahead while her
children cling to her, looking away. The three figures
form a pyramidal shape. The angle of the mother's

right arm, paralleling the strong line of her nose,
implies determination and resolution; but the fur-
rowed brow reveals anxiety. The formal elements
cohere much more in this photograph than in the
other four shots Lange took of this family.

Manuel Alvarez Bravo (b. 1902) took photographs
in Mexico in the 1930s and 1940s; he was always
looking for the revealing gesture and for the patterns
of intense light and dark that characterize the Mexican landscape. His *Man from Papantla* (Figure 18-18)
is unabashed, direct, and frank. Bravo has photographed this young man at an instant of inattention,
when his eye had been caught by something more
interesting than the photographer. The young man
seems impatient, and he has stopped to be photographed as a courtesy. Bravo has placed him directly
in the center of an almost square rectangle, permit-

Figure 18-18
Manuel Alvarez Bravo. *Man from Papantla.* 1934–1935.
Photograph. (Manuel Alvarez Bravo.)

ting the light and shade to fall across his figure as they will and even including the extraneous detail of the stone cornice at the right, which is either a window or a reliquary niche. Stone dominates the composition, except for the softness of the clothing and the human presence. Everything is carefully balanced.

Sculpture

ORGANIC MASS, VOLUME, AND SPACE

Sculpture after Rodin took not just one but several experimental routes. Sculptors began to free themselves from the obligation to be purely representational. When Aristide Maillol (1861–1944) came to Paris to study painting, he found the teaching old-fashioned and stultifying. But he was excited by Gauguin and the postimpressionists. He turned to sculpture in middle age, and his first show earned the praise of Rodin. Yet his work was very different from Rodin's. *Mediterranean* (Figure 18-19) is a result of his efforts at simplification of form. He purposely tried to avoid Rodin's intense psychological reality and his tortured emotional anxiety. Instead, he turned to a simpler, but nonetheless refined, style that achieved a much cooler emotional statement. *Mediterranean* did not please everyone—many, such as the great writer André Gide, found it unacceptable.

Maillol does not idealize this nude by making the model seem more beautiful than she might have been. His distortions make her more bulky and weighty— essentially more sculptural—than a living woman would be. As seen from the angle shown in Figure 18-19, the basic forms of the sculpture are triangular. The triangle and the resulting pyramid help Maillol achieve an emotional stasis, a totally arresting sense of stability and completeness. Gide said that this sculpture "signified nothing"; but in a very important way it signifies a volume—a relationship of spaces and forms whose mass and weight add intensity to the image of the woman and abstract a great power from her basic shape. A comparison with ritual Egyptian sculpture, in terms of mass and stylization, may be reasonable. Maillol's stylization is modern, but no less effective. *Mediterranean* is the icon of nudeness, a sculpture that stands for the nude as well as for being a nude.

Constantin Brancusi (1876–1957), a Romanian sculptor, went further than Maillol in the simplifica-

Figure 18-19
Aristide Maillol. *Mediterranean.* c. 1901. Bronze, 41 inches high. (Collection, Museum of Modern Art, New York; gift of Stephen C. Clark.)

tion of form. He was noticed by Rodin, who invited him to work with him. But Brancusi, a patient craftsman and an admirer of Rodin's *Balzac*, declined, saying that nothing grows in the shadow of a great tree. And he worked in Paris on his own.

Brancusi personally cut and dressed his own marble sculptures and polished and formed his metal sculptures. He analyzed his subject for its most elemental forms, preferring the organic to the geometric. We find no triangles, rectangles, or squares: rather, we see ovoids, egg-shaped masses, and other natural forms. *Bird in Space* (Figure 18-20) suggests flight in the most essential form that Brancusi could imagine. By simplifying forms he discovered essence. His religious beliefs, like those of Kandinsky and some other artists, were connected with theosophy, a combination of religion and philosophy that was concerned with essences.

Brancusi's discovery of essence moved us toward abstract sculpture. Unlike many other sculptors, Brancusi often reinterpreted the same piece in different materials. *Bird in Space* exists in numerous versions in bronze as well as in marble of different colors. Brancusi made subtle changes in each version, but he was interested primarily in seeing how different materials affected his concept.

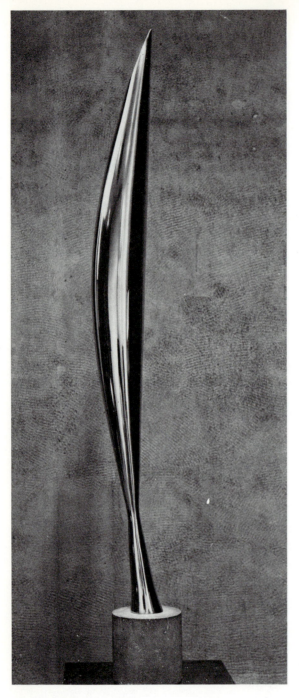

Figure 18-20
Constantin Brancusi. *Bird in Space.* 1928. Bronze, 54 inches high. (Collection, Museum of Modern Art, New York; given anonymously.)

Figure 18-21
Umberto Boccioni. *Unique Forms of Continuity in Space.* 1913. Bronze, 43 ½ inches high. (Collection, Museum of Modern Art, New York, Lillie P. Bliss Bequest.)

Umberto Boccioni, who wrote the futurist manifesto, might have gone on to greater things had he not died in a riding accident in 1916. His *Unique Forms of Continuity in Space* (Figure 18-21) captures some of the essence of speed; the forms now seem associated with streamlining and aerodynamics. A figure strides forward with immense confidence, suggesting speed, thrust, and power. Its lyrical qualities make it seem like a hymn to metal and machinery, the great forces of futurism.

THE CONSTRUCTIVISTS: A MODERN ANALYSIS OF SPACE

The sculpture we have examined so far is a sculpture of mass. It has volume and weight. It refers to —if it does not represent— objects in life. Another school of sculpture, constructivism, was influenced by modern engineering and developed in the work of two brothers, Antoine Pevsner (1886–1962) and Naum Gabo (1890–1977). They were Russian and were

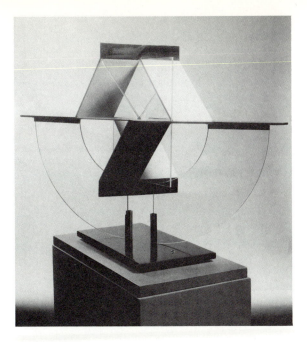

Figure 18-22
Naum Gabo. *Construction in Space with Balance on Two Points.* 1925. Painted bronze, glass, and clear plastic. 50 inches high, 40 inches long. (Yale University Art Gallery, gift of H. Wade White.)

influenced by a number of like-minded artists. Their constructivist manifesto (Moscow, 1920) grounded their work in real life, which was composed of space and time; they said, "We deny volume as an expression of space," and they praised the engineer's solution to space, citing in particular the power of railroad tracks. They especially delighted in thinking that "We have freed ourselves from the age-old errors of the Egyptians, according to whom the basic element of art could only be a static rhythm." Unfortunately, Pevsner and Gabo were not encouraged by the Russian authorities, who considered their work to be sterile formalism, not appropriate to building the revolution. They left Russia in 1922.

Gabo's *Construction in Space with Balance on Two Points* (Figure 18-22) is typical of his experimentation with clear materials such as plastic and celluloid, which make the concept of space doubly complex and interesting. Later, in the 1940s and 1950s, Gabo's constructions using plastic structures covered with nylon thread became well known and spawned a popular thread art.

Gabo never denied sculptural mass, but he insisted on maintaining a dynamic rhythm in his works. They change as we move around them because their transparency complicates the relationship of volume to mass and of line to space. If Gabo claims reality for his work because it is grounded in space and time and because, like life, it has a rhythmic dynamic, then it is also true that he helps us retain a sense of mystery about the relativity of space and time. The constant shifts and changes in light, shadow, line, and relationship establish the vitality of Gabo's forms. They may be geometric, but they are not severe. They are subtle and sometimes suggest the organic.

Piet Mondrian (1872–1944) was a painter, not a sculptor, but his work influenced later constructivist sculpture and architecture. He was in Paris during the heyday of cubism and changed his style from a fauvist intensity to a linearity that developed into a powerful and expressive style that is virtually his alone. In *Broadway Boogie-Woogie* (Color Plate 44), the vibrating, scintillating colors evoke the mood of Broadway and the jazz rhythms of the 1940s. The grid suggests the rigor of the city, as a plan might do, but the careful balance of the colors and of white in the square and rectangular elements results in an unusually intense design. Mondrian's earlier works, such as his "Composition" series, are more relaxed and almost static in their perfect restfulness.

Mondrian experimented with balance, form, and structure. Each of the color planes in *Broadway Boogie-Woogie* is calculated mathematically to balance the entire surface volume as well as the other color planes. The precision with which Mondrian worked out the balance of given volumes in relation to one another and the whole is so exact as to constitute an aesthetic science in and of itself. And like the mathematical efforts of the Greeks, Mondrian's are not boring or wooden. Instead, they are endlessly fascinating and mysterious. Mondrian's work bridges painting, constructivist sculpture, and architecture.

Architecture: Form, Function, and Freedom

The revivalist tendency in nineteenth-century architecture continued into the twentieth century, augmented by a revolution in building techniques made possible by new materials. The older styles did not die out; they thrived in an atmosphere of change.

Figure 18-23
Louis Sullivan. Guaranty Building, Buffalo, New York. 1895. (Buffalo and Erie County Historical Society.)

LOUIS SULLIVAN: PROPHET OF THE NEW AGE OF FORM AND FUNCTION

Louis Sullivan (1856–1924) did not invent the skyscraper, but his Guaranty Building in Buffalo (Figure 18-23) signaled the coming of a new age in construction, characterized by the use of steel I beams and of exterior masonry that does not bear weight. Instead of using huge piers at the base of this building and tapering to small piers above, Sullivan treats all the floors equally, both visually and structurally. The first level is two stories high, but for aesthetic reasons, not structural ones. The top level uses circular windows because they integrate the decorations and soften the rising vertical shafts. Sullivan incorporated romanesque curves into the design of this building, as well as simplified, organic decorative details of his own creation.

The thirteen-story Guaranty Building has powerful vertical lines. Sullivan chose a democratic material: brick, with terra-cotta decorative panels. The building, which is simple but not severe, resembles a pile of bank notes. Sullivan believed in democracy and felt that architecture should reflect democratic values. His views were strengthened by his reading of Whitman, Emerson, and Thoreau.

We are used to seeing such structures and so might not observe the weightlessness in the design of the Guaranty Building. We are virtually unaware of the structure because the visible stonework is not the structure, not even the key to the structure. Sullivan's view that "form follows function" is revealed in this building: we would never confuse it with a home, a church, or an amphitheater. The regularity of the vertical and horizontal lines set the standard for a generation of office buildings that imitated the rhythm, proportion, and harmony of Sullivan's work.

ANTONIO GAUDI: ART NOUVEAU AND EXPRESSIONIST ARCHITECTURE

Gaudi (1852–1926), who did not share Sullivan's concerns for form and function, was absorbed by the fluidity of the interiors of the buildings of the French architect Victor Horta (1861–1947), whose ribwork, filled in with glass or wood, inspired the brief movement known as "art nouveau." This was an exciting, eccentric approach to design that is still appealing and romantic in its abandonment of the straight line. The curve was its most impressive articulation.

Gaudi's Casa Milá (Figure 18-24), situated on a corner, features fairy-tale rhythmic contours; it is built of cut stone made to look fluid. Gaudi left the stone natural and unpolished. The effect is similar to that of a canyon wall into which living spaces have been cut. The only straight lines are in the mullions of the windows. In the center of the building are three irregularly shaped courtyards, which admit light into the dwelling spaces. Like all Gaudi's projects in Barcelona, this one offers a very personal vision.

One of the most individual buildings of the century, the Church of the Holy Family (Figure 18-25), in Barcelona, is as dramatic as any rococo masterpiece. Gaudi never lived to see the four towers erected, and the church is not yet finished. He constructed elaborate models in his studio, suspended upside down so that he could study the effects of structural stress on his design. The surfaces of the building contain embedded pieces of ceramic tile. Looking at it we see the traditional gothic forms of naves and aisles, and yet they seem almost to be melted, resulting in a new sense of fluidity.

Figure 18-24
Right: Antonio Gaudi. Casa Milá, Barcelona. 1907. (Photo, Ampliaciones y Reproducciones MAS, Barcelona.)

Figure 18-25
Below: Antonio Gaudi. Church of the Holy Family (Sagrada Familia). 1883–1926. (Photo, Ampliaciones y Reproducciones MAS, Barcelona.)

WALTER GROPIUS AND THE BAUHAUS: LESS IS MORE

Walter Gropius (1883–1969) founded the Bauhaus design school in 1919. It was in many ways a socialist experiment. Gropius's view was that no one had yet taken advantage of the techniques of mass production, which were a natural gift of the new machine age. The Bauhaus sought to simplify and clarify the design of furniture and many other everyday objects for the general public. Simplicity and the absence of ornamentation resulted from Gropius's doctrine that in good design, less is more.

Gropius often said that rationality, which seemed to be the guiding principle of Bauhaus design, was only part of the approach. Finding the soul of simplicity was just as important. Gropius avoided ornamentation and anything else that might distract from straightforward design based on modern principles of building and the use of modern materials: steel, glass, and light masonry. The results of his theories are evident in the buildings that housed the Bauhaus, constructed in 1925 and 1926 (Figure 18-26).

Figure 18-26
Walter Gropius. Bauhaus Buildings, Dessau. 1925–1926. (By permission of Max Protech Gallery; collection Centre Canadien d'Architecture/Canadian Centre for Architecture, Montreal; photo, Klaus Hertig.)

PERCEPTION KEY

Gropius and Early-Twentieth-Century Architects

1. Analyze each building discussed so far in this chapter (see Figures 18-23 through 18-26) in terms of expression of mass and weightiness. Which is least massive? Which is most massive?

2. What is the function of ornamentation in these buildings?

3. A building is both horizontal and vertical. Which of these buildings seems most to reveal its verticality? Which seems most to reveal its horizontality? Which does neither?

4. The relation of form to function is important in all architecture. In which of these buildings are form and function best matched? Remember that Casa Milá is an apartment house; the Bauhaus was a school of design.

5. The style which grew from Gropius's work is called the "international style." Does it seem to have any recognizable national origins? Does it seem to be Germanic? European? What does it mean for a style to be international?

6. Examine the buildings in your neighborhood. Are any of them indebted to the buildings discussed here?

Gropius said:

The liberation of architecture from a welter of ornament, the emphasis on its structural functions, and the
concentration on concise and economical solutions,
represent the purely mathematical side of that formaliz-
ing process on which the *practical* value of the New
Architecture depends. The other, the aesthetic satisfaction of the human soul, is just as important as the
material. Both find their counterpart in that unity
which is life itself. What is far more important than this
structural economy and its functional emphasis is the
intellectual achievement which has made possible a new
spatial vision. For whereas building is merely a matter of
methods and materials, architecture implies the mastery
of space.

Gropius expresses mastery of space in his decision
to reveal its existence—for example, in the pillarless
corners that let us look through the glass skin of the
building, which encompasses at once the interior and
the exterior space. The roof is flat, in keeping with
his theory that pitched roofs waste space and are a fire
hazard. The bridge which joins sections of the building on either side of the road further implies space by
its transparency—above and below as well as through
the windows. There is no trace of ornamentation, no
effort to suggest an earlier style. Space is evident, but
mass is not. We have no sense of weight. The
building is delicate, almost gossamer. Gropius
achieved enormous savings by doing away with
weighty materials in this structure.

The Bauhaus was too liberal for Nazi Germany.
When Hitler came to power, Gropius was forced to
leave. The Nazis put a pitched roof on the building
and then closed the school in 1933. Fascist architecture—and there was much of it—demanded a
different approach to space and mass. It looked back
to the monolithic designs of the Romans and the
Egyptians, designs marked by colossal mass whose purpose was to awe people, to urge them to respect authority. It was totally opposed to Bauhaus simplicity.

FRANK LLOYD WRIGHT:
THE AMERICAN FRONTIER

Frank Lloyd Wright (1867–1959), one of Louis Sullivan's students and his heir to dominance in American architecture, developed independently of the
influence of the Bauhaus style. An American maver-
ick, Wright—like Sullivan—read Jefferson, Thoreau,
and other important American writers, from whom
he absorbed a philosophy of frontier individualism
that dominated his thought and work.

Wright felt that ornamentation added important
dimensions to buildings. Some practitioners of the
international style (derived from the Bauhaus style),
such as Adolf Loos, declared that ornamentation was
a "crime" in architecture and that it pointed to sexual
deviance on the part of the architect. Wright drew
his ornamentation from numerous sources: Asian,
Celtic, Mayan, and Amerindian patterns. His earliest work, which was still influenced by Sullivan, was
in the so-called "prairie style." Wright said: "The
Prairie has a beauty of its own and we should
recognize and accentuate this natural beauty, its
quiet level." The houses of this period were, like
much of Wright's work, one-family homes; they were
low to the ground and had low-pitched roofs and
rambling floor plans. Wright made a point of integrating his houses with the environment so that they
became almost part of nature. This was true even of
his urban houses, most of which were built of
masonry and had considerable overhang in the roofs.
The cantilevered roof—which juts out from the main
part of the house the way a limb juts out from a
tree—became a Wright trademark.

Some of Wright's greatest work was done in the
1930s and 1940s, after he had given up the sprawling
prairie style. Falling Water (Figure 18-27) is marked
by its integration with the natural setting, with
concrete blocks cantilevered over a waterfall. The
building, from virtually any position, seems at one
with its environment, and yet the strong proportions
of the basic rectangular shapes create a rhythm that is
unique in American architecture. It is not only a
piece of architecture, but also a piece of sculpture.
The integration with nature, the cantilevering, and
the linear look—all these are developments of the
prairie style. Yet their overall effect is dramatically
different. This is an architecture of mass as well as of
space, but the mass is defiant of gravity. Its solidity is
counterpointed by the fluidity of the waterfall, and
the cantilevering echoes the surrounding trees.

The Guggenheim Museum in New York (Figure
18-28), which was conceived in the 1940s and built
in the 1950s, is futuristic: a huge white tower looms
out over Fifth Avenue, with horizontal "slits" that
make it look almost like a gun emplacement. The
exterior is dramatic and in stark contrast to the
neighboring rectangular buildings. The interior space

Figure 18-27
Left: Frank Lloyd Wright. *Falling Waters;* the Kaufmann house, Bear Run, Pennsylvania. (Photo, Bill Hedrich, Hedrich-Blessing.)

Figure 18-28
Right: Frank Lloyd Wright. Solomon R. Guggenheim Museum. 1943–1959. (Solomon R. Guggenheim Museum, New York; photo, Robert E. Mates.)

is baffling to many people. A single ramp winds upward around the walls, providing curious vistas from which one can see huge modern paintings, both close up and from a distance, across the width of the building. It remains the most futuristic-looking, if not the most successful, building in New York.

LE CORBUSIER: MODERNISM AND THE MACHINE AGE

Like Frank Lloyd Wright, Charles-Édouard Jeanneret (1887–1965), known as Le Corbusier, was something of a loner. He was born in Switzerland, where he was trained as an architect; after studying in Paris, he went on a ten-year pilgrimage throughout Europe, finally returning to Paris in 1917. At one time he spent six solitary months drawing important buildings —he spent six weeks on the Acropolis alone. He never lost his affection for Greek architecture and other architecture of careful proportions. His theories included the concept of a "regulating line," which is invisible to the average eye but which governs our emotional response to a building. A regulating line might be a series of intersecting half circles, a pattern of proportional rectangles built on one another, or a rhythm of vertical or simply parallel lines that tie together various design elements of a building.

In 1927 he took the name Le Corbusier. There has been considerable speculation about his sense of identity. He behaved like a split personality. Politically, the right thought of him as a leftist, while the left thought of him as a rightist. At times he espoused fascist views, and when he went to Russia in the 1930s, he became involved with communism. He argued in his youth that a house was "a machine for living in," and he insisted on the most careful adherence to principles of simplicity, rectilinearity, and rationality in design. He proclaimed the dominance of mass, surface, and plan in architecture, particularly emphasizing plan—which prevented "willfulness" and eccentricity. Yet some of his most impressive work seems poetic rather than rational, biomorphic instead of rectilinear. It is not simply that he was a man of contradictions, but rather that he was a man of dialectical views. He was contentious with others as well as with himself.

The apartment building in Marseilles, Unité d'Habitation (Figure 18-29), which is derived from Le Corbusier's work in the 1920s and 1930s, is a rectangular box raised on pillars so as to separate it dramatically from the ground and give it an airy feeling. The play of smaller rectangles is consistent, but not monotonous. The building principles are consistent with mass production and with Le Corbusier's essential faith in the benefits to be reaped from the machine age (a faith that was somewhat shaken late in his life). Le Corbusier included shops, restaurants, and entertainment centers in the Unité.

Figure 18-29
Le Corbusier. Unité d'Habitation, Marseilles. 1946–1952. (© Ezra Stoller, ESTO.)

Today hotels around the world follow this pattern. Ironically, most of the inhabitants of this modern building decorate their apartments with antimodern, ornate, and patterned lamps, sofas, draperies, and other furniture.

The dramatic, very different church at Ronchamp, Notre-Dame-du-Haut (Figure 18-30), in which there is no sense of prefabrication, rectilinearity, or interchangeability, dates from about the same period as the Unité. The soaring roofline—not flat, like most of Le Corbusier's roofs—gives a feeling of airiness, but the building is solidly rooted in the earth, like an organic growth. Yet this is not a contradiction of his principles; it is a different way of adhering to them. In 1923 he praised the design achievements of automobiles, ships, and airplanes. And here he found a way to "describe" the church as a means of transport. Not only does the roof remind us of a wing, but from many angles it looks like the hull of a ship. The three towers have been compared to periscopes, but they, too, are primitive rounded

Figure 18-30
Le Corbusier. Notre-Dame-du-Haut, Ronchamp, France. 1950–1955. (© Ezra Stoller, ESTO.)

COMPARISON KEY

Wright and Le Corbusier

1. Have you seen any buildings that were influenced by the work of either Wright or Le Corbusier? Which man do you feel is more likely to influence later architects?

2. Which of the works of Wright and Le Corbusier shown in Figures 18-27 through 18-30 is closest in feeling to Gropius's Bauhaus style? Which is least like Bauhaus architecture?

3. Wright's Guggenheim Museum (Figure 18-28) has been described as futuristic-looking, like something from science fiction. Can Le Corbusier's Notre-Dame-du-Haut (Figure 18-30) be described this way?

4. Which of the buildings discussed in this section on architecture has the most power to "move" you, which Le Corbusier believed architecture should do? Which has the least such power?

5. In which of these buildings are you most aware of special architectural qualities? Which has the fewest architectural qualities? This question naturally invites you to define the term "architectural qualities." What is the difference between construction and architecture?

hulls. The strut holding the highest point of the roof resembles a biplane strut, which Le Corbusier frequently illustrated in his books. The windows are placed in the walls in a pattern which shows the influence of Mondrian but which still imitates the spare fenestration of the superliner or the airliner. The curves and the angling in of the walls suggest speed and the experience of going around curves in a racing car. All this lends modern significance to religion as expressed in this church, and yet Le Corbusier said: "The requirements of religion have had little effect on the design; the form was an answer to a psychophysiology of the feelings." Le Corbusier always said that "The purpose of construction is to make things hold together; of architecture TO MOVE US." If that is so, then Notre-Dame-du-Haut is architecture.

Literature: The Search for Values

POETRY

English poetry of World War I is traditional in form, is usually rhymed, and repeats stanzas of the same length and form. Rupert Brooke (1887–1915), Isaac Rosenberg (1890–1918), and Wilfred Owen (1893–1918), poets who died in the war, left a rich legacy of work. Like poets who survived, they wrote detailed descriptions of army life, of their feelings about battle, and of their fears of death. Among the best-known lines of these poets are Owen's:

> What passing-bells for these who die as cattle?
> Only the monstrous anger of the guns.
> Only the stuttering rifles' rapid rattle
> Can patter out their hasty orisons.

That funerals could be held for these mass-produced dead to mark their individual passing, with the bells common in English villages and elsewhere in peacetime, is out of the question. Machines have reduced men to cattle, passively feeding the war.

Among the poets not associated with the war, there are three whose genius was so extraordinary as to set them apart: William Butler Yeats (1865–1939), an Irishman; Wallace Stevens (1879–1955), an American; and T. S. Eliot (1888–1965), an Englishman.

William Butler Yeats: The Last Romantic

Yeats called himself the "last romantic." His concerns with political matters, with the nature of the self, with an easiness of style, and yet with traditional verse forms and rhyme all sound romantic. But late in his career, his style is marked by certain oblique qualities, some of which are due to his use of personal symbols derived from occult beliefs presented in *A Vision* (second edition, 1937). His use of such personal mythic material is similar to Blake's, as is the resultant obscurity. Yeats, under the influence of the American poet Ezra Pound (1885–1972), also began to use some of the techniques of the imagists (among whom T. S. Eliot was a leader). The image, a direct appeal to the senses, was capable of expressing through emotional means the feelings that the poet wished to control. Yeats never shared the imagists' views completely, although some of his images are among the most powerful in modern poetry.

Yeats also absorbed certain Nietzschean views regarding the cyclic nature of history and the recurrence of events. Nietzsche suggested that because history repeats itself, humans are doomed to live the same lives again and again. This view fit in with Yeats's occult concepts, which he incorporated into his poems. Unlike Wordsworth, Coleridge, and other romantics, Yeats did not address a general audience. Rather, he spoke to those who could understand him, which is one reason he felt a kinship with the poet Milton, who once described himself as addressing a "fit audience, though few."

Yeats believed in the capacity of poetry to be prophetic. He thought that "The Second Coming," which contains his best-known lines, foresaw not only the Russian Revolution but also the rise of fascism and the Second World War:

> Turning and turning in the widening gyre
> The falcon cannot hear the falconer;
> Things fall apart; the centre cannot hold;
> Mere anarchy is loosed upon the world,
> The blood-dimmed tide is loosed, and everywhere
> The ceremony of innocence is drowned;
> The best lack all conviction, while the worst
> Are full of passionate intensity.
>
> Surely some revelation is at hand;
> Surely the Second Coming is at hand.
> The Second Coming! Hardly are those words out
> When a vast image out of Spiritus Mundi

Yeats, "The Second Coming"

1. Because "The Second Coming" is a difficult poem, we must ask some basic questions: What does the term "Second Coming" imply? To whom do "the best" and "the worst" seem to refer in the seventh line? What is the "shape" in the desert, and why does Yeats refer to a desert? What does the "rocking cradle" refer to?

2. Which images in the poem are the most powerful? Remember that an image is a vivid description designed to appeal directly to the senses.

3. Is it clear whether the poem is optimistic or pessimistic regarding the future of humankind?

4. Why does Yeats begin by speaking about a falcon, whereas he speaks later of "indignant desert birds"? What is the difference between them?

5. Are there any clear references to current events in the poem? To historical events?

Troubles my sight: somewhere in sands of the desert
A shape with lion body and the head of a man
A gaze blank and pitiless as the sun,
Is moving its slow thighs, while all about it
Reel shadows of the indignant desert birds.
The darkness drops again; but now I know
That twenty centuries of stony sleep
Were vexed to nightmare by a rocking cradle,
And what rough beast, its hour come round at last,
Slouches towards Bethlehem to be born?

Yeats held that history repeats itself in cycles. The "widening gyre" is the corkscrew motion of the falcon, a carefully trained bird and a symbol of aristocratic stateliness, as it obeys its master. The gyre is a visual image of the historical cycle of repetition; when the breakdown of one stable era occurs, it is as if the center—the falconer—dissolves, and in place of order there is "anarchy" and chaos.

In this poem Yeats speaks of the entirety of Christian civilization. The title refers to the second coming of Christ and the end of the present era. It will not be pleasant and cheering. Instead, it is a threat. The "image out of Spiritus Mundi"—the world spirit or world soul—is the Sphinx, which threatened Thebes and which Oedipus outwitted, only to meet his awful fate. The desert is the desert of beginnings: Mary and Joseph crossed a desert to reach Bethlehem; the Egyptian culture grew in proximity to a desert. And the threatening Sphinx is as much in contrast to the Christ of the nativity as the disciplined, sleek, obedient falcon is to the ravaging, annoyed desert birds, who are as irascible and unteachable as crows. Yeats feared that the Sphinx—having had to wait out this 2000-year Christian era—was especially vexed and that the tide of blood would be the worse for this.

The first stanza reviews world conditions, which are marked by revolution in Russia, economic collapse in Germany, rebellion in Yeats's Ireland, and the terrible waste of World War I—which obviously did not make Europe safer or better. It points out that the best politicians do not know what to do —they "lack all conviction"—and the worst are "full of passionate intensity." In light of the failures of Wilson and Chamberlain and the successes of Mussolini and Hitler, the poem did prove prophetic.

Wallace Stevens: The Poem of Aesthetic Value

Just as the cubists concentrated on the purely aesthetic values of painting, apart from other humanist values, Wallace Stevens wrote poetry in which aesthetic considerations are foremost. He studied the ways in which art transforms experience, and he produced a poetry of extreme complexity and extreme spareness. "The Emperor of Ice-Cream," from his first book, *Harmonium* (1923), was his favorite among his poems. He said, in a letter, that it "deliberately wears a commonplace costume, and yet seems to me to contain something of the essential gaudiness of poetry":

> Call the roller of big cigars,
> The muscular one, and bid him whip
> In kitchen cups concupiscent curds.
> Let the wenches dawdle in such dress
> As they are used to wear, and let the boys
> Bring flowers in last month's newspapers.
> Let be be finale of seem.
> The only emperor is the emperor of ice-cream.
>
> Take from the dresser of deal,
> Lacking the three glass knobs, that sheet
> On which she embroidered fantails once
> And spread it so as to cover her face.
> If her horny feet protrude, they come
> To show how cold she is, and dumb.
> Let the lamp affix its beam.
> The only emperor is the emperor of ice-cream.

To appreciate the poem, one should hear it read well aloud. It is musical in form, consisting of two strophic verses whose last two lines are rhymed couplets, with an exact repetition of the final line. The metrical patterns of the verses are symmetrical, and Stevens uses many musical effects, such as alliteration (the "k" sound in the third line) and assonance (close juxtaposition of vowel sounds, as in the fourth line). What is not provided is the identification of the people in the poem or its setting. We must deduce those for ourselves, much as we might deduce the subject of a cubist painting from the clues given in the title.

Stevens's letter helps us understand the poem, but even without it some things are clear. There is a woman, dead, who is to be covered with a sheet on which she herself has embroidered complex designs. There will be a wake at which people will gather and for which the cigar roller will whip up a treat. That the treat is concupiscent (sexy) simply helps contrast the event with death. In Freud's view, sex and death were the two strongest drives; in the work of seventeenth-century poets, such as Donne, they were often metaphors for each other. The enigmatic line "Let be be finale of seem" echoes Hamlet's line to his mother: "I know not seems." In *Hamlet*, appearances —seems—are not at all trustworthy. Stevens is ask-ing for appearances to be trustworthy. Seem and be should be one. Ice cream should be thought of as an absolute good: it tastes good, it satisfies, it is good. We contrast the dead woman with the living wenches, the boys, and the muscular cigar roller and their implied concupiscence. Life is good. It must be lived; it stands in stark contrast with death.

Unraveling this poem is one thing, but experiencing it is another. Read it aloud or hear it read out loud again. Regard it as a painting in sound, an artifact whose elements are ordered in such a way as to produce a new experience and a new reality.

T. S. Eliot: Poetry and Religious Renovation

The most influential poet of the period, T. S. Eliot, was born in the United States but chose to live in England and become a British subject. His work revives traditional religious values while reacting against the lack of spirituality in modern life.

Eliot's poem *The Waste Land* (1922) is in five sections: I, *The Burial of the Dead*; II, *A Game of Chess*; III, *The Fire Sermon*; IV, *Death by Water*; V, *What the Thunder Said*. It is immensely difficult because Eliot's intent was to write a poem of extreme significance and because he addressed only the most intelligent, cultivated, and literate readers. His allusions to world literature, to art, and to opera and his quotations in foreign languages all restricted his readership, although he included a large group of explanatory footnotes at the end of the poem.

The poem is an examination of postwar life, focusing on the crassness of commerce, the cheapening of sex, and the materialism that swept religious and spiritual values aside. The land is waste—Europe is waste—because the people did not honor spiritual values. The land is cursed like the Thebes of Oedipus: parched, arid, and unrenewed. In the final section, all of Europe waits for the thunder to speak:

> What is that sound high in the air
> Murmur of maternal lamentation
> Who are those hooded hordes swarming
> Over endless plains, stumbling in cracked earth
> Ringed by the flat horizon only
> What is the city over the mountains
> Cracks and reforms and burst in the violet air
> Falling Towers
> Jerusalem Athens Alexandria
> Vienna London
> Unreal

The thunder finally speaks, telling us, like the word of God, to give, sympathize, and control. Generosity makes us unselfish; sympathy makes us more humane; control makes us less wanton, less apt to be victims of passion. Eliot saw a loss of godliness as the cause of Europe's destruction. A return to Christian values was Europe's only hope, and "The Waste Land" was his effort to make the world realize that there was a curse on the land—the curse of materialism—and that until the curse was lifted, Europe would be arid and sterile. On the one hand, the "hooded hordes" sound like Dante's vision in hell, sufferers whose commitment to lust condemns them to perpetual disorder and passion. On the other hand, they are the helmeted hordes who swarmed over Europe in 1914 and would do so again in 1939.

The Waste Land is a landmark in poetic technique as well as in substance. Eliot's method is based on imagism—juxtaposing and organizing images to create a strong emotional language. Eliot also alludes to esoteric literature, abandoning conventional linking passages which would clarify comments, lines, statements, and images. We must cope with difficulties such as those of the last stanza:

> I sat upon the shore
> Fishing, with the arid plain behind me
> Shall I at least set my lands in order?
> London Bridge is falling down falling down falling
>   down
> Poi s'ascose nel foco che gli affina
> Quando fiam uti chelidon—O swallow swallow
> Le Prince d'Aquitaine a la tour abolie
> These fragments I have shored against my ruins
> Why then Ile fit you. Hieronymo's mad againe.
> Datta. Dayadhvam. Damyata.
> > Shantih   shantih   shantih

The "I" character (not Eliot) can do nothing. Fishing in the waste land is futile, and yet he has little else to do. He decides to gather some fragments, perhaps these quotations from various literary sources, and set his house in order, a biblical reference to preparing for death. The children's song, "London Bridge Is Falling Down," can be taken literally here, as destruction seems imminent. The Italian words that follow are a quotation from Dante—"he hid himself in the fire which refines them"—reminding us that in purgatory, the fire refines and purifies. The Latin words are from an obscure hymn to spring associated with Venus, and the swallow is the bird

that ushers in the spring—which in the waste land of the poem has not come. The Prince of Aquitaine is symbolic of the old traditions of aristocratic Europe—now useless and left behind. Mad Hieronymo, from the *Spanish Tragedie,* by the Elizabethan playwright Thomas Kyd, "fits" an audience with an entertainment (like this poem). "Datta. Dayadhvam. Damyata" are the words the thunder spoke: give, sympathize, control. The final "shantih" comes from the Indian religious books the Upanishads and means something close to "the peace that passeth understanding."

Such difficulties mean that only well-prepared readers can understand and respond to the poem. Given Eliot's critique of materialism, it was natural for him to address an audience that shared his affection for art, literature, and spiritual concerns. He offered a large-scale cultural challenge to Europe: return to spiritual values, or continue into the waste and arid land of matter without spirit, without humanity, and without god. The brilliance of his vision made him the most important poet of his time.

THE MODERN NOVEL

Like the poetry of the first part of the twentieth century, the novels of the period were marked by brilliance, difficulty, and obscurity. The three finest were written within approximately the same ten-year period. *À la recherche du temps perdu (Remembrance of Things Past),* by Marcel Proust (1871–1922), was published in sixteen volumes between 1913 and 1927; *Der Zauberberg (The Magic Mountain),* by Thomas Mann (1875–1955), was published in 1924; and *Ulysses,* by James Joyce (1882–1941), was published in 1922. These three masterpieces share many qualities: they are all very long books centering on a character who resembles the author; they are extremely demanding and cannot be considered simple entertainments; they offer a liberal emotional education in return for the reader's patience; and they all reflect Freud's theories of psychoanalysis and focus on central issues of humanity.

They are untraditional novels. Proust begins in the present time, but very soon Marcel, the main character, dips a small cookie, a madeleine, into his tea, and its taste brings an involuntary rush of memories from childhood. This sets the stage for long, complex narratives of events that were important in shaping the person he has become. The texture of the prose is so rich as to be lush. Sentences and paragraphs are unusually long. Proust achieves his effects by a slow, inexorable accretion of sensual details. There is no other novel like this one. The method is internal: it depends on reflection and thought and centers on Marcel's remembered affection for his mother; his memories of Combray, where he spent summers during his childhood; and his recollections of Swann, a friend of his family. Proust is slow in telling his story and makes few, if any, concessions to his reader concerning dramatic pacing or the speed of the narrative. When one reads Proust, one is immersed and carried along in a world of rich, intense, very personal experience.

Thomas Mann's novel is structured quite different-ly. It does not rely on the interior consciousness of his character, Hans Castorp, and its plot is more traditional—at least it can be described. On the eve of World War I, Castorp, a young German, goes to a sanatorium in Switzerland to visit a cousin who has tuberculosis; while there, he learns that he himself is infected. During his years in the sanatorium—the "magic mountain"—he learns not just who he is, but also what the materials of his culture are. The novel includes remarkable dialogues between a Christian humanist, Settembrini, and an atheistic social-materialist, Naphta. Castorp, listening to these arguments, is exposed to the social forces which have shaped modern values. He also discovers the power of sex as a result of his intense affection for Clavdia

PERCEPTION KEY:

The Modern Novel

The novels discussed here are probably too long to be read in a humanities course. However, Joyce's *Portrait of the Artist as a Young Man* is certainly short enough to be read and will serve as an introduction to the modern novel. Use it as the basis for considering these questions.

1. What is Stephen Dedalus like? Is he heroic in a traditional sense or in some new sense? Do you identify with him?

2. The stream-of-consciousness technique (which depicts the psychological, subjective life of a character) is used in the first section of the novel. Establish where it is used and what its characteristics are. What problems does it create? What advantages does it offer in terms of narration? Is it fair to compare it to van Eyck's and Velásquez' technique of putting the viewer in the position of the artist or the subject of a portrait?

3. What problems does an artist who grows up in a middle-class environment face? What middle-class standards are presented in the novel, and what is Stephen's position on them? Is Stephen class-conscious? Is he antagonistic toward the middle class?

4. Stephen struggles with the demands made by his family. What are those demands? Does Stephen behave correctly? He struggles with religion, with Irish nationalism, and with basic questions of art. What stands does he take, and how sympathetic are you to his position?

5. Do you feel that there is a reasonable connection between the fragmentation of images in modern painting and the fragmentation of narrative in this novel? What are the similarities and the differences between these two kinds of fragmentation?

Chauchat. All the while he is lured by the lotuslike attraction of the sanatorium, which is like the land of the dead. The novel ends with Castorp returning to society and to the holocaust of the war. As an analysis of the values of Mann's generation, *The Magic Mountain* stands as a monument. Mann was deeply committed to the values of his culture, and when Hitler came to power he was among those who protested and left Germany.

James Joyce is known for three important novels: *A Portrait of the Artist as a Young Man* (1916), *Ulysses* (1922), and *Finnegans Wake* (1939). His most accessible novel is the first; his least accessible is the last. *Ulysses* is among the most influential pieces of literature of the century. As its title implies, it is an epic, but a modern epic with a modern hero. It is not neoclassical, but rather constitutes a total revision of basic Greek and classical values. Instead of a warlike Ulysses fighting his way homeward, Joyce chooses a very humble character, Leopold Bloom, as his hero. The novel tells of the events of a single day in the lives of its leading characters. Bloom walks about the city of Dublin, placing an ad for a client and worrying about his wife, Molly, who in the afternoon expects the amorous attentions of Blazes Boylan. Bloom also thinks about his daughter, Millie, who has gone off to start a new job, and about his son, Rudy, who died years before at the age of eleven days.

By choosing Bloom as his hero, Joyce creates a totally modern epic. The values of Homeric heroism were destroyed in 1914, and so was the concept of a hero who is larger than life. Instead, we have a hero who is no greater than we are. The teachings of Freud appear in the novel in many ways—in echoes from Freud's cases, in the dominance of stream of consciousness, in an episode that dips into the subconscious, and in a commitment to the Freudian view that everything has meaning. Joyce is said to have been one of two people in Dublin in 1904 who had read Freud. The other was Yeats.

The technical innovation in this novel, begun in *A Portrait of the Artist as a Young Man,* is stream of consciousness. It influenced virtually all succeeding generations of novelists, particularly William Faulkner in America and Virginia Woolf in England. It was a baffling technique in 1922 and still baffles some readers. Because Joyce attempts to reproduce the consciousness of an individual, with its quirks and its sudden unexplained leaps of thought, we are often disconcerted. We read the dialogue and respond to the description, but only with great effort do we understand that we have been placed inside a character's mind without being told that this has happened. Joyce's readers are expected to know their Homer, Virgil, Dante, Milton, and Blake—all the major epic poets of the past. Like the novels of Proust and Mann, *Ulysses* is written for the most mature and the best-prepared reader that Joyce could imagine.

Film: Drama of the Masses

In terms of reaching an audience and affecting its behavior, the most powerful art form of the twentieth century is the film. Motion pictures, invented in the late nineteenth century, became a mass medium in the decade of the First World War. There is a tempting comparison to be made between film and the mass-produced Ford automobile: one brought cheap transportation to the masses, and the other brought cheap entertainment, virtually at the same time. The world of the average person has not been the same since.

THE SILENT FILM

D. W. Griffith: Epic Vision

The American D. W. Griffith (1875–1948) was first a writer, then an actor in films, and then a director at a time when no one was quite sure what a director did. He and his ace cameraman, Billy Bitzer, worked together.

Birth of a Nation (1915; three scenes are shown in Figures 18-31, 18-32, and 18-33) was a full-scale epic based on *The Clansmen,* by the Reverend Thomas Dixon, who was vastly better known than Griffith. Like its source, the film looked favorably on the Ku Klux Klan and offered an unsympathetic view of black Americans. Griffith, a southerner, said that he had done his best to "tell the truth about the War between the States"; but the reaction to the film in America was marked by intense dispute. Northern legislators actually tried to invoke a law to prevent its being distributed; they claimed that it would contribute to conflict between the races because it portrayed blacks unfavorably. Griffith was shocked at the film's reception—he said that he had never meant to be

Figure 18-31
Right: D. W. Griffith. *Birth of a Nation,* battle
sequence. 1915. (Museum of Modern Art Film
Stills Archive, New York.)

Figure 18-32
Left: Griffith. *Birth of a Nation.*
(Museum of Modern Art Film
Stills Archive, New York.)

Figure 18-33
Right: Griffith. *Birth of a Nation.* (Museum of Modern
Art Film Stills Archive, New York.)

unfair to blacks—yet the film has never lost its original reputation. In the 1940s Griffith was quoted as having said that despite his intentions, he could understand why the film would be inflammatory, and he agreed that it probably ought not to be displayed in its existing form.

Griffith's treatment of blacks is more closely tied to the attitudes of Americans in the first part of the century than to any personal feelings. He felt that he was being factual, even though he portrayed a renegade black, Gus, who is captured by the Klan because he tried to rape Flora Cameron, the sister of the heroine. In what seems today to be an obviously racist sequence, Gus stalks Flora, who in desperation leaps over a cliff to her death.

The power of *Birth of a Nation* to project and interpret social values was startling in 1915. However, Griffith's technique is what made it a success. Griffith was a determined realist. His plot was fiction, but it was intertwined closely with actual historical events.

Charlie Chaplin: The Clown of Subversion

Chaplin (1889–1977), born in extreme poverty in England, started in vaudeville as a child. He was offered a film contract by Mack Sennett, famous as the originator of the Keystone Kops. It took Chaplin a while to agree to make films, but when he did in 1913, he invented a character—the lovable tramp, the butt of everyone's ill humor—that still reveals his genius. The tramp became the most famous character in the world and made Chaplin the world's most famous actor.

At the time, very few people realized that great films like *The Floorwalker* (1916), *Easy Street* (1917), *The Immigrant* (1917), *A Dog's Life* (1918), *The Kid* (1921; Figure 18-34), and the classic *Gold Rush* (1925) were contributing to the extraordinary change in values that marked the period of the First World War and the 1920s. The widespread loss of faith in the authority of the ruling class and other institutions, including government and politics, was certainly not caused by Chaplin's films, but they added to the speed with which the old values and the old authorities were overthrown.

The masses identified with the tramp, who was one of them: he bore their indignities, suffered their humiliations, and eventually achieved their victor-

Figure 18-34
Charles Chaplin in *The Kid,* with Jackie Coogan. 1921. (Museum of Modern Art Film Stills Archive, New York.)

ies. The great power of film to involve the masses totally with art—some for the first time—is still one of its most impressive qualities. Chaplin's films provided a participative experience that, for most people, was among the most intense they had known.

Chaplin, like Griffith, worked his magic in silence. These films had no sound. There was usually a musical score, played by a single pianist or sometimes a small orchestra. The titles made the action understandable—there was no dialogue. Everything was achieved by visual effect, selection of camera angles, movement of the camera, selection of shots, and editing.

Sergey Eisenstein: Genius of the Proletariat

After the Russian Revolution of 1917, Soviet authorities encouraged the making of films as a way of educating the masses in the principles of the revolution. They were uncannily accurate in their judgment of the power of film, and they were fortunate enough to produce a large number of gifted filmmakers in the Soviet film school. One of these, Sergey Eisenstein (1898–1948), was a brilliant man. He read the works of Shakespeare, Dickens, and Balzac and many more of the world's classics—usually in the original language. He lectured in Berlin in German, in London in English, and in Paris in French. He traveled to Hollywood, where he could not make films (despite his efforts and despite psychoanalysis), and he traveled to Mexico, where his film on the Mexican revolution, *Que viva Mexico!* (1931–1932), was never shown. His knowledge of art, music, and literature was immense, and he was acquainted with most of the important figures of his age.

Battleship Potemkin (1925; Figures 18-35 and 18-36) is repeatedly cited as one of the greatest films of all time. It began as a project to make a film on the subject of the revolution of 1905, which had failed. Eisenstein had done only one film before this, *Strike* (1924), but it was powerful enough for him to be given full control of the project. The episode of the *Potemkin*, he began to see, could be the subject of a full-length film. Eisenstein had studied cubist and futurist painting carefully, and—possibly as a result of his study—he experimented with a relatively violent form of montage. Montage is the joining together of two different shots or frames—in other words, a form of film editing.

The Marxist dialectic of thesis, antithesis, and synthesis may have inspired him; he may also have been influenced by the work of other filmmakers, such as Abel Gance (1889–1981). Wherever it came from, his concept of the montage became such an exciting emotional language for him that he had to be careful not to overwhelm his audience with it. Today we think of its sudden cuts and jumps as functional, but they were such a shock in 1925 that the reception of the film was mixed.

Eisenstein later said:

> I am accused of making *Battleship Potemkin* too emotional. Are we not all people? Don't we have human feelings? Don't we have passions? Don't we have our own tasks and purposes in life?

As his student, Jay Leyda, tells us, Eisenstein wanted to stimulate the emotions, but not as an end in itself:

> The purposive direction of the spectator's emotion is a social responsibility, and all art in the Soviet Union is conscious of that responsibility . . . . This social function . . . underlies every word of Eisenstein's film theory.

In 1925 a full-length film was produced in several reels. A showing was stopped after each reel so that the next reel could be loaded onto the projector. Films were constructed with an eye to these breaks, which lasted twelve to fifteen minutes. Thus, for *Potemkin*, a five-reel film, it is easy to see why Eisenstein chose the structure of a five-act tragedy.

Figure 18-35
Sergey Eisenstein. *Battleship Potemkin,* scene on the quarterdeck. 1925. (Museum of Modern Art Film Stills Archive, New York.)

He described the film's structure as follows:

Act 1. "Men and Maggots." The sailors are fed rotten meat with Dr. Smirnov's approval. The czar's contempt for them is the last straw for the crew members.

Act 2. "The Drama on the Quarterdeck" (Figure 18-35). The crew members refuse to eat the soup. Vakulinchuk takes the first step toward revolt. When the marines are ordered to shoot down the mutineers, they refuse. The crew members throw the officers overboard. Vakulinchuk dies.

Act 3. "The Blood Cries Vengeance." The ship makes for the port of Odessa to bury Vakulinchuk's body. The people greet the ship in a sign of brotherhood. After the funeral, the red flag of communist revolution is raised.

Act 4. "The Odessa Steps." In the most memora- ble scenes of the film, the czar's soldiers arrive and shoot down innocent civilians on the broad steps of Odessa. The montage of collision (Figure 18-36) is overwhelming in this section.

Act 5. "The Passing of the Fleet." The crew members hold a vigil through the night. They spot the czar's fleet pursuing them and rev up the engines, preparing to flee. The fleet does not fire on them, but breaks out with sympathetic cheers, and the *Potemkin* goes on to freedom.

In the last scene, the intercutting of long shots of the fleet with medium shots of the crew and then with close-up shots of the engines throbbing, the water crashing across the bow, and other details of intense activity builds emotional tension. The last shot shows the bow of the ship coming directly at the audience, as if it were running it down.

Figure 18-36
Eisenstein. *Battleship Potemkin,* selected frames showing the violence of the montage.
(Museum of Modern Art Film Stills Archive, New York.)

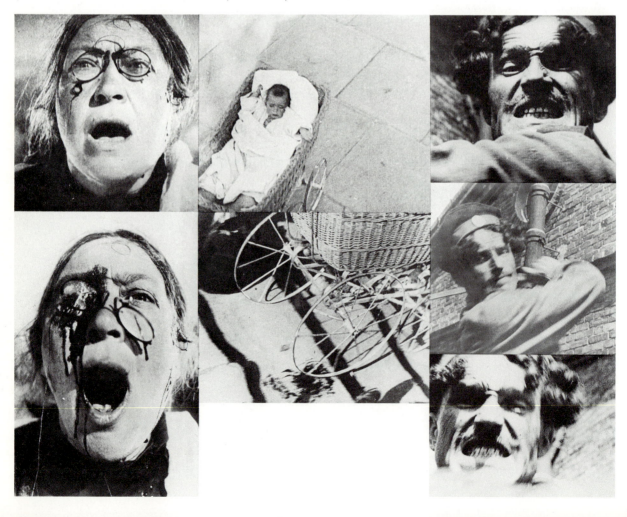

The Silent Film

Note: Many silent films are now available on video cassette. *Birth of a Nation* and others can be obtained from Kartes Video in Indianapolis.

1. If possible, see a silent film. As you watch, use the following as a checklist, noting each appearance of a long shot, a medium shot, and a close-up shot.

2. Observe the instances of the following uses of the camera: fixed camera shot, moving camera shot, and sharp camera angle.

3. Keep a record of the changes of scene or the montage of shots. Note slow transitions, abrupt transitions, and shocking transitions.

4. Is the editing, or montage work, generally done for emotional effect, or is it neutral? What emotional effects, if any, seem to be achieved by the editing?

5. You may perform this experiment using a television film with the sound turned off. If you use a modern film, consider the relative value of its visual elements. Would this film communicate with its audience on a visual level to the same extent that silent films did?

SOUND FILMS

Citizen Kane and the Indictment of Materialism

The visual qualities of films generally declined in the 1930s, despite the production of many very amusing, bright, and charming commercial films. A number of directors experimented with surrealism, and Luis Buñuel had some notable successes. But most films were made with soft-focus lenses and unnatural lighting, and the acting was hardly relaxed. When Orson Welles directed and starred in his first film, *Citizen Kane* (1941; a scene is shown in Figure 18-37), from a script by Herman Mankiewicz, filmmakers went to study it.

The story was explosive: it seemed to be an unauthorized biography of the powerful and vindictive newspaper tycoon William Randolph Hearst. Welles denied the connection between Hearst and Kane; but Kane was a newspaper tycoon who, like Hearst, began as a populist, became a fascist sympathizer, ran for public office, kept a pretty young woman as his mistress (the singer Susan Alexander in the film; the film star Marion Davies in real life),

lived in a castle filled with works of art, and became an enigma to everyone. Mankiewicz had been in Hearst's inner circle; had dined with him and Marion Davies at his "castle," San Simeon; and had conceived the script as Welles's first project in Hollywood.

Because of Hearst's attacks, the film failed to make much money, and Welles never again had a free hand in directing. Yet *Citizen Kane* was so innovative that it remains a milestone. Welles's concern for the visual image is as great as Eisenstein's, even though Welles once said: "I know that in theory the word is secondary in cinema but the secret of my work is that everything is based on the word. I do not make silent films."

Because Welles knew nothing of the technical problems of film, he did things which were believed to be impossible. He used a wide-angle lens that produced an image close to what is seen by the normal human eye, and as a result he had to build ceilings in all the rooms he used as settings; this was unheard-of. He also kept distant and close objects more in focus than had been done in earlier films.

Figure 18-37
Orson Welles. *Citizen Kane;* Kane listening to Susan at the piano. 1941.
(By permission of RKO General Pictures.)

Because he used very fast film emulsions, he was able to stop his lenses down even more and maintain very sharp images throughout—no more soft focus. That was analogous to the revolution in Stieglitz's Photo-Secession. In order to get the camera angles he wanted, Welles often built pits in the floor of the set so that the camera was looking up at the characters; the effect for the viewer is like being a child looking up at adults.

Welles began *Citizen Kane* with what appears to be a newsreel and merged the story of Kane with it, using flashbacks to provide different points of view analogous to those in the stream-of-consciousness novel. Welles's choice of flashbacks—the memories of several "witnesses" commenting on Kane after his funeral—presented a fragmentation of point of view similar to what was being done by experimental writers of the day. It was too unusual for an audience who expected a single, author-controlled point of view and a single, chronological, continuous narrative. But Welles's experiment is so vital that even forty years later, the film seems fresh and impressive.

Casablanca: Existentialism and the "Marseillaise"

We now turn to a film designed to stir the patriotism of even the most cynical audience. *Casablanca* (1942;

Figure 18-38) was distributed only months before President Roosevelt and Winston Churchill met in Casablanca to discuss the progress of the European campaign of World War II. It made many world-weary Americans take the cause of the European war seriously.

Technically, there is little to recommend the visual sequences of the film. They are professional, polished, and ordinary. *Casablanca* was a team project typical of studio mass production. Warner Brothers had Julius and Philip Epstein write the screenplay with Howard Koch. They began with a thoroughly undistinguished novel. Hal Wallis produced it, and Michael Curtiz directed it: all seasoned, workaday professionals. The stars, Humphrey Bogart and Ingrid Bergman, seem more the source of the film's genius than anything else.

The story sounds tired. Rick, an American expatriate, disappointed in his love for Ilsa, avoids the war by running a nightclub in Casablanca, which is occupied by the Vichy French (the government of occupied France). By staying out of politics and the war, he can continue to live as he has been. When Ilsa arrives with her husband, Victor Laszlo, a patriot who has escaped from Prague, Rick does not want to become involved. But, like the existentialist philosopher Albert Camus, who was Algerian, Rick finally

Figure 18-38
Humphrey Bogart and Ingrid Bergman in
Casablanca. 1942. (From the United Artists
release *Casablanca,* © 1943 Warner Brothers
Pictures, Inc; renewed 1970 United Artists
Television, Inc.; photo, Wisconsin Center for
Film and Theater Research.)

PERCEPTION KEY

Sound Films

1. Listen to a film on television without the picture. How difficult is it to follow the narrative? Make some comparisons with silent films. Is their narrative easier to follow?

2. Two of the most memorable films ever made are arguments in favor of a political view: the silent film *Battleship Potemkin* and *Casablanca.* If you have seen a film which attempts to defend a political view, try to decide whether your memory of its visual qualities or its sound qualities is more distinct.

3. If you feel that a film is compromised artistically by the addition of a sound track, what are some of your reasons? How can a sound track compromise the artistic integrity of a film?

4. What artistic advantages would a film whose photography is artistically on a par with excellent still photography be likely to have? What disadvantages might it have? Is splendid photography essential in a good film?

5. Analyze a film of your choice in terms of its visual and aural qualities. Consider quality of photography, types of shots, editing, camera movement, and lighting. Consider also the use of dialogue, music, and any emotional sound qualities (special effects of any sort). Establish the relationship between the visual and aural effects. Is either clearly dominant? Is there an effective marriage of both elements in the film?

sees that principles are more important than his own hurt pride. Life is not worth living if one does not shape it through principles of honor and dignity.

We discover that Rick ran guns to the Ethiopians when Italy waged war and that he fought in 1936 for the Spanish republicans. In Paris he fell in love with Ilsa the day the Nazis marched in; when they separated, Rick thought he had lost her to the war. He fled to Casablanca, part of a French African colony. To Victor Laszlo, who knows that Rick is at heart a patriot, he says: "I'm not interested in politics. The problems of the world are not in my department. I'm a saloon keeper." Moments later German officers, gathered around the piano, start singing a German song. Laszlo calls out for the French national anthem, the "Marseillaise." As the anthem is sung, everyone in the cafe rises except the Germans. All sing, some with tears in their eyes. It is an emotionally stirring moment which only a sound film could portray.

However, this scene "cheats" a little. As critics have pointed out, the French ought not to have been in Morocco any more than the Germans, and if the Moroccan national anthem had been played, neither American nor European audiences would have been moved at all. Moreover, war is at root a nationalistic phenomenon, and anthems are part of the reason we have wars. But despite all this, the anthem works. We see it as an international protest against the forces not of a nation, but of ideological fascism, which seemed to have declared war on everyone who was not German or Aryan.

When Rick finally agrees to help, and when his counterpart in the French government, Renault, helps too, we cheer. The film ends with the sound of the airplane that will take Laszlo and Ilsa to freedom. The two former world-weary cynics, Rick and Renault, both realize that they must leave Casablanca and become part of the larger world.

Music

THE CRISIS IN TONALITY

The twentieth century began with a series of crises in values that were undefined, but not unnoticed. In music the crisis centered on tonality. The concept of the tonal center—the sense of expectation that is created when a piece begins in the tonic, or "home" key, and then moves purposely away from the tonic, only to come decisively back to it—began to break down at the turn of the century.

Musicologists point to the influence of Wagner, particularly his *Tristan und Isolde* (1859), in which long delays of the expected tonal resolution produce passages that seem to lack the tonal center of traditional music. One of the most significant experiments in music of the early twentieth century was the abandonment of key-centered composition. Atonal music and twelve-tone music treat all twelve tones in the octave as equal, denying dominance to a given tone and denying the listener the satisfaction of tension, expectation, and release caused by moving away from, and then back to, the tonic.

IGOR STRAVINSKY: PRIMITIVISM AND NEOCLASSICISM

Igor Stravinsky (1882–1971) is widely regarded as the most important composer of the twentieth century. His work, like Picasso's, went through numerous styles and "periods," and like Picasso he maintained freshness and originality in his creations throughout his life. He was born near Saint Petersburg, in Russia, into a well-to-do family. He gave up an education in the law to pursue his studies in music and rapidly came to the notice of important Russian musicians. His life changed when his music was heard by Sergey Diaghilev, the impresario of the Russian ballet (which was based primarily in Paris). At that time, Diaghilev was establishing a ballet repertory that would change the course of dance and clarify a thoroughly modern style. The choreographers Michel Fokine and George Balanchine produced dances which the great Vaslav Nijinsky realized. Diaghilev persuaded Stravinsky to compose music for the Ballets Russes. *The Firebird* (1910) and *Petrushka* (1911) are based on Russian folktales and contain snatches of Russian folk melodies. They became immediately popular and are still in the repertory today. *The Rite of Spring* was first performed in 1913, the year Freud's *Totem and Taboo* was published. Freud analyzed primitive attitudes toward sexuality and ritual. Just as Picasso had been fascinated by African masks, and just as the colonization of Africa had made Europeans aware of African artifacts, anthropologists became

Figure 18-39
Igor Stravinsky. *The Rite of Spring,* opening melody. 1913. (© copyright 1921 by Edition Russe de Musique, renewed 1958. Copyright and renewal assigned to Boosey & Hawkes, Inc. Revised edition copyright 1947 by Boosey and Hawkes, Inc. New edition, 1967.)

aware of unusual cultural practices that Freud thought provided insight into the nature of the human psyche.

The audiences that first saw *The Rite of Spring* were as outraged by its obvious sexuality and its probing of psychological depths as those who saw the Armory Show were disturbed by Duchamp's *Nude Descending a Staircase* and, earlier, as people had been disturbed by Picasso's *Demoiselles d'Avignon.* Stravinsky's ballet explored an emotional territory that music had never before touched directly. His method was to use powerful rhythmic motifs, repeated almost incessantly. He began with a solo bassoon stating a now-famous and haunting folk melody (shown in Figure 18-39, above).

What was technically alarming about the music was the abrupt breaks and movements, which defied any kind of anticipation on the part of the audience. Whereas even romantic symphonic structures were built on the normal expectations of form, or of tone structure and melodic or harmonic development, this piece stopped abruptly, substituted violent motifs for orderly transitions, and generally defied the standards that the audiences of 1913 expected at the ballet. Yet it also depended on many of Debussy's techniques: the use of ostinato, a persistent piling up of rhythmic figures, and carefully planned silences. A modern performance of *The Rite of Spring* is shown in Figure 18-40.

Stravinsky's neoclassical period began in 1919, although he never limited himself exclusively to music which took its structure and tonalities from classical compositions. He used symmetrical structures and melodic borrowings from classical composers. Among other things, he chose classical subjects, as in *Oedipus Rex* (1927) and *Apollo Musagetes* (1928). His *Symphony of Psalms* (1930) and Symphony in C (1940) show classical influences. Stravinsky has said that he wrote the Symphony in C during one of the worst periods of his life. He had tuberculosis when he began the work, and while he was compos-

Figure 18-40
Igor Stravinsky and Maurice Béjart. *Rite of Spring.* (ICM Artists, Ltd.; photo, William Dupont.)

ing it his daughter, wife, and mother died. The act of writing, he said, kept him from despair, but none of the emotions he felt were used in the work.

Stravinsky was only one of several contemporary composers working in a neoclassical style. Maurice Ravel (1875–1937) was capable of impressionistic work in *Rhapsodie Espagnole* ("Spanish Rhapsody"; 1907), and some of the primitivism of Stravinsky is suggested in his *Boléro* (1928). But he was also capable of more strict neoclassical expression in works such as *Pavane pour une enfante défunte* ("Pavane for a Dead Princess"; 1899) and *Le Tombeau de Couperin* ("The Tomb of Couperin"; 1917), in which he alludes distinctly to eighteenth-century styles.

BÉLA BARTÓK

Béla Bartók (1881–1945) was interested in folk melodies and in percussive techniques; his six string quartets demonstrate that the modern ear has much to learn from classical principles. Naturally, like most moderns experimenting with the traditional tonal structures, Bartók worked with unexpected dissonances, shifting tonalities, and novel relationships.

ATONAL MUSIC: A NEW EXPRESSIONISM

Arnold Schoenberg

The most revolutionary changes were produced by abandoning key-based music entirely. Arnold Schoenberg (1874–1951) began as a romantic composer, but under the influence of Wagner he began to devise unusual approaches to harmonic coloring, particularly in the extensive use of chromaticism. In 1908 he began to construct a new theory of music, basing each work on a predetermined order of the twelve notes within the octave rather than on the standard eight-tone scale. In order to avoid the problem of lapsing into a conventional tonal structure, his tones were given an absolute order—the "tone row"—to ensure that no single tone was repeated enough to produce the illusion of a key base.

The tone row for the Suite for Piano, Opus 25, illustrated in Figure 18-41 suggests that the piece would begin on E, with the next tone F, and all subsequent tones following the order shown. The notes do not stay in the same octave, and thus there are often considerable leaps from high to low or low to high. Such sudden movement is often characteristic of atonality, and its unsettling effect is usually very unpleasant for the general listener. In reality, the tone row can be played whole or in fragments, backward, upside down, even inside out, producing an astonishing variety and range of possibilities. *Five Pieces for Orchestra*, Opus 16 (1909), retains certain impressionistic aspects in its use of tone clusters. "Klangfarben," the sounding of individual tones by different instruments in succession and in different pitches, was one of its distinguishing features, and remains an important atonal technique.

Atonal music lacks the sense that what one hears at any given moment is the result of what one has just heard. Even when a tone row determines what happens, the ear cannot establish the tone row well enough to know what to expect. Similarly, the dissonances which naturally result in the music are not resolved into consonance, as happens in key-centered music. This produces a sense of freshness, but also a feeling of uneasiness on the part of many listeners.

Schoenberg's Followers

Even though Schoenberg's own work was neither extensive nor well received, the works of two of his

Figure 18-41
Arnold Schoenberg. Example of a tone row, from *Suite for Piano*, Opus 25. 1925. The basic twelve-tone series is stated in full in the right hand at the start of the first movement. (Vienna: Universal Edition A. G., 1925; copyright renewed, 1952. By permission of Belmont Music, Inc.)

students, Alban Berg (1885–1935) and Anton Webern (1883–1945), were widely heard and widely admired. They have sometimes been described as the "popular" atonal composers. Berg is the better known of the two. His operas *Wozzeck* (composed 1917–1921) and *Lulu* (composed 1928–1935) have become part of the standard repertory. Berg was Viennese and served in the Austrian army in World War I (he was in the army when he began *Wozzeck*). *Wozzeck* is adapted from a nineteenth-century novel about a soldier, but the story is told in a very modern way. Berg's Wozzeck is mistreated by the army, deceived by his mistress, driven to madness and murder. He drowns while trying to wash the blood of his mistress from his hands. Those who hear the splash when he falls into the water think nothing of it.

The quality of disconnected nightmare in *Wozzeck* resembles portions of Joyce's *Ulysses*. The music has the same kind of apparent disconnectedness as the novel, but here it emphasizes the stark, modern theme of a young man driven to self-destruction by a society that asks the wrong things of him. The ending is overwhelming. Children—the victims of the next war—are playing on hobbyhorses when Marie's body is discovered nearby. The children tell her son that she is dead, and then ride off to have a look. After an instant's hesitation, Marie's son follows them. It is an impressive, taut, and emotional ending.

Berg's unfinished opera *Lulu* has, like *Wozzeck*, had fine recent performances in America, and has even been shown on television. Lulu, earth mother and whore, drifts from one sexual relationship to another, taking Jack the Ripper as her final lover. Atonality is extremely effective in this work, intensifying the unreal and terrifying atmosphere that haunts the entire opera.

Webern, although much less popular than Berg, composed a number of works which are played frequently today. Many of them depend on a variant of Schoenberg's klangfarben, in which the shifting of tone color from instrument to instrument is a key element. Several of Webern's pieces for orchestra are praised as extraordinary miniatures (some last only a few minutes). Their delicacy is one of their most distinctive features.

JAZZ: POPULAR EXPRESSIONISM

American jazz is rooted in black gospel music, work songs, plantation refrains, and marching music. The cultural blend that created the music of Jelly Roll Morton (who claimed to have invented jazz single-handed), King Oliver, Louis Armstrong, Bix Beiderbecke, Fletcher Henderson, Count Basie, Benny Goodman, and Duke Ellington, to name only a few jazz innovators, was explicitly American.

Jazz is a virtuoso performance medium for the improviser; it relies on a strong tonality and on chords that follow predictable patterns or "changes." Its powerful and insistent rhythmic base gives the weak beats (the second and third beats in 4/4 time) extra stress, and the player's insinuation of the beat produces a "swing" to the otherwise rigid time signature. The complex rhythmic insinuations, based on syncopation—in which a note is played "off," or against, the beat—have west African origins. The musical heritage of African Americans was rich in polyrhythms, complex and contrapuntal patterns of extraordinary sophistication. The subtle patterning of rhythms associated with jazz were developed through the adaptation of some of that heritage to western music. The harmonic patterns of jazz were derived from march music, hymns, gospel music, and possibly some European art music. For example, in the ragtime compositions of Scott Joplin (1868–1917) one can hear harmonic echoes of certain pieces by Chopin.

Jazz began in public halls in New Orleans frequented by blacks as well as in whorehouses frequented by whites. The association with prostitution, drinking, gambling, and the underworld gave jazz a bad name in polite society, and its development was thus basically a form of cultural subversion, promoting values which bourgeois society could not accept, but which it could not stay away from. During prohibition (1920–1932) jazz was associated with rumrunners, speakeasys, and the "flappers," all as anti-bourgeois as dadaism, although less intellectual. These phenomena seemed to have sprung from cultural forces and vague historical thrusts—the changing times. They were an expression of disagreement with older values.

Louis Armstrong (1900–1971; Figure 18-42), a great trumpet player who influenced all subsequent jazz, played in Storyville, the red-light district of New Orleans and the center of jazz development, until it was closed down by the navy in 1917. Like other musicians, when Storyville died, he sailed up the Mississippi to Chicago, which, like Kansas City and New York, developed distinct jazz styles. Armstrong's

Figure 18-42
Louis Armstrong and
the Hot Five.
(Institute of Jazz
Studies, Rutgers
University.)

style is often called "hot jazz"; it was characterized by a small group, usually including a lead trumpet, sometimes a second trumpet, a trombone, a clarinet, and a rhythm section consisting of piano, drums, and bass. The horns played aggressive counterpoint, with the trumpet carrying the tune, the trombone developing a throaty and essential harmonic support, and the clarinet weaving and darting through the melodic lines of the trumpet and trombone. The piano furnished a powerful rhythmic line, supported by the bass and drums. Increasingly, the horns—as well as the piano and sometimes a banjo or guitar—were expected to play extended solos (mainly in the 1920s), and thus jazz permitted instrumentalists to shape their own emotional statements as they saw fit.

The blues, popular in the 1920s and 1930s, built its melody on 12-bar sections with the following chord pattern: tonic, subdominant, dominant (in the key of F the chord pattern would be F, B flat, C). The lyrics made liberal use of the refrain. The blues has been equated with an emotional mood (we often

have the "blues"), and its capacity to express disappointment over love, loss, and betrayal has made it a universal form of musical expression.

The contrapuntal energies of Louis Armstrong's style are based on the individual performers' working within a limited framework and developing a characteristic improvisation on a familiar, often popular, tune. The development of jazz in the late 1920s and the 1930s followed a pattern. The essentially black music was imitated by white players (who were the first to record jazz) and was eventually made less "subversive" by white bandleaders, such as Gene Goldkette and Paul Whiteman. Inevitably, black jazz inspired some good white players even before the advent of integrated bands. Bix Beiderbecke (1903–1931), a white cornetist from Davenport, Iowa, was a fine player; but he was hampered because he did not play with a first-class black band. Instead, he spent his last years with the Whiteman band, creating a version of jazz for dancing.

The great years of the dance band produced Count

Basie, Benny Goodman, and Duke Ellington—who influenced one another and began to make jazz an integrated art form. The big bands could not follow the New Orleans style of rugged improvisation; instead, they developed "charts," or arrangements, that featured brilliant ensemble playing, riffs (short, repeated passages), and opportunities for brilliant soloists—like Harry Carney, Benny Carter, Harry James, Gene Krupa, and Cat Anderson—to improvise a set number of choruses (patterns of 8 bars), with the orchestra playing backup. Because this was dance music, it maintained regular rhythmic patterns and expectations. Sometimes the bands would "let go" and play listening music, and once, in 1938, the Goodman band gave a concert in Carnegie Hall, the first of its kind. The Carnegie Hall concert, in which Count Basie and some of his rhythm section played with Goodman on "Honeysuckle Rose," was fashioned as a "history of jazz," with imitations of Armstrong, Beiderbecke, and other early innovators. The next to the last number that was played at the concert, "Sing, Sing, Sing," is considered one of the high points of jazz in the period before the Second World War.

LISTENING KEY

Early Jazz

The best source of jazz recordings of this period is the Smithsonian Institution's record album *Anthology of American Jazz.*

1. Listen to one of Louis Armstrong's singles of the 1920s—his Hot Five or Hot Seven group. Compare the ensemble playing and the solo playing. How much of the recording is devoted to each?

2. Establish the expressive content of the music. Try to describe Armstrong's trumpet style.

3. Listen to a single by a blues singer, such as Ma Rainey, Bessie Smith, or Billie Holiday. What is the subject of the song? Can you make out the words? Do the singer's style and the style of the accompaniment help establish the expressive context of the piece? What do you feel is being expressed?

4. Listen to a recording of Paul Whiteman's band and compare it with a recording of the band of Fletcher Henderson, Count Basie, Duke Ellington, or another black band of the period. Can you understand why Whiteman would be more acceptable to a middle-class white audience?

5. Listen to "Sing, Sing, Sing," from the recording of Benny Goodman's 1938 jazz concert at Carnegie Hall (Columbia SL 160), which showcased the talents of Harry James (trumpet), Gene Krupa (drums), Goodman (clarinet), and Jess Stacy (piano). Is the melodic line easy to follow? Do the soloists have "space" in which to be individually expressive? Does the music excite any emotions that might be considered "subversive"? The piano solo near the end of the piece was unexpected, even by Goodman, and it has been hailed as a great moment in jazz. Is its emotional expression different from that of the rest of the composition?

Summary

The first half of the twentieth century was marked by a profusion of art movements—not just in painting, but in other arts as well. Cubism, dadaism, futurism, imagism, and many more "-isms" established theories and practices which drew many adherents. Most of these tended to be unconcerned with attracting a wide audience among the middle classes in Europe, the Americas, or other parts of the world. Instead, the adherents of these movements took the view that since it was the middle classes who were primarily responsible for the wholesale slaughter of the mechanized First World War, there was no point trying to communicate with them. To pander to their taste and their intelligence would be to tacitly acknowledge their worthiness, and the artists who reacted against the war were unwilling to take such a position. Freud's theories concerning the existence in the mind of an unconscious and his methods of handling guilt through psychoanalysis were widely accepted by writers, painters, and other artists. Einstein's theory of relativity, which produced a physics that was totally unlike the durable Newtonian views of the eighteenth and early nineteenth centuries, was also accepted; as a result, "relativity" became a catchword, and the concept of static forms disappeared in styles such as cubism, which treated a form as a subject to be analyzed and rearranged. Film, both silent and sound, tended to replace popular drama for the masses. It was one art that did not follow the lead of the dadaists and others whose work was aimed only at a highly educated audience. Because films were introduced as commercial rather than exclusively aesthetic enterprises, their evolution was unusual. However, the genius of Griffith, Eisenstein, Chaplin, Welles, and others soon revealed the vitality of the form. The century began with war and disturbance, and the period discussed in this chapter ended with the detonation of atom bombs over Japan, signaling the beginning of yet another new age of change and bafflement.

Concepts in Chapter 18

The twentieth century began relatively prosperously, with European nations in possession of vast colonial territories in Africa and Asia.

World War I was unexpected in its ferocity and in the destruction of life; it shattered the values of the preceding century.

The postwar years were often marked by social upheaval, particularly in regard to attitudes toward morality and traditional social structures.

The Russian Revolution resulted in the first communist nation in Europe's history.

The great depression gave Mussolini and Hitler the opportunity to win over the middle classes of Italy and Germany, thus forging a fascist axis.

World War II was a modern war fought with machines at lightning speed; the death toll was upward of 30 million people.

In just moments, the atom bombing of Hiroshima and Nagasaki made the technology of World War II outmoded.

China joined the communist sphere of influence in 1949.

The cold war years intensified anxieties in the west, creating an atmosphere of uncertainty.

Freudian psychology and the discovery of the unconscious became a major intellectual force in the period.

Einstein's theory of relativity, which made the atom bomb possible, was accepted by the public in various ways, among which was the social application of relativity to values: values were no longer thought of as absolute.

Painting in the first half of the twentieth century underwent numerous stylistic changes.

The first movement in painting in the century was fauvism, led by Henri Matisse; the fauves stressed dynamism, strong colors, and intense energy in their canvases.

Malevich's suprematism emphasized aesthetic emotions as being most important in a work of art.

Kandinsky and other painters began the exploration of the unconscious in abstract expressionist works which stressed the expression of the painter's emotional, or inner, life rather than the interpretation of a visual reality.

Cubism developed as an analytic approach to visual space: the cubists used multiple perspectives, rather than the traditional single perspective.

Picasso and other painters were influenced by African sculpture and nonwestern art.

Social protest was possible in the work of the cubists, as Picasso demonstrated in *Guernica.*

Dada developed as a reaction to World War I; the dadaists produced an essentially irrational art.

Surrealism was based partly on Freudian thought; the surrealists dug into the unconscious to find symbols that would have profound meaning.

Alfred Stieglitz began the Photo-Secession to free photography from the influence of painting.

Sculpture, in the hands of Maillol and others, began to address itself to mass, volume, and space.

Sculpture reacted to trends in futurism, dadaism, cubism, and surrealism.

Gabo, Pevsner, and others developed constructivism; a constructivist sculpture was not representational but was a structure in its own right.

Louis Sullivan and Frank Lloyd Wright insisted on the unity of form and function in architecture.

Walter Gropius developed the international style in the Bauhaus; his doctrine of "less is more" resulted in a spare, economical style.

Le Corbusier defined a house as a machine for living; he held that architecture should "move us."

The poetry of the first half of the twentieth century was marked by unusual complexities and obscurities, removing it from the province of the average reader.

Imagism spoke to the reader directly and emotionally through images that appealed to the senses, rather than through discursive language.

Yeats brought the development of romantic poetry to a conclusion; Stevens created an aestheticism in his poems; Eliot attempted a poetry of religious experience.

The modern novel, as exemplified by the works of Proust, Mann, and Joyce, tended to be epic in length, complex and demanding, and experimental.

The stream-of-consciousness technique, which places the reader inside the consciousness of a character, replaced the older, author-based perspective.

Film developed as the most popular artistic medium of the century, replacing literature as the entertainment of the masses.

D. W. Griffith adapted literary works to film, creating visual epics.

Russian techniques of montage became part of the visual language of film.

Orson Welles used innovative camera work and editing to further the development of film language.

There were numerous movements in music, ranging from the neoclassicism of Stravinsky to the atonality of Schoenberg and Webern.

Atonal music treats all twelve notes in the octave as equal; no group of notes predominates, as in key-based music.

American jazz, sometimes said to be this country's one genuine art form, developed in New Orleans around the turn of the century.

The New Orleans jazz style of Jelly Roll Morton and Louis Armstrong gave way to the Chicago and Kansas City styles of Bix Beiderbecke and Count Basie and then developed into swing, the style of Duke Ellington and Benny Goodman.

Jazz became a popular subversive art form; it developed in brothels and speakeasies, undermining the official values of the society.

Suggested Readings

Andrew, J. Dudley. *The Major Film Theories: An Introduction.* New York: Oxford University Press, 1976.

Apollinaire, Guillaume. *The Cubist Painters.* L. Abel, trans. New York: Wittenborn, 1949.

Arnason, H. H. *History of Modern Art: Painting, Sculpture, Architecture.* 2d ed. Englewood Cliffs, N.J.: Prentice-Hall, 1977.

Beaver, Frank E. *On Film: A History of the Motion Picture.* New York: McGraw-Hill, 1983.

Blunt, Anthony, and P. Pool. *Picasso, the Formative Years: A Study of His Sources.* Greenwich, Conn.: New York Graphic Society, 1958.

Breton, André. *Surrealism and Painting.* New York: Harper & Row, 1972.

Dorival, Bernard. *Twentieth Century Painters.* 2 vols. New York: Universe Books, 1958.

Elderfield, John. *The "Wild Beasts": Fauvism and Its Affinities.* New York: Museum of Modern Art, 1976.

Frampton, Kenneth. *Modern Architecture: A Critical History*. New York: Oxford University Press, 1980.

Fry, Edward F. *Cubism*. London: Thames and Hudson, 1966.

Fry, Maxwell. *Art in a Machine Age*. London: Methuen, 1969.

Geduld, Harry M., ed. *Focus on D. W. Griffith*. Englewood Cliffs, N.J.: Prentice-Hall, 1971.

Giedion, Sigfried. *Space, Time and Architecture: The Growth of a New Tradition*. Cambridge, Mass.: Harvard, 1962.

Giedion-Welcker, Carola. *Contemporary Sculpture: An Evaluation in Volume and Space*. New York: Wittenborn, 1961.

Gottesman, Ronald, ed. *Focus on Citizen Kane*. Englewood Cliffs, N.J.: Prentice-Hall, 1977.

Gould, Michael. *Surrealism and the Cinema*. New York: Barnes, 1976.

Grohmann, Will. *Wassily Kandinsky: Life and Work*. N. Guterman, trans. New York: Abrams, 1958.

Gropius, Walter. *The New Architecture and the Bauhaus*. London: Faber, 1935.

Hamilton, George Heard. *Painting and Sculpture in Europe 1880–1940*. Baltimore: Penguin, 1967.

Hitchcock, Henry Russell. *Architecture: Nineteenth and Twentieth Centuries*. 3d ed. Baltimore: Penguin, 1971.

——— and Philip Johnson. *The International Style*. New York: Norton, 1932 (originally published in 1922).

Hughes, Robert. *The Shock of the New*. New York: Knopf, 1980.

Jacobus, John. *Henri Matisse*. New York: Abrams, 1973.

Jencks, Charles. *Modern Movements in Architecture*. Garden City, N.Y.: Doubleday, Anchor Books, 1973.

Jeanneret, Charles-Édouard (Le Corbusier). *Towards a New Architecture*. New York: Praeger, 1960 (originally published in 1927).

Johnson, Paul. *Modern Times*. New York: Macmillan, 1983.

Kael, Pauline. *The Citizen Kane Book*. Boston: Little, Brown, 1971.

Koch, Howard. *Casablanca: Script and Legend*. Woodstock, N.Y.: Overlook, 1973.

Lockspeiser, Edward. *Debussy: His Life and Mind*. New York: Macmillan, 1962.

Motherwell, Robert, ed. *The Dada Painters and Poets: An Anthology*. New York: Wittenborn, 1951.

Newhall, Beaumont. *Photographic Essays and Images*. New York: Museum of Modern Art, 1980.

Pevsner, Nikolaus. *The Sources of Modern Architecture and Design*. New York: Praeger, 1968.

Read, Herbert. *A Concise History of Modern Painting*. New York: Oxford University Press, 1974.

———. *A Concise History of Modern Sculpture*. New York: Oxford University Press, 1964.

Rubin, William, ed. *Pablo Picasso: A Retrospective*. New York: Museum of Modern Art, 1980.

Salzman, Eric. *Twentieth-Century Music: An Introduction*. Englewood Cliffs, N.J.: Prentice-Hall, 1974.

Schuller, Gunther. *Early Jazz*. New York: Oxford University Press, 1968.

Scully, Vincent. *Modern Architecture: The Architecture of Democracy*. Rev. ed. New York: George Braziller, 1974.

Silva, Fred, ed. *Focus on Birth of a Nation*. Englewood Cliffs, N.J.: Prentice-Hall, 1971.

Stravinsky, Igor. *An Autobiography*. New York: Norton, 1962.

Swallow, Norman. *Eisenstein: A Documentary Portrait*. New York: Dutton, 1977.

Tafuri, Manfredo, and Francesco Dal Co. *Modern Architecture*. New York: Abrams, 1970.

Vogel, Amos. *Film as a Subversive Art*. New York: Random House, 1974.

CHAPTER 19

AN UNEASY PEACE: 1945 TO THE PRESENT

Historical Background

THE COLD WAR

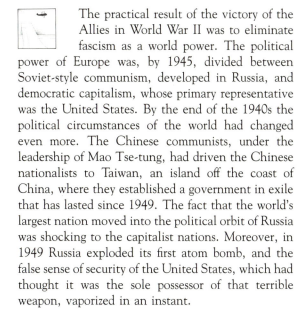 The practical result of the victory of the Allies in World War II was to eliminate fascism as a world power. The political power of Europe was, by 1945, divided between Soviet-style communism, developed in Russia, and democratic capitalism, whose primary representative was the United States. By the end of the 1940s the political circumstances of the world had changed even more. The Chinese communists, under the leadership of Mao Tse-tung, had driven the Chinese nationalists to Taiwan, an island off the coast of China, where they established a government in exile that has lasted since 1949. The fact that the world's largest nation moved into the political orbit of Russia was shocking to the capitalist nations. Moreover, in 1949 Russia exploded its first atom bomb, and the false sense of security of the United States, which had thought it was the sole possessor of that terrible weapon, vaporized in an instant.

Colonies, such as India and Egypt, were granted independence during the first years after World War II. The British mandate to govern Palestine gave way when, after a brief but fierce war, Palestinian Jews, aided by American and European Jews, established the nation of Israel in May 1948. War with the Arabs in 1949 resulted in the displacement of hundreds of thousands of Arab Palestinians. This political disturbance has yet to be settled and has resulted in a series of Arab-Jewish wars that threaten to continue.

During the cold war of the 1950s the United States and the Soviet Union seemed to be testing each other. The Soviet Union closed Berlin to rail and land traffic, despite postwar treaties. Meanwhile, the United Nations was drawn into a "peacekeeping" activity in South Korea when the North Koreans invaded on June 25, 1950. South Korea was in the political sphere of the capitalists, while North Korea was in the political sphere of the communists. The burden of fighting in Korea fell on the United States, which supplied most of the troops.

In the 1960s communism moved to Cuba, establishing its first foothold in the western hemisphere. The Soviet Union installed missile bases there, and the world was at the brink of war when President Kennedy forced Chairman Kruschev to remove them. The threat of nuclear annihilation had never been greater since the dropping of the first atom bombs.

Protest against the Vietnamese war (1961–1975) was matched by protest by black Americans, led by Martin Luther King and others, who sought equal rights and improved conditions. A wave of assassinations—John F. Kennedy in 1963, Martin Luther King in 1967, and Robert Kennedy in 1968 — demonstrated the intensity of the emotions and energies that were directed toward fundamental change in American society. The protest for black equality was in its turn matched by a resurgence of the feminist movement, which had been particularly intense in England before the First World War.

The end of the Vietnamese war coincided with the development of a generally conservative trend in the western democracies. Liberalism was associated with the unrest that had characterized the energetic period of the previous decade. The widespread use of contraceptives, leading to a profound change in sexual mores, as well as the invasion of drugs such as heroin and cocaine into schools, businesses, and other walks of life, contributed to a sudden shift from a liberal political atmosphere, which had dominated western political philosophies since the time of Roosevelt, to a conservative and traditional atmosphere. The western democracies are now undergoing changes that have been compared to the industrial revolution: the postindustrial revolution, in which the west is deindustrializing in the face of competition from Asia in the manufacture and design of goods. The results of such changes are evident in the arts.

Painting

DE KOONING, HOFMANN, AND POLLOCK: ABSTRACT EXISTENTIALISTS

The first generation of New York painters called themselves the "New York school" partly as a joke, alluding to the overwhelming influence of the school of Paris. Yet the term was appropriate. New York had replaced Paris as the center of artistic activity.

Among the influential Europeans who settled in New York were Willem de Kooning (b. 1904) and Hans Hofmann (1880–1966). Hofmann is generally considered a greater teacher than a painter, while the reverse is true of de Kooning. Both advocated liberation of technique and approach. Both were strongly influenced by cubism and the freedom it offered from exact imitation of the objective world. Both were concerned with color and its emotional impact. Both were expressionistic in their painting; they agreed that the artist's job was to probe the inner consciousness and embark on a voyage of genuine self-discovery, in which no recesses would be hidden from view.

An American painter, Jackson Pollock (1912–1956), from Cody, Wyoming, began attracting attention with his first show in 1943. He was the least European of the younger painters, even though his first work was obviously influenced by the expressionistic agony of Picasso's *Guernica* (Figure 18-8). The energy, daring, risk taking, and almost jazzlike affection for improvisation and discovery through action of Pollock and de Kooning made them seem like existentialist deities. Between them they divided the art world of the 1940s and much of the 1950s. They were known for their regard for existentialism.

Existentialism had developed in France during the Second World War and had spread quickly after it. The novelists André Gide, Jean-Paul Sartre, and Albert Camus had asserted that people had no essential nature—that people were nothing more or less than what they did. Action, therefore, was all. What people did was what they were. Existentialism totally contradicted medieval wisdom, which, by contrast, asserted that what people did was relatively unimportant in comparison with their essence as persons. In addition, the issue of action related to a process, described by Sartre and the religious philosopher Søren Kierkegaard, which involved passing through a period of personal anguish and suffering. The agony associated with the discovery of self in existentialist terms was related to the work of the abstract expressionists. In their personal involvement with their work, their insistence on the value of action, and their intensity, they tended to live out the existentialist philosophy. Their work came to be known as "action painting" or "gesture painting," indicating that it existed in terms of gesture, as if gesture were the only expressive action available to an artist.

The energy of de Kooning's series "Woman" (*Woman I* is shown in Color Plate 45) is revealed in its intense brushstrokes, the power of the line, and the willingness to leave portions of the canvas "in process," as an indication of the painter's unconcern with finish. De Kooning ignored the modernist insistence on maintaining the flatness of the canvas and suggested a three-dimensional illusionism. There is nothing idealized about the representation; we are easily convinced that de Kooning is giving vent to present—and pressing—emotions which are expressed directly on the canvas. As Harold Rosenberg, an important contemporary critic, said, "The canvas began to appear . . . as an arena in which to act." For de Kooning, the canvas was not only an arena but also an adversary, and he attacked it until it bent to his will.

De Kooning's connection with cubism is apparent in the liberties he takes with the figure represented in *Woman I*. He is not inclined to disintegrate it entirely, as Picasso does in *Ma Jolie*, but he also does not want even an approximate likeness. The lines fall where they must, dictated more by energy than by the demands of the subject. He forces the subject to yield to him, using the cubist technique of abstracting from life.

The complexity of emotions revealed in the painting produces an ambiguity of attitude. The womanliness of the figure is apparent only in the gigantic breasts, which are also the most three-dimensional elements in the canvas. The eyes are oversize, almost like those in Picasso's *Demoiselles d'Avignon*. The teeth seem crude and threatening; the thrashing lines at the right suggest power, but terror as well. Some viewers see this as a totemic painting, a blend of the primitive and the iconic. It represents a psychological idea of woman, almost like Carl Jung's famous "mother archetype." Jung suggests that we are imprinted with an image of the mother with which we must come to terms if we are to be psychologically healthy. In addition, Jung says that men have within them the seeds of the "anima," their potential female nature, with which they must also come to terms. It is tempting to see some of these popular psychological

PERCEPTION KEY

De Kooning and Earlier Painters of Women

1. De Kooning has admitted that cubism was a powerful influence on his work. What kinds of influence are apparent in the painting shown in Color Plate 45? Refer to Picasso's *Ma Jolie* (Figure 18-7), a portrait of a woman playing a zither or guitar.

2. Compare de Kooning's *Woman I* (Color Plate 45) with Picasso's *Demoiselles d'Avignon* (Figure 18-6) and *Girl Before a Mirror* (Color Plate 41). What are the emotional differences between these works? In which painting is the subject matter most or least recognizable?

3. What new approaches does de Kooning use in his portrayal of his subject? What are the formal ingredients? Does he rely on centrality of composition? Geometry? Balance? Symmetry?

4. Which portions of *Woman I* make you least aware that you are looking at a flat surface? Which portions are most clearly painted surfaces and little more?

5. If painting was a voyage of self-discovery for the abstract expressionists and if nothing, however raw, was to be held back, what do you think de Kooning discovered in making *Woman I*?

theories expressed in *Woman I*, particularly in view of the obsessive nature of the imagery of the series.

Pollock's first one-man show in 1943 was made possible by Peggy Guggenheim, who championed the work of the new abstract expressionists. In 1943 Pollock was influenced by numerous European and South American painters, among them Matta, a Chilean surrealist. This influence produced in Pollock's work recognizable images of figures that were often as totemic as de Kooning's. But Pollock was to become the most daring of the abstract expressionists when he developed his style of "drip" painting—something that Hans Hofmann had experimented with a decade earlier.

Pollock's drip paintings represented a totally new direction. His discussion of what he was doing correlates with the surrealists' concepts of "automatism"—an automatic psychic process which does not censor itself, but which reaches into the deepest part of the mind. Pollock said:

> When I am *in* my painting, I'm not aware of what I'm doing. It is only after a sort of "get acquainted" period that I see what I have been about. I have no fears of making changes, destroying the image, etc., because the painting has a life of its own.

Those who watched Pollock paint were amazed at his intensity. The enormous canvas was placed flat on the floor of the studio; Pollock walked around it, not only dripping paint from a can held in his hand but also pouring it and splashing it with a stick or a housepainter's brush.

Number 2 (Figure 19-1) is predominantly red, with dripped lines of blue and white paint. The rhythms of the lines are so regular and so lyric that it is easy to see why some critics have insisted on a connection with music, particularly jazz, and with dance. In doing this painting, Pollock was forced into a kind of performance which was much like a dance, moving his body as he applied the paint.

In *Number 2*, painting has come close to music in that there is no recognizable object anywhere in the canvas. It is form without reference to anything outside itself. The doctrine of flatness has been adhered to, and the painting has become an object in itself. One regards it in a new way. The sensa of color and line have become its subject matter and have fused with its form, which, because it has no predetermining necessities, seems to grow out of the necessities of the act of painting.

The work of Hans Hofmann contrasts powerfully with the paintings of both de Kooning and Pollock. *The Gate* (Color Plate 46), essentially a color study, would be relatively meaningless reproduced in black and white. The aggressive brushwork of earlier abstract expressionists is absent in Hofmann's work. Instead of activity, motion, restlessness, and searching, Hofmann reveals a serenity—a sense of having made a discovery rather than a sense of making it. The term "stasis" is often used in describing his work, suggesting that it achieves a state of spiritual rest. In *The Gate*, sharply defined blocks of color are set against a shifting background of less sharply defined shapes of greens, blacks, and yellows. The two dominating forms are the gold rectangle at the top and the red rectangle in the center. They are in turn balanced by other color patches. The composition may suggest stasis, but Hofmann demonstrates that there is a psychological intensity to the color relationships he has discovered, and in that sense the painting is a voyage of discovery.

Figure 19-1

Jackson Pollock. *Number 2.* 1949. Oil, duco, and aluminum paint on canvas, 38 ½ by 189 ½ inches. (Munson-Williams-Proctor Institute, Utica, New York.)

KLINE AND MOTHERWELL:
ABSTRACT EXPRESSIONISTS

The abstract expressionists often gathered to talk at the Cedar Bar or at their club on Eighth Street. Among them were Franz Kline (1910–1962) and Robert Motherwell (b. 1915). Kline was a figurative painter until, in 1949, he studied one of his paintings in extreme detail in an enlargement on a slide. This inspired him to paint in a new way, and he began his series of bold patterns of black and white applied to the canvas with a housepainter's brush (Figure 19-2 is an example). The vigor of his style inspired other painters and led him to new avenues of discovery.

Motherwell helped organize shows and wrote important documents establishing the theoretical bases of what the abstract expressionists were doing. His monumental series of huge canvases, for the most part in black and white, are, like Kline's work, completely nonobjective. Many of the paintings in the "Elegy" series, like *Number LV* (Figure 19-3), resemble a flag. The series consists of more than 100 works, and anyone familiar with it will respond instantly to the two elliptical forms, with the bold pillar between them. They are the "elegy" to the Spanish Republic, which, under General Franco, became the world's longest-lived fascist government. Picasso's *Guernica* was a response to Franco's violence against his own people, and Motherwell's series is a

Figure 19-3
Robert Motherwell. *Elegy to the Spanish Republic Number LV.* 1955–1960. Oil on canvas, 70 by 76 ⅛ inches. (Cleveland Museum of Art, purchase, General Reserve Fund.)

reminder that the abstract expressionists often had a social conscience. However, it is true that, like most Americans in the 1950s, the painters of the New York school felt that politics was a deadening rather than an enlivening subject for art.

Figure 19-2
Franz Kline. *Chief.* 1950. 58 ⅜ by 73 ½ inches. (Collection, Museum of Modern Art, New York; gift of Mr. and Mrs. David M. Solinger.)

PERCEPTION KEY

The Abstract Expressionists

1. Which of the paintings shown in Figures 19-2 and 19-3 is more nonobjective? On the other hand, which painting more clearly alludes to an object outside itself?

2. Which of the paintings seems to depend more on primitive art for its inspiration? Which of the paintings seems more iconic or magical? Which painting do you think would have a stronger appeal to someone unfamiliar with western culture?

3. What is the subject of de Kooning's painting shown in Color Plate 45? What is the subject of Pollock's, shown in Figure 19-1? What is the subject of Kline's (Figure 19-2)? If you did not know the title of Motherwell's painting (Figure 19-3), what would you think its subject matter was?

4. One intention of the abstract expressionists was to force us to look closely at the canvas—to accept the painting on its own terms as an object. Does Figure 19-2 or 19-3 do this more effectively? How does it call attention to itself as an object and avoid references to other objects that we might be familiar with?

5. Recall that Kazimir Malevich, in the early decades of the twentieth century, attempted to excite only emotions connected with art. Can it be said that the abstract expressionists have much the same kind of goal? Which of these paintings seems to achieve what Malevich himself tried to achieve?

COLOR GESTURE AND COLOR FIELD PAINTERS

The New York painters visited one another's studios and argued with one another at their club and in taverns. When Helen Frankenthaler (b. 1928) saw Pollock's new work, she conceived a liberating style of her own. She decided to work directly on the untreated canvas, keeping a recognizable object as referent but also permitting herself considerable latitude in the statement of color and its organization.

Jacob's Ladder (Color Plate 47) reveals her approach: the use of color which is so thin as to suggest a staining rather than a painting of the canvas. The luminous quality of her color inspired other painters to follow in this direction. On her huge canvas (it is almost 10 feet high) the paint has been permitted to spread and drip. Both control and freedom are evident in the application of the paint, and Frankenthaler felt that her gestures in the act of painting had become "her mark," her signature.

Barnett Newman (1905–1970) was also moving in new directions. *Vir Heroicus Sublimis* (loosely translated as "Sublime Hero"; Color Plate 48) represents the beginning of a style that absorbed Newman for the rest of his life. He insisted that the stripes dividing or interrupting his huge color planes were not mathematical and that they did not refer to anything in nature. They were abstracted from the imagination and represented—as some critics thought—a gestalt pattern: a psychological pattern based on primary perception. However, many of Newman's paintings in this mode relied on symmetry and balance, and the rhythms of the stripes in *Vir Heroicus Sublimis* are close to those of the Greek ideal proportion, the ratio of 3:5. The offset white stripe at the left falls in a rhythm echoed by the two light-red offset lines. The panel can be analyzed as a triptych: the center is an 8-foot square, and the two end "panels" are each three-fifths of that dimension. If Newman had "intuited" these relationships, it only shows the power of simple mathematical formulas.

The emotional power of Newman's work cannot be conveyed very accurately in reproductions. The scale of this painting, which is almost 18 feet long, is an immense part of its effect. Just as Pollock felt that he was "in" his work when he painted, viewers feel that they are in Newman's work. Moving in front of the canvas, one perceives the dynamic intensity of the stripes. The saturation of color—red—becomes an insistent emotional statement. The stripes refuse to "stay still," and the painting operates like spectrograph analyzing our inner life.

Mark Rothko (1903–1970) was born in Russia and was brought to America as a child. At first his work derived from Kandinsky, but in the early 1950s he began painting on a gigantic scale and concentrating on huge areas of color—rectangles whose edges blurred, much as watercolors do on wet paper. (Color Plate 50 is an example.)

Rothko was a deeply contemplative man whose work was based on theories of sublimity and meditation. The viewer, in the presence of his massive color structures, is struck by a sense of solemnity induced by the psychological absorption of the colors and their subtle interaction. Rothko's painting is seen to its best advantage in a room or gallery which contains nothing but his work. The Tate Gallery, in London, has such a room, and some say that standing in it produces something close to a religious experience. This room is certainly a hushed and intensely silent part of the museum. Such an effect is also achieved in the Rothko Chapel at Saint Thomas University, in Houston, an appropriately religious setting.

In addition to sublimity, Rothko's work also communicates an experience of color sensa in ways that no other painter's work does. Our insight into the intensity of the color experience, gained through contemplation of his areas of color, constitutes part of the content of the work, just as our own psychological transformation as we view his paintings constitutes part of their expressive function. We submit to a work by Rothko and find ourselves subtly changed, but not in terms of our relationship to objects or events outside the painting. Rather, we are changed in terms of our relationship to the inner psychological world evoked within us by deep perception of the sensa of the work.

Frank Stella (b. 1936), the youngest of the painters of the New York school, was thought in 1960 to be rejecting the aesthetics of the older members of the group. His intention was to create works which would be simply objects of contemplation. In commenting on conservativism in painting, he said that those who are backward-thinking about art always want to assert that a painting is something else "besides paint on the canvas"; that is, they expect to see something in the painting other than its component parts.

Stella's early canvases were severe and irregularly shaped. In the mid-1960s, in the "Protractor" series —of which *Tahkt-I-Sulayman I* (Figure 19-4) is a part—he developed a new style. This is a powerful

Figure 19-4
Frank Stella. *Tahkt-I-Sulayman I.* 1967. Polymer and fluorescent paint on canvas, 10 feet ¼ inch by 20 feet 2 ¼ inches. (Private collection, United States; photo, Rudolph Burckhardt.)

and intriguing work, although its qualities are not fully apparent in a monochrome reproduction; one must see the actual painting. It is playful, permitting the eye to roam line by line and section by section in response to the rhythms and movements of color and shape. Although this work seems to derive from a decorative motif, it is not decoration—partly, perhaps, because of its size (it is 20 feet long), but also because of the patterns of variety—of movement of color and of shape—within the basic patterns of the composition. Newman and Rothko depend partly on a "magicality" of color interaction to evoke a psychological response in viewers, and Stella does much the same. This work is vigorous and exciting, despite its self-imposed limitations.

REACTIONS AGAINST THE ABSTRACT EXPRESSIONISTS

In the 1950s *Fortune* magazine noted that corporations were identifying the fine arts as "growth areas." The reaction to this trend was complex. The fact that art is now part of the marketplace has tended to accelerate the search for new, independent styles which would make the works of individual painters unusually valuable. But such an atmosphere can produce its share of irony and humor, since artists are likely to be disdainful of money and commercial success and contemptuous of a ravening public.

Pop Art

Reactions against abstract expressionism began in the early 1960s with Stella's work. Jasper Johns (b. 1930) began working with found images. Two of the most persistent and best known are the American flag and targets. Johns sometimes presented a "cake" of flags: a bottom flag would have another, smaller flag, an inch or so thick, superimposed on it. The effect was both humorous and serious. In the era of the Vietnamese war and its attendant disturbances, this was a quizzical effect.

Johns's work is often interrogative. We cannot look at his flags or his targets without observing how they blur the distinction between art and life. After all, we can go to places other than an art gallery to see flags and targets. Yet the fact that these flags and targets clearly were made by the hand of an artist, rather than by a machine, contributed to making them seem totally novel.

Figure 19-5
Jasper Johns. *Painted Bronze (Ale Cans)*. 1960. Bronze, 5 ½ by 8 by 4 ¾ inches. (Oeffentliche Kunstsammlung Basel, Depositum.)

Painted Bronze (Ale Cans), shown in Figure 19-5, is a sculpture rather a painting—but then, so are the flags and targets, since each of them is a three-dimensional painted object in relief. As noted above, one aspect of Johns's work is interrogation. *Painted Bronze* seems to pose at least two questions: Why look at this as an art object? And: Why not? What we see is not two ale cans. In fact, we are looking at a genuine work of art—an artificial construction, with great attention paid to every detail—which has represented these objects just as any realistic portrait might represent the sitter. The painting of the labels is obviously the work of a person, not a machine, and so we are reminded constantly that this is a handmade object.

The interrogative nature of Johns's work has another aspect: What difference would it make if these *were* ale cans rather than bronze representations? The answer lies in a subtle contradiction of some basic principles of the abstract expressionists. The difference between Johns's ale cans and those we buy in a store is in their essence. The act of representation, or presentation, is illusory; but the reality has to do with the genuine differences between the object and its representation, their essentially different nature. The insistence of the abstract expressionists on looking inward so as to make painting an act of discovery is virtually nonexistent in Johns's work. He presents us with a work in bronze which is totally dependent on objects that lie outside himself and which reveals nothing of himself to us. We have no sense of angst, of struggle, or of a search for an inner psychological world of symbols. Instead, we see a playful, object-bound experiment similar to some of the dadaist experiments of the period between the two world wars. Johns did this work after he met Marcel Duchamp in 1960.

Robert Rauschenberg (b. 1925) also used found objects in his work. In *Monogram* (1955–1959) he presents us with a stuffed goat with a tire around its middle. It became known as a gesture of contempt and whimsy. Later, Rauschenberg became famous for taking images from magazines and newspapers and silk-screening them onto canvas, making them part of a painting. He once said that pop art was "the use of commercial art as subject matter in painting. . . . It was hard to get a painting that was despicable enough so that no one would hang it—everybody was hanging everything. . . ."

In *Illustrations for Dante's Inferno, Canto XXXI: The Giants* (Figure 19-6), Rauschenberg has taken images from the popular media (including photographs of Olympic weight lifters), silk-screened them, and used them in a collage of resonant images. All the images are covered with a wash of lines, which tends on the one hand to unify them and on the other hand to keep the work from having a sense of finish. We see not just an artistic product, but an artistic process.

High finish is frequently an important part of pop art, however, as we can see in a whimsical work by Roy Lichtenstein (b. 1923) done in 1974, *The Artist's Studio: The Dance* (Figure 19-7). The technique derives from the comic book; the clear, finished lines might have been produced by a machine. In the foreground there is a typical still life: a plate of lemons, a cup, paintbrushes, some driftwood, and a Chianti bottle. Music comes in through the window, and on the wall is a humorous version of Matisse's *Dance* (see Color Plates 37 and 38).

Earlier, Lichtenstein did a comic strip series, often working directly from a comic strip panel, but altering it in important ways. *Whaam!* (Color Plate 51) is enormous; it dominates the wall on which it hangs in the Tate Gallery. One feels its dynamics instantly. It

Figure 19-6
Robert Rauschenberg. Illustrations for Dante's *Inferno, Canto XXXI: The Giants.* 1959–1960. 14 ½ by 11 ½ inches. (Collection, Museum of Modern Art, New York; given anonymously.)

is colorful and intense, and Lichtenstein uses the principles of the hard-edge minimalists to achieve his effect. The dominant colors, yellow and red, are applied in a flat, mechanical fashion, as they would appear in a newspaper. There is little effort to model the form of the airplane at the left; its three-dimensionality is taken for granted. Yet it is clear that the flatness of the objects in the painting contributes to the work's matter-of-factness, which is what we expect in the comics and perhaps in life as well.

Larry Rivers (b. 1923) was a particularly good draftsman, but in the 1950s such a gift was not as much of an advantage as it was in the 1850s or earlier. The abstract expressionists did not value draftsmanship. Rivers threw himself into the pop scene with a painting of Washington crossing the Delaware that was a mockery and a kind of realistic buffoonery. He said that "nothing could be dopier" than painting a portrait of Washington, and he did it to bemuse older painters and the general public.

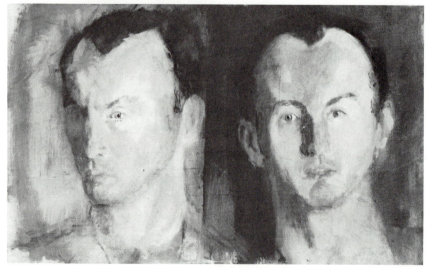

Figure 19-7
Left: Roy Lichtenstein. *The Artist's Studio: The Dance.* 1974. Oil and magma on canvas, 96 by 128 inches. (Permission courtesy of S. I. Newhouse, Leo Castelli Gallery, New York; photo, Eric Pollitzer.)

Figure 19-8
Right: Larry Rivers. *Double Portrait of Frank O'Hara.* 1955. 15 ¼ by 19 ⅛ inches. (Collection, Museum of Modern Art, New York; gift of Stuart Preston.)

Rivers's *Double Portrait of Frank O'Hara* (Figure 19-8) is done in a different vein from that of his more humorous pieces. Frank O'Hara (1926–1966) was a poet and a curator at the Museum of Modern Art. He was also an inspiration to numerous painters of the New York school. O'Hara and Rivers worked together on a series of lithographs. (O'Hara worked with many artists, supplying words for their visual designs).

There is a sense of indecision in the *Double Portrait* of *Frank O'Hara.* Nothing is finished. Such qualities are more common in the work of the abstract expressionists than in that of the pop artists, and it is appropriate that Rivers, with his gifts of draftsmanship and of ironic whimsy, should float in an ambiguous space between them. Rivers did many double portraits in a style that Irving Sandler calls "gestural realism," which is a useful distinction, particularly in relation to the superrealism of certain later artists.

Andy Warhol (b. 1925), a strangely charismatic artist, is often said to have chosen the subject of boredom as his professional domain. He made several films in which the camera focuses on an object for hours—but nothing happens. One, for example, shows a man sleeping. Warhol scoured the culture for images and objects which, because of their banality, were almost totally ignored— or at least were never thought of as subjects for works of art. He also reproduced Campbell's soup cans and Brillo boxes (which were designed by an aspiring abstract expressionist) and displayed them in galleries, much as they might be on display in a grocery store. But when he took actual soup cans and autographed them for resale at $5 apiece, he pushed the entire question of the merging of art and life to its limits.

If Jasper Johns's ale cans were baffling because they were so like the real thing, the genuine autographed soup cans were even more baffling. Many people insist that what they want most from art is realism, but Warhol demonstrated that there is a limit to the amount of realism that is acceptable.

Marilyn Monroe Diptych (Figure 19-9) also treats the question of merging art and life. For one thing, the image of Marilyn Monroe, a film superstar, was familiar to most moviegoing Americans when Warhol did this portrait. The work, which reproduces a photograph, is not the same sort of work as Larry

PERCEPTION KEY

Pop Art and the Reaction to Abstract Expressionism

1. Warhol's *Marilyn Monroe Diptych* (Figure 19-9) has a subject very close to that of de Kooning's *Woman I* (Color Plate 45). Does the repetition of the portrait in Figure 19-9 make it easier or more difficult for us to think about woman in general rather than about the particular woman, Marilyn Monroe? Is it possible that the subjects of the two paintings are totally different?

2. How do those artists who reacted against the ideals of the abstract expressionists— Stella, Johns, Rauschenberg, Lichtenstein, Rivers, and Warhol—handle the problem of representation, or figurative imagery, in their work? What are their attitudes toward figurative imagery in painting? Do they have minimum requirements in terms of representation?

3. Merging life and art—blurring the lines between the two—seems to be an ideal of the pop artists. Does each handle this ideal differently?

4. To what extent do the works of the pop artists reveal an interest in expressionism? Which of the works shown in Figures 19-5 through 19-9 and Color Plate 51 is most expressionistic, and which is least expressionistic? Do any of these works compare with the most intense works of the abstract expressionists or the color field painters?

5. What problems do you see posed by Johns's ale cans (Figure 19-5) and Warhol's autographed soup cans? Does it really matter that the soup cans were manufactured by a machine and actually contained a product, while the ale cans were made by hand and are a solid piece of sculpture? Does it really matter that the "labels" on the ale cans are obviously inferior in representation to the labels on the soup cans? The labels on the soup cans are "prints," like an etching or like Warhol's silk screens of Marilyn Monroe. Are they any less a work of art?

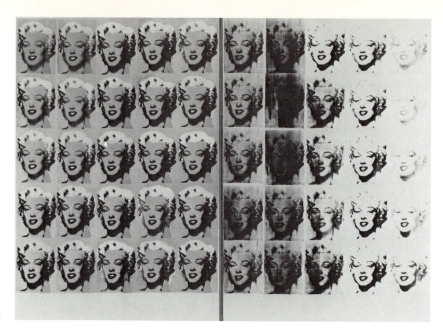

Figure 19-9
Andy Warhol. *Marilyn Monroe Diptych.* 1962. Acrylic and silkscreen on canvas, 82 by 144 inches. (Tate Gallery, London.)

Rivers's portrait of Frank O'Hara. Warhol's contribution has been to "find" the image the way Schwitters "found" the elements of his collages. The organization into a series of repetitions—fifty in color and fifty in black and white—has no apparent purpose other than mechanical restatement, which relates Monroe to the soup can: a reproducible product for consumption by an eager and insatiable public. For critics who were touched by Monroe's innocence and vulnerability, Warhol's portrait is an important statement. For others, the work says something about our appetite for popular imagery: there is no end to it.

Op Art

Among the many minor movements in art in the 1960s, op art has attracted the most attention, in part because it is both successful in its aims and novel in its approach. It is based on the work of artists who studied the physiology of sight and the interaction of colors. Op art is fascinating because of its kinetic qualities and its capacity to involve us in its complexities. Its subject matter can be said to be our emotional responses to the "action" we perceive and our growing awareness of our capacities for perception.

Bridget Riley (b. 1931) has been among the most widely accepted of the op artists; her work is inventive and painstakingly done. *Fall* (Figure 19-10)

produces illusions of height and depth on a flat surface. The title refers to the apparently descending rhythm that the eye perceives as it moves down the canvas. The most abrupt curves insinuate themselves dynamically because of their moiré effect: a predictable interference that we perceive in patterns of parallel lines merging with one another. As is true of the work of the color field painters, the effect is purely visual; there is no reference to anything outside the painting.

Figure 19-10
Bridget Riley. *Fall.* 1963. Emulsion on board, 55 ½ by 55 ½ inches. (By permission of the artist; Tate Gallery, London; © by ADAGP, Paris, 1986.)

One of the most commanding presences among the op artists was Josef Albers (1888–1976). Like Hans Hofmann, Albers was a refugee from Europe; he was also, like Hofmann, better known and more influential as a teacher than as a painter. His series of colored squares within squares, carefully calculated for their effect, was his primary work between 1949 and his death. (One of this series is shown in Color Plate 52.) The image of the squares is talismanic. Albers's training was at the Bauhaus, and the doctrine of "less is more" is apparent in the simplicity of the forms he chose to work with. Because of his extraordinary theoretical understanding of color and its interactions and effects, the "Homage to the Square" series is surprisingly inexhaustible. We constantly seem to be penetrating into a mystery—a perceptual mystery—with rules that we discover by looking.

Realism and Superrealism

Among recent stylistic developments in painting has been a resurgence of realism, but with several "twists." Realism never disappeared entirely from American painting, but during the 1940s, and 1950s the dominance of abstract expressionism was so great that major critics could say, as Clement Greenberg did in 1954, that most efforts at realism "seem to result in second-hand, second-rate painting."

The realism of Courbet contained feeling, but one of its aims was to avoid sentimentality. Realists wanted to inform the emotional life rather than merely to stroke it. Andrew Wyeth (b. 1917), the son of a book illustrator, was among the steadiest of the realist painters during the heyday of abstract expressionism.

Christina's World (Figure 19-11) is one of the most popular American paintings of the period, although it has been criticized for its sentimentality. There is an implied narrative: the crippled girl, Christina, exists in a world which is large and spacious but limited and barren. An obvious reason for Wyeth's popular success is his technical skill; by comparison, the public hardly knew what to make of the heirs of the dadaists and suprematists who were working at the time.

Wyeth's work includes many realistic studies of Chadd's Ford, his home in Pennsylvania. When these are seen in the aggregate, they are susceptible to the charge of sentimentality. Wyeth is not in the same realist camp as Courbet, although the world he reveals in Pennsylvania has some of the starkness and immediacy of Courbet's Ornans.

But other artists in the late 1950s and early 1960s were beginning to turn away from abstract expressionism and toward a realistic style, looking for a new way to approach realism and avoid clichés, sentimentality, literary narratives, and anecdotes. Philip Pearlstein (b. 1924) returned to figurative painting in the early 1960s and has been in the forefront of a new movement. He felt that he had to combat two forces in contemporary theory: the flatness of the canvas and the cubistic roving point of view. He produced a three-dimensional illusion from a single point of view, like that of the camera. Figure 19-12 is an example.

Figure 19-11
Andrew Wyeth. *Christina's World.* 1948. Tempera on gesso panel, 32 ¼ by 47 ¾ inches. (Collection, Museum of Modern Art, New York; purchase.)

Pearlstein avoids sentiment in this painting by refusing to place the figures in circumstances about which a viewer could fantasize: their only "narrative" is their appearance. Pearlstein crops off parts of their bodies with the apparent indifference of a camera. Thus he shares Degas's fascination with the camera's point of view, but not Degas's romantic coloration or subject matter. Pearlstein's coloration is intense but emotionally flat. The contrast between the highlighted surfaces and those which are in relative shadow is one of the distinguishing features of his style. Pearlstein forces us to concentrate on the visual present and not on extraneous, or "outside," considerations. There is something brutal about his approach, but that, too, is a factor of the psychology of the viewer—who is usually susceptible to a softening sentimentality that Pearlstein absolutely refuses to indulge in.

Alfred Leslie (b. 1927), with Pearlstein, is one of the pioneers of the new realism. He, too, is uninterested in clichés and sentimentality. Yet he is concerned with the evocation of emotion, and his subject matter is sometimes emotionally charged. *The Killing Cycle Number 6: Loading Pier* (Figure 19-13) is

typical of his work; it shows people carrying the body of Frank O'Hara, who died in a dune-buggy crash on Fire Island in 1966. The composition of the painting, with the action in a sharp diagonal across the canvas, is suggestive of the depositions of Christ (such as Rubens's in Figure 14-20). The strong chiaroscuro lighting is characteristic of Leslie, as it was of Caravaggio and Joseph Wright of Derby. And despite the fact that a photograph would treat light differently, the expression on the face of the young woman at the bottom of the canvas, who bears most of the weight of the body, as well as that of the woman leaning over the body from above, is photographic in the sense of showing an awareness of being suddenly observed. Even the chiaroscuro suggests the invasion of the flashbulb. Emotion seems to be bottled up in the painting, and one cannot help participating in the intensity of the moment.

Photorealism

The photograph is the source of the photorealists' imagery. Their paintings are more detailed and exact than a photograph of comparable size would be. Realists of all kinds, including those whose work adorns magazine covers, have used photographs as aids in painting for several hundred years—if we include the camera obscura. Modern photorealists not only depend on the photograph, but also try to make their work superior to it. They might be said to be responding to Paul Delaroche, who in 1839 said that photography meant the end of painting. Their response is simply that painting can outdo photography and that photography has become a useful servant of painting.

Chuck Close (b. 1940) startled viewers in the early 1970s with his painstaking reproductions of photographs of himself and his friends. Each canvas was huge; some were 8 feet high. The process of transferring "photographic information," as he described it, took months of careful work.

In *Susan,* an early work (Figure 19-14), some sections—the ears and the hair—are out of focus because the camera was so close and the aperture was open so far. The image is naive, but its scale is such that we cannot avoid participating with it. We are "in" this painting, much as we are in Pollock's or Newman's work. That experience, in relation to a portrait, is novel. The fact that Close chose a

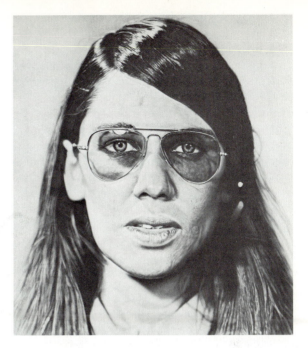

Figure 19-14
Chuck Close. *Susan.* 1972. Oil on canvas, 91 ¼ by 89 ¼ inches. (Pace Gallery, New York.)

photograph that has no special photographic or technical subtleties is important because it helps us concentrate totally on the image and not on an interpretation of it. The complexity of the work is increased by our wondering what its true subject is: Susan or the photograph of Susan.

Although she does not work on the same scale, Idelle Weber (b. 1932) produces canvases of exacting realism. She relies on photographic slides, which she takes in abundance.

Weber works and lives in New York, where she has been developing a group of paintings called the "Trash" series. New York, she says, is the undisputed king of trash, and many of her canvases have developed from slides that she took only a block or so from her studio. In *Gutter I* (Color Plate 53) we see just what we might expect to find in a gutter in a big city. The yellow paint meant to mark curbs and dividing lines is splashed over a sewer grate; assorted pieces of paper and paper bags, as well as bits of food and old oil cans, take on an almost glamorous quality in the painting.

But the choice of subject is also important for what it achieves in our own consciousness of the canvas. The most important problem is that, as with any realistic image, people relate to the subject matter instantly, without being aware of the mediation of the medium and the formal values that transform the image. Thus, when they look at a serious photograph, people often ignore the photograph *as* photograph and respond instead to what is represented. They look at a portrait and recognize a celebrity. *Susan* addresses this problem by presenting us with a woman we do not know. In some cases photographers have lavished enormous technical efforts on a trivial subject in order to help us see its visual value. Weber's "Trash" series does the same. We participate with the work itself, not with a fantasy that it may excite in us. This is the same distinction that led Kazimir Malevich to his suprematist theories. He used pure geometric forms to excite pure aesthetic responses.

The same approach, but on a different scale, is taken by Richard Estes (b. 1936) in *Baby Doll Lounge* (Color Plate 54). Philip Pearlstein has said: "I have learned to look at what is in front of me without idealization, a consuming experience in itself. Most of us really don't want to see things as they are." *Baby Doll Lounge* seems to share this approach.

Estes works from photographs and often studies the visual demands made by storefront windows and their reflections—things which we do not always notice. The absence of people in his cityscapes sometimes produces a quality characterized by some observers as an illusion of silence. With a clarity that makes us uneasy, Estes reveals "things as they are." After looking at his work, we see our everday world with a different eye.

PERCEPTION KEY

After the Abstract Expressionists

1. Larry Rivers's painting of Washington crossing the Delaware does not treat trivial subject matter, and yet he felt that it was vapid and stupid. Are any of the pop artists' works vapid in the same way? Why would the subject of de Kooning's *Woman I* (Color Plate 45) not be vapid?

2. Major critics regarded realistic works of the 1940s and 1950s as "second-hand, second-rate" paintings. Do you agree? Do you agree with the critic who found *Christina's World* (Figure 19-11) "obvious and contrived"? What is Wyeth's attitude toward sentimentality in painting?

3. The dadaists had contempt for the general public; is this true of the abstract expressionists? The pop artists? The op artists?

4. The abstract expressionists were content to have their work appear unfinished. For the existentialist philosophers, life itself is always unfinished. The work of the photorealists has a high degree of finish. Do you prefer paintings that have a high degree of finish, such as Estes' *Baby Doll Lounge* (Color Plate 54), or do you find a painting like Rivers's *Double Portrait of Frank O'Hara* (Figure 19-8) just as satisfying?

5. The abstract expressionists were agonized painters who examined an inner, psychological "landscape." Does the object-dependent work of realists such as Idelle Weber (Color Plate 53) strike you as having given up on the inner self? Do the realists avoid emotion— or do they simply avoid sentimentality?

Figure 19-15
Jean Dubuffet. *The Cow with the Subtile Nose.* 1954. Oil on enamel on canvas, 35 by 45 ¾ inches. (Collection, Museum of Modern Art, New York.)

IMPORTANT EUROPEAN INFLUENCES: DUBUFFET AND BACON

Jean Dubuffet (1901–1985) began an exploration of images drawn from works done by insane people and by children. He was able to find both the immediacy and the naiveté present in such sources. His first show, in 1945 after the liberation of Paris, helped begin a form of expressionism called "tachisme," which refers to the way in which the paint was built up—almost as clay, mud, or cement might be. Colors took on an earthenware quality—mottled and expressive. The subject of *The Cow with the Subtile Nose* (Figure 19-15) is, like that of Rivers's painting of Washington, deliberately "dopey." But the painting's directness and its lack of three-dimensionality and proportion at once gave it a strong appeal—which it maintains today. Dubuffet demonstrated that the imagery of children is filled with potential for expression. Taking a cow as a subject was an act of considerable daring. A comparison with the paintings in the caves of southern France (see Chapter 1) may help us understand why this work has the force that it does.

Francis Bacon (b. 1909) developed a style whose nightmarish quality can be associated with World War II and its aftermath. It is figurative, but it is also abstract and expressive. In some of his canvases gestures of paint seem not to be controlled entirely by conscious decisions. Bacon's paintings also seem unfinished, which in some cases gives them a strange hallucinatory quality. Many of his early works show generals, popes, and other important people with their mouths open, as if screaming. *Dog* (Color Plate 49) is based on a series of photographs of dogs by the nineteenth-century photographer Eadweard Muybridge, whose works inspired many of Bacon's paintings. The setting, Bacon said, was inspired by Albert Speer's Zeppelinfeld (Figure 19-30), a Nazi building in which storm troopers rallied. This image is haunting in the way that dreams can be haunting. Bacon's works are filled with innumerable metaphors for suffering. As Edward Lucie-Smith put it, a Bacon retrospective can be an oppressing experience.

Sculpture

THE MIDDLE YEARS: EXPERIMENTS IN FORM AND SPACE

Sculpture has experienced the same intense stylistic changes as painting and other arts. In mid-century, the distinction between sculpture and painting, as well as between sculpture and life, were relatively clear, but they have grown dim. Experimenters who

Figure 19-16
Henry Moore. *Three-Piece Reclining Figure Number 2: Bridge Prop.* Bronze, 1972–1973. (Hirshhorn Museum and Sculpture Garden, Smithsonian Museum.)

used to be considered radical, such as Henry Moore (b. 1898), now seem traditional and familiar in comparison with certain contemporary sculptors. Much of Moore's early work is figurative with expressionistic distortions. Since the 1960s his work has become spare, expressive, and almost skeletal. His experiments are with space. His subject is space and volume, and his revelations are about the effects of form in space. A work such as *Large Three Piece Reclining Figure* (Figure 19-16) is a lyric study of forms which allude to the articulation of animals' joints, natural forms rarely visible to us.

As with his sculptural group in Lincoln Center, in New York, and most of his late works, one can walk around this piece and observe the rhythms of the curves, the shifting attitudes of the bulking bronze, and the subtle movement of light and shadow over the smooth, polished surfaces. These forms blend into the landscape in which they are set. They are a sensual and emotional experience, a way of perceiving space and volume directly; and yet they have a mobile, light quality that defies their weight.

Walking Man (Figure 19-17), by Alberto Giacometti (1901–1966), is part of a series of works which became symbols in the 1960s for the isolation and striving of existentialist men and women. They stood, as stylized Egyptian sculpture had stood, for the spirit of the times. Giacometti abstracted from natural forms, as Moore and others did, but in these works he maintained the link with the human form, reviving memories of the shrunken, skeletal figures of the concentration camps.

Figure 19-17
Alberto Giacometti. *Walking Man.* 1962. Bronze. (Hirshhorn Museum and Sculpture Garden, Smithsonian Museum.)

Figure 19-18
David Smith. Above left: *Cubi XVII*. 1963. Middle: *Cubi XVIII*. 1964. Right: *Cubi XIX*. 1964.
(Permission courtesy of the Collection of Candida and Rebecca Smith; photo, David Smith Papers,
on deposit at Archives of American Art, Smithsonian Institution.)

David Smith (1906–1965) was to sculpture what Pollock was to painting. His early work reflected his wartime experience welding tanks. The connection of the "Cubi" series with cubism may be only in the name, but Smith worked with genuine cubes—arranging them, balancing them, and analyzing their relationships (see Figure 19-18). Smith usually left the marks of industrial wire brushing on the surfaces of his works so that we would remain aware of their industrial origins. He took special pleasure in the play of light—the reflection of sky, grass, or snow— on their surfaces. The surroundings of his works—which are best viewed outdoors—are integrated into the experience of them. Like Moore's work, they can be walked around and studied, but they tend to have a clearer sense of what F. David Martin calls "the privileged position" from which they should be viewed. They have, for all their abstraction, a frontality that helps integrate the forms.

One of Smith's studios, Terminal Iron Works, was named after the plant in which he once worked. It was a reminder that his work stemmed from a new source of energy and inspiration in sculpture: the age of industry and the machine.

Alexander Calder (1898–1976) was also interested in using the power of the industrial age. His mobiles, which consist of forms reminiscent of the work of Miró are, suspended delicately on wires so that they move gently in the air. Mobiles have become household items, hung, for example, above children's cribs. Calder's *Stegosaurus* (Figure 19-19) is an example of his huge public stabiles, works that show evidence of their fabrication in an industrial shop. The general public has often protested works of this sort because they do not resemble traditional sculpture of the nineteenth century. Yet a work like *Stegosaurus* is a considerable presence; it is located in a bricked plaza between two large office buildings, and one can walk close to it and watch its towering, curved forms loom overhead and shift in their relationships to one another. Its tapering curves slice into the air, and moving close to it one gets a sense of

Figure 19-19
Alexander Calder. *Stegosaurus.* 1973. Steel plates, 50 feet high. (Alfred E. Burr Mall, Hartford, Connecticut; gift of the Trustees of the Ella Burr McManus Fund.)

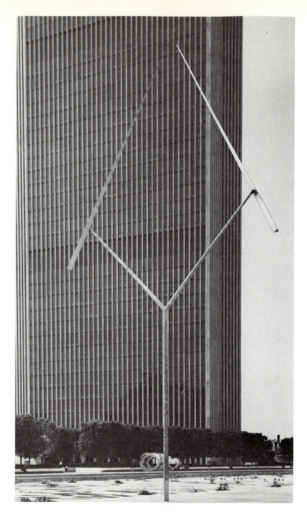

Figure 19-20
George Rickey. *Two Lines Oblique.* 1968–1971. Stainless steel, about 10 feet high. (Empire State Center, Albany; New York State Office of General Services.)

"impending space": a sense that Calder has discovered relationships that would not exist unless the work defined volume and space. The form—which is painted red—is dynamic, exciting, and in profound contrast to the rectilinear shapes of the nearby architecture. The fact that dinosaurs once walked on the very spot where the work is placed helps establish its poetic rationale.

The influences of both industry and the machine are evident in the work of George Rickey (b. 1907), whose approach to kinetic sculpture has been singular and effective. *Two Lines Oblique* (Figure 19-20) moves in response to the wind. The long, pointed arms sometimes move in the same direction and sometimes move in opposite directions, always changing their relationship with the surroundings. In its current setting, the sculpture contrasts sharply with the intense verticality of the distant buildings; occasionally it creates a moiré effect, like an illusion in a work of op art, producing a momentary visual confusion. Rickey's work generally depends on motion for its effect. Like Smith's, it retains the machine finish, reminding us of its origins.

The sculptors of the 1950s and 1960s obviously changed the nature of the medium; much of their work would hardly be recognized by a nineteenth-century sculptor. Louise Nevelson (b. 1900) added her own vocabulary to modernism in a series of wall sculptures composed of boxes in which parts of old furniture, mill ends, and other wooden objects are arranged to produce a series of visual rhythms of remarkable orginality and intensity. *Royal Tide IV* (1960; Figure 19-21) is filled, like most of her works, with machined or mass-produced forms that are repeated throughout the composition; this work is punctuated by the shape of the oval frame. Table legs, newel-posts, and other forms produced on a turning lathe fascinate her and show up in this work at rhythmic intervals, always accentuating the work's verticality—its pyramidal ascension. Nevelson paints her works in monochrome: all black, white, or, as in this case, gold. She is in the tradition of Gabo, a constructivist, and Schwitters, a dadaist. Like many of the sculptors of the period, she found a vocabulary in which she could do her work, and she has remained within it.

Nevelson's power derives from her success in integrating cubist ideas with those of the collagists and assemblagists. But most critics who have responded positively to her work see other qualities, such as a penetrating psychological vision. Her constructions of boxes are as mysterious and symbolic as some of the images in surrealist paintings. Because of their uniform color—usually black—they tend to be even more mysterious, suggesting meanings which are ineffable. Many of her works suggest not only walls but also altars, as if their contents were icons of an inexplicable religion. The most common emotional reaction to her work is an unnamed awe—perhaps a

Freudian dread. The sexual connotations of boxes and newel-posts are inescapable.

Mark di Suvero (b. 1933) also works in an assemblage technique, often on a large scale, and usually produces sculptures for public spaces. Because his work is rough and unfinished in appearance, and because he often includes in them huge creosoted blocks of wood similar to railroad ties, di Suvero has often stirred intense controversy.

Federico García Lorca was a Spanish poet who fled fascist Spain to live in exile in America, where he wrote *The Poet in New York*. Tragically, his protests were silenced by an assassin's bullet. Di Suvero's *New York Dawn (for Lorca)*, shown in Figure 19-22, in which the ice tongs and the rod resemble a bull, suggests his Spanish origins, while the chains at the end of the rod suggest the rigid prison atmosphere that Lorca left. Lorca had written about the dark inner spirit—duende—of inspiration and the irrational. A gesture, he said, could mean more than an uninspired edifice. Di Suvero's work is all gesture, with form balancing form, a simplicity of contrasting materials, and a directness of statement that suggests a memorial.

Figure 19-21
Louise Nevelson. *Royal Tide IV.* 1960. Gold and wood, 11 by 14 feet. This work has been destroyed. (Pace Gallery, New York.)

Figure 19-22
Mark di Suvero. *New York Dawn (for Lorca)*. 1965. Wood, steel, and iron, 936 by 888 by 600 inches. (Collection, Whitney Museum of American Art, New York; photo, Geoffrey Clements.)

Sculpture—The Middle Years

1. Which of the works shown in Figures 19-16 through 19-22 seem most indebted to cubism? Is sculpture more limited than painting in its capacity to conduct a cubistic analysis of experience?

2. Which of these works demonstrate the influence of abstract expressionism? Can any of these sculptures be said to be the product of a gesture? Can any of them be said to reach into the "uncensored" psyche? Is instantaneity possible in sculpture of the kind discussed above?

3. People generally concern themselves with the problem of beauty in sculpture. Which of these works is least concerned with beauty? Which can be said to be completely concerned with beauty? Is beauty a relevant issue in relation to works of this kind?

4. Why would sculptors such as Calder and Smith want us to be aware of the contributions of industry to their works? Can it be said that the appearance of industrial influences is part of the subject matter of their works?

5. Establish the subject matter of at least one of the works shown here. Then, if possible, establish the subject of a piece of sculpture in your own vicinity—preferably one created in the period 1945–1965. To what extent does the work employ space, volume, or weight as part of its subject matter? What kinds of revelations about space, volume, or weight are you aware of as you move around the piece?

POP ART AND MINIMALISM

The connection of George Segal (b. 1924) with pop art has been tenuous because his imagery is not as wry or as unsympathetic to society as that of others in the movement. *Bus Riders* (Figure 19-23) has a ghostly quality that results from the placement of the white plaster figures in an environment built from real objects. The monochrome treatment resembles black-and-white photography: it distances the lifelike figures enough so that what we see is abstract and quite different from actual experience.

Minimalist sculpture was as vital in the mid-1960s as pop sculpture. It depended on observation concerning real space and real time, while avoiding

Figure 19-23
George Segal. *Bus Riders.* 1964. Plaster and bus seats, 69 by 40 by 76 inches. (Hirshhorn Museum and Sculpture Garden, Smithsonian Museum.)

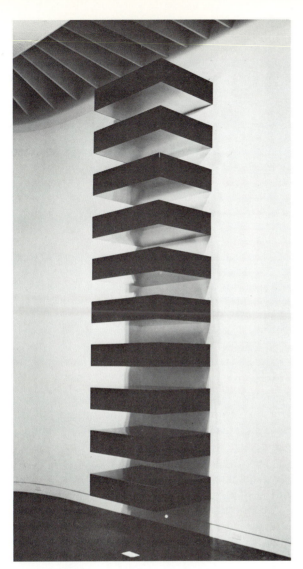

Figure 19-24
Donald Judd. *Untitled.* 1965. Galvanized iron and aluminum, 33 by 141 by 30 inches. (Leo Castelli Gallery, New York.)

movements of reflections on the polished surfaces. A confrontation with such simple forms is a novel experience in sculpture; such confrontations were explored in some depth during the period. The power of the minimalists to order experience through the use of primary shapes was a revelation.

SOME CURRENT DEVELOPMENTS IN SCULPTURE

Earth Sculpture

With the shift in thought that accompanied the exploration into what could actually constitute a sculpture came a new freedom. A recent movement, sometimes called "earth sculpture," involves colossal projects that require bulldozers and earthmovers. One might say that the sculptor is carving on the earth itself. Robert Smithson (1938–1973) was a leader of this movement until he died in an airplane crash while examining a site from the air.

Spiral Jetty (Figure 19-25), 1500 feet long and 15 feet wide, is a coil of rocks that can be seen from almost nowhere except the air, like the giant earth sculptures of certain primitive peoples. Other sculptors working in this mode have piled rocks in straight lines, carved matching notches in facing mountains, and built trenches and wells. In some cases, such works can be seen and appreciated only in photographs. Most of them are in very isolated areas.

The Romanian artist Christo (Christo Jaracheff, b. 1935) became famous for wrapping buildings and even coastlines; he once attempted to place a fabric screen across the Grand Canyon. One of his most

narrative and illusion. A minimalist work is nothing other than what it seems to be. In one sense, it is "purist" sculpture, using volume and space as its primary subject matter. Donald Judd's *Untitled* (1965; Figure 19-24) explores the repetition of simple forms: seven boxes affixed to a wall. It depends on lighting for some of its effects, but Judd exploits the spaces between the boxes as well as the space occupied by each box. As one moves past the work, one perceives unexpected relationships: shifts of light and dark and

Figure 19-25
Robert Smithson. *Spiral Jetty,* Great Salt Lake, Utah. 1970. (Photo, Gian Franco Gorgoni/Contact, New York.)

Figure 19-26
Christo. *Running Fence.* California, lasting two weeks. Nylon and steel, 24 ½ miles long, 18 feet high. (© Running Fence Corporation, 1976; photo, Jeanne-Claude.)

successful works was *Running Fence* (Figure 19-26), a snakelike nylon fence put up near Sonoma, California; more than 24 miles long, it went up and down the sides of the hills, finally ending in the ocean. Once erected, it began to wave in the wind, giving off the snapping sounds of gigantic flags or banners. For this work, Christo had to mobilize an enormous crew of people, raise a great deal of money, and cope with legal problems and the resistance of property owners. The documentary film made of the project is a testimony to the excitement it engendered and to its ultimate aesthetic power.

Works such as Christo's and Smithson's are often called "conceptual" or "environmental": they last, like a performance, for only a short time. A work by Christo is a work of art largely by virtue of Christo's declaring and willing it to be one. Further, the process (rather than the product) and the idea (rather than the object itself) are what interest the creator.

Superrealist Sculpture

Duane Hanson (b. 1925) and John De Andrea (b. 1941) produce works that comment on the relation of the artist to society and to the model. *Bowery Derelicts*

(Figure 19-27) was done during what Hanson calls his early "expressionist" phase. During this period he also did a number of works which might be considered social protest: a gathering of American soldiers, dead and dying, for example, and a group of violent football players. His later—and current—work has a satirical edge.

A connection with Courbet and his followers is apparent. Courbet detested sentimentality and falsity; his realism was designed to help people see things as they are. For many artists, the new realism seems to pose the threat of a return to sentimentality and easy responses to art—what the novelist John Barth calls the return to "middle-class ease and vulgarity." Hanson's later work forces us to examine the ugliness of ordinary life. He has achieved what the early realists had hoped for: a representation of reality that does not invoke automatic emotional responses.

Western sculptors are not alone in working in a superrealist mode. *The Rent Collection Courtyard* (Figure 19-28) is installed in the actual courtyard of a former rent collector. The life-size figures, modeled in clay, appear to have been snatched from an instant in real life. The social commentary is as clear as Hanson's: the people are suffering while the indiffer-

Figure 19-27
Left: Duane Hanson. *Bowery Derelicts*. 1969–1970. Polyester and fiberglass, polychromed; life-size. (Neue Galerie, Samlung Ludwig, Aachen; photo © Klaus Herzog.)

Figure 19-28
Right: Anonymous Chinese sculptors. *The Rent Collection Courtyard*. Yayi, Szechuan. c. 1974. Life-size figures in clay. (Photo, © Wan-go H. C. Weng.)

ent landlord grows rich. Made by a team of sculptors, this work is typical of realistic styles in both China and Russia, where communism dictates that all art must be intelligible to the masses and must serve the political well-being of the state. In China no art can be exhibited unless it is formally approved by a government commission. Art is screened on the basis of its political content.

Current Developments in Sculpture

1. Should George Segal's work (Figure 19-23, for example) be associated with the new realism?

2. What can one expect in terms of emotional impact from the work of Donald Judd (as in Figure 19-24)? Does it have a clear emotional focus? Is there a connection with the suprematist ambitions of Kazimir Malevich?

3. What problems about the definition of sculpture are raised by the work of Robert Smithson (as in Figure 19-25) and Christo (as in Figure 19-26)? Does confusion concerning the definition of sculpture produce confusion about how one should respond to sculpture?

4. Does the "wax museum reality" of the work of Hanson and De Andrea (as in Figures 19-27 and 19-29) call into question the proper definition of sculpture? How do these sculptors seem to use illusionistic techniques in their work? Would you value these works more or less if the sculptors had used other techniques? How much of the effect of *The Rent Collection Courtyard* (Figure 19-28) depends on illusionistic techniques?

5. The Soviet Union, China, and other nations that use art for political purposes insist that artists use a realistic technique. Abstract expressionism is thought to be subversive and dangerous because it does not communicate with the masses. Consider the sculptures shown in Figures 19-23 through 19-29. Which would appeal most to the masses? Why? Which would appeal least to the masses? Why is realistic technique so universally preferred by artists whose work is ideological? Can works such as those by Judd make a political comment?

The subject of *Self-Portrait with Sculpture*, by John De Andrea (Figure 19-29), is a traditional one: the relationship of the artist to the self-portrait and to the model has been central to art since the Renaissance. The psychological qualities of *Self-Portrait with Sculpture* are part of its subject matter. At first sight, if this work is set in an informal environment, one is certain that the figures are real. One must study De Andrea's self-portrait for some time before being convinced that it will not turn and speak. No painting could induce the same kind of bafflement.

Being able to explore the spaces around a work such as *Self-Portrait with Sculpture*—realizing that there are many vantage points from which to see them—makes us uneasy. We are not informed about space, volume, or shape, as we are when examining a minimalist sculpture. Rather, we are informed about our own emotional relationship to objects which appear lifelike, but are not. We become part of the experience. Just as Pollock was excited by being "in" his paintings, we are excited by being in the sculptural group.

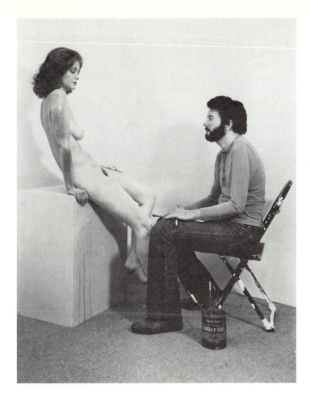

Figure 19-29
John De Andrea. *Self-Portrait with Sculpture.* 1980. Polyvinyl, oil-painted, life-size. (Collection of Foster and Monique Goldstrom, Oakland, California.)

Figure 19-30
Albert Speer. Zeppelinfeld, Nuremberg, Germany. 1934. (Reproduced from Collections of Library of Congress.)

Architecture

THE VALUE OF MONUMENTALITY

Critics have praised late modern architecture for its simplicity and directness, and occasionally for its eloquence. But they have also complained about its starkness, pointing particularly to the glass skyscrapers that dominate the New York skyline. Such buildings are inefficient to operate and anonymous in appearance. Critics have also noted that postwar architecture tends to resemble buildings in fascist states, designed to awe and impress viewers with the power of an institution. Fascist architecture is not unlike the monolithic structures of Egypt, the early civilizations of Sumer, and Rome.

Hitler depended on Albert Speer for tactical innovations in the German effort to conquer Europe. Speer was resourceful and original. His Zeppelinfeld (Figure 19-30), like the Louvre (Figure 14-10), is long and low, with a central entrance dominating two balanced wings. The vertical lines give it strength and solidity, but it differs from the Louvre in that these lines are not Greek, nor are they rounded. The humanizing effects of such details in Greek architecture are absent in the Zeppelinfeld, which presents us with brutal starkness.

The Zeppelinfeld was a huge arena in which the Nazis held nighttime rallies, with torchlight parades suggestive of pagan rituals. The building and the events that took place inside it mesmerized much of a nation and articulated the rhetoric of power.

Figure 19-31
Top, left: Oscar Niemeyer.
1957–1960. Senate, Secretariat,
and Congress. Brasília, Brazil.
(Photo, Lucien Hervé; © SPADEM,
Paris/VAGA, New York, 1984.)

Figure 19-32
Top, right: Ludwig Mies van der
Rohe and Philip Johnson. Seagram
Building, New York. (Joseph E.
Seagram and Sons, Inc.; photo,
Ezra Stoller/ESTO.)

Figure 19-33
Right, above: Louis Kahn. First
Unitarian Church, Rochester, New
York. 1964. (Photo, courtesy of
Dorrie Meeker, Rochester.)

Figure 19-34
Right: Philip Johnson, Wallace K.
Harrison, and Max Abramowitz.
Lincoln Center for the Performing
Arts, New York. 1963. (Photo,
Ronald L. C. Kienhuis, Brooklyn.)

INSTITUTIONAL ARCHITECTURE

The buildings shown in Figures 19-31 to 19-34 represent institutions: a government in the Secretariat at Brasília (Figure 19-31); a corporation in the Seagram Building (Figure 19-32); religion in the First Unitarian Church (Figure 19-33); and a cultural complex in Lincoln Center (Figure 19-34).

Monolithic architecture is generally characterized by stone masonry or reinforced concrete, but the Seagram Building is made, like most modern skyscrapers, of steel and glass sheathing. Lincoln Center is sheathed with marble (now corroded by urban air pollution). The short walls of the Secretariat at Brasília are made of stone, and the long walls are made of glass and steel. Mies and Johnson celebrated industry; Niemeyer, the future (Brasília was a brand-new, "ideal" city); Kahn, religion; and Johnson, Harrison, and Abramowitz, the performing arts. Each building has a different function and a different approach to construction.

Speer's Zeppelinfeld (Figure 19-30) emphasizes strength, linearity, and symmetry. It is barren of ornamentation, solid in its masonry, and exacting in its repetition of vertical detailing. Unlike most of the later buildings shown here, it is low to the ground and impresses one with its earth-clinging bulk.

Kahn's Unitarian Church (Figure 19-33) does the same, and its repetition of vertical lines suggests the ziggurat at Ur (Figure 2-2) or the temple compound at Saqqara (Figure 2-5), both of which impress the viewer with their solidity and strength. Kahn's strong lines are exact, unsoftened by curves, simple, efficient, and expressive of the rationality that characterizes Unitarianism.

Lincoln Center (Figure 19-34) has often been compared to Nazi buildings, including Speer's. It is low to the ground, dominated by thin vertical lines, severe, and simple. Harrison's five curves—suggestive of the Roman baths—are the only softening lines in the complex. The marble surfaces allude to the classical origins of drama and art.

PERCEPTION KEY

Institutional Architecture—Four Examples

1. Speer's Zeppelinfeld (Figure 19-30) is only one example of Nazi architecture, and comparisons with it are naturally limited. With this thought in mind, determine which of the four examples of institutional architecture in Figures 19-31 through 19-34 is most like Speer's. What qualities (size, dominant lines, symmetry, attitude toward materials, or specific motifs) are most comparable in the two buildings?

2. How do the buildings shown in Figures 19-31 through 19-34 differ in terms of their approach to use of space around them or in terms of their relation to other buildings?

3. Which building is most clearly identifiable as to its function? Which is least identifiable? What makes it difficult for you to determine what the function of this building is? If you had not been told, would you have known the function of the Zeppelinfeld by looking at it?

4. Which of these buildings is most expressive of power? What kind of power? What else do these buildings seem to express? Is any of the buildings explicitly humane or apparently concerned with humane values? Is any of them concerned with values of tenderness? Does any of the buildings suggest feelings of sensitivity or responsiveness to human needs?

5. What might the presence of ornamentation imply for any of these buildings?

The two columns of Niemeyer's Secretariat (Figure 19-31) contrast with the dome of the Senate and its opposite, the "saucer" of the Congress. The function of buildings of this sort would be difficult to imagine simply by looking at them. Except for the fact that other government buildings have used such a design—the United Nations headquarters and the Empire State Plaza in Albany, for example—we would not think it appropriate. Yet its roots—the severity of line and the dominating verticality—are in the architecture of the 1930s.

Probably the building whose function is most easily identifiable is the Seagram Building (Figure 19-32), by Mies van der Rohe (1896–1969). Like the United Nations headquarters, it has come to define what a corporate structure ought to look like. It is efficient and rational. The materials from which it is constructed are quite economical: steel girders, steel exterior trim, and a glass skin on metal bones. The most dramatic quality of the building is its placement: it is set back from the street, permitting it to be viewed as a piece of sculpture. As Figure 19-32 shows, it is dominating—lean, sleek, and dark, like a storm trooper. The buildings around it look dumpy and trivial by comparison. This was Le Corbusier and the international style brought up to date; and, not surprisingly, it at once established the rationale for most corporate skyscrapers. It was a visual symbol of corporate values: the most space for the money, the greatest return on the dollar, and gray-suited conservatism. This building is expressive of power, but quiet power: the power that gets things done.

LATE MODERN ARCHITECTURE: EMPHASIS ON STRUCTURAL ELEMENTS

One striking feature of contemporary architecture is a willingness to exhibit the structural elements of the building—rather than hiding them with a decorative skin. This derives from the geodesic dome buildings of R. Buckminster Fuller (1895–1983). Leaving the structural elements bare is sometimes referred to as "high tech," and it has become a design cliché.

Another important legacy of Fuller is the interchangeability of basic structural elements. In the years before his dome experiments, he proposed prefabricated cellular units which could be moved anywhere. They were sometimes sheathed with metal and were always easy to assemble and care for. Two examples of contemporary use of those ideas are the celebrated Habitat, by Moshe Safdie (Figure 19-35), and the Georges Pompidou Center in Paris, by Enzo Piano and Richard Rogers (Figure 19-36).

Safdie solved the problem of building urban housing units by using some of Fuller's concepts. Each unit is basically identical, prefabricated, and erected on the site. Because of the flexibility of the individual units, they can be placed in different relationships with one another; this makes it possible to maintain visual interest and variety, while also permitting unusual views from the interior and providing a reasonable amount of privacy. The connection with the pueblo concept, and thus with a legitimate tradition, helps establish the validity of the work.

The exterior of the Pompidou Center is covered with brightly painted pipes and tubing, all functional

Figure 19-35
Moshe Safdie. Habitat, Montreal. 1967. (Photo, Canadian Consulate General, New York.)

Figure 19-36
Enzo Piano and Richard
Rogers. Georges Pompidou
Center, Paris. 1977.

and all visible. Its interior is unusually flexible because of 165-foot trusses that permit the interior walls to be moved almost anywhere. The Pompidou Center is a modern art museum, an art library, and a performing arts center; but it does not really look like any of these. Its design has been controversial from the first. Yet it is very popular. Each day, 30,000 people visit Beauborg, as it is known. In the plazas below, musicians, acrobats, mimes, and other performers entertain the crowds. On one side of the building are huge glassed-in escalators that take people to heights which rival the Eiffel Tower.

I. M. Pei (b. 1917), a Chinese-born American architect, was commissioned to fit a major museum wing—the east building of the National Gallery of Art, in Washington— onto a small triangle of land next to a Jeffersonian classical building. Pei, sensitive to materials appropriate to a given locale and responsive to light and complex siting, chose to retain the triangular motif: he used two opposing triangles, connected the wing to the museum with a tunnel, and repeated the triangulations in the interior (Figure 19-37). Pei, like Piano and Rogers, reveals some of the structural elements, particularly the triangulation of the trussing. He used the same technique effectively in the John F. Kennedy Library, in Boston.

Figure 19-37
I. M. Pei. East wing, National
Gallery, Washington. 1980.
(National Gallery of Art,
Washington.)

Figure 19-38
Kevin Roche and John Dinkeloo. College Insurance Building, Indiana. 1969. (Photo, Kevin Roche, John Dinkeloo and Associates.)

TWO CONTEMPORARY DIRECTIONS IN ARCHITECTURE

The problem of monumentality naturally plagues large projects. Solutions are possible other than those inspired by Albert Speer. Two architectural groups—John Portman Associates and Kevin Roche and John Dinkeloo—have designed and built huge projects which do not have the severity associated with monolithic architecture.

The temptation to build on a monumental scale is clear in the pyramidal structures of the College Insurance Company Building (Figure 19-38). However, the slanting walls, and the fact that glass and steel are the principal building materials, make them appear much more natural in their setting. The walls reflect the skies in ever-changing patterns, and the shapes of the structures, which are wider at the bottom than at the top, make them seem a part of the site—like mountains rather than like buildings.

The four round pillars of the Knights of Columbus Building (Figure 19-39) suggest a medieval fortress. They are covered with brown ceramic tiles, and glass and steel walls at every level house offices. Below are the New Haven Civic Center and two parking garages with circular drives. The steel is designed to rust, and so the color of the building is predominantly brown. Because of the way the building is sited, it is dominant from several directions along the throughway; yet because its forms are rounded rather than severe, it is not intimidating.

Figure 19-39
Kevin Roche and John Dinkeloo. Knights of Columbus Building, New Haven, Connecticut. 1980.

Figure 19-40
John Portman. Renaissance
Center, Detroit. 1979. (Photo,
Ford Motor Land Development
Corporation.)

John Portman has been criticized for the lavish drama of the interior of the Hyatt House Hotel in Atlanta, which features a glass elevator rising through a huge interior lobby. Renaissance Center, on the shore of Lake Michigan, features circular towers and more traditional business towers in a group (Figure 19-40). The primary structure is a hotel; the lobby is five stories high, with hanging gardens reaching two or three stories below their roots. It is all Babylonian, but in a Hollywood sense. One is not awed, but amused. The ramps of the interior (Figure 19-41) seem to fan out in numerous directions, reminding one of the fantasized interiors of science-fiction writers. People get lost here. Because the main building is circular, there are no "landmarks" by which to get one's bearings. Escalators rise to great heights, increasing the drama, and openings in the walls produce interesting visual illusions which are part of the psychological qualities of the architecture.

The complex is a city within a city. Banks, restaurants, shops, theaters, cafes, and exercise facilities abound. One could conceivably live within Renaissance Center permanently. This is a form of monumentality which even Albert Speer did not imagine.

Figure 19-41
Portman. Renaissance Center, interior.

Late Modern Architecture

1. Which of the buildings shown in Figures 19-35 through 19-41 seems to be most deserving of the description "futuristic"? Bear in mind that there is no one definition of this vague term, and thus you should establish criteria for making your decision.

2. Select a recently constructed building near you. Does it emphasize or deemphasize monumentality? What means does it use to deal with the question of its effect on a viewer?

3. Consider the examples of buildings by Portman and by Roche and Dinkeloo (Figures 19-38 through 19-41). How important is it for these buildings to reveal their function? Which reveals its function most successfully? Which reveals it least successfully?

4. Of all the buildings shown in this chapter, which is the most severe in appearance? Which is the least severe? What technical qualities—structural details, materials, siting, and shapes—influenced your decision?

5. Do any of the buildings shown in Figures 19-35 through 19-41 seem to point to the future development of architecture? If you had to choose one of these buildings as a model that architects for the remainder of this century would follow, which building would it be? What are your reasons?

Photography

W. EUGENE SMITH AND THE TRADITION

W. Eugene Smith (1918–1979) worked in the tradition of straight photography, emphasizing balance, lighting, symmetry, centrality of composition, high finish, and theme. Smith was also a socially conscious photographer who felt that his work could affect public thought and public policy.

Spanish Village (Figure 19-42) portrays life in the last fascist nation (in 1951). The stark lighting on the dark figures; their black leather hats, which contrast with the stucco wall; and their rifle barrels, sinister and at the ready—all this communicates a harsh reality. These police are guarding the state, not the individual. Smith does not soften their significance or excuse their function, but he also permits them to retain their humanity. Smith was always interested in the humane implications of his images. While he was working at a factory in Japan, photo-graphing the extraordinary "Minimata" series, hired thugs beat and temporarily blinded him because they feared the power of photographs of people who had been deformed by mercury poisoning.

OTHER PHOTOGRAPHERS

Aaron Siskind (b. 1903) was influenced by straight photography, but he broke through to a new style under the influence of abstract expressionism. The influence of junk art and found art combined to produce a body of work that discovered abstract expressionist images in torn paper and urban grafitti; an example is *Chicago* (Figure 19-43), which is one of the works that made a new kind of photography possible. Siskind's subject matter is not like Smith's; his concern is not people or social circumstances. His subject matter is the objects themselves, not what they remind us of, or what they mean beyond themselves.

Figure 19-42
W. Eugene Smith. *Spanish Village*. 1951. (W. Eugene Smith, *Life* Magazine, © 1951 Time Inc.)

Diane Arbus (1928–1972) and Ralph Gibson (b. 1939) headed in different directions from those taken by Smith and Siskind. Arbus was interested in subconscious processes. Her images, like *Child with a Toy Hand Grenade in Central Park* (Figure 19-44), contain people, but they are often outsiders or freaks.

This little boy, who may be perfectly ordinary, has momentarily transformed himself for the camera. He has become surrealistic. Like the surrealists, who sometimes used freaks in their paintings and films, Arbus found a means of riveting our attention to the image without offering any interpretation of its meaning.

Figure 19-43
Aaron Siskind. *Chicago*. 1952. (Museum of Modern Art, New York, John Parkinson III Fund.)

Figure 19-44
Above: Diane Arbus. *Child with Toy Hand Grenade in Central Park.* (Museum of Modern Art, New York; purchase.)

Figure 19-45
Above: Jerry Uelsmann. *Untitled,* from *Silver Meditations.*

Figure 19-46
Below: Duane Michals. *Things Are Queer,* from *Real Dreams.*

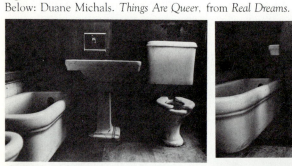
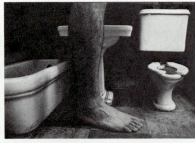

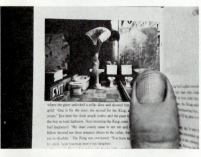

Modern Photography

1. Which of the photographs shown in Figures 19-42 through 19-46 seems most in the humanist tradition of the Renaissance? Which is least in that tradition?

2. Which photograph seems most concerned with the organization of its formal elements?

3. Which photograph is most influenced by the abstract expressionists? Consider gesture; action; investing the image with personal emotion; and abstracting forms from nature. Which photograph seems most passionate?

4. How many of these photographs succeed in forcing you to look at them as photographs—as aesthetic objects rather than as records of an event or a person?

5. If you were to define "seeing photographically" on the basis of these images, what would your definition be? How would your definition differ if you used only the photographs shown in Chapter 18 (Figures 18-15 through 18-18)?

Jerry Uelsmann (b. 1929) and Duane Michals (b. 1929) have delved into surrealist imagery. Uelsmann uses manipulated prints—the result of merging two negative images or a positive and a negative image. The technique imparts an inside-out feeling that heightens the mystery of the photograph. Mystery is essential to surrealism. Surrealist meanings are as obscure as the meanings of our dreams. Uelsmann's images, when successful, play on unnamed fears and anxieties (Figure 19-45 is an example). Many of his images are of dreamlike situations that we can associate with nightmares. By playing on subconscious implications, Uelsmann distracts us from making conscious connections between the images and life. The images stand alone.

Duane Michals's "storyboard" technique uses images which would be unremarkable alone. But together, they narrate impossible events. *Things Are Queer* (Figure 19-46) presents a surrealist "endless loop" of experience. This narrative is a whimsical work which succeeds because we are so used to accepting the "reality" of photographs that it jolts our emotional expectations.

Film

BERGMAN'S CHRISTIAN EXISTENTIALISM: THE 1950s

The most striking postwar films of the 1940s were made in Italy by Vittorio De Sica (1901–1974) and Roberto Rossellini (1906–1977). The Italian realists concentrated on the harsh existence of people who were rebuilding after the war. Ingmar Bergman (b. 1918) brought Swedish films into world prominence with a series of dark studies of human anxiety and searching. Unlike the Italian realists, he did not portray the rigors of postwar society or concentrate on social issues. Instead, his films have a mythic quality; the characters' journeys imply a religious search for individual meaning and satisfaction.

Bergman's most important films in the 1950s were *The Seventh Seal* (1956), *Wild Strawberries* (1957), *The Magician* (1958), and *The Virgin Spring* (1960). Each concerns an individual's inward search for self-knowledge and religious knowledge. The existentialist nature of the films lies in the characters' realization that one's actions create one's nature—

Figure 19-47
Ingmar Bergman. *The Seventh Seal.* 1956. (By permission of Janus Films.)

that every gesture and every moment are of importance to the understanding of self. Each focuses on the individual's struggle for self-definition.

In *The Seventh Seal* (a scene is shown in Figure 19-47), a knight returns from the Crusades to a corrupt society. Religion has decayed into fanaticism and self-flagellation; the land suffers a real plague and also inward rot; and death, rather than life, rules all. His vision of the world is dark; nevertheless, when Death comes to claim him he proposes a game of chess. Eventually, he sacrifices himself for a family of wandering jugglers—he distracts Death by losing the game so that the young family can escape unnoticed. Bergman's chiaroscuro film (it was shot in black and white) establishes the sense of life in the jugglers and contrasts them with the knight as their dark, doomed champion. Despite its medieval setting, the film is a modern allegory of life struggling to overcome death, if only for the little while humankind stands in the sun.

TRUFFAUT AND FELLINI: THE WORLD BETWEEN THEM—THE 1960s

Many important films were made in the 1960s, but François Truffaut (1932–1984) in France and Federico Fellini (b. 1920) in Italy were perhaps the most influential figures of the decade. In 1959, Truffaut's *Four Hundred Blows* won first prize at the Cannes Film Festival. Somewhat autobiographical, it tells of An-

toine, whose free spirit brings him into conflict with the world of home and school, causing him to break the law and jeopardize his future. The boy's hope for genuine freedom is dim at the end of the film—which suggests that some people pay dearly for not being able to fit the mold society makes for them.

Truffaut's most successful film is *Jules and Jim* (1961; Figure 19-48), in which Catherine, a free spirit who loves both Jules and Jim, refuses to live except at the pitch of intensity that she displays in her moments of whimsy. When it becomes clear that she cannot live as intensely as she must, she drives her car off a pier, killing herself and Jim, who is with her. Jules, like the audience, looks on horrified, but powerless. Truffaut's later work includes a number of studies of film artists and the particular kinds of illusions with which they deal.

Federico Fellini (b. 1920) was the dominant influence in Italian films in the 1960s. Like Truffaut, his best films have been autobiographical. *La Dolce Vita* (1959), loosely translated as "The Sweet Life," concerns a recovered and affluent Rome. He makes use of its reputation as the center of the church as well as the historical center of fleshly excess. Spiritual matters are drowned in the Rome of *La Dolce Vita.* His characters, all celebrities, are empty and unhappy, drifting from one "amusement" to another, with no means of sustaining a serious inner life. Even the most spiritual of the characters in the film—a professor who plays Bach on the organ, whose family is

Figure 19-48
François Truffaut. *Jules and Jim.*
1961. (By permission of Janus
Films and Gades Films
International.)

loving and beautiful, and whose work is fulfilling—
ends by killing himself. As depicted in *La Dolce Vita*,
postwar Rome had found material wealth and spiritual poverty.

Fellini's 8½ (1963; Figure 19-49) is not just about
making films, but also about the process of making
8½ itself. Marcello Mastroianni, the actor who has
repeatedly played Fellini's alter ego on film, is a
director making a film about a director making a film.
8½ begins with Mastroianni in a traffic jam in Rome.
Suddenly he suffers an attack of claustrophobia and
imagines himself flying above the traffic, freed on the
wings of his imagination—like all poets. The rest of
the film, which is filled with flashbacks, explores the
relationship of the director to himself and his work.
Suffering from emotional strain, he repairs to a spa,
greets his actors and collaborators, and begins to see
himself more fully. The film is a voyage of self-
discovery—but unlike most films and other dramatic
fictions, it bares the process of both self-creation (the
film) and self-discovery (Fellini). Fellini's theme has
been said to be the conflict between the flesh and the
spirit, but in another sense it might be said that his
subject is Rome and his place in it. Rome—the
"eternal city"—naturally encompasses all the themes
that would be central to a Roman. His later films,
Fellini-Satyricon (1969), *The Clowns* (1970), *Roma*
(1972), and *Amarcord* (1974), all involve his own
search for self, his own quest for meaning.

Figure 19-49
Federico Fellini, 8 ½. 1963. (By permission of Corinth
Films.)

THE 1970s AND 1980s: NEW DIRECTIONS

American films demonstrated a new vitality in the 1970s; after the breakup of the major studios, a number of serious independent producers, who understood how to appeal to an audience, addressed themselves to the problem of reaching people who had deserted theaters for the television set. The answer was to use the big screen to show the sex and sometimes the violence that could not be shown on television. Most films made in the 1970s and later were in color; black and white was reserved for special effects, such as suggesting the past.

Woody Allen (b. 1935) constantly parodies Ingmar Bergman, but he uses the autobiographical tools of Fellini. His films are invariably about a character who resembles himself—sometimes to the point, as in *Annie Hall* (1977), of recreating his current experiences. His character Alvie Singer appears under different names in other films. He is usually divorced, a comic writer, and a "schlemiel." By choosing such a character, Allen turns the autobiographical film inside out. Usually portraits of artists are portraits of heroes who overcome odds to "make it." Allen's character, in films like *Take the Money and Run* (1969), *Sleeper* (1973), *Manhattan* (1979; Figure 19-50), *Stardust Memories* (1980), *Zelig* (1983), and

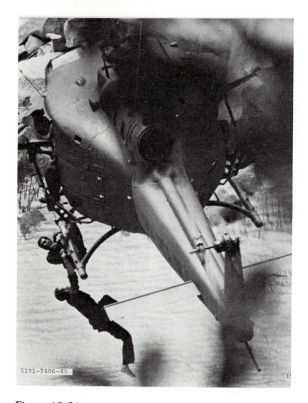

Figure 19-51
Michael Cimino. *The Deer Hunter.* 1978. (By permission of Universal Studios.)

Modern Film

1. If you have the chance, see one of the films discussed here. Do you agree with the judgments made here about this film? As you watch, pay attention to the shots: Are they primarily close-up shots, long shots, or medium shots? Is the choice of shots appropriate to the subject matter of the film? Is the camera generally stationary, or is it often in motion?

2. See a recent film in the realist mode—which includes most that are being shown. Does it court sentiment and easy emotional response?

3. If possible, see a film that contains surrealistic elements—essentially unreal situations and dreamlike sequences. Establish which portions of the film are surrealistic, how they contribute to suggesting dreamlike significance, and whether they seem to penetrate to subconscious meanings.

4. If you have seen a film in which some scenes appear to be "found," in the sense that the dialogue was improvised or accidental events were included for effect, describe the results. Is it reasonable to call such scenes "found"?

5. Consider the most recent film you have seen. Is it realistic in the sense of showing life as it is or in the sense of showing unpleasant aspects of life? Is it mythic—alluding to events in literature—or does it rely on the conventions of the journey of self-discovery?

Broadway Danny Rose (1984), is usually a self-depreciating Chaplinesque victim.

The Vietnamese war inspired a number of important films in the late 1970s. Hal Ashby's *Coming Home,* Michael Cimino's *Deer Hunter* (Figure 19-51), both from 1978, and Francis Ford Coppola's *Apocalypse Now* (1979) explored the domestic and foreign agonies of the war.

The Deer Hunter recreates the three levels of Dante's *Divine Comedy.* The inferno is suggested in the rivers of molten steel in Clairton, Pennsylvania, where the film begins, as well as in the rivers of Saigon and in the prisons of the countryside and the blackened, burning city as Mike, played by Robert De Niro, searches for his friend, Nick, whom he left behind playing Russian roulette in the ruins of

Vietnam. The film is realistic, but it is also mythic in its suggestions of levels of meaning and life. The scenes showing the comradeship of deer hunters, high in the West Virginia mountains, are a glimpse of paradise, as is the scene of revelry at the Russian Orthodox wedding. Everyday life in Clairton represents the purgatory in which most people live, a life demarked by mobile homes, supermarkets, and automobiles.

A number of distinguished films, with important American directors, were produced during the 1970s. Stanley Kubrick directed *2001: A Space Odyssey* (1968), *A Clockwork Orange* (1973), and *Barry Lyndon* (1975). Martin Scorsese directed *Mean Streets* (1973) and *Taxi Driver* (1974), which examined the levels of violence common in American cities.

Literature

EXISTENTIALISM

Existentialism had its roots in the philosophy of Søren Kierkegaard (1813–1855), a Danish writer whose works were rediscovered in the 1920s. His attack on the systematic philosophical theories of Hegel left a legacy of distrust for all philosophical systems. His chief complaint was that Hegel had neglected the most important aspect of a person's life: existence. The German philosophers Edmund Husserl (1859–1938), Martin Heidegger (1889–1976), and Karl Jaspers (1883–1969) espoused existentialist views, emphasizing the value of experience over a priori theories. Existentialism never became a systematic philosophy; it encompassed a range of philosophical attitudes based on certain principles.

After World War II the French writers Albert Camus (1913–1960) and Jean-Paul Sartre (1905–1980) brought existentialism to world prominence in works such as Sartre's play *No Exit* (1944) and Camus's novels *The Plague* (1947) and *The Fall* (1956). Sartre's *Being and Nothingness* (1943) and his essay "Existentialism is a Humanism" (1946) and Camus's philosophical discourse on suicide, "The Myth of Sisyphus" (1942), helped establish the major existentialist positions.

"Existence precedes essence" expressed Sartre's view that people are defined by their actions, not their essential nature. Doctrines of essence were products of the analysis of objects: a knife's essence was defined by cutting; a piano's by playing; an automobile's by driving. But people are not objects. They exist in terms of infinite potential. The medieval view insisted that humankind clarify its essential nature—which was to worship God—and devalue everyday experience. Thus, essences counted, not actions. Kierkegaard complained that Hegel viewed development of intellect as the primary goal of the individual, whereas he should have focused equally on development of personality—which includes not just thought but action, or existence.

Camus emphasized the principles of the absurd, which influenced—and still influences—a wide body of literature. "The Myth of Sisyphus" explores the tale of Sisyphus, who, in Greek mythology, offended the gods and was sentenced to spend eternity in Hades pushing a rock up a hill, only to have it tumble back down each time. Sisyphus then pushed the rock back up the hill; this went on forever. The parable is clear: people are like Sisyphus. The world is without meaning; life is absurd. Whatever meaning there is, the existentialists tell us, is created by humankind. In an absurd world, every gesture must take on—create —meaning. People are the makers of meaning.

Camus felt that Sisyphus was happy—that absurdity and happiness were aspects of the same thing. Because Sisyphus understood the absurdity of his circumstances, and because he understood himself, he was content to continue his efforts, even forever.

> There is no sun without shadow, and it is essential to know the night. The absurd man says yes and his effort will henceforth be unceasing. . . . For the rest, he knows himself to be the master of his days. At that subtle moment when man glances backward over his life, Sisyphus returning toward his rock, in that slight pivoting he contemplates that series of unrelated actions which become his fate, created by him, combined under his memory's eye and soon sealed by his death.

The absurdity of Camus's death, in a high-speed car crash, has often been seen as an ironic comment on his philosophy.

BEAT WRITERS AND THE INCURSIONS OF ZEN

The "beat movement" began in the United States in the late 1950s and persisted until the early 1970s. The origins of the term "beat" are unclear. It may have derived from an allusion to jazz or from the beat or beaten look of bohemian writers (the hippies embellished on the style in the late 1960s), or perhaps—and this interpretation is accepted by some beat writers—it referred to beatitude: the holiness sometimes associated with the priestlike poet.

The influence of jazz was apparent immediately in the long lines of the beat poets' verse, which resembled the long lines of a Charley Parker saxophone solo. It was also apparent in the impromtu or improvised "feel" of much of the literature. Like the abstract expressionists, the beat writers felt that they were their art; that anything they did was art; and that art was inspiration and freedom. Zen Buddhism emphasized a beatific state as essential for creation as well as an openness to experience, a kind of passivity in the face of life forces. One accepted one's dharma, or fate. One of Jack Kerouac's first novels after his explosive *On the Road* (1956) was *The Dharma Bums* (1958), which celebrated a sensual life in which sex was an ecstatic and religious experience. The inspiration for the beat view of life came from an eastern religion, and thus its novelty was one of its great sources of power. The beat writers were constantly defining themselves in their works and their lifestyle, which was soon imitated by a generation of young people whose beatitude was connected more with drugs than with art.

On the Road was a different novel for critics to judge in 1957. The commanding American writers were Ernest Hemingway (1889–1961) and William Faulkner (1897–1962). Hemingway's novel *The Sun Also Rises* (1926) was credited as having defined the "lost generation." Kerouac's novel was, according to some critics, a successor which would define the "beat generation." Faulkner's novels centered on the moral dilemmas of the south, associated with slavery and its aftermath. Kerouac's work, in comparison, seemed slapdash, and yet he too was deeply interested in the black experience, particularly as evidenced in jazz. His own moral views were liberal compared with those of the classic American writers.

THE REALIST TRADITION

The literature of the 1970s and 1980s has reached back to the realist traditions associated with turn-of-the-century authors. The work of John Updike, Kingsley Amis, William Trevor, Anne Tyler, Anne Beatty, J. P. Donleavy, John McGahern, and Gabriel Garcia Marquez—and other novelists of equal quality—indicates that the century will end with a return to tradition. The age of experimentation in literature that existed between the two world wars is at an end. The same appears to be true of poetry, with writers such as Seamus Heaney, Ted Hughes, Anne Sexton, Adrienne Rich, W. S. Merwin, Philip Larkin, and Denise Levertov—in the English language—all writing essentially traditional verse.

DRAMA: FROM GODOT TO HAPPENINGS

European drama before the war was experimental; through the theories of Bertolt Brecht (1898–1956) and others, a theater developed in which the comfort of distance was dissolved. Distance—being separate from the action on stage and safe from its implications—was the protection of the middle class.

Beckett: Theater of the Absurd

Some of the plays of Samuel Beckett (b. 1906) have no apparent setting; some have no players ("lips" appear to speak the lines); some have no apparent plot. His most influential play is *Waiting for Godot* (1955; Figure 19-52), in which Vladimir and Estragon, tramps who bear a resemblance to Chaplin, wait on a deserted plain for Godot. Each day Godot sends a boy to tell them that he will come the next day; he never does. What the tramps say is often incoherent and meaningless. Only two passersby interrupt their random babblings—Pozzo, a rich man, and his slave,

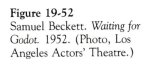

Figure 19-52
Samuel Beckett. *Waiting for Godot*. 1952. (Photo, Los Angeles Actors' Theatre.)

Lucky. Lucky is an idiot who speaks a semitechnical language that is thoroughly absurd, although at times it sounds sensible. They are unimpressed by Vladimir and Estragon's interest in Godot and eventually leave them. The boy ends Act 1 by explaining that Godot is sorry, but he cannot come today and will come tomorrow. In Act 2 Pozzo returns; he is blind and is led by Lucky, who is now dumb. He is unable to remember Vladimir and Estragon. The play ends with the boy coming again to apologize for Godot's absence. Vladimir and Estragon must wait. They are afraid not to wait, although they cannot be sure that Godot will ever come.

Grotowski and Schechner

Jerzy Grotowski's "poor theater" in Poland and Richard Schechner's "environmental theater" in New York both flourished in the 1960s. Grotowski's actors, like Schechner's, were very near—sometimes in—the audience. In each of his productions Grotowski looks for new relationships with the audience. There is no "comfort zone," no distance from the action. His poor theater creates magical worlds with simple props. He contrasts what he does with "rich theater," the theater of the commercial stage, in which expensive props and costumes create the dramatic world. In his work, the actors create this world with their imaginations. His most successful plays are *The Constant Prince* (Figure 19-53), a powerful, stark drama that alludes to the life of Christ; and *Akropolis* (1968), a turn-of-the-century

Polish drama adapted to wartime Poland and set in Auschwitz. *Akropolis* ends with the prisoners following a headless corpse, Christ, into an afterlife. They march in a ritual procession offstage into the waiting ovens of the concentration camp.

Richard Schechner (b. 1939) had one great success in *Dionysus in 69* (1969). His company performed in a garage among the audience, which was included in the play's ecstatic finale. The reference in the title is to Dionysus, the Greek god of wine and the inspirer of passion and ecstasy. Schechner's environmental theater helped change the way plays are produced. The proscenium, with its arch—which separates the stage from the audience—has all but disappeared in theaters built since the late 1960s. Now the stage projects into the audience, which sits around it, feeling more a part of the action.

The breakdown of the distance between audience and actor was not limited to the works of Grotowski and Schechner. The Living Theater of Julian Beck and Judith Malina produced *Paradise Now* in 1972, in which the actors roamed through the theater talking with the audience, apparently at random. Peter Weiss's *Persecution and Assassination of Marat as Performed by the Inmates of the Asylum at Charenton under the Direction of the Marquis de Sade* (1965)—usually called *Marat/Sade*—also broke down this distance by being performed in the round, permitting the actors to establish contact with the audience. Weiss was developing Artaud's theories of the "theater of cruelty," and he remains among those who did so most successfully.

Figure 19-53
Jerzy Grotowski. *The Constant Prince.* (Photo, Max Waldman; © 1984 Waldman Archives, Westport, Connecticut.)

Happenings

Happenings, which were dadaist events, usually took place in a nontheatrical environment. They differed from ordinary drama in that they were not usually repeated, nor was there ever a clear sense of what was part of a happening and what was not. Like found art, happenings often included happy accidents and spontaneous outbursts. The sculptor Claes Oldenburg was almost as well known as Alan Kaprow, the inventor of happenings, for his productions of *The Street* and *The Store*. Happenings were multimedia events, incorporating music, film, paint, dance, and anything else that could be brought to bear. They were exuberant, intense, and unstructured.

The connection of happenings with abstract expressionist theories, with existentialism, and with the absurd is to be expected. Happenings were characterized by the abstract expressionist emphasis on action, spontaneity, immediacy, energy, and the intensity of the moment. Conceptual artists—whose work is not a product, but a production—naturally responded to happenings. Just as the abstract expressionists wished to break down the distinctions between art and life, happenings sometimes broke down all the traditional distinctions—such as those between painting and sculpture, music and drama, and theater and architecture.

Dance

MODERN DANCE

Martha Graham: Movement and Myth

In 1900 Isadora Duncan (1878–1927) began to free dance from the rules of ballet. She was joined by Doris Humphrey, Ted Shawn, Ruth St. Denis, and her student Martha Graham (b. 1893), who created a powerful body of works interpreting Greek tragedy, particularly the stories of great women, such as Phaedra. Her *Night Journey* (1958; Figure 19-54) is an interpretation of Sophocles's *Oedipus Rex*. Graham's explorations of Greek myth reflect an interest in Freudian and Jungian psychology and imply an exploration of the dream state, which also inspired surrealism.

Alvin Ailey

Alvin Ailey's American classic, *Revelations* (Figure 19-55), first produced in 1960, draws its subject

Figure 19-54
Martha Graham. *Night Journey*. 1958. (Martha Graham Studio.)

matter from black spirituals. Performed by an almost entirely black company, it is an electrifying dance in three large sections. "Rocka My Soul in the Bosom of Abraham," the finale, inevitably invites rhythmic participation from the audience. *Revelations* narrates sketches of the lives of blacks from the time of slavery, and the theme of endurance and faith is central to the story. But the story is not told directly; it is implied. And the movement is shaped by the powerful black spiritual music.

Alwin Nickolais

Alwin Nikolais, with Murray Louis, created a dance theater using a wide variety of stage props, unusual and futuristic costuming, electronic music, and dramatic lighting. Nikolais's dances ignore narrative: they present movement in the abstract, but explicit movement that is obviously shaped and planned. Nikolais avoids chance events and untrained dancers;

Figure 19-56
Alwin Nikolais. *Imago.* (By permission of Nikolais Dance
Theatre; photo, Robert Sosenko.)

his approach produces an exciting theatrical experience. The emotions we experience while watching
these dances must be like those which Malevich
valued in his suprematist compositions: they are
related to the dance alone, and not to any suggestions
of life or experience beyond the dance. Nickolais's
Imago is shown in Figure 19-56.

Twyla Tharp

Twyla Tharp (b. 1939) avoids narratives and concentrates on movement as interpretation of music. Her
most popular pieces have used black jazz, such as the
music of Fats Waller and Jelly Roll Morton (*Eight Jelly
Rolls* is shown in Figure 19-57), and the music of the
white cornetist and pianist Bix Beiderbecke in *Bix
Pieces*. Tharp's dancers sometimes appear very casual,
undulating against one another in what seem to be
improvised passages. Some of her dances contain
"cadenzas" in which the dancers work from a basic
premise, but improvise as jazz musicians do. Yet the
overall concept is tightly controlled and completely
imagined.

Figure 19-57
Above: Twyla Tharp. *Eight Jelly Rolls.* 1981. (By permission of Twyla Tharp Dance Foundation; photo, Tony Russell.)

Figure 19-58
Below: Bolshoi Ballet, *Don Quixote.* (Society for Cultural Relations with the U.S.S.R., London.)

BALLET

Modern ballet derives from French traditions continued in Russia and carried on by the Bolshoi in Moscow. (A performance of *Don Quixote* by the Bolshoi is shown in Figure 19-58.) Some of the best-known dancers and choreographers in modern ballet in the United States and other western countries are Russians who defected: George Balanchine (he defected in 1924), Rudolf Nureyev (in 1961), Natalia Makarova (in 1970), Mikhail Baryshnikov (in 1973), and Valery Panov (in 1974).

One of the legacies of Balanchine's work is an emphasis on the priority of movement over narrative. The Royal Ballet in London, directed by Kenneth Macmillan, has produced sumptuous stagings of dramatic narratives, such as *Manon* and *Mayerling,* in which the dancing is sometimes subservient to the story. But Balanchine was careful to avoid such staging and to concentrate closely on the most demanding, most refined movement, making it primary in his compositions. *Agon,* for example, is danced in simple leotards.

The style of classical ballet dominates the Bolshoi. But some ballets, such as *Mutations* (Figure 19-59), by Glen Tetley for the Netherlands Dance Theater, show the influence of modern dance. They draw their movements from sources other than the basic vocabulary of classical ballet. In *Mutations,* the movement is designed to be expressive in intense psychosexual ways. Costuming has given way to nudity, as in sculpture. Movement is primary; the lavish sets and costumes of traditional ballet have been eliminated.

Figure 19-59
Glenn Tetley. *Mutations,* Netherlands Dance
Theater. 1970. Shown are Anger Licher and
Gerard Lemaitre. (By permission of
Netherlands Dance Theater; photo, Anthony
Crickmay.)

Music

APPROACHING THE TONAL CONTINUUM

Music, like the other arts, has experienced many movements and many styles in the postwar years. The twelve-tone revolution continued, with the legacy of Schoenberg and Webern making itself felt even in popular music. But certain new influences began to be felt as well. The twelve-tone system depended on a tone row with twelve fixed-pitch tones corresponding to those in the octave. The techniques of establishing the row of tones, reversing them, and playing them upside down or in parts resemble the techniques of cubism and thus were analytic and striking. But with the advent of electronic techniques in composition and with the growing interest in nonwestern music, some composers began to think in terms of sound as a continuum and of the possibilities of pitch as being infinite.

ELECTRONIC MUSIC

Electronic instruments and tape recorders revolutionized both serious music and popular music. The electric guitar made it possible for three or four musicians to emulate an orchestra. The tape recorder and synthesizer made it possible for serious composers to break away from the limitations of conventional tonality and treat all tone as a continuum. The period 1952–1962 saw intense experimentation in the Columbia-Princeton Electronic Music Laboratories and the Magnetic Tape Music Project in New York, with John Cage. The avant-garde composer Karlheinz Stockhausen worked in the Electronic Music Studio in Cologne; and there were similar studios in Milan, Brussels, and other European cities.

Such experiments are analogous to the efforts of the abstract expressionists to emphasize sensa, the details of immediate perception. Just as Pollock, Kline, Rothko, and others worked to make us aware of the power of line and color in and of themselves, Cage, Stockhausen, and others worked to make us hear sound in a new way.

JOHN CAGE: ZEN INDETERMINACY

John Cage (b. 1912) has been deeply influenced by Zen Buddhism. He has said that his "purpose is to eliminate purpose," by which he means that his music is open to the forces of chance. For him all sounds, including random coughs and movements in an audience, are part of the composition. The distinction between art and life becomes blurred in some of Cage's works. In the 1940s and early 1950s he was noted for his compositions for prepared piano—an instrument in which the hammers were altered, the strings were changed in pitch, and objects were placed on the strings to change the character of the sound. But for Cage the most important point was that music could be made using any sounds the composer chose, not just the twelve tones in the conventional diatonic scale. By rejecting fixed pitch and tone, Cage introduced his audiences to noise and its potential for use in composition. Several European composers used everyday sounds in an approach they called "musique concrète."

EDGARD VARÈSE

Edgard Varèse (1883–1965) was among the pioneers in the use of taped sounds. His *Ionisations* (1933) used percussion and instrumental sound for their own sake. But when tape recording became a possibility, he experimented eagerly, producing *Deserts* in 1954, when he was seventy-one. It begins with a peal of bells, followed by a pointillistic use of horns, trumpets, and percussion instruments. The texture of sound is open, anticipatory, and apprehensive. The piece is scored for orchestra and tape recorder, which appears three distinct times, acting antiphonally to the orchestral sounds. At first, the tape is broad in spectrum, with considerable "white noise" (a hiss: all audible tones sounded at once). In its last appearance it seems to be offering an electronic interpretation of the instrumental sections, with distinct "notes" and durations.

KRZYSZTOF PENDERECKI

The Soviet Union and other communist nations have been exceptionally conservative in their music. Not only is experimentation frowned on, but those who write atonal or synthesized music can expect expulsion from the Society of Composers. Some of the most important Russian composers, such as Sergey Prokofiev (1891–1953) and Dmitry Shostakovich (1906–1975), were severely criticized for producing works that were considered depressing or beyond the understanding of the masses. If such a standard had been maintained in the rest of the world, it would have effectively stifled three generations of avant-garde music. Predictably, Russian art adheres to·a standard of ideologically approved realism.

In the more liberal atmosphere of Poland, Krzysztof Penderecki (b. 1933) has produced a body of important work. As a young boy he saw the Nazis round up and take away Jews in his own town. In some of his compositions the emotional reservoir of his experiences is apparent. *Dies Irae (Auschwitz Oratorio;* 1967) uses a subtle irony in setting parts of the Christian mass to commemorate the Jews killed by a special form of Christian fanaticism. *Threnody for the Victims of Hiroshima* (1960) is scored for fifty-two strings (a B-52 dropped the bomb) which often play at their highest pitch. The opening tone (a high B) is chilling, as if the earth were protesting. The intensity of the piece is psychologically much greater than its duration of only 9½ minutes. Alluding to electronic technique, the instruments sometimes play a "band" of tones—from B flat to B sharp, say—so that we hear not the precise tone, but rather all the tones associated with it. The result is a throbbing, resonant quality that deeply underscores the subject matter of the composition.

GEORGE CRUMB

Among those who have stayed with traditional means of composition, George Crumb (b. 1929) has created a genuinely modern statement that, like Penderecki's shows awareness of electronic techniques. Crumb has used texts of poems by Federico García Lorca, the Spanish poet who was assassinated in 1936, as the basis of a cycle of songs. *Night Music I* (1963), *Madrigals* (consisting of four books composed between 1965 and 1969), *Night of the Four Moons* (1969), and *Ancient Voices of Children* (1970) use Lorca's texts. Crumb was sympathetic to Lorca's emphasis on basic values relating to the earth and on deep primal feelings, which imply a starting point for the restructuring of human feeling in art. "Duende," a Spanish concept of primal feeling—a dark, soulful spirit rising from the earth—inspired Lorca. Crumb responds by using flamenco rhythms and dark-timbred vocal passages in his work: screams, whispers, and a variety of instruments— oboe, harp, mandolin, drums, bells, and others. *Ancient Voices of Children* uses an amplified piano, into which the soprano sometimes sings and whispers, creating eerie, primitive effects. The songs have an intensely dramatic, psychological quality, depending occasionally on vocalise (a vocalized passage without words). A boy soprano also sings offstage.

Late-Twentieth-Century Music

1. Listen to an electronic composition by Ussachevsky, Babbitt, Varèse, Erb, Subotnick, Stockhausen, or any other contemporary composer. Try to list the different kinds of sounds you hear (this is difficult), such as glissandos; percussive sound; long, sustained sounds; soft, loud, or sudden sounds; and reverberating or echoing sounds. Try to identify what the composer's resources are. Is the piece you listened to emotionally expressive? Is sound its subject matter? Some available recordings are listed in a special section of the Schwann catalog. Desto 6466 has Ussachevsky's *Sonic Contours;* Columbia M-32741 contains Subotnick's *4 Butterflies;* and CRI 268 has Varèse's *Deserts,* Babbitt's *Vision and Prayer,* and Davidowsky's *Synchronisms 5.* Also, some individual works by Erb and Stockhausen are available on Nonesuch recordings.

2. Listen to Penderecki's *Threnody for the Victims of Hiroshima,* available on RCA-Victrola VICS-1239. If you did not know the title, could you tell what the subject matter is? Knowing that there are allusions within the composition to the B-52 that dropped the bomb, is it possible to "hear" the sound of an airplane in the piece? Is there an explosion? Could you call this program music?

3. Listen to George Crumb's *Ancient Voices of Children* (Nonesuch 71255). First, listen only to the music without reading Lorca's poems. Then read the poems while listening to the music. Which of the poems is most successfully interpreted in the music? Which is interpreted least successfully? What musical techniques are most appropriate for interpreting Lorca's poems? How different would the musical experience be if you had no knowledge of the poems? To what extent is sound part of the subject matter of this composition?

The last song is set to the following text:

My silken heart
is filled with light,
lost bells,
lilies and bees.
And I will go many miles—
farther than these mountains,
farther than those seas,
beyond the stars,
to ask Christ
the Lord to give me back
my ancient soul of a child.

Technically, *Ancient Voices of Children* is not daunting. Crumb is very direct, expressive, and controlled. Yet he does not depend on traditional tonal structures. Instead, he uses modern concepts of the tonal continuum, including sounds as part of his work. The coloration is emotional, and many of the songs create a distinct mood. Lorca's texts generally control that mood by defining the emotional range and establishing limits, within which Crumb moves easily. The subject matter of the songs goes beyond the texts, but includes the emotions implied by them as expressed through the music.

POPULAR MUSIC

Jazz and Bop

Bop, born during the Second World War, was influential in the 1950s. It delighted in musical complexity and produced several great saxophonists: Lester "Prez" Young, Flip Phillips, Sonny Stitt, Lee Konitz, the great Charlie "Yardbird" Parker, and—in the 1960s—Eric Dolphy and John Coltrane. Other great performers included Dizzy Gillespie and Miles Davis (trumpet), Max Roach (drums), and Art Tatum, Lenny Tristano, and Thelonious Monk (piano). Yet postwar jazz was dominated by the saxophone: first the improvisatory ingenuity of Charlie Parker, from Kansas City; then the saxophone wars of Jazz at the Philharmonic, which toured throughout the 1950s; and finally the huge, free-form explorations of Coltrane, whose theme was mother Africa.

Jazz in the 1930s and 1940s was generally designed for dancing, but bop was designed for listening. That change produced subtleties, especially when bop musicians played to impress one another. The result was that, to be appreciative, an audience had to be sophisticated: "hip" to what was happening. Jazz lost its large audience and became a kind of chamber music played in small clubs like Birdland, the Five Spot, and the Jazz Gallery in New York. These clubs were intimate and filled with informed listeners. Miles Davis and his quartet brought avid listeners to these clubs. Some players insisted that they were creating a black classical music.

John Coltrane, particularly in his album *Africa/Brass* and in tunes such as "A Love Supreme," demonstrates one natural evolution of the expressive potential of jazz. In *Africa*, recorded in 1961, Coltrane used western instruments, including french horns and other brasses, but he began with African rhythms, expressed with two basses and percussion. His own saxophone lead is a lugubrious wail, an expressive call—as if across the sea—to mother Africa. The music is filled with complex polyrhythms and adventurous dissonances, which have an expressive effect. The rising tide of black consciousness in the 1960s found expression in Coltrane's music, which rides waves of intense emotion unlike anything heard in jazz before. Coltrane demonstrated that when not constrained by prescribed chord changes or other artificial formal demands, jazz could be as expressive as any modern music. He found the source of that expression deep in jazz: the yearning after African roots and the memory of the suffering of African forebears.

Rock: The Mass Appeal

When jazz began to acquire the complexity of bop, it lost its general audience. Rock music found a popular audience when Bill Haley and His Comets produced "Rock Around the Clock," featured in the 1955 film *The Blackboard Jungle*. The film is about violence and rebelliousness in city schools; symbolically, in one scene a teacher's collection of jazz recordings is ruthlessly destroyed. "Rock Around the Clock" gave the movement its name and also contributed certain elements of style: extremely loud music based on blues chords, insistent 4/4 rhythm with loud accents on the offbeat, and simple, repetitious lyrics.

Elvis Presley appeared on the scene in 1953. Many of his most popular songs were written by a black singer, Otis Blackwell, whose voice was remarkably like Presley's. The explicitly sexual nature of Presley's singing and his gyrations on stage made him immensely popular with people his own age, but he was completely rejected by people in their thirties and forties. It was the beginning of a youth revolution which swept the western world and which used rock music as its universal language. Rock is a prime example of a subversive art form. The title of a Janis Joplin song—"Sex, Drugs, and Rock and Roll"—was a universal message throughout the 1960s. Timothy Leary and others were telling young people to "tune in, turn on, and drop out." To some extent, the same message was delivered in rock music.

The Beatles

The 1960s and 1970s were dominated by an English group, the Beatles: John Lennon (killed in 1980), George Harrison, Paul McCartney, and Ringo Starr. They first appeared in America in 1964, toured until 1966, and then proceeded to make one smash album after another, using multiple track effects that could not be duplicated on the road. *Sgt. Pepper's Lonely Hearts Club Band*, *The Magical Mystery Tour* (both 1967), *The White Album* (1968), and *Abbey Road* (1969) are still influencing popular music. The Beatles' music was characterized by pleasing melody and sometimes complex lyrics, and it was available to a large audience. Their own experiments with drugs are reflected in tunes such as "Lucy in the Sky with Diamonds," which alludes to taking LSD. *Sgt. Pepper's Lonely Hearts Club Band* uses the special electronic effects of a synthesizer, unusual combinations of instruments (such as harpsichord and sitar), and musical parodies ("When I'm Sixty-Four").

The album began as an effort to capture some of Paul McCartney's memories of his childhood in Liverpool. "Strawberry Fields" referred to the local Salvation Army. All the songs that eventually found their way into the album had a personal significance for Paul, George, or John. The concept of a unified album of interrelated songs was not completely novel, although it was unusual. The lyrics were printed on the inner sleeve, and novelty items, such as a false mustache, were included in the record jacket, increasing the wackiness of the effect. Yet serious critics asserted that the album had made musical history. The record was treated more as a classical song cycle than as a popular vehicle. *The New York Times Book Review* claimed that it was the beginning of a renaissance of song.

The Beatles' experiments with LSD—which they insist they ended when LSD was made illegal—achieved two things. They brought the group closer together at a time when it was close to fragmenting entirely under the strain of adulation and business disagreements. Second, they introduced a surrealistic, dreamlike quality to the Beatles' songs which placed them in the mainstream of an important artistic development. The "tangerine trees," "marmalade skies," and "newspaper taxis" were only some of their surrealistic visions.

In 1967, after the *Sgt. Pepper* album, the Beatles replaced LSD with a commitment to eastern religion and transcendental meditation. Turning from drug use to the "emptiness" of meditation and the practice of an eastern religion became the "way" for many Beatle fans. The spiritual benefits proved limited, however, and with the exception of George Harrison, the Beatles abandoned such religious commitments. They disbanded in 1970, having, as John Lennon was to say, given everything—"themselves"—for ten years. When he was asked to get the group together one more time, he complained that they would simply be "four rusty old men."

Rock and Protest

In the 1960s rock music expressed a wide range of protest. Janis Joplin and Jimmy Hendrix—who, like many other rock stars, died young as a result of drug use—expressed a general protest against the mainstream of culture in America, which was threatening to send young people to fight in Vietnam, a war they

---

LISTENING KEY

Popular Music

1. Listen to a recording by Charlie Parker or John Coltrane. Establish what seem to be the expressive qualities of the music. Which instruments and which passages seem most expressive? Does the music seem to come close to losing control at any time?

2. Listen to a Beatles album. Which of the songs is most melodic? Are the lyrics serious? Whimsical? Political? What aspects of the song would specifically appeal to a young audience? Which would appeal to an older audience?

3. Choose a contemporary rock group that you feel is currently advancing the genre. Using a representative tune, demonstrate how the group you have chosen is taking a novel approach to the musical qualities of melody, harmony, rhythm, dynamics, lyrics, tone color, and sound.

could not understand. Groups such as Country Joe and the Fish, the Grateful Dead, and the Mommas and the Poppas, as well as Bob Dylan, Simon and Garfunkel, Joan Baez, Arlo Guthrie, and others, protested the war. The huge rock concert at Woodstock, New York, where 300,000 young people came together in 1969, marked the peak of both antiwar protest and rock music.

Summary

The abstract expressionists, influenced by existentialist philosophy and literature, particularly the work of the French writers Jean-Paul Sartre and Albert Camus, translated painting into action. Their gestures on canvas were existentialist moments, personal and agonized statements. The abstract expressionists were champions of sensa in painting, the perception of line, form, and color in the abstract. The influence of Freud— dreams and the unconscious— continued to be felt in the work of painters, photographers, filmmakers, and musicians. The idea that the unconscious reveals our innermost nature produced an interest in dreams as well as an interest in drugs.

The years of protest, particularly in America, coincided with a burgeoning young population which expressed itself in pop art and popular music. The black protest of the 1960s produced a new consciousness of African roots, which in turn was expressed in jazz, particularly the work of John Coltrane in the mid-1960s. The views of feminist groups, war protestors, and others were all heard in rock music. Electronics transformed serious music, leading to experiments with the sensa of music: pure sound. Social issues found their way into serious music as well; in the music of Krzysztof Penderecki, for example, there are references to the Nazi concentration camps and to the bombing of Hiroshima. The trend toward emphasizing the elements of a medium, such as the photographic values of a photograph and the painterly values of a painting, is visible in the experiments of the superrealists of the late 1970s. The era has produced almost unparalleled ferment in the arts, reflecting a similar social ferment; the years since World War II have witnessed the discovery of the extent of the horrors of the Nazi concentration camps, the Vietnamese war and protests against it, racist and sexist injustices, and the fear of nuclear holocaust. The arts remain indomitable, inexhaustible.

Concepts in Chapter 19

The period following World War II was marked by the tensions of the cold war, disillusionment over the holocaust in Nazi Germany, and fears engendered by the explosion of the first atom bomb.

The expansion of the communist nations—in particular China— changed the balance of power between east and west.

Social protest centering on the Vietnamese war and on nuclear testing and the threat of nuclear war has been significant during the period both in Europe and in the United States.

Abstract expressionism developed in New York right after the war; it was informed to a large extent by the existentialist thought of Sartre and Camus, who wrote in response to the disillusionment of Europe during and after the war.

The abstract expressionists saw painting as a gesture —an act that defined existence and an attack on the canvas—rather than as an effort to represent a scene or a figure.

Reactions against abstract expressionism in the late 1950s and early 1960s took the form of a return to realistic approaches to painting as well as the amusing explorations of pop art and op art.

Pop art often blurred the distinction between art and reality.

Pop art made extensive use of prefabricated images drawn from popular media, including advertisements, films, and comic books.

Realism in painting never disappeared completely during the postwar period, but it became most significant in the late 1960s and the 1970s.

The superrealists depended largely on the aesthetic established by contemporary photography.

Sculpture has continued its experiments in space, bulk, and form and has also continued in certain constructivist directions.

Earth sculpture and environmental sculpture, such as the work of Robert Smithson and Christo, have helped redefine sculpture in our time.

Superrealist sculpture often produces confusions between the work of art and its environment.

Superrealist sculpture is particularly suited to political statement, both in the east and in the west.

The monumentality of Nazi architecture of the late

1930s has been a powerful influence on the architecture of the period.

The international style evolved into the glass and steel skyscrapers of Mies van der Rohe.

The Georges Pompidou Center represents a development in high tech.

Among the current developments in architecture are spaces calculated to have a psychological effect, including the awe inspired by futuristic art.

Modern photography has evolved a number of styles in response to developments in modern art; among them are efforts to make us aware of the photograph itself, rather than what it represents.

The post-World War II era has seen relatively few new techniques in film (color may be the most important), but it has produced directors who have created important oeuvres: Bergman, Fellini, and Truffaut.

The power of film to deliver messages of social protest and to evoke social concern has developed in this period.

Existentialist thought has been powerfully expressed in the literature of the period—in the works of Sartre and Camus, as well as in certain novels by Hemingway and Faulkner.

The basis of existentialist thought lies in the rubric of Sartre: existence precedes essence.

The literature of the beat generation of the late 1950s and the 1960s represents a postromantic celebration of inherent creativity.

Beat literature was inspired to some extent by Zen Buddhism, which promoted the value of "emptiness" and nondirected thought; Zen produced a "beatific" state based on meditation.

Theater in the round and theaters in which the stage extends into the audience have largely supplanted the traditional theater, with proscenium and arch.

Schechner's environmental theater and Grotowski's poor theater attempted to rob the audience of its sense of comfort and aesthetic distance.

Happenings were a form of drama which involved the audience and the environment in activities that blurred the distinction between theater and life.

Modern dance has flowered in the second half of the century, producing numerous innovators, such as Martha Graham, Alvin Ailey, Alwin Nikolais, and Twyla Tharp.

Ballet has developed a number of modern variations, particularly those of Kenneth Macmillan, George Balanchine, and the Bolshoi Ballet.

In music, electronic developments and novel approaches to instrumentation have made it possible to treat all sound as possessing potential for tonal use.

Modern jazz, particularly as it has been influenced by bop and other developments, has become refined, complex, and expressive.

Rock music has captured the popular audiences, as jazz once did.

Rock music has been largely subversive, as jazz was before it, attempting to subvert the values of the young; it represents a form of protest against an official social order.

The tensions of the period are immense, but the arts demonstrate a capacity for inexhaustibility and continued vitality.

Suggested Readings

Ashton, Dore. *American Art since 1945*. New York: Oxford, 1979.

———. *The New York School: A Cultural Reckoning*. New York: Viking, 1972.

Austin, William. *Music in the Twentieth Century*. New York: Norton, 1966.

Battcock, Gregory, ed. *Super Realism*. New York: Dutton, 1975.

Beaver, Frank. *On Film: A History of the Motion Picture*. New York: McGraw-Hill, 1983.

Brockett, Oscar G., and Robert B. Findlay. *Century of Innovation: A History of European and American Theatre and Drama since 1870*. Englewood Cliffs, N.J.: Prentice-Hall, 1973.

Brown, Milton W., Sam Hunter, John Jacobus, Naomi Rosenblum, and David M. Sokol. *American Art*. Englewood Cliffs, N.J.: Prentice-Hall, 1979.

Buettner, Stewart. *American Art Theory: 1945–1970*. Ann Arbor, Mich.: UMI Research Press, 1981.

Clarke, Mary, and Clement Crisp. *The History of Dance*. New York: Crown, 1981.

Cowie, Peter. *Eighty Years of Cinema*. New York: Barnes, 1977.

Curtis, William J. *Modern Architecture since 1900*. Englewood Cliffs, N.J.: Prentice-Hall, 1983.

Goodyear, Frank, Jr. *Contemporary American Realism since 1960.* Boston: New York Graphic Society, 1981.

Gridley, Mark C. *Jazz Styles.* Englewood Cliffs, N.J.: Prentice-Hall, 1978.

Johnson, Paul. *Modern Times.* London: Macmillan, 1983.

Kerouac, Jack. *On the Road.* Scott Donaldson, ed. (text and criticism). New York: Viking, 1979.

Krauss, Rosalind E. *Passages in Modern Sculpture.* Cambridge, Mass.: M.I.T., 1977.

Lucie-Smith, Edward. *Art in the Seventies.* Ithaca, N.Y.: Cornell, 1980.

———. *Late Modern: The Visual Arts since 1945.* 2d ed. New York: Praeger, 1976.

Malcolm, Janet. *Diana and Nikon: Essays on the Aesthetic of Photography.* Boston: David Godine, 1980.

Mast, Gerald. *A Short History of the Movies.* 3d ed. Indianapolis: Bobbs-Merrill, 1981.

Meyer, Leonard B. *Music, the Arts, and Ideas.* Chicago: University of Chicago Press, 1967.

Norman, Philip. *Shout: The Beatles in Their Generation.* New York: Simon and Schuster, 1981.

Real, Really Real, Superreal: Directions in Contemporary American Realism. San Antonio, Tex.: San Antonio Museum, 1981.

Roose-Evans, James. *Experimental Theatre.* New York: Avon, 1970.

Salzman, Eric. *Twentieth-Century Music: An Introduction.* Englewood Cliffs, N.J.: Prentice-Hall, 1974.

Sandler, Irving. *The New York School: The Painters and Sculptors of the Fifties.* New York: Harper & Row, 1978.

Sorrell, Walter. *Dance in Its Time.* Garden City, N.Y.: Doubleday, Anchor Books, 1981.

Stangos, Nikos, ed. *Concepts of Modern Art.* 2d ed. New York: Harper & Row, 1974.

Waldman, Max. *Waldman on Theater.* Garden City, N.Y.: Doubleday, 1971.

GLOSSARY

Abstract expressionism A twentieth-century artistic movement in which the image was abstracted from nature, but not always recognizably. Often, the distortion was so great that only the title could establish the original subject. The style is profoundly expressionistic, portraying the deep emotional feelings of the artist.

Academy A professional association that maintained artistic standards. The French Academy was established formally in 1632 by the king, but it had existed informally earlier. In other countries, similar academies developed, both for the arts and for literature. The purpose of such academies was usually to preserve existing values in the arts; the work of radical artists was often rejected.

Action painting A style of painting of the New York school in the 1950s in which the actions of the painter, almost like dance gestures before the canvas, helped dictate the ultimate look of the canvases.

Aerial perspective The use of color—lighter tones for nearer objects—to produce the illusion of three dimensions in painting.

Aesthetics The philosophy of art.

Agnosticism The belief that no genuine knowledge of God is possible.

Agora A marketplace in an ancient Greek city.

Allegory A representation in which a person, place, or thing stands for an abstract value or for another person, place, or thing. Dante is noted for his use of allegory. (See Chapter 10.)

Animism A belief in the spirit world; the doctrine that all objects—particularly natural objects, such as trees—are inhabited by spirits.

Antinomies Arguments that can be equally well defended and attacked. (See the section on Kant in Chapter 16.)

Apse The semicircular recess at the end of a church. It usually contains the altar.

Arch A curved architectural construction spanning an opening. The Roman arch is rounded on top, while the gothic and Islamic arches are pointed.

Architectonic Resembling an architectural design; inspired by architecture.

Arête The Homeric term for personal honor, an important Greek value.

Aria A solo vocal passage in an opera or other composition in which many voices participate. It is usually expressive and moving.

Arianism The belief that Christ was mortal and that his body did not ascend to heaven after the resurrection.

Ars antiqua The "old style" in music, referring to polyphonic music used in church liturgies in the twelfth and thirteenth centuries. (See Chapter 10.)

Ars nova The "new art" in music, referring to the beginnings of monophonic music, in which a single melodic line is dominant, supported by chordal notes in other voices.

Art nouveau A twentieth-century artistic movement greatly influenced by the natural forms of plants. It was a fluid, line-dominated style that took special pleasure in the curve, often appearing in architectural details made of wood, glass, and metal.

Asymmetry Lack of balance in an artistic composition. Symmetrical compositions give the viewer a sense of balance, completeness, and relaxation. Asymmetrical compositions produce a sense of unbalance and of emotional tension and demand an aesthetic resolution—sometimes to be provided by the viewer.

Atonal music Music in which no tone is dominant and which therefore is not in a key.

Avant-garde A group of artists—usually highly experimental artists—who are ahead of their time. Literally, the term means "forward guard."

Ba   The Egyptian word for "spirit."

Ballad   A narrative song, usually with a traditional tune and a refrain.

Baptistry   A separate, usually octagonal, building next to a church where baptisms take place.

Baroque   The artistic style characterized by the exuberance of Bernini, who has been credited with being one of its inventors. Baroque art is florid, intense, dynamic, asymmetrical, and grand. It is often marked by a confusion of genres designed to have a powerful psychological effect on the viewer. (See Chapter 14.)

Basilica   A large meeting room, such as those in which the Christians met during the Roman period. Early Christian churches were built in the style of the basilica, but with a wide aisle on each side.

Bas-relief   (Pronounced "bah-relief".) Sculpture which is neither freestanding nor completely carved away from the background.

Bauhaus design   An extremely simple design associated with the Bauhaus school, under the direction of Walter Gropius. His dictum that "less is more" expresses the core of this approach to design.

Ben-ben   In Egyptian religion, the mound from which the first god rose. It was the model for the first pyramid.

Bharata natya   Indian dance drama.

Blank verse   Unrhymed iambic pentameter verse: "To be, or not to be. That is the question. / Whether 'tis nobler in the mind to suffer / The slings and arrows of outrageous fortune, / Or to take arms against a sea of troubles, / And by opposing, end them." (*Hamlet*, Act 3, Scene 1, lines 55–59.)

Blues   Emotionally expressive music, closely related to jazz. It is based on special blues "scales" and chord progressions within a 12-bar format.

Bodhisattva   A Buddhist saint.

Bop   A form of jazz developed in the 1940s. It was extremely cerebral, well thought out, and complex, developing unusual and unexpected harmonies built on melodic lines which were not "singable" or popular.

Bust   A sculptural representation of a figure, including the head, the shoulders, and part of the chest.

Buttress   A support for an architectural structure, usually on the outside of the building.

Cadence   A tonal structure in music which leads to a sense of conclusiveness or finality.

Calvinism   The theological system developed by John Calvin. It stressed determinism in human behavior—a loss of the freedom of will—predestination, and the guilt of all humankind.

Camera obscura   Literally, "dark room." The camera obscura was a box fitted with a lens and a viewing panel that created an upside-down image of everything in front of the lens. It was well known in the fifteenth century.

Campanile   The bell tower of a romanesque church.

Cantata   An extended musical composition featuring a text sung by soloists and chorus.

Canzona   An instrumental composition derived from the French chanson.

Capital   The usually decorative top of a pier or pillar in architecture.

Cella   An interior space in a temple, usually designed to hold an image.

Chamber music   Music played by a small group —a trio or quartet, for example—meant to be heard in a room rather than a concert hall.

Chanson   A French song popular during the Renaissance.

Ch'i   The underlying spirit or vitality of a scene as revealed in a Chinese landscape painting.

Chiaroscuro   The sharp contrast of light and dark elements in a painting.

Chord   Several tones sounded together.

Choreographer   A composer of dances.

Chromaticism   In music, the use of "color," or unexpected sharps and flats that would not normally appear in the base key of the composition.

Cliché-verre   A photograph made from a glass-plate negative.

Clip   A section of filmed material.

Closet drama   A play intended to be read rather than performed.

Coffer   A recessed section in a ceiling. (See Figure 5-12.)

Collage   An assembled work of art. The French word "coller" means "to glue"; most collages are made of various materials that are glued to the picture surface.

Color field painting   A twentieth-century artistic development exemplified by the work of Hans Hofmann and Mark Rothko. Large areas of color interact with one another in unexpected ways, and the sensa of the colors and their interactions are the subject matter of the painting.

Comedy   Drama which is light and amusing, usually ending in a marriage. The comedy of manners criticizes society in order to encourage improvements and reform. Farce is raucous comedy, often relying on slapstick "violence" and improbable situations.

Commedia dell'arte   Stylized Italian drama performed by wandering players. It was largely unwritten, improvised farce relying on a body of stock characters, such as Harlequin. It was at its height in the seventeenth century.

Conceptual art   Art in which the idea which underlies it is as important as the work itself. The idea underlying conceptual art is perhaps the most important part of its subject matter.

Concertato An Italian composition featuring conflict among the instruments or voices resulting in a musical resolution.

Consonance A relaxing effect produced by simultaneously sounded musical tones, sometimes thought of as pleasing harmony.

Constructivism A sculptural movement of the twentieth century influenced by machines and open-work structures. Constructivist sculptures are sculptures not of mass or weight, but of space and movement. They were influenced by engineering constructions. (See the section on Pevsner and Gabo in Chapter 18.)

Contraposto A pose in which the axes of the shoulders and hips are opposed: if the right shoulder is raised, the left hip is raised. (See the section on Botticelli's *Birth of Venus* in Chapter 11.)

Corbeled roof A roof formed from stones (or sometimes wood blocks) which are laid stepwise; each successive course projects farther inward until the top courses meet.

Corinthian order One of the Greek architectural orders; it is elaborate and detailed. It was favored by the Romans and became associated with imperial grandeur. (See Figure 4-10.)

Council of Trent A Roman Catholic council which, in 1563, began the Counterreformation, which stressed a spiritual revival in religion. It was reflected almost immediately in religious art centering on emotional involvement and expression.

Counterpoint Music in which several different melodies are combined into a single harmonic texture.

Counterreformation The effort by the Roman Catholic church to combat the Protestant schism of the sixteenth century. Counterreformation art addressed the emotions of viewers and tried to move them toward the faith.

Cubism A twentieth-century artistic movement based on the analysis of visual forms from more than one point of view simultaneously. It grew from the work of Cézanne, but was developed by Picasso and Braque. It established a hierarchy of aesthetic values. Cubist paintings always refer to a subject drawn from life, although the viewer may need to know the title of a work in order to determine its subject.

Da capo aria An aria consisting of three parts (ABA) in which the first part is repeated.

Dada An artistic movement developed in Switzerland during World War I; it stressed nonsense in art. The dadaists were strongly opposed to the middle-class values of Europe, which they felt were largely materialistic, nationalistic, and selfish. These were the values that had led to the war. Nonsense was unintelligible to the middle classes, and thus dada ignored them.

Daguerreotype The process of producing photographs using salts of mercury to reveal an image on a prepared copper plate. Invented in 1839, it proved to be the first practical photographic method and spurred interest in photography all over the world. Also, a photograph produced in this manner.

Development In music, the exploration of thematic material previously stated in the exposition of a piece.

Dialectic In the Renaissance, dialectic was logic. In the work of Hegel—and then later in the work of Marx—dialectic was a process, both intellectual and social, by which a position is proposed, countered, re-formed, and re-presented. Each thesis has an antithesis; the "combat" between them produces a synthesis, which in turn becomes a new thesis. (See the section on Hegel in Chapter 16.)

Dialectical materialism A Marxist view opposing German idealism. Marx stressed not the ideal world of things which could not be perceived, but the real world of perception and matter. His views are the basis of modern communism.

Dissonance A tension-producing effect of simultaneously sounded musical tones whose harmonic relationship may be grating or irritating.

Distortion Stylization or exaggeration for artistic and emotional effect.

Divisionism Sometimes called "pointillism," a technique of painting in which separate dabs of paint "meld" into a color effect in the eyes of the viewer. (See the section on Seurat in Chapter 17.)

Dominant The note a fifth above the tonic note in a key. In the key of C it is G; in the key of F it is C; etc.

Doric order A Greek architectural order marked by restraint, clarity, and simplicity. (See Figure 4-10.)

Earth sculpture Twentieth-century sculpture in which the artist works directly on the surface of the earth rather than on a part of it (such as a marble slab).

Engraving A printing process in which a metal plate is incised with an image and then inked, after which the plate is wiped, leaving the ink in the incised grooves. Paper is then placed on the plate, and pressure is applied. The resulting print is highly detailed.

Enlightenment A period of intellectual development in France in the eighteenth century, characterized by a new secularism in which the values of the dark ages (largely theological) were replaced or augmented by values associated with learning and the advancement of science. The French philosophes, who helped Diderot produce his *Encyclopedia*, were its leaders.

En pointe In ballet, referring to dancing done on the tips of the toes.

Entasis The bulging in the center of Doric pillars; it is designed to "correct" the tendency of straight pillars to seem thinner in the center than at the top and bottom when viewed from a distance.

Epic A long poem centering on a single hero and often telling of significant wars and the beginnings of new empires. The most notable are by Homer, Virgil, and Milton.

Epicureanism A classical philosophy based on the view that happiness is the greatest good; it was a pleasure-based philosophy and valued sensual delight. Epicureanism was self-centered and rarely included the concept of public service.

Étude A study piece. Those by Chopin are among the best-known musical études.

Evangelists Matthew, Mark, Luke, and John, authors of the gospels of the New Testament. Their symbols are, respectively, an angel, a lion, a bull or an ox, and an eagle. These are also symbols associated with Christ.

Existentialism A twentieth-century philosophy which holds that a person is defined in terms of existence—his or her actions—rather than in terms of essence, or unobservable basic nature.

Exposition In music, the first presentation of thematic material, which is developed in the rest of the composition.

Expressionism A nineteenth-century artistic movement which continues today. It places a special value on the expression of the artist's emotions through the medium of painting or other art forms.

Facade The face or front of a building.

Fauvism The first twentieth-century movement in painting. The term was given in derision; it means "wild beasts." It refers to the fauves' intense and sometimes unlikely uses of color. (See Chapter 18.)

Fertility cult A religious cult celebrating the fertility of the land, animals, or people. Sexual distortions in ice age art sometimes reveal an interest in promoting or praising fertility.

Fêtes galantes Elegant entertainments for seventeenth- and eighteenth-century aristocrats in France. (See the section on Watteau in Chapter 15.)

Flat In music, to lower a note in pitch by half a tone, or the note so lowered.

Fluting Vertical incisions on Greek or Roman pillars; used to help maintain the visual sense of roundness when seen from a distance.

Foreshortening A technique in painting whereby a form, such as an arm or leg, is represented in such a way as to create the illusion that it extends or projects in space.

Form In all works of art, the final organization of individual elements. Formal analysis implies analysis of the relationships between the elements of a work and their organization into a whole.

"Form follows function" The theory that the architectural form of a building should reflect its function.

Formulaic art Art which follows a prescribed formula.

Found art Art which uses discarded materials for its composition.

Fresco A wall painting. The usual method of producing a fresco is to mix the paint with plaster and apply the wet plaster to the wall.

Frieze A section above the pillars of a Greek temple, usually running along the outside of the building and decorated with bas-relief carvings narrating a continuous action.

Fugue A contrapuntal musical composition in which a specific number of voices enter successively, imitating one another and developing a single theme.

Futurism An artistic movement, greatly influenced by speed and machines, that developed in Italy before World War I. (See Chapter 18.)

Futuristic Referring to a style of the future, usually to the changes which will be brought about by technology and which can only be imagined at the time.

Genre paintings Paintings of scenes from everyday life, without symbols or religious implications.

Gnosticism The beliefs of various early Christian cults which professed that special learning and knowledge were necessary to salvation.

Gothic A northern architectural style exemplified by the great cathedrals of the medieval period. It was based on the elongated ogival arch and was marked by considerable daring and risk taking.

Gregorian chant A choral chant having a single melodic line, sung in church. Gregorian chant was established by Pope Gregory I (540–604). (See Chapter 9.)

Guild An association of merchants, manufacturers, or businesspeople, somewhat like modern trade unions. The guilds were most powerful during the Renaissance in Italy.

Happenings Dramatic performances, popular in the 1960s, usually improvised and featuring a mixture of media and dadaist incoherence. They were usually one-time-only performances featuring amateurs and artists.

Hard-edge painting Painting in which flat color planes meet sharply defined edges, but with no outlining.

Hastas Hand gestures in Indian dance.

Heb-sed An ancient Egyptian ritual of renewal, when the king was expected to demonstrate his continued youthful vigor.

Hieroglyphics In Egypt and the Americas, a system of writing that used a picture script and was expressly designed to be understood by priests and others high in the social hierarchy.

Hinayana The lesser vehicle, or lesser way, of Buddhism.

Hindu trinity Brahma, the creator; Shiva, the destroyer; and Vishnu, the preserver.

Holy Roman Empire The titular rule of the western Roman empire since the time of Charlemagne. In the seventeenth century it was associated with the German principalities and had very little authority or power. It was a commonplace to say that the Holy Roman Empire was not holy, Roman, or an empire. The Hapsburgs' control of the empire survived in Germany. (See Chapter 14.)

Homophony Music in which the primary melodic line is supported by chordal harmony, as contrasted with polyphony.

Hue The attribute of colors that makes it possible to class them as red, yellow, or blue (the primary hues) or as green, orange, or violet (the secondary hues).

Icon A work of art that has a symbolic, usually religious, value. The term is usually used in reference to Byzantine painting, but has been extended to sculpture of several periods. Most frequently, it refers to images of the holy family.

Iconography The use of symbolic emblems within a painting to give it a meaning intelligible only to those who recognize the symbols. (See the section on van Eyck in Chapter 12.)

Idealism A German philosophical school, led by Immanuel Kant, that reinterpreted Platonic thought, which had placed the highest value on ideas rather than on things. Idealism is an antimaterialistic philosophy because it places a higher value on the pure world of thought than on sensory perceptions. (See Chapter 16.)

Idealization "Improving" the subject to make it correspond with an ideal form. Neoclassical art often idealizes its subject, whereas realistic art does not.

Illumination The colorful, often elaborate, decoration of a manuscript.

Impressionism An artistic movement of the second half of the nineteenth century which stressed the subjective responses of the artist. The painter concentrated on his or her impression of a scene, while the composer tried to represent in music an emotional impression of an event, object, or place. Impressionist paintings often look unfinished; they are concerned with the effects of light and color.

Ionic order One of the Greek architectural orders, marked by gracefulness and elegant decoration. (See Figure 4-10.)

Jazz An improvisational musical form developed by black American musicians at the turn of the century. It is an expressive form which depends on insinuating rhythms, flights of melodic and harmonic invention, and often great subtlety of effect. The instrumentation has been traditionally acoustic, including all families of instruments.

Junk art Art that uses trash or other discarded materials for its composition.

Ka The Egyptian word for "soul" or "essence."

Key A system of seven notes based on their relationship to the tonic, or keynote, which dominates that scale. The scale in the key of C is C-D-E-F-G-A-B-C.

Kithera A Greek musical instrument with seven strings, resembling a lyre.

Klangfarben Literally, "painting with tones." It is a twentieth-century technique in which instruments play different tones in succession and in different pitches. The effect is surprising because one cannot predict how the tones will be sounded. Since each tone is usually sounded alone, the technique results in a certain "bareness."

La Tène art Celtic art of the first and second centuries after Christ.

Leitmotif In music, a motif that is closely associated with a specific idea, person, or thing. When it is repeated, whatever it represents is supposed to be automatically suggested. The technique, a form of repetition, is also used in literature, particularly in the novels of Gustave Flaubert and James Joyce.

Lieder German art songs, especially of the nineteenth century. Perhaps the best known are those of Franz Peter Schubert, whose song cycles are among the greatest lieder ever composed. "Lieder" is the plural form; one art song is called a "lied."

Lithograph A print, usually black and white. Oil-based markers are used to draw an image on a stone or metal plate, and ink is applied that adheres only to the drawn lines. Damp paper is pressed against the plate to make the print.

Lyric A poem expressing deep personal emotion, usually suggestive of a song.

Madonna The Italian term for the Virgin Mary; literally, "my lady."

Madrigal A secular, usually unaccompanied, song for several voices singing contrapuntally. It was developed in the thirteenth century.

Mahayana The greater vehicle, or greater way, of Buddhism.

Manichaean A member of a mystery cult which taught that the universe had two opposing forces: good and evil. Manichaeans were on the side of good and fought against evil. Manichaeanism was also called "dualism" and led to fire worship.

Manipulated print   In photography, an image that is made up of combined negatives or negatives which have been significantly altered. It is not a "straight" print, made directly from a single negative.

Mannerism   An artistic style characterized by extreme distortion or stylization, often with visually contradictory elements and evoking an anticipated response in the viewer. It is a highly psychological approach to the arts because it depends on a shock effect. The term derives from "maniera," a word used by Vasari.

Mass   The gathering of Catholics and certain Protestants for the purpose of taking holy communion and celebrating the eucharist, the symbolic reenactment of the last supper of Christ. The mass is divided into segments, each of which has music and prayers specifically appropriate to it.

Mastaba   An Egyptian mud bench, often built in front of a home.

Melismatic composition   Usually a religious composition in which many musical notes are set to a single syllable of text.

Melody   A horizontal succession of single notes organized into a pattern.

Metaphor   An implied comparison between two unlike things, such as "You are a rose that blooms but once and fadeth away." As another example, in "Strether maneuvered between them," "maneuvered" is a military term, and so metaphorically it makes Strether a soldier. Metaphor is one of the most important literary devices.

Metaphysical poetry   Seventeenth-century poetry that, like mannerist painting, is energetic, distorted, psychological, and in some ways outrageous. Its chief device was the conceit (related to the metaphor), in which two otherwise unrelated things are forcibly compared with each other. (See the section on John Donne in Chapter 14.)

Metopes   Square panels, usually decorated with a narrative scene; they were part of the frieze on a Greek temple.

Mihrab   An arched doorway used in Islamic mosques to give an exact orientation toward Mecca.

Minaret   A tower from which the muezzin calls the faithful to prayer in Islamic communities.

Minimalism   A twentieth-century style in painting, sculpture, dance, and other media. Minimalist works rely on the least gesture, the least color, or the least line possible to achieve an effect. Minimalism is an extension of Gropius's doctrine that "less is more."

Minuet   A stately dance of aristocratic society in the seventeenth and eighteenth centuries.

Mobile sculpture   Portable, usually small sculpture, such as the ice age "Venus" of Willendorf. Also, sculpture that moves, as in the work of Alexander Calder (Chapter 19).

Modes   Scales in Greek music. Each mode was said to have a special emotional aura. Medieval church music used the Greek modes in chants and liturgical services.

Montage   A film technique of switching from one scene to another without warning. It was used by early filmmakers to build emotional tension in the audience. It is still popular.

Mosaic   A composition made of small pieces of material of various colors, such as stones or pieces of glass or ceramic.

Motet   A short, unaccompanied contrapuntal choral composition used in church services.

Movement   A section of a large musical composition, such as a symphony or concerto.

Muezzin   An Islamic priest who calls the faithful to prayer.

Mullions   Wooden or metal dividers of panes of glass in a window.

Muqarna   Downward-projecting forms in Islamic architecture in which bricks are layered one over the other.

Mystery cults   Religious groups of ancient Greece and the period shortly before and after the time of Christ. The core of a cult was a group of mysteries that were slowly revealed to initiates as they progressed more deeply in the religion.

Mysticism   Belief in communion with the divine through contemplation, meditation, and intuition.

Myth   A traditional narrative concerning ostensibly historical events or explaining natural phenomena or the practices or beliefs of a people. Greek and Roman myths are stories of gods and goddesses such as Zeus, Apollo, Venus, and Athena. All cultures have myths, which act as repositories of wisdom or express religous values. The psychologist Carl Jung suggested that a culture's myths are its "collective unconscious" and thus are of preeminent cultural value.

Nave   The long body of a church, situated on an east-west axis. The term comes from the Latin word for "ship."

Necropolis   A city of the dead; a structure that houses tombs.

Neoclassicism   An artistic movement, usually associated with eighteenth-century painting, architecture, and literature, that revived classical artistic values but centered more on the Roman republican values of honor, self-sacrifice, and public service as interpreted by the arts. (See Chapter 15.)

Neo-Platonism   A philosophy developed by Plotinus in the first century after Christ, based on the teachings of Plato and designed to help Christianize classical and

Asian religious teachings. In Italy, the Florentine academy in the 1400s was deeply influenced by the mystical and spiritual teachings of Plotinus and helped revive neo-Platonism. It emphasized the connection between the perceived material world and the unperceived spiritual world and was sometimes marked by an interest in magic and numerology.

Neumatic composition   A musical composition in which a syllable of the text is set to two notes. This is typical of Gregorian chant.

New comedy   Classical comedy of manners and social comment.

Oculus   Literally, "eye"; it is an opening in a domed ceiling, usually at the center.

Ode   A poem which, while relatively loose and open in form, draws on deep emotions and sometimes reflects, in successive stanzas, a shift from intense feeling to reflection, and then back to intense feeling. Odes were popular in the romantic period; John Keats is probably best known for his. Horace, a Roman poet, was justly famous for his odes, which the romantics knew well. (See the section on Keats in Chapter 16.)

Ogival arch   An arch that is slightly pointed at the top, as in Islamic architecture.

Old comedy   Classical slapstick, raucous comedy, similar to modern farce.

Op art   A twentieth-century style in painting in which the kinetic interaction of lines and colors is the primary subject matter.

Opera   A drama set to music, in which the lines are sung to the accompaniment of an orchestra and chorus. Opera was invented in Italy in the sixteenth century.

Opus   A musical composition numbered according to the order in which it appears in the composer's published work. Opus 1, then, would refer to the first published work of a composer, not necessarily to the first work that he or she composed.

Oratorio   A religious musical composition featuring soloists, orchestra, and chorus.

Ostinato   Constant repetition of a musical phrase or note.

Pantheon   The Greek gods. "Pan" means "all"; "theo" means "god". The Pantheon in Rome was a temple built to honor all the gods.

Participation   The loss of self in the process of becoming involved with a work of art.

Pediment   A triangular space above the frieze in the front and back of a Greek temple. Life-size sculptures were often placed on a pediment.

Perspective   The technique of representing three dimensions on a two-dimensional surface and thus creating the illusion of reality, made possible by the Renaissance discovery of vanishing-point perspective. A single point was drawn on the canvas; lines radiating from it to the edges allowed the painter to gauge the proportions of near and distant objects and figures.

Pietà   A scene depicting the Virgin Mary with the dead Christ.

Pilaster   An attached—not freestanding—pillar. It is sometimes decorative and sometimes structural.

Polyphony   Music in which several melodic lines are played simultaneously. Polyphonic music may be orchestral or vocal; it was developed in the twelfth and thirteenth centuries in France.

Pop art   A twentieth-century artistic movement including many media. It is highly irreverent both of previous art and of society. (See Chapter 19.)

Positivism   A philosophy developed by August Comte which asserts that some basic questions can never be answered. Thus, people should concentrate on what they can know positively and should carry on with their lives, trusting perception and the relationships between things that can be perceived. (See the section on Comte in Chapter 16.)

Pretext   The narrative story line of a ballet or dance.

Primitive art   Art produced by a preindustrial people or culture, or a naive artist. Western culture views African, Oceanic, Amerindian, and tribal art as primitive because it does not reflect western thought and training. It has become a major resource of western artists in the twentieth century.

Program music   Music that describes or suggests a story (such as a play by Shakespeare, a classical myth, or another narrative) or a locale (such as a nation or a landscape). *La Mer*, by Debussy, describes the ocean; Mendelssohn's Scotch Symphony uses melodies suggestive of Scotch folk music to help describe the locale.

Psychotherapy   The treatment of a mental or emotional illness by psychological means. Psychotherapy is associated with the views of Sigmund Freud, whose psychiatric practice was based on the analysis of his patients' dreams and other subconscious manifestations. It affected the development of surrealism in art.

Pure music   Music which does not have a program and which does not describe a narrative or a locale. Bach's *Art of Fugue* is an example of pure music.

Raga   The melodic plan for an Indian musical composition.

Ramesside tomb   A tomb of one of the many pharaohs named Rameses.

Realism   An artistic movement which turned its back on historical, mythical, and other imagined subjects. Realist art was often socially conscious, depicting the conditions of ordinary people in everyday situations.

Recapitulation In music, the return to thematic material which was previously presented in the exposition and the development. Usually the material is changed and enlarged in the recapitulation.

Recitative Speechlike singing, usually in an opera, in which words are half spoken and half sung.

Reformation A religious movement, beginning with Martin Luther in the sixteenth century, marked by the rejection or modification of Roman Catholic doctrines and the establishment of Protestantism.

Relic An object that is valued or considered holy because of its association with a saint or a martyr.

Reliquary A container in which relics are kept.

Representational art Art that portrays recognizable objects or scenes.

Resolution In music, the following of an unstable or dissonant section by a stable or consonant section.

Rock Popular music of the twentieth century played on electronically amplified instruments and characterized by great sound mass and a 12-bar blues structure with a conventional blues harmonic base. (See Chapter 19.)

Rococo An artistic style that developed after the baroque, sometimes described as a decadent or overblown baroque. Rococo is sensual, aims at giving pleasure, and is justly associated with abundance. (See Chapter 15.)

Romanesque An artistic style developed in the tenth, eleventh, and twelfth centuries. It is characterized by a revival and adaptation of Roman techniques and styles. (See Chapter 10.)

Romanticism A worldwide artistic movement which began in the late eighteenth century in Europe and stressed the imagination and the emotions. An emphasis on the individual, social progress, and deep emotional responses characterized the romantic style. (See Chapter 16.)

Salon An annual show of artists' works. The French Salons of the 1840s are the best known. The works of members of the Academy would be hung, but nonmembers could expect their work to be rejected if it was not pleasing to the Academy.

Salon des Refusés The "Salon of the Refused," set up by order of Napoléon III in 1863 in Paris, as an alternative to the official Salon. So many important works of art had been turned down by the Academy that a separate show was needed to exhibit the paintings of such artists as Manet, a leader of the impressionist movement. It marked the first recognition of an avant-garde movement in modern art.

Sarcophagus A stone coffin, usually decorated and often designed to stand above the ground or in a crypt. Literally, the term means "flesh-eating stone."

Satire A literary work that ridicules or scorns human foibles or vices in an effort to reform society.

Scale In western music, a graduated series of notes within the octave used as a basis for composition.

Scherzo A lively movement in a musical composition. Literally, the term means "joke." A scherzo is whimsical and playful.

Scholasticism A philosophical movement that began in the ninth century and combined religious dogma with the teachings of Aristotle. Saint Thomas Aquinas is one of the most important of the scholastics.

Sensa The elements of a work of art which appeal directly to the senses. In certain works, such as color field paintings, the sensa are the subject matter of the work.

Sharp In music, to raise a note in pitch by half a tone; or the note so raised.

Shot In film, a single sequence shot by one camera without interruption. Shots are edited together to form the completed film.

Sidhe (Pronounced "shee.") An Irish term for the world of the spirits, particularly those who change their shape.

Significant form The organization of elements in such a manner as to excite only the aesthetic emotions. Clive Bell and other art theorists of the early twentieth century asserted that the only art worth examining was art which achieved significant form.

Sikhara The pointed "steeple" on Indian temples.

Sistrum An ancient Egyptian musical instrument consisting of a metal frame and metal loops or rods that make a jingling noise when shaken. It is still used today in some compositions.

Soliloquy A dramatic monologue spoken by a character who is alone onstage. Because the character is alone, we are meant to believe that he or she is speaking the truth.

Sonata form (Also called "sonata allegro" form.) A musical construction usually used in the first movement of a classical symphony, sonata, or concerto. It is also used in other movements. There are three sections: the exposition, the development, and the recapitulation. The movement is from the tonic, or keynote, to the dominant, to a variety of keys, and then back to the tonic.

Sonnet A fourteen-line rhymed poem on a single theme. The Italian sonnet consists of an octave (eight lines) followed by a sestet (six lines). The Shakespearean sonnet consists of three quatrains (abab, cdcd, efef) followed by a couplet (gg). The sonnet originated during the Renaissance; sonnets are still written today.

Stoicism A Roman philosophy of acceptance; stoics believed in public service and self-sacrifice as well as in discipline and seriousness.

Straight photography A twentieth-century documentary

photographic style. The photograph is not permitted to resemble a painting, nor is it softened so as to evoke a sentimental response. (See the section on Stieglitz in Chapter 18.)

Stream of consciousness A literary technique that places the reader within the consciousness of a character, including all the wanderings and misdirections of his or her thought. The technique is associated particularly with the novels of James Joyce and William Faulkner.

String quartet A group of four performers playing first and second violin, viola, and cello. Also, a composition written for such a group.

Strophic song A song in which the same music is used for all the stanzas. In such a composition, the music is not likely to perfectly reflect the different emotional situations of the stanzas.

Stupa An Indian burial mound. (See Figure 6-4.)

Sturm und drang A German literary movement, developed by Goethe and other eighteenth-century writers, which centered on evoking profound emotional responses in the reader by depicting intense emotional suffering of the characters. The movement contributed to romanticism, of which it is a part. Literally, the term means "storm and stress."

Sufism An Islamic religion which is exceptionally mystical.

Superrealism A twentieth-century artistic movement in which realistic techniques were revived.

Suprematism An artistic movement of the early twentieth century developed by Kazimir Malevich. It considered aesthetic values in art to be of supreme importance, disregarding social, political, and other values not related to art.

Sura A chapter of the Koran.

Surrealism A twentieth-century artistic movement dominated by dreamlike fantasy and imagination. It was greatly influenced by psychotherapy and Freudian analysis.

Syllabic composition A musical piece in which each syllable of the text is set to one note.

Symmetry Balance in a work of art, usually achieved by repetition of similar elements in a rhythmic pattern; for example, elements on the left side of a work of art are balanced by similar elements on the right side. Symmetry is characteristic of classical art and of art influenced by it.

Tala The tempo scheme of an Indian musical composition.

Talisman An object thought to have magical powers.

Taoism A Chinese religion stressing personal virtue and mysticism.

Tempo The speed at which a musical composition is played.

Terra-cotta A ceramic medium used for pots, vases, statuettes, and sometimes relief sculptures.

Terribilità An overpowering force of will; Michelangelo, who made the pope back down in face of his demands, is said to have had terribilità.

Theme In music, the melodic subject of a composition. In literature, the theme is the dominant subject matter of a work.

Theocentrism The belief that God is the central meaning and concern in life.

Tholos A circular Greek or Roman building derived from early Greek tombs.

Through-composed song A song in which different music is used for each stanza, as contrasted with a strophic song.

Tone color The quality of sound produced by an instrument; stringed instruments and brass instruments have different tone colors, even when they play the same notes.

Tone poem A piece of programmatic music which interprets an emotional state or mood.

Tonic The keynote of a given key signature (C in the key of C, F in the key of F, etc.).

Totemic A term referring to images which have a symbolic value for an artist. The term derives from the belief of Northwest Amerindians that certain animal images were related to the tribe; totem poles clarified the images and their relationship to the tribe.

Tragedy A drama in which a highborn figure falls from a great height because of a flaw in his or her character. Tragedies were played during the feasts of Dionysus in ancient Greece.

Tragicomedy A drama which is serious in tone but which does not have the specific qualities of tragedy. Much modern drama is of this type.

Transept A cross aisle in a church, situated on a north-south axis. The dome (or if there is no dome, the steeple) is often built where it intersects the nave.

Triadic harmony Harmony based on two intervals of thirds (F-A-C; C-E-G; etc.). This is the basic harmony of popular music and most classical music.

Tribhanga A serpentine posture derived from Indian dance; literally, "thrice-bent."

Trilothon At Stonehenge, two upright stones and a lintel.

Triptych A work of art consisting of three panels or sections.

Twelve-tone music Music in which all twelve tones of the scale are equal in value. They are established in an ordered relationship which prevents any one group of notes from predominating, as in a key-based composition.

Tympanum The face of the pediment, usually triangular, above the doorway of a church or above the columns and below the roofline of a Greek temple. It is usually decorated with either bas-relief or freestanding sculpture.

Vault An arched structure forming a ceiling or roof over an aisle or corridor.

Villa In early Roman times, a country house.

Vocalise A vocalized passage sung without words; the voice imitates a musical instrument.

Wide-angle lens A photographic lens which captures a wide field of vision. A normal lens is as long, from film plane to lens surface, as the diagonal of the final negative; thus, a 50-mm lens is normal for 35-mm film (standard for movies). The lens of the normal human eye is wide-angle.

Woodcut A print made from a wooden block on which a design has been incised or carved. Ink is rolled onto the surface and remains on the raised portions of the block; paper is pressed against the block to produce a print. The print is the mirror opposite of the design on the block.

Zen Buddhism A form of Buddhism stressing spiritual tranquility, an end to striving, and a beatific inner calm. Zen Buddhism influenced twentieth-century artistic styles; the beat writers were deeply interested in Zen.

Ziggurat An ancient Mesopotamian tower, such as the ziggurat at Ur, which dates from 2100 B.C.

ACKNOWLEDGMENTS
FOR QUOTED MATERIAL

Chapter 1

References to (1) Abbé Henri Breuil. *Four Hundred Centuries of Cave Art*. Montignac: Centre études et de documentation préhistoriques. 1952. (2) Paul Leroi-Gourhan. *Treasures of Prehistoric Art*. New York: Abrams, 1967.

Chapter 2

"Hymn to Osiris." Joseph Kaster, trans. In *The Literature and Mythology of Ancient Egypt*. London: Allen Lane, 1968. Reprinted by permission of Holt, Rinehart, and Winston.

H. A. Groenwegen-Frankfort, in H. A. Groenwegen-Frankfort and Bernard Ashmole. *Art of the Ancient World*. New York: Abrams, 1977. Reprinted by permission of the publisher.

"Hymn to Aton." From K. Lange. *Egypt*. 4th ed. London: Phaidon, 1968.

Chapter 3

Diodorus Siculus. *Bibliotheca Historica*. Vol. 3, on Caesar's Gallic wars.

Gerald Hawkins. *Stonehenge Decoded*. Copyright © 1965 by Gerald S. Hawkins and John B. White. Reprinted by permission of Doubleday and Co., Inc.

The Tain Bo Cualinge. Thomas Kinsella, trans. Copyright 1970 by Oxford University Press. Reprinted by permission of Oxford University Press.

Ian Finlay. *Celtic Art*. London: Faber, 1973. Reprinted by permission of Faber and Faber, Ltd.

N. K. Sandars. *Prehistoric Art in Europe*. Baltimore: Penguin Books, 1968.

Chapter 4

Homer. *Iliad*. Richmond Lattimore, trans. Reprinted by permission of University of Chicago Press.

Homer. *Odyssey*. Robert Fitzgerald, trans. Reprinted by permission of Doubleday, Inc.

Excerpt from Plato. *Crito*. Benjamin Jowett, trans. Oxford: Oxford University Press, 1871.

Chapter 5

Catullus, "Lesbia Speaks"; Propertius, "Passion's Flower" and "Beyond the Grave"; Sulpicia, "An Avowal." James Grainger, trans. All are reprinted from *Roman Poetry*. New York: Random House, 1946. Reprinted by permission of the publisher.

Virgil. *Aeneid*. Book 1. Patrick Dickinson, trans. New York: New American Library, 1961. Reprinted by permission of New American Library.

Seneca. *The Trojan Women*. Frank Justus Miller, trans. In *Complete Roman Drama*. New York: Random House, 1942. Reprinted by permission of the publisher.

John Ferguson. *The Religions of the Roman Empire*. Ithaca: Cornell University Press, 1970.

Tertullian. *Apologetical Works of Tertullian*. Sr. Emily Joseph Daly, C.S.J., trans. Washington: Catholic University Press, 1950. Reprinted by permission of Catholic University Press.

Suetonius. "Life of Caligula." Sec. 54. From *Lives of the Caesars*.

Chapter 6

"Song of Creation." From *The Rigveda*. Ralph H. Griffith, trans. Reprinted by permission of Random House, Inc.

John Irwin. "Sanchi Torso," *Victoria and Albert Museum Yearbook*. No. 3. London: Phaidon, 1972.

Bhagavad-Gita. Swami Prabhavananda, Christopher Isherwood, and Marcel Rodd, trans. New York: New American Library, 1944. Reprinted by permission of the publisher.

Bengali poem, "Oh Madhava." Edward C. Dimock and Denise Levertov, trans. Reprinted by permission of *Poetry*, Modern Poetry Society, copyright 1965.

The Ramayana. Romesh Dutt, trans.

Ananda Coomaraswamy. *The Dance of Shiva*, New York: Sunwise Turn, 1918.

Enakshi Bhavnani. *The Dance in India.* 2d ed. Bombay: D. B. Tarapoleva, 1970.

Chapter 7

Confucius. *The Analects.* In *The Wisdom of China and India.* New York: Random House, 1948. Reprinted by permission of Random House, Inc.

Lao-Tze. *The Book of Tao.* Wisdom of China and India, trans. New York: Random House, 1948. Reprinted by permission of Random House, Inc.

Wang Wei. From Michael Sullivan. *The Arts of China.* Berkeley: University of California Press, 1973. P. 97.

Paraphrase of Alexander Soper. From Laurence Sickman and Alexander Soper. *The Art and Architecture of China.* 3d ed. Baltimore: Penguin Books, 1968.

Tu Fu. "The Emperor." E. Powys Mather, trans. Originally published by Houghton Mifflin, 1911. Reprinted by permission of Blackwell, Ltd.

Poem, "Spring View." David Lattimore, trans. In *The Harmony of the World: Chinese Poems.* Providence: Copper Beech Press, 1980. Reprinted by permission of the Copper Beech Press.

Poem from "Seven Songs Written while Living at T'ung-ku in 1759." Geoffry Waters, trans. Published in *Sunflower Splendor.* Wu-Chi Liu and Irving Yucheng Lo, eds. Bloomington: Indiana University Press, 1975. Reprinted by permission of Geoffry Waters.

Poem, from "Autumn Thoughts." Wu-Chi Liu, trans. In *Sunflower Splendor.* Wu-Chi Liu and Irving Yucheng Lo, eds. Bloomington: Indiana University Press, 1975. Reprinted by permission of Indiana University Press.

Chapter 8

The Koran. Suras 25, 31, and 33. From *The Koran Interpreted.* A. J. Arberry, trans. Reprinted by permission of George Allen and Unwin, Ltd.; McGraw-Hill, Inc.

Poem, "Appearance and Reality." R. A. Nicholson, trans. In *Persian Poems.* A. J. Arberry, ed. London: Dutton, 1954. Reprinted by permission of J. M. Dent and Sons (George Allen and Unwin, Ltd.).

Excerpts from *The Rubaiyat of Omar Khayyam.* Edward FitzGerald, trans. As included in Nicholson and Arberry's *Persian Poems.*

The Rubai-yat of 'Umar Khayyam. Paricher Kasra, trans. Reprinted by permission of the Bibliotheca Persica, Persian Heritage Series.

Bernard Lewis. *The Arabs in History.* New York: Harper and Row, 1966. Reprinted by permission of Harper and Row, Inc.

Note

There are no acknowledgments for Chapter 9.

Chapter 10

Bernard de Ventadour's song. D. W. Robertson, trans. In *The Literature of Medieval England.* New York: McGraw-Hill, 1970. Reprinted by permission of the publisher.

Dante Alighieri. *The Divine Comedy.* H. R. Huse, trans. New York: Holt, Rinehart, and Winston, 1954. Reprinted by permission of Holt, Rinehart, and Winston.

Geoffrey Chaucer. *The Canterbury Tales.* Theodore Morrison, trans. New York: Viking Press, 1949. Reprinted by permission of Viking Press, Inc.

Thomas Aquinas. *Summa Theologica.* Encyclopedia Britannica, trans. Reprinted by permission of Benziger Publishing Company.

Chapter 11

Quotation from Giorgio Vasari. *Lives of the Most Eminent Painters, Sculptors, and Architects.* Mrs. Jonathan Foster, trans.; E. H. Blashfield, E. W. Blashfield, and A. A. Hopkins, eds. New York: Scribners, 1911.

Poetry by Lorenzo de' Medici. Ł. R. Lind, trans. In *Lyric Poetry of the Italian Renaissance.* New Haven: Yale University Press, 1954. Reprinted by permission of Yale University Press and L. R. Lind.

Niccolò Machiavelli. *The Prince.* From *The Portable Machiavelli.* Peter Bondanella and Mark Musa, eds. and trans. Copyright © 1979 by Viking Penguin, Inc. Reprinted by permission of Viking Penguin, Inc.

Song by Marchetto Cara. From *Collegium Musicum: Yale.* 2d series. Madison, Wisconsin: A-R Editions, 1972.

Chapter 12

Charles Cuttler. *Northern Painting from Pucelle to Breughel.* New York: Holt, Rinehart, and Winston, 1968.

François Rabelais. *The Five Books of Gargantua and Pantagruel.* Jacques Le Clergue, trans. Copyright Limited Editions Club, New York, 1936.

Michel de Montaigne. *Montaigne: Complete Works.* Donald Frame, trans. Stanford: Stanford University Press, 1948, 1957. Reprinted by permission of Stanford University Press.

Christopher Marlowe. *The Tragicall History of Doctor Faustus,* modernized and annotated by Hallett Smith. Copyright © 1962, 1968, by W. W. Norton and Company, Inc.

Martin Luther. *On Christian Liberty.*

Howard Mayer Brown. *Music in the Renaissance.* Englewood Cliffs, N. J.: Prentice-Hall, 1976.

Chapter 13

Giorgio Vasari's life of Michelangelo. In *Lives of the Most Eminent Painters, Sculptors, and Architects.* Mrs. Jonathan Foster, trans.; E. H. Blashfield, E. W. Blashfield, and A. A. Hopkins, eds. New York: Scribners, 1911.

Howard Hibbard. *Michelangelo: Painter, Sculptor, Architect.* New York: Vendome, 1974.

Michelangelo, letter. *Michelangelo.* Robert W. Carden, trans. London: Constable, 1913. Reprinted by permission of Constable and Co.

Quotations from Shakespeare: Sonnet 73; *Taming of the Shrew; Henry IV, Part I; Hamlet; The Tempest.* From *The Riverside Shakespeare.* G. Blakemore Evans, ed. Boston: Houghton-Mifflin, 1974.

Quotation from Queen Elizabeth I. In Muriel C. Bradbrook. *Shakespeare: The Poet in His World.* New York: Columbia University Press, 1978.

Chapter 14

John Donne. *Collected Poems.* Herbert J. Grierson, ed. London: Oxford University Press, 1912. "Come Madam," from "Elegy 19: Going to Bed." "Batter my heart" is Holy Sonnet 14.

Richard Crawshaw. *Collected Poems.* L. C. Martin, ed. London: Oxford University Press, 1927. Quotations are from "A Hymn to the Name and Honor of the Admirable Saint Teresa," 1652.

John Milton. Selections from *Paradise Lost.* London: 1695.

Claude Palisca. *Baroque Music.* Englewood Cliffs, N. J.: Prentice-Hall, 1968. Pp. 4–5.

Claudio Monteverdi. Quoted in *Source Readings in Music History.* Oliver Strunk, trans. and ed. New York: Norton, 1950. Pp. 409 and 413.

Claudio Monteverdi. Stanza 2 of "Possente Spirto," Act 3 of *Orfeo.* Accademia Monteverdiana, trans.

Chapter 15

Edward Lucie-Smith. *Concise History of French Painting.* London: Oxford, 1974.

Julien la Mettrie. *Man the Machine.* Paris, 1748.

Alexander Pope. *The Rape of the Lock.* 1713. Lines 121–134.

Alexander Pope. *An Essay on Man.* 1733. Lines 282–294. *Epistle II: Of the Nature and State of Man with Respect to Himself, as an Individual.* 1733. Lines 1–2.

Voltaire (François-Marie Arouet). *Candide.* Robert Martin Adams, trans. New York: Norton. Reprinted by permission of W. W. Norton, Inc.

Samuel Johnson. Opening of *Rasselas.* London: 1759.

Antonio Vivaldi. *The Four Seasons.* Abraham Veinus (for Bach Guild), trans. Reprinted by permission of Vanguard Records, Inc.

Chapter 16

James Engell. *The Creative Imagination.* Cambridge, Mass.: Harvard University Press, 1981.

Samuel Taylor Coleridge. From *Biographia Literaria.* London, 1817.

William Blake. "The Lamb" and "The Tyger." From *Songs of Innocence and Experience.* London, 1794. Proverbs from *The Marriage of Heaven and Hell.* London, 1790–1793.

William Wordsworth. Preface to *Lyrical Ballads.* London, 1800. "Ode: Intimations of Immortality." 1807.

Samuel Taylor Coleridge. "The Rime of the Ancient Mariner." From *Lyrical Ballads.* London, 1798.

George Gordon, Lord Byron. *Childe Harold's Pilgrimage.* London, 1812. *Manfred.* London, 1817.

John Keats. "Ode on a Grecian Urn." From *The Poems of John Keats.* Jack Stillinger, ed. Cambridge, Mass.: Belknap Press of Harvard University Press. Copyright © 1978 by the President and Fellows of Harvard College.

Ludwig van Beethoven's letter. Quoted in Irving Kolodin. *The Interior Beethoven.* New York: Knopf, 1975.

Quotation from Franklin L. Baumer. *Intellectual Movements in Modern European History.* London: Macmillan, 1965.

Chapter 17

Charles Baudelaire. *The Mirror of Art.* Jonathan Mayne, trans. New York: Anchor Books, Doubleday and Co., Inc., 1956. The passage is from "The Salon of 1846." Quoted in Elizabeth Gilmore Holt, ed. *A Documentary History of Art.* Vol. 3. New York: Doubleday, 1966. P. 185.

Edmond and Jules de Goncourt. "Painting at the Exposition of 1855." Reprinted in Elizabeth Gilmore Holt. *The Art of All Nations: 1850–1873.* New York: Doubleday, 1981. P. 134.

Gustave Courbet's letter to Champfleury (Jules Husson). January 1855. Elizabeth Gilmore Holt, trans. From R. Huyghé, G. Bazin, and H. Adhémar. *L'Atelier du Peintre.* Paris, 1944. Reprinted in Elizabeth Gilmore Holt, ed. *A Documentary History of Art.* Vol. 3. New York: Doubleday, 1966. P. 349.

Paraphrase of Hélène Toussaint. "The Dossier on 'The Studio' by Courbet." Published in *Courbet.* London: Royal Academy of the Arts, 1978.

Courbet, quoted in *Courbet*, catalog of the exhibition of Gustave Courbet. Royal Academy of Art: London, 1978. P. 210.

Maurice Denis. From "Definition of Neo-Traditionalism." Elizabeth Gilmore Holt, trans. From *Théories: 1890–1910.* Paris: L'Occident, 1912. Reprinted in Elizabeth Gilmore Holt, ed. *A Documentary History of Art.* Vol. 3. New York: Doubleday, 1966. P. 509.

Karl Joris Huysmans. "L'exposition des independants en 1880." Reprinted in *L'art moderne.* Paris, 1883. P. 90. Quoted from Barbara Ehrlich White. *Impressionism in Perspective.* Englewood Cliffs, N. J.: Prentice-Hall, 1978. P. 39. Reprinted by permission of Prentice-Hall, Inc.

Walt Whitman. from *Leaves of Grass.* 1891. Beginning of Stanza 32. The hymn also comes from *Leaves of Grass.*

Charles Baudelaire. from "Metamorphosis of the Vampire." Richard Howard, trans. *Les Fleurs du Mal.* Boston: David Godine, 1982. Reprinted by permission of David Godine, Inc.

Charles Darwin, from paragraph 1 of "Natural Selection" in *Origin of Species.* 1859.

Chapter 18

Roger Fry. *The Nation*, August 2, 1913. P. 677. Quoted in George Heard Hamilton. *Painting and Sculpture in Europe: 1880–1940.* Harmondsworth: Penguin, 1972. P. 208.

Wassily Kandinsky. *Concerning the Spiritual in Art and Painting in Particular.* M. T. H. Sadleir, trans. New York: Wittenborn, Schultz, 1947. Quoted in George Heard Hamilton. *Painting and Sculpture in Europe: 1880–1940.* Harmondsworth: Penguin, 1972. P. 209. See footnote 54, p. 531. Reprinted by permission of Wittenborn Publishers.

Umberto Boccioni. *Manifesto of Futurist Painters.* 1910. Quoted in Herbert Read. *A Concise History of Modern Painting.* Oxford University Press, 1974. P. 110.

André Breton. "Manifesto of Surrealism." In *La Révolution surréaliste.* December 15, 1929. Quoted in George Heard Hamilton. *Painting and Sculpture in Europe: 1880–1940.* Harmondsworth: Penguin, 1972. P. 289.

Alfred Stieglitz. "The Photo Secession." From *The Bausch and Lomb Lens Souvenir.* Rochester, N. Y.: Bausch and Lomb Optical Company, 1903. Reprinted in Beaumont Newhall, ed. *Photography: Essays and Images.* New York: Museum of Modern Art, 1980. P. 167.

Walter Gropius. *The New Architecture and the Bauhaus 8.* London: Faber and Faber, 1935. Reprinted by permission of Faber and Faber, Ltd.

Frank Lloyd Wright. Reprinted in Kenneth Frampton. *Modern Architecture: A Critical History.* New York: Oxford University Press, 1980.

Le Corbusier. Reprinted in Kenneth Frampton. *Modern Architecture: A Critical History.* New York: Oxford University Press, 1980.

Wilfred Owen. "Anthem for Doomed Youth." Lines 1–4. From *The Collected Poems of Wilfred Owen.* C. Day Lewis, ed. Copyright 1963 by Chatto and Windus Ltd. Reprinted by permission of New Directions Publishing Corporation.

William Butler Yeats. "The Second Coming." Reprinted by permission of Macmillan Publishing Company from *The Poems of William Butler Yeats.* Richard J. Finneran, ed. Copyright 1924 by Macmillan Publishing Co.; renewed 1952 by Bertha Georgie Yeats.

Wallace Stevens. "The Emperor of Ice-Cream." Copyright 1923 and renewed 1951 by Wallace Stevens. From *Collected Poems.* Alfred A. Knopf, Inc.

T. S. Eliot. "The Waste Land." Published 1922. From *Collected Poems 1909–1962.* Copyright 1936 by Harcourt Brace Jovanovich, Inc.; copyright © 1963, 1964, by T. S. Eliot. Reprinted by permission of Harcourt Brace Jovanovich, Inc., and Faber and Faber Ltd.

Quotation from Jay Leyda. *The Film Sense.* London: Faber and Faber, 1943.

Orson Welles. Quoted in Pauline Kael. *The Citizen Kane Book.* Boston: Atlantic–Little, Brown, 1971.

Chapter 19

Harold Rosenberg. Quoted in Dore Ashton. *American Art since 1945.* New York: Oxford, 1982. P. 13.

Jackson Pollock. "My Painting." *Possibilities.* Vol. 1 (Winter 1947/480). P. 79.

Robert Rauschenberg. Quoted in Dore Ashton. *American Art since 1945.* New York: Oxford, 1982. P. 117. By permission of Oxford University Press.

Clement Greenberg. Quoted in Irving Sandler. *The New York School: The Painters and Sculptors of the Fifties.* New York: Harper and Row, 1978. P. 95.

Milton Brown et al. Comment on *Christina's World.* In Milton Brown, Sam Hunter, John Jacobus, Naomi Rosenblum, and David Sokol. *American Art.* Englewood Cliffs, N. J.: Prentice-Hall. P. 453.

Philip Pearlstein. *Real, Really Real, Superreal: Directions in Contemporary American Realism.* San Antonio: San Antonio Museum, 1981. P. 39.

F. David Martin. In F. David Martin and Lee A. Jacobus. *The Humanities through the Arts.* 3d ed. New York: McGraw-Hill, 1983. P. 132.

Albert Camus. from "The Myth of Sisyphus." In *The Myth of Sisyphus and Other Essays.* Justin O'Brien, trans. Copyright © 1955 by Alfred A. Knopf, Inc. Reprinted by permission of the publisher.

Federico García Lorca. *Selected Poems.* J. L. Gili, trans. Copyright 1955 by New Directions Publishing Co.

INDEX

Pyramids, 25; in the Americas, 37–39; at Giza, 28–29, illus. 29
Pythagoras, 85

Qualities of romantic music, 439
Quetzalcoat1, 20

Ra, 26
Ra-Amen, 34, 36
Ra-Atum-Khepri, 26
Rabelais, François, *Gargantua and Pantagruel*, 278, 282
Rabirius, 98
Radha and Krishna in a Grove, illus. 132
Ragas, 133, 172
Rainey, Ma, 549
Ramayana, 131
Rameses, King, 36
Raphael, 302–304, 422; *Pope Leo X with Cardinals Giulio de'Medici and Luigi de'Rossi*, illus. 303; *The School of Athens*, 303, Color Plate 14
Rauschenberg, Robert, *Illustrations for Dante's Inferno*, illus. 561
Ravel, Maurice, *Le Tombeau de Couperin*, 546
Ravenna, Italy, 184–186; church mosaics, 185–186
Realism, 247, 409–410, 452ff.; and superrealism, 565–567
Realist tradition in modern literature, 595
Realistic sculpture, politics and, 575–576
Reason, 432–433; age of, 423, 432
Reformation, 275, 281–284; in England, 282–284
Regulus, 107
Reims, cathedral at, 209
Relief sculpture of the ceremonial hunt at Ur, 21, illus. 22
Religion, early Christian, 199; eighteenth-century, 373ff.; the growth of scholasticism, 227; Indian, 124
Rembrandt van Rijn, 351–354; *Blinding of Sampson*, illus. 352; *Descent from the Cross*, illus. 352; *Night Watch*, illus. 354; *Self-Portrait*, Color Plate 23
Renaissance, 234ff.; allegory, 254; architecture, 237; the church, 237; dance and music, 257; guilds, 238; humanism, 255; literature, 255–257; painting, 247ff.; portraits, 251, illus. 252; scholarship, 256; sculpture, 238
Renaissance Center, Detroit, illus. 585
Reni, Guido, *Saint John the Baptist*, 345, Color Plate 19
Renoir, Pierre-Auguste, 410; *Luncheon of the Boating Party*, Color Plate 34; *Monet Painting in His Garden*, illus. 464
Rent Collection Courtyard, The, sculpture, illus. 577
Repetition in literature, 479
Revolutions of 1848, 409

Reynolds, Sir Joshua, 386, 388, 389, 422; *Mrs. Siddons as the Tragic Muse*, illus. 388
Rickey, George, *Two Lines Oblique*, illus. 572
"Ride of the Valkyries," leitmotif, illus. 484
Rigaud, Hyacinthe, *Portrait of Louis XIV*, illus. 339
Rigveda, 123
Riley, Bridget, *Fall*, illus. 564
Rise of Christianity, 181
Rise of humanism (1375 to 1500), 237ff.
Ritornello, 394
Rivers, Larry, 561–564; *Double Portrait of Frank O'Hara*, illus. 562, 564; *Washington Crossing the Delaware*, 561
Roche, Kevin, College Insurance Building, illus. 584; Knights of Columbus Building, illus. 584
"Rock Around the Clock," 603
Rock music, 603–605; and protest, 604–605; as a subversive art form, 603
Rococo, 371, 380ff.
Rococo architecture, 373–374
Rococo music, 398
Rodin, Auguste, 473–477; *Balzac*, illus. 476; *The Burghers of Calais*, illus. 476; *Gates of Hell*, illus. 474–475; *The Kiss*, illus. 474; *The Thinker*, illus. 475
Rogers, Richard, 582; Georges Pompidou Center, illus. 583
Rolin, Nicholas, illus. 269
Roman arch, 93–95
Roman architecture, 91, 182
Roman dramatists, 110
Roman empire, 178
Roman forum, 91–92, illus. 92
Roman love lyrics, 106–108
Roman music and dance, 114
Roman myth and religion, 111
Roman sculpture, 103, illus. 103–106
Roman wall paintings, 196
Romanesque architecture and sculpture, 203
Romanesque church, 205
Romanesque dome, 207
Romanesque sculpture, 204
Romantic classicism, 429
Romantic dance, 446–447
Romantic gothicism, 430
Romantic opera, 439
Romantic philosophy, 447–449
Romantic poetry, 409
Romantic style in painting, 414–416
Romanticism, 409
Rome, decay of, 181; model in A.D. 350, illus. 92; sack of, 178
Romulus and Remus, 87, 93, 110
Rosenberg, Harold, 555
Rosenberg, Isaac, 531
Rossellini, Roberto, 589